THE
PREACHER'S
OUTLINE & SERMON
BIBLE®

THE
PREACHER'S
OUTLINE & SERMON
BIBLE®

OLD TESTAMENT

_____
_____

KING JAMES VERSION

Leadership Ministries Worldwide
Chattanooga, TN

THE PREACHER'S OUTLINE & SERMON BIBLE® - 2 KINGS

KING JAMES VERSION

Please address all requests for information or permission to:

Leadership Ministries Worldwide
Ph.# (800) 987-8790   E-Mail: info@lmw.org
Web: lmw.org

Library of Congress Catalog Card Number: 96-75921
ISBN Softbound Edition: 978-1-57407-172-6

Printed in the United States of America

DEDICATED

To all the men and women of the world who preach and teach the Gospel of our Lord Jesus Christ and to the Mercy and Grace of God

- Demonstrated to us in Christ Jesus our Lord.

  "In whom we have redemption through His blood, the forgiveness of sins, according to the riches of His grace." (Ep.1:7)

- Out of the mercy and grace of God, His Word has flowed. Let every person know that God will have mercy upon him, forgiving and using him to fulfill His glorious plan of salvation.

  "For God so loved the world, that he gave His only begotten Son, that whosoever believeth in Him should not perish, but have everlasting life. For God sent not his son into the world to condemn the world, but that the world through him might be saved." (Jn.3:16-17)

  "For this is good and acceptable in the sight of God our Saviour; who will have all men to be saved, and to come unto the knowledge of the truth." (1 Ti.2:3-4)

10/22

The Preacher's Outline & Sermon Bible®

is written for God's servants to use in their study, teaching, and preaching of God's Holy Word...

- to share the Word of God with the world.
- to help believers, both ministers and laypersons, in their understanding, preaching, and teaching of God's Word.
- to do everything we possibly can to lead men, women, boys, and girls to give their hearts and lives to Jesus Christ and to secure the eternal life that He offers.
- to do all we can to minister to the needy of the world.
- to give Jesus Christ His proper place, the place the Word gives Him. Therefore, no work of Leadership Ministries Worldwide will ever be personalized.

ACKNOWLEDGMENTS AND BIBLIOGRAPHY

Every child of God is precious to the Lord and deeply loved. And every child as a servant of the Lord touches the lives of those who come in contact with him or his ministry. The writing ministries of the following servants have touched this work, and we are grateful that God brought their writings our way. We hereby acknowledge their ministries to us, being fully aware that there are so many others down through the years whose writings have touched our lives and who deserve mention, but the weaknesses of our minds have caused them to fade from memory. May our wonderful Lord continue to bless the ministry of these dear servants, and the ministry of us all as we diligently labor to reach the world for Christ and to meet the desperate needs of those who suffer so much.

THE REFERENCE WORKS

Archer, Gleason L. *A Survey of Old Testament Introduction*. Chicago, IL: Moody Bible Institute of Chicago, 1974.

_____. *Encyclopedia of Bible Difficulties*. Grand Rapids, Michigan: Zondervan Publishing House, 1982.

Atlas of the World. Hammond Concise Edition. Maplewood, NJ: Hammond Inc., 1993.

Baker's Dictionary of Theology. Everett F. Harrison, Editor-in-Chief. Grand Rapids, MI: Baker Book House, 1960.

Barker, William P. *Everyone in the Bible*. Westwood, NJ: Fleming H. Revell Co., 1966.

Brown, Francis. *The New Brown-Driver-Briggs-Gesenius Hebrew-English Lexicon*. Peabody, MA: Hendrickson Publishers, 1979.

Cruden's Complete Concordance of the Old & New Testament. Philadelphia, PA: The John C. Winston Co., 1930.

Dake, Finis Jennings. *Dake's Annotated Reference Bible, The Holy Bible*. Lawrenceville, GA: Dake Bible Sales, Inc., 1963.

Easton's 1897 Bible Dictionary. Database NavPress Software, 1996.

Enhanced Nave's Topics. Database NavPress Software, 1991, 1994.

Frank, Harry Thomas, ed. *Atlas of the Bible Lands*. Maplewood, NJ: Hammond Incorporated, 1977.

Freedman, David Noel, ed., et. al. *The Anchor Bible Dictionary*. New York: Doubleday, 1992.

Funk & Wagnalls Standard Desk Dictionary. Lippincott & Crowell, Publishers, 1980, Vol.2.

Geisler, Norman. *A Popular Survey of the Old Testament*. Grand Rapids, MI: Baker Book House, 1977.

Good News Bible. Old Testament: © American Bible Society, 1976. New Testament: © American Bible Society, 1966, 1971, 1976. Collins World.

Good News for Modern Man, The New Testament. New York, NY: American Bible Society, 1971.

Goodrick, Edward W. and John R. Kohlenberger, III. *The NIV Exhaustive Concordance*. Grand Rapids, MI: Zondervan Publishing House, 1990.

Grun, Bernard. *The Timetables of History*. 3rd ed. New York: Simon & Schuster, 1991.

Harrison, Roland Kenneth. *Introduction to the Old Testament*. Grand Rapids, MI: Eerdmans Publishing Co., 1969.

Holman Bible Dictionary. Nashville, TN: Broadman & Holman Publishers, 1991. Database NavPress Software.

Hooper, Jerry L., ed. *The Holman Bible Atlas*. Philadelphia, PA: A.J. Holman Company, 1978.

Jauchen, John S., ed., et. al. *NIV Thompson Student Bible*. Indianapolis, IN: Kirkbride Bible Company, 1999.

Josephus, Flavius. *Complete Works*. Grand Rapids, MI: Kregel Publications, 1981.

Kaiser, Walter C. *A History of Israel*. Nashville, Tennessee: Broadman and Holman Publishers, 1998.

Kipfer, Barbara Ann, Ph.D. *Roget's 21st Century Thesaurus*. New York, NY: Dell Publishing, 1992.

Kohlenberger, John R. III. *The Interlinear NIV Hebrew-English Old Testament*. Grand Rapids, MI: Zondervan Publishing House, 1987.

Kouffman, Donald T. *The Dictionary of Religious Terms*. Westwood, NJ: Fleming H. Revell Co., 1967.

Life Application® Bible. Wheaton, IL: Tyndale House Publishers, Inc., 1991.

Life Application® Study Bible. New International Version. Tyndale House Publishers, Inc.: Wheaton, IL 1991, and Zondervan Publishing House: Grand Rapids, MI, 1984.

Lindsell, Harold and Woodbridge, Charles J. *A Handbook of Christian Truth*. Westwood, NJ: Fleming H. Revell Company, A Division of Baker Book House, 1953.

Living Quotations For Christians. Edited by Sherwood Eliot Wirt and Kersten Beckstrom. New York, NY: Harper & Row, Publishers, 1974.

Lockyer, Herbert. *All the Books and Chapters of the Bible*. Grand Rapids, MI: Zondervan Publishing House, 1966.

_____. *All the Men of the Bible*. Grand Rapids, MI: Zondervan Publishing House, 1958.

_____. *All the Miracles of the Bible*. Grand Rapids, MI: Zondervan Publishing House, 1961.

_____. *All the Parables of the Bible*. Grand Rapids, MI: Zondervan Publishing House, 1963.

_____. *The Women of the Bible*. Grand Rapids, MI: Zondervan Publishing House, 1967.

Martin, Alfred. *Survey of the Scriptures*, Part I, II, III. Chicago, IL: Moody Bible Institute of Chicago, 1961.

McDowell, Josh. *Evidence That Demands a Verdict*, Vol.1. San Bernardino, CA: Here's Life Publishers, Inc., 1979.

Miller, Madeleine S. & J. Lane. *Harper's Bible Dictionary*. New York, NY: Harper & Row Publishers, 1961.

Nave, Orville J. *Nave's Topical Bible*. Nashville, TN: The Southwestern Company. Copyright © by J.B. Henderson, 1921.

Nelson's Complete Book of Bible Maps & Charts. Nashville, TN: Thomas Nelson Publishers, Inc., 1996.

New American Standard Bible, Reference Edition. La Habra, CA: The Lockman Foundation, 1975.

New American Standard Bible, Updated Edition. La Habra, CA: The Lockman Foundation, 1995.

New Bible Dictionary, 3rd Edition. Leicester, England: Universities & Colleges Christian Fellowship, 1996.

New International Version Study Bible. Grand Rapids, MI: Zondervan Bible Publishers, 1985.

New Living Translation, Holy Bible. Wheaton, IL: Tyndale House Publishers, Inc., 1996.

Orr, William. *How We May Know That God Is*. Wheaton, IL: Van Kampen Press, n.d.

Owens, John Joseph. *Analytical Key to the Old Testament,* Vols.1, 2, 3. Grand Rapids, MI: Baker Book House, 1989.

Payne, J. Barton. *Encyclopedia of Biblical Prophecy.* New York, NY: Harper & Row, Publishers, 1973.

Pilgrim Edition, Holy Bible. New York, NY: Oxford University Press, 1952.

Ridout, Samuel. *Lectures on the Tabernacle.* New York, NY: Loizeaux Brothers, Inc., 1914.

Silverman, David P. ed. *Ancient Egypt.* New York: Oxford University Press, 1997.

Smith, William. *Smith's Bible Dictionary.* Peabody, MA: Hendrickson Publishers, n.d.

Stone, Nathan J. *Names of God.* Chicago, IL: Moody Press, 1944.

Strong, James. *Strong's Exhaustive Concordance of the Bible.* Nashville, TN: Thomas Nelson, Inc., 1990.

———. *The Tabernacle of Israel.* Grand Rapids, MI: Kregel Publications, 1987.

Strong's Greek and Hebrew Dictionary as compiled by iExalt Software. Database NavPress Software, 1990-1993.

The Amplified Bible. Scripture taken from THE AMPLIFIED BIBLE, Old Testament copyright © 1965, 1987 by the Zondervan Publishing House. The Amplified New Testament copyright © 1958, 1987 by The Lockman Foundation. Used by permission.

The Evangelical Dictionary of Theology. Elwell, Walter A., Editor. Grand Rapids, MI: Baker Book House, 1984.

The Hebrew-Greek Key Study Bible, New International Version. Spiros Zodhiates, Th.D., Executive Editor. Chattanooga, TN: AMG Publishers, 1996.

The Holy Bible in Four Translations. Minneapolis, MN: Worldwide Publications. Copyright © The Iversen-Norman Associates: New York, NY, 1972.

The Illustrated Bible Atlas, with Historical Notes by F. F. Bruce. Grand Rapids, MI: Kregel Publications, 1994.

The Interlinear Bible, Vols.1, 2, 3. Translated by Jay P. Green, Sr. Grand Rapids, MI: Baker Book House, 1976.

The International Standard Bible Encyclopaedia, Edited by James Orr. Grand Rapids, MI: Eerdmans Publishing Co., 1939.

The NASB Greek/Hebrew Dictionary and Concordance. La Habra, CA: The Lockman Foundation, 1988.

The Nelson Study Bible, New King James Version. Nashville, TN: Thomas Nelson Publishers, Inc., 1997.

The New Compact Bible Dictionary. Edited by T. Alton Bryant. Grand Rapids, MI: Zondervan Publishing House, 1967. Used by permission of Zondervan Publishing House.

The New Scofield Reference Bible. Edited by C.I. Scofield. New York, NY: Oxford University Press, 1967.

The New Thompson Chain Reference Bible. Indianapolis, IN: B.B. Kirkbride Bible Co., Inc., 1964.

The New Unger's Bible Dictionary. Chicago, IL: Moody Press, 1998. Database NavPress Software, 1997.

The NIV Study Bible, New International Version. Grand Rapids, MI: Zondervan Publishing House, 1985.

The Open Bible. Nashville, TN: Thomas Nelson Publishers, 1975.

The Quest Study Bible. New International Version. Grand Rapids, MI: Zondervan Publishing House, 1994.

The Zondervan Pictorial Encyclopedia of the Bible, Vol.1. Merrill C. Tenney, Editor. Grand Rapids, MI: Zondervan Publishing House, 1982.

Theological Wordbook of the Old Testament. Edited by R. Laird Harris. Chicago, IL: Moody Bible Institute of Chicago, 1980.

Unger, Merrill F. & William White, Jr. *Nelson's Expository Dictionary of the Old Testament.* Nashville, TN: Thomas Nelson Publishers, 1980.

Vine, W.E., Merrill F. Unger, William White, Jr. *Vine's Complete Expository Dictionary of Old and New Testament Words.* Nashville, TN: Thomas Nelson Publishers, 1985.

Walton, John H. *Chronological and Background Charts of the Old Testament.* Grand Rapids, MI: Zondervan Publishing House, 1978.

Webster's Seventh New Collegiate Dictionary. Springfield, MA: G. & C. Merriam Company, Publishers, 1971.

Wilmington. Harold L. *The Outline Bible.* Wheaton, IL: Tyndale House Publishers, Inc., 1999.

Wilson, William. *Wilson's Old Testament Word Studies.* McLean, VA: MacDonald Publishing Company, n.d.

Wood, Leon. *A Survey of Israel's History.* Grand Rapids, MI: Zondervan Publishing House, 1982.

Young, Edward J. *An Introduction to the Old Testament.* Grand Rapids, MI: Eerdmans Publishing Co., 1964.

Young, Robert. *Young's Analytical Concordance to the Bible.* Grand Rapids, MI: Eerdmans Publishing Co., n.d.

Zondervan NIV Bible Library. Version 2.5. Grand Rapids, MI: Zondervan Publishing House.

THE COMMENTARIES

Baldwin, Joyce G. *1 & 2 Samuel.* "The Tyndale Old Testament Commentaries." Downers Grove, IL: Inter-Varsity Press, 1988.

Barnes' Notes, Exodus to Esther. F.C. Cook, Editor. Grand Rapids, MI: Baker Book House, n.d.

Bergen, Robert D. *1, 2 Samuel.* "The New American Commentary," Vol.7. Nashville, TN: Broadman & Holman Publishers, 1996.

Brueggemann, Walter. *1 Kings.* "Knox Preaching Guides." Atlanta, GA: John Knox Press, 1982.

———. *2 Kings.* "Knox Preaching Guides." Atlanta, GA: John Knox Press, 1982.

Burroughs, P.E., D.D. *Old Testament Studies.* Nashville, TN: Sunday School Board, Southern Baptist Convention, 1915.

Chafin, Kenneth. *1, 2 Samuel.* "Mastering the Old Testament," Vol.8. Dallas, TX: Word Publishing, 1989.

Crockett, William Day. *A Harmony of Samuel, Kings, and Chronicles.* Grand Rapids, MI: Baker Book House, 1985.

Denton, Robert C. *The First and Second Books of the Kings. The First and Second Books of the Chronicles.* "The Layman's Bible Commentary," Vol.7. Atlanta, GA: John Knox Press, 1964.

DeVries, S.J. *1 Kings.* WBC. Waco, TX: Word, 1985.

ACKNOWLEDGMENTS AND BIBLIOGRAPHY
THE COMMENTARIES (continued)

Dilday, Russell. *The Preacher's Commentary on 1, 2 Kings.* Nashville, TN: Word Publishing, 1987, 2003.

Evans, Mary J. *1 and 2 Samuel.* "New International Biblical Commentary." Peabody, MA: Hendrickson Publishers, Inc., 2000.

Farrar, F.W. *The First Book of Kings.* Minneapolis, MN: Klock & Klock Christian Publishers, Inc., n.d.

———. *The Second Book of Kings.* Minneapolis, MN: Klock & Klock Christian Publishers, Inc., n.d.

Gill, John. *Gill's Commentary*, Vol.2. Grand Rapids, MI: Baker Book House, 1980.

Gray, John. *I & II Kings.* Second, Fully Revised, Edition. "The Old Testament Library." Philadelphia, PA: The Westminster Press, 1970.

Henry, Matthew. *Matthew Henry's Commentary*, 6 Vols. Old Tappan, NJ: Fleming H. Revell Co., n.d.

Hertzberg, Hans Wilhelm. *I & II Samuel.* Philadelphia, PA: Westminster Press, 1964.

Hobbs, T.R. *2 Kings.* "Word Biblical Commentary," Vol.13. Waco, TX: Word Books, 1985.

House, Paul R. *1, 2 Kings.* "The New American Commentary," Vol.8. Nashville, TN: Broadman & Holman Publishers, 1995.

Kaiser, Walter C., Jr. *A History of Israel.* Nashville, TN: Broadman & Holman Publishers, 1998.

Keil-Delitzsch. *Commentary on the Old Testament*, Vol.3. Grand Rapids, MI: Eerdmans Publishing Co., n.d.

Maclaren, Alexander. *Expositions of Holy Scripture*, 11 Vols. Grand Rapids, MI: Eerdmans Publishing Co., 1952-59.

McGee, J. Vernon. *Thru the Bible*, Vol.2. Nashville, TN: Thomas Nelson Publishers, 1981.

Morgan, G. Campbell. *Living Messages of the Books of the Bible*, Vol.1. Old Tappan, NJ: Fleming H. Revell, 1912.

Newsome, James D., Jr. *1 Samuel, 2 Samuel.* Atlanta, GA: John Knox Press, 1982.

Patterson, Richard D. and Hermann J. Austel. *1, 2 Kings.* "The Expositor's Bible Commentary," Vol.4. Grand Rapids, MI: Zondervan Publishing House, 1988.

Payne, D.F. *I and II Samuel*, DSB. Philadelphia, PA: Westminster Press, 1982.

Poole, Matthew. *Matthew Poole's Commentary on the Holy Bible.* Peabody, MA: Hendrickson Publishers, n.d.

Provan, Iain W. *1 and 2 Kings.* "New International Biblical Commentary." Peabody, MA: Hendrickson Publishers, Inc., 1995.

Rust, Eric C. *The First and Second Books of Samuel.* "The Layman's Bible Commentary," Vol.6. Atlanta, GA: John Knox Press, 1961.

Spurgeon, C.H. *Spurgeon's Sermon Notes. Genesis to Malachi.* Westwood, NJ: Fleming H. Revell Co., n.d.

The Interpreter's Bible, 12 Vols. New York, NY: Abingdon Press, 1956.

The Pulpit Commentary. 23 Vols. Edited by H.D.M. Spence & Joseph S. Exell. Grand Rapids, MI: Eerdmans Publishing Co., 1950.

Walvoord, John F. and Roy B. Zuck, Editors. *The Bible Knowledge Commentary, Old Testament.* Colorado Springs, CO: Chariot Victor Publishing, 1985.

Wiersbe, Warren W. *Be Responsible.* Colorado Springs, CO: Victor Books, 2000.

———. *Be Successful.* Colorado Springs, CO: Victor Books, 2001.

Wiseman, Donald J. *1 & 2 Kings.* "The Tyndale Old Testament Commentaries." Downers Grove, IL: Inter-Varsity Press, 1993.

Youngblood, Ronald F. *1 Samuel. 2 Samuel.* "The Expositor's Bible Commentary," Vol.3. Grand Rapids, MI: Zondervan Publishing House, 1990.

ABBREVIATIONS

&	= and	O.T.	= Old Testament
Bc.	= because	p./pp.	= page/pages
Concl.	= conclusion	Pt.	= point
Cp.	= compare	Quest.	= question
Ct.	= contrast	Rel.	= religion
e.g.	= for example	Rgt.	= righteousness
f.	= following	Thru	= through
Illust.	= illustration	v./vv.	= verse/verses
N.T.	= New Testament	vs.	= versus

THE BOOKS OF THE OLD TESTAMENT

Book	Abbreviation	Chapters	Book	Abbreviation	Chapters
GENESIS	Gen. or Ge.	50	Ecclesiastes	Eccl. or Ec.	12
Exodus	Ex.	40	The Song of Solomon	S. of Sol. or Song	8
Leviticus	Lev. or Le.	27	Isaiah	Is.	66
Numbers	Num. or Nu.	36	Jeremiah	Jer. or Je.	52
Deuteronomy	Dt. or De.	34	Lamentations	Lam.	5
Joshua	Josh. or Jos.	24	Ezekiel	Ezk. or Eze.	48
Judges	Judg. or Jud.	21	Daniel	Dan. or Da.	12
Ruth	Ruth or Ru.	4	Hosea	Hos. or Ho.	14
1 Samuel	1 Sam. or 1 S.	31	Joel	Joel	3
2 Samuel	2 Sam. or 2 S.	24	Amos	Amos or Am.	9
1 Kings	1 Ki. or 1 K.	22	Obadiah	Obad. or Ob.	1
2 Kings	2 Ki. or 2 K.	25	Jonah	Jon. or Jona.	4
1 Chronicles	1 Chron. or 1 Chr.	29	Micah	Mic. or Mi.	7
2 Chronicles	2 Chron. or 2 Chr.	36	Nahum	Nah. or Na.	3
Ezra	Ezra or Ezr.	10	Habakkuk	Hab.	3
Nehemiah	Neh. or Ne.	13	Zephaniah	Zeph. or Zep.	3
Esther	Est.	10	Haggai	Hag.	2
Job	Job or Jb.	42	Zechariah	Zech. or Zec.	14
Psalms	Ps.	150	Malachi	Mal.	4
Proverbs	Pr.	31			

THE BOOKS OF THE NEW TESTAMENT

Book	Abbreviation	Chapters	Book	Abbreviation	Chapters
MATTHEW	Mt.	28	1 Timothy	1 Tim. or 1 Ti.	6
Mark	Mk.	16	2 Timothy	2 Tim. or 2 Ti.	4
Luke	Lk. or Lu.	24	Titus	Tit.	3
John	Jn.	21	Philemon	Phile. or Phm.	1
The Acts	Acts or Ac.	28	Hebrews	Heb. or He.	13
Romans	Ro.	16	James	Jas. or Js.	5
1 Corinthians	1 Cor. or 1 Co.	16	1 Peter	1 Pt. or 1 Pe.	5
2 Corinthians	2 Cor. or 2 Co.	13	2 Peter	2 Pt. or 2 Pe.	3
Galatians	Gal. or Ga.	6	1 John	1 Jn.	5
Ephesians	Eph. or Ep.	6	2 John	2 Jn.	1
Philippians	Ph.	4	3 John	3 Jn.	1
Colossians	Col.	4	Jude	Jude	1
1 Thessalonians	1 Th.	5	Revelation	Rev. or Re.	22
2 Thessalonians	2 Th.	3			

HOW TO USE
The Preacher's Outline & Sermon Bible®
Follow these easy steps to gain maximum benefit from The POSB.

① SUBJECT HEADING - - - -

② MAJOR POINTS - - - -

③ SUBPOINTS - - - - -
&
SCRIPTURE - - - - -

④ COMMENTARY - - - -

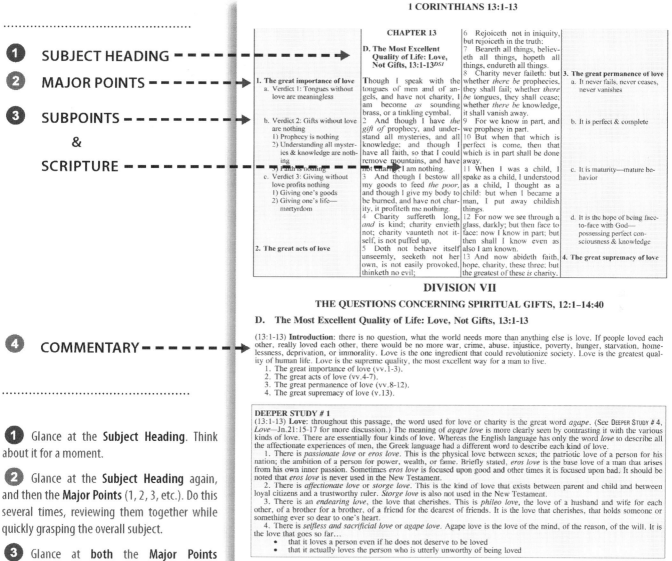

1 CORINTHIANS 13:1-13

CHAPTER 13

D. The Most Excellent Quality of Life: Love, Not Gifts, 13:1-13[DS1]

1. **The great importance of love**
   a. Verdict 1: Tongues without love are meaningless
   b. Verdict 2: Gifts without love are nothing
      1) Prophecy is nothing
      2) Understanding all mysteries & knowledge are nothing
      3) Faith is nothing
   c. Verdict 3: Giving without love profits nothing
      1) Giving one's goods
      2) Giving one's life—martyrdom

2. **The great acts of love**

Though I speak with the tongues of men and of angels, and have not charity, I am become *as* sounding brass, or a tinkling cymbal.
2 And though I have *the gift of* prophecy, and understand all mysteries, and all knowledge; and though I have all faith, so that I could remove mountains, and have not charity, I am nothing.
3 And though I bestow all my goods to feed *the poor,* and though I give my body to be burned, and have not charity, it profiteth me nothing.
4 Charity suffereth long, *and* is kind; charity envieth not; charity vaunteth not itself, is not puffed up,
5 Doth not behave itself unseemly, seeketh not her own, is not easily provoked, thinketh no evil;

6 Rejoiceth not in iniquity, but rejoiceth in the truth;
7 Beareth all things, believeth all things, hopeth all things, endureth all things.
8 Charity never faileth: but whether *there be* prophecies, they shall fail; whether *there* be tongues, they shall cease; whether *there be* knowledge, it shall vanish away.
9 For we know in part, and we prophesy in part.
10 But when that which is perfect is come, then that which is in part shall be done away.
11 When I was a child, I spake as a child, I understood as a child, I thought as a child: but when I became a man, I put away childish things.
12 For now we see through a glass, darkly; but then face to face: now I know in part; but then shall I know even as also I am known.
13 And now abideth faith, hope, charity, these three; but the greatest of these *is* charity.

3. **The great permanence of love**
   a. It never fails, never ceases, never vanishes
   b. It is perfect & complete
   c. It is maturity—mature behavior
   d. It is the hope of being face-to-face with God—possessing perfect consciousness & knowledge

4. **The great supremacy of love**

DIVISION VII
THE QUESTIONS CONCERNING SPIRITUAL GIFTS, 12:1–14:40

D. The Most Excellent Quality of Life: Love, Not Gifts, 13:1-13

(13:1-13) **Introduction:** there is no question, what the world needs more than anything else is love. If people loved each other, really loved each other, there would be no more war, crime, abuse. injustice, poverty, hunger, starvation, homelessness, deprivation, or immorality. Love is the one ingredient that could revolutionize society. Love is the greatest quality of human life. Love is the supreme quality, the most excellent way for a man to live.
1. The great importance of love (vv.1-3).
2. The great acts of love (vv.4-7).
3. The great permanence of love (vv.8-12).
4. The great supremacy of love (v.13).

DEEPER STUDY # 1
(13:1-13) **Love:** throughout this passage, the word used for love or charity is the great word *agape*. (See DEEPER STUDY # 4, *Love*—Jn.21:15-17 for more discussion.) The meaning of *agape love* is more clearly seen by contrasting it with the various kinds of love. There are essentially four kinds of love. Whereas the English language has only the word *love* to describe all the affectionate experiences of men, the Greek language had a different word to describe each kind of love.
1. There is *passionate love* or *eros love*. This is the physical love between sexes; the patriotic love of a person for his nation; the ambition of a person for power, wealth, or fame. Briefly stated, *eros* love is the base love of a man that arises from his own inner passion. Sometimes *eros love* is focused upon good and other times it is focused upon bad. It should be noted that *eros love* is never used in the New Testament.
2. There is *affectionate love* or *storge love*. This is the kind of love that exists between parent and child and between loyal citizens and a trustworthy ruler. *Storge love* is also not used in the New Testament.
3. There is an *endearing love*, the love that cherishes. This is *phileo love*, the love of a husband and wife for each other, of a brother for a brother, of a friend for the dearest of friends. It is the love that cherishes, that holds someone or something ever so dear to one's heart.
4. There is *selfless and sacrificial love* or *agape love*. Agape love is the love of the mind, of the reason, of the will. It is the love that goes so far...
   • that it loves a person even if he does not deserve to be loved
   • that it actually loves the person who is utterly unworthy of being loved

① Glance at the **Subject Heading**. Think about it for a moment.

② Glance at the **Subject Heading** again, and then the **Major Points** (1, 2, 3, etc.). Do this several times, reviewing them together while quickly grasping the overall subject.

③ Glance at **both** the **Major Points** and **Subpoints** together while reading the **Scripture**. Do this slower than Step 2. Note how these points sit directly beside the related verse and simply restate what the Scripture is saying—in Outline form.

④ Next read the **Commentary**. Note that the *Major Point Numbers* in the Outline match those in the Commentary. A small raised number (**DS1, DS2, etc.**) at the end of a Subject Heading or Outline Point, directs you to a related **Deeper Study** in the Commentary.

Finally, read the **Thoughts** and **Support Scripture** (not shown).

As you read and re-read, pray that the Holy Spirit will bring to your attention exactly what you should preach and teach. May God bless you richly as you study and teach His Word.

The POSB contains everything you need for sermon preparation:

1. **The Subject Heading** describes the overall theme of the passage, and is located directly above the Scripture (keyed *alphabetically*).

2. **Major Points** are keyed with an outline *number* guiding you to related commentary. Note that the Commentary includes *"Thoughts"* (life application) and abundant Supporting Scriptures.

3. **Subpoints** explain and clarify the Scripture as needed.

4. **Commentary** is fully researched and developed for every point.
   • **Thoughts** (in bold) help apply the Scripture to real life.
   • **Deeper Studies** provide in-depth discussions of key words.

"Woe is unto me, if I preach not the gospel"
(1 Co.9:16)

TABLE OF CONTENTS
2 KINGS

THE
SECOND BOOK OF THE KINGS

COMMONLY CALLED
THE FOURTH BOOK OF THE KINGS

AUTHOR: Uncertain. There is no direct claim to authorship. However, there is strong evidence that a prophet wrote the books of *First* and *Second Kings*.

1. *First* and *Second Kings* are written from the perspective of a prophet. Time and again the destructive results of an evil life of immorality, wickedness, lawlessness, violence, idolatry, and false worship are seen and warned against. In addition, there is a strong emphasis upon the temple and other religious subjects. The very purpose of the book is to give the Israelites a permanent history of their monarchy, a history of their kings from a *moral and spiritual* perspective. These facts point toward a prophet's having written *First* and *Second Kings*.

2. *First* and *Second Kings* were apparently written before the exile of the Southern Kingdom by Babylon. This fact is known because the phrase "to this day" is used repeatedly (1 K.8:8; 9:13, 21; 10:12; 12:19; 2 K.2:22; 8:22; 10:27; 14:7; 16:6; 17:23, 41; 20:17; 21:15). Although some scholars claim that this phrase could have easily been copied from one of the original sources, this seems most unlikely. For if the fact being spoken about was not true in his day, it seems far more logical to think he would have either worded the fact as *past history* or else just omitted the phrase from his record. Thus it seems that the bulk of *First* and *Second Kings* was written before the exile.

3. The focus of the book is the *moral and spiritual* evaluation of the kings and the ministries of the prophets. Every king is measured against the righteous reign of David to which they should have all aspired. Every king is judged either as righteous or "evil in the sight of the LORD."

4. Jewish tradition actually says that Jeremiah the prophet wrote the book of *Kings*. Jeremiah lived during the days of Josiah and the other kings of Judah up to the destruction of Jerusalem and the Babylonian captivity. Some scholars say that the style of writing is like that in the book of *Jeremiah* and that much of the content of *First* and *Second Kings* actually sounds like the book of *Jeremiah*. In fact, 2 Kings 24:18–25:30 is the same as Jeremiah 52. However, other scholars claim that the differences in writing styles between *Jeremiah* and *Kings* are significant.

Whatever the case concerning writing styles, Jeremiah was a priest and prophet who had access to the royal records of his day. He was also present and personally involved in the circles of government during the days of Jerusalem's fall. Among all the known persons of his day, he was certainly capable of writing a permanent history of the nation from a moral and spiritual perspective. However, it must be kept in mind that Jeremiah died in Egypt, not in Babylon (Je.43:6-7). Therefore, if he was the author, the historical fact mentioned at the end of *Second Kings* was obviously written and added to the book by someone in Babylon (2 K.25:27-30).

Although the author cannot be known for certain, the Divine Author is clearly known. The Holy Spirit of God *breathed* or *inspired* the great books of *First* and *Second Kings*. Through His inspiration, the Holy Spirit has given to the world a history of the very events God wanted recorded about the kings of Israel and the people they served. A study of these events shows us the great hope we can have in the LORD, for they were written to be both an example and a warning to us.

> **"For whatsoever things were written aforetime were written for our learning, that we through patience and comfort of the scriptures might have hope" (Ro.15:4).**
>
> **"Now all these things happened to them for examples: and they are written for our admonition, upon whom the ends of the world are come" (1 Co.10:11).**

DATE: Some of the book was written before 586 B.C., and the rest was written before 538 B.C. The Babylonian captivity took place in 586 B.C., so the major portion of *Kings* was written before this date, as is indicated by the above-mentioned phrase "to this day."

The return of King Jehoiachin from Babylon, which took place in the 37th year of his imprisonment (c.568 B.C.), is also mentioned. Hence the latter part of *Second Kings* was written sometime later. In determining just when, note that nothing whatsoever is mentioned about the return of the exiles from the Babylonian captivity in 538 B.C. Thus the books of *First* and *Second Kings* were probably written before 586 and 538 B.C.

TO WHOM WRITTEN: The Israelites in particular and the human race in general. *First* and *Second Kings* were written in a time of civil, moral, and spiritual decline. Political unrest and disunity gripped the people and their leaders. Furthermore, the nation had split asunder, dividing into the Northern Kingdom of Israel and the Southern Kingdom of Judah. *First* and *Second Kings* were written to the Israelites...

- to teach them the utter necessity of building their lives and society upon the LORD and His commandments.
- to warn them of judgment to come unless they repented and returned to the LORD.

PURPOSE: Three purposes can be gleaned from the books of *First* and *Second Kings*:

1. The *Historical Purpose*:
   a. To record a permanent history of Israel's monarchy or kings from a moral, spiritual perspective. Beginning with Solomon and the tragic division of the nation, the author covers all the kings of both the Northern and Southern Kingdoms. He then ends with the utter destruction of Jerusalem and the Babylonian captivity.
   b. To explain the decline and utter destruction of Israel as a nation, pointing out why the people lost the promised land and were exiled, suffering a terrible plight.
   c. To turn the Israelites back to the LORD, teaching both leaders and people the importance of building their lives and society upon the LORD. To be successful as a nation and people they must...
      - obey God's law, His commandments

1

- reject all false worship, worshipping the LORD and Him alone
- govern with compassion, executing true justice and righteousness throughout the land

2. The *Doctrinal* or *Spiritual Purpose*:
   a. To explain the reason for the plight of the Israelite people and their nation. The author shows that the wickedness of the kings and the people led to the destruction of their nation and the loss of their land, the promised land of God. The rulers and the people committed all forms of immorality, lawlessness, violence, idolatry, and false worship. Consequently, the LORD was left with no choice but to execute judgment upon the people.
   b. To teach the importance of obedience to God. In covering the history of the kings, the author points out how obedience to God's law led to God's blessing, but disobedience led to His judgment. If the ruler and the people kept the covenant—their promise to believe and obey the LORD—they would be blessed by God. But if the people broke their covenant (promise), they would be judged and suffer the curses spelled out in the covenant (see outline and notes—Le.26:1-46; De.28:1-68).
   c. To give the people hope and assurance that God would fulfill His wonderful promise to David (the Davidic covenant), the promise that David's kingdom would be an eternal kingdom. Despite the apostasy of various rulers and the people and the eventual destruction of the nation, the LORD had always kept His promises. Thus He would fulfill His promise to David, giving an eternal kingdom to those who truly believed and obeyed the LORD. This promise, of course, was to be fulfilled in Christ.
   d. To stress the sovereignty of God. The author shows how God works behind the scene of world history. He uses the chain of natural events and the actions of men to bless the obedient and to judge the wicked.

3. The *Christological* or *Christ-Centered Purpose*: To stress the faithfulness of God in continuing the royal line of David despite the unbelief and sin of the people. God was faithful to His promise, the promise of the Davidic covenant (see outline and note—2 S.7:11-17 for more discussion). God was going to continue the dynasty, the royal line of David, just as He had promised. As the New Testament tells us, from the line of David arose the Messiah or Savior of the world. David's kingdom will last forever through the Lord Jesus Christ and the eternal kingdom He has established.

SPECIAL FEATURES:

1. *First* and *Second Kings* are "The Great Books That Were Originally One Book in the Hebrew Scriptures." The two books were known as *The Book of Kings*. However, when the Old Testament was translated into Greek (about 150 B.C.), the four books of *Samuel* and *Kings* were combined to give a complete history of Israel's kings and monarchy (titled *First, Second, Third* and *Fourth Kingdom*). Later, the two books of Samuel were again separated from *First and Second Kings,* which is the way the books are divided in many Bibles today. However, in the Vulgate and Latin Bibles they are called *First, Second, Third*, and *Fourth Kings*.

2. *First* and *Second Kings* are "The Great Books That Made Use of Other Written Sources in Recording the History of the Kings and the Divided Monarchy." The author used at least these sources:
   ⇒ *The Book of the Acts of Solomon* (1 K.11:41).
   ⇒ *The Book of the History of the Kings of Judah* (1 K.14:29; 15:7, 23; 22:45; 2 K.8:23; 12:19; 14:18; 15:6, 36; 16:19; 20:20; 21:17, 25; 23:28; 24:5).
   ⇒ *The Book of the History of the Kings of Israel* (1 K.15:31; 16:5, 14, 20, 27; 22:39; 2 K.1:18; 10:34; 13:8, 12; 14:15, 28; 15:21).

The author probably used other sources as well, such as the four sources used by the author of *First Chronicles*:
   ⇒ The court records of King David (1 Chr.27:24).
   ⇒ The records of Samuel the seer (1 Chr.29:29).
   ⇒ The records of Nathan the prophet (1 Chr.29:29).
   ⇒ The records of Gad the seer (1 Chr.29:29).

3. *First* and *Second Kings* are "The Great Books That Give the Official Account of the Monarchy's History, Its Rise to Glory Under Solomon and Its Division and Decline Under Various Kings."

4. *First* and *Second Kings* are "The Great Books That Cover Solomon's Wisdom, Wealth, and Wickedness" (1 K.1-11).

5. *First* and *Second Kings* are "The Great Books That Cover the Division of the Nation" (1 K.12–16).

6. *First* and *Second Kings* are "The Great Books That Lift Up the Reign of David as the Standard by Which All Other Kings Are to Be Measured" (1 K.9:4; 11:4, 6, 33, 38; 14:8; 15:3, 5, 11; 2 K.16:2; 18:3; 22:2).

7. *First* and *Second Kings* are "The Great Books That Stress Prophecy and Its Fulfillment" (2 S.7:13 with 1 K.8:20; 1 K.11:29-39 with 12:15; 1 K.13:1-34 with 2 K.23:16-18; and many others).

8. *First* and *Second Kings* are "The Great Books That Cover the Ministry of Elijah" (1 K.17–19).

9. *First* and *Second Kings* are "The Great Books That Stress the Prophets and Their Ministry."
   ⇒ Elijah, 1 K.17–19
   ⇒ Elisha, 2 K.1–13
   ⇒ Ahijah, 1 K.11:29-40; 14:5-18
   ⇒ Shemaiah, 1 K.12:22-24
   ⇒ Micaiah, 1 K.22:8-28
   ⇒ Jonah, 2 K.14:25
   ⇒ Isaiah, 2 K.19:1-7, 20-34
   ⇒ Huldah, 2 K.22:14-20

10. *First* and *Second Kings* are "The Great Books That Cover the Spiritual Erosion of Israel and Judah and the Result of Their Apostasy: The Great Captivity and Exile" (1 K.20–2 K.25).

11. *First* and *Second Kings* are "The Great Books That Stress the People's Disobedience to God—and Their Insane Rush to the Inevitable Judgment of Utter Destruction."

12. *First* and *Second Kings* are "The Great Books That Show That Society Reaps What It Sows." As long as the people of Israel lived righteous lives, obeying the commandments of God and worshipping God alone, they were successful. They were blessed more and more by God. But when the people committed sin and continued on in their sin, they stepped ever closer to the day when they would face the judgment of God (1 K.2:3; 8:33-34; 9:6-7).

13. *First* and *Second Kings* are "The Great Books That Teach a Necessary Truth: We Must Base Our Lives, Government, and Society upon the Word of God" (1 K.3:14; 6:12; 8:61; 11:38; 18:26; 21:26).

14. *First* and *Second Kings* are "The Great Books That Show the Faithfulness of God." Even when the people of Israel were not faithful to God, God was faithful to continue the royal line of David. And through the royal line of David, God sent His Son into the world. Jesus Christ is the promised Son of David, the King of kings and LORD of lords, the Messiah and Savior of the world (1 K.9:5; Mt.1:20; Re.22:16).

TIMELINE OF KINGS, PROPHETS AND HISTORY*

HISTORY

DATE BC	FOREIGN KINGS	WORLD EVENTS
1000	Ashur-Rabi II (1010–970) (Assyria); Hiram (1003–966) (Tyre); Tiglath-Pileser II (960–935) (Assyria)	David captures Jerusalem (1004); Foundation for the Temple (966); 22nd Egyptian Dynasty (945)
950		
930		Kingdom Divided (930)
	Shishak I (945–924) (Egypt)	Assyria makes peace with Babylon (915)
900	Ben-Hadad I (900) (Syria); Eth-Baal (887–856) (Sidon)	Jehoshaphat leads a revival (865); Elijah's contest with prophets of Baal (857); Elijah's mantle passed to Elisha (845)
850	Hazael (840) (Syria)	
800	Ben-Hadad II (798) (Syria)	Carthage established (814); Joash repairs Temple (812); 23rd Egyptian dynasty (800)
	Ben-Hadad III (773) (Syria)	Olympic games begin (776); Rome founded (753)
750	Rezin (750) (Syria)	Babylonian and Chinese calendar (750)

THE UNITED KINGDOM

BIBLE REF.	KINGS (Years Reigned)	PROPHETS
1 S.16:1–1 K.2:11; 1 Chr.11:1-30	David (40) (1011–971)	Samuel (1095–1015); Gad (1015–950); Asaph (1004)
1 K.2:12-11:43; 1 Chr.28:1–2 Chr.9:31	Solomon (40) (971–931)	Nathan (1003–931); Heman (971)

THE DIVIDED KINGDOM

NORTHERN KINGDOM OF ISRAEL

PROPHETS	KINGS (Years Reigned)	BIBLE REF.
Ahijah (931–910); Man from Judah (930); Shemaiah (927)	Jeroboam I (22) (931–910)	1 K.12:1-24; 12:25-14:20; 2 Chr.10:1-16
Jehu (886)	Nadab (2) (910–909)	1 K.15:25-31
	Baasha (24) (909–886)	1 K.15:16-16:7; 2 Chr.16:1-6
	Elah (2) (886–885)	1 K.16:6-14
Hanani (870)	Zimri (7 days) (885)	1 K.16:9-20
	Omri (12) (885–874)	1 K.16:21-28
Elijah (860–845)	Ahab (22) (874–853)	1 K.16:28-22:40; 2 Chr.18:1-34
Micaiah (853); Elisha (850–795); Eliezer (849–48)	Ahaziah (2) (853–852); Joram/Jehoram (12) (852–841)	1 K.22:49-51; 2 K.1:1-18; 2 Chr.20:35-37; 22:1-11; 2 K.1:17; 3:1-8:15
	Jehu (28) (841–814)	2 K.9:1-10:36; 2 Chr.22:7-9
	Jehoahaz (17) (814–798)	2 K.13:1-9
Zechariah (797); Jonah (780–765)	Jehoash (16) (798–782)	2 K.13:9-25; 14:8-16
Amos (750)	Jeroboam II (41) (793–753)	2 K.14:23-29
	Zechariah (6 mos) (753); Shallum (1 mo) (752); Menahem (10) (752–742)	2 K.15:8-12; 2 K.15:13-15; 2 K.15:16-22

SOUTHERN KINGDOM OF JUDAH

BIBLE REF.	KINGS (Years Reigned)	PROPHETS
1 K.12:1-24; 14:21-31; 2 Chr.9:31-12:16	Rehoboam (17) (931–913)	
1 K.15:1-8; 2 Chr.12:16-14:1	Abijah (3) (913–911)	
1 K.15:9-24; 2 Chr.14:1-16:14	Asa (3) (911–870)	Iddo (910); Azariah (896)
1 K.22:41-50; 2 K.3:6-14; 2 Chr.17:1-21:1	Jehoshaphat (25) (873–848)	
2 K.8:16-24; 2 Chr.21:1-20	Jehoram (8) (853–841)	Obadiah (845)
2 K.8:25-29; 9:27-29; 2 Chr.22:1-10	Ahaziah (2) (841)	
2 K.11:1-16; 2 Chr.22:10-23:21	Athaliah (7) (841–835)	
2 K.11:17-12:21; 2 Chr.22:11-12; 24:1-27	Joash/Jehoash (40) (835–796)	Joel (830)
2 K.14:1-20; 2 Chr.24:27-25:28	Amaziah (29) (796–767)	
2 K.14:21-22; 15:1-7; 2 Chr.26:1-23	Azariah/Uzziah (52) (792–740)	Hosea (788–723); Jonah (780–765)
2 K.15:32-38; 2 Chr.26:23-27:9	Jotham (16) (750–731)	

THE DIVIDED KINGDOM

SOUTHERN KINGDOM OF JUDAH			NORTHERN KINGDOM OF ISRAEL			DATE	FOREIGN KINGS	HISTORY
BIBLE REF.	KINGS (YEARS REIGNED)	PROPHETS	BIBLE REF.	KINGS (YEARS REIGNED)	PROPHETS	BC	FOREIGN KINGS	WORLD EVENTS
			2 K.15:23-26	Pekahiah (2) (742-740)			Tiglath-Pil[n]eser III [or Pul] (745-727) (Assyria)	Assyria takes control of Northern Kingdom (745-627)
2 K.15:38-16:20; 2 Chr.27:9-27; Is.7:1-9:1	Ahaz (16) (735-715)	Isaiah (740-690)	2 K.15:27-31	Pekah (20) (752-732) (752-740) (ruled only in Gilead) (740-732) (ruled in Samaria)			Shalmaneser V (727-722) (Assyria)	Assyria invades Northern Israel (732)
2 K.18:1-20:21; 2 Chr.28:27-32:33; Pr.25:1; Is.36:1-39:8	Hezekiah (29) (729-686)	Micah (735-725) Oded (733)	2 K.17:1-23	Hoshea (9) (732-722)			So (727-716) (Egypt) Sargon II (710-705) (Assyria)	Fall of Northern Kingdom (722)
							Sennacherib (705-681) (Assyria) Merodach-Baladan (721-710, 705-704) (Assyria)	Sennacherib defeats Egypt (701) Hezekiah's tunnel (701)
						700	Tirhakah (690-664) (Egypt)	185,000 Assyrians killed by God (701)
2 K.20:21-21:18; 2 Chr.32:33-33:20	Manasseh (55) (696-642)	Nahum (663-612)						Sennacherib destroys Babylon (689)
2 K.21:18-26; 2 Chr.33:20-25	Amon (2) (642-640)					650	Esarhaddon (681-669) (Assyria) Nabopolassar (626-605) (Assyria) Neco (610-595) (Egypt)	Josiah's reform (621) Nineveh destroyed (612)
2 K.21:26-23:30; 2 Chr.33:25-35:27	Josiah (31) (640-609)	Zephaniah (640-609) Jeremiah (627-562)					Nebuchadnezzar II (605-562) (Babylon)	Battle of Carchemish (605) 1st group of exiles from Judah taken to Babylon (605)
2 K.23:31-33; 2 Chr.36:1-4	Jehoaz/Jehoahaz (3 mos) (609)	Habakkuk (615-598)				600		2nd group of exiles from Judah taken to Babylon (597)
2 K.23:34-24:7; 25:27-30; 2 Chr.36:5-8	Jehoiakim (11) (608-598)	Daniel (605-535)						Fall of Judah—Third group of exiles from Judah taken to Babylon (586)
2 K.24:8-17; 25:27-30; 2 Chr.36:8-10;	Jehoiachin (3 mos) (598-597)	Ezekiel (593-571)					Evil-Merodach (562-560) (Babylon)	Fall of Babylon to Medo-Persian Empire (539)
2 K.24:18-25:21; 2 Chr.36:10-14; Je.21:1-52:11	Zedekiah/Mattaniah (11) (597-586)					550	Cyrus II (559-530) (Medo-Persia)	Cyrus II decrees that the Jews may return to the Holy Land (538)
2 K.25:22-26; Je.40:5-41:18	Gedaliah (2 mos) (Appointed by Nebuchadnezzar) (586)						Belshazzar (552-539) (Babylon)	1st exiles return to Holy Land with Zerubbabel (537)
		Haggai (520) Zechariah (520-518)						1st Temple foundation laid (536) 2nd Temple foundation laid (520)
						500	Darius I (521-486) (Medo-Persia)	Temple completed (516) Republic of Rome est. (509)
		Malachi (430)				450	Artaxerxes (465-425) (Persia)	2nd return under Ezra (458)
								3rd return under Nehemiah (445)

*Some dates are approximate.

The resources used for the Timeline in addition to the *Bible* are as follows:
1 Archer, Gleason L. *Encyclopedia of Bible Difficulties.* (Grand Rapids, Michigan: Zondervan Publishing House), 1982.
2 Freedman, David Noel, ed., et. al. *The Anchor Bible Dictionary.* (New York: Doubleday), 1992.
3 Grun, Bernard. *The Timetables of History.* 3rd ed. (New York: Simon & Schuster), 1991.
4 Kaiser, Walter C. *A History of Israel.* (Nashville, Tennessee: Broadman & Holman Publishers), 1998.
5 Silverman, David P., ed. *Ancient Egypt.* (New York: Oxford University Press), 1997.

2 KINGS

THE PREACHER'S OUTLINE AND SERMON BIBLE® is *unique*. It differs from all other Study Bibles and Sermon Resource Materials in that every Passage and Subject is outlined right beside the Scripture. When you choose any *Subject* below and turn to the reference, you have not only the Scripture but also an outline of the Scripture and Subject *already prepared for you—verse by verse*.

For a quick example, choose one of the subjects below and turn over to the Scripture; you will find this to be a marvelous help for more organized and streamlined study.

In addition, every point of the Scripture and Subject is *fully developed in a Commentary with supporting Scripture* at the end of each point. Again, this arrangement makes sermon preparation much simpler and more efficient.

Note something else: the Subjects of *2 Kings* have titles that are both Biblical and *practical*. The practical titles are often more appealing to people. This *benefit* is clearly seen for use on billboards, bulletins, church newsletters, etc.

A suggestion: for the *quickest* overview of *2 Kings*, first read *all the Division titles* (I, II, III, etc.), then come back and read the individual outline titles.

OUTLINE OF 2 KINGS

I. THE FINAL DAYS OF ELIJAH'S MINISTRY: A FAITHFUL SERVANT WHO PERSEVERED TO THE VERY END, 1:1–3:27

    A. The Confrontation of Elijah with King Ahaziah: The Danger of Rejecting the Only Living and True God, 1:1-18
    B. The Ascension of Elijah and the Transfer of His Ministry to Elisha: A Picture of Total Commitment to God and God's Power, 2:1-25
    C. The Evil Reign of Joram in Israel and Elisha's Call Proven to the World's Rulers: The Proof of a Prophet, 3:1-27

II. THE MINISTRY AND MIRACLES OF ELISHA: A DRAMATIC DEMONSTRATION OF GOD'S POWER AND CARE FOR HIS PEOPLE, 4:1–13:25

    A. The Poor Widow, a Wealthy Shunammite Woman, and a School of Prophets Miraculously Delivered: God's Power to Meet the Desperate Needs of His People, 4:1-44
    B. The Syrian Army Commander Naaman Miraculously Healed: God's Power to Convert and Heal a Person, 5:1-27
    C. The Lost Ax Head Miraculously Recovered and a Syrian Military Force Miraculously Blinded: God's Power to Help and to Defend His People, 6:1-23
    D. The Syrian Blockade Against Samaria Miraculously Broken: God's Power to Deliver His People, 6:24–7:20
    E. The Political Influence of Elisha and the Evil Reigns of Jehoram and Ahaziah in Judah: Being a Strong Godly Example and Witness for the LORD, 8:1-29
    F. The Secret Anointing of Jehu As King of Israel and His Bloody Purge: Misguided Justice Due to Self-Interest, 9:1–10:36
    G. The Evil Reign of Queen Athaliah in Judah: The Desperate Need for a Just, Righteous Leader, 11:1-21
    H. The Good Reign of Jehoash (Joash) in Judah: A Strong and Righteous Beginning but a Weak and Sinful Ending, 12:1-21
    I. The Evil Reigns of Jehoahaz and Jehoash in Israel and the Final Days of Elisha: A Contrast Between Weak and Strong Character, 13:1-25

III. THE UTTER DISINTEGRATION AND FALL OF ISRAEL, THE NORTHERN KINGDOM: A TRAGIC END DUE TO AN UNBROKEN STREAM OF WICKEDNESS AND LAWLESSNESS, 14:1–17:41

    A. The Reign of Amaziah in Judah and His Provoking War with Israel: Losing One's Opportunity to Serve, 14:1-22
    B. The Long Reigns of Jeroboam II in Israel and Azariah (Uzziah) in Judah: God's Blessing the People and Giving Them One Last Chance to Repent, 14:23–15:7
    C. The Reigns of Five Kings in Israel, Four of Whom Were Assassinated: Political Disorder Due to the People's Continued Wickedness and Rejection of God, 15:8-31
    D. The Reigns of Two Kings in Judah, Jotham and Ahaz: A Sharp Contrast Between Righteousness and Wickedness, 15:32–16:20
    E. The Tragic Fall of Israel, Its Conquest and Deportation of the People by the Assyrians (722 BC): The End of God's Long-Suffering and the Execution of His Judgment, 17:1-41

DIVISION I

THE FINAL DAYS OF ELIJAH'S MINISTRY: A FAITHFUL SERVANT WHO PERSEVERED TO THE VERY END, 1:1–3:27

(1:1–3:27) **DIVISION OVERVIEW**: In the dark days of the Northern Kingdom of Israel, God had sent a prophet to proclaim the most basic truth of the universe: there is only one true and living God, the LORD Himself (Jehovah, Yahweh). There is no other God, not Baal nor any other so-called god. All so-called gods are the mere creations of man's imaginations, his ideas and his hands. Elijah was one of the greatest prophets of all time; and if there had ever been a day when a true prophet was needed, it was the dark, dismal days in which he lived. For these were the days of the evil king Ahab and his infamous wife Jezebel. These two rulers were savage oppressors of the people who unleashed a flood of wickedness and brutality seldom seen in any society. Despite Elijah's constant warnings that the nation's two rulers and people must turn to the LORD or else face the judgment of God, they had all rejected his appeals. Ahab, Jezebel, and the people—all had continued to live wicked lives and to worship false gods. Consequently, as the book of *First Kings* closed, God's judgment fell upon King Ahab. He was violently killed in battle as he fought against the Syrians. And just as Elijah had earlier predicted, the dogs licked up the blood of this evil, unrepentant king (1 K.21:17-19; 22:29-40, esp.v.38).

Now, *Second Kings* continues the story of the rulers of Israel and Judah, right up until the tragic collapse of both nations and the exile of the citizens. As this great book of Holy Scripture opens, both Elijah and Jezebel are aged, but still living. The infamous Jezebel will continue in her wicked ways for about eight more years, but then God's judgment will fall upon her. Just as Elijah had predicted, she would die a grizzly death at the hands of Jehu and dogs would devour her flesh (1 K.21:23; 2 K.9:36-37).

Standing in stark contrast to the wicked lives and violent deaths of Ahab and Jezebel is the righteous life and ascension of Elijah into God's presence. No more stark contrast could be drawn than the lives and departures of these three people from the earth.

The great book of *Second Kings* opens with the final days of Elijah's ministry. After twenty plus years of ministry, Elijah had two more tasks to complete before leaving the earth. He had to issue a strong warning to Ahaziah, Ahab's son who had assumed the throne upon his fathers' death (1:1-18). And he had to prepare the student prophets whom he was training, especially Elisha his replacement, for his departure (2:1-25). Immediately upon his departure, the LORD began to prove to the kings and leaders of this world that Elisha was His appointed prophet to replace Elijah (3:1-27).

The great prophet Elijah left this earth without passing through death. He will be seen once more on earth at the transfiguration of the greatest prophet of all, the Lord Jesus Christ Himself (Mt.17:1-3).

As a person studies this division of Scripture, he or she is inspired by the faithfulness of Elijah. The reader is challenged to persevere to the end of life just as Elijah did.

THE FINAL DAYS OF ELIJAH'S MINISTRY: A FAITHFUL SERVANT WHO PERSEVERED TO THE VERY END, 1:1–3:27

A. The Confrontation of Elijah with King Ahaziah: The Danger of Rejecting the Only Living and True God, 1:1-18
B. The Ascension of Elijah and the Transfer of His Ministry to Elisha: A Picture of Total Commitment to God and God's Power, 2:1-25
C. The Evil Reign of Joram in Israel and Elisha's Call Proven to the World's Rulers: The Proof of a Prophet, 3:1-27

THE
SECOND BOOK OF KINGS

COMMONLY CALLED

THE FOURTH BOOK OF THE KINGS

CHAPTER 1

I. THE FINAL DAYS OF ELIJAH'S MINISTRY: A FAITHFUL SERVANT WHO PERSEVERED TO THE VERY END, 1:1–3:27

A. The Confrontation of Elijah with King Ahaziah of Israel: The Danger of Rejecting the Only Living & True God, 1:1-18

1. The king's two major problems, a revolt & a serious accident: Rejecting the only living LORD & turning to a false deliverer (god)
a. The revolt by Moab, 1; 3:1-27
b. The accident of King Ahaziah
c. The messengers sent by the king to the false god Baal-Zebub: Seeking encouragement, healing
d. The interception of the messengers by Elijah
   1) Elijah was sent by God
   2) Elijah condemned the king
      • For turning away from the living LORD
      • For consulting a false god

   3) Elijah pronounced God's judgment upon the king: Death

e. The messengers' quick return to King Ahaziah
   1) The king questioned why they had returned
   2) The messengers reported the whole episode of the prophet's confrontation
      • Elijah's condemnation of the king
      • Elijah's pronouncement of judgment upon the king

   3) The king asked who the man was, what he looked like

Then Moab rebelled against Israel after the death of Ahab. 2 And Ahaziah fell down through a lattice in his upper chamber that *was* in Samaria, and was sick: and he sent messengers, and said unto them, Go, enquire of Baal-zebub the god of Ekron whether I shall recover of this disease. 3 But the angel of the LORD said to Elijah the Tishbite, Arise, go up to meet the messengers of the king of Samaria, and say unto them, *Is it* not because *there is* not a God in Israel, *that* ye go to enquire of Baal-zebub the god of Ekron? 4 Now therefore thus saith the LORD, Thou shalt not come down from that bed on which thou art gone up, but shalt surely die. And Elijah departed. 5 And when the messengers turned back unto him, he said unto them, Why are ye now turned back? 6 And they said unto him, There came a man up to meet us, and said unto us, Go, turn again unto the king that sent you, and say unto him, Thus saith the LORD, *Is it* not because *there is* not a God in Israel, *that* thou sendest to enquire of Baal-zebub the god of Ekron? therefore thou shalt not come down from that bed on which thou art gone up, but shalt surely die. 7 And he said unto them, What manner of man *was he* which came up to meet you, and told you these words?

8 And they answered him, *He was* an hairy man, and girt with a girdle of leather about his loins. And he said, It *is* Elijah the Tishbite. 9 Then the king sent unto him a captain of fifty with his fifty. And he went up to him: and, behold, he sat on the top of an hill. And he spake unto him, Thou man of God, the king hath said, Come down. 10 And Elijah answered and said to the captain of fifty, If I *be* a man of God, then let fire come down from heaven, and consume thee and thy fifty. And there came down fire from heaven, and consumed him and his fifty. 11 Again also he sent unto him another captain of fifty with his fifty. And he answered and said unto him, O man of God, thus hath the king said, Come down quickly. 12 And Elijah answered and said unto them, If I *be* a man of God, let fire come down from heaven, and consume thee and thy fifty. And the fire of God came down from heaven, and consumed him and his fifty. 13 And he sent again a captain of the third fifty with his fifty. And the third captain of fifty went up, and came and fell on his knees before Elijah, and besought him, and said unto him, O man of God, I pray thee, let my life, and the life of these fifty thy servants, be precious in thy sight. 14 Behold, there came fire down from heaven, and burnt up the two captains of the former fifties with their fifties: therefore let my life now be precious in thy sight. 15 And the angel of the LORD said unto Elijah, Go down with him: be not afraid of him. And he arose, and went down with him unto the king. 16 And he said unto him, Thus saith the LORD, Forasmuch as thou hast sent messengers to enquire of *is it*

4) The messengers described the prophet's appearance
5) The king then knew it was Elijah who had made the stern prediction of judgment

2. The king's enraged attempts to arrest Elijah: God's protection of His servant
a. The first attempt by a captain & 50 soldiers
   1) They demanded Elijah surrender to the king
   2) Elijah called out for God's protection: For fire to consume the threatening soldiers
   3) God answered Elijah's prayer

b. The second attempt by a captain & 50 soldiers
   1) Insisted Elijah surrender to the king

   2) Elijah again called out for God's protection: For fire to consume the threatening soldiers
   3) God again answered Elijah's prayer

c. The third attempt by a captain & 50 soldiers
   1) The captain acknowledged the supreme authority of Elijah's LORD
      • Fell to his knees & showed humility
      • Asked Elijah to spare their lives

      • Acknowledged that the consuming fire had come from heaven, from Elijah's God
      • Begged for his life

   2) The LORD gave Elijah two instructions
      • To go with the captain
      • Not to fear the captain
   3) Elijah obeyed the LORD

3. The king's death: Judgment due to sin
a. The confrontation between Elijah & the king

1) Elijah condemned the king • For turning away from the living LORD • For consulting a false god 2) Elijah pronounced God's judgment: Death b. The king's death: Just as predicted by Elijah	Baal-zebub the god of Ekron, not because *there is* no God in Israel to enquire of his word? therefore thou shalt not come down off that bed on which thou art gone up, but shalt surely die. 17 So he died according to the word of the LORD which Elijah had spoken. And	Jehoram reigned in his stead in the second year of Jehoram the son of Jehoshaphat king of Judah; because he had no son. 18 Now the rest of the acts of Ahaziah which he did, *are* they not written in the book of the chronicles of the kings of Israel?	c. The king's successor: Joram (Jehoram), his brother d. The king's achievements: Recorded in the book *The History of the Kings of Israel*

DIVISION I

THE FINAL DAYS OF ELIJAH'S MINISTRY: A FAITHFUL SERVANT WHO PERSEVERED TO THE VERY END, 1:1–3:27

A. The Confrontation of Elijah with King Ahaziah: The Danger of Rejecting the Only Living and True God, 1:1-18

(1:1-18) **Introduction—God, Living, Only—God, One and Only—God, Supreme—God, Helper—God, Works of—Needs, Met by**: there is only one living and true God, only one Creator, one LORD and Majesty of the universe. He is the LORD God Almighty (Jehovah, Yahweh), who alone possesses supreme knowledge (omniscience) and supreme power (omnipotence) and is present everywhere (omnipresent). Because He is the LORD God of the universe, He is able to help us as we walk day-by-day throughout life. No matter what difficult circumstance, problem, trial, or temptation may face us—the LORD loves us and wants to help us. And He will help us if we will simply trust Him and follow Him. This is the great practical message of this Scripture.

But keep this fact in mind: although this is the beginning passage of *Second Kings*, there is no real division between the books of *First Kings* and *Second Kings*. In the Hebrew Bible, the two books were originally combined as one book (see Introduction to 2 Kings). In fact, a brief summary of King Ahaziah was covered in the last three verses of *First Kings*. Now his reign is continued in the first chapter of *Second Kings*. Sadly, Ahaziah had been reared by two very ungodly parents, King Ahab and the infamous Jezebel. Due to their wicked, evil lives, Ahaziah was influenced to walk in their sinful steps. This is: *The Confrontation of Elijah with King Ahaziah of Israel: The Danger of Rejecting the Only Living and True God, 1:1-18.*

1. The king's two major problems, a revolt and a serious accident: rejecting the only living LORD and turning to a false deliverer (god) (vv.1-8).
2. The king's enraged attempts to arrest Elijah: God's protection of His servant (vv.9-15).
3. The king's death: judgment due to sin (vv.16-18).

1 (1:1-8) **Rejection, of God—Turning Away, from God—God, Rejection of—Ahaziah, King of Israel, Evil Reign of—Influence, of Parents—Children, Tragedy of, Following Evil Example—Parents, Evil Influence of—God, False, Baal-Zebub—Baal-Zebub, False God**: immediately after being crowned king, Ahaziah was confronted with two major problems, a revolt and a serious accident. Remember that Ahaziah served the god Baal just as Ahab and Jezebel, his father and mother, had (1 K.22:53). His rejection of the living LORD is clearly seen in the present passage:

OUTLINE	SCRIPTURE	SCRIPTURE	OUTLINE
1. The king's two major problems, a revolt & a serious accident: Rejecting the only living LORD & turning to a false deliverer (god) a. The revolt by Moab, 1; 3:1-27 b. The accident of King Ahaziah c. The messengers sent by the king to the false god Baal-Zebub: Seeking encouragement, healing d. The interception of the messengers by Elijah 1) Elijah was sent by God 2) Elijah condemned the king • For turning away from the living LORD	Then Moab rebelled against Israel after the death of Ahab. 2 And Ahaziah fell down through a lattice in his upper chamber that *was* in Samaria, and was sick: and he sent messengers, and said unto them, Go, enquire of Baalzebub the god of Ekron whether I shall recover of this disease. 3 But the angel of the LORD said to Elijah the Tishbite, Arise, go up to meet the messengers of the king of Samaria, and say unto them, *Is it* not because *there is* not a God in Israel, *that* ye go to	enquire of Baal-zebub the god of Ekron? 4 Now therefore thus saith the LORD, Thou shalt not come down from that bed on which thou art gone up, but shalt surely die. And Elijah departed. 5 And when the messengers turned back unto him, he said unto them, Why are ye now turned back? 6 And they said unto him, There came a man up to meet us, and said unto us, Go, turn again unto the king that sent you, and say unto him, Thus saith the LORD, *Is it* not	• For consulting a false god 3) Elijah pronounced God's judgment upon the king: Death e. The messengers' quick return to King Ahaziah 1) The king questioned why they had returned 2) The messengers reported the whole episode of the prophet's confrontation • Elijah's condemnation of the king

OUTLINE	SCRIPTURE	SCRIPTURE	OUTLINE
• Elijah's pronouncement of judgment upon the king	because *there is* not a God in Israel, *that* thou sendest to enquire of Baal-zebub the god of Ekron? therefore thou shalt not come down from that bed on which thou art gone up, but shalt surely die.	What manner of man *was he* which came up to meet you, and told you these words?	man was, what he looked like
		8 And they answered him, *He was* an hairy man, and girt with a girdle of leather about his loins. And he said, It *is* Elijah the Tishbite.	4) The messengers described the prophet's appearance
3) The king asked who the	7 And he said unto them,		5) The king then knew it was Elijah who had made the stern prediction of judgment

a. Immediately after being crowned king, Ahaziah was confronted with a revolt by the nation Moab (v.1; 3:1-27). The Moabites were the descendants of Lot's grandson Moab. They occupied the land just south of the East Jordan tribes of Israel where the Jordan River runs into the Dead Sea (Ge.19:30-38). Years before David had conquered the Moabite nation and required the people to pay tribute or taxation (2 S.8:2). But most likely, when the northern tribes revolted from Judah, Jeroboam their king subjected the Moabites under the political rule of the Northern Kingdom.[1]

Now hearing of Ahab's death, Misha, King of Moab, knew that Israel would be politically weakened. He knew that this would be an opportune time to revolt against Ahab's son. At last he could throw off the oppression and taxation imposed upon his people by the Northern Kingdom. Just how serious a problem the revolt was is discussed in detail in chapter three. Here it is mentioned only briefly to show that Ahaziah was confronted with two major problems right after being inaugurated as the new king of Israel.

b. But far more serious than the revolt of Moab, Ahaziah suffered severe injuries in an unusual accident (v.2). He fell through the lattice framework of an upper room at his palace in Samaria, severely injuring himself. In those days the upper stories of palaces and large houses had balconies that were enclosed with wood railings or some form of lattice work. This allowed the flow of air, just as the balconies and decks of modern housing do. Obviously, the king leaned against the wood railing, and due to faulty construction or deterioration, the railing broke. He fell to the ground below suffering very serious internal injuries.

c. Knowing the seriousness of his injuries, the king did what most people do: he began to seek the help of his god. Remember, Ahaziah was the son of Ahab and Jezebel who were worshipers of false gods, in particular the false god Baal. Following in the footsteps of his parents, Ahaziah sent messengers to the false god Baal-Zebub. This false god's major temple was located in Ekron, a Philistine city only about forty miles away. Note that Ahaziah was so seriously injured he was not himself able to travel. He had to send messengers to seek encouragement and healing and to find out if he would recover from the injury. Deceiving himself, Ahaziah was putting his trust and faith in a false god, a mere creation of man's mind that could offer no help and no hope to the king.

d. But this is not true with the LORD (Jehovah, Yahweh). He is the living and true God, the One who holds the power of life and death in the palm of His hand. Thus, He is the One who should be sought for healing. To teach this lesson, the LORD sent Elijah to intercept the messengers (vv.3-4). Following the instructions of the LORD, Elijah caught up with the messengers shortly after they had left the city of Samaria. Standing face-to-face with the royal messengers, Elijah condemned the king for turning away from the living LORD and for seeking the help of a false god. Then he pronounced God's inevitable judgment upon sin: death. The king would not recover. Because he had rejected the LORD, he would surely die.

e. Not knowing that the man standing before them was Elijah, but being fully aware that he was a prophet, the royal delegation quickly returned to King Ahaziah (vv.5-8). Surprising the king by their quick return from what should have been a long journey, the king immediately questioned why they had returned and not completed their journey. No doubt somewhat fearful, the royal messengers reported the whole episode of the prophet's confrontation with them. They related that the prophet had condemned the king for rejecting the LORD and for seeking the help of the false god of the Philistines. Consequently, the king would die.

Somewhat stunned, the king asked who the man was and what he looked like (v.7). When hearing that the prophet was a hairy man and that he wore a leather belt around his waist, the king immediately knew that it was Elijah. The LORD had sent the stern prediction of judgment through Elijah the prophet. How did he know? Because Elijah had often confronted Ahaziah's parents, Ahab and Jezebel (1 K.17:1-21:29). Obviously, growing up as a child in the royal court of his father, Ahaziah had seen and heard the rugged prophet condemn his father and mother for their wickedness and false worship.

Thought 1. A person who rejects the LORD and turns to a false god is foolish. This person makes the most grievous error in all of life, for no false god is living. False gods are made or created by people. They are nothing more than a figment of people's imaginations. Possessing no life, ability, power, or knowledge, false gods are unable to meet any needs. They are nothing more than pieces of wood or metal or stone or some other element that has been formed by the hands of men. People imagine who God is and what God is like, and they worship their own ideas.

The result is tragic, for when people need help, their false gods are powerless to help them in their hour of need. Their false gods have no life or consciousness or power to help.

But this is not true with the living LORD (Jehovah, Yahweh). God loves the world; therefore, He has revealed Himself to us. Although man cannot penetrate the spiritual world to discover God, God has revealed Himself to the human race. For God so loved the world that He sent His Son *into the world* to reveal the truth of Himself to us. God loves us so much that He would never leave us in the dark, grasping and groping around to find our way through life, never knowing whether or not He truly lives. Because of His love, He has revealed the truth to us through the coming of the Lord Jesus Christ into the world. And one of the great truths Christ teaches is just this: He is the living and true God, the only God who can help us and meet our needs.

---

[1] *The NIV Study Bible, New International Version.* (Grand Rapids, MI: Zondervan Publishing House, 1985), 1:1.

This was the tragic error of Ahaziah: rejecting the Lord God and turning to a false god for help. Likewise, when we need help, if we reject the Lord and turn to a false god, there will be no help. For only the Lord is living. Only the Lord has the power and ability to help us. No matter what the crisis, He wants to help us, whether coping with a serious accident and internal injuries such as Ahaziah faced or the needs brought about by such problems as…
- disease
- financial difficulty
- unemployment
- emotional instability
- the death of a loved one
- enslavement to some sin
- constant temptation

Whatever the need, God loves us and will meet our needs. This is one of the great truths shown to us by the Lord Jesus Christ. He is the living Lord who can help us in our time of desperate need.

"And saying, Sirs, why do ye these things? We also are men of like passions with you, and preach unto you that ye should turn from these vanities unto the living God, which made heaven, and earth, and the sea, and all things that are therein" (Ac.14:15).

"For they themselves show of us what manner of entering in we had unto you, and how ye turned to God from idols to serve the living and true God; And to wait for his Son from heaven, whom he raised from the dead, *even* Jesus, which delivered us from the wrath to come" (1 Th.1:9-10).

"Forasmuch then as the children are partakers of flesh and blood, he also himself likewise took part of the same; that through death he might destroy him that had the power of death, that is, the devil; And deliver them who through fear of death were all their lifetime subject to bondage. For verily he took not on *him the nature of* angels; but he took on *him* the seed of Abraham. Wherefore in all things it behooved him to be made like unto *his* brethren, that he might be a merciful and faithful high priest in things *pertaining* to God, to make reconciliation for the sins of the people. For in that he himself hath suffered being tempted, he is able to succour them that are tempted" (He.2:14-18).

"For we have not an high priest which cannot be touched with the feeling of our infirmities; but was in all points tempted like as *we are, yet* without sin. Let us therefore come boldly unto the throne of grace, that we may obtain mercy, and find grace to help in time of need" (He.4:15-16).

"When I consider thy heavens, the work of thy fingers, the moon and the stars, which thou hast ordained; What is man, that thou art mindful of him? and the son of man, that thou visitest him?" (Ps.8:3-4).

"My soul thirsteth for God, for the living God: when shall I come and appear before God?" (Ps.42:2).

"Because I have called, and ye refused; I have stretched out my hand, and no man regarded; But ye have set at nought all my counsel, and would none of my reproof: I also will laugh at your calamity; I will mock when your fear cometh; When your fear cometh as desolation, and your destruction cometh as a whirlwind; when distress and anguish cometh upon you. Then shall they call upon me, but I will not answer; they shall seek me early, but they shall not find me: For that they hated knowledge, and did not choose the fear of the Lord: They would none of my counsel: they despised all my reproof. Therefore shall they eat of the fruit of their own way, and be filled with their own devices" (Pr.1:24-31).

2 (1:9-15) **Protection, of God—God, Protection of—Elijah, Miracles of—Miracles, of Elijah—Ahaziah, Sins of, Attempted to Arrest Elijah**: Ahaziah became enraged at Elijah's stern condemnation and began his efforts to arrest the prophet. He should have repented at Elijah's stern rebuke. But instead he stubbornly reacted, launching three different attempts to arrest and execute God's prophet. This is a clear picture of God's power to protect His dear servant:

OUTLINE	SCRIPTURE	SCRIPTURE	OUTLINE
2. The king's enraged attempts to arrest Elijah: God's protection of His servant	9 Then the king sent unto him a captain of fifty with his fifty. And he went up to him: and, behold, he sat on the top of an hill. And he spake unto him, Thou man of God, the king hath said, Come down.	him another captain of fifty with his fifty. And he answered and said unto him, O man of God, thus hath the king said, Come down quickly.	captain & 50 soldiers 1) Insisted Elijah surrender to the king
a. The first attempt by a captain & 50 soldiers 1) They demanded Elijah surrender to the king			
2) Elijah called out for God's protection: For fire to consume the threatening soldiers 3) God answered Elijah's prayer	10 And Elijah answered and said to the captain of fifty, If I *be* a man of God, then let fire come down from heaven, and consume thee and thy fifty. And there came down fire from heaven, and consumed him and his fifty.	12 And Elijah answered and said unto them, If I *be* a man of God, let fire come down from heaven, and consume thee and thy fifty. And the fire of God came down from heaven, and consumed him and his fifty.	2) Elijah again called out for God's protection: For fire to consume the threatening soldiers 3) God again answered Elijah's prayer
b. The second attempt by a	11 Again also he sent unto	13 And he sent again a captain of the third fifty with his fifty. And the third captain of	c. The third attempt by a captain & 50 soldiers

OUTLINE	SCRIPTURE	SCRIPTURE	OUTLINE
1) The captain acknowledged the supreme authority of Elijah's LORD • Fell to his knees & showed humility • Asked Elijah to spare their lives 1) Acknowledged that the consuming fire had	fifty went up, and came and fell on his knees before Elijah, and besought him, and said unto him, O man of God, I pray thee, let my life, and the life of these fifty thy servants, be precious in thy sight. 14 Behold, there came fire down from heaven, and burnt	up the two captains of the former fifties with their fifties: therefore let my life now be precious in thy sight. 15 And the angel of the LORD said unto Elijah, Go down with him: be not afraid of him. And he arose, and went down with him unto the king.	come from heaven, from Elijah's God • Begged for his life 2) The LORD gave Elijah two instructions • To go with the captain • Not to fear the captain 3) Elijah obeyed the LORD

a. In his first attempt to arrest Elijah, the king sent a captain and a force of fifty crack soldiers (vv.9-10). Sending such a large band of soldiers shows just how much contempt Ahaziah held for Elijah. No doubt in the king's mind, Elijah was a criminal who stood opposed to the throne; consequently, the prophet was to be arrested by *force* and drug back to the palace to be sentenced and put to death.

When the troops found Elijah, he was sitting on the top of a hill. Confronting him, they addressed him as "man of God" and demanded that he surrender to the king. Courageously and sternly, Elijah called out for God's protection. Obviously sensing the movement of God's spirit in his heart, he called for fire to come down from heaven to consume the threatening soldiers. And God answered his prayer, protecting His dear servant. Suddenly fire fell from heaven and consumed the fifty soldiers and their captain.

b. When the troops failed to return, the king sent out another captain with his detachment of fifty crack soldiers to find out what had happened (vv.11-12). As this officer approached Elijah, he was no doubt wondering what had happened to the other troops. For that reason, when he confronted Elijah, he insisted that the prophet surrender to the king *at once*. But just as before, Elijah cried out for God's protection. And a second time fire fell from heaven and consumed the threatening regiment. God again answered the prayer of His servant.

c. When the time had long passed for some of the troops to return, the king sent out a third captain with his fifty crack soldiers (vv.13-15). As this captain approached Elijah, he perhaps saw a huge black area of scorched earth. Whatever the case, something made him approach Elijah carefully. Humbly, he fell to his knees and begged Elijah to spare his life and the lives of his men. At that point, the angel of the LORD spoke to Elijah's heart and gave him two instructions: he was to go with the soldiers, and he was not to fear them nor the king. Obediently, Elijah allowed the soldiers to arrest him and take him to the king.

Thought 1. God protected His dear servant from the threat of the king. So it is with us. If we truly follow and trust God, He will protect us also. But like Elijah, we must boldly approach God, asking great things of Him and acknowledging His mighty power. No matter what may threaten us, the protective hand of God will look after us and take care of us. God loves us; therefore, whatever happens to us concerns God. It may be some person who threatens us, or an accident, disease, or terrible loss. But no matter what the trial or temptation, the hardship or misfortune, God cares. And God will protect us, looking after and taking care of the threat against us. This is the clear teaching of God's Holy Word:

"**But there shall not an hair of your head perish**" (Lu.21:18).

"**There hath no temptation taken you but such as is common to man: but God is faithful, who will not suffer you to be tempted above that ye are able; but will with the temptation also make a way to escape, that ye may be able to bear it**" (1 Co.10:13).

"**For the which cause I also suffer these things: nevertheless I am not ashamed: for I know whom I have believed, and am persuaded that he is able to keep that which I have committed unto him against that day**" (2 Ti.1:12).

"**And the Lord shall deliver me from every evil work, and will preserve me unto his heavenly kingdom: to whom be glory for ever and ever. Amen**" (2 Ti.4:18).

"**So that we may boldly say, The Lord is my helper, and I will not fear what man shall do unto me**" (He.13:6).

"**Who are kept by the power of God through faith unto salvation ready to be revealed in the last time**" (1 Pe.1:5).

"**The eternal God *is thy* refuge, and underneath *are* the everlasting arms: and he shall thrust out the enemy from before thee**" (De.33:27).

"**For the eyes of the LORD run to and fro throughout the whole earth, to show himself strong in the behalf of *them* whose heart *is* perfect toward him. Herein thou hast done foolishly: therefore from henceforth thou shalt have wars**" (2 Chr.16:9).

"**For in the time of trouble he shall hide me in his pavilion: in the secret of his tabernacle shall he hide me; he shall set me up upon a rock**" (Ps.27:5).

"**Thou shalt hide them in the secret of thy presence from the pride of man: thou shalt keep them secretly in a pavilion from the strife of tongues**" (Ps.31:20).

"**Thou *art* my hiding place; thou shalt preserve me from trouble; thou shalt compass me about with songs of deliverance. Selah**" (Ps.32:7).

"**The angel of the LORD encampeth round about them that fear him, and delivereth them**" (Ps.34:7).

"I waited patiently for the LORD; and he inclined unto me, and heard my cry. He brought me up also out of an horrible pit, out of the miry clay, and set my feet upon a rock, and established my goings. And he hath put a new song in my mouth, even praise unto our God: many shall see it, and fear, and shall trust in the LORD" (Ps.40:1-3).

"God is our refuge and strength, a very present help in trouble" (Ps.46:1).

"Be thou my strong habitation, whereunto I may continually resort: thou hast given commandment to save me; for thou *art* my rock and my fortress" (Ps.71:3).

"He shall cover thee with his feathers, and under his wings shalt thou trust: his truth *shall be thy* shield and buckler" (Ps.91:4).

"Thou *art* my hiding place and my shield: I hope in thy word" (Ps.119:114).

"As the mountains *are* round about Jerusalem, so the LORD *is* round about his people from henceforth even for ever" (Ps.125:2).

"Deliver me, O LORD, from mine enemies: I flee unto thee to hide me" (Ps.143:9).

"In the fear of the LORD *is* strong confidence: and his children shall have a place of refuge" (Pr.14:26).

"The name of the LORD *is* a strong tower: the righteous runneth into it, and is safe" (Pr.18:10).

"For thou hast been a strength to the poor, a strength to the needy in his distress, a refuge from the storm, a shadow from the heat, when the blast of the terrible ones *is* as a storm *against* the wall" (Is.25:4).

---

3 (1:16-18) **Judgment, Cause of—Sin, Penalty of—Ahaziah, Death of**: as soon as Elijah was escorted before the bed-ridden king, he shared the message from the LORD. The king stood condemned for having turned away from the living LORD and for seeking help from a false god. Consequently, the king was never to leave his bed. He would surely die (v.16).

OUTLINE	SCRIPTURE	SCRIPTURE	OUTLINE
3. The king's death: Judgment due to sin	16 And he said unto him, Thus saith the LORD, Forasmuch as thou hast sent messengers to enquire of *is it* Baal-zebub the god of Ekron, not because *there is* no God in Israel to enquire of his word? therefore thou shalt not come down off that bed on which thou art gone up, but shalt surely die.	the word of the LORD which Elijah had spoken. And Jehoram reigned in his stead in the second year of Jehoram the son of Jehoshaphat king of Judah; because he had no son.	predicted by Elijah
a. The confrontation between Elijah & the king			c. The king's successor: Joram (Jehoram), his brother
1) Elijah condemned the king			
• For turning away from the living LORD			
• For consulting a false god			
2) Elijah pronounced God's judgment: Death		18 Now the rest of the acts of Ahaziah which he did, *are* they not written in the book of the chronicles of the kings of Israel?	d. The king's achievements: Recorded in the book *The History of the Kings of Israel*
b. The king's death: Just as	17 So he died according to		

Just as Elijah prophesied, the king soon died (v.17). And because he had no son, his brother Joram or Jehoram succeeded him as king. A complete record of Ahaziah's brief two-year reign was recorded in the book *The History of the Kings of Israel* (v.18).

Thought 1. Judgment is due to sin. Or to state the truth another way, sin causes death. The penalty of sin is death. But when God created us, He never intended us to die. Keep in mind what death means. When the Bible speaks of death, it means not only physical death, but also spiritual and eternal death. The root meaning of death is *separation*. Because of sin, we are *spiritually separated* from God, dead to God. A person who is living a life of selfishness and sin is not focused upon God. He is focused upon himself and his sin. He is dead to God and alive to himself and whatever sinful obsessions he has. He is living for this world, focused upon the things of this world, dead to God and separated from God. This is what *spiritual death* means. Many people who are walking upon this earth are *spiritually dead*, separated from God.

But as earlier stated, spiritual death is not the only death caused by sin. So is physical death. Sin makes us unholy, unrighteous, imperfect. Consequently, we can never—not on our own—live in God's presence. We can never be allowed into heaven, for God is holy, righteous, and perfect. If He allowed a sinful, wicked person to live in heaven, then heaven would become contaminated. It would no longer be perfect. This is the reason for God's judgment of *physical death* and of *eternal death*. If we choose not to worship and serve God throughout this life, choose to be separated from Him, then we will continue to be separated from Him throughout all eternity. As we walk throughout life, we either choose to walk with God or without God. What we choose determines where we will live. If we choose to walk with God, we will be with God. But if we choose to walk without God, then we have made our choice. We will not be with God. If we choose to walk in death, that is, to walk separated from God, then we will die eternally. That is, we will live without God forever and ever. Just as Ahaziah chose to walk without God and bore the judgment of God, the judgment of death, so we will bear the judgment of death, for the penalty of sin is death.

"Wherefore, as by one man sin entered into the world, and death by sin; and so death passed upon all men, for that all have sinned" (Ro.5:12).

"For the wages of sin *is* death; but the gift of God *is* eternal life through Jesus Christ our Lord" (Ro.6:23)

"For to be carnally minded *is* death; but to be spiritually minded *is* life and peace" (Ro.8:6).

"Now the works of the flesh are manifest, which are *these;* Adultery, fornication, uncleanness, lasciviousness, Idolatry, witchcraft, hatred, variance, emulations, wrath, strife, seditions, heresies, Envyings, murders, drunkenness, revellings, and such like: of the which I tell you before, as I have also told *you* in time past, that they which do such things shall not inherit the kingdom of God" (Ga.5:19-21).

"Be not deceived; God is not mocked: for whatsoever a man soweth, that shall he also reap. For he that soweth to his flesh shall of the flesh reap corruption; but he that soweth to the Spirit shall of the Spirit reap life everlasting" (Ga.6:7-8).

"And you *hath he quickened,* who were dead in trespasses and sins" (Ep.2:1).

"Wherefore he saith, Awake thou that sleepest, and arise from the dead, and Christ shall give thee light" (Ep.5:14).

"And you, being dead in your sins and the uncircumcision of your flesh, hath he quickened together with him, having forgiven you all trespasses" (Col.2:13).

"But she that liveth in pleasure is dead while she liveth" (1 Ti.5:6).

"For if the word spoken by angels was stedfast, and every transgression and disobedience received a just recompence of reward; How shall we escape, if we neglect so great salvation; which at the first began to be spoken by the Lord, and was confirmed unto us by them that heard *him*" (He.2:2-3).

"Then when lust hath conceived, it bringeth forth sin: and sin, when it is finished, bringeth forth death" (Js.1:15).

"And unto the angel of the church in Sardis write; These things saith he that hath the seven Spirits of God, and the seven stars; I know thy works, that thou hast a name that thou livest, and art dead" (Re.3:1).

"But the fearful, and unbelieving, and the abominable, and murderers, and whoremongers, and sorcerers, and idolaters, and all liars, shall have their part in the lake which burneth with fire and brimstone: which is the second death" (Re.21:8).

"But of the tree of the knowledge of good and evil, thou shalt not eat of it: for in the day that thou eatest thereof thou shalt surely die" (Ge.2:17).

"If I regard iniquity in my heart, the Lord will not hear *me*" (Ps.66:18).

"As righteousness *tendeth* to life: so he that pursueth evil *pursueth it* to his own death" (Pr.11:19).

"He, that being often reproved hardeneth *his* neck, shall suddenly be destroyed, and that without remedy" (Pr.29:1).

"But your iniquities have separated between you and your God, and your sins have hid *his* face from you, that he will not hear" (Is.59:2).

"And *there is* none that calleth upon thy name, that stirreth up himself to take hold of thee: for thou hast hid thy face from us, and hast consumed us, because of our iniquities" (Is.64:7).

"Behold, all souls are mine; as the soul of the father, so also the soul of the son is mine: the soul that sinneth, it shall die" (Eze.18:4).

"The soul that sinneth, it shall die. The son shall not bear the iniquity of the father, neither shall the father bear the iniquity of the son: the righteousness of the righteous shall be upon him, and the wickedness of the wicked shall be upon him" (Eze.18:20).

Thought 2. Russell Dilday, who was at one time president of Southwestern Baptist Theological Seminary in Fort Worth, Texas, gives an application on Ahaziah's sin that is well worth quoting:

> *One reason so many in contemporary society are miserable is that they have repeated Ahaziah's worst mistake: seeking help in the wrong place. They are searching for strength, fulfillment, and comfort in the wrong places. Some look for help in chemical reinforcement, mistakenly assuming that a prescription, a pill, a bottle, or an injection can provide life's missing ingredient. The worldwide epidemic of heroin and cocaine addiction has shocked us. Alcoholism continues to take its toll in traffic deaths and broken homes. These are painful reminders that the remedy for personal emptiness is not a chemical substance.*
>
> *A popular black preacher in America warns his congregation from time to time: "Some of you think you can drown your troubles in drink. But I want to remind you, 'Troubles can swim!'" Those who seek help in drugs are, like Ahaziah, looking in the wrong place.*
>
> *Paul pointed to the only source that can fill man's emptiness. He said that God is the "God of all comfort" (2 Cor. 1:3). Genuine comfort comes only through faith in God. It cannot be found anywhere else. Ahaziah failed to understand this basic truth.*[2]

---

2 Russell Dilday. *The Preacher's Commentary on 1, 2 Kings.* (Nashville, TN: Word Publishing, 1987, 2003), p.262.

CHAPTER 2

B. The Ascension of Elijah & the Transfer of His Ministry to Elisha: A Picture of Total Commitment to God & of God's Power, 2:1-25

1. Elijah's last day on earth & his ascension into heaven: A lesson on commitment to service
a. Elijah tested Elisha, sought to confirm & strengthen his commitment to God's call
   1) Elijah suggested that Elisha stay behind in Gilgal while he visited the school in Bethel
   2) Elisha refused to stay: Insisted he continue his service to Elijah
b. Elijah spent some final moments of exhortation with the young prophets at Bethel
   1) They were aware of Elijah's imminent departure
   2) Elisha, also aware, instructed them to say nothing
c. Elijah tested Elisha a second time, seeking to strengthen his commitment to God's call even more: Again, Elisha proved his commitment by accompanying Elijah to Jericho
d. Elijah spent some final moments of exhortation with the young prophets at Jericho
   1) They, too, were aware of Elijah's imminent departure
   2) Elisha instructed them to keep silent
e. Elijah tested Elisha a third time, seeking to use every opportunity to strengthen his commitment: Elisha proved that his commitment was strong by remaining with his tutor
f. Elijah sought to spend his final moments alone with his chosen disciple: To reinforce God's power upon his mind
   1) Fifty prophets followed from a distance
   2) Elijah rolled up his cloak & struck the water of the Jordan River: The waters divided & the two prophets crossed over on dry ground
g. Elijah wanted to meet whatever final need Elisha felt

And it came to pass, when the LORD would take up Elijah into heaven by a whirlwind, that Elijah went with Elisha from Gilgal. 2 And Elijah said unto Elisha, Tarry here, I pray thee; for the LORD hath sent me to Bethel. And Elisha said *unto him, As* the LORD liveth, and as thy soul liveth, I will not leave thee. So they went down to Bethel. 3 And the sons of the prophets that *were* at Bethel came forth to Elisha, and said unto him, Knowest thou that the LORD will take away thy master from thy head to day? And he said, Yea, I know *it;* hold ye your peace. 4 And Elijah said unto him, Elisha, tarry here, I pray thee; for the LORD hath sent me to Jericho. And he said, *As* the LORD liveth, and *as* thy soul liveth, I will not leave thee. So they came to Jericho. 5 And the sons of the prophets that *were* at Jericho came to Elisha, and said unto him, Knowest thou that the LORD will take away thy master from thy head to day? And he answered, Yea, I know *it;* hold ye your peace. 6 And Elijah said unto him, Tarry, I pray thee, here; for the LORD hath sent me to Jordan. And he said, *As* the LORD liveth, and *as* thy soul liveth, I will not leave thee. And they two went on. 7 And fifty men of the sons of the prophets went, and stood to view afar off: and they two stood by Jordan. 8 And Elijah took his mantle, and wrapped *it* together, and smote the waters, and they were divided hither and thither, so that they two went over on dry ground. 9 And it came to pass, when Elijah said to Elisha, "Tell me

what can I do for you before I am taken from you?" "Let me inherit a double portion of your spirit," Elisha replied. 10 And he said, Thou hast asked a hard thing: *nevertheless,* if thou see me *when I am* taken from thee, it shall be so unto thee; but if not, it shall not be so. 11 And it came to pass, as they still went on, and talked, that, behold, *there appeared* a chariot of fire, and horses of fire, and parted them both asunder; and Elijah went up by a whirlwind into heaven. 12 And Elisha saw *it,* and he cried, My father, my father, the chariot of Israel, and the horsemen thereof. And he saw him no more: and he took hold of his own clothes, and rent them in two pieces. 13 He took up also the mantle of Elijah that fell from him, and went back, and stood by the bank of Jordan; 14 And he took the mantle of Elijah that fell from him, and smote the waters, and said, Where *is* the LORD God of Elijah? and when he also had smitten the waters, they parted hither and thither: and Elisha went over. 15 And when the sons of the prophets which *were* to view at Jericho saw him, they said, The spirit of Elijah doth rest on Elisha. And they came to meet him, and bowed themselves to the ground before him. 16 And they said unto him, Behold now, there be with thy servants fifty strong men; let them go, we pray thee, and seek thy master: lest peradventure the Spirit of the LORD hath taken him up, and cast him upon some mountain, or into some valley. And he said, Ye shall not send. 17 And when they urged him till he was ashamed, he said, Send. They sent therefore fifty men; and they sought three days, but found him not. 18 And when they came again to him, (for he tarried at Jericho,) he said unto them, Did I not say unto you,

he had

   1) Elisha asked for a double portion of Elijah's spirit
   2) Elijah's response: His disciple's request would be granted if he witnessed the LORD's taking him

h. Elijah was transported into heaven
   1) The event: Elijah was transported in a chariot of fire pulled by horses of fire while he & Elisha walked along together
   2) The impact upon Elisha
      • Cried out a tribute to Elijah, his spiritual father & Israel's protector
      • Expressed sorrow: Tore his clothes

2. Elisha's call to replace Elijah proven: A picture of God's power
a. Proof 1—Elisha picked up Elijah's fallen cloak: A symbol of God's equipping His servant
b. Proof 2—dividing the Jordan River: God's power to guide His servant
   1) Elisha took the cloak & struck the Jordan River
      • He cried out to the LORD
      • The LORD divided the water
   2) The fifty prophets from Jericho witnessed the miracle
      • Acknowledged Elisha's call to replace Elijah
      • Bowed in respect: Accepted Elisha's leadership
c. Proof 3—verifying Elisha's word: God's power to give His servant spiritual knowledge & insight
   1) The prophets insisted on looking for Elijah
      • Elisha protested & refused their request

      • The prophets repeatedly insisted until Elisha gave in to their request
      • The fifty prophets failed to find Elijah after a three-day search
   2) The word & spiritual knowledge of God's servant was proven, verified

OUTLINE	SCRIPTURE	SCRIPTURE	OUTLINE
d. Proof 4—purifying the contaminated water of Jericho: God's power to provide the basic needs of life 1) The bad water problem was presented to Elisha 2) The prophet requested a new bowl with salt in it 3) The prophet went to the spring & threw the salt into the water 4) The prophet declared the LORD's miraculous power • He had purified the bad water • He had purified the wa-	Go not? 19 And the men of the city said unto Elisha, Behold, I pray thee, the situation of this city *is* pleasant, as my lord seeth: but the water *is* naught, and the ground barren. 20 And he said, Bring me a new cruse, and put salt therein. And they bring *it* to him. 21 And he went forth unto the spring of the waters, and cast the salt in there, and said, Thus saith the LORD, I have healed these waters; there shall not be from thence any more death or barren *land.* 22 So the waters were healed	unto this day, according to the saying of Elisha which he spake 23And he went up from thence unto Bethel: and as he was going up by the way, there came forth little children out of the city, and mocked him, and said unto him, Go up, thou bald head; go up, thou bald head. 24 And he turned back, and looked on them, and cursed them in the name of the LORD. And there came forth two she bears out of the wood, and tare forty and two children of them. 25 And he went from thence to mount Carmel, and from thence he returned to Samaria.	ter permanently, up to the time of writing Second Kings e. Proof 5—pronouncing judgment upon a large, threatening gang of hoodlums: God's power to protect & deliver His servant 1) The gang mocked, threatened Elisha the prophet 2) The prophet cursed them in the name of the LORD (Le.26:21-22; 2 Chr. 36:16) 3) The hoodlums—42 of them—were mauled by two bears 4) The prophet traveled safely home to Mt. Carmel then to Samaria (4:23; 5:3)

DIVISION I

THE FINAL DAYS OF ELIJAH'S MINISTRY: A FAITHFUL SERVANT WHO PERSEVERED TO THE VERY END, 1:1–3:27

B. The Ascension of Elijah and the Transfer of His Ministry to Elisha: A Picture of Total Commitment to God and of God's Power, 2:1-25

(2:1-25) **Introduction—Crises, How to Conquer—Circumstances, Bad, Listed—Desperation, Experiences of, Listed**: bad circumstances are faced by every one of us. Sometimes a bad circumstance becomes a severe crisis, even life threatening. Just think of the severe accidents some of us have experienced and others of us have barely escaped. Think of the threatening diseases, the periods of economic slump and unemployment and financial crisis that so many of us experience. And think of broken relationships within marriages and families and among business partners. Finally think of death, the loss of a child or spouse or loved one or friend. During these bad circumstances and severe crisis of life, we often feel helpless and hopeless. No matter who we are—how much knowledge or authority we have—there is an inability to handle the situation. There are severe crises that no person can prevent or stop.

In such times, the power of God is needed, and the wonderful news is that God's power is available to us. If we will turn to God, trusting and calling upon Him, He promises to help us through any bad circumstance. This is the wonderful message of this passage. It is a demonstration of God's power that is exercised in behalf of those who are totally committed to Him.

For over twenty years the great prophet Elijah had been ministering to the nation Israel. Now the close of his ministry had arrived, and he knew it. The LORD had revealed to Elijah that he was to depart this earth. And the very day of his departure had arrived. This was to be the last day of Elijah's life upon earth. He was confronted with the question that would grip any of us who knew it was our last day: What was he to do? How was he to spend the last hours of his life? This is the gripping subject of the present passage of Scripture: *The Ascension of Elijah and the Transfer of His Ministry to Elisha: A Picture of Total Commitment to God and of God's Power, 2:1-25.*

1. Elijah's last day on earth and his ascension into heaven: a lesson on commitment to service (vv.1-12).
2. Elisha's call to replace Elijah proven: a picture of God's power (vv.13-25).

1 (2:1-12) **Service, Commitment to—Commitment, to Ministry—Ascension, of Elijah—Elijah, Last Day on Earth—Prophets, Schools of—Elisha, Commitment of**: Elijah's last day on earth and his ascension into heaven is one of the most astounding and dramatic stories in all of Scripture. Scripture immediately says that Elijah was to leave this earth, and he was to leave it in a spectacular fashion. He was not to experience death; instead, he was to be dramatically swept up alive into heaven by a whirlwind.

OUTLINE	SCRIPTURE	SCRIPTURE	OUTLINE
1. **Elijah's last day on earth & his ascension into heaven: A lesson on commitment to service** a. Elijah tested Elisha, sought to confirm & strengthen his	And it came to pass, when the LORD would take up Elijah into heaven by a whirlwind, that Elijah went with Elisha from Gilgal.	2 And Elijah said unto Elisha, Tarry here, I pray thee; for the LORD hath sent me to Bethel. And Elisha said *unto him, As* the LORD liveth, and	commitment to God's call 1) Elijah suggested that Elisha stay behind in Gilgal while he visited the school in Bethel

OUTLINE	SCRIPTURE	SCRIPTURE	OUTLINE
2) Elisha refused to stay: Insisted he continue his service to Elijah b. Elijah spent some final moments of exhortation with the young prophets at Bethel 1) They were aware of Elijah's imminent departure 2) Elisha, also aware, instructed them to say nothing c. Elijah tested Elisha a second time, seeking to strengthen his commitment to God's call even more: Again, Elisha proved his commitment by accompanying Elijah to Jericho d. Elijah spent some final moments of exhortation with the young prophets at Jericho 1) They, too, were aware of Elijah's imminent departure 2) Elisha instructed them to keep silent e. Elijah tested Elisha a third time, seeking to use every opportunity to strengthen his commitment: Elisha proved that his commitment was strong by remaining with his tutor f. Elijah sought to spend his final moments alone with his chosen disciple: To reinforce	as thy soul liveth, I will not leave thee. So they went down to Bethel. 3 And the sons of the prophets that *were* at Bethel came forth to Elisha, and said unto him, Knowest thou that the LORD will take away thy master from thy head to day? And he said, Yea, I know *it;* hold ye your peace. 4 And Elijah said unto him, Elisha, tarry here, I pray thee; for the LORD hath sent me to Jericho. And he said, *As* the LORD liveth, and *as* thy soul liveth, I will not leave thee. So they came to Jericho. 5 And the sons of the prophets that *were* at Jericho came to Elisha, and said unto him, Knowest thou that the LORD will take away thy master from thy head to day? And he answered, Yea, I know *it;* hold ye your peace. 6 And Elijah said unto him, Tarry, I pray thee, here; for the LORD hath sent me to Jordan. And he said, *As* the LORD liveth, and *as* thy soul liveth, I will not leave thee. And they two went on. 7 And fifty men of the sons of the prophets went, and stood to view afar off:	and they two stood by Jordan. 8 And Elijah took his mantle, and wrapped *it* together, and smote the waters, and they were divided hither and thither, so that they two went over on dry ground. 9 And it came to pass, when Elijah said to Elisha, "Tell me what can I do for you before I am taken from you?" "Let me inherit a double portion of your spirit," Elisha replied. 10 And he said, Thou hast asked a hard thing: *nevertheless,* if thou see me *when I am* taken from thee, it shall be so unto thee; but if not, it shall not be so. 11 And it came to pass, as they still went on, and talked, that, behold, *there appeared* a chariot of fire, and horses of fire, and parted them both asunder; and Elijah went up by a whirlwind into heaven. 12 And Elisha saw *it,* and he cried, My father, my father, the chariot of Israel, and the horsemen thereof. And he saw him no more: and he took hold of his own clothes, and rent them in two pieces.	God's power upon his mind 1) Fifty prophets followed from a distance 2) Elijah rolled up his cloak & struck the water of the Jordan River: The waters divided & the two prophets crossed over on dry ground g. Elijah wanted to meet whatever final need Elisha felt he had 1) Elisha asked for a double portion of Elijah's spirit 2) Elijah's response: His disciple's request would be granted if he witnessed the LORD's taking him h. Elijah was transported into heaven 1) The event: Elijah was transported in a chariot of fire pulled by horses of fire while he & Elisha walked along together 2) The impact upon Elisha • Cried out a tribute to Elijah, his spiritual father & Israel's protector • Expressed sorrow: Tore his clothes

a. Knowing this was to be his last day upon earth, Elijah wanted to confirm and strengthen the faith of his young disciple Elisha (vv.1-2). The burden of his ministry was soon to be upon the shoulders of Elisha. Thus Elijah wanted to do everything he could to strengthen the commitment of Elisha. This he did by testing the young disciple's sense of God's call upon his life. He suggested that Elisha stay behind in Gilgal while he personally visited the school of prophets in Bethel. But Elisha knew beyond doubt that he was to replace Elijah, so he refused to stay behind. He insisted that he be allowed to continue the trip and continue to serve the aged prophet.

Somehow, Elisha and the student prophets knew that the departure of Elijah was near at hand (vv.3-7). Most likely, Elijah had earlier shared that his departure was to be soon or else the LORD had revealed the fact to Elisha and the other prophets. Whatever the case, the young disciple Elisha had a deep sense that he was chosen by God to succeeded Elijah, so he wanted to be with his master to the very end.

b. On his final day upon earth, Elijah also wanted to spend some final moments of exhortation with the young prophets at Bethel (v.3). As stated, somehow they knew that Elijah's departure was to be this particular day. Approaching Elisha, the prophets asked him if he was aware of the fact. He acknowledged his awareness, but instructed them to say absolutely nothing about it. They must not bring up the subject. Just why Elisha gave these instructions is not stated.

c. Note that Elijah tested his young disciple's sense of call a second time. He suggested that Elisha stay behind at Bethel while he personally traveled on to Jericho (v.4). Once again he was seeking to strengthen the commitment of Elisha. But the young disciple again proved his commitment by accompanying Elijah to Jericho.

d. Elijah's purpose for going to Jericho was the same as it had been for going to Bethel: to exhort the young prophet's in the school at Jericho (v.5). Note, they too were aware of Elijah's departure, and they also asked Elisha if he was aware of the fact. Again, Elisha instructed them to keep silent about the matter just as he had the young students at Bethel.

e. For a third time Elijah tested his young disciple Elisha by suggesting he stay behind in Jordan (v.6). Sensing ever so deeply the burden of his mission, Elijah was driven to use every opportunity to strengthen the commitment of the young disciple. Responding emphatically to his master, Elisha made a solemn promise: as surely as the LORD lives and as Elijah himself lived, he would not leave his teacher Elijah. Beyond any question, he proved his commitment to God's call. He remained with Elijah as the two of them walked on.

f. With the hour of his departure from this earth drawing ever so near, Elijah sought to spend his final moments alone with his chosen disciple and replacement. He wanted to reinforce God's power upon the mind of the young disciple (vv.7-8). Note as the two men left Jericho, walking to the Jordan River, fifty prophets followed behind from a distance. When the two prophets reached the river, Elijah rolled up his cloak and struck the water of the Jordan River. Immediately the waters divided and the two prophets crossed over on dry ground to be alone. Note the similarity between this event and the dividing of the Red Sea by Moses through the power of God (Ex.14:16-28).

g. On reaching the other side of the Jordan and finding a comfortable spot, Elijah's heart reached out in love and compassion to his young disciple. This young man had been appointed by God to be his replacement, and Elisha had faithfully walked with him and served him for years. In love and compassion, sensing deeply the awesome weight of the mission that was to be placed upon Elisha's shoulders, the aged prophet wanted to know what final need he might meet for his young disciple.

No doubt taking a few moments to think through what he needed most, the young disciple ultimately asked for a double portion of Elijah's spirit (vv.9-10). By making this request, he showed that he knew the importance of God's Spirit working both in and through the heart of a prophet. Above all else, Elisha wanted spiritual power, a power far beyond his own abilities. He was undoubtedly gripped by the awesome task that lay before him, and he knew that he could never fulfill the shoes of Elijah nor the call of God without the fullness of God's Spirit. God's Spirit had forcefully dwelt and worked through his famed teacher and prophet Elijah. He desperately needed the very same Spirit and power working within and through him. Knowing that he was far less capable than Elijah, and being gripped by a sense of inadequacy, he knew that he needed far more help than Elijah ever needed. Thus, he asked for a double portion of Elijah's spirit, a spirit that was controlled by God's Spirit.

Note Elijah's response: his disciple's request was a difficult thing for him to grant. In fact, he did not personally have the power to grant such a request. Only God could give His Spirit to people. But Elijah did give him a sign that would indicate whether or not the LORD was going to grant his request. If Elisha actually witnessed Elijah's departure from this earth, then he would be receiving a double portion of Elijah's spirit. But if he was not a personal witness of the departure, then his request would not be granted.

h. As the mentor and disciple continued to walk along together and talk, a chariot of fire suddenly appeared, drawn by several horses of fire. Then the aged prophet Elijah was swept away from Elisha up into heaven in a whirlwind of fire (vv.11-12).

Stunned! Amazed! The young disciple cried out, "My father! My father! The chariot and horsemen of Israel!" This was the cry of a young man's heart after his father, a father who was being swept away from him forever. Elijah had been a spiritual mentor who had meant so much to him.

The reference to Elijah's being the chariot and horsemen of Israel meant that he was Israel's true protector. Israel's defense and protection had not rested in its army and military might but, rather, in the God of the great prophet Elijah himself. The LORD had used this prophet to demonstrate that God alone had been the true strength and power, the defender and protector of the nation. In a dramatic expression of his sorrow, Elisha took hold of his own clothes and tore them apart.

Thought 1. This is a strong lesson on commitment to one's call in life. During the remaining hours of his last day on earth, Elijah tested the commitment of his young disciple time and again. And on each occasion, Elisha proved faithful. He was totally committed to his call and to the task God had given him upon this earth. In his commitment to service, Elisha is a dynamic example for us.

Whatever our call in life, whatever our task, we must be committed. Nothing gets done apart from commitment. A worker's labor is often unacceptable and incomplete if he or she is only partially committed to the job. A farmer reaps little if any crop if he is only partially committed. A business suffers financial loss and perhaps bankruptcy if the management is only partially committed. Workers are not rewarded and often lose their jobs if they are not committed. Homes disintegrate if husbands and wives or children are not committed to one another. Students suffer and fail to learn if teachers are not committed.

No matter what the task, no matter what our hands work at every day, our efforts and the job suffer unless there is commitment. Ministers of the gospel must be committed to the LORD and to the task God has given them. Christian believers must also be committed to the LORD and to the task assigned them. And the workers of the world must be committed and diligent in the employment provided by the businesses of this world. All of us—as citizens of this world—are called to be committed individuals and servants of one another. We are to minister to the needs of one another and to serve each other by providing the goods to sustain life and to provide pleasure and joy upon this earth. This is the clear teaching of Holy Word.

(1) Listen to what God says about being committed to Him personally:

> "I beseech you therefore, brethren, by the mercies of God, that ye present your bodies a living sacrifice, holy, acceptable unto God, which *is* your reasonable service" (Ro.12:1).
> "I am crucified with Christ: nevertheless I live; yet not I, but Christ liveth in me: and the life which I now live in the flesh I live by the faith of the Son of God, who loved me, and gave himself for me" (Ga.2:20).
> "And thou shalt love the LORD thy God with all thine heart, and with all thy soul, and with all thy might" (De.6:5).
> "Trust in the LORD with all thine heart; and lean not unto thine own understanding. In all thy ways acknowledge him, and he shall direct thy paths" (Pr.3:5-6).
> "My son, give me thine heart, and let thine eyes observe my ways" (Pr.23:26).
> "And ye shall seek me, and find *me,* when ye shall search for me with all your heart" (Je.29:13).

(2) Listen to what God says to all the citizens of this world about being diligently committed to the task and work at hand:

> "Moreover it is required in stewards, that a man be found faithful" (1 Co.4:2).
> "Bear ye one another's burdens, and so fulfil the law of Christ" (Ga.6:2).

"But let every man prove his own work, and then shall he have rejoicing in himself alone, and not in another" (Ga.6:4).

"And let us not be weary in well doing: for in due season we shall reap, if we faint not. As we have therefore opportunity, let us do good unto all *men*, especially unto them who are of the household of faith" (Ga.6:9-10).

"And whatsoever ye do in word or deed, *do* all in the name of the Lord Jesus, giving thanks to God and the Father by him" (Col.3:17).

"And whatsoever ye do, do *it* heartily, as to the Lord, and not unto men" (Col.3:23).

"For we hear that there are some which walk among you disorderly, working not at all, but are busybodies. Now them that are such we command and exhort by our Lord Jesus Christ, that with quietness they work, and eat their own bread" (2 Th.3:11-12).

"But ye, brethren, be not weary in well doing" (2 Th.3:13).

"Nevertheless we, according to his promise, look for new heavens and a new earth, wherein dwelleth righteousness. Wherefore, beloved, seeing that ye look for such things, be diligent that ye may be found of him in peace, without spot, and blameless" (2 Pe.3:13-14).

"He becometh poor that dealeth *with* a slack hand: but the hand of the diligent maketh rich" (Pr.10:4).

"The soul of the sluggard desireth, and *hath* nothing: but the soul of the diligent shall be made fat" (Pr.13:4).

"He also that is slothful in his work is brother to him that is a great waster" (Pr.18:9).

"I went by the field of the slothful, and by the vineyard of the man void of understanding; And, lo, it was all grown over with thorns, *and* nettles had covered the face thereof, and the stone wall thereof was broken down" (Pr.24:30-31).

"Whatsoever thy hand findeth to do, do *it* with thy might; for *there is* no work, nor device, nor knowledge, nor wisdom, in the grave, whither thou goest" (Ec.9:10).

Thought 2. Why did God take Elijah up into heaven in a whirlwind? Why did He honor this great prophet in such a way as to escape death? Why did He not let Elijah go through the normal, common, natural passage of death? Matthew Henry suggests three possible reasons:

(1) God wanted to encourage and challenge His people to trust Him more and more, to seek after Him with the zeal that Elijah demonstrated throughout his life. Elijah had been faithful, persevering to the very end, sometimes at great cost. He had to bear constant threats of persecution and death. The implication is, a person who is wholly committed and faithful to the LORD will be greatly honored by the LORD.

(2) Elijah was taken up into heaven by the whirlwind to demonstrate a great reward for those who truly trust the LORD and are faithful to Him. By taking Elijah up into heaven without his experiencing death, God demonstrated that heaven and eternal life are realities. Elijah was taken up to live eternally in heaven, serving God forever and ever. His ascension is strong evidence of a great reward for those who live righteously and godly, looking for the blessed hope and the glorious appearing of the great God and Savior, the Lord Jesus Christ (Tit.2:12-13).

(3) The ascension of Elijah is a type of the ascension of the Lord Jesus Christ. It is also a type of believer who will rise to meet the Lord in the air when He returns at the climax of the age (Acts 1:9-11; 1 Th.4:13-18). Elijah was a man of righteousness and strong prayer, a man who communed and fellowshipped with God. Apparently, he gained an unbroken communion with God, a communion that never ceased. Thus, God was able to use him as a dynamic example to all people of all generations of all time. Moreover, the LORD was able to use him as a type of the Lord Jesus Christ and of the coming resurrection of the believer at the return of Christ. What an example of righteousness and prayer, of unbroken communion and fellowship with God!

2 (2:13-25) **Power, of God, Example of—Call, Example of, Elisha—Elisha, Call of**: Elisha's call to replace Elijah was clearly proven and demonstrated by the power of God. This is a clear picture of God's power to act in behalf of His people and to meet their needs. God gave five very specific proofs that Elisha was the replacement for the great prophet Elijah:

OUTLINE	SCRIPTURE	SCRIPTURE	OUTLINE
2. Elisha's call to replace Elijah proven: A picture of God's power a. Proof 1—Elisha picked up Elijah's fallen cloak: A symbol of God's equipping His servant b. Proof 2—dividing the Jordan River: God's power to guide His servant 1) Elisha took the cloak & struck the Jordan River • He cried out to the LORD • The LORD divided the	13 He took up also the mantle of Elijah that fell from him, and went back, and stood by the bank of Jordan; 14 And he took the mantle of Elijah that fell from him, and smote the waters, and said, Where *is* the LORD God of Elijah? and when he also had smitten the waters, they parted hither and thither: and Elisha went	over. 15 And when the sons of the prophets which *were* to view at Jericho saw him, they said, The spirit of Elijah doth rest on Elisha. And they came to meet him, and bowed themselves to the ground before him. 16 And they said unto him, Behold now, there be with thy servants fifty strong men; let them go, we pray thee,	water 2) The fifty prophets from Jericho witnessed the miracle • Acknowledged Elisha's call to replace Elijah • Bowed in respect: Accepted Elisha's leadership c. Proof 3—verifying Elisha's word: God's power to give His servant spiritual knowledge & insight

OUTLINE	SCRIPTURE	SCRIPTURE	OUTLINE
1) The prophets insisted on looking for Elijah • Elisha protested & refused their request • The prophets repeatedly insisted until Elisha gave in to their request • The fifty prophets failed to find Elijah after a three-day search 2) The word & spiritual knowledge of God's servant was proven, verified d. Proof 4—purifying the contaminated water of Jericho: God's power to provide the basic needs of life 1) The bad water problem was presented to Elisha 2) The prophet requested a new bowl with salt in it 3) The prophet went to the	and seek thy master: lest peradventure the Spirit of the LORD hath taken him up, and cast him upon some mountain, or into some valley. And he said, Ye shall not send. 17 And when they urged him till he was ashamed, he said, Send. They sent therefore fifty men; and they sought three days, but found him not. 18 And when they came again to him, (for he tarried at Jericho,) he said unto them, Did I not say unto you, Go not? 19 And the men of the city said unto Elisha, Behold, I pray thee, the situation of this city is pleasant, as my lord seeth: but the water is naught, and the ground barren. 20 And he said, Bring me a new cruse, and put salt therein. And they bring it to him. 21 And he went forth unto	the spring of the waters, and cast the salt in there, and said, Thus saith the LORD, I have healed these waters; there shall be not from thence any more death or barren land. 22 So the waters were healed unto this day, according to the saying of Elisha which he spake 23 And he went up from thence unto Bethel: and as he was going up by the way, there came forth little children out of the city, and mocked him, and said unto him, Go up, thou bald head; go up, thou bald head. 24 And he turned back, and looked on them, and cursed them in the name of the LORD. And there came forth two she bears out of the wood, and tare forty and two children of them. 25 And he went from thence to mount Carmel, and from thence he returned to Samaria	spring & threw the salt into the water 4) The prophet declared the LORD's miraculous power • He had purified the bad water • He had purified the water permanently, up to the time of writing Second Kings e. Proof 5—pronouncing judgment upon a large, threatening gang of hoodlums: God's power to protect & deliver His servant 1) The gang mocked, threatened Elisha the prophet 2) The prophet cursed them in the name of the LORD (Le.26:21-22; 2 Chr. 36:16) 3) The hoodlums—42 of them—were mauled by two bears 4) The prophet traveled safely home to Mt. Carmel then to Samaria (4:23; 5:3)

a. The first proof of Elisha's call was the fallen cloak of Elijah (v.13). It had fallen at the feet of Elisha. Using a dramatic symbol, God showed that the very mantle of His Spirit that had covered Elijah was now to clothe the young disciple Elisha. Earlier, when God first led Elijah to the young man Elisha, the prophet had thrown his cloak around the shoulders of the young man who was to become his disciple. This had been a clear symbol that God was choosing the young Elisha to replace the prophet some day in the future. The mantle of leadership was eventually to be placed upon his shoulders. Now that day had come. Elisha was now to pick up the mantle of prophetic leadership to the nation Israel. The fallen cloak at the feet of Elisha was proof that he was appointed by God to replace the great prophet Elijah.

b. The second proof of Elisha's call was the dividing of the Jordan River (v.14). This was a clear symbol of God's power to guide his servant through whatever difficulties lay in his path. Knowing that he was chosen by God, Elisha picked up the cloak of his teacher and walked back to the Jordan River, returning to the school of prophets waiting on the other side. When he arrived at the Jordan, he struck the water with the cloak and cried out from the depths of his lungs, "Where is the LORD God of Elijah?" This was not a cry questioning where God was, but rather a cry for God to demonstrate His power through him just as He had done through Elijah. Immediately the water divided, piling up on the inflowing side and flowing out on the outflowing side. Subsequently Elisha, God's newly appointed prophet to the nation, crossed over on dry ground.

Note that the fifty prophets from Jericho witnessed the miracle. They immediately acknowledged God's call for Elisha to replace Elijah, and they knew that Elijah's spirit was definitely resting on the young disciple. Therefore, they bowed in respect, accepting his leadership. The proof of Elisha's call had been given in a specific miracle.

c. The third proof of Elisha's call was the verification of his word (v.16). God's power to give His servant spiritual knowledge and insight was to be demonstrated. The young prophets who had followed Elijah and Elisha had witnessed the whirlwind on the other side of the Jordan River. When Elisha shared that Elijah had been taken up into heaven by the whirlwind, the young disciples had difficulty understanding just how this could be. After some discussion, they approached Elisha about sending fifty of the prophets back across the Jordan to look for Elijah. They felt that perhaps the Spirit of the LORD had picked him up and set him down some place close by. Despite Elisha's objections, the prophets repeatedly insisted until the new leader finally gave in to their request (v.17).

For three days the fifty prophets searched all over the countryside trying to find Elijah. But of course, they failed. Eventually, they came to the conclusion that the LORD had actually taken Elijah up into heaven in the whirlwind, just as Elisha had said. When they returned to their new leader, the word and the spiritual knowledge of Elisha were proven, verified to them. Their conviction that he was God's appointed replacement for Elijah was reinforced. They could totally trust his word and spiritual knowledge, for God had given him the unusual privilege of witnessing the actual ascension of Elijah, and he had faithfully declared the truth of the fact to them.

d. Elisha's call needed to be demonstrated to the people as well as to the prophets of the nation (vv.19-22). Thus, as a fourth proof, God immediately empowered Elisha to purify the contaminated water of Jericho. By performing this miracle, Elisha demonstrated God's power to provide the basic needs of life. Before Elisha left Jericho and the school of the prophets, some men from the city approached him about the polluted water of the city. The water made the land unproductive and apparently had caused some deaths and barrenness among the women and animals of the city (see v.21). To meet the need, Elisha requested a new bowl with salt in it (v.20). Once the bowl with salt had been brought to him, he walked out to the source of the water and cast the salt into it. He then cried out that the LORD had healed the water. Never again would it be unproductive or cause the death of any person or animal. The bad water was purified permanently, which was verified at the time of the writing of *Second Kings* (vv.21-22).

e. Sometime later Elisha traveled up to Bethel, where God was to give a fifth proof of His call to replace the prophet Elijah. His ministry needed to be demonstrated to the wicked unbelievers of the nation. This was done by judgment being pronounced upon a large, threatening gang of hoodlums. God used the event to demonstrate His power to protect and deliver His servant.

As Elisha was approaching Bethel, this large gang of hoodlums began to surround him, mocking and threatening him. They mocked the fact that he was bald, using his baldness to publicly insult him and his prophetic ministry. They were ridiculing, insulting Elisha as God's representative. By being the newly appointed prophet of the nation, Elisha's very ministry was at stake. If the youthful hoodlums had been allowed to persecute Elisha without being punished, the people would never have accepted his ministry as the prophet to the nation. Sensing this fact from the Spirit of God, Elisha whipped around to confront the gang: he called down a curse upon them in the name of the LORD (Lev.26:21-22). They were like so many down through the ages who have "mocked the messengers of God, and despised his words, and misused his prophets, until the wrath of the LORD arose against [them]" (2 Chron.36:16).

Soon after the curse had been pronounced, the judgment of God fell upon the thugs. Two bears came out of the woods and mauled forty-two of them (v.24). From there, Elisha traveled safely home to Mount Carmel and then later made a trip to Samaria (4:23; 5:3).

Thought 1. God had the power to take care of His servant Elisha. And He has the power to take care of any servant of His, whether minister or lay person. If a minister's call is being questioned or doubted, God has the power to prove that call, that he is a true minister of God.

God does not use His power just to help the minister, but to help us all. Whenever we need help, God's power is present to help us. No matter what our need, whether for water as the people of Jericho needed or for safety as Elisha needed when he confronted the hoodlums, God's power is available to help us. God loves us and will meet whatever need we have. If we will do what Elisha did—turn to the LORD and cry out for His help—the LORD will help us. He has the power to help. No matter what the problem or difficulty, trial or temptation, nothing is too hard for the LORD. He can do anything, and He longs to use His power to help us. This is the clear teaching of God's Holy Word:

> "But Jesus beheld *them,* and said unto them, With men this is impossible; but with God all things are possible" (Mt.19:26).
>
> "For with God nothing shall be impossible" (Lu.1:37).
>
> "But ye shall receive power, after that the Holy Ghost is come upon you: and ye shall be witnesses unto me both in Jerusalem, and in all Judaea, and in Samaria, and unto the uttermost part of the earth" (Ac.1:8).
>
> "Now to him that is of power to stablish you according to my gospel, and the preaching of Jesus Christ, according to the revelation of the mystery, which was kept secret since the world began, But now is made manifest, and by the Scriptures of the prophets, according to the commandment of the everlasting God, made known to all nations for the obedience of faith: To God only wise, *be* glory through Jesus Christ for ever. Amen" (Ro.16:25-27).
>
> "That he would grant you, according to the riches of his glory, to be strengthened with might by his Spirit in the inner man" (Ep.3:16).
>
> "Now unto him that is able to do exceeding abundantly above all that we ask or think, according to the power that worketh in us" (Ep.3:20).
>
> "For God hath not given us the spirit of fear; but of power, and of love, and of a sound mind" (2 Ti.1:7).
>
> "For thou hast girded me with strength to battle: them that rose up against me hast thou subdued under me" (2 S.22:40).
>
> "Both riches and honour *come* of thee, and thou reignest over all; and in thine hand *is* power and might; and in thine hand *it is* to make great, and to give strength unto all" (1 Chr.29:12).
>
> "I know that thou canst do every *thing,* and *that* no thought can be withholden from thee" (Jb.42:2).
>
> "But they that wait upon the LORD shall renew *their* strength; they shall mount up with wings as eagles; they shall run, and not be weary; *and* they shall walk, and not faint" (Is.40:31).
>
> "Fear thou not; for I *am* with thee: be not dismayed; for I *am* thy God: I will strengthen thee; yea, I will help thee; yea, I will uphold thee with the right hand of my righteousness" (Is.41:10).
>
> "Yea, before the day *was* I *am* he; and *there is* none that can deliver out of my hand: I will work, and who shall let [hinder] it?" (Is.43:13).

1. The evil reign of Joram (Jehoram), son of Ahab (1 K. 22:51): A leader carries out a halfhearted reformation
   a. His background: Reigned 12 years
   b. His partial reformation
      1) He lived a wicked life
      2) He destroyed the idol of his parents, Ahab & Jezebel
      3) He clung, however, to the false worship of Jeroboam, 1 K.12:25-33
      4) He was a stumbling block, causing Israel to sin
2. The revolt of Moab against Joram: A ruler desperately seeks the true prophet of God
   a. The cause of the revolt
      1) Moab had been subject to Israel & forced to pay taxes
      2) Moab grasped the chance to rebel after King Ahab's death
   b. The reaction of Joram
      1) He mobilized the army
      2) He formed an alliance with King Jehoshaphat of Judah & the king of Edom, 9
   c. The strategy of the alliance: To march south through the Desert of Edom in a large, half-circle pattern to launch a surprise attack
   d. The seven-day march through the desert & the crisis faced by the alliance: A drought, no water
      1) Joram became terrified: Complained & blamed the LORD
      2) Jehoshaphat suggested they find a prophet who could seek the LORD on their behalf

CHAPTER 3

C. The Evil Reign of Joram in Israel & Elisha's Call Proven to the World's Rulers: The Proof of a True Prophet, 3:1-27

Now Jehoram the son of Ahab began to reign over Israel in Samaria the eighteenth year of Jehoshaphat king of Judah, and reigned twelve years.
2 And he wrought evil in the sight of the LORD; but not like his father, and like his mother: for he put away the image of Baal that his father had made.
3 Nevertheless he cleaved unto the sins of Jeroboam the son of Nebat, which made Israel to sin; he departed not therefrom.
4 And Mesha king of Moab was a sheepmaster, and rendered unto the king of Israel an hundred thousand lambs, and an hundred thousand rams, with the wool.
5 But it came to pass, when Ahab was dead, that the king of Moab rebelled against the king of Israel.
6 And king Jehoram went out of Samaria the same time, and numbered all Israel.
7 And he went and sent to Jehoshaphat the king of Judah, saying, The king of Moab hath rebelled against me: wilt thou go with me against Moab to battle? And he said, I will go up: I am as thou art, my people as thy people, and my horses as thy horses.
8 And he said, Which way shall we go up? And he answered, The way through the wilderness of Edom.
9 So the king of Israel went, and the king of Judah, and the king of Edom: and they fetched a compass of seven days' journey: and there was no water for the host, and for the cattle that followed them.
10 And the king of Israel said, Alas! that the LORD hath called these three kings together, to deliver them into the hand of Moab!
11 But Jehoshaphat said, Is there not here a prophet of the LORD, that we may enquire of the LORD by him?

And one of the king of Israel's servants answered and said, Here is Elisha the son of Shaphat, which poured water on the hands of Elijah.
12 And Jehoshaphat said, The word of the LORD is with him. So the king of Israel and Jehoshaphat and the king of Edom went down to him.
13 And Elisha said unto the king of Israel, What have I to do with thee? get thee to the prophets of thy father, and to the prophets of thy mother. And the king of Israel said unto him, Nay: for the LORD hath called these three kings together, to deliver them into the hand of Moab.
14 And Elisha said, As the LORD of hosts liveth, before whom I stand, surely, were it not that I regard the presence of Jehoshaphat the king of Judah, I would not look toward thee, nor see thee.
15 But now bring me a minstrel. And it came to pass, when the minstrel played, that the hand of the LORD came upon him.
16 And he said, Thus saith the LORD, Make this valley full of ditches.
17 For thus saith the LORD, Ye shall not see wind, neither shall ye see rain; yet that valley shall be filled with water, that ye may drink, both ye, and your cattle, and your beasts.
18 And this is but a light thing in the sight of the LORD: he will deliver the Moabites also into your hand.
19 And ye shall smite every fenced city, and every choice city, and shall fell every good tree, and stop all wells of water, and mar every good piece of land with stones.
20 And it came to pass in the morning, when the meat offering was offered, that, behold, there came water by the way of Edom, and the country was filled with water.
21 And when all the Moabites heard that the kings were come up to fight against them, they gathered all that were able to put on armour, and upward, and stood in the border.
22 And they rose up early in the morning, and the sun

3) An officer of Israel informed the kings about Elisha, a prophet who had been the aide of Elijah
4) The kings, facing the crisis of utter defeat, humbled themselves & went to Elisha to seek his help & godly counsel
   e. The confrontation of the three kings with the prophet Elisha
      1) Elisha sternly rebuked Joram for his idolatry, for following false prophets & false worship
      2) Joram again blamed the LORD
      3) Elisha, with disgust in his voice against Joram, agreed to seek the LORD for Jehoshaphat's sake (the sake of the true believer)
   f. The promise of God's provision by Elisha
      1) Elisha requested a harpist while praying
      2) Elisha instructed the kings to dig ditches throughout the valley
      3) Elisha shared the promises of God
         • God would flood the valley with water—without wind or rain
         • God would give them victory over Moab
      4) Elisha revealed how devastating their destruction would be: They would destroy all the cities & the food & water supply—to prevent resettlement
3. The victory of Israel over Moab: God fulfills His promises & validates the true prophet
   a. The promise of God fulfilled: Flash floods in the hills flowed into the valley
   b. The army of Moab was mobilized & stationed at the southern border
   c. The fatal mistake of the Moabite forces

1) They saw the sun shining on the water in the ditches • Mistook it for blood • Concluded the coalition armies had turned against & killed each other 2) They rushed to seize the plunder 3) The coalition rushed out & attacked, scattering the Moabites, sending them fleeing for their lives d. The invasion of Moab by the Israelite coalition 1) Slaughtered the population 2) Destroyed the major cities & the land: To prevent re-settlement • Covered the fields with stones	shone upon the water, and the Moabites saw the water on the other side *as* red as blood: 23 And they said, This *is* blood: the kings are surely slain, and they have smitten one another: now therefore, Moab, to the spoil. 24 And when they came to the camp of Israel, the Israelites rose up and smote the Moabites, so that they fled before them: but they went forward smiting the Moabites, even in *their* country. 25 And they beat down the cities, and on every good piece of land cast every man his stone, and filled it; and they stopped all the wells	of water, and felled all the good trees: only in Kir-haraseth left they the stones thereof; howbeit the slingers went about *it,* and smote it. 26 And when the king of Moab saw that the battle was too sore for him, he took with him seven hundred men that drew swords, to break through *even* unto the king of Edom: but they could not. 27 Then he took his eldest son that should have reigned in his stead, and offered him *for* a burnt offering upon the wall. And there was great indignation against Israel: and they departed from him, and returned to *their own* land.	• Stopped up the springs • Cut down the good trees 3) Attacked Kir-Hareseth where the Moabites made a final stand e. The Moabite king's strategy to turn back the invaders 1) He courageously took 700 swordsmen to break through the coalition line defended by the Edomites (the weakest forces) 2) He offered his son as a human sacrifice—in sight of all: To appease, remove the anger of his false god f. The withdrawal of the coalition: Due to a passionate fury rising against Israel

DIVISION I

THE FINAL DAYS OF ELIJAH'S MINISTRY: A FAITHFUL SERVANT WHO PERSEVERED TO THE VERY END, 1:1–3:27

C. The Evil Reign of Joram in Israel and Elisha's Call Proven to the World's Rulers: The Proof of a True Prophet, 3:1-27

(3:1-27) **Introduction—Philosophy, of the World, Seven Listed—Secularism, Described—Humanism, Described—Relativism, Described—Materialism, Described—Pragmatism, Described—Mindlessness, Described—Christianity, Described—Truth, Proof of**: within every generation there are several philosophies, mindsets, and lifestyles that seek the attention and loyalty of people. As different philosophies and ideas are presented to us, how can we tell which is true? To what and to whom should we give our loyalty and allegiance? Whom should we follow and pattern our lives after, seeking to please?

First, there is the philosophy or voice of *secularism* that seeks our allegiance. Secularism claims this world is all there is. There is no divine being behind the scenes of this world. Look at the universe, the earth, this age in which you live, for this is all there is. So live it up, do what you want, and do it now—for today is the only day you are sure of living. The emphasis of secularism is the here and now, including the elimination of any thought of God. Hence, secularism allows us to live as we wish. "If it feels good, do it"—no consequences, no responsibility, no guilt. This is the philosophy and the blatant message splashed across the television, movie screens, and most other forms of media in the world today.

Second is the philosophy or idea of *humanism* that bombards us as we walk day-by-day. Humanism claims that this is a man-centered world. Man is the center of the universe, his own savior. When it comes to life, man must save himself by eliminating conflict and war and by developing technology, science, and medicine to extend his life and to make life more comfortable. There is no god or power beyond man himself. Our health and life and future rest in our own hands. We are the determining masters of our own fate. Humanism is the philosophy being taught so widely that it is weakening the Christian faith of multitudes worldwide.

The third philosophy or thought that solicits our loyalty is *relativism*. Relativism is taught by people who say there are no moral absolutes. The Ten Commandments are only suggestions, not commandments. Each situation determines what is right or wrong. An action may be wrong today, but right tomorrow. Then on another occasion and at a different time, it may be wrong again. This is what is known as *situation ethics*. This philosophy allows man to change the rules according to each situation. Therefore, there really are no rules. Nothing is ever "always right" or "always wrong"—for all behavior is relative. There simply are no moral absolutes.

Materialism is the fourth philosophy or voice that cries out for our attention. Materialism focuses only upon the material possessions and pleasures of this world. Our primary focus should therefore be a life of ease, comfort, and pleasure. Sensual pleasure and material possessions become the focus of a person's life. There is nothing beyond this material universe; consequently, a person should enjoy the sensual pleasures and the comforts of this world every day of his life. This philosophy is eating away at individuals and societies, arousing people to crave more and more possessions and more and more power. As a result, the work ethic and integrity of millions are being destroyed and the very stability of nations is being affected.

Fifth, *pragmatism* is always a major voice bidding for our attention. Pragmatism claims that truth is determined by practical results. If it works, it is truth and it should be done. Therefore, if you find that some behavior or action works for you, if it produces the results you want, then do it. It is practical and pragmatic for you. Even if it means disobeying God's commandments or God's Word, do it. "The end justifies the means" is a good example of this philosophy. For instance, if a salesperson or a company stretches the truth in advertising its product and as a result sells many more of the item, then the sales gimmick worked. Therefore it is the right thing to do—even though the truth was stretched and the public was deceived.

Sixth, *mindlessness* is a path of life followed by many. Mindlessness indicates that a person walks through life thoughtlessly, seldom if ever giving attention to proper behavior, the future, God, or to any possibility of life beyond this world. The mindless person lives just for today, wrapped up in his own life and thoughts, his own desires and wants. Little if anything concerns the person other than his own self-centered world. A person with this mindset simply gets up each day and goes about his activities with no thought as to consequences or outcome or how his behavior might affect others. There is no plan, no structure, no purpose to the person's life other than to plow through another day.

Seventh, there is the truth of *Christianity*, the fact that there is a living and true God who created the universe and who loves us and has a plan for our lives. In the midst of a corruptible, depraved world that pulls every living thing down into the grave of death, there is the truth that God loves.

Man has sinned and brought corruption and death into the world, but Christianity declares God's love for the world. He is not a God of hate who has left man in the dark, groping and grasping about, trying to discover the truth about life: its source, purpose, and end. But He is a God of love. He so loves the world that He has sent His very own Son into the world to reveal the truth of life to man. His son is the Lord Jesus Christ who came into the world to show and provide the way, the truth, and the life God expects people to live.

How do we know which philosophy, which mindset, which lifestyle, which voice to follow in this life? So many prophetic voices are screaming for our attention, claiming to be the truth and the way to a complete, fulfilled, and fruitful life. But which voice is correct? How can we prove whether a prophetic voice is truthful or lying?

This present Scripture will tell us how to prove whether or not a prophetic voice is telling the truth. Remember, Elisha had been appointed by God to replace the great prophet Elijah. But in replacing such a great servant, there was a problem that first had to be handled, the problem of proving Elisha's ministry. In the last chapter we saw Elisha's ministry proven to three groups of people: the prophets, the general public, and the unbelievers of the world. Now it was time for God to prove to the kings and leaders of this world that Elisha was His appointed servant to replace Elijah. And in proving that Elisha was His true prophet, God was proving that He is the only living and true God. God proclaimed His Word and promises through Elisha and then fulfilled His Word and promises. By this we test the prophets and philosophies of this world, by their word and the fulfillment of their word. If a philosophy or prophet or fortune-teller or mind reader promises anything and that promise fails to come true, that philosophy or individual is false. Their word is proven false. But if a person or philosophy makes promise after promise and those promises always come true, that person or philosophy is true. This is the way God proved the ministry of Elisha.

King Ahaziah of Israel (the Northern Kingdom) had just died from a freak accident. Having no sons, his brother Joram was crowned king of Israel. This is the subject of the present passage of Scripture: *The Evil Reign of Joram in Israel and Elisha's Call Proven to the World's Rulers: The Proof of a True Prophet, 3:1-27.*

1. The evil reign of Joram (Jehoram), son of Ahab (1 K. 22:51): a leader carries out a halfhearted reformation (vv.1-3).
2. The revolt of Moab against Joram: a ruler desperately seeks the true prophet of God (vv.4-19).
3. The victory of Israel over Moab: God fulfills His promises and validates the true prophet (vv.20-27).

1 (3:1-3) **False Worship, Example of—Stumbling, Example of—Idolatry, Example of—Halfheartedness, Example of—Double-Mindedness, Example of—Neglect, Example of—Reformation, Halfhearted or Partial—Joram or Jehoram, Reign of**: there was the evil reign of Joram (Jehoram), the son of wicked Ahab and the infamous Jezebel. Remember that King Ahaziah, another son of Ahab and Jezebel, had just died as a result of a freak accident (2 K.1:2-18). Because Ahaziah had no sons, his brother Joram was crowned king. In these three brief verses a summary of his reign is given:

OUTLINE	SCRIPTURE	SCRIPTURE	OUTLINE
1. The evil reign of Joram (Jehoram), son of Ahab (1 K. 22:51): A leader carries out a halfhearted reformation	Now Jehoram the son of Ahab began to reign over Israel in Samaria the eighteenth year of Jehoshaphat king of Judah, and reigned twelve years.	his father, and like his mother: for he put away the image of Baal that his father had made. 3 Nevertheless he cleaved unto the sins of Jeroboam the son of Nebat, which made Israel to sin; he departed not therefrom.	2) He destroyed the idol of his parents, Ahab & Jezebel
a. His background: Reigned 12 years			3) He clung, however, to the false worship of Jeroboam, 1 K.12:25-33
b. His partial reformation	2 And he wrought evil in the sight of the LORD; but not like		4) He was a stumbling block, causing Israel to sin
1) He lived a wicked life			

a. Joram began his reign during the eighteenth year of Jehoshaphat, who was king of Judah (v.1). He reigned for a period of twelve years (852–841 B.C.).

b. A spiritual evaluation is given of Joram's reign. He launched a reformation in the nation, but it was only partial and halfhearted (vv.2-3). His mother Jezebel was living and was most likely exerting a strong, evil influence over him. However, note what Scripture says about the spiritual life of Joram: he lived an evil, wicked life in the eyes of the LORD, yet he did not commit as much evil as did his father and mother. For some reason Joram got rid of the idol that had been made by his father and placed in the temple Ahab had built for Jezebel in Samaria (1 K.16:30-32). It should be noted that Joram apparently did not destroy this idol, for Scripture says that it was later destroyed in the purge by King Jehu (2 K.10:26-27). Obviously, this particular idol or statue of Baal was the focus of worship for many in the capital of Samaria and throughout the Northern Kingdom. Thus, Joram did a commendable thing in removing it. But his reformation was limited, halfhearted. For Joram still clung to the sins and false worship of Jeroboam (1 K.12:25-33). Remember, Jeroboam had instituted a statewide political religion that had nothing to do with the worship of Baal. When the northern tribes broke off from the southern kingdom of Judah, Jeroboam feared the people's loyalty and attachment to the temple in Jerusalem. If the people continued to make their annual pilgrimages to the temple in Jerusalem, they might seek political reunification with Judah and rebel against him. They might seek to restore *all Israel* into a unified nation under the royal house of David. Thus Jeroboam had erected two calf images, one in the south at Bethel and one in the north at Dan, claiming that the calves were representations of the LORD. He made the utterly false claim that by worshipping the calves the people would be worshipping the LORD. In addition, he encouraged the people to focus their worship in Dan and Bethel instead of making the long journey to Jerusalem.

Because of the great political advantage of keeping the people's loyalty focused in the Northern Kingdom, the kings of Israel strongly encouraged the false worship instituted by Jeroboam. Note that this was one of the terrible acts of evil and wickedness committed by the newly crowned King Joram. He was a shameful stumbling block, causing Israel to commit apostasy against God. He refused to repent of this terrible evil, refused to turn the people away from false worship back to God.

Thought 1. Scripture clearly says that Joram was not as evil as his father and mother. He did a commendable thing by removing the statue of Baal from the temple in the capital of Samaria. But the king was only halfheartedly committed to reformation, to turning people back to God. Sadly, he still clung to the false worship instituted by the state.

There have always been and always will be many people who have only partial, halfhearted commitments to Christ. They worship on Sundays, offer grace at meals, never use profanity or tell dirty or off-colored jokes, never read or watch pornography, never steal, cheat, or lie. Yet, despite living moral and just lives, they are not totally committed to the LORD. They are double-minded, have a divided allegiance, keeping one foot in the world and one foot in the service of the LORD and His righteousness. They seek to follow the LORD, but they also seek the pleasures and possessions of the world. They try to fellowship with God while still fellowshipping with the wicked of the world. They continually subject themselves to the enticements and seductions of a corrupt style of living. And the more they become companions in fellowship with the wicked of this world, the more likely they are to begin living unrighteous lives themselves. Listen to what God says about a person who is halfhearted and double-minded and whose allegiance to Him is divided.

"And every one that heareth these sayings of mine, and doeth them not, shall be likened unto a foolish man, which built his house upon the sand: And the rain descended, and the floods came, and the winds blew, and beat upon that house; and it fell: and great was the fall of it" (Mt.7:26-27).

"He that is not with me is against me; and he that gathereth not with me scattereth abroad" (Mt.12:30).

"Then he which had received the one talent came and said, Lord, I knew thee that thou art an hard man, reaping where thou hast not sown, and gathering where thou hast not strawed: And I was afraid, and went and hid thy talent in the earth: lo, there thou hast that is thine. His lord answered and said unto him, Thou wicked and slothful servant, thou knewest that I reap where I sowed not, and gather where I have not strawed: Thou oughtest therefore to have put my money to the exchangers, and then at my coming I should have received mine own with usury. Take therefore the talent from him, and give it unto him which hath ten talents. For unto every one that hath shall be given, and he shall have abundance: but from him that hath not shall be taken away even that which he hath. And cast ye the unprofitable servant into outer darkness: there shall be weeping and gnashing of teeth" (Mt.25:24-30).

"And Jesus said unto him, No man, having put his hand to the plough, and looking back, is fit for the kingdom of God" (Lu.9:62).

"And that servant, which knew his lord's will, and prepared not himself, neither did according to his will, shall be beaten with many stripes" (Lu.12:47).

"And if ye have not been faithful in that which is another man's, who shall give you that which is your own?" (Lu.16:12).

"No servant can serve two masters: for either he will hate the one, and love the other; or else he will hold to the one, and despise the other. Ye cannot serve God and mammon" (Lu.16:13).

"A double minded man is unstable in all his ways" (Js.1:8).

"What doth it profit, my brethren, though a man say he hath faith, and have not works? can faith save him?" (Js.2:14).

"Draw nigh to God, and he will draw nigh to you. Cleanse your hands, ye sinners; and purify your hearts, ye double minded" (Js.4:8).

"Therefore to him that knoweth to do good, and doeth *it* not, to him it is sin" (Js.4:17).

"I know thy works, that thou art neither cold nor hot: I would thou wert cold or hot. So then because thou art lukewarm, and neither cold nor hot, I will spue thee out of my mouth" (Re.3:15-16).

"And Elijah came unto all the people, and said, How long halt ye between two opinions? if the LORD *be* God, follow him: but if Baal, *then* follow him. And the people answered him not a word" (1 K.18:21).

"Cursed *be* he that doeth the work of the LORD deceitfully, and cursed *be* he that keepeth back his sword from blood" (Je.48:10).

"Their heart is divided; now shall they be found faulty" (Ho.10:2)

---

2 (3:4-19) **Promises, of God—Word of God, Duty—Prophet, Proof of—Moab, Revolt Against Israel—Mesha, King of Moab—Taxation, Example of—Tribute, Example of—Revolt, Example of, Moab Against Israel—Elisha, Proof of Ministry—Joram, War Against Moab—War, of Israel, Against Moab—Israel, Northern Kingdom, Wars of**: when Joram was crowned king, he immediately faced the uprising of the Moabites against the Northern Kingdom. Scripture clearly paints a picture of what happened:

OUTLINE	SCRIPTURE	SCRIPTURE	OUTLINE

2. The revolt of Moab against Joram: A ruler desperately seeks the true prophet of God
a. The cause of the revolt
  1) Moab had been subject to Israel & forced to pay taxes
  2) Moab grasped the chance to rebel after King Ahab's death
 	
b. The reaction of Joram
  1) He mobilized the army
 	
  2) He formed an alliance with King Jehoshaphat of Judah & the king of Edom, 9
 	
c. The strategy of the alliance: To march south through the Desert of Edom in a large, half-circle pattern to launch a surprise attack
d. The seven-day march through the desert & the crisis faced by the alliance: A drought, no water
 	
  1) Joram became terrified: Complained & blamed the LORD
 	
  2) Jehoshaphat suggested they find a prophet who could seek the LORD on their behalf
  3) An officer of Israel informed the kings about Elisha, a prophet who had been the aide of Elijah
	4 And Mesha king of Moab was a sheepmaster, and rendered unto the king of Israel an hundred thousand lambs, and an hundred thousand rams, with the wool.
	5 But it came to pass, when Ahab was dead, that the king of Moab rebelled against the king of Israel.
	6 And king Jehoram went out of Samaria the same time, and numbered all Israel.
	7 And he went and sent to Jehoshaphat the king of Judah, saying, The king of Moab hath rebelled against me: wilt thou go with me against Moab to battle? And he said, I will go up: I *am* as thou *art,* my people as thy people, *and* my horses as thy horses.
	8 And he said, Which way shall we go up? And he answered, The way through the wilderness of Edom.
	9 So the king of Israel went, and the king of Judah, and the king of Edom: and they fetched a compass of seven days' journey: and there was no water for the host, and for the cattle that followed them.
	10 And the king of Israel said, Alas! that the LORD hath called these three kings together, to deliver them into the hand of Moab!
	11 But Jehoshaphat said, *Is there* not here a prophet of the LORD, that we may enquire of the LORD by him? And one of the king of Israel's servants answered and said, Here *is* Elisha the son of Shaphat, which poured water on the hands of Elijah.
		12 And Jehoshaphat said, The word of the LORD is with him. So the king of Israel and Jehoshaphat and the king of Edom went down to him.
		13 And Elisha said unto the king of Israel, What have I to do with thee? get thee to the prophets of thy father, and to the prophets of thy mother. And the king of Israel said unto him, Nay: for the LORD hath called these three kings together, to deliver them into the hand of Moab.
		14 And Elisha said, *As* the LORD of hosts liveth, before whom I stand, surely, were it not that I regard the presence of Jehoshaphat the king of Judah, I would not look toward thee, nor see thee.
		15 But now bring me a minstrel. And it came to pass, when the minstrel played, that the hand of the LORD came upon him.
		16 And he said, Thus saith the LORD, Make this valley full of ditches.
		17 For thus saith the LORD, Ye shall not see wind, neither shall ye see rain; yet that valley shall be filled with water, that ye may drink, both ye, and your cattle, and your beasts.
		18 And this is *but* a light thing in the sight of the LORD: he will deliver the Moabites also into your hand.
		19 And ye shall smite every fenced city, and every choice city, and shall fell every good tree, and stop all wells of water, and mar every good piece of land with stones.
			4) The kings, facing the crisis of utter defeat, humbled themselves & went to Elisha to seek his help & godly counsel
			e. The confrontation of the three kings with the prophet Elisha
			  1) Elisha sternly rebuked Joram for his idolatry, for following false prophets & false worship
			  2) Joram again blamed the LORD
			
			  3) Elisha, with disgust in his voice against Joram, agreed to seek the LORD for Jehoshaphat's sake (the sake of the true believer)
			
			f. The promise of God's provision by Elisha
			  1) Elisha requested a harpist while praying
			
			  2) Elisha instructed the kings to dig ditches throughout the valley
			  3) Elisha shared the promises of God
			    • God would flood the valley with water—without wind or rain
			
			    • God would give them victory over Moab
			
			  4) Elisha revealed how devastating their destruction would be: They would destroy all the cities & the food & water supply—to prevent resettlement

a. The cause of the revolt had been the heavy taxation imposed upon Moab by the kings and rulers of Israel. For years Moab had been subjected by Israel and forced to pay a heavy tribute or taxation. Two years earlier the Northern Kingdom had been defeated in a battle at Ramoth-Gilead by the Syrians and King Ahab of Israel had been killed. Seeking to take advantage of the weakened condition of Israel, Moab had revolted. Fortifying its northern border, Moab sought to protect itself against any attempt by Israel to enforce its rule and heavy taxation. Ahab's son Ahaziah had succeeded him as king, but he had suffered a freak accident from which he died. Thus his brief two-year reign had weakened Israel or the Northern Kingdom and Moab's rebellion continued.

b. When Joram took the throne, one of his first acts was to tackle the problem of Moab's rebellion. He knew the nation Israel needed the taxes from Moab in order to sustain the economy of the Northern Kingdom. Note that the taxes paid by Moab was a huge amount: 100,000 lambs and the wool from 100,000 rams. Without this tax, the economy of Israel would be adversely affected. However, Joram faced another potentially serious problem with Moab: during the two years of turmoil within the Northern Kingdom, Moab had had the opportunity to strengthen its forces on the southern border. Consequently, the Northern Kingdom needed help to put down the rebellion. While mobilizing his own army, Joram sought to form an alliance with the king of Judah, Jehoshaphat, and Jehoshaphat agreed to the terms of the alliance.

c. In planning their military strategy, Jehoshaphat suggested they march south instead of north through the Desert of Edom. This meant they would march in a large half-circle pattern and then launch a surprise attack from the south below the Dead Sea (v.8). This particular strategy of attack seemed to be brilliant, for the forces of Moab were mobilized along the northern border above the Dead Sea. Also, by going around the southern end of the Dead Sea, the army of the alliance not only would catch Moab by surprise, but they could also enlist the support of Edom. Since the alliance had to march through the land of Edom, the Edomites, with a smaller army than the alliance, would join Israel and Judah instead of fighting against them.

d. Although the southern strategy would be far more difficult because of having to march through the desert, the alliance adopted this strategy of assault against Moab. But after marching seven days through the desert, the alliance army faced a severe, life-threatening crisis: they ran out of water. There was no water for the soldiers or for the animals.

Note the reaction of King Joram of the Northern Kingdom: he became terrified. He complained and blamed the LORD, accusing Him of bringing the crisis upon them in order to defeat them before the power of Moab. But note the response of Jehoshaphat, who, despite some spiritual weaknesses, was a true believer in the LORD: he suggested they find a prophet who could seek the LORD on their behalf (v.11).

Thankfully and providentially, one of the officers of Israel knew about Elisha and informed the kings that he was actually accompanying their army into battle. Furthermore, the officer informed the three kings that Elisha had been the aide of the great prophet Elijah. Obviously, the LORD had moved upon the heart of Elisha to accompany the troops and to minister to them. Facing the crisis of utter defeat due to lack of water, the three kings humbled themselves and went personally to Elisha to seek his help and godly counsel (v.12).

e. When the three kings confronted Elisha, appealing for his help, Elisha boldly and sternly rebuked Joram for his idolatry. The king was following false prophets and engaging in false worship (vv.13-14). Thus, King Joram should go to the prophets of his father and mother for help, the prophets of Ahab and the infamous Jezebel.

But note the response of King Joram: he again blamed the LORD for their severe, life-threatening crisis. He accused the LORD of having led the three kings to form an alliance in order to bring about their defeat by the king of Moab.

With disgust in his voice toward Joram, Elisha responded bluntly: he would not help them if it were not for the presence of Jehoshaphat, king of Judah. In fact, he would not even bother to look at them at all if it were not for Jehoshaphat, the only true believer associated with the alliance. But for the sake of Jehoshaphat he would seek the counsel of the LORD on behalf of the three armies of the alliance.

f. Note God's wonderful promise to meet the needs of the three-nation alliance—all because of the presence of the true believer Jehoshaphat (vv.15-19). Elisha requested a harpist to play music while he was praying. No doubt, this was for the purpose of quieting his mind and his thoughts from the disturbance of the confrontation with Joram. He needed to focus and concentrate in prayer, and the music would help him.

At some point, the LORD spoke to Elisha and gave him instructions for the three kings. Turning back to the kings, Elisha declared the Word of God to them, instructing them to dig ditches throughout the valley (v.16). If they would dig ditches in the dry sand of the desert—believe the promise of God—the LORD would fill the valley with water. And note: they would see neither wind nor rain; yet the valley would be filled with water for both their soldiers and their livestock (v.17). Furthermore, the LORD would give them victory over Moab (v.18). And the victory would be a great one, for they would be able to overrun the entire land. They would conquer all the major cities and, once again, subject the Moabites under the control of the Northern Kingdom. They were to cut down all of Moab's fruit trees and stop up all their springs in order to limit the nation's water supply. All this would prevent immediate resettlement and the ability to retaliate.

By devastating the land and conquering the major cities, Moab would once again be subjected and forced to pay tribute or taxation to the Northern Kingdom. Apparently, the other two parties of the alliance would most likely be rewarded with the spoils and plunder of Moab.

Thought 1. This was the first nationwide ministry of Elisha. God was using this particular war to show the kings of the world that Elisha was His appointed replacement for the great prophet Elijah. Hereafter the kings of the world were to deal with Elisha, looking to him as God's major representative and prophet to whom they should listen.

Elisha proved his ministry by proclaiming the Word, the promises of God to the kings. This was the task of Elisha, and he proved faithful to the task. Boldly, even sternly, he rebuked King Joram for his false worship and idolatry. Then following the rebuke, he sought the face of the LORD and proclaimed the wonderful promises of God.

This is the task of every prophet and preacher, every teacher and minister of God: to proclaim the Word of God, His wonderful promises…

• to a world in constant conflict, strife, turmoil, distress, pressure, and pain
• to a world that is gripped by a spirit of false worship, idolatry, hopelessness, lawlessness, and violence

Every minister, every servant of God must bear strong testimony and witness to the promises of God. Bearing strong testimony and witness is the duty of every believer, minister and layperson alike. This is the forceful command of God's Holy Word. And it is the fundamental proof of a person's call and ministry, that a person is a true disciple of the Lord Jesus Christ:

> **"Go ye therefore, and teach all nations, baptizing them in the name of the Father, and of the Son, and of the Holy Ghost: Teaching them to observe all things whatsoever I have commanded you: and, lo, I am with you alway, even unto the end of the world. Amen" (Mt.28:19-20).**

> **"And he said unto them, Go ye into all the world, and preach the gospel to every creature" (Mk.16:15).**

> **"But ye shall receive power, after that the Holy Ghost is come upon you: and ye shall be witnesses unto me both in Jerusalem, and in all Judaea, and in Samaria, and unto the uttermost part of the earth" (Ac.1:8).**

> **"Go, stand and speak in the temple to the people all the words of this life" (Ac.5:20).**

> **"We having the same spirit of faith, according as it is written, I believed, and therefore have I spoken; we also believe, and therefore speak" (2 Co.4:13).**

> **"Preach the word; be instant in season, out of season; reprove, rebuke, exhort with all longsuffering and doctrine" (2 Ti.4:2).**

"But sanctify the Lord God in your hearts: and *be* ready always to *give* an answer to every man that asketh you a reason of the hope that is in you with meekness and fear" (1 Pe.3:15).

3 (3:20-27) **Needs, Met, Example of—Promises, of God, Fulfilled—Victory, of Israel, over Moab—Israel, Victories of, over Moab—Northern Kingdom, Victories, over Moab—Moab, Defeated by Israel**: just as God had promised, Israel and its alliance defeated Moab. God met the desperate needs of the alliance exactly as He had promised. Scripture graphically describes the scene:

OUTLINE	SCRIPTURE	SCRIPTURE	OUTLINE

3. The victory of Israel over Moab: God fulfills His promises & validates the true prophet
a. The promise of God fulfilled: Flash floods in the hills flowed into the valley
 	
b. The army of Moab was mobilized & stationed at the southern border
 	
c. The fatal mistake of the Moabite forces
  1) They saw the sun shining on the water in the ditches
    • Mistook it for blood
 	
    • Concluded the coalition armies had turned against & killed each other
  2) They rushed to seize the plunder
  3) The coalition rushed out & attacked, scattering the Moabites, sending them fleeing for their lives
	20 And it came to pass in the morning, when the meat offering was offered, that, behold, there came water by the way of Edom, and the country was filled with water.
	21 And when all the Moabites heard that the kings were come up to fight against them, they gathered all that were able to put on armour, and upward, and stood in the border.
	22 And they rose up early in the morning, and the sun shone upon the water, and the Moabites saw the water on the other side *as* red as blood:
	23 And they said, This *is* blood: the kings are surely slain, and they have smitten one another: now therefore, Moab, to the spoil.
	24 And when they came to the camp of Israel, the Israelites rose up and smote the Moabites, so that they fled
		before them: but they went forward smiting the Moabites, even in *their* country.
		25 And they beat down the cities, and on every good piece of land cast every man his stone, and filled it; and they stopped all the wells of water, and felled all the good trees: only in Kir-haraseth left they the stones thereof; howbeit the slingers went about *it,* and smote it.
		26 And when the king of Moab saw that the battle was too sore for him, he took with him seven hundred men that drew swords, to break through *even* unto the king of Edom: but they could not.
		27 Then he took his eldest son that should have reigned in his stead, and offered him *for* a burnt offering upon the wall. And there was great indignation against Israel: and they departed from him, and returned to *their* own land.
			d. The invasion of Moab by the Israelite coalition
			  1) Slaughtered the population
			  2) Destroyed the major cities & the land: To prevent re-settlement
			    • Covered the fields with stones
			    • Stopped up the springs
			    • Cut down the good trees
			  3) Attacked Kir-Hareseth where the Moabites made a final stand
			
			e. The Moabite king's strategy to turn back the invaders
			  1) He courageously took 700 swordsmen to break through the coalition line defended by the Edomites (the weakest forces)
			  2) He offered his son as a human sacrifice—in sight of all: To appease, remove the anger of his false god
			f. The withdrawal of the coalition: Due to a passionate fury rising against Israel

a. Everything unfolded just as God had promised through His dear servant Elisha (v.20). Flash floods in the hills flowed down into the valley, and the ditches that had been dug by the soldiers were filled with water. There was no question, Elisha was God's prophet and the kings had clear evidence of his appointment by God. Hereafter, the kings were to look to Elisha as God's messenger and prophet.

b. At some point in time, border guards stationed by the Moabites along the southern border spotted the invasion force led by Israel. They were able to get word to the Moabite officials that an alliance led by Israel was launching a southern assault. As quickly as possible, the Moabite king mobilized a citizen-army by drafting every man who was able to bear arms and positioned them on the southern border.

c. But the Moabite army made a fatal mistake (vv.22-24). When they arose in the morning, they saw in the distance the sun shining on the water in the ditches, and the water reflected a red color that the Moabites mistook for blood. Concluding that the coalition parties had turned against each other and suffered a great massacre among themselves, the Moabite forces rushed to finish the massacre and to seize the plunder. But as they neared the campsite of the Israelite coalition, the alliance forces rushed out and attacked the Moabite army, scattering them and sending them fleeing for their lives.

d. The Israelite forces began pursuing the fleeing citizen-army and, just as prophesied, they slaughtered the population and destroyed the major cities. In order to prevent resettlement of the land, they covered the fields with stones, stopping up the springs, and cutting down the fruit-producing trees. When the allied forces reached the capital of Moab, Kir-Hareseth, they set up a siege around the city. They then attacked with a corps of special forces skilled in the use of slings, for the Moabites were making a final stand within the capital city (v.25).

e. Seeking to turn back the invaders, the Moabite king launched a courageous strategy (vv.26-27). He took seven hundred swordsmen and boldly rushed out the city gate to attack the weakest forces of the alliance, which were the Edomites. But his strategy failed, and he had to retreat back behind the city walls.

As the desperate struggle for the capital city continued, the Moabite king Mesha became frantic, sacrificing his firstborn son as a human sacrifice. This was an attempt to satisfy or appease the false god Chemosh, the major Moabite deity. Obviously, the Moabite king felt that he and his forces had for some reason displeased their god. Consequently, Mesha sought to pacify the anger of his false god by making the most valuable sacrifice he could, which was, of course, the sacrifice of his oldest son and heir apparent. Note that the sacrifice had taken place on the city wall in full view of everyone: the alliance forces, Mesha's own Moabite forces, and the citizenry finding refuge behind the city walls.

f. Note the reference to a passionate fury rising against Israel, a fury so fierce that it forced the Israelites to withdraw and return to their own land (v.27). What was this intense fury? Had the Moabite army become so aroused and motivated by the human sacrifice that they were consumed with rage—a rage so intense that they arose and ended up defeating the Israelite forces, causing them to retreat? Or does it mean that the Israelite coalition was so disgusted, shocked, and indignant with the human sacrifice that they simply withdrew on their own? Scripture does not say. But whatever the reason, some burning passion arose that caused the Israelite coalition to retreat and to return to their own lands.

Thought 1. God fulfills His promises. He did exactly what He had promised through His dear servant Elisha. And Elisha's call and ministry were validated, proven by the fulfillment of God's promises. God will always do exactly what He promises us. The unconditional promises of God will take place, and nothing can stop them. Other promises have conditions attached to them. If we meet the conditions, God will fulfill these promises as well. If a person walks righteously before God, seeking God, and trusting God, God will work in the person's life and fulfill every promise He has made. Listen to what Scripture says about the promises of God.
(1) God's promises are unfailing.

> **"Blessed *be* the LORD, that hath given rest unto his people Israel, according to all that he promised: there hath not failed one word of all his good promise, which he promised by the hand of Moses his servant" (1 K.8:56).**

(2) God has the power to do what He promises.

> **"He staggered not at the promise of God through unbelief; but was strong in faith, giving glory to God; And being fully persuaded that, what he had promised, he was able also to perform" (Ro.4:20-21).**
> **"Now unto him that is able to do exceeding abundantly above all that we ask or think, according to the power that worketh in us" (Ep.3:20).**

(3) God's promises are great and precious, of infinite value.

> **"Whereby are given unto us exceeding great and precious promises: that by these ye might be partakers of the divine nature, having escaped the corruption that is in the world through lust" (2 Pe.1:4).**

(4) God's promises are rooted in Jesus Christ and reach their summit in the gift of eternal life.

> **"For God so loved the world, that he gave his only begotten Son, that whosoever believeth in him should not perish, but have everlasting life" (Jn.3:16).**
> **"And Jesus said unto them, I am the bread of life: he that cometh to me shall never hunger; and he that believeth on me shall never thirst" (Jn.6:35).**
> **"Let not your heart be troubled: ye believe in God, believe also in me. In my Father's house are many mansions: if *it were* not so, I would have told you. I go to prepare a place for you" (Jn.14:1-2).**
> **"For all the promises of God in him *are* yea, and in him Amen, unto the glory of God by us" (2 Co.1:20).**
> **"And this is the promise that he hath promised us, *even* eternal life" (1 Jn.2:25).**
> **"And God shall wipe away all tears from their eyes; and there shall be no more death, neither sorrow, nor crying, neither shall there be any more pain: for the former things are passed away" (Re.21:4).**

(5) God's promises have one primary purpose: to work all things out for the good of the believer.

> **"And we know that all things work together for good to them that love God, to them who are the called according to *his* purpose" (Ro.8:28).**
> **"For our light affliction, which is but for a moment, worketh for us a far more exceeding *and* eternal weight of glory" (2 Co.4:17).**

DIVISION II

THE MINISTRY AND MIRACLES OF ELISHA: A DRAMATIC DEMONSTRATION OF GOD'S POWER AND CARE FOR HIS PEOPLE, 4:1–13:25

(4:1–13:25) **DIVISION OVERVIEW**: With this division, a new period of history begins for both Israel and Judah. When Ahab died, he left Israel somewhat weakened militarily, economically, politically, and socially. And true spiritual direction was totally absent from the nation's soul. Ahab had died on the battlefield in a losing cause against Syria and was succeeded by his wicked son Ahaziah. Sadly, Ahaziah continued the detestable policies of his father and mother (Jezebel), the policies of oppressing the people and of enforcing the worship of false gods upon them, in particular the worship of Baal and the state religion instituted by Jeroboam I (see outline and note—1 K.12:25-33 for more discussion). Tragically, throughout this entire period of the Northern Kingdom's history, not a single king stepped forth to turn the tide of wickedness and false worship that flooded the nation.

Nevertheless, God did not yet forsake the Northern Kingdom. He had already appointed Elisha to replace Elijah. And while using Elisha to reach out and warn the nation as a whole, God raised up other prophets to minister in specific places or on special occasions. But the focus of this division of Scripture is upon Elisha and his miraculous works both within and without the borders of the Northern Kingdom. God used Elisha in an attempt to arouse the kings and people to trust the LORD and to turn away from their immoral, lawless behavior and from their false worship. Through the messages and miraculous signs of Elisha, the LORD proclaimed His love for the people, demonstrating that He is the only living and true God and that He cares deeply for them. But God's pleas and warnings through His dear prophet were to no avail. The Israelites, both kings and people, continued to reject the LORD. Within the Northern Kingdom, the unbroken stream of wickedness, lawlessness and corrupt worship rushed madly to its inevitable judgment. Since the division of Israel into two kingdoms, the Northern Kingdom had never had a good, righteous king. Even during this period of their history, no righteous king stepped forth to turn the Israelites back to God. If the unbroken stream continued, there was only one inevitable end lying over the horizon: judgment. The Northern Kingdom of Israel would fall and the people would be exiled just as predicted by the prophets (1 K.14:15-16).

So far as Judah is concerned during this period of history, the pattern of inconsistent reigns continued. Both good and evil rulers took the throne in Judah:

⇒ Jehoram and Ahaziah, who were both evil kings. (8:1-29).
⇒ Queen Athaliah, who was the only woman to rule in either Judah or Israel and was one of the most brutal, violent rulers of either kingdom (11:1-21).
⇒ Jehoash who was the only good ruler during this entire period, and even he slipped away from the LORD during the latter years of his life (12:1-21).

This period of history covers about fifty-five years (850-795). These were years when both Israel and Judah continued their downward spiral of disintegration, a spiral that would lead to utter destruction and exile. Israel's collapse would merely come sooner, because not a single king of the Northern Kingdom ever trusted—or led his people to trust—the LORD.

As a person studies this section of Scripture, a challenge confronts the person with an awesome truth: he or she must turn away from wickedness and false worship. A person must turn to the LORD or else face the inevitable consequence of terrifying judgment.

THE MINISTRY AND MIRACLES OF ELISHA: A DRAMATIC DEMONSTRATION OF GOD'S POWER AND CARE FOR HIS PEOPLE, 4:1–13:25

A. The Poor Widow, a Wealthy Shunammite Woman, and a School of Prophets Miraculously Delivered: God's Power to Meet the Desperate Needs of His People, 4:1-44

B. The Syrian Army Commander Naaman Miraculously Healed: God's Power to Convert and Heal a Person, 5:1-27

CHAPTER 4

II. THE MINISTRY & MIRA-
CLES OF ELISHA: A
DRAMATIC DEMONSTRA-
TION OF GOD'S POWER
& CARE FOR HIS PEO-
PLE, 4:1–13:25

A. The Poor Widow, a
Wealthy Shunammite
Woman, & a School of
Prophets Miraculously
Delivered: God's Power
to Meet the Desperate
Needs of His People,
4:1-44

**1. The poor widow's oil miracu-
lously multiplied: God's power to
meet the needs of poor widows**
a. The crisis: A prophet had
died & left his widow with
heavy debt
1) Creditors demanded payment: To enslave her sons

2) All food & supplies had
been depleted: Only a little olive oil for cooking &
heating was left
b. The solution
1) Seeking the counsel of the
prophet, 1-2
2) Seeking the help of neighbors: To ask for empty
jars; not to ask for just a
few, but many
3) Seeking privacy, the glory
of God, not attention for
self
4) Working—personally do-
ing all she could

5) Doing exactly what the
prophet instructed & trusting God to meet the need

c. The provision
1) The small amount of olive
oil was multiplied, filling
many jars: A lesson on
great faith

2) The miraculous oil was
sold to pay the widow's
debt & to save taking care of
one's debts
**2. The Shunammite's son mi-
raculously restored to life:
God's power to give life & to
raise the dead**
a. The rich woman's hospitality
1) She entertained Elisha
when he passed by

bread.
9 And she said unto her husband, Behold now, I perceive
that this *is* an holy man of
God, which passeth by us
continually.
10 Let us make a little chamber, I pray thee, on the wall;
and let us set for him there a
bed, and a table, and a stool,
and a candlestick: and it shall
be, when he cometh to us,
that he shall turn in thither.
11 And it fell on a day, that
he came thither, and he
turned into the chamber, and
lay there.
12 And he said to Gehazi his
servant, Call this Shunammite. And when he had called
her, she stood before him.
13 And he said unto him,
Say now unto her, Behold,
thou hast been careful for us
with all this care; what *is* to
be done for thee? wouldest
thou be spoken for to the
king, or to the captain of the
host? And she answered, I
dwell among mine own peo-
ple.
14 And he said, What then *is*
to be done for her? And
Gehazi answered, Verily she
hath no child, and her husband is old.
15 And he said, Call her.
And when he had called her,
she stood in the door.
16 And he said, About this
season, according to the time
of life, thou shalt embrace a
son. And she said, Nay, my
lord, *thou* man of God, do
not lie unto thine handmaid.
17 And the woman con-
ceived, and bare a son at that
season that Elisha had said
unto her, according to the
time of life.
18 And when the child was
grown, it fell on a day, that
he went out to his father to
the reapers.
19 And he said unto his father, My head, my head. And
he said to a lad, Carry him to
his mother.
20 And when he had taken
him, and brought him to his
mother, he sat on her knees
till noon, and *then* died.
21 And she went up, and laid
him on the bed of the man of
God, and shut *the door* upon
him, and went out.
22 And she called unto her
husband, and said, Send me, I

Now there cried a certain
woman of the wives of the
sons of the prophets unto Elisha, saying, Thy servant
my husband is dead; and
thou knowest that thy servant
did fear the LORD: and the
creditor is come to take unto
him my two sons to be
bondmen.
2 And Elisha said unto her,
What shall I do for thee? tell
me, what hast thou in the
house? And she said, Thine
handmaid hath not any thing
in the house, save a pot of
oil.
3 Then he said, Go, borrow
thee vessels abroad of all thy
neighbours, *even* empty vessels; borrow not a few.
4 And when thou art come
in, thou shalt shut the door
upon thee and upon thy sons,
and shalt pour out into all
those vessels, and thou shalt
set aside that which is full.
5 So she went from him, and
shut the door upon her and
upon her sons, who brought
the vessels to her; and she
poured out.
6 And it came to pass, when
the vessels were full, that she
said unto her son, Bring me
yet a vessel. And he said unto
her, *There is* not a vessel
more. And the oil stayed.
7 Then she came and told the
man of God. And he said,
Go, sell the oil, and pay thy
debt, and live thou and thy
children of the rest.
8 And it fell on a day, that
Elisha passed to Shunem,
where *was* a great woman;
and she constrained him to
eat bread. And so it was,
that as oft as he passed
by, he turned in thither to eat

2) She encouraged her husband to add a room to
their house where Elisha
could stay when he came
to their city, Shunem

b. The woman's wonderful reward: A child
1) Elisha wanted to do something for the kind & gen-
erous woman
• He sent his servant
Gehazi to summon the
woman so he could ask
what he could do to re-
pay her: Could he re-
quest a special political
or legal favor for her or
a military guard to pro-
tect her?

• The woman replied that
she had no special needs

2) Elisha asked his servant
for a gift suggestion for
the woman: Discovered
she was childless

3) Elisha summoned the
childless woman: Prom-
ised that God would give
her a child within one year

• She objected: Feared
disappointment, a bro-
ken heart
• She soon became preg-
nant & bore a son—just
as Elisha promised

c. The woman's broken heart &
overwhelming sorrow
1) The child suffered a violent headache one day
• Was with his father in
the fields
• Was sent home to his
mother in the arms of a
servant
2) The mother tenderly held
the child on her lap until
noon: He then died
3) The mother kept the
child's death a secret
• She laid him on Elisha's
bed
• She asked her husband
for a servant & donkey

so she could make a quick visit to Elisha

- She was questioned why, since it was not a religious holiday
- She assured her husband

4) The mother rushed to Elisha

d. The woman's faith in God & in His prophet Elisha

1) The mother rushed to Mt. Carmel where Elisha lived
2) Elisha saw her coming in the distance

- He sent his servant to meet & greet her

- She refused to be delayed by conversation with the servant

3) The mother rushed up to Elisha & knelt to the ground, grabbing his feet
  - Gehazi went over to push her away
  - Elisha stopped him, sensing the mother's bitter grief & sorrow

4) The mother poured out her soul to Elisha: Her pain was worse than having no child at all
5) Elisha instructed his servant Gehazi to rush to the boy & to lay Elisha's staff on the dead child's face: A symbol of God's power

- The mother refused to leave unless Elisha went back with her: A picture of persistent faith in God
- Elisha returned with her
- Gehazi rushed on ahead & laid the staff on the boy's face, but there was no response

- Gehazi went back to meet Elisha to report what had happened

pray thee, one of the young men, and one of the asses, that I may run to the man of God, and come again.
23 And he said, Wherefore wilt thou go to him to day? *it is* neither new moon, nor sabbath. And she said, *It shall be* well.
24 Then she saddled an ass, and said to her servant, Drive, and go forward; slack not *thy* riding for me, except I bid thee.
25 So she went and came unto the man of God to mount Carmel. And it came to pass, when the man of God saw her afar off, that he said to Gehazi his servant, Behold, *yonder is* that Shunammite:
26 Run now, I pray thee, to meet her, and say unto her, *Is it* well with thee? *is it* well with thy husband? *is it* well with the child? And she answered, *It is* well.
27 And when she came to the man of God to the hill, she caught him by the feet: but Gehazi came near to thrust her away. And the man of God said, Let her alone; for her soul *is* vexed within her: and the LORD hath hid *it* from me, and hath not told me.
28 Then she said, Did I desire a son of my lord? did I not say, Do not deceive me?
29 Then he said to Gehazi, Gird up thy loins, and take my staff in thine hand, and go thy way: if thou meet any man, salute him not; and if any salute thee, answer him not again: and lay my staff upon the face of the child.
30 And the mother of the child said, *As* the LORD liveth, and *as* thy soul liveth, I will not leave thee. And he arose, and followed her.
31 And Gehazi passed on before them, and laid the staff upon the face of the child; but *there was* neither voice, nor hearing. Wherefore he went again to meet him, and told him, saying, The child is not awaked.
32 And when Elisha was come into the house, behold, the child was dead, *and* laid upon his bed.

33 He went in therefore, and shut the door upon them twain, and prayed unto the LORD.
34 And he went up, and lay upon the child, and put his mouth upon his mouth, and his eyes upon his eyes, and his hands upon his hands: and he stretched himself upon the child; and the flesh of the child waxed warm.
35 Then he returned, and walked in the house to and fro; and went up, and stretched himself upon him: and the child sneezed seven times, and the child opened his eyes.
36 And he called Gehazi, and said, Call this Shunammite. So he called her. And when she was come in unto him, he said, Take up thy son.
37 Then she went in, and fell at his feet, and bowed herself to the ground, and took up her son, and went out.
38 And Elisha came again to Gilgal: and *there was* a dearth in the land; and the sons of the prophets *were* sitting before him: and he said unto his servant, Set on the great pot, and seethe pottage for the sons of the prophets.
39 And one went out into the field to gather herbs, and found a wild vine, and gathered thereof wild gourds his lap full, and came and shred *them* into the pot of pottage: for they knew *them* not.
40 So they poured out for the men to eat. And it came to pass, as they were eating of the pottage, that they cried out, and said, O *thou* man of God, *there is* death in the pot. And they could not eat *thereof.*
41 But he said, Then bring meal. And he cast *it* into the pot; and he said, Pour out for the people, that they may eat. And there was no harm in the pot.
42 And there came a man from Baal-shalisha, and brought the man of God bread of the firstfruits, twenty loaves of barley, and full ears of corn in the husk thereof. And he said, Give unto the people, that they may eat.

e. The woman's persistent faith rewarded
1) Elisha found the boy lying dead on his bed
2) Elisha shut the door & prayed to the LORD

3) Elisha stretched his body out upon the boy, face-to-face: The dead child's body began to grow warm
4) Elisha got up & paced the floor, continuing to pray
5) Elisha again stretched his body out upon the boy, & the boy sneezed seven times: God revived the dead child
6) Elisha sent his servant to summon the woman
  - He instructed her to take her son

- She fell at his feet in gratitude & bowed in worship before the LORD

3. **The prophets miraculously fed: God's power to meet the basic needs of His people**
a. A bad stew was miraculously purified
1) Elisha visited the school of prophets in Gilgal

2) A stew was prepared
3) A student gathered wild gourds & cut them up in the stew

4) The students—tasting the stew—immediately knew it was poisonous: Informed Elisha

5) Elisha instructed them to add flour to the pot
6) The stew was suddenly purified, edible

b. One hundred prophets were miraculously fed
1) An unknown believer brought supplies to the school: 20 loaves of bread & some fresh grain
2) Elisha ordered the food distributed

3) Elisha's servant protested, questioning how so little could be used to feed 100 young men 4) Elisha assured the servant of God's promise: He	43 And his servitor said, What, should I set this before an hundred men? He said again, Give the people, that they may eat: for thus saith the LORD, They	shall eat, and shall leave *thereof.* 44 So he set *it* before them, and they did eat, and left *thereof,* according to the word of the LORD.	would feed His people, meet their need 5) Elisha's servant obeyed & all the prophets had food: God's Word was fulfilled

DIVISION II

THE MINISTRY AND MIRACLES OF ELISHA: A DRAMATIC DEMONSTRATION OF GOD'S POWER AND CARE FOR HIS PEOPLE, 4:1–13:25

A. The Poor Widow, a Wealthy Shunammite Woman, and a School of Prophets Miraculously Delivered: God's Power to Meet the Desperate Needs of His People, 4:1-44

(4:1-44) Introduction—Circumstances, Described—Circumstances, How to Conquer—Crises, Described—Desperation, Experiences of, Described: circumstances sometimes arise that create a sense of desperation. Take death, for example. We have no control over death. Consequently, when a loved one is snatched from our presence—whether child, parent, or some other close friend—a sense of helplessness grips us. A deep, agonizing void fills the human heart, an emptiness that is sometimes almost unbearable.

When a person loses everything he or she has financially or materially, becoming destitute and perhaps unemployed, the same sense of desperation grips the human heart. An intense stress afflicts the mind and heart, provoking the person to question: "What am I to do? How can I live with no money and no job to earn a living?"

Almost any human activity can create moments of desperation for us: eating can cause choking; swimming can end in drowning; and the home or workplace or even the playground may be the site of a serious injury. A serious crisis can occur in almost any place at any time, creating an urgent need in the life of any one of us.

This is the practical message of the present Scripture, the message that answers the gnawing question: Where is the power to meet the desperate needs of human life? This is: *The Poor Widow, a Wealthy Shunammite Woman, and a School of Prophets Miraculously Delivered: God's Power to Meet the Desperate Needs of His People*, 4:1-44.

1. The poor widow's oil miraculously multiplied: God's power to meet the needs of poor widows (vv.1-7).
2. The rich Shunammite's son miraculously restored to life: God's power to give life and to raise the dead (vv.8-37).
3. The prophets miraculously fed: God's power to meet the basic needs of His people, (vv.38-44).

1 (4:1-7) **Faith, Kinds of, Great—Debt, Duty—Stewardship, Duty—Money, Duty—Bills, Duty—Widow's Oil, Miracle of—Widow, Poor, Needs Met**: the first miracle was a very special case, that of a poor widow's oil being miraculously multiplied. Note the desperate condition of this poverty-stricken widow:

OUTLINE	SCRIPTURE	SCRIPTURE	OUTLINE

1. **The poor widow's oil miraculously multiplied: God's power to meet the needs of poor widows**
a. The crisis: A prophet had died & left his widow with heavy debt
  1) Creditors demanded payment: To enslave her sons
 	
  2) All food & supplies had been depleted: Only a little olive oil for cooking & heating was left
b. The solution
  1) Seeking the counsel of the prophet, 1-2
  2) Seeking the help of neighbors: To ask for empty jars; not to ask for just a few, but many
  3) Seeking privacy, the glory
	Now there cried a certain woman of the wives of the sons of the prophets unto Elisha, saying, Thy servant my husband is dead; and thou knowest that thy servant did fear the LORD: and the creditor is come to take unto him my two sons to be bondmen.
	2 And Elisha said unto her, What shall I do for thee? tell me, what hast thou in the house? And she said, Thine handmaid hath not any thing in the house, save a pot of oil.
	3 Then he said, Go, borrow thee vessels abroad of all thy neighbours, *even* empty vessels; borrow not a few.
	4 And when thou art come
		in, thou shalt shut the door upon thee and upon thy sons, and shalt pour out into all those vessels, and thou shalt set aside that which is full.
		5 So she went from him, and shut the door upon her and upon her sons, who brought *the vessels* to her; and she poured out.
		6 And it came to pass, when the vessels were full, that she said unto her son, Bring me yet a vessel. And he said unto her, *There is* not a vessel more. And the oil stayed.
		7 Then she came and told the man of God. And he said, Go, sell the oil, and pay thy debt, and live thou and thy children of the rest.
			of God, not attention for self
			4) Working—personally doing all she could
			
			5) Doing exactly what the prophet instructed & trusting God to meet the need
			
			c. The provision
			  1) The small amount of olive oil was multiplied, filling many jars: A lesson on great faith
			
			  2) The miraculous oil was sold to pay the widow's debt & to save her sons: A lesson on taking care of one's debts

a. The widow faced a severe and urgent crisis. Her husband, a prophet, had died and left her with heavy debt (vv.1-2). She was destitute, having no money whatsoever to pay off the debts nor to meet payments demanded by the creditors. As a result, the creditors were threatening to enslave her two sons. Ancient Jewish law demanded that debt be paid off by *labor* if a person could not pay his creditor. The debtor was to become a servant, a worker for his creditor, but never a slave. Furthermore, the creditor was to treat the debtor as a worker, not as a slave (see outline and notes—Ex.21:1-2;

Le.25:35-55; De.15:1-11 for more discussion). However, as is so often the case, the law of God was abused and some creditors within Jewish society apparently enslaved others who owed them money. Apparently this was the case with the widow and her two sons. Note that she was utterly destitute, without any food or supplies whatsoever. All she had was a little olive oil that could be used for cooking or perhaps heating.

b. In seeking for a way to solve her critical problem, the widow did the only thing she could: she sought the counsel of the prophet Elisha (vv.2-5). Note the five steps she took, and how the very same steps can apply to any widow or any individual who is facing a serious crisis:

1) In desperation the widow went to the prophet Elisha to appeal for help (vv.1-2). As simply as she could, she explained her circumstances, how desperately she needed help to pay off her debts and to keep her boys from being enslaved by the creditor. She informed Elisha that she was destitute, with no means whatsoever to pay off the debts, nothing except a little oil.

2) With a heart full of compassion, the prophet told her to seek the help of her neighbors (v.3). She was to go around to all her neighbors and borrow all the jars they would lend her. She was not to ask for just a few jars, but for many, just as many as they would lend.

3) She and her sons were then to seek privacy, get all alone by going inside their home and shutting the door behind them (v.4). Whatever miracle took place was to be to the glory of God. The miracle of meeting her need was not to attract attention to her, not to point to her as a super-spiritual person, but rather to honor God. Out of a heart of compassion, God would be meeting her need. But He and He alone was to be praised, for He and He alone could meet her need.

4) Once inside her home, the widow was to begin working, personally doing all she could (v.4). She was to take the little oil she had and begin to pour it in the jars she had borrowed. She was to continue to pour until each jar was completely full and to continue pouring until all the jars were full.

5) If the widow believed Elisha, she would do exactly as he instructed, trusting God to meet the need (v.5). Just imagine the great faith this took: to take the little bit of oil she had in a small jar and to begin to pour it, believing that God would multiply the oil until all the jars were full. But this is exactly what this poor, destitute widow did: she obeyed the prophet and trusted the LORD to multiply the oil enough to fill all the containers she had borrowed.

c. The result was miraculous: the small amount of olive oil was multiplied, filling a large number of jars (vv.6-7). Excitedly rushing to the prophet Elisha, she explained just what had happened. There was not a jar left that was not full and overflowing with oil. Hearing this, Elisha instructed the woman to go and sell the oil to pay off her debts and to save her sons from enslavement. Note how much the oil had been multiplied: not only enough for her to pay off her debts, but also enough to meet the living expenses for her and her sons for the rest of their lives (v.7).

Thought 1. The lesson for us is simple and straightforward: widows and widowers can look to God to have their needs met. No matter what need a widow or widower is facing, God's heart is full of compassion and reaches out to meet that need. Just like this widow in Scripture, if the need is financial, God wants to help meet the need for money. If the crisis is loneliness, lack of companionship, insecurity, disobedient or rebellious children, poverty, lack of food, clothing, or housing, unemployment, or a job that pays too little—whatever the need is, God's heart reaches out in compassion for the widow or widower. And He wants to help meet the need.

But there is a condition: the same five steps taken by this widow should be taken by any widow or widower facing a grave need:

⇒ that of informing a true minister of the gospel and seeking his counsel
⇒ that of seeking the help of neighbors, humbly asking for assistance
⇒ that of seeking privacy in the sense of giving the glory to God and not pointing to oneself as being super spiritual or deserving of help
⇒ that of working personally to solve the problem
⇒ that of following the counsel and advice of the minister and trusting God to help meet the need

In each of these five steps the widow or widower must take the initiative. The person following these steps and trusting God will be helped.

"But seek ye first the kingdom of God, and his righteousness; and all these things shall be added unto you" (Mt.6:33).
"And there was one Anna, a prophetess, the daughter of Phanuel, of the tribe of Aser: she was of a great age, and had lived with an husband seven years from her virginity; And she *was* a widow of about fourscore and four years, which departed not from the temple, but served *God* with fastings and prayers night and day. And she coming in that instant gave thanks likewise unto the Lord, and spake of him to all them that looked for redemption in Jerusalem" (Lu.2:36-38).
"But my God shall supply all your need according to his riches in glory by Christ Jesus" (Ph.4:19).
"He doth execute the judgment of the fatherless and widow, and loveth the stranger, in giving him food and raiment" (De.10:18).
"Thou hast seen *it;* for thou beholdest mischief and spite, to requite *it* with thy hand: the poor committeth himself unto thee; thou art the helper of the fatherless" (Ps.10:14).
"A father of the fatherless, and a judge of the widows, *is* God in his holy habitation" (Ps.68:5).
"Blessed *be* the Lord, *who* daily loadeth us *with benefits, even* the God of our salvation. Selah" (Ps.68:19).
"I will abundantly bless her provision: I will satisfy her poor with bread" (Ps.132:15).
"The LORD openeth *the eyes of* the blind: the LORD raiseth them that are bowed down: the LORD loveth the righteous: The LORD preserveth the strangers; he relieveth the fatherless and widow: but the way of the wicked he turneth upside down" (Ps.146:8-9).

2 KINGS 4:1-44

"Trust in the LORD with all thine heart; and lean not unto thine own understanding. In all thy ways acknowledge him, and he shall direct thy paths" (Pr.3:5-6).

"The LORD will destroy the house of the proud: but he will establish the border of the widow" (Pr.15:25).

"Leave thy fatherless children, I will preserve *them* alive; and let thy widows trust in me" (Je.49:11).

2 (4:8-37) **Life, Source of—Dead, Raised—Resurrection, Example of—Miracles, Raised from the Dead—Shunammite's Son, Raised from the Dead—God, Power of, to Raise the Dead—Restoration, from the Dead, Example of—Faith, Kinds of, Persistent**: there was the Shunammite's son who was miraculously restored to life. This is a clear demonstration of God's power to give life and to raise the dead. Exactly what happened is dramatically pictured by Scripture:

OUTLINE	SCRIPTURE	SCRIPTURE	OUTLINE
2. The Shunammite's son miraculously restored to life: God's power to give life & to raise the dead a. The rich woman's hospitality 1) She entertained Elisha when he passed by 2) She encouraged her husband to add a room to their house where Elisha could stay when he came to their city, Shunem b. The woman's wonderful reward: A child 1) Elisha wanted to do something for the kind & generous woman • He sent his servant Gehazi to summon the woman so he could ask what he could do to repay her: Could he request a special political or legal favor for her or a military guard to protect her? • The woman replied that she had no special needs 2) Elisha asked his servant for a gift suggestion for the woman: Discovered she was childless 3) Elisha summoned the childless woman: Promised that God would give her a child within one year • She objected: Feared disappointment, a broken heart • She soon became preg-	8 And it fell on a day, that Elisha passed to Shunem, where *was* a great woman; and she constrained him to eat bread. And so it was, *that* as oft as he passed by, he turned in thither to eat bread. 9 And she said unto her husband, Behold now, I perceive that this *is* an holy man of God, which passeth by us continually. 10 Let us make a little chamber, I pray thee, on the wall; and let us set for him there a bed, and a table, and a stool, and a candlestick: and it shall be, when he cometh to us, that he shall turn in thither. 11 And it fell on a day, that he came thither, and he turned into the chamber, and lay there. 12 And he said to Gehazi his servant, Call this Shunammite. And when he had called her, she stood before him. 13 And he said unto him, Say now unto her, Behold, thou hast been careful for us with all this care; what *is* to be done for thee? wouldest thou be spoken for to the king, or to the captain of the host? And she answered, I dwell among mine own people. 14 And he said, What then *is* to be done for her? And Gehazi answered, Verily she hath no child, and her husband is old. 15 And he said, Call her. And when he had called her, she stood in the door. 16 And he said, About this season, according to the time of life, thou shalt embrace a son. And she said, Nay, my lord, *thou* man of God, do not lie unto thine handmaid. 17 And the woman con-	ceived, and bare a son at that season that Elisha had said unto her, according to the time of life. 18 And when the child was grown, it fell on a day, that he went out to his father to the reapers. 19 And he said unto his father, My head, my head. And he said to a lad, Carry him to his mother. 20 And when he had taken him, and brought him to his mother, he sat on her knees till noon, and *then* died. 21 And she went up, and laid him on the bed of the man of God, and shut *the door* upon him, and went out. 22 And she called unto her husband, and said, Send me, I pray thee, one of the young men, and one of the asses, that I may run to the man of God, and come again. 23 And he said, Wherefore wilt thou go to him to day? *it is* neither new moon, nor sabbath. And she said, *It shall be* well. 24 Then she saddled an ass, and said to her servant, Drive, and go forward; slack not *thy* riding for me, except I bid thee. 25 So she went and came unto the man of God to mount Carmel. And it came to pass, when the man of God saw her afar off, that he said to Gehazi his servant, Behold, *yonder is* that Shunammite: 26 Run now, I pray thee, to meet her, and say unto her, *Is it* well with thee? *is it* well with thy husband? *is it* well with the child? And she answered, *It is* well. 27 And when she came to the man of God to the hill, she caught him by the feet: but Gehazi came near to	nant & bore a son—just as Elisha promised c. The woman's broken heart & overwhelming sorrow 1) The child suffered a violent headache one day • Was with his father in the fields • Was sent home to his mother in the arms of a servant 2) The mother tenderly held the child on her lap until noon: He then died 3) The mother kept the child's death a secret • She laid him on Elisha's bed • She asked her husband for a servant & donkey so she could make a quick visit to Elisha • She was questioned why, since it was not a religious holiday • She assured her husband 4) The mother rushed to Elisha d. The woman's faith in God & in His prophet Elisha 1) The mother rushed to Mt. Carmel where Elisha lived 2) Elisha saw her coming in the distance • He sent his servant to meet & greet her • She refused to be delayed by conversation with the servant 3) The mother rushed up to Elisha & knelt to the ground, grabbing his feet • Gehazi went over to

38

OUTLINE	SCRIPTURE	SCRIPTURE	OUTLINE
push her away	thrust her away. And the man	come into the house, behold,	rewarded
• Elisha stopped him, sensing the mother's bitter grief & sorrow	of God said, Let her alone; for her soul *is* vexed within her: and the LORD hath hid *it* from me, and hath not told me.	the child was dead, *and* laid upon his bed.	1) Elisha found the boy lying dead on his bed
		33 He went in therefore, and shut the door upon them twain, and prayed unto the LORD.	2) Elisha shut the door & prayed to the LORD
4) The mother poured out her soul to Elisha: Her pain was worse than having no child at all	28 Then she said, Did I desire a son of my lord? did I not say, Do not deceive me?	34 And he went up, and lay upon the child, and put his mouth upon his mouth, and his eyes upon his eyes, and his hands upon his hands: and he stretched himself upon the child; and the flesh of the child waxed warm.	3) Elisha stretched his body out upon the boy, face-to-face: The dead child's body began to grow warm
5) Elisha instructed his servant Gehazi to rush to the boy & to lay Elisha's staff on the dead child's face: A symbol of God's power	29 Then he said to Gehazi, Gird up thy loins, and take my staff in thine hand, and go thy way: if thou meet any man, salute him not; and if any salute thee, answer him not again: and lay my staff upon the face of the child.		
• The mother refused to leave unless Elisha went back with her: A picture of persistent faith in God	30 And the mother of the child said, *As* the LORD liveth, and *as* thy soul liveth, I will not leave thee. And he arose, and followed her.	35 Then he returned, and walked in the house to and fro; and went up, and stretched himself upon him: and the child sneezed seven times, and the child opened his eyes.	4) Elisha got up & paced the floor, continuing to pray
• Elisha returned with her			5) Elisha again stretched his body out upon the boy, & the boy sneezed seven times: God revived the dead child
• Gehazi rushed on ahead & laid the staff on the boy's face, but there was no response	31 And Gehazi passed on before them, and laid the staff upon the face of the child; but *there was* neither voice, nor hearing. Wherefore he went again to meet him, and told him, saying, The child is not awaked.	36 And he called Gehazi, and said, Call this Shunammite. So he called her. And when she was come in unto him, he said, Take up thy son.	6) Elisha sent his servant to summon the woman
• Gehazi went back to meet Elisha to report what had happened			• He instructed her to take her son
		37 Then she went in, and fell at his feet, and bowed herself to the ground, and took up her son, and went out.	• She fell at his feet in gratitude & bowed in worship before the LORD
e. The woman's persistent faith	32 And when Elisha was		

a. Note the Shunammite woman's hospitality to Elisha on one of his trips to her city (vv.8-10). While ministering there, she invited the prophet to join her and her family for a meal. He accepted her kindness, and a close bond of friendship was developed between him and her family. As a result, she left an open invitation for him to stop by anytime he was passing through their city, and this was quite often. For Elisha frequently passed through Shunem as he traveled to Jezreel and other cities in the surrounding area of Israel. His visits became so frequent that the Shunammite woman encouraged her husband to add a room to their house where Elisha could stay when he needed overnight accommodations.

b. Note the Shunammite woman's wonderful reward for her kindness and hospitality shown to Elisha (vv.11-17). Because of her generosity, Elisha wanted to do something very special for her. Sending his servant to summon her, he asked if he could request a special political or legal favor from the king for her? Or, knowing that her husband was quite aged, could he perhaps request a special military guard from the army commander to protect her?

Graciously the woman declined, informing Elisha that she had no special needs, for she lived among her relatives and both they and her neighbors were caring. With the issue settled in the woman's mind, she left Elisha and returned to her household duties.

But soon after leaving, Elisha turned to his servant and asked for a gift suggestion from him (v.14). The servant replied that the woman was childless and her husband was very elderly, so she probably would never have children. Immediately Elisha summoned the childless woman and promised that God would give her a child within one year (vv.15-17). Standing in the doorway, the woman was utterly shocked, but no doubt flooded with a sense of excitement. Nevertheless, she objected to Elisha's promise because she feared disappointment, a broken heart. She objected, asking for Elisha not to mislead her, not to break her heart with such a promise. But she soon became pregnant and bore a son just as Elisha had promised.

c. However, some years later the woman's heart was to be broken with an overwhelming sorrow (vv.18-24). The child suffered a violent headache while he was out playing in the fields where his father was working. Immediately the father put the child in the arms of a servant and instructed him to carry the child home to his mother. All morning the mother tenderly held the child in her lap, but he died at noon (v.20). In faith, trusting God with all her heart, she kept the child's death a secret. Taking him upstairs to Elisha's room, she laid the child on the prophet's bed. As quickly as she could, she asked her husband for a servant and donkey so she could make a quick visit to Elisha. Somewhat perplexed, the husband asked why she needed to make the visit since it was not a religious holiday. Obviously, she gave assurance that it was a spiritual matter that needed to be handled immediately, for he gave her permission to make the quick trip. As rapidly as she could, she rushed to Elisha, the prophet of God, from whom she would seek help in her desperate and helpless hour of need.

d. The woman's faith in God and in His prophet Elisha was apparently unlimited (vv.24-31). The mother rushed to Mt. Carmel where Elisha lived. Spotting her off in the distance rushing toward him, Elisha sent his servant to meet and greet her. But she refused to be delayed by conversation with the servant (vv.25-26). As soon as she reached Elisha, she quickly slipped off her donkey and rushed up to him, kneeling to the ground and grabbing his feet (v.27). Gehazi rushed over to push her away, but Elisha stopped him. For he sensed the mother's bitter grief and sorrow. Pouring out her soul to Elisha, she expressed that her pain was worse than having no child at all. In fact, when Elisha had promised the child, she had asked him not to raise her hopes (v.28).

Without even taking time to respond to his dear friend, Elisha turned to his servant Gehazi and instructed him to rush to the boy. Reaching the boy as soon as possible was critical. The servant was to allow no one to interfere with his journey, not even for greeting a passerby. Once reaching the boy, the servant was to lay Elisha's staff on the dead child's face (v.29).

But the mother refused to leave unless Elisha himself went back with her (v.30). Note her *persistent faith*: her faith was in the LORD and in His prophet, not in the prophet's servant. Filled with *persistent faith*, she swore, taking an oath before the LORD that she would not leave Elisha unless he went back with her. Filled with compassion for this dear mother, Elisha arose and followed her to the home he had visited so often, the home where death now ruled.

Rushing on ahead, the servant Gehazi reached the dead child and laid the staff on the boy's face. But there was no response. The boy was not restored to life. So the servant rushed back to meet Elisha and the boy's mother to report what had happened.

e. Now note the miraculous reward of the woman's *persistent faith* (vv.32-37). Finally arriving at the home, Elisha found the boy lying on the bed in the room that had been prepared for the prophet's visits. Shutting the door, the prophet began to pray to the LORD. At some point he stretched his body out upon the boy face-to-face, and the dead child's body began to grow warm (vv.33-34). Getting up off the child, Elisha began to pace the floor, continuing to pray (v.35). Then once again he stretched out his body upon the boy. Immediately the boy sneezed seven times, and God revived the dead child. At that point, Elisha instructed his servant to summon the woman (vv.36-37). As she entered the room, her first sight was of Elisha holding the child in his arms; then she heard the prophet instruct her to take the child. But this she did not do. Rushing toward the prophet and her son, she fell at Elisha's feet and bowed to the ground showing gratitude and worship to the LORD. Before long she arose and tenderly took her son into her arms. She then went out to spend some precious moments with the son who had been raised from the dead and given life by the power of God (vv.36-37).

Thought 1. What a hope! To be raised from the dead! This is the wonderful lesson for us in this passage. God is going to raise the dead: all believers to live with Him eternally and all unbelievers to be separated from Him eternally. The wonderful hope of believers is the glorious resurrection when the Lord Jesus Christ returns to this earth. When we are raised from the dead we will receive our *permanent bodies*, bodies that will be perfected, free of all disease and aging, pain and suffering, deformity and defect. Just as this small child was raised from the dead and returned to the Shunammite mother, so we will be raised from the dead. Listen to what God's Holy Word says:

"Verily, verily, I say unto you, He that heareth my word, and believeth on him that sent me, hath everlasting life, and shall not come into condemnation; but is passed from death unto life. Verily, verily, I say unto you, The hour is coming, and now is, when the dead shall hear the voice of the Son of God: and they that hear shall live. For as the Father hath life in himself; so hath he given to the Son to have life in himself; And hath given him authority to execute judgment also, because he is the Son of man. Marvel not at this: for the hour is coming, in the which all that are in the graves shall hear his voice, And shall come forth; they that have done good, unto the resurrection of life; and they that have done evil, unto the resurrection of damnation" (Jn.5:24-29).

"And this is the will of him that sent me, that every one which seeth the Son, and believeth on him, may have everlasting life: and I will raise him up at the last day" (Jn.6:40).

"Jesus said unto her, I am the resurrection, and the life: he that believeth in me, though he were dead, yet shall he live: And whosoever liveth and believeth in me shall never die. Believest thou this" (Jn.11:25-26).

"And have hope toward God, which they themselves also allow, that there shall be a resurrection of the dead, both of the just and unjust" (Ac.24:15).

"But now is Christ risen from the dead, *and* become the firstfruits of them that slept. For since by man *came* death, by man *came* also the resurrection of the dead. For as in Adam all die, even so in Christ shall all be made alive. But every man in his own order: Christ the firstfruits; afterward they that are Christ's at his coming" (1 Co.15:20-23).

"But some man will say, How are the dead raised up? and with what body do they come? Thou fool, that which thou sowest is not quickened, except it die: And that which thou sowest, thou sowest not that body that shall be, but bare grain, it may chance of wheat, or of some other grain: But God giveth it a body as it hath pleased him, and to every seed his own body. All flesh is not the same flesh: but there is one kind of flesh of men, another flesh of beasts, another of fishes, and another of birds. There are also celestial bodies, and bodies terrestrial: but the glory of the celestial *is* one, and the *glory* of the terrestrial *is* another. *There is* one glory of the sun, and another glory of the moon, and another glory of the stars: for *one* star differeth from *another* star in glory. So also *is* the resurrection of the dead. It is sown in corruption; it is raised in incorruption: It is sown in dishonour; it is raised in glory: it is sown in weakness; it is raised in power: It is sown a natural body; it is raised a spiritual body. There is a natural body, and there is a spiritual body" (1 Co.15:35-44).

"Behold, I show you a mystery; We shall not all sleep, but we shall all be changed, In a moment, in the twinkling of an eye, at the last trump: for the trumpet shall sound, and the dead shall be raised incorruptible, and we shall be changed. For this corruptible must put on incorruption, and this mortal must put on immortality. So when this corruptible shall have put on incorruption, and this mortal shall have put on immortality, then shall be brought to pass the saying that is written, Death is swallowed up in victory" (1 Co.15:51-54).

"Knowing that he which raised up the Lord Jesus shall raise up us also by Jesus, and shall present us with you" (2 Co.4:14).

"But I would not have you to be ignorant, brethren, concerning them which are asleep, that ye sorrow not, even as others which have no hope. For if we believe that Jesus died and rose again, even so them also which sleep in Jesus will God bring with him. For this we say unto you by the word of the Lord, that we which are alive and remain unto the coming of the Lord shall not prevent them which are asleep. For the Lord himself shall descend from heaven with a shout, with the voice of the archangel, and with the trump of God: and the dead in Christ shall rise first: Then we which are alive *and* remain shall be caught up together with them in the clouds, to meet the Lord in the air: and so shall we ever be with the Lord. Wherefore comfort one another with these words" (1 Th.4:13-18).

"But God will redeem my soul from the power of the grave: for he shall receive me. Selah" (Ps.49:15).

3 (4:38-44) **Needs, Met and Provided for, by God—Needs, Basic, Provision for—Miracles, Provision of Food—Ministers, Provisions for**: there were the prophets being miraculously fed. In these two miracles, God's power to meet the needs of His people was clearly demonstrated:

OUTLINE	SCRIPTURE	SCRIPTURE	OUTLINE
3. The prophets miraculously fed: God's power to meet the basic needs of His people a. A bad stew was miraculously purified 1) Elisha visited the school of prophets in Gilgal 2) A stew was prepared 3) A student gathered wild gourds & cut them up in the stew 4) The students—tasting the stew—immediately knew it was poisonous: Informed Elisha 5) Elisha instructed them to	38 And Elisha came again to Gilgal: and *there was* a dearth in the land; and the sons of the prophets *were* sitting before him: and he said unto his servant, Set on the great pot, and seethe pottage for the sons of the prophets. 39 And one went out into the field to gather herbs, and found a wild vine, and gathered thereof wild gourds his lap full, and came and shred *them* into the pot of pottage: for they knew *them* not. 40 So they poured out for the men to eat. And it came to pass, as they were eating of the pottage, that they cried out, and said, O *thou* man of God, *there is* death in the pot. And they could not eat *thereof.* 41 But he said, Then bring	meal. And he cast *it* into the pot; and he said, Pour out for the people, that they may eat. And there was no harm in the pot. 42 And there came a man from Baal-shalisha, and brought the man of God bread of the firstfruits, twenty loaves of barley, and full ears of corn in the husk thereof. And he said, Give unto the people, that they may eat. 43 And his servitor said, What, should I set this before an hundred men? He said again, Give the people, that they may eat: for thus saith the LORD, They shall eat, and shall leave *thereof.* 44 So he set *it* before them, and they did eat, and left *thereof,* according to the word of the LORD.	add flour to the pot 6) The stew was suddenly purified, edible b. One hundred prophets were miraculously fed 1) An unknown believer brought supplies to the school: 20 loaves of bread & some fresh grain 2) Elisha ordered the food distributed 3) Elisha's servant protested, questioning how so little could be used to feed 100 young men 4) Elisha assured the servant of God's promise: He would feed His people, meet their need 5) Elisha's servant obeyed & all the prophets had food: God's Word was fulfilled

a. A bad and poisonous stew was miraculously purified by God through His prophet Elisha (vv.38-41). During a famine, Elisha visited the school of prophets at Gilgal (v.38). Noticing how hungry some of the students seemed to be, he instructed his servant to prepare a large pot of stew and cook it for the prophets. In obedience to Elisha's instructions, the servant went out to gather some vegetables and ran across a wild vine from which he picked some *gourds*. When he returned back to the school, he sliced the gourds into the stew, although no one knew exactly what they were.

As the students began to taste the stew, they immediately knew it was poisonous and informed Elisha (v.40). Trusting the provision of the LORD, Elisha calmly instructed them to add some flour or meal to the stew and then re-serve it. Miraculously, the LORD purified the poisonous stew and the students were able to eat it.

b. On another occasion a hundred prophets were miraculously fed (vv.42-44). An unknown believer brought food supplies to the school, including 20 loaves of baked bread and some fresh grain (v.42). Immediately Elisha ordered the food distributed, but his servant protested, questioning how so little food could be used to feed 100 young men (vv.42-43). Assuring the servant that the LORD would fulfill His promise to meet the needs of His people, Elisha instructed the servant to begin to pass out the food to the people. The servant obeyed and all the prophets had not only enough food to eat, but they had some left over. The promise of the LORD was fulfilled: the food was multiplied just as the five loaves of bread and two fish were to be multiplied by Christ in feeding the multitude (Mt.14:13-21; Mk.6:30-42; 8:1-21; Lu.9:10-17; Jn.6:5-14).

Thought 1. God has the power to meet the *basic needs* of human life. In the case of the students, He met the basic need for food. God possesses omnipotent, unlimited power, the power to meet any and every need. Whatever need may confront us, God can meet it. And if God has the power to meet all needs, He will surely meet the *basic needs* of human life:
⇒ the need for food, shelter, and clothing
⇒ the need for purpose, meaning, and significance in life
⇒ the need for a sense of fulfillment and satisfaction

⇒ the need for conquering the trials and temptations of life
⇒ the need for either health or the strength to bear the sufferings, pain, and infirmities of life

God has the power to meet our needs. But there is a condition: we must seek first the kingdom of God and His righteousness. We must love—truly love—the LORD, obeying His commandments and faithfully worshipping Him. And we must strengthen our relationship, our daily walk with the LORD, taking care of our bodies, which are the temple of the Holy Spirit. This is the clear declaration of God's Holy Word:

"Give us this day our daily bread" (Mt.6:11).

"Therefore I say unto you, Take no thought for your life, what ye shall eat, or what ye shall drink; nor yet for your body, what ye shall put on. Is not the life more than meat, and the body than raiment? Behold the fowls of the air: for they sow not, neither do they reap, nor gather into barns; yet your heavenly Father feedeth them. Are ye not much better than they" (Mt.6:25-26).

"Wherefore, if God so clothe the grass of the field, which to day is, and to morrow is cast into the oven, shall he not much more clothe you, O ye of little faith? Therefore take no thought, saying, What shall we eat? or, What shall we drink? or, Wherewithal shall we be clothed? (For after all these things do the Gentiles seek:) for your heavenly Father knoweth that ye have need of all these things. But seek ye first the kingdom of God, and his righteousness; and all these things shall be added unto you. Take therefore no thought for the morrow: for the morrow shall take thought for the things of itself. Sufficient unto the day is the evil thereof" (Mt.6:30-34).

"But seek ye first the kingdom of God, and his righteousness; and all these things shall be added unto you" (Mt.6:33).

"There hath no temptation [trial] taken you but such as is common to man: but God is faithful, who will not suffer you to be tempted above that ye are able; but will with the temptation also make a way to escape, that ye may be able to bear it" (1 Co.10:13).

"But my God shall supply all your need according to his riches in glory by Christ Jesus" (Ph.4:19).

"And God said, Behold, I have given you every herb bearing seed, which is upon the face of all the earth, and every tree, in the which is the fruit of a tree yielding seed; to you it shall be for meat" (Ge.1:29).

"And ye shall serve the LORD your God, and he shall bless thy bread, and thy water; and I will take sickness away from the midst of thee" (Ex.23:25).

"That I will give you the rain of your land in his due season, the first rain and the latter rain, that thou mayest gather in thy corn, and thy wine, and thine oil" (De.11:14).

"Thou visitest the earth, and waterest it: thou greatly enrichest it with the river of God, which is full of water: thou preparest them corn, when thou hast so provided for it" (Ps.65:9).

"Who giveth food to all flesh: for his mercy endureth for ever" (Ps.136:25).

"Then shall he give the rain of thy seed, that thou shalt sow the ground withal; and bread of the increase of the earth, and it shall be fat and plenteous: in that day shall thy cattle feed in large pastures" (Is.30:23).

CHAPTER 5

B. The Syrian Army Commander Naaman Miraculously Healed: A Lesson on God's Power to Convert & Heal a Person, 5:1-27

1. **The hope aroused in the brilliant but sick army commander: He listened to a strong witness for the LORD**
   a. Naaman's noble character: Great, honorable, victorious, valiant (brave)

   b. Naaman's disease: Leprosy
   c. Naaman's hope aroused: A young slave girl from Israel bore strong testimony to the LORD
      1) She served Naaman's wife
      2) She strongly urged her mistress to send Naaman to the prophet in Samaria: She believed the LORD would heal Naaman through Elisha
   d. Naaman's belief in the young girl's testimony
      1) He secured permission from the king to go to Samaria: Was given a letter of introduction to Israel's king & a large gift for the king, assuming the prophet served the king

      2) He traveled to Samaria & presented the letter to Joram the king: Requested Joram to heal Naaman, obviously through his prophet

      3) He was feared & detained by Israel's king
         • Joram reacted: So worldly-minded, he never thought of Elisha
         • Joram concluded Syria was seeking an excuse to invade Israel

2. **The healing & conversion of Naaman: He laid aside his pride & obeyed God's Word**
   a. Elisha's offer to help
      1) Heard about Naaman's need & the king's fear
      2) Saw an opportunity to bear strong witness

   b. Naaman's arrival at Elisha's house: An impressive

Now Naaman, captain of the host of the king of Syria, was a great man with his master, and honourable, because by him the LORD had given deliverance unto Syria: he was also a mighty man in valour, *but he was* a leper.
2 And the Syrians had gone out by companies, and had brought away captive out of the land of Israel a little maid; and she waited on Naaman's wife.
3 And she said unto her mistress, Would God my lord *were* with the prophet that *is* in Samaria! for he would recover him of his leprosy.
4 And *one* went in, and told his lord, saying, Thus and thus said the maid that *is* of the land of Israel.
5 And the king of Syria said, Go to, go, and I will send a letter unto the king of Israel. And he departed, and took with him ten talents of silver, and six thousand *pieces* of gold, and ten changes of raiment.
6 And he brought the letter to the king of Israel, saying, Now when this letter is come unto thee, behold, I have *therewith* sent Naaman my servant to thee, that thou mayest recover him of his leprosy.
7 And it came to pass, when the king of Israel had read the letter, that he rent his clothes, and said, *Am* I God, to kill and to make alive, that this man doth send unto me to recover a man of his leprosy? wherefore consider, I pray you, and see how he seeketh a quarrel against me.
8 And it was *so,* when Elisha the man of God had heard that the king of Israel had rent his clothes, that he sent to the king, saying, Wherefore hast thou rent thy clothes? let him come now to me, and he shall know that there is a prophet in Israel.
9 So Naaman came with his horses and with his chariot,

and stood at the door of the house of Elisha.
10 And Elisha sent a messenger unto him, saying, Go and wash in the Jordan seven times, and thy flesh shall come again to thee, and thou shalt be clean.
11 But Naaman was wroth, and went away, and said, Behold, I thought, He surely will come out to me, and stand, and call on the name of the LORD his God, and strike his hand over the place, and recover the leper.
12 *Are* not Abana and Pharpar, rivers of Damascus, better than all the waters of Israel? may I not wash in them, and be clean? So he turned and went away in a rage.
13 And his servants came near, and spake unto him, and said, My father, *if* the prophet had bid thee *do some great thing,* wouldest thou not have done *it?* how much rather then, when he saith to thee, Wash, and be clean?
14 Then went he down, and dipped himself seven times in Jordan, according to the saying of the man of God: and his flesh came again like unto the flesh of a little child, and he was clean.
15 And he returned to the man of God, he and all his company, and came, and stood before him: and he said, Behold, now I know that *there is* no God in all the earth, but in Israel: now therefore, I pray thee, take a blessing of thy servant.
16 But he said, *As* the LORD liveth, before whom I stand, I will receive none. And he urged him to take *it;* but he refused.
17 And Naaman said, Shall there not then, I pray thee, be given to thy servant two mules' burden of earth? for thy servant will henceforth offer neither burnt offering nor sacrifice unto other gods, but unto the LORD.
18 In this thing the LORD pardon thy servant, *that* when my master goeth into the house of Rimmon to worship there, and he leaneth on my hand, and I bow myself in the house of Rimmon: when I bow down myself in the

entourage of power & wealth

   c. Elisha's response & instructions: Sent a messenger out, telling Naaman to wash seven times in the Jordan

   d. Naaman's prideful, self-centered reaction: Anger, rage
      1) He expected Elisha personally to come out, wave his hand over his leprosy, pray, & heal him

      2) He considered the suggestions be those of a quack: He was more likely to be healed by washing in the cleaner rivers of Damascus

   e. Naaman's healing & conversion
      1) He was encouraged to calm down by his servants
         • To do the simple thing suggested
         • To consider that he would gladly do any difficult task
      2) He reluctantly obeyed the instructions of Elisha, the man of God
         • His flesh was restored
         • He was immediately cleansed, healed

   f. Naaman's confession & dedication
      1) He returned to Elisha & confessed his belief: He now knew there was only one true & living God
      2) He tried to pay Elisha

      3) He was informed that payment could not be accepted: Salvation was free, by God's grace, & could not be purchased
      4) He asked for some dirt from Elisha's property: To take back home to build an altar
         • To offer sacrifices to the LORD
         • To never again sacrifice to a false god
      5) He informed Elisha of his official duties as commander of the Syrian army, see 1 K.18:1-15
         • He was required to join his king in religious ceremonies in the temple Rimmon

• He would ask for forgiveness at such times	house of Rimmon, the LORD pardon thy servant in this thing.	talents of silver in two bags, with two changes of garments, and laid *them* upon	(150 pounds) & two sets of clothing
g. Naaman was told by Elisha to "go [home] in peace"	19 And he said unto him, Go in peace. So he departed from him a little way.	two of his servants; and they bare *them* before him.	• Two servants to carry the wealth back
3. The greed of Elisha's servant Gehazi: He exposed a heart filled with worldly lusts & covetousness	20 But Gehazi, the servant of Elisha the man of God, said, Behold, my master hath	24 And when he came to the tower, he took *them* from their hand, and bestowed	4) He took the gifts from the servants before they reached Elisha's house & sent the servants back to Naaman: He hid the money & clothing
a. Gehazi's lustful, craving thoughts: Wanted some of Naaman's wealth that he had offered to Elisha	spared Naaman this Syrian, in not receiving at his hands that which he brought: but, *as* the LORD liveth, I will run after him, and take somewhat of him.	*them* in the house: and he let the men go, and they departed.	c. Gehazi's greed uncovered & his judgment
b. Gehazi's covetous action: Rushed to catch Naaman	21 So Gehazi followed after Naaman. And when Naaman	25 But he went in, and stood before his master. And Elisha said unto him, Whence	1) Elisha confronted his servant: Gehazi lied about where he had been
1) He was spotted by Naaman: Naaman got out of his chariot, asking if everything was all right	saw *him* running after him, he lighted down from the chariot to meet him, and said, *Is* all well?	*comest thou*, Gehazi? And he said, Thy servant went no whither.	2) Elisha revealed that he knew Gehazi had taken the money & clothing
2) He lied, deceived Naaman	22 And he said, All *is* well. My master hath sent me, saying, Behold, even now there	26 And he said unto him, Went not mine heart *with thee,* when the man turned again from his chariot	3) Elisha rebuked his servant: This was not the time to receive payment—
• Said Elisha had sent him	be come to me from mount Ephraim two young men of	to meet thee? *Is* it a time to receive money, and to receive	salvation & healing were to be free, not to be offered for profit
• Said two young prophets needed financial aid	the sons of the prophets: give them, I pray thee, a talent of	garments, and oliveyards, and vineyards, and sheep,	
• Said Elisha was requesting a talent of silver (75 pounds) & 2 sets of clothing	silver, and two changes of garments.	and oxen, and menservants, and maidservants?	4) Elisha pronounced the judgment of God: Gehazi & his descendants (through their genes) would be stricken with leprosy
3) He was generously given more than he requested	23 And Naaman said, Be content, take two talents. And	27 The leprosy therefore of Naaman shall cleave unto thee, and unto thy seed for ever. And he went out from	
• Two talents of silver	he urged him, and bound two	his presence a leper *as white* as snow.	

DIVISION II

THE MINISTRY AND MIRACLES OF ELISHA: A DRAMATIC DEMONSTRATION OF GOD'S POWER AND CARE FOR HIS PEOPLE, 4:1–13:25

B. The Syrian Army Commander Naaman Miraculously Healed: A Lesson on God's Power to Convert and Heal a Person, 5:1-27

(5:1-27) **Introduction—Power of God, Described, Examples**: think of this fact: God's power is so forceful, so energizing that it can heal a person of any disease or any affliction. But that is not all: God has the power to convert a person, to change a life totally. No matter how depraved or sad a life has become, God can turn that life around and give the person a new beginning, a new start, a brand new life. God's power is omnipotent and unlimited. No matter how high a person is exalted in this life or how low a person has been debased, if he or she senses emptiness or loneliness or purposelessness, or faces one of the many crises, trials, or temptations of this life—if the person craves a new beginning, a fresh start—God's power can meet the need of that person's heart. This is the practical message of the present story.

Actually, this Scripture is one of the most well-known stories in the Old Testament. It is the story of Naaman, the chief commander of the Syrian army who was stricken with the dreaded disease of leprosy. In a story that reaches the height of drama, Naaman confronts the prophet Elisha and is both healed of his leprosy and converted to the LORD. This is the compelling story of a military commander who reached the summit of power in one of the greatest nations of his day and time, the story of a man who was second only to his king. This is: *The Syrian Army Commander Naaman Miraculously Healed: A Lesson on God's Power to Convert and Heal a Person,* 5:1-27

1. The hope aroused in the brilliant but sick army commander: he listened to a strong witness for the LORD (vv.1-7).
2. The healing and conversion of Naaman: he laid aside his pride and obeyed God's Word (vv.8-19).
3. The greed of Elisha's servant Gehazi: he exposed a heart filled with worldly lusts and covetousness (vv.20-27).

1 (5:1-7) **Hope, for Healing—Witnessing, Duty—Witnessing, Example of, a Young Slave Girl—Testimony, Example of—Naaman, Syrian Commander, Character—Naaman, Hope Aroused for Healing**: hope was aroused in the brilliant but sick commander of the Syrian army, Naaman. Somehow Naaman had caught leprosy, a very serious skin disease that would eventually disable him. But great hope was aroused within Naaman. And note why: because he listened to a strong witness for the LORD. The story is compelling and dramatic:

OUTLINE	SCRIPTURE	SCRIPTURE	OUTLINE
1. The hope aroused in the brilliant but sick army commander: He listened to a strong witness for the LORD	Now Naaman, captain of the host of the king of Syria, was a great man with his master, and honourable, because by him the LORD had given deliverance unto Syria: he was also a mighty man in valour, *but he was* a leper.	said, Go to, go, and I will send a letter unto the king of Israel. And he departed, and took with him ten talents of silver, and six thousand *pieces* of gold, and ten changes of raiment.	of introduction to Israel's king & a large gift for the king, assuming the prophet served the king
a. Naaman's noble character: Great, honorable, victorious, valiant (brave)			
b. Naaman's disease: Leprosy	2 And the Syrians had gone out by companies, and had brought away captive out of the land of Israel a little maid; and she waited on Naaman's wife.	6 And he brought the letter to the king of Israel, saying, Now when this letter is come unto thee, behold, I have *therewith* sent Naaman my servant to thee, that thou mayest recover him of his leprosy.	2) He traveled to Samaria & presented the letter to Joram the king: Requested Joram to heal Naaman, obviously through his prophet
c. Naaman's hope aroused: A young slave girl from Israel bore strong testimony to the LORD			
1) She served Naaman's wife			
2) She strongly urged her mistress to send Naaman to the prophet in Samaria: She believed the LORD would heal Naaman through Elisha	3 And she said unto her mistress, Would God my lord *were* with the prophet that *is* in Samaria! for he would recover him of his leprosy.	7 And it came to pass, when the king of Israel had read the letter, that he rent his clothes, and said, *Am* I God, to kill and to make alive, that this man doth send unto me to recover a man of his leprosy? wherefore consider, I pray you, and see how he seeketh a quarrel against me.	3) He was feared & detained by Israel's king • Joram reacted: So worldly-minded, he never thought of Elisha • Joram concluded Syria was seeking an excuse to invade Israel
d. Naaman's belief in the young girl's testimony	4 And *one* went in, and told his lord, saying, Thus and thus said the maid that *is* of the land of Israel.		
1) He secured permission from the king to go to Samaria: Was given a letter	5 And the king of Syria		

a. Naaman was a man of noble character, an honorable commander who had won victory after victory on the battlefield for the Syrians. He was a courageous and heroic soldier. Furthermore, in the eyes of the king and the Syrian citizens, he was a great man held in the highest esteem.

b. But Naaman had leprosy. The Hebrew word "leprosy" (*tsara* or *sara*) refers to some form of skin disease that was incurable and that eventually incapacitated the victim. Because of his wealth and his royal position as commander, Naaman had access to the best medical help and technology of that day; but he could find no cure. Apparently the disease would ultimately be fatal. Sadly, this man of noble character was caught in a helpless and hopeless situation due to his incurable disease.

c. Yet suddenly, from the most unexpected source, Naaman's hope was aroused (v.2). Several small groups of Syrian soldiers had raided some of the border towns of Israel and taken captive a young girl. When the combat troops returned to Syria, they gave the young girl to Naaman, who assigned her the task of serving his wife. On one occasion when Naaman was home from fighting, the young slave girl strongly urged her mistress to encourage Naaman to visit the prophet Elisha who lived in Samaria (v.3). She believed the LORD would heal Naaman through Elisha.

d. Naaman believed the young girl's testimony, at least enough to seek out Elisha (vv.4-7). Appealing to the Syrian king, he secured permission to go to Samaria. The king, who was probably Ben-Hadad II, gave Naaman a letter of introduction to the king of Israel and a large gift to pay for the services of the prophet. Note that the Syrian king assumed that the prophet served in the royal court of Israel's king Joram and that the gift he sent was huge: 750 pounds of silver, 150 pounds of gold, and 10 sets of royal clothing which no doubt were very expensive (v.5).

With a heart full of great hope and expectation, Naaman traveled to Samaria and presented the letter of introduction to King Joram (vv.6-7). The letter requested Joram to heal Naaman of his leprosy, no doubt by assigning the task to Elisha, whom he thought served as one of the royal prophets. But as soon as Joram read the letter, he was gripped by a dreadful fear, for he knew that neither he nor any of the royal prophets had the power to heal the Syrian commander. And he feared when the commander returned unhealed from Samaria, Syria would have an excuse to invade Israel. In fact, Joram thought this was the very purpose of the letter: to give Syria an excuse to attack. So much fear and anxiety gripped Joram's heart that he never even thought of seeking the help of the prophet Elisha.

Thought 1. Hope was aroused within Naaman, the hope of being healed of an incurable, disabling disease. But Naaman's hope was aroused for one reason and one reason only: he listened to the testimony, the witness of a young slave girl, and he accepted what she said. He believed that the LORD, the God of the prophet Elisha, could heal him. Believing the message of the LORD's power was what aroused hope within Naaman. The same hope can be ours if we will simply believe in the LORD, trusting His power to take effect in our lives. No matter what circumstances or crises we may face, we too can have hope. If we will just believe the witness, the testimony about the LORD, then we will be saved and delivered from the bondages and enslavements of this world. No matter what may attack us or grip our lives, God will infuse His power within us to conquer and to deliver us. But the condition is faith: we must believe, trust the message, the witness about the LORD.

> **"But that on the good ground are they, which in an honest and good heart, having heard the word, keep *it,* and bring forth fruit with patience" (Lu.8:15).**

> **"That whosoever believeth in him should not perish, but have eternal life. For God so loved the world, that he gave his only begotten Son, that whosoever believeth in him should not perish, but have everlasting life" (Jn.3:15-16).**

"Verily, verily, I say unto you, He that heareth my word, and believeth on him that sent me, hath everlasting life, and shall not come into condemnation; but is passed from death unto life" (Jn.5:24).

"Then said they unto him, What shall we do, that we might work the works of God? Jesus answered and said unto them, This is the work of God, that ye believe on him whom he hath sent" (Jn.6:28-29).

"But these are written, that ye might believe that Jesus is the Christ, the Son of God; and that believing ye might have life through his name" (Jn.20:31).

"Therefore being justified by faith, we have peace with God through our Lord Jesus Christ" (Ro.5:1).

"Even as Abraham believed God, and it was accounted to him for righteousness" (Ga.3:6).

"Above all, taking the shield of faith, wherewith ye shall be able to quench all the fiery darts [temptations, trials] of the wicked" (Ep.6:16).

"But without faith it is impossible to please him: for he that cometh to God must believe that he is, and that he is a rewarder of them that diligently seek him" (He.11:6).

"And this is his commandment, That we should believe on the name of his Son Jesus Christ, and love one another, as he gave us commandment" (1 Jn.3:23).

"For whatsoever is born of God overcometh the world: and this is the victory that overcometh the world, even our faith. Who is he that overcometh the world, but he that believeth that Jesus is the Son of God" (1 Jn.5:4-5).

"And they rose early in the morning, and went forth into the wilderness of Tekoa: and as they went forth, Jehoshaphat stood and said, Hear me, O Judah, and ye inhabitants of Jerusalem; Believe in the LORD your God, so shall ye be established; believe his prophets, so shall ye prosper" (2 Chr.20:20).

"The ear that heareth the reproof of life abideth among the wise" (Pr.15:31).

---

2 (5:8-19) **Pride, Example of—Conversion, Example of—Healing, Example of—Obedience, Example of—Naaman, Conversion of—Confession, Example of—Self-centeredness, Example of:** Naaman's hope was fully realized and completely fulfilled: he was healed and converted. The event is drama at its best, and most exciting:

OUTLINE	SCRIPTURE	SCRIPTURE	OUTLINE

2. The healing & conversion of Naaman: He laid aside his pride & obeyed God's Word
a. Elisha's offer to help
  1) Heard about Naaman's need & the king's fear
  2) Saw an opportunity to bear strong witness
 	
b. Naaman's arrival at Elisha's house: An impressive entourage of power & wealth
 	
c. Elisha's response & instructions: Sent a messenger out, telling Naaman to wash seven times in the Jordan
 	
d. Naaman's prideful, self-centered reaction: Anger, rage
  1) He expected Elisha personally to come out, wave his hand over his leprosy, pray, & heal him
 	
  2) He considered the suggestions be those of a quack: He was more likely to be healed by washing in the cleaner rivers of Damascus
 	
e. Naaman's healing & conversion
  1) He was encouraged to calm down by his servants
    • To do the simple thing
	8 And it was *so,* when Elisha the man of God had heard that the king of Israel had rent his clothes, that he sent to the king, saying, Wherefore hast thou rent thy clothes? let him come now to me, and he shall know that there is a prophet in Israel. 9 So Naaman came with his horses and with his chariot, and stood at the door of the house of Elisha. 10 And Elisha sent a messenger unto him, saying, Go and wash in the Jordan seven times, and thy flesh shall come again to thee, and thou shalt be clean. 11 But Naaman was wroth, and went away, and said, Behold, I thought, He will surely come out to me, and stand, and call on the name of the LORD his God, and strike his hand over the place, and recover the leper. 12 *Are* not Abana and Pharpar, rivers of Damascus, better than all the waters of Israel? may I not wash in them, and be clean? So he turned and went away in a rage. 13 And his servants came near, and spake unto him, and said, My father, *if* the prophet had bid thee *do some*	great thing, wouldest thou not have done *it?* how much rather then, when he saith to thee, Wash, and be clean? 14 Then went he down, and dipped himself seven times in Jordan, according to the saying of the man of God: and his flesh came again like unto the flesh of a little child, and he was clean. 15 And he returned to the man of God, he and all his company, and came, and stood before him: and he said, Behold, now I know that *there is* no God in all earth, but in Israel: now therefore, I pray thee, take a blessing of thy servant. 16 But he said, *As* the LORD liveth, before whom I stand, I will receive none. And he urged him to take *it;* but he refused. 17 And Naaman said, Shall there not then, I pray thee, be given to thy servant two mules' burden of earth? for thy servant will henceforth offer neither burnt offering nor sacrifice unto other gods, but unto the LORD. 18 In this thing the LORD pardon thy servant, *that* when my master goeth into the house of Rimmon to worship	suggested
			  • To consider that he would gladly do any difficult task
			  2) He reluctantly obeyed the instructions of Elisha, the man of God
			    • His flesh was restored
			    • He was immediately cleansed, healed
			f. Naaman's confession & dedication
			  1) He returned to Elisha & confessed his belief: He now knew there was only one true & living God
			  2) He tried to pay Elisha
			  3) He was informed that payment could not be accepted: Salvation was free, by God's grace, & could not be purchased
			  4) He asked for some dirt from Elisha's property: To take back home to build an altar
			    • To offer sacrifices to the LORD
			    • To never again sacrifice to a false god
			  5) He informed Elisha of his official duties as commander of the Syrian army, see 1 K.18:1-15
			    • He was required to join his king in religious ceremonies in the temple

46

OUTLINE	SCRIPTURE	SCRIPTURE	OUTLINE
Rimmon • He would ask for forgiveness at such times	there, and he leaneth on my hand, and I bow myself in the house of Rimmon: when I bow down myself in the house of Rimmon, the LORD	pardon thy servant in this thing. 19 And he said unto him, Go in peace. So he departed from him a little way.	g. Naaman was told by Elisha to "go [home] in peace"

a. Elisha heard about Naaman's visit and the king's fearful reaction, so he sent an offer to help the king in his distress (v.8). Somewhat rebuking the king, Elisha encouraged him to send Naaman to him and he would prove there was a true prophet in Israel, a prophet who could call upon the LORD to heal this Syrian commander. In referring to himself as a real prophet, Elisha was claiming that the LORD whom he serves is the only living and true God. Elisha saw a unique opportunity to bear strong witness to this commander of the Syrian forces. If he could lead Naaman to a saving knowledge of the LORD, the commander would become a strong witness to many throughout Syria.

b. Naaman's arrival at Elisha's house was an impressive entourage of power and wealth (v.9). He obviously rode up in a caravan of chariots with all the pomp and ceremony of a commander, stopping at the very door of Elisha's house.

c. But Elisha's response was that of a man unimpressed with worldly glory and display (v.10). In fact, he did not personally go out to meet the commander. Instead, he sent a messenger out instructing Naaman to go and wash seven times in the Jordan River (v.10). If Naaman would follow these instructions, he would be healed and cleansed of his leprosy.

d. In contrast, note Naaman's disrespectful and arrogant reaction. He was filled with rage, feeling that Elisha had slighted him. He had expected Elisha to personally come out, wave his hand over his leprosy, pray, and heal him (v.11). In his mind he considered the suggestions of Elisha to be those of a quack. He was more likely to be healed by washing in the cleaner rivers of Damascus than in the dirtier waters of the Jordan. Filled with fury, the commander turned and rode off.

e. However, God was at work in the hearts of both Naaman and his servants, and the commander was still to be healed and converted (vv.13-14). As soon as Naaman's servants felt it was safe to approach the commander, they began encouraging him to calm down and to get control of his emotions. Then they began to suggest that he would have paid any price and undertaken any difficult task demanded by the prophet. Why, then, would he not do the simple thing suggested?

Finally being convinced by his servants, the prideful and self-centered commander reluctantly obeyed the instructions of Elisha, the man of God (v.14). He went down to the Jordan River and dipped himself seven times, exactly as Elisha had instructed. Immediately after the seventh dip, he was healed. Surprisingly, his flesh became as healthy and looked as young as that of a child.

f. Excited and filled with a heart of thanksgiving, Naaman quickly returned to Elisha and made a strong confession of faith in the LORD (vv.15-18). He now knew there is only one true and living God, that there is no God other than the LORD God worshipped in Israel. He and He alone is the true and living LORD.

In appreciation for the help Elisha had been, Naaman attempted to pay the prophet (vv.15-16). But Elisha informed the commander that payment could not be accepted. Salvation—both deliverance and healing—was free, by God's grace alone. Salvation could not be purchased. After some urging, Naaman finally accepted Elisha's refusal for payment.

Before he left, though, Naaman asked two favors of Elisha. First, he requested enough dirt from Elisha's property to take back home so he could build an altar (v.17). He needed the altar to offer sacrifices to the LORD, for he would never again sacrifice to a false god. Second, Naaman wanted Elisha to pray and ask the LORD to continually forgive him for this one thing: in his official duties as commander of the Syrian army, he was required to join his king in religious services in the temple of the false god Rimmon (v.18). At such times, he would ask for forgiveness, but he also wanted Elisha to pray for the LORD to forgive him. Naaman was confessing that he would be present with the king only in an official capacity, not in heart. He would not personally be worshipping, not at all, for he knew that the LORD is the only living and true God. And it was the LORD alone whom he would personally worship. Note that his dilemma was somewhat the same as that faced by Obadiah during the days of Ahab (see outline and note 1 K.18:2-16 for more discussion).

g. Assuring Naaman of his prayers, Elisha announced his blessing upon Naaman. He told the commander to go in peace of conscience and mind.

No doubt, Elisha charged Naaman to make every opportunity he could to be a strong witness for the LORD. Keep in mind that Naaman's conversion and witness for the LORD were already far stronger than the vast majority of professing believers in Israel itself. The day of the kings was a period when people lived sinful and wicked lives. Contrary to the false profession of most people, Naaman experienced a true conversion and would be a far stronger witness for the LORD.

Thought 1. Before this commander of the Syrian army could be converted, he had to lay aside his pride, arrogance, and self-exaltation. No doubt, this was difficult to do, for Naaman was second only to the king of Syria. He was not only the chief commander of the armed forces, but he was also the second leader over the entire nation, one of the most powerful nations of the earth during that time. Power, authority, honor, praise, recognition, esteem, adoration—all that lifts a person up in the minds of people and causes a person to feel prideful and exalted—all this had become the daily experience of Naaman. As a result, he had become prideful, self-centered, and self-exalting. But when he confronted the LORD, he had to empty himself of pride and humble himself before the LORD. So it is with us. Before God can save us or meet our needs, we must lay aside our pride, selfishness, and self-exaltation. Pride is excessive, uncontrolled self-esteem. It is exalting oneself over others, exalting our...

- appearance
- position
- achievement
- health

- authority
- ability or skill
- knowledge or intellect
- friends or social circle

We can take anything that concerns us and exalt it above others. We should take pride in how God has made, blessed, and gifted us. We should esteem ourselves highly, but we should never exalt ourselves over other people. Pride becomes sin when we become arrogant and exalt ourselves over others. Listen to what the Word of God says about pride, arrogance, and self-exaltation.

> **"And whosoever shall exalt himself shall be abased; and he that shall humble himself shall be exalted" (Mt.23:12).**
> **"But he giveth more grace. Wherefore he saith, God resisteth the proud, but giveth grace unto the humble" (Js.4:6).**
> **"Love not the world, neither the things that are in the world. If any man love the world, the love of the Father is not in him. For all that is in the world, the lust of the flesh, and the lust of the eyes, and the pride of life, is not of the Father, but is of the world" (1 Jn.2:15-16).**
> **"These six things doth the LORD hate: yea, seven are an abomination unto him: A proud look, a lying tongue, and hands that shed innocent blood, An heart that deviseth wicked imaginations, feet that be swift in running to mischief, A false witness that speaketh lies, and he that soweth discord among brethren" (Pr.6:16-19).**
> **"When pride cometh, then cometh shame: but with the lowly is wisdom" (Pr.11:2).**
> **"Pride goeth before destruction, and an haughty spirit before a fall" (Pr.16:18).**
> **"He loveth transgression that loveth strife: and he that exalteth his gate seeketh destruction" (Pr.17:19).**
> **"An high look, and a proud heart, and the plowing of the wicked, is sin" (Pr.21:4).**
> **"Evil men understand not judgment: but they that seek the LORD understand all things" (Pr.28:5).**
> **"A man's pride shall bring him low: but honour shall uphold the humble in spirit" (Pr.29:23).**
> **"Though thou exalt thyself as the eagle, and though thou set thy nest among the stars, thence will I bring thee down, saith the LORD" (Ob.4).**

Thought 2. J. Vernon McGee has an excellent application dealing with pride that is worth quoting in its entirety.

> *God declares that He hates the pride in man's heart. Proverbs 6:16-19 lists seven things that God hates. First on His list are these: "A proud look, a lying tongue, and hands that shed innocent blood." Do you see what is number one on God's hate parade? It is a proud look. God says he hates that. He hates that as much as He hates murder.*
> ⇒ *James 4:6 says, "But he giveth more grace. Wherefore he saith, God resisteth the proud, but giveth grace unto the humble."*
> ⇒ *Pride is the undoing of man. It is a great sin. In Proverbs 16:18 we read, "Pride goeth before destruction, and an haughty spirit before a fall."*
> ⇒ *Proverbs 11:2 says, "When pride cometh, then cometh shame: but with the lowly is wisdom."*
> ⇒ *Finally, Proverbs 29:23 says, "A man's pride shall bring him low: but honour shall uphold the humble in spirit."*
>
> *Why does God hate pride? The definition of pride is "excessive self-esteem." It is inordinate self-esteem. It is more than reasonable delight in one's position and achievement. Paul put it like this, "For I say, through the grace given unto me, to every man that is among you, not to think of himself more highly than he ought to think; but to think soberly, according as God hath dealt to every man the measure of faith" (Rom. 12:4). Pride is placing an excessive price on self. It is demanding more than you are worth. Have you ever heard it said, "I wish I could buy that man for what he is worth?" Pride is the difference between what you are and what you think you are. It was the pride of Satan that brought him down. That was his sin. Pride was also the sin of Edom. Of Edom God said, "Though thou exalt thyself as the eagle, and though thou set thy nest among the stars, thence will I bring thee down, saith the LORD" (Obad. 4).*
> *Man's pride runs counter to God's plan; and, whenever they meet, there is friction. There is no compromise. It is always a head-on collision. You see, God's plan of salvation is the supreme answer to man's pride. God lays man low. God takes nothing from man. Paul could say of himself when he met Jesus Christ, "But what things were gain to me, those I counted loss for Christ" (Phil. 3:7). Paul gave up religion. Paul gave up everything he had been; he rated it as dung—he said, "I just flushed it down." Christ and pride do not go together. You cannot be proud and at the same time trust Christ as your Savior. If you trust Him, my friend, you will lay all of your pride in the dust.[1]*

3 (5:20-27) **Greed, Example of—Materialism, Example of—Worldliness, Example of—Gehazi, Greed of**: although Elisha had turned down Naaman's offer of payment, Elisha's servant Gehazi was filled with greed. And his greed exposed a heart flooded with worldly lusts and covetousness.

OUTLINE	SCRIPTURE	SCRIPTURE	OUTLINE
3. The greed of Elisha's servant Gehazi: He exposed a heart filled with worldly lusts & covetousness a. Gehazi's lustful, craving	20 But Gehazi, the servant of Elisha the man of God, said, Behold, my master hath spared Naaman this Syrian, in not receiving at his hands	that which he brought: but, *as* the LORD liveth, I will run after him, and take somewhat of him. 21 So Gehazi followed after	thoughts: Wanted some of Naaman's wealth that he had offered to Elisha b. Gehazi's covetous action:

---

1 J. Vernon McGee. *Thru the Bible, Vol.II.* (Nashville, TN: Thomas Nelson Publishers, 1982), p.312. (Arrows by us for clarity.)

OUTLINE	SCRIPTURE	SCRIPTURE	OUTLINE
Rushed to catch Naaman 1) He was spotted by Naaman: Naaman got out of his chariot, asking if everything was all right 2) He lied, deceived Naaman • Said Elisha had sent him • Said two young prophets needed financial aid • Said Elisha was requesting a talent of silver (75 pounds) & 2 sets of clothing • 3) He was generously given more than he requested • Two talents of silver (150 pounds) & two sets of clothing Two servants to carry the wealth back 4) He took the gifts from the servants before they reached Elisha's house &	Naaman. And when Naaman saw *him* running after him, he lighted down from the chariot to meet him, and said, *Is* all well? 22 And he said, All *is* well. My master hath sent me, saying, Behold, even now there be come to me from mount Ephraim two young men of the sons of the prophets: give them, I pray thee, a talent of silver, and two changes of garments. 23 And Naaman said, Be content, take two talents. And he urged him, and bound two talents of silver in two bags, with two changes of garments, and laid *them* upon two of his servants; and they bare *them* before him. 24 And when he came to the tower, he took *them* from their hand, and bestowed	*them* in the house: and he let the men go, and they departed. 25 But he went in, and stood before his master. And Elisha said unto him, Whence *comest thou,* Gehazi? And he said, Thy servant went no whither. 26 And he said unto him, Went not mine heart *with thee,* when the man turned again from his chariot to meet thee? *Is it* a time to receive money, and to receive garments, and oliveyards, and vineyards, and sheep, and oxen, and menservants, and maidservants? 27 The leprosy therefore of Naaman shall cleave unto thee, and unto thy seed for ever. And he went out from his presence a leper *as white* as snow.	sent the servants back to Naaman: He hid the money & clothing c. Gehazi's greed uncovered & his judgment 1) Elisha confronted his servant: Gehazi lied about where he had been 2) Elisha revealed that he knew Gehazi had taken the money & clothing 3) Elisha rebuked his servant: This was not the time to receive payment—salvation & healing were to be free, not to be offered for profit 4) Elisha pronounced the judgment of God: Gehazi & his descendants (through their genes) would be stricken with leprosy

a. Standing nearby during the conversation between Naaman and Elisha, Gehazi's mind was racing. He wanted some of the wealth that Naaman had offered Elisha (v.20). So while the two men were still talking, he was already working out a deceitful plan by which he could secure some of the money for himself.

b. As soon as Naaman had ridden off in the distance, Gehazi put into motion his greedy scheme and rushed to catch Naaman (vv.21-24). Soon thereafter, Naaman spotted the servant rushing after him. Stopping the caravan, Naaman got out of his chariot to meet him. Once face-to-face, the commander asked the servant if everything was all right.

Gehazi quickly and convincingly lied to Naaman by saying that Elisha had sent him (v.22). He declared that Elisha had remembered two young student prophets who did need some financial aid, and he would appreciate the commander making a contribution of 75 pounds of silver and two sets of clothing to the students. Grateful for the help Elisha had been to him, Naaman doubled the requested money and gave the clothing to the servant Gehazi. Moreover, since Gehazi was traveling alone, Naaman assigned two soldiers to accompany him back in the event he was attacked by thieves. But Gehazi took the gifts from the soldiers before they reached Elisha's house and sent the guards back to Naaman. He then hid the money and the clothing (v.24).

c. But soon thereafter, when the servant again faced his master Elisha, his greed was uncovered and judgment was pronounced upon him (vv.25-27). Elisha asked him where he had been, and Gehazi lied, stating that he had not gone anywhere. But Elisha revealed to the servant that he knew the truth, that Gehazi had taken the money and clothing from Naaman (v.26). Rebuking his servant, Elisha stated that this was not the time to receive payment for having ministered to a person, for salvation and healing were to be free. Salvation and healing were not to be offered for profit.

Elisha then pronounced the judgment of God upon Gehazi: the deceitful servant and all his descendants (through their genes) would be stricken with severe cases of leprosy, the very leprosy from which Naaman had just been delivered. Apparently quicker than the eye can blink, Gehazi was afflicted with leprosy. For when he departed from Elisha's presence, his skin was already diseased and as white as snow (v.27).

Thought 1. Greed and covetousness are terrible evils. A grudging and self-indulgent person becomes so consumed with money and wealth that he hoards what he has. Regardless of the needs around him, he piles up more and more, giving little if any to help meet the needs of this world.

In addition, a covetous person will, at times, steal, scheme, or manipulate to get more and more, sometimes even twisting the rules or law to get more of what he wants. Even if it means bankrupting other persons, taking all they have and causing them to become destitute and unemployed, a greedy person will do whatever it takes to secure every dime or piece of property he can. God warns the covetous and greedy. Listen to what God says:

"And he said unto them, Take heed, and beware of covetousness: for a man's life consisteth not in the abundance of the things which he possesseth. And he spake a parable unto them, saying, The ground of a certain rich man brought forth plentifully: And he thought within himself, saying, What shall I do, because I have no room where to bestow my fruits? And he said, This will I do: I will pull down my barns, and build greater; and there will I bestow all my fruits and my goods. And I will say to my soul, Soul, thou hast much goods laid up for many years; take thine ease, eat, drink, *and* be merry. But God said unto him, *Thou* fool, this night thy soul shall be required of thee: then whose shall those things be, which thou hast provided? So *is* he that layeth up treasure for himself, and is not rich toward God" (Lu.12:15-21).

"For the wrath of God is revealed from heaven against all ungodliness and unrighteousness of men, who hold the truth in unrighteousness;...Being filled with all unrighteousness, fornication, wickedness, covetousness, maliciousness; full of envy, murder, debate, deceit, malignity; whisperers;...Who knowing the judgment of God, that they which commit such things are worthy of death, not only do the same, but have pleasure in them that do them" (Ro.1:18, 29, 32).

"Know ye not that the unrighteous shall not inherit the kingdom of God? Be not deceived: neither fornicators, nor idolaters, nor adulterers, nor effeminate, nor abusers of themselves with mankind, Nor thieves, nor covetous, nor drunkards, nor revilers, nor extortioners, shall inherit the kingdom of God" (1 Co.6:9-10).

"But fornication, and all uncleanness, or covetousness, let it not be once named among you, as becometh saints; Neither filthiness, nor foolish talking, nor jesting, which are not convenient: but rather giving of thanks. For this ye know, that no whoremonger, nor unclean person, nor covetous man, who is an idolater, hath any inheritance in the kingdom of Christ and of God. Let no man deceive you with vain words: for because of these things cometh the wrath of God upon the children of disobedience" (Ep.5:3-6).

"Mortify therefore your members which are upon the earth; fornication, uncleanness, inordinate affection, evil concupiscence, and covetousness, which is idolatry: For which things' sake the wrath of God cometh on the children of disobedience" (Co.3:5-6).

"Let your conversation [behavior, conduct] be without covetousness; and be content with such things as ye have: for he hath said, I will never leave thee, nor forsake thee" (He.13:5).

"But the fearful, and unbelieving, and the abominable, and murderers, and whoremongers, and sorcerers, and idolaters [coveters], and all liars, shall have their part in the lake which burneth with fire and brimstone: which is the second death" (Re.21:8).

CHAPTER 6

C. The Lost Ax Head Miraculously Recovered & a Syrian Military Force Miraculously Blinded: A Lesson on God's Power to Help & to Defend His People, 6:1-23

1. A borrowed ax head lost but miraculously recovered: A lesson on God's power to help the faithful, diligent laborer

a. The school of prophets requested permission to build additional space: At the Jordan River

   1) Elisha granted the request

   2) Elisha was asked to join the prophets at the construction site: He agreed

b. The prophets themselves did the work: A picture of diligence

c. The prophets faced an immediate problem: An ax head flew off the handle into the river
   1) Was borrowed by a poor student
   2) Was iron, very expensive

d. The man of God, Elisha, demonstrated God's power to help the diligent worker
   1) Used a stick to show what he wanted the ax head to do
   2) Threw the stick into the river & watched it & the ax head rise to the top
   3) Instructed the student to lift the ax head out

2. A Syrian military force miraculously blinded: A lesson on God's power to defend His people

a. The secret plan of attack by Syrian raiding parties was miraculously revealed to Elisha: He warned Israel's king where the attacks were to take place

   1) The information proved true time & again
   2) The army of Israel was always prepared: Prevented the attacks, frustrating the Syrians
   3) The king of Syria became enraged, suspecting that one of his officers was a spy
      • He summoned & demanded that they expose the spy

And the sons of the prophets said unto Elisha, Behold now, the place where we dwell with thee is too strait for us.
2 Let us go, we pray thee, unto Jordan, and take thence every man a beam, and let us make us a place there, where we may dwell. And he answered, Go ye.
3 And one said, Be content, I pray thee, and go with thy servants. And he answered, I will go.
4 So he went with them. And when they came to Jordan, they cut down wood.
5 But as one was felling a beam, the axe head fell into the water: and he cried, and said, Alas, master! for it was borrowed.
6 And the man of God said, Where fell it? And he showed him the place. And he cut down a stick, and cast *it* in thither; and the iron did swim.
7 Therefore said he, Take *it* up to thee. And he put out his hand, and took it.
8 Then the king of Syria warred against Israel, and took counsel with his servants, saying, In such and such a place *shall be* my camp.
9 And the man of God sent unto the king of Israel, saying, Beware that thou pass not such a place; for thither the Syrians are come down.
10 And the king of Israel sent to the place which the man of God told him and warned him of, and saved himself there, not once nor twice.
11 Therefore the heart of the king of Syria was sore troubled for this thing; and he called his servants, and said unto them, Will ye not show me which of us *is* for the king of Israel?

12 And one of his servants said, None, my lord, O king: but Elisha, the prophet that *is* in Israel, telleth the king of Israel the words that thou speakest in thy bedchamber.
13 And he said, Go and spy where he *is,* that I may send and fetch him. And it was told him, saying, Behold, *he is* in Dothan.
14 Therefore sent he thither horses, and chariots, and a great host: and they came by night, and compassed the city about.
15 And when the servant of the man of God was risen early, and gone forth, behold, an host compassed the city both with horses and chariots. And his servant said unto him, Alas, my master! how shall we do?
16 And he answered, Fear not: for they that *be* with us *are* more than they that *be* with them.
17 And Elisha prayed, and said, LORD, I pray thee, open his eyes, that he may see. And the LORD opened the eyes of the young man; and he saw: and, behold, the mountain *was* full of horses and chariots of fire round about Elisha.
18 And when they came down to him, Elisha prayed unto the LORD, and said, Smite this people, I pray thee, with blindness. And he smote them with blindness according to the word of Elisha.
19 And Elisha said unto them, This *is* not the way, neither *is* this the city: follow me, and I will bring you to the man whom ye seek. But he led them to Samaria.
20 And it came to pass, when they were come into Samaria, that Elisha said, LORD, open the eyes of these *men,* that they may see. And the LORD opened their eyes, and they saw; and, behold, *they were* in the midst of Samaria.
21 And the king of Israel said unto Elisha, when he saw them, My father, shall I smite *them?* shall I smite *them?*
22 And he answered, Thou

• One officer informed the king that it was not any of them but Elisha the prophet who was giving the Israelite king information: He had supernatural knowledge

b. The king of Syria sought to capture Elisha
   1) He learned Elisha was in Dothan

   2) He sent *special forces* to capture Elisha
      • Marched by night
      • Surrounded the city

c. The LORD miraculously delivered the man of God
   1) Elisha's servant arose early the next morning & saw the Syrian troops
      • Was terrified, alarmed
      • Cried out in dismay
   2) Elisha sought to calm & assure the servant: Declared God's forces were stronger & more numerous than the enemy's forces
   3) Elisha prayed for God to open the eyes of the servant
      • The LORD answered Elisha's prayer
      • The servant saw a heavenly, angelic host surrounding & protecting God's dear servant

   4) Elisha saw the soldiers advancing toward him & asked God to strike the enemy soldiers with blindness
   5) Elisha's prayer was answered: The enemy was stricken blind
   6) Elisha led the blinded enemy soldiers to Samaria, Israel's capital: A trip of about eleven miles

      • He prayed, asking God to restore their eyesight
      • God answered his prayer

d. The king of Israel showed mercy to the enemy soldiers
   1) He asked Elisha if they should be executed

   2) Elisha advised that they be

treated humanely, given food & water & then sent home: To signify that he wished for a peace treaty with Syria	shalt not smite *them:* wouldest thou smite those whom thou hast taken captive with thy sword and with thy bow? set bread and water before them, that they may eat and drink, and go to their master.	23 And he prepared great provision for them: and when they had eaten and drunk, he sent them away, and they went to their master. So the bands of Syria came no more into the land of Israel.	3) Elisha's advice was accepted: The enemy was generously provided for & sent home e. The result: The Syrian army stopped their raiding of Israelite territory

DIVISION II

THE MINISTRY AND MIRACLES OF ELISHA: A DRAMATIC DEMONSTRATION OF GOD'S POWER AND CARE FOR HIS PEOPLE, 4:1–13:25

C. The Lost Ax Head Miraculously Recovered and a Syrian Military Force Miraculously Blinded: A Lesson on God's Power to Help and to Defend His People, 6:1-23

(6:1-23) **Introduction—Circumstances, Opportunities of, to Grow—Growth, Mature, How to Achieve—Maturity, How to Achieve—God, Power of, to Conquer—Conquest, Source, God**: every circumstance in life is a test. Whether good or bad, the circumstance gives us a unique opportunity to grow stronger in character and fruitfulness of life. Good circumstances give us—among other benefits—the opportunity to joy and rejoice in the Lord, giving thanks to God for the privilege of life. For every good and perfect gift comes from above, from the Father of lights, the LORD Himself.

In contrast, bad circumstances give us the unique opportunity to be a good testimony to others, especially unbelievers. It is during these times that we learn conquer, rise above, and be victorious over whatever bad or evil thing has happened to us or is confronting us. In dealing with the bad circumstances of life, we must remember one truth: the power to permanently conquer is found in God Himself. The LORD alone has the power to infuse within us the strength to overcome any circumstance, no matter how devastating or evil. The LORD will even deliver us from the bondage of death itself, immediately transferring us into His presence to live with Him eternally in the new heavens and earth that is to come.

God's power to help and defend His people through all the troubling circumstances of life is the practical subject of this Scripture. Two astounding miracles are performed by Elisha, miracles that demonstrate God's amazing power. This is: *The Lost Ax Head Miraculously Recovered and a Syrian Military Force Miraculously Blinded: A Lesson on God's Power to Help and to Defend His People,* 6:1-23.

1. A borrowed ax head lost but miraculously recovered: a lesson on God's power to help the faithful, diligent laborer (vv.1-7).
2. A Syrian military force miraculously blinded: a lesson on God's power to defend His people (vv.8-23).

[1] (6:1-7) **Laborer, Example of, Students—Students, Duty—Ministers, Duty—Diligence, Example of, Students—Prophets, School of, Needs Met—Ax Head, Miracle of—Miracles, Example of—Elisha, Miracles of**: a borrowed ax head was lost in the Jordan River, but Elisha miraculously made it float to the surface. Why would God perform such a miracle? To demonstrate His power to help the faithful, diligent worker. Note how Scripture describes what happened:

OUTLINE	SCRIPTURE	SCRIPTURE	OUTLINE
1. A borrowed ax head lost but miraculously recovered: A lesson on God's power to help the faithful, diligent laborer a. The school of prophets requested permission to build additional space: At the Jordan River 1) Elisha granted the request 2) Elisha was asked to join the prophets at the construction site: He agreed b. The prophets themselves did the work: A picture of diligence	And the sons of the prophets said unto Elisha, Behold now, the place where we dwell with thee is too strait for us. 2 Let us go, we pray thee, unto Jordan, and take thence every man a beam, and let us make us a place there, where we may dwell. And he answered, Go ye. 3 And one said, Be content, I pray thee, and go with thy servants. And he answered, I will go. 4 So he went with them. And when they came	to Jordan, they cut down wood. 5 But as one was felling a beam, the axe head fell into the water: and he cried, and said, Alas, master! for it was borrowed. 6 And the man of God said, Where fell it? And he showed him the place. And he cut down a stick, and cast *it* in thither; and the iron did swim. 7 Therefore said he, Take *it* up to thee. And he put out his hand, and took it.	c. The prophets faced an immediate problem: An ax head flew off the handle into the river 1) Was borrowed by a poor student 2) Was iron, very expensive d. The man of God, Elisha, demonstrated God's power to help the diligent worker 1) Used a stick to show what he wanted the ax head to do 2) Threw the stick into the river & watched it & the ax head rise to the top 3) Instructed the student to lift the ax head out

Apparently, the school of prophets at Jericho had outgrown its facilities, so the prophets requested permission of Elisha to build additional space at the Jordan River (vv.1-3; 2:1-25). After granting their request, Elisha was asked to join the prophets at the construction site. Note that the prophets did not hire contractors to do the work, but they themselves constructed the buildings. This is a clear picture of diligent labor and of hard, industrious workers (v.4). As the students were chopping down trees for beams, an immediate problem arose. One student was swinging an ax when the ax head flew off the handle and into the Jordan River (v.5). Deeply concerned about the loss, the student cried out to Elisha that the ax was borrowed. The student was apparently poor and had no way to replace the ax head, for iron was very expensive in that day.

Simply asking where the ax head had fallen into the river, Elisha set out to demonstrate God's power to help the faithful, diligent worker (vv.6-7). He then cut a stick from a nearby bush, threw it into the water, and watched it quickly rise again to the surface, showing (symbolizing) what he wanted the ax head to do. Miraculously, the ax head floated to the top of the river just as the stick had done, and Elisha instructed the student to grab the ax head and lift it out.

Thought 1. Whatever we, as believers, do, we are to do it well and do it diligently. Whenever we undertake a task, we are to be faithful and complete the work.

In our jobs and employment, we are to be committed. We are to be hardworking, conscientious, and steadfast, doing the very best work we can. It is a privilege to have a job and to have the health to perform the job—a privilege for which we should be thankful, a privilege that demands our very best. Yet think of all of the lazy, apathetic workers and all the sloppy work that goes on around us—all the people who think that society and others owe them a livelihood. Then think what a different society this would be if everyone were hardworking and did his or her very best, if every worker was diligent and steadfast at his or her employment.

But it is not only our jobs and employment that concern God: it is every task we undertake in life. No matter what we put our hands to—whether employment or volunteer work or an activity that we freely undertake for our own benefit—God cares about how we approach the tasks. Never are we to be slothful, slacking and doing tasks halfheartedly. On the contrary, we are to be attentive and take an active interest in whatever task we undertake: we are to be industrious and persistent, pressing on until the work of our hands has been completed. And once the task has been finished, God will give us a sense of satisfaction and fulfillment. Listen to what God says about being diligent and hardworking:

"Not slothful in business; fervent in spirit; serving the Lord" (Ro.12:11).

"Let him that stole steal no more: but rather let him labour, working with *his* hands the thing which is good, that he may have to give to him that needeth" (Ep.4:28).

"And whatsoever ye do in word or deed, *do* all in the name of the Lord Jesus, giving thanks to God and the Father by him" (Co.3:17).

"And whatsoever ye do, do *it* heartily, as to the Lord, and not unto men" (Co.3:23).

"And the LORD God took the man, and put him into the garden of Eden to dress it and to keep it" (Ge.2:15).

"Now them that are such we command and exhort by our Lord Jesus Christ, that with quietness they work, and eat their own bread" (2 Th.3:12).

"Nevertheless we, according to his promise, look for new heavens and a new earth, wherein dwelleth righteousness. Wherefore, beloved, seeing that ye look for such things, be diligent that ye may be found of him in peace, without spot, and blameless" (2 Pe.3:13-14).

"Go to the ant, thou sluggard; consider her ways, and be wise" (Pr.6:6).

"He becometh poor that dealeth *with* a slack hand: but the hand of the diligent maketh rich" (Pr.10:4).

"He that gathereth in summer *is* a wise son: *but* he that sleepeth in harvest *is* a son that causeth shame" (Pr.10:5).

"He that tilleth his land shall be satisfied with bread: but he that followeth vain *persons is* void of understanding" (Pr.12:11).

"The soul of the sluggard desireth, and *hath* nothing: but the soul of the diligent shall be made fat" (Pr.13:4).

"Wealth *gotten* by vanity shall be diminished: but he that gathereth by labour shall increase" (Pr.13:11).

"Love not sleep, lest thou come to poverty; open thine eyes, *and* thou shalt be satisfied with bread" (Pr.20:13).

"In all labour there is profit: but the talk of the lips *tendeth* only to penury" (Pr.14:23).

"Whatsoever thy hand findeth to do, do *it* with thy might; for *there is* no work, nor device, nor knowledge, nor wisdom, in the grave, whither thou goest" (Ec.9:10).

2 (6:8-23) **Defense, of God—Protection, of God—Shield, Divine—Miracles, Purpose, to Protect—Elisha, Miracles of—Power, of God, to Defend—Syria, Attacks or Wars Against the Northern Kingdom—Elisha, Delivered From, Syria**: a Syrian (Aramean) military force was miraculously blinded by God, blinded in order to save Elisha from being captured and possibly executed by the king of Syria (Aram). This is a dramatic, suspenseful story of God's power to defend His people.

OUTLINE	SCRIPTURE	SCRIPTURE	OUTLINE
2. A Syrian military force miraculously blinded: A lesson on God's power to defend His people a. The secret plan of attack by Syrian raiding parties was miraculously revealed to Elisha: He warned Israel's king where the attacks were to take place 1) The information proved true time & again 2) The army of Israel was always prepared: Prevented the attacks, frustrating the Syrians 3) The king of Syria became enraged, suspecting that one of his officers was a spy • He summoned & demanded that they expose the spy • One officer informed the king that it was not any of them but Elisha the prophet who was giving the Israelite king information: He had supernatural knowledge b. The king of Syria sought to capture Elisha 1) He learned Elisha was in Dothan 2) He sent *special forces* to capture Elisha • Marched by night • Surrounded the city c. The LORD miraculously delivered the man of God 1) Elisha's servant arose early the next morning & saw the Syrian troops • Was terrified, alarmed • Cried out in dismay 2) Elisha sought to calm & assure the servant: Declared God's forces were stronger & more numerous than the enemy's forces	8 Then the king of Syria warred against Israel, and took counsel with his servants, saying, In such and such a place *shall be* my camp. 9 And the man of God sent unto the king of Israel, saying, Beware that thou pass not such a place; for thither the Syrians are come down. 10 And the king of Israel sent to the place which the man of God told him and warned him of, and saved himself there, not once nor twice. 11 Therefore the heart of the king of Syria was sore troubled for this thing; and he called his servants, and said unto them, Will ye not show me which of us *is* for the king of Israel? 12 And one of his servants said, None, my lord, O king: but Elisha, the prophet that *is* in Israel, telleth the king of Israel the words that thou speakest in thy bedchamber. 13 And he said, Go and spy where he *is,* that I may send and fetch him. And it was told him, saying, Behold, *he is* in Dothan. 14 Therefore sent he thither horses, and chariots, and a great host: and they came by night, and compassed the city about. 15 And when the servant of the man of God was risen early, and gone forth, behold, an host compassed the city both with horses and chariots. And his servant said unto him, Alas, my master! how shall we do? 16 And he answered, Fear not: for they that *be* with us *are* more than they that *be* with them.	17 And Elisha prayed, and said, LORD, I pray thee, open his eyes, that he may see. And the LORD opened the eyes of the young man; and he saw: and, behold, the mountain *was* full of horses and chariots of fire round about Elisha. 18 And when they came down to him, Elisha prayed unto the LORD, and said, Smite this people, I pray thee, with blindness. And he smote them with blindness according to the word of Elisha. 19 And Elisha said unto them, This *is* not the way, neither *is* this the city: follow me, and I will bring you to the man whom ye seek. But he led them to Samaria. 20 And it came to pass, when they were come into Samaria, that Elisha said, LORD, open the eyes of these *men,* that they may see. And the LORD opened their eyes, and they saw; and, behold, *they were* in the midst of Samaria. 21 And the king of Israel said unto Elisha, when he saw them, My father, shall I smite *them?* shall I smite *them?* 22 And he answered, Thou shalt not smite *them:* wouldest thou smite those whom thou hast taken captive with thy sword and with thy bow? set bread and water before them, that they may eat and drink, and go to their master. 23 And he prepared great provision for them: and when they had eaten and drunk, he sent them away, and they went to their master. So the bands of Syria came no more into the land of Israel.	3) Elisha prayed for God to open the eyes of the servant • The LORD answered Elisha's prayer • The servant saw a heavenly, angelic host surrounding & protecting God's dear servant 4) Elisha saw the soldiers advancing toward him & asked God to strike the enemy soldiers with blindness 5) Elisha's prayer was answered: The enemy was stricken blind 6) Elisha led the blinded enemy soldiers to Samaria, Israel's capital: A trip of about eleven miles • He prayed, asking God to restore their eyesight • God answered his prayer d. The king of Israel showed mercy to the enemy soldiers 1) He asked Elisha if they should be executed 2) Elisha advised that they be treated humanely, given food & water & then sent home: To signify that he wished for a peace treaty with Syria 3) Elisha's advice was accepted: The enemy was generously provided for & sent home e. The result: The Syrian army stopped their raiding of Israelite territory

a. The Syrian king, conferring with his officers, planned a series of secret attacks against Israel by several groups of his special forces. The strategy of attacks by the raiding parties was to take place over an extended period of time. But God miraculously revealed the secret attacks to Elisha. Elisha then forewarned the king of Israel where the attacks were to take place (vv.8-9). Time and again the information proved true, and the army of Israel was always prepared. They prevented the attacks and utterly frustrated the Syrian raiding parties (v.10). Enraged and suspicious, the king of Syria suspected that one of his officers had become a spy for Israel (vv.11-12). Summoning his officers, the Syrian king demanded that they expose the spy. Stepping forth, one officer informed the king that it was not any of them who had betrayed the Syrian king. Rather, Elisha the prophet was giving the secret information to the king of Israel. The prophet not only had supernatural knowledge, but also a knowledge so detailed he knew what the Syrian king spoke in his bedroom.

b. Hearing this, the Syrian king immediately sent out a unit of spies to find out where Elisha was (vv.13-14). As soon as the reconnaissance report came back that he was in Dothan, the king sent a group of special forces to capture Elisha. Marching under the cover of darkness, the troops reached and surrounded the city of Dothan.

c. But was with Elisha, just as He is always with His dear people; and He was now going to deliver Elisha, the man of God (vv.15-20). Arising early the next morning, Elisha's servant saw the Syrian troops. Stricken with terror, he cried out to Elisha in utter dismay: "Oh my lord, what shall we do?"

Looking out and seeing the troops himself, Elisha sought to calm and assure his servant. He declared that God's forces were stronger and more numerous than the enemies' forces (v.16). Then Elisha began to pray for God to open the eyes of his servant so that he could see how God was protecting them from the Syrian forces. Hearing Elisha's prayer, God enabled the servant to see a heavenly, angelic host surrounding and protecting Elisha, God's dear servant (v.17).

Soon thereafter, Elisha saw the soldiers advancing toward him and once again he began to pray, asking God to strike the enemies' forces with blindness (v.18). Elisha's prayer was immediately answered and the enemy was stricken blind by the power of God. Courageously, Elisha walked out to the blinded soldiers and informed them that this was not the place where they belonged, neither the road nor the city. Elisha was not lying in telling them this. He was simply referring to the fact that this was not where God intended them to go. He then offered to lead them to the city and the man they were supposed to find. Being blind, they gladly accepted his offer. Therefore Elisha led them to Samaria, a trip of about 11 miles (vv.19-20). After they entered the city, Elisha prayed and asked God to restore their eyesight. God answered his prayer and opened the eyes of the soldiers. When they looked about, they saw they were inside enemy territory, inside Samaria, the very capital of the Northern Kingdom of Israel.

d. When Joram, the king of Israel, saw the captured Syrian soldiers, he asked Elisha if they should be executed (vv.21-23). But Elisha advised that, instead of executing them, the king should treat the Syrian soldiers humanely. He should give them food and water and then send them home. By treating the soldiers with such dignity, Joram would be signifying his desire for a peace treaty with Syria. Sensing the wisdom of this advice, Joram generously provided for the enemy soldiers and sent them home.

e. When the Syrian troops arrived back in Damascus, the result was just as Elisha had predicted. The Syrian attacks against Israelite territory stopped. At least for the present time, no other Syrian gorilla forces raided the border towns of Israel.

Thought 1. The lesson for us is most reassuring. God has the power to defend us, to protect us from the attack of any enemy. No matter who the enemy is, God will defend us, deliver us *through* the attack. He will carry us *through* any crushing or overwhelming circumstances such as...

- people ridiculing, scoffing, or poking fun at us
- people persecuting, attacking, or assaulting us
- people cursing, falsely accusing, or spreading rumors about us
- people hating, showing contempt, or reacting against us with disgust and hostility

Some people merely *speak* cruelly to us. Others become archenemies who take a stand against us, seeking to harm us. But in addition to human enemies there are spiritual enemies who stand opposed to us, who seek to defeat and destroy us. Spiritual enemies seduce and entice us, tempt and arouse passions within us, passions to commit evil and wickedness. Spiritual enemies are behind all the corruption and evil in this world, behind all the murder, rape, lawlessness, immorality, broken hearts, and broken bodies.

But God has the power to defend and protect us from all enemies, whether human or spiritual. When we are attacked spiritually or physically, our deliverance is found in the LORD. The LORD is our protector, defender, fortress, shield, shelter, and hiding place. Listen to what the Word of God says:

(1) God is our protector.

> "But there shall not an hair of your head perish" (Lu.21:18).
> "Finally, my brethren, be strong in the Lord, and in the power of his might. Put on the whole armour of God, that ye may be able to stand against the wiles of the devil. For we wrestle not against flesh and blood, but against principalities, against powers, against the rulers of the darkness of this world, against spiritual wickedness in high *places*. Wherefore take unto you the whole armour of God, that ye may be able to withstand in the evil day, and having done all, to stand" (Ep.6:10-13; see also 6:14-18).
> "The LORD shall fight for you, and ye shall hold your peace" (Ex.14:14).
> "For the eyes of the LORD run to and fro throughout the whole earth, to show himself strong in the behalf of *them* whose heart *is* perfect toward him" (2 Chr.16:9).
> "The angel of the LORD encampeth round about them that fear him, and delivereth them" (Ps.34:7).
> "He shall cover thee with his feathers, and under his wings shalt thou trust: his truth *shall be thy* shield and buckler" (Ps.91:4).
> "As the mountains *are* round about Jerusalem, so the LORD *is* round about his people from henceforth even for ever" (Ps.125:2).

(2) God is our defense.

> "But let all those that put their trust in thee rejoice: let them ever shout for joy, because thou defendest them: let them also that love thy name be joyful in thee" (Ps.5:11).
> "Bow down thine ear to me; deliver me speedily: be thou my strong rock, for an house of defence to save me" (Ps.31:2).

(3) God is our fortress.

"And he said, The LORD is my rock, and my fortress, and my deliverer" (2 S.22:2).

"The LORD is my rock, and my fortress, and my deliverer; my God, my strength, in whom I will trust; my buckler, and the horn of my salvation, and my high tower" (Ps.18:2).

"I will say of the LORD, He is my refuge and my fortress: my God; in him will I trust" (Ps.91:2).

"My goodness, and my fortress; my high tower, and my deliverer; my shield, and he in whom I trust; who subdueth my people under me" (Ps.144:2).

"The LORD is good, a strong hold in the day of trouble; and he knoweth them that trust in him" (Na.1:7).

(4) God is our shield.

"After these things the word of the LORD came unto Abram in a vision, saying, Fear not, Abram: I am thy shield, and thy exceeding great reward" (Ge.15:1).

"Our soul waiteth for the LORD: he is our help and our shield" (Ps.33:20).

"For the LORD God is a sun and shield: the LORD will give grace and glory: no good thing will he withhold from them that walk uprightly" (Ps.84:11).

"O Israel, trust thou in the LORD: he is their help and their shield" (Ps.115:9).

"Every word of God is pure: he is a shield unto them that put their trust in him" (Pr.30:5).

(5) God is our refuge.

"The eternal God is thy refuge, and underneath are the everlasting arms: and he shall thrust out the enemy from before thee; and shall say, Destroy them" (De.33:27).

"For in the time of trouble he shall hide me in his pavilion: in the secret of his tabernacle shall he hide me; he shall set me up upon a rock" (Ps.27:5).

"Thou shalt hide them in the secret of thy presence from the pride of man: thou shalt keep them secretly in a pavilion from the strife of tongues" (Ps.31:20).

"God is our refuge and strength, a very present help in trouble" (Ps.46:1).

"Be thou my strong habitation, whereunto I may continually resort: thou hast given commandment to save me; for thou art my rock and my fortress" (Ps.71:3).

"In the fear of the LORD is strong confidence: and his children shall have a place of refuge" (Pr.14:26).

"The name of the LORD is a strong tower: the righteous runneth into it, and is safe" (Pr.18:10).

"For thou hast been a strength to the poor, a strength to the needy in his distress, a refuge from the storm, a shadow from the heat, when the blast of the terrible ones is as a storm against the wall" (Is.25:4).

(6) God is our hiding place.

"Keep me as the apple of the eye, hide me under the shadow of thy wings" (Ps.17:8).

"For in the time of trouble he shall hide me in his pavilion: in the secret of his tabernacle shall he hide me; he shall set me up upon a rock" (Ps.27:5).

"Thou shalt hide them in the secret of thy presence from the pride of man: thou shalt keep them secretly in a pavilion from the strife of tongues" (Ps.31:20).

"Thou art my hiding place; thou shalt preserve me from trouble; thou shalt compass me about with songs of deliverance. Selah" (Ps.32:7).

"Hide me from the secret counsel of the wicked; from the insurrection of the workers of iniquity" (Ps.64:2).

"Thou art my hiding place and my shield: I hope in thy word" (Ps.119:114).

"Deliver me, O LORD, from mine enemies: I flee unto thee to hide me" (Ps.143:9).

1. The Syrian blockade & its effects: A picture of utter hopelessness & depravity

a. The first effects: Famine, starvation, & the greed of inflated prices
  1) A donkey's head: Cost about two pounds of silver
  2) A cup of dove dung: Cost about two ounces of silver

b. The second effects: The worst atrocity & depravity imaginable: Murder & cannibalism
  1) A woman cried out to the king for help
  2) The king, frustrated, responded bitterly: If the LORD did not help her, how could he
  3) The king softened & asked how he could help her
  4) The woman shared a dilemma, a case of cannibalism
    • She & another woman had agreed to kill & eat their sons
    • She had killed & cooked her son first, but the other woman was now hiding & refusing to give up her son
  5) The king was horrified & tore his robes in an act of anguish & despair: The torn robes exposed the fact that he was wearing sackcloth as a sign of grief

c. The third effect: The terrible sin of blaming God's prophet & even God Himself, 27
  1) The king swore to execute Elisha that very day
    • He was apparently unaware that Elisha was home attending a meeting with the leaders
    • He sent an executioner to kill Elisha
  2) The plot was revealed to Elisha by God: He instructed the leaders to lock the door, for the king would soon follow right behind to stop the assassination attempt

D. The Syrian Blockade Against Samaria Miraculously Broken: A Lesson on God's Power to Deliver His People, 6:24–7:20

24 And it came to pass after this, that Ben-hadad king of Syria gathered all his host, and went up, and besieged Samaria.
25 And there was a great famine in Samaria: and, behold, they besieged it, until an ass's head was *sold* for fourscore *pieces* of silver, and the fourth part of a cab of dove's dung for five *pieces* of silver.
26 And as the king of Israel was passing by upon the wall, there cried a woman unto him, saying, Help, my lord, O king.
27 And he said, If the LORD do not help thee, whence shall I help thee? out of the barnfloor, or out of the winepress?
28 And the king said unto her, What aileth thee? And she answered, This woman said unto me, Give thy son, that we may eat him to day, and we will eat my son to morrow.
29 So we boiled my son, and did eat him: and I said unto her on the next day, Give thy son, that we may eat him: and she hath hid her son.
30 And it came to pass, when the king heard the words of the woman, that he rent his clothes; and he passed by upon the wall, and the people looked, and, behold, *he had* sackcloth within upon his flesh.
31 Then he said, God do so and more also to me, if the head of Elisha the son of Shaphat shall stand on him this day.
32 But Elisha sat in his house, and the elders sat with him; and *the king* sent a man from before him: but ere the messenger came to him, he said to the elders, See ye how this son of a murderer hath sent to take away mine head? look, when the messenger cometh, shut the door, and hold him fast at the door: *is* not the sound of his master's feet behind him?

33 And while he yet talked with them, behold, the messenger came down unto him: and he said, Behold, this evil *is* of the LORD; what should I wait for the LORD any longer?

CHAPTER 7

Then Elisha said, Hear ye the word of the LORD; Thus saith the LORD, To morrow about this time *shall* a measure of fine flour *be sold* for a shekel, and two measures of barley for a shekel, in the gate of Samaria.
2 Then a lord on whose hand the king leaned answered the man of God, and said, Behold, *if* the LORD would make windows in heaven, might this thing be? And he said, Behold, thou shalt see *it* with thine eyes, but shalt not eat thereof.
3 And there were four leprous men at the entering in of the gate: and they said one to another, Why sit we here until we die?
4 If we say, We will enter into the city, then the famine *is* in the city, and we shall die there: and if we sit still here, we die also. Now therefore come, and let us fall unto the host of the Syrians: if they save us alive, we shall live; and if they kill us, we shall but die.
5 And they rose up in the twilight, to go unto the camp of the Syrians: and when they were come to the uttermost part of the camp of Syria, behold, *there was* no man there.
6 For the Lord had made the host of the Syrians to hear a noise of chariots, and a noise of horses, *even* the noise of a great host: and they said one to another, Lo, the king of Israel hath hired against us the kings of the Hittites, and the kings of the Egyptians, to come upon us.
7 Wherefore they arose and fled in the twilight, and left their tents, and their horses, and their asses, even the camp as it *was,* and fled for their life.
8 And when these lepers came to the uttermost part of

d. The fourth effect: Utter hopelessness
  1) The assassin & king soon arrived
  2) The king—in despair—asked Elisha: "Why should I not surrender?"

2. The blockade's end promised by God: A message of hope & deliverance

a. Elisha seized on the king's hopelessness & shared the Word of God: The blockade would end the next day & food would be plentiful
b. The king's chief official ridiculed God's promise: Doubted & spoke sarcastically about it
c. Elisha made a prediction about the chief official: He would see the promise fulfilled, but not share in it

3. The blockade miraculously ended by God: The power of God to deliver His people

a. The blockade's end discovered by four lepers
  1) They had been expelled as lepers, forced to live outside the city & to beg for food
  2) In desperation, they made the decision to go over to the Syrians & to appeal for mercy
  3) They made their way to the Syrian camp at dusk: Surprisingly, they discovered the camp still there, intact but abandoned

b. The cause of the blockade's end: GOD's miraculous work
  1) The LORD had caused the Syrians to hear a noise like that of a massive army attacking them, 6:16-17
  2) The Syrians concluded that Israel had hired the Hittites & Egyptians as mercenary armies
  3) The Syrians panicked & fled into the night, running for their lives. They abandoned their camp & left everything behind intact

c. They rush of the lepers to gorge themselves & to hide

as much of the plunder as they could

d. The changed hearts & decision of the lepers to share the good news of their discovery
- Admitted their selfishness & greed
- Made a decision to immediately share the good news of their discovery (God's deliverance)

4. The blockade's end shared by the four lepers: A picture of sharing the good news with the starving masses (spiritually)

a. The good news shouted out, spread by a *chain of sharing*
1) By the lepers to the gatekeepers

2) By the gatekeepers to the people & officials
3) By the officials to the king
b. The questioning, doubting of the good news: The king suspected a strategic plot by the Syrian army, an attempt to lure him & his people out of the city so they could capture them

c. The verifying of the incredible news
1) The suggestion was made by an officer to send out several spies to find out exactly where the Syrians were

the camp, they went into one tent, and did eat and drink, and carried thence silver, and gold, and raiment, and went and hid *it;* and came again, and entered into another tent, and carried thence *also,* and went and hid *it.*

9 Then they said one to another, We do not well: this day *is* a day of good tidings, and we hold our peace: if we tarry till the morning light, some mischief will come upon us: now therefore come, that we may go and tell the king's household.

10 So they came and called unto the porter of the city: and they told them, saying, We came to the camp of the Syrians, and, behold, *there was* no man there, neither voice of man, but horses tied, and asses tied, and the tents as they *were.*

11 And he called the porters; and they told *it* to the king's house within.

12 And the king arose in the night, and said unto his servants, I will now show you what the Syrians have done to us. They know that we *be* hungry; therefore are they gone out of the camp to hide themselves in the field, saying, When they come out of the city, we shall catch them alive, and get into the city.

13 And one of his servants answered and said, Let *some* take, I pray thee, five of the horses that remain, which are left in the city, (behold, they *are* as all the multitude of Israel that are left in it: behold, *I say,* they *are* even as all the multitude of the Israelites that are consumed:) and

let us send and see.

14 They took therefore two chariot horses; and the king sent after the host of the Syrians, saying, Go and see.

15 And they went after them unto Jordan: and, lo, all the way *was* full of garments and vessels, which the Syrians had cast away in their haste. And the messengers returned, and told the king.

16 And the people went out, and spoiled the tents of the Syrians. So a measure of fine flour was *sold* for a shekel, and two measures of barley for a shekel, according to the word of the LORD.

17 And the king appointed the lord on whose hand he leaned to have the charge of the gate: and the people trode upon him in the gate, and he died, as the man of God had said, who spake when the king came down to him.

18 And it came to pass as the man of God had spoken to the king, saying, Two measures of barley for a shekel, and a measure of fine flour for a shekel, shall be to morrow about this time in the gate of Samaria:

19 And that lord answered the man of God, and said, Now, behold, *if* the LORD should make windows in heaven, might such a thing be? And he said, Behold, thou shalt see it with thine eyes, but shalt not eat thereof.

20 And so it fell out unto him: for the people trode upon him in the gate, and he died.

2) The king approved the suggestion: He had two chariots & their horses selected & sent the scouts out to locate the Syrians
3) The spies followed the Syrians as far as the Jordan River (about 25 miles): Found equipment & clothing scattered all along the road by the Syrians as they fled in panic
4) The spies returned & verified the good news
d. The claiming of God's deliverance by the people: The people rushed out to secure food & to claim the plunder
e. The Word of God was fulfilled
1) The cost of food was lowered
2) The king's chief aide was trampled to death in the gateway

- The fact: He died just as Elisha had predicted

- The reason: He had ridiculed & spoken sarcastically concerning God's promise of deliverance

- The conclusion: God's Word was fulfilled exactly as predicted

DIVISION II

THE MINISTRY AND MIRACLES OF ELISHA: A DRAMATIC DEMONSTRATION OF GOD'S POWER AND CARE FOR HIS PEOPLE, 4:1–13:25

D. The Syrian Blockade Against Samaria Miraculously Broken: A Lesson on God's Power to Deliver His People, 6:24–7:20

(6:24–7:20) **Introduction—Helplessness, Feelings of, Examples—Deliverance, from What, Helplessness—Hopelessness, Feelings of, Example—Power of God, Results, Conquest of Helplessness**: Have you ever felt helpless, unable to handle a situation? Something happened that aroused within you an overwhelming sense of despair, grief, or desperation? And in the face of the overwhelming circumstance, you felt unable to cope or deal with the problem? Many people go through such gripping or paralyzing moments, experiencing extreme emotional upheaval, feeling that things are completely out of control.

But there is wonderful news for all who face intense hopelessness and helplessness. No matter what happens to us, God loves us. He cares for us and wants to help us. There is even a verse of Scripture that says, "Cast all your anxiety on Him because He cares for you" (1 Pe.5:7). When things are beyond our control—even death itself—God will infuse power in us, enough power to conquer and overcome whatever confronts us.

This is the good news of this wonderful Scripture. In dramatic fashion, it shows how the good news of God's deliverance must be proclaimed to the masses whose hearts are gripped by despair and depression. This passage paints one of the greatest and most powerful pictures of evangelism and missions in all of Scripture. It is a passage that should be preached and taught by every minister in the world. This is: *The Syrian Blockade Against Samaria Miraculously Broken: A Lesson on God's Power to Deliver His People,* 6:24–7:20.

1. The Syrian blockade and its effects: a picture of utter hopelessness and depravity (ch.6:24-33).
2. The blockade's end promised by God: a message of hope and deliverance (ch.7:1-2).
3. The blockade miraculously ended by God: the power of God to deliver His people (vv.3-9).
4. The blockade's end shared by the four lepers: a picture of sharing the good news with the starving masses (spiritually), (vv.10-20).

1 (6:24-33) **Hopelessness, Example of—Depravity, Example of—Corruption, Example of—Siege, Example of—Syria, Wars of, Against Israel—Israel, Wars of—Blockade, Example of—Israel, Northern Kingdom, Wars of:** sometime later, Syria once again invaded the Northern Kingdom and set up a siege or blockade around Samaria itself, the capital. No longer was the Syrian king, Ben-Hadad, interested in just raiding the border towns of Israel (6:8-10); he wanted to conquer the entire nation of the Northern Kingdom. Mobilizing his army, he marched up to Samaria and laid siege to or blockaded the capital. The effects of the siege upon the Samarians were catastrophic, a picture of utter hopelessness and depravity.

OUTLINE	SCRIPTURE	SCRIPTURE	OUTLINE

1. The Syrian blockade & its effects: A picture of utter hopelessness & depravity
a. The first effects: Famine, starvation, & the greed of inflated prices
  1) A donkey's head: Cost about two pounds of silver
  2) A cup of dove dung: Cost about two ounces of silver
 	
b. The second effects: The worst atrocity & depravity imaginable: Murder & cannibalism
  1) A woman cried out to the king for help
  2) The king, frustrated, responded bitterly: If the LORD did not help her, how could he
 	
  3) The king softened & asked how he could help her
  4) The woman shared a dilemma, a case of cannibalism
   • She & another woman had agreed to kill & eat their sons
   • She had killed & cooked her son first, but the other woman was now hiding & refusing
	24 And it came to pass after this, that Ben-hadad king of Syria gathered all his host, and went up, and besieged Samaria.
	25 And there was a great famine in Samaria: and, behold, they besieged it, until an ass's head was *sold* for fourscore *pieces* of silver, and the fourth part of a cab of dove's dung for five *pieces* of silver.
	26 And as the king of Israel was passing by upon the wall, there cried a woman unto him, saying, Help, my lord, O king.
	27 And he said, If the LORD do not help thee, whence shall I help thee? out of the barnfloor, or out of the winepress?
	28 And the king said unto her, What aileth thee? And she answered, This woman said unto me, Give thy son, that we may eat him to day, and we will eat my son to morrow.
	29 So we boiled my son, and did eat him: and I said unto her on the next day, Give thy son, that we may eat him: and
		she hath hid her son.
		30 And it came to pass, when the king heard the words of the woman, that he rent his clothes; and he passed by upon the wall, and the people looked, and, behold, *he had* sackcloth within upon his flesh.
		31 Then he said, God do so and more also to me, if the head of Elisha the son of Shaphat shall stand on him this day.
		32 But Elisha sat in his house, and the elders sat with him; and *the king* sent a man from before him: but ere the messenger came to him, he said to the elders, See ye how this son of a murderer hath sent to take away mine head? look, when the messenger cometh, shut the door, and hold him fast at the door: *is* not the sound of his master's feet behind him?
		33 And while he yet talked with them, behold, the messenger came down unto him: and he said, Behold, this evil *is* of the LORD; what should I wait for the LORD any longer?
			to give up her son
			5) The king was horrified & tore his robes in an act of anguish & despair: The torn robes exposed the fact that he was wearing sackcloth as a sign of grief
			
			c. The third effect: The terrible sin of blaming God's prophet & even God Himself, 27
			  1) The king swore to execute Elisha that very day
			   • He was apparently unaware that Elisha was home attending a meeting with the leaders
			   • He sent an executioner to kill Elisha
			  2) The plot was revealed to Elisha by God: He instructed the leaders to lock the door, for the king would soon follow right behind to stop the assassination attempt
			d. The fourth effect: Utter hopelessness
			  1) The assassin & king soon arrived
			  2) The king—in despair—asked Elisha: "Why should I not surrender?"

a. The first effects of the siege were that of famine, starvation, and the greed of inflated prices (v.25). The siege lasted so long and the blockade was so effective that the food supplies dried up completely. The famine that swept through the city was so terrible that the most revolting, nauseating garbage was being sold for scandalous black market prices.[1] As an example, the head of a donkey cost about two pounds of silver and, as nauseating as the thought is, a cup of dove dung

---

[1] Russell Dilday. *1, 2 Kings,* p. 321.

cost about two ounces of silver. To think that people would be starving to the point that they would consume animal waste is repulsive. Nevertheless, Scripture does report such incidences (2 K.18:27). Few experiences show the tragedy and repulsiveness of war as that of starvation, often by the innocent citizens of a nation.

b. The second effects of the blockade were the worst atrocity and depravity imaginable, that of murder and cannibalism (vv.26-30). One day, as the king was walking on the wall of the city inspecting his troops and assessing the critical situation facing the capital, a woman cried out to him for help. Frustrated at the severity of the circumstances, the king responded bitterly to the woman: If the LORD did not help her, how could he? He had no power to grow crops for bread or grapes for wine (vv.26-27).

Having blurted out his accusation against God, the king's emotions calmed down somewhat and he softly asked the woman how he could help her (vv.28-29). Shockingly, the woman shared a dilemma, a case of cannibalism that shook the king. She and another woman had agreed to kill and eat their sons. She had agreed to kill and cook her son first, but the other woman was now hiding her son and refusing to give him up. Utterly horrified, the king took hold of his robes and tore them in an act of total anguish and despair. The torn robes exposed the fact that he was wearing sackcloth underneath as a sign of grief (probably in an attempt to gain God's favor).

c. The third effect of the blockade was the terrible sin of blaming God and His prophet Elisha (vv.31-32). In responding to the woman, the king had just blamed God (v.27). Now he swore to execute Elisha that very day, either because he felt Elisha had been encouraging the people to trust God and to hold out against the siege, or because the prophet's prayers for the siege to be broken were not being answered. Or, knowing that the Syrians had attempted to capture and execute Elisha earlier, perhaps the king felt that if he executed and turned the body of Elisha over to the Syrians, they might withdraw and return home to Damascus.

Whatever the case, King Joram swore to execute Elisha that same day. Apparently, he was unaware that at that very moment Elisha was attending a meeting with the elders discussing the critical situation. Following through with his plans, the king sent an executioner to assassinate Elisha. But the plot was revealed to the prophet by God. Consequently, Elisha instructed the leaders to lock the door and not to harm the assassin, for the king himself would soon follow right behind in order to stop the assassination attempt.

d. The fourth effect of the siege was that of utter hopelessness (v.33). While Elisha was still talking and before the leaders could lock the door, the assassin burst through the door, not knowing that the leaders were present with the prophet. Because of their presence, he was unable to kill Elisha. Soon thereafter the king arrived, and in utter despair he asked Elisha why he should not go ahead and surrender to the Syrians? Why should he wait any longer for the LORD's deliverance?

Thought 1. The people of Samaria had forsaken God, turned away from and denied Him. As a result, they had sunk to the depths of depravity and corruption and were gripped by a sense of hopelessness and despair. So it is with us. If we reject and deny God, we too can fall into utter hopelessness and despair, sinking into the depths of depravity and corruption. For if there is no God, the Ten Commandments are not really His Word. They are merely irrelevant laws of an ancient society that do not have to be obeyed. In fact, without God, there are no moral absolutes, no morality that we truly have to follow except the laws that society might feel are essential for us to live together in peace. And if there is no God, there is no future life beyond this life, no heaven and no judgment where perfect justice will be executed by God. If there is no God, no heaven, and no judgment in the future that we have to face, we can live as we want, doing what we want when we want just as we want.

In reality, this is the way many people live all over the world. This is the reason for lawlessness, murder, war, rape, and assaults. Down deep within, great numbers of people simply do not believe that God exists or that He will hold them accountable in a day of judgment. For this reason, they live as they want no matter how selfish their lives may be. Consequently, when a severe crisis arises that is beyond their control, a spirit of helplessness and hopelessness grips their hearts and lives. For they have no hope or help beyond this world. They have no hope of life after their earthly pilgrimage. Thus if the crisis becomes severe enough, many will sink to the depths of depravity and corruption. They will steal, assault, kill, and commit any act of wickedness or evil in order to escape the crisis. Look at all the evil and wickedness in the world: it comes from the depravity of the human heart, either from the selfish passions and lusts of the heart or from a sense of hopelessness and despair. Look at the picture painted by God's Holy Word, the picture of hopelessness and depravity.

(1) Scripture paints the picture of utter hopelessness that grips the hearts of some people.

> **"That at that time ye were without Christ, being aliens from the commonwealth of Israel, and strangers from the covenants of promise, having no hope, and without God in the world: But now in Christ Jesus ye who sometimes were far off are made nigh by the blood of Christ" (Ep.2:12-13).**
>
> **"My days are swifter than a weaver's shuttle, and are spent without hope" (Jb.7:6).**
>
> **"So that my soul chooseth strangling, and death rather than my life" (Jb.7:15).**
>
> **"And where is now my hope? as for my hope, who shall see it" (Jb.17:15).**
>
> **"How then comfort ye me in vain, seeing in your answers there remaineth falsehood" (Jb.21:34).**
>
> **"So I returned, and considered all the oppressions that are done under the sun: and behold the tears of such as were oppressed, and they had no comforter; and on the side of their oppressors there was power; but they had no comforter" (Ec.4:1).**
>
> **"Withhold thy foot from being unshod, and thy throat from thirst: but thou saidst, There is no hope: no; for I have loved strangers, and after them will I go" (Je.2:25).**
>
> **"They have heard that I sigh: there is none to comfort me: all mine enemies have heard of my trouble; they are glad that thou hast done it: thou wilt bring the day that thou hast called, and they shall be like unto me" (Lam.1:21).**
>
> **"And I said, My strength and my hope is perished from the LORD" (Lam.3:18).**

(2) Scripture paints the picture of hearts being gripped by utter depravity and corruption.

"Woe unto you, scribes and Pharisees, hypocrites! for ye are like unto whited sepulchres, which indeed appear beautiful outward, but are within full of dead *men's* bones, and of all uncleanness" (Mt.23:27).

"For from within, out of the heart of men, proceed evil thoughts, adulteries, fornications, murders" (Mk.7:21).

"For the invisible things of him from the creation of the world are clearly seen, being understood by the things that are made, *even* his eternal power and Godhead; so that they are without excuse: Because that, when they knew God, they glorified him not as God, neither were thankful; but became vain in their imaginations, and their foolish heart was darkened. Professing themselves to be wise, they became fools, And changed the glory of the uncorruptible God into an image made like to corruptible man, and to birds, and fourfooted beasts, and creeping things. Wherefore God also gave them up to uncleanness through the lusts of their own hearts, to dishonour their own bodies between themselves: Who changed the truth of God into a lie, and worshipped and served the creature more than the Creator, who is blessed for ever. Amen. For this cause God gave them up unto vile affections: for even their women did change the natural use into that which is against nature: And likewise also the men, leaving the natural use of the woman, burned in their lust one toward another; men with men working that which is unseemly, and receiving in themselves that recompence of their error which was meet. And even as they did not like to retain God in their knowledge, God gave them over to a reprobate mind, to do those things which are not convenient; Being filled with all unrighteousness, fornication, wickedness, covetousness, maliciousness; full of envy, murder, debate, deceit, malignity; whisperers, Backbiters, haters of God, despiteful, proud, boasters, inventors of evil things, disobedient to parents, Without understanding, covenantbreakers, without natural affection, implacable, unmerciful: Who knowing the judgment of God, that they which commit such things are worthy of death, not only do the same, but have pleasure in them that do them" (Ro.1:20-32).

"And GOD saw that the wickedness of man *was* great in the earth, and *that* every imagination of the thoughts of his heart *was* only evil continually" (Ge.6:5).

"And God looked upon the earth, and, behold, it was corrupt; for all flesh had corrupted his way upon the earth" (Ge.6:12).

"How much more abominable and filthy is man, which drinketh iniquity like water" (Jb.15:16).

"The fool hath said in his heart, There is no God. They are corrupt, they have done abominable works, *there is* none that doeth good" (Ps.14:1).

"They are all gone aside, they are all together become filthy: there is none that doeth good, no, not one" (Ps.14:3).

"For your hands are defiled with blood, and your fingers with iniquity; your lips have spoken lies, your tongue hath muttered perverseness" (Is.59:3).

"But we are all as an unclean thing, and all our righteousnesses are as filthy rags; and we all do fade as a leaf; and our iniquities, like the wind, have taken us away" (Is.64:6).

2 (7:1-2) **Hope, Source of, God's Promise—Deliverance, Source of, God's Promise—Promise, of God, Example of—Deliverance, by God, Promised**: the end of the Syrian blockade was promised by God through His prophet Elisha. Remember the utter despair and hopelessness of King Joram. He had just asked Elisha why he should not go ahead and surrender to the Syrian army? Why he should wait any longer on God to deliver them? Hearing the king express his hopelessness and despair, Elisha seized the opportunity to share the Word of God, the wonderful promises of the LORD. Elisha immediately announced that the blockade would end on the very next day, and food would be plentiful (v.1). The very idea that the siege could end and food be plentiful within one day was incomprehensible, unbelievable. And the king's chief official blurted out his unbelief. He ridiculed, doubting and speaking sarcastically about the promise. He exclaimed that such could not happen. It could not happen even if the LORD opened the floodgates of heaven itself. Countering the sarcastic disbelief of the chief official, Elisha turned to him and predicted that he would indeed see the promise fulfilled. But he would not personally share in it. He would not eat one mouthful of the plentiful food that would be provided.

OUTLINE	SCRIPTURE	SCRIPTURE	OUTLINE
2. The blockade's end promised by God: A message of hope & deliverance a. Elisha seized on the king's hopelessness & shared the Word of God: The blockade would end the next day & food would be plentiful b. The king's chief official	Then Elisha said, Hear ye the word of the LORD; Thus saith the LORD, To morrow about this time *shall* a measure of fine flour *be sold* for a shekel, and two measures of barley for a shekel, in the gate of Samaria. 2 Then a lord on whose	hand the king leaned answered the man of God, and said, Behold, *if* the LORD would make windows in heaven, might this thing be? And he said, Behold, thou shalt see *it* with thine eyes, but shalt not eat thereof.	ridiculed God's promise: Doubted & spoke sarcastically about it c. Elisha made a prediction about the chief official: He would see the promise fulfilled, but not share in it

Thought 1. In the midst of hopelessness and despair, there is the message of God, a message of hope and deliverance. No matter how helpless we may feel or how hopeless a situation may seem, there is always hope. There is hope in God and in His power to deliver us. Just as the Northern Kingdom of Israel was facing war, so war and conflict may face us. Starvation may confront us. Bankruptcy, financial difficulties, broken relationships, divorce, a severe accident or disease, or even death itself may stare us in the face. But there is always the message of God's

Holy Word, the message of hope. There is hope in God and His power to deliver us. Listen to what God's Holy Word says about the message of His hope and deliverance.

"For when we were yet without strength, in due time Christ died for the ungodly" (Ro.5:6).

"And he said unto me, My grace is sufficient for thee: for my strength is made perfect in weakness. Most gladly therefore will I rather glory in my infirmities, that the power of Christ may rest upon me" (2 Co.12:9).

"Above all, taking the shield of faith, wherewith ye shall be able to quench all the fiery darts of the wicked" (Ep.6:16).

"If any of you lack wisdom, let him ask of God, that giveth to all men liberally, and upbraideth not; and it shall be given him. But let him ask in faith, nothing wavering. For he that wavereth is like a wave of the sea driven with the wind and tossed" (Js.1:5-6).

"And they rose early in the morning, and went forth into the wilderness of Tekoa: and as they went forth, Jehoshaphat stood and said, Hear me, O Judah, and ye inhabitants of Jerusalem; Believe in the LORD your God, so shall ye be established; believe his prophets, so shall ye prosper" (2 Chr.20:20).

"Behold, the eye of the LORD is upon them that fear him, upon them that hope in his mercy" (Ps.33:18).

"Trust in the LORD, and do good; so shalt thou dwell in the land, and verily thou shalt be fed" (Ps.37:3).

"Commit thy way unto the LORD; trust also in him; and he shall bring it to pass" (Ps.37:5).

"And now, Lord, what wait I for? my hope is in thee" (Ps.39:7).

"Why art thou cast down, O my soul? and why art thou disquieted within me? hope thou in God: for I shall yet praise him, who is the health of my countenance, and my God" (Ps.42:11).

"For thou art my hope, O Lord GOD: thou art my trust from my youth" (Ps.71:5).

"The LORD preserveth the simple: I was brought low, and he helped me" (Ps.116:6).

"Happy is he that hath the God of Jacob for his help, whose hope is in the LORD his God" (Ps.146:5).

"Trust in the LORD with all thine heart; and lean not unto thine own understanding" (Pr.3:5).

"Trust ye in the LORD for ever: for in the LORD JEHOVAH is everlasting strength" (Is.26:4).

"Who is among you that feareth the LORD, that obeyeth the voice of his servant, that walketh in darkness, and hath no light? let him trust in the name of the LORD, and stay upon his God" (Is.50:10).

"Blessed is the man that trusteth in the LORD, and whose hope the LORD is" (Je.17:7).

---

3 (7:3-9) **Deliverance, of God, Example—Miracle, Listed, Deliverance from an Enemy Siege**: the blockade or siege was miraculously ended by God, and the message of hope was proven true. Through the power of God, the people were delivered from their enemy.

OUTLINE	SCRIPTURE	SCRIPTURE	OUTLINE
3. The blockade miraculously ended by God: The power of God to deliver His people	3 And there were four leprous men at the entering in of the gate: and they said one to another, Why sit we here until we die?	Hittites, and the kings of the Egyptians, to come upon us.	that Israel had hired the Hittites & Egyptians as mercenary armies
a. The blockade's end discovered by four lepers	4 If we say, We will enter into the city, then the famine is in the city, and we shall die there: and if we sit still here, we die also. Now therefore come, and let us fall unto the host of the Syrians: if they save us alive, we shall live; and if they kill us, we shall but die.	7 Wherefore they arose and fled in the twilight, and left their tents, and their horses, and their asses, even the camp as it *was*, and fled for their life.	3) The Syrians panicked & fled into the night, running for their lives: They abandoned their camp & left everything behind intact
1) They had been expelled as lepers, forced to live outside the city & to beg for food			
2) In desperation, they made the decision to go over to the Syrians & to appeal for mercy		8 And when these lepers came to the uttermost part of the camp, they went into one tent, and did eat and drink, and carried thence silver, and gold, and raiment, and went and hid *it;* and came again, and entered into another tent, and carried thence *also,* and went and hid *it.*	c. The rush of the lepers to gorge themselves & to hide as much of the plunder as they could
3) They made their way to the Syrian camp at dusk: Surprisingly, they discovered the camp still there, intact but abandoned	5 And they rose up in the twilight, to go unto the camp of the Syrians: and when they were come to the uttermost part of the camp of Syria, behold, there was no man there.		
b. The cause of the blockade's end: GOD's miraculous work	6 For the Lord had made the host of the Syrians to hear a noise of chariots, and a noise of horses, *even* the noise of a great host: and they said one to another, Lo, the king of Israel hath hired against us the kings of the	9 Then they said one to another, We do not well: this day *is* a day of good tidings, and we hold our peace: if we tarry till the morning light, some mischief will come upon us: now therefore come, that we may go and tell the king's household.	d. The changed hearts & decision of the lepers to share the good news of their discovery
1) The LORD had caused the Syrians to hear a noise like that of a massive army attacking them, 6:16-17			• Admitted their selfishness & greed
2) The Syrians concluded			• Made a decision to immediately share the good news of their discovery (God's deliverance)

a. Four lepers were the first to discover that the blockade had ended (vv.3-5). Being lepers, the four men had been expelled from the city, forced to live outside the city gate to beg for food. But ever since the siege, no food had been provided for them. In desperation, they made the decision to go over to the camp of the Syrians to appeal for mercy. Although they knew they might be executed immediately by the enemy, they also knew that they would be starving to death within just a few days. Consequently, they felt they stood a better chance of being shown mercy by the Syrians than remaining at the city gates and starving. At dusk, they struck out and made their way to the Syrian camp (v.5). When they arrived, they discovered the camp still there intact but, surprisingly, it was abandoned. The Syrian army was just not there, but the camp and all the food and plunder was.

b. What caused the blockade to end, the enemy soldiers to become so frightened that they fled leaving all their possessions behind? God's miraculous power and deliverance. The LORD had caused the Syrians to hear the sound of chariots and horses, a sound just like that of a massive army rushing to attack them (6:16-17). Concluding that Israel had hired the Hittites and Egyptians as mercenary armies, the Syrian forces panicked. They fled into the night, running for their lives. They abandoned their camp and left everything there unharmed, including the food and all the plunder.

c. Coming upon the deserted camp, the lepers rushed about gorging themselves and hiding as much of the plunder as they could (v.8). Once their stomachs were full and they had hidden enough plunder to make them wealthy, they became conscious-stricken.

d. The lepers realized how selfish and greedy they were acting. It was a day of good news, and they were keeping the good news to themselves. The lepers also realized that the king would later punish them if they kept the good news to themselves. Thus, they made a decision to share right away their discovery, the good news of God's wonderful deliverance.

Thought 1. A strong confidence in God's power is the lesson for us. God has the power to deliver us from any circumstance or crisis. He delivered Samaria from an impossible situation, and God will deliver us from whatever confronts us. Whatever it is that may besiege us, attempt to block us from living fruitful lives, it is not beyond the power of God's deliverance. Nothing, absolutely nothing, can defeat or conquer us if we only trust God and walk righteously before Him, loving and obeying Him. If we live godly lives and call upon the LORD as Elisha did, God will deliver us just as He did Elisha and the Samaritan people.

"There hath no temptation taken you but such as is common to man: but God *is* faithful, who will not suffer you to be tempted above that ye are able; but will with the temptation also make a way to escape, that ye may be able to bear *it*" (1 Co.10:13).

"For we would not, brethren, have you ignorant of our trouble which came to us in Asia, that we were pressed out of measure, above strength, insomuch that we despaired even of life: But we had the sentence of death in ourselves, that we should not trust in ourselves, but in God which raiseth the dead: Who delivered us from so great a death, and doth deliver: in whom we trust that he will yet deliver *us*" (2 Co.1:8-10).

"And the Lord shall deliver me from every evil work, and will preserve *me* unto his heavenly kingdom: to whom *be* glory for ever and ever. Amen" (2 Ti.4:18).

"Forasmuch then as the children are partakers of flesh and blood, he also himself likewise took part of the same; that through death he might destroy him that had the power of death, that is, the devil; And deliver them who through fear of death were all their lifetime subject to bondage" (He.2:14-15).

"Let your conversation [behavior, conduct] *be* without covetousness; *and be* content with such things as ye have: for he hath said, I will never leave thee, nor forsake thee. So that we may boldly say, The Lord *is* my helper, and I will not fear what man shall do unto me" (He.13:5-6).

"The Lord knoweth how to deliver the godly out of temptations, and to reserve the unjust unto the day of judgment to be punished" (2 Pe.2:9).

"And he said, The LORD *is* my rock, and my fortress, and my deliverer" (2 S.22:2).

"He shall deliver thee in six troubles: yea, in seven [the ultimate number of times] there shall no evil touch thee" (Jb.5:19).

"But I *am* poor and needy; *yet* the Lord thinketh upon me: thou *art* my help and my deliverer; make no tarrying, O my God" (Ps.40:17).

"Surely he shall deliver thee from the snare of the fowler, *and* from the noisome pestilence" (Ps.91:3).

"Fear thou not; for I *am* with thee: be not dismayed; for I *am* thy God: I will strengthen thee; yea, I will help thee; yea, I will uphold thee with the right hand of my righteousness" (Is.41:10).

"Fear not: for I have redeemed thee, I have called thee by thy name; thou art mine. When thou passest through the waters, I will be with thee; and through the rivers, they shall not overflow thee: when thou walkest through the fire, thou shalt not be burned; neither shall the flame kindle upon thee" (Is.43:1-2).

"And *even* to *your* old age I *am* he; and *even* to hoar [gray] hairs will I carry *you:* I have made, and I will bear; even I will carry, and will deliver *you*" (Is.46:4).

"Behold, the Lord GOD will help me; who is he that shall condemn me? lo, they all shall wax old as a garment; the moth shall eat them up" (Is.50:9).

"Be not afraid of their faces: for I *am* with thee to deliver thee, saith the LORD" (Je.1:8).

"He delivereth and rescueth, and he worketh signs and wonders in heaven and in earth, who hath delivered Daniel from the power of the lions" (Da.6:27).

4 (7:10-20) **Gospel, Duty—Witnessing, Duty—Testimony, Duty—Evangelism, Duty—Soul-Winning, Duty—Church, Duty—Missions, Duty**: the good news of God's wonderful deliverance was shared by the four lepers. This is a clear picture of sharing the good news of the gospel with the masses who are starving spiritually. Note how the drama painted by Scripture emphasizes the importance of missions. Those who are starving, hungering, and thirsting for life must be fed spiritually. Only God can feed their souls and give them life—abundant life—both now and eternally. For this reason, the good news of God's deliverance must be proclaimed to the starving masses.

OUTLINE	SCRIPTURE	SCRIPTURE	OUTLINE
4. The blockade's end shared by the four lepers: A picture of sharing the good news with the starving masses (spiritually) a. The good news shouted out, spread by a *chain of sharing* 1) By the lepers to the gate-keepers 2) By the gatekeepers to the people & officials 3) By the officials to the king b. The questioning, doubting of the good news: The king suspected a strategic plot by the Syrian army, an attempt to lure him & his people out of the city so they could capture them c. The verifying of the incredible news 1) The suggestion was made by an officer to send out several spies to find out exactly where the Syrians were 2) The king approved the suggestion: He had two chariots & their horses selected & sent the scouts out to locate the Syrians 3) The spies followed the Syri-	10 So they came and called unto the porter of the city: and they told them, saying, We came to the camp of the Syrians, and, behold, *there was* no man there, neither voice of man, but horses tied, and asses tied, and the tents as they *were*. 11 And he called the porters; and they told *it* to the king's house within. 12 And the king arose in the night, and said unto his servants, I will now show you what the Syrians have done to us. They know that we *be* hungry; therefore are they gone out of the camp to hide themselves in the field, saying, When they come out of the city, we shall catch them alive, and get into the city. 13 And one of his servants answered and said, Let *some* take, I pray thee, five of the horses that remain, which are left in the city, (behold, they *are* as all the multitude of Israel that are left in it: behold, *I say,* they *are* even as all the multitude of the Israelites that are consumed:) and let us send and see. 14 They took therefore two chariot horses; and the king sent after the host of the Syrians, saying, Go and see. 15 And they went after	them unto Jordan: and, lo, all the way *was* full of garments and vessels, which the Syrians had cast away in their haste. And the messengers returned, and told the king. 16 And the people went out, and spoiled the tents of the Syrians. So a measure of fine flour was *sold* for a shekel, and two measures of barley for a shekel, according to the word of the LORD. 17 And the king appointed the lord on whose hand he leaned to have the charge of the gate: and the people trode upon him in the gate, and he died, as the man of God had said, who spake when the king came down to him. 18 And it came to pass as the man of God had spoken to the king, saying, Two measures of barley for a shekel, and a measure of fine flour for a shekel, shall be to morrow about this time in the gate of Samaria. 19 And that lord answered the man of God, and said, Now, behold, *if* the LORD should make windows in heaven, might such a thing be? And he said, Behold, thou shalt see it with thine eyes, but shalt not eat thereof. 20 And so it fell out unto him: for the people trode upon him in the gate, and he died.	ans as far as the Jordan River (about 25 miles): Found equipment & clothing scattered all along the road by the Syrians as they fled in panic 4) The spies returned & verified the good news d. The claiming of God's deliverance by the people: The people rushed out to secure food & to claim the plunder e. The Word of God was fulfilled 1) The cost of food was lowered 2) The king's chief aide was trampled to death in the gateway • The fact: He died just as Elisha had predicted • The reason: He had ridiculed & spoken sarcastically concerning God's promise of deliverance • The conclusion: God's Word was fulfilled exactly as predicted

a. The lepers did not wait until morning to rush back to the famished people with the news, for the news of God's deliverance was too important to wait for daybreak. Rushing back in the middle of the night, they shouted out the good news to the gatekeepers (vv.10-11). Afterward the *chain of sharing* was launched: the lepers to the gatekeepers, the gatekeepers to the people and royal officials, and the royal officials to the king. All of the starving people heard the good news that food was available. The Syrians had broken their siege and left their camp intact, including all the food and plunder.

b. But note the response of King Joram: he questioned and doubted the good news. He suspected a strategic plot by the Syrian army, an attempt to lure him and his people out of the city in order to capture them (v.12).

c. In consultation with his cabinet officials, King Joram accepted the advice of an officer to verify the incredible news. Several spies were to be sent out to determine exactly where the Syrians were (vv.13-15). Reconnaissance was critically needed before the king could risk letting the starving populace flood out of the city gates to gather the food and plunder from the Syrian camp. Approving the suggestion, King Joram had two chariots prepared and then sent several scouts out to locate the Syrians (v.14). The scouting party followed the Syrians as far as the Jordan River, which was about 25 miles from the capital Samaria. All along the road and everywhere they looked, they found equipment and clothing scattered by the Syrians as they fled in panic (v.15). Returning to Samaria, the spies gave their report verifying the good news.

d. Upon hearing the good news, the people rushed out to secure food and to claim the plunder. This is a clear picture of people hearing the good news of God's deliverance and rushing to lay claim to His wonderful salvation (v.16).

e. Note that the Word of God was fulfilled exactly as predicted by Elisha:

⇒ the cost of food was lowered: five quarts of flour was sold that day for one-half an ounce of silver.

⇒ ten quarts of barley grain were sold for one-half an ounce of silver.

In addition, the king's chief official was killed at the city gate where he had been stationed to control the traffic (v.17). Obviously, he was somehow knocked down in the mad rush and trampled to death. He died just as Elisha had predicted (vv.3, 18). Because he had ridiculed and spoken sarcastically about God's promise of deliverance, he was condemned to die (v.19). And this is exactly what happened to him. God's Word was fulfilled exactly as predicted by God's prophet (v.20).

Thought 1. Russell Dilday has an excellent application to this point that is well worth quoting in its entirety:

> *To have any great gift—wealth, education, freedom—and not share it is evil. Using such gifts only for selfish purposes without regard for the needs of others is a serious sin. Never is that more true than with the gift of salvation. Do we think we are important enough that we are the ultimate end of God's mercy? Do we dare assume that God loved us enough that He sent Jesus to die for* our *sins alone? No, He saves us and empowers us so that we can become channels through which His blessings may flow to others. Paul wrote, "[God] comforts us...that we may be able to comfort those who are in any trouble, with the comfort with which we ourselves are comforted by God" (2 Cor.1:4). We are to become links in His great chain of transmission, passing on our experience with the Lord to others.*
>
> *As witnesses, we should also remember it is the message, not the messenger, that is important. God does not always choose great people to be His messengers. The Samaritan lepers were weak and unlikely instruments for God. They could only tell what they had seen and tasted, but that was enough. Just because you consider yourself ordinary and inadequate doesn't mean you are therefore excused from the responsibility of personal witnessing. God never requires His witnesses to be walking encyclopedias of theological knowledge, or champion debaters, or persuasive salesmen. He only expects us to be faithful conveyers of the message, the good news. No matter how weak or untalented you consider yourself to be, this passage reminds you, it is a sin to remain silent.*[2]

"For we cannot but speak the things which we have seen and heard" (Ac.4:20).

"Go, stand and speak in the temple to the people all the words of this life. And when they heard *that,* they entered into the temple early in the morning, and taught. But the high priest came, and they that were with him, and called the council together, and all the senate of the children of Israel and sent to the prison to have them brought" (Ac.5:20-21).

"We having the same spirit of faith, according as it is written, I believed, and therefore have I spoken; we also believe, and therefore speak" (2 Co.4:13).

"To wit, that God was in Christ, reconciling the world unto himself, not imputing their trespasses unto them; and hath committed unto us the word of reconciliation. Now then we are ambassadors for Christ, as though God did beseech *you* by us: we pray *you* in Christ's stead, be ye reconciled to God. For he hath made him *to be* sin for us, who knew no sin; that we might be made the righteousness of God in him" (2 Co.5:19-21).

"And the things that thou hast heard of me among many witnesses, the same commit thou to faithful men, who shall be able to teach others also" (2 Ti.2:2).

"These things speak, and exhort, and rebuke with all authority. Let no man despise thee" (Ti.2:15).

"Come *and* hear, all ye that fear God, and I will declare what he hath done for my soul" (Ps.66:16).

"Ye *are* my witnesses, saith the LORD, and my servant whom I have chosen: that ye may know and believe me, and understand that I *am* he: before me there was no God formed, neither shall there be after me" (Is.43:10).

"I will mention the lovingkindnesses of the LORD, *and* the praises of the LORD, according to all that the LORD hath bestowed on us, and the great goodness toward the house of Israel, which he hath bestowed on them according to his mercies, and according to the multitude of his lovingkindnesses" (Is.63:7).

"Then they that feared the LORD spake often one to another: and the LORD hearkened, and heard *it,* and a book of remembrance was written before him for them that feared the LORD, and that thought upon his name" (Ma.3:16).

---

[2] Russell Dilday. *1, 2 Kings,* p.328.

CHAPTER 8

E. The Political Influence of Elisha & the Evil Reigns of Jehoram & Ahaziah in Judah: A Picture of Being a Strong Godly Example & Witness for the LORD, 8:1-29

8:16-24; see 2 Chr.21:1-20

8:25-29; see 2 Chr.22:1-6

1. The Shunammite woman's land restored due to Elisha's political influence: The impact of a godly example for the LORD

a. The woman's relocation
   1) She had been warned by Elisha to flee a coming famine
   2) She & her family did as instructed
      • Fled to the land of the Philistines
      • Lived there seven years

b. The woman's return: She discovered that her property had been confiscated or stolen

c. The woman's appeal to the king for her home & land

d. The woman's land restored: Due to Elisha's testimony & political influence
   1) The LORD had prepared the way for her
      • The king had summoned Elisha's servant Gehazi to discuss the miracles performed by the prophet
      • The woman entered the royal court just as Gehazi was sharing the miracle of her son being raised from the dead

      • The king asked her about the miracle: She verified the fact
   2) The king restored her property
      • Her home & land
      • All the monies earned off the land

2. The new king of Syria predicted by Elisha: The need to bear strong witness to the entire world

a. Elisha's trip to Damascus, Syria

b. King Ben-Hadad's appeal for Elisha's help
   1) He was deathly sick
   2) He sent his trusted official Hazael to Elisha, asking

Then spake Elisha unto the woman, whose son he had restored to life, saying, Arise, and go thou and thine household, and sojourn wheresoever thou canst sojourn: for the LORD hath called for a famine; and it shall also come upon the land seven years.

2 And the woman arose, and did after the saying of the man of God: and she went with her household, and sojourned in the land of the Philistines seven years.

3 And it came to pass at the seven years' end, that the woman returned out of the land of the Philistines: and she went forth to cry unto the king for her house and for her land.

4 And the king talked with Gehazi the servant of the man of God, saying, Tell me, I pray thee, all the great things that Elisha hath done.

5 And it came to pass, as he was telling the king how he had restored a dead body to life, that, behold, the woman, whose son he had restored to life, cried to the king for her house and for her land. And Gehazi said, My lord, O king, this is the woman, and this is her son, whom Elisha restored to life.

6 And when the king asked the woman, she told him. So the king appointed unto her a certain officer, saying, Restore all that was hers, and all the fruits of the field since the day that she left the land, even until now.

7 And Elisha came to Damascus; and Ben-hadad the king of Syria was sick; and it was told him, saying, The man of God is come hither.

8 And the king said unto Hazael, Take a present in thine hand, and go, meet the man of God, and enquire of the LORD by him, saying, Shall

I recover of this disease?

9 So Hazael went to meet him, and took a present with him, even of every good thing of Damascus, forty camels' burden, and came and stood before him, and said, Thy son Ben-hadad king of Syria hath sent me to thee, saying, Shall I recover of this disease?

10 And Elisha said unto him, Go, say unto him, Thou mayest certainly recover: howbeit the LORD hath showed me that he shall surely die.

11 And he settled his countenance stedfastly, until he was ashamed: and the man of God wept.

12 And Hazael said, Why weepeth my lord? And he answered, Because I know the evil that thou wilt do unto the children of Israel: their strong holds wilt thou set on fire, and their young men wilt thou slay with the sword, and wilt dash their children, and rip up their women with child.

13 And Hazael said, But what, is thy servant a dog, that he should do this great thing? And Elisha answered, The LORD hath showed me that thou *shalt be* king over Syria.

14 So he departed from Elisha, and came to his master; who said to him, What said Elisha to thee? And he answered, He told me *that* thou shouldest surely recover.

15 And it came to pass on the morrow, that he took a thick cloth, and dipped *it* in water, and spread *it* on his face, so that he died: and Hazael reigned in his stead.

16 And in the fifth year of Joram the son of Ahab king of Israel, Jehoshaphat *being* then king of Judah, Jehoram the son of Jehoshaphat king of Judah began to reign.

17 Thirty and two years old was he when he began to reign; and he reigned eight years in Jerusalem.

18 And he walked in the way of the kings of Israel, as did the house of Ahab: for the daughter of Ahab was his wife: and he did evil in the sight of the LORD.

19 Yet the LORD would

for spiritual help
   3) He sent 40 camel loads of the finest products as a gift to Elisha

c. Hazael's audience with Elisha
   1) He presented the king's request for spiritual help

   2) Elisha stunned Hazael: Revealed that the king would die by the hand of an assassin, not from his sickness

d. Elisha's icy stare & confrontation with Hazael
   1) Hazael became uneasy
   2) Elisha began to weep
   3) Hazael asked why he was weeping
   4) Elisha bore strong witness about the sinful, evil heart of Hazael: The official would commit horrible atrocities against the Israelites (an instrument of God's judgment upon His sinful people, 10:32-33; 13:3)

   5) Hazael, stunned & insulted, denied his sinful heart, that he would do such gross evil
   6) Elisha revealed that Hazael was soon to become king of Syria

e. Hazael's sinful, wicked heart proven
   1) He returned to King Ben-Hadad & lied to him: Stated that Elisha had assured the king of a complete recovery
   2) He assassinated the king on the very next day: Smothered him to death
   3) He seized the throne of Syria

3. The evil reign of Jehoram exposed—during Elisha's ministry: The danger of marrying an unbelieving spouse

a. His background
   1) He was the son of a good ruler, Jehoshaphat, 1 K.22:41-50
   2) He became king at age 32 & reigned eight years

b. His evil life, 2 Chr.21:2-4, 11
   1) He walked after the evil ways of Ahab & Israel's kings, not his own father
   2) He married Ahab's daughter, Athaliah, 26; 11:1-3

c. His experience of God's mercy

1) The LORD was not willing to totally destroy Judah in judgment
2) The reason: God's promise to David, 1 S.7:11-17
d. His two major foreign crises
  1) Edom rebelled against Judah
 	
   • Edomite soldiers surrounded Jehoram & almost succeeded in killing him & his chariot commanders
   • Edom had remained independent of Judah at the writing of *Second Kings*
  2) Libnah revolted
e. His achievements & the summary of his life
  1) His reign: Recorded in the book *The History of the Kings of Judah*
  2) His death & burial in Jerusalem
  3) His successor: Ahaziah, his son
4. The evil reign of Ahaziah ex-
	not destroy Judah for David his servant's sake, as he promised him to give him alway a light, *and* to his children.
	20 In his days Edom revolted from under the hand of Judah, and made a king over themselves.
	21 So Joram went over to Zair, and all the chariots with him: and he rose by night, and smote the Edomites which compassed him about, and the captains of the chariots: and the people fled into their tents.
	22 Yet Edom revolted from under the hand of Judah unto this day. Then Libnah revolted at the same time.
	23 And the rest of the acts of Joram, and all that he did, *are* they not written in the book of the chronicles of the kings of Judah?
	24 And Joram slept with his fathers, and was buried with his fathers in the city of David: and Ahaziah his son reigned in his stead.
	25 In the twelfth year of Jo-
		ram the son of Ahab king of Israel did Ahaziah the son of Jehoram king of Judah begin to reign.
		26 Two and twenty years old *was* Ahaziah when he began to reign; and he reigned one year in Jerusalem. And his mother's name *was* Athaliah, the daughter of Omri king of Israel.
		27 And he walked in the way of the house of Ahab, and did evil in the sight of the LORD, as *did* the house of Ahab: for he *was* the son in law of the house of Ahab.
		28 And he went with Joram the son of Ahab to the war against Hazael king of Syria in Ramoth-gilead; and the Syrians wounded Joram.
		29 And king Joram went back to be healed in Jezreel of the wounds which the Syrians had given him at Ramah, when he fought against Hazael king of Syria. And Ahaziah the son of Jehoram king of Judah went down to see Joram the son of Ahab in Jezreel, because he was sick.
			posed—during Elisha's ministry: The danger of following in the footsteps of an evil parent
			
			a. His background
			  1) He reigned only one year
			  2) He was the son of Athaliah, a granddaughter of Omri, king of Israel
			
			b. His evil life & reign
			  1) He followed the evil example of Ahab & Israel's kings
			  2) He was related by marriage to Ahab's family
			c. His fatal alliance with Israel against Syria
			  1) Joram, Israel's king, was wounded in battle & returned to Jezreel to recover
			
			  2) Ahaziah went to visit him as soon as possible: Was to be a fatal visit, for he & Joram would later be killed by Jehu, 9:14-29

DIVISION II

THE MINISTRY AND MIRACLES OF ELISHA: A DRAMATIC DEMONSTRATION OF GOD'S POWER AND CARE FOR HIS PEOPLE, 4:1–13:25

E. The Political Influence of Elisha and the Evil Reigns of Jehoram and Ahaziah in Judah: A Picture of Being a Strong Godly Example and Witness for the LORD, 8:1-29

(8:1-29) **Introduction—Sin, Power of, Described—Power, of Sin, Described—Disappointment, Caused by, Examples—Shame, Caused by, Examples—Starting Anew, Difficult, Reasons—New Start, Difficult, Reasons—Fresh Start, Difficult, Reasons—New Beginnings, Difficult, Reasons—Examples, Godly, Need for—Witnesses, Godly, Need for**: the world is full of sin and wickedness, gripped by the darkness of disappointment and shame. How often we have become disappointed because of some failure or sin in our lives, embarrassed and shamed by our weaknesses, finding it difficult to arise and gain a fresh start. In fact, the more we sin and commit wickedness, the more difficult it is to get up and start anew. The more we sin, the more enslaved we become to sin. Sin sows more sin; wickedness reaps more wickedness. Unless we are careful, we can be captured by sin and become enslaved to a life of wickedness. We can become addicted to the iron grip of drugs, alcohol, sex, food, anger, greed, money, fame or almost any other human activity, possession, or behavior.

Because of the power of sin, there is a crying need for strong, godly examples and for a strong witness for the Lord. Only the Lord can break the bondages of sin and shame. Only He can deliver the human soul from the despair of disappointment and wickedness. Godly examples and strong witnesses are needed to proclaim the power of the Lord to conquer sin and shame, wickedness and disappointment.

This is the good news proclaimed by the present Scripture. This is: *The Political Influence of Elisha and the Evil Reigns of Jehoram and Ahaziah in Judah: A Picture of Being a Strong Godly Example and Witness for the LORD,* 8:1-29.

  1. The Shunammite woman's land restored due to Elisha's political influence: the impact of a godly example for the LORD (8:1-6).

  2. The new king of Syria predicted by Elisha: the need to bear strong witness to the entire world (8:7-15).

  3. The evil reign of Jehoram exposed—during Elisha's ministry: the danger of marrying an unbelieving spouse (8:16-24).

  4. The evil reign of Ahaziah exposed—during Elisha's ministry: the danger of following in the footsteps of an evil parent (8:25-29).

1 (8:1-6) **Testimony, of Life, Results of—Witness, of Life, Results of—Elisha, Political Influence of—Shunammite Woman, Testimony of—Joram, King of Israel, Good Deeds**: there was the restoration of land that belonged to the Shunammite woman, restoration that occurred because of Elisha's political influence. Remember who the Shunammite woman was: she was the woman of hospitality, the woman whose family had become close, dear friends of Elisha. They had even added a room to their home where Elisha could stay when he visited their city. Because of her kindness to Elisha the LORD had given her a son who later became critically ill and died. However, he had been restored to life by the LORD through the prophet Elisha (see outline and note—2 K.48-37 for more discussion). Now once again, Scripture gives us a story about the Shunammite woman, a story that shows the impact of a strong testimony for the LORD.

OUTLINE	SCRIPTURE	SCRIPTURE	OUTLINE
1. **The Shunammite woman's land restored due to Elisha's strong influence: The impact of a godly example for the LORD**	Then spake Elisha unto the woman, whose son he had restored to life, saying, Arise, and go thou and thine household, and sojourn wheresoever thou canst sojourn: for the LORD hath called for a famine; and it shall also come upon the land seven years.	Gehazi the servant of the man of God, saying, Tell me, I pray thee, all the great things that Elisha hath done.	Due to Elisha's testimony & political influence
a. The woman's relocation		5 And it came to pass, as he was telling the king how he had restored a dead body to life, that, behold, the woman, whose son he had restored to life, cried to the king for her house and for her land. And Gehazi said, My lord, O king, this *is* the woman, and this *is* her son, whom Elisha restored to life.	1) The LORD had prepared the way for her
1) She had been warned by Elisha to flee a coming famine	2 And the woman arose, and did after the saying of the man of God: and she went with her household, and sojourned in the land of the Philistines seven years.		• The king had summoned Elisha's servant Gehazi to discuss the miracles performed by the prophet
2) She & her family did as instructed			• The woman entered the royal court just as Gehazi was sharing the miracle of her son being raised from the dead
• Fled to the land of the Philistines			
• Lived there seven years			
b. The woman's return: She discovered that her property had been confiscated or stolen	3 And it came to pass at the seven years' end, that the woman returned out of the land of the Philistines: and she went forth to cry unto the king for her house and for her land.	6 And when the king asked the woman, she told him. So the king appointed unto her a certain officer, saying, Restore all that *was* hers, and all the fruits of the field since the day that she left the land, even until now.	• The king asked her about the miracle: She verified the fact
c. The woman's appeal to the king for her home & land			2) The king restored her property
			• Her home & land
d. The woman's land restored:	4 And the king talked with		• All the monies earned off the land

a. Due to a coming famine, Elisha warned the Shunammite woman to escape the crisis by moving to some other location (vv.1-2). Knowing the serious consequences of a famine—the hunger, suffering, and in some cases death of both people and livestock—the woman and her family fled to the land of the Philistines, where they lived for seven years. Note that nothing is said about her husband, indicating that he had most likely died. She was now head of the family, and the heavy responsibility of overseeing family affairs and property rested entirely upon her shoulders. Whatever pressure, anxiety, and demands a widow bears in looking after a family and taking care of business affairs, this woman now experienced.

b. At the end of the seven-year famine, the woman moved back home to Shunem. As soon as she arrived, she discovered that her property had either been confiscated or stolen, possibly by greedy relatives or a land-grabbing stranger. Or perhaps the king now owned the land. For during that day and time, land that had been abandoned was taken over by the estate of the king.

c. Whatever the case, the woman appealed to the king for the return of her home and land (v.3).

d. Note how God maneuvered and worked out events to have the woman's land restored (vv.4-6). God used Elisha's testimony and political influence to prepare the way for her audience before the king. Immediately prior to her audience, the king had summoned Elisha's servant Gehazi to discuss the miracles performed by Elisha (vv.4-5). Just as the woman entered the royal court, Elisha's servant was sharing the miracle of her son's being raised from the dead. Turning to the Shunammite woman, the king asked about the miracle. She quickly verified the fact that it had actually happened. Hearing this, the king was moved to restore her home, including the land and all the income that had been earned off the land during her seven-year absence (v.6).

Thought 1. The political influence of Elisha can be seen in this passage. His strong testimony for the LORD reached the halls of government and influenced the king to restore the Shunammite woman's property.

Our testimony for God may not impact the rulers of nations, but God will use our godly examples in the lives of people around us. But for people to see a godly example in us, we must live godly lives.

Ask yourself: What kind of example am I setting before my family, friends, fellow workers, or schoolmates? A godly example or a wicked example? God wants us living righteous lives so that we too will be godly examples to all with whom we come in contact. To a large extent the example we set before others exposes about us...

- a productive or unproductive life
- a purposeful or purposeless life
- a victorious or defeated life
- a righteous or wicked life
- a joyful or sad life
- a life with God or without God
- a life that will live with God eternally or be separated from God eternally

The importance of living righteous lives and of setting godly examples before our family and others cannot be overemphasized. Wherever God has placed us—wherever we are living and moving about day by day—we are to set godly examples before others just as Elisha did. Listen to what God's Holy Word says:

"Ye are the salt of the earth: but if the salt have lost his savour, wherewith shall it be salted? it is thenceforth good for nothing, but to be cast out, and to be trodden under foot of men" (Mt.5:13).

"For what knowest thou, O wife, whether thou shalt save *thy* husband? or how knowest thou, O man, whether thou shalt save *thy* wife" (1 Co.7:16).

"Let no man despise thy youth; but be thou an example of the believers, in word, in conversation, in charity, in spirit, in faith, in purity" (1 Ti.4:12).

"In all things showing thyself a pattern of good works: in doctrine *showing* uncorruptness, gravity, sincerity" (Tit.2:7).

"Let us labour therefore to enter into that rest, lest any man fall after the same example of unbelief" (He.4:11).

"By faith Abel offered unto God a more excellent sacrifice than Cain, by which he obtained witness that he was righteous, God testifying of his gifts: and by it he being dead yet speaketh" (He.11:4).

"Take, my brethren, the prophets, who have spoken in the name of the Lord, for an example of suffering affliction, and of patience" (Js.5:10).

"For even hereunto were ye called: because Christ also suffered for us, leaving us an example, that ye should follow his steps: Who did no sin, neither was guile found in his mouth: Who, when he was reviled, reviled not again; when he suffered, he threatened not; but committed *himself* to him that judgeth righteously" (1 Pe.2:21-23).

"Ye therefore, beloved, seeing ye know *these things* before, beware lest ye also, being led away with the error of the wicked, fall from your own stedfastness. But grow in grace, and *in* the knowledge of our Lord and Saviour Jesus Christ. To him *be* glory both now and for ever. Amen" (2 Pe.3:17-18).

"But I said unto their children in the wilderness, Walk ye not in the statutes of your fathers, neither observe their judgments, nor defile yourselves with their idols" (Ez.20:18).

2 (8:7-15) **Witnessing, Duty—Evangelism, Duty—Elisha, Political Influence of—Elisha, Prediction of—Syria, King of, Predicted by Elisha—Politics, Influenced by, Elisha**: there was the political influence of Elisha upon Syria, his prediction of the new king. This story illustrates the need to bear a strong witness to the entire world.

OUTLINE	SCRIPTURE	SCRIPTURE	OUTLINE

2. The new king of Syria predicted by Elisha: The need to bear strong witness to the entire world
a. Elisha's trip to Damascus, Syria
b. King Ben-Hadad's appeal for Elisha's help
  1) He was deathly sick
  2) He sent his trusted official Hazael to Elisha, asking for spiritual help
  3) He sent 40 camel loads of the finest products as a gift to Elisha
c. Hazael's audience with Elisha
  1) He presented the king's request for spiritual help
 	
  2) Elisha stunned Hazael: Revealed that the king would die by the hand of an assassin, not from his sickness
d. Elisha's icy stare & confrontation with Hazael
  1) Hazael became uneasy
  2) Elisha began to weep
	7 And Elisha came to Damascus; and Ben-hadad the king of Syria was sick; and it was told him, saying, The man of God is come hither.
	8 And the king said unto Hazael, Take a present in thine hand, and go, meet the man of God, and enquire of the LORD by him, saying, Shall I recover of this disease?
	9 So Hazael went to meet him, and took a present with him, even of every good thing of Damascus, forty camels' burden, and came and stood before him, and said, Thy son Ben-hadad king of Syria hath sent me to thee, saying, Shall I recover of this disease?
	10 And Elisha said unto him, Go, say unto him, Thou mayest certainly recover: howbeit the LORD hath showed me that he shall surely die.
	11 And he settled his countenance stedfastly, until he was ashamed: and the man of God wept.
		12 And Hazael said, Why weepeth my lord? And he answered, Because I know the evil that thou wilt do unto the children of Israel: their strong holds wilt thou set on fire, and their young men wilt thou slay with the sword, and wilt dash their children, and rip up their women with child.
		13 And Hazael said, But what, *is* thy servant a dog, that he should do this great thing? And Elisha answered, The LORD hath showed me that thou *shalt be* king over Syria.
		14 So he departed from Elisha, and came to his master; who said to him, What said Elisha to thee? And he answered, He told me *that* thou shouldest surely recover.
		15 And it came to pass on the morrow, that he took a thick cloth, and dipped *it* in water, and spread *it* on his face, so that he died: and Hazael reigned in his stead.
			3) Hazael asked why he was weeping
			4) Elisha bore strong witness about the sinful, evil heart of Hazael: The official would commit horrible atrocities against the Israelites (an instrument of God's judgment upon His sinful people, 10:32-33; 13:3)
			5) Hazael, stunned & insulted, denied his sinful heart, that he would do such gross evil
			6) Elisha revealed that Hazael was soon to become king of Syria
			e. Hazael's sinful, wicked heart proven
			  1) He returned to King Ben-Hadad & lied to him: Stated that Elisha had assured the king of a complete recovery
			  2) He assassinated the king on the very next day: Smothered him to death
			  3) He seized the throne of Syria

a. For some unknown reason, Elisha made a trip to Damascus, the capital of Syria (v.7). While Elisha was there, King Ben-Hadad of Syria became gravely ill. The king was very old, having ruled the nation for about 40 years.

b. Thus Ben-Hadad, feeling deathly sick and remembering the miraculous healing of his former commander Naaman, appealed to Elisha for help (vv.8-9). He sent his trusted official Hazael to seek spiritual help from Elisha. Knowing that the relationship between him and Elisha had earlier been strained, the king sent 40 camel-loads of the finest products in an attempt to bribe or buy Elisha's immediate help.

c. As soon as Hazael secured an audience with Elisha, he presented the king's request for immediate spiritual help (vv.9-10). But Elisha stunned the official with a strange statement, a statement that seemed contradictory. He said that the king would certainly recover from his illness, but that he would indeed die. What Elisha meant was that the king would die by the hand of an assassin, not from his sickness. Scripture later reveals that that assassin would be Hazael himself.

d. Standing face-to-face with the chief official, Elisha stared at him with a fixed gaze, saying absolutely nothing. After what undoubtedly seemed a long time, Hazael began to feel uneasy and ashamed. Then suddenly Elisha began to weep (vv.11-13). Hazael, sensing an uneasy embarrassment, asked the prophet why he was weeping. Seizing the opportunity, Elisha bore a strong witness about the sinful, evil heart of Hazael. The chief official would commit horrible atrocities against the Israelites, destroying their fortified cities, killing their young men, dashing their children to the ground, and ripping open their pregnant women (10:32-33; 13:3).

Stunned and insulted by Elisha's accusations, Hazael denied his sinful heart, denied that he would do such gross, horrendous evil (v.13). But Elisha revealed that Hazael was already plotting Ben-Hadad's assassination and that he was soon to become king of Syria.

e. Hazael's sinful and wicked heart was immediately proven upon his return to the palace. Lying to King Ben-Hadad, he stated that Elisha had assured the king of a complete recovery (vv.14-15). But Hazael returned the very next day to assassinate the king, smothering him to death with a thick cloth soaked in water. He then seized the throne of Syria just as Elisha had predicted.

Thought 1. Elisha courageously bore strong witness to Hazael. And he bore strong witness standing face-to-face with the chief official, knowing full-well that Hazael could react, arresting and imprisoning or executing him.

We, too, must be courageous and bear strong witness to the world. The only hope for the world's salvation is the Lord. All the great gifts of life come from the Lord:

⇒ peace and security
⇒ purpose, meaning, and significance
⇒ fulfillment and a permanent sense of satisfaction
⇒ assurance and confidence of the future
⇒ true love, joy, and rejoicing
⇒ a victorious, conquering life
⇒ strength to bear all the trials of life
⇒ power to conquer all temptations

Consider all the pain and suffering in the world, the hardships and misfortunes, the trials and tribulations, the temptations and evil. The power to overcome and conquer all these and more can be found only in the Lord Jesus Christ Himself. For this reason, we must bear strong witness about the Lord. Even in the face of opposition, whether mild ridicule or the threat of death, we must proclaim the gospel to the whole world. For the world's only answer is found in the gospel of the Lord. Listen to the constraint of God's Word that is laid upon us, a powerful constraint to proclaim the gospel to all mankind:

"**And this gospel of the kingdom shall be preached in all the world for a witness unto all nations; and then shall the end come**" (Mt.24:14).

"**Go ye therefore, and teach all nations, baptizing them in the name of the Father, and of the Son, and of the Holy Ghost: Teaching them to observe all things whatsoever I have commanded you: and, lo, I am with you alway,** *even* **unto the end of the world. Amen**" (Mt.28:19-20).

"**And the gospel must first be published among all nations**" (Mk.13:10).

"**And they went and told** *it* **unto the residue: neither believed they them**" (Mk.16:13).

"**And that repentance and remission of sins should be preached in his name among all nations, beginning at Jerusalem**" (Lu.24:47).

"**But ye shall receive power, after that the Holy Ghost is come upon you: and ye shall be witnesses unto me both in Jerusalem, and in all Judaea, and in Samaria, and unto the uttermost part of the earth**" (Ac.1:8).

"**For we cannot but speak the things which we have seen and heard**" (Ac.4:20).

"**Go, stand and speak in the temple to the people all the words of this life**" (Ac.5:20).

"**And he said, The God of our fathers hath chosen thee, that thou shouldest know his will, and see that Just One, and shouldest hear the voice of his mouth. For thou shalt be his witness unto all men of what thou hast seen and heard**" (Ac.22:14-15).

"**We having the same spirit of faith, according as it is written, I believed, and therefore have I spoken; we also believe, and therefore speak**" (2 Co.4:13).

"**Be not thou therefore ashamed of the testimony of our Lord, nor of me his prisoner: but be thou partaker of the afflictions of the gospel according to the power of God**" (2 Ti.1:8).

"**These things speak, and exhort, and rebuke with all authority. Let no man despise thee**" (Tit.2:15).

"**But sanctify the Lord God in your hearts: and** *be* **ready always to** *give* **an answer to every man that asketh you a reason of the hope that is in you with meekness and fear**" (1 Pe.3:15).

"Then I said, I will not make mention of him, nor speak any more in his name. But *his word* was in mine heart as a burning fire shut up in my bones, and I was weary with forbearing, and I could not *stay*" (Je.20:9).

3 (8:16-24) **Marriage, of an Unbeliever—Intermarriage, Evil Influence upon—Compromise, Duty—Separation, Spiritual—Unbelievers, Duty Toward—Believers, Duty—Jehoram, King of Judah, Reign of**: there was the exposure of the evil reign of Jehoram during Elisha's ministry in the Northern Kingdom. For some time now, the author of *Kings* has set aside the story of the kings in order to cover the ministries of Elijah and Elisha. Now the author returns to the royal reigns of the kings and focuses upon them. First, he covers the evil reign of King Jehoram in Judah, which took place during Elisha's ministry. In briefly covering Jehoram's life, the author shows the danger of marrying an unbelieving spouse. He uses the king's reign to teach that we must not compromise with sinners and unbelievers. Note how the Scripture stresses his evil life in describing his reign:

OUTLINE	SCRIPTURE	SCRIPTURE	OUTLINE

3. The evil reign of Jehoram exposed—during Elisha's ministry: The danger of marrying an unbelieving spouse
a. His background
  1) He was the son of a good ruler, Jehoshaphat, 1 K.22:41-50
  2) He became king at age 32 & reigned eight years
b. His evil life, 2 Chr.21:2-4, 11
  1) He walked after the evil ways of Ahab & Israel's kings, not his own father
  2) He married Ahab's daughter, Athaliah, 26; 11:1-3
c. His experience of God's mercy
  1) The LORD was not willing to totally destroy Judah in judgment
  2) The reason: God's promise to David, 1 S.7:11-17
d. His two major foreign crises
  1) Edom rebelled against Judah
	16 And in the fifth year of Joram the son of Ahab king of Israel, Jehoshaphat *being* then king of Judah, Jehoram the son of Jehoshaphat king of Judah began to reign.
	17 Thirty and two years old was he when he began to reign; and he reigned eight years in Jerusalem.
	18 And he walked in the way of the kings of Israel, as did the house of Ahab: for the daughter of Ahab was his wife: and he did evil in the sight of the LORD.
	19 Yet the LORD would not destroy Judah for David his servant's sake, as he promised him to give him alway a light, *and* to his children.
	20 In his days Edom revolted from under the hand of Judah, and made a king
		over themselves.
		21 So Joram went over to Zair, and all the chariots with him: and he rose by night, and smote the Edomites which compassed him about, and the captains of the chariots: and the people fled into their tents.
		22 Yet Edom revolted from under the hand of Judah unto this day. Then Libnah revolted at the same time.
		23 And the rest of the acts of Joram, and all that he did, *are* they not written in the book of the chronicles of the kings of Judah?
		24 And Joram slept with his fathers, and was buried with his fathers in the city of David: and Ahaziah his son reigned in his stead.
			• Edomite soldiers surrounded Jehoram & almost succeeded in killing him & his chariot commanders
			• Edom had remained independent of Judah at the writing of *Second Kings*
			  2) Libnah revolted
			e. His achievements & the summary of his life
			  1) His reign: Recorded in the book *The History of the Kings of Judah*
			  2) His death & burial in Jerusalem
			  3) His successor: Ahaziah, his son

a. The author points out that Jehoram was the son of King Jehoshaphat, a good ruler who had reigned over the Southern Kingdom of Judah (1 K.22:41-50). Thus, Jehoram had a godly influence to follow; however, as the next point reveals, he chose to follow a wicked example (vv.16-17). Jehoram was crowned king of Judah in the fifth year of the reign of Israel's King Joram, who was the son of Ahab. Becoming king at age 32, Jehoram had only a brief reign in Jerusalem, ruling for only eight years.

b. Instead of following the godly example of his father Jehoshaphat, Jehoram walked in the evil ways of Ahab and of Israel's kings (v.18). In fact, he married into the wicked family of Ahab himself, marrying Ahab's daughter Athaliah. Apparently, it was her evil influence that caused Jehoram to turn away from the LORD and become so violent and wicked. In the parallel passage in *Second Chronicles*, Jehoram is seen killing all of his brothers as well as some other leaders of the nation in order to consolidate his power (2 Chr.21:1-4). *Second Chronicles* also points out that he became a stumbling block to the Southern Kingdom. Building high places or false worship centers, he led the people to commit spiritual adultery by engaging in false worship (2 Chr.21:11). Marrying an unbeliever had made a catastrophic impact on Jehoram, leading him and the nation away from the LORD.

c. But God had mercy upon Judah, for He was not willing to totally destroy the nation (v.19). Note why: because of His promise to David. God had made a covenant, a great promise to David: He would keep the light of David's throne shining forever. That is, David and his descendants would reign upon the throne of God's people forever (see outline and note—1 S.7:11-17 for more discussion). Of course, this promise is still being fulfilled in the person of the Lord Jesus Christ, who alone reigns forever over the people of God.

d. Two major crises confronted Jehoram during his reign: the rebellion of the Edomites against Judah and the revolt by Libnah at the same time (vv.20-22). Ever since the days of King David, the nation Edom had been subjected by neighboring Judah and forced to pay tribute or taxes. But as soon as Jehoram took the throne of Judah, the Edomites saw the opportunity to rebel. They knew Jehoram's attention would be diverted, focusing upon consolidating his power. And note, their judgment proved correct, for they remained independent of Judah up until the very time the author was writing *Second Kings* (v.22).

e. A record of Jehoram's achievements and a summary of his life are recorded in the book *The History of the Kings of Judah* (vv.23-24). After his death, he was buried in Jerusalem. *Second Chronicles* says that he was given a dishonorable burial. The people did not build a ceremonial fire to honor his life and reign, and they did not mourn his passing nor bury him in the royal tombs (2 Chr.21:19-20). As the author of *Kings* says, he simply died and was buried someplace in the city of David. He was succeeded by his son Ahaziah.

Thought 1. There is a strong lesson for us in Jehoram's reign: we must not compromise with sinners and unbelievers. King Jehoram compromised; he married an unbeliever and became heavily influenced by her wicked life. But God's Holy Word is clear: we must live lives of spiritual separation, never becoming associated with or tied to unbelievers. We must never be unequally yoked with unbelievers, not in anything. If we fellowship with unbelievers, their sinful and wicked behavior will influence us.

God knows that we are not strong enough to resist the worldly influence of unbelievers if we are always associating with them. Eventually, their worldly ways will wear down our resistance. Then we will find ourselves committing spiritual adultery, that is, turning away from God to the gods of this world—the attractions, possessions, and pleasures of this world. Moreover, if we are constantly fellowshipping and forming permanent alliances with unbelievers, many of us will end up marrying those who live sinful and wicked lives.

We must always remember: it is difficult to remain pure, to live righteous and holy lives day after day after day. It is difficult to be alert at all times to the lust of the flesh, the lust of the eyes, and the pride of life (1 Jn.2:15-16). It is difficult to focus upon growing and maturing in Christ if we are fellowshipping with the unbelievers of this world. For this reason, we need the constant help of other believers, in particular the help of a spouse or other family members who know the Lord. This is the reason believers absolutely must not carry on close fellowships with the carnal, fleshly unbelievers of this world.

> **"But now I have written unto you not to keep company, if any man that is called a brother be a fornicator, or covetous, or an idolater, or a railer, or a drunkard, or an extortioner; with such an one no not to eat" (1 Co.5:11).**

> **"Be ye not unequally yoked together with unbelievers: for what fellowship hath righteousness with unrighteousness? and what communion hath light with darkness? And what concord hath Christ with Belial? or what part hath he that believeth with an infidel? And what agreement hath the temple of God with idols? for ye are the temple of the living God; as God hath said, I will dwell in them, and walk in *them;* and I will be their God, and they shall be my people" (2 Co.6:14-16).**

> **"Wherefore come out from among them, and be ye separate, saith the Lord, and touch not the unclean *thing;* and I will receive you, And will be a Father unto you, and ye shall be my sons and daughters, saith the Lord Almighty" (2 Co.6:17-18).**

> **"And have no fellowship with the unfruitful works of darkness, but rather reprove *them*" (Ep.5:11).**

> **"Love not the world, neither the things *that are* in the world. If any man love the world, the love of the Father is not in him. For all that *is* in the world, the lust of the flesh, and the lust of the eyes, and the pride of life, is not of the Father, but is of the world" (1 Jn.2:15-16).**

> **"Take heed to yourselves, that your heart be not deceived, and ye turn aside, and serve other gods, and worship them" (De.11:16).**

> **"Thou shalt not follow a multitude to *do* evil; neither shalt thou speak in a cause to decline after many to wrest *judgment*" (Ex.23:2).**

> **"Take heed to thyself, lest thou make a covenant with the inhabitants of the land whither thou goest, lest it be for a snare in the midst of thee" (Ex.34:12).**

> **"Blessed *is* the man that walketh not in the counsel of the ungodly, nor standeth in the way of sinners, nor sitteth in the seat of the scornful" (Ps.1:1).**

> **"I *am* a companion of all *them* that fear thee, and of them that keep thy precepts" (Ps.119:63).**

> **"Enter not into the path of the wicked, and go not in the way of evil *men*" (Pr.4:14).**

> **"He that walketh with wise *men* shall be wise: but a companion of fools shall be destroyed" (Pr.13:20).**

> **"Be not thou envious against evil men, neither desire to be with them" (Pr.24:1).**

4 (8:25-29) **Parents, Evil Example of—Children, Following Evil Parents—Ahaziah, King of Judah, Reign of**: there was the exposure of the evil reign of Ahaziah during Elisha's ministry. Ahaziah succeeded his father upon the throne of Judah in the twelfth year of King Joram's reign over the Northern Kingdom. Ahaziah was only 22 years old when he was crowned, and he reigned over Judah only one year. Remember, he was the son of Queen Athaliah who was the daughter of Ahab and the granddaughter of Omri, two wicked kings who did more evil in the eyes of the LORD than all those who reigned before them (v.26; also see 1 K.16:21-34, in particular v.25, 30).

Although Ahaziah ruled for only one year, he lived an evil life and his one-year reign was judged evil by the LORD (v.27). Growing up, he had followed the evil example of his father. And now he began his rule by walking in the ways of the house of Ahab and Israel's kings. He turned away from the righteous walk of the kings of Judah and of David his ancestor. Keep in mind that Ahaziah was related by marriage to Ahab's family through his mother, who was the daughter of Ahab himself.

Following the counsel of his evil mother and the wicked counselors who were still ruling in the Northern Kingdom, Ahaziah joined King Joram in war against the king of Syria (vv.28-29). This alliance was to prove fatal for the young King Ahaziah. During the raging conflict of the battle, King Joram of Israel was wounded and quickly returned to Jezreel to recover. Soon thereafter, Ahaziah, having escaped being captured by the Syrians, went to visit King Joram. However, the visit was to prove fatal, for both he and Joram would later be killed in the rebellion led by the Commander Jehu in his violent seizure of Israel's throne. This will be seen in chapter 9 (9:14-29).

OUTLINE	SCRIPTURE	SCRIPTURE	OUTLINE

4. The evil reign of Ahaziah exposed—during Elisha's ministry: The danger of following in the footsteps of an evil parent
 	
a. His background
  1) He reigned only one year
  2) He was the son of Athaliah, a granddaughter of Omri, king of Israel
 	
b. His evil life & reign
  1) He followed the evil ex ample of Ahab & Israel's kings
  2) He was related by
	25 In the twelfth year of Joram the son of Ahab king of Israel did Ahaziah the son of Jehoram king of Judah begin to reign.
	26 Two and twenty years old *was* Ahaziah when he began to reign; and he reigned one year in Jerusalem. And his mother's name *was* Athaliah, the daughter of Omri king of Israel.
	27 And he walked in the way of the house of Ahab, and did evil in the sight of the LORD, as *did* the house of Ahab: for he *was* the son in law of the
		house of Ahab.
		28 And he went with Joram the son of Ahab to the war against Hazael king of Syria in Ramoth-gilead; and the Syrians wounded Joram.
		29 And king Joram went back to be healed in Jezreel of the wounds which the Syrians had given him at Ramah, when he fought against Hazael king of Syria. And Ahaziah the son of Jehoram king of Judah went down to see Joram the son of Ahab in Jezreel, because he was sick.
			marriage to Ahab's family
			c. His fatal alliance with Israel against Syria
			
			1) Joram, Israel's king, was wounded in battle & returned to Jezreel to recover
			
			2) Ahaziah went to visit him as soon as possible: Was to be a fatal visit, for he & Joram would later be killed by Jehu, 9:14-29

Thought 1. Ahaziah had a wicked father and a wicked mother. Both parents set sinful, evil examples for their son. And he walked right in the steps of his parents, following their evil ways. Using our imagination, we can see him as a small child running around playing day by day, living in a home that was focused upon the world and the things of the world. Just like him, so many of us have lived in homes where our parents were focused upon this world:

⇒ its pleasures and stimulations
⇒ its possessions and wealth
⇒ its passions and urges
⇒ its immorality and perversions
⇒ its addictions and obsessions
⇒ its foul mouth and vulgarity
⇒ its greed and covetousness
⇒ its false worship and idolatry
⇒ its denial of God and His commandments
⇒ its rejection of Christ and His salvation

Living in such a home and atmosphere of unholy, wicked behavior, a child is likely to follow in the same footsteps. Failing to know Christ, the child is doomed to never know permanent peace of heart and mind, lacking full assurance and security of living forever with God. Without God, there is no permanent peace or security within the human heart and mind. Regardless of what a person may claim, he experiences a sense of emptiness and unfulfillment and lacks assurance of living eternally with God.

Following in the steps of an evil parent is dangerous. Listen to the warning of God's Holy Word:

"**For as in the days that were before the flood they were eating and drinking, marrying and giving in marriage, until the day that Noe entered into the ark, And knew not until the flood came, and took them all away; so shall also the coming of the Son of man be**" (Mt.24:38-39).

"**And take heed to yourselves, lest at any time your hearts be overcharged with surfeiting, and drunkenness, and cares of this life, and so that day come upon you unawares**" (Lu.21:34).

"**Know ye not that the unrighteous shall not inherit the kingdom of God? Be not deceived: neither fornicators, nor idolaters, nor adulterers, nor effeminate, nor abusers of themselves with mankind, Nor thieves, nor covetous, nor drunkards, nor revilers, nor extortioners, shall inherit the kingdom of God**" (1 Co.6:9-10).

"**Wherefore come out from among them, and be ye separate, saith the Lord, and touch not the unclean *thing;* and I will receive you, And will be a Father unto you, and ye shall be my sons and daughters, saith the Lord Almighty**" (2 Co.6:17-18).

"**Be ye therefore followers of God, as dear children; And walk in love, as Christ also hath loved us, and hath given himself for us an offering and a sacrifice to God for a sweetsmelling savour. But fornication, and all uncleanness, or covetousness, let it not be once named among you, as becometh saints; Neither filthiness, nor foolish talking, nor jesting, which are not convenient: but rather giving of thanks. For this ye know, that no whoremonger, nor unclean person, nor covetous man, who is an idolater, hath any inheritance in the kingdom of Christ and of God**" (Ep.5:1-5).

"**Ye adulterers and adulteresses, know ye not that the friendship of the world is enmity with God? whosoever therefore will be a friend of the world is the enemy of God**" (Js.4:4).

Thought 2. Tumultuous events were taking place all over the known world when Ahaziah was crowned king. *The Expositor's Bible Commentary* covers the secular events, political events that are well worth noting:

Ahaziah succeeded his father, Jehoram, in the critical year 841 B.C. He was not to survive the momentous waves of political events that were to inundate the ancient Near East in that year. Indeed in 841 B.C. Shalmaneser III of Assyria (859–824 B.C.) at last was able to break the coalition of western allies with whom he had previously fought a long series of battles (853, 848, 845). While all these complex details were part of God's teleological processes in the government of the nations and his dealing with Israel, doubtless the long-standing controversy and the growing specter of Assyrian power could be felt in the political intrigues that bought about the death of Ben-Hadad II of Damascus and the downfall of the Omride Dynasty in Israel. Before 841 had ended Hazael would be master of Damascus (where Shalmaneser had set him up after having defeated him in battle), the pro-Assyrian Jehu would initiate the fourth dynasty in Israel (chs. 9–10), and the wicked Athaliah would sit as usurper on the throne of Judah (ch. 11).[1]

---

1   Richard D. Patterson and Hermann J. Austel. *1, 2 Kings.* "The Expositor's Bible Commentary," Vol.4. (Grand Rapids, MI: Zondervan Publishing House, 1988), p.203.

CHAPTER 9

F. The Secret Anointing of Jehu As King of Israel & His Bloody Purge: A Picture of Misguided Justice Due to Self-Interest, 9:1–10:36

1. Jehu's anointing as king of Israel: A picture of rulers being appointed as ministers of justice

a. The anointing was executed by Elisha
  1) He summoned one of the prophets to go quickly to Ramoth Gilead to find the army commander Jehu
  2) He instructed the prophet
     • To anoint Jehu in private

     • To declare that God had appointed him king over Israel
     • To quickly flee the scene

b. The instructions of Elisha were obeyed
  1) The prophet traveled to Jehu's camp & found him in a council meeting with his commanders

     • He asked to see Jehu alone

     • Jehu took him into the house
  2) The prophet anointed the commander, declaring that God had appointed him king over Israel

c. The purpose for Jehu's special appointment was then spelled out: To execute justice upon the family of Ahab for their murder of God's prophets & people, 1 Ki.18:4; 21:13, 17-26
  1) The family members to be executed
     • To execute all males

     • To end the house, dynasty of Ahab just as the dynasties of Jeroboam & Baasha ended, 1 Ki.14:7-12; 15:27-30; 16:1-4, 8-12
  2) The death & fate of Jezebel predicted

And Elisha the prophet called one of the children of the prophets, and said unto him, Gird up thy loins, and take this box of oil in thine hand, and go to Ramoth-gilead:
2 And when thou comest thither, look out there Jehu the son of Jehoshaphat the son of Nimshi, and go in, and make him arise up from among his brethren, and carry him to an inner chamber;
3 Then take the box of oil, and pour it on his head, and say, Thus saith the LORD, I have anointed thee king over Israel. Then open the door, and flee, and tarry not.
4 So the young man, even the young man the prophet, went to Ramoth-gilead.
5 And when he came, behold, the captains of the host were sitting; and he said, I have an errand to thee, O captain. And Jehu said, Unto which of all us? And he said, To thee, O captain.
6 And he arose, and went into the house; and he poured the oil on his head, and said unto him, Thus saith the LORD God of Israel, I have anointed thee king over the people of the LORD, even over Israel.
7 And thou shalt smite the house of Ahab thy master, that I may avenge the blood of my servants the prophets, and the blood of all the servants of the LORD, at the hand of Jezebel.
8 For the whole house of Ahab shall perish: and I will cut off from Ahab him that pisseth against the wall, and him that is shut up and left in Israel:
9 And I will make the house of Ahab like the house of Jeroboam the son of Nebat, and like the house of Baasha the son of Ahijah:
10 And the dogs shall eat Jezebel in the portion of Jez-

reel, and there shall be none to bury her. And he opened the door, and fled.
11 Then Jehu came forth to the servants of his lord: and one said unto him, Is all well? wherefore came this mad fellow to thee? And he said unto them, Ye know the man, and his communication.
12 And they said, It is false; tell us now. And he said, Thus and thus spake he to me, saying, Thus saith the LORD, I have anointed thee king over Israel.
13 Then they hasted, and took every man his garment, and put it under him on the top of the stairs, and blew with trumpets, saying, Jehu is king.
14 So Jehu the son of Jehoshaphat the son of Nimshi conspired against Joram. (Now Joram had kept Ramoth-gilead, he and all Israel, because of Hazael king of Syria.
15 But king Joram was returned to be healed in Jezreel of the wounds which the Syrians had given him, when he fought with Hazael king of Syria.) And Jehu said, If it be your minds, then let none go forth nor escape out of the city to go to tell it in Jezreel.
16 So Jehu rode in a chariot, and went to Jezreel; for Joram lay there. And Ahaziah king of Judah was come down to see Joram.
17 And there stood a watchman on the tower in Jezreel, and he spied the company of Jehu as he came, and said, I see a company. And Joram said, Take an horseman, and send to meet them, and let him say, Is it peace?
18 So there went one on horseback to meet him, and said, Thus saith the king, Is it peace? And Jehu said, What hast thou to do with peace? turn thee behind me. And the watchman told, saying, The messenger came to them, but he cometh not again.
19 Then he sent out a second on horseback, which came to them, and said, Thus saith the king, Is it peace? And Jehu answered, What hast thou

3) The prophet immediately fled

d. The commander cautiously, carefully revealed the anointing to his officers: Lest they oppose & arrest him for treason
  1) They questioned him about the visit
  2) He dodged their questioning
  3) They pressed him for an explanation
  4) He sensed their support & loyalty: Revealed the anointing

e. The army enthusiastically accepted & proclaimed Jehu as king

2. Jehu's bloody purge—executions that exceeded true justice & became atrocities (Ho.1:4-5): A picture of murder & of sin's wages, "the judgment of death"

a. Jehu executed justice upon Joram, Israel's evil king
  1) Jehu planned a conspiracy against King Joram
     • Joram was in Jezreel recovering from his wounds
     • The wounded king had been defending Ramoth-Gilead
     • Jehu issued strict orders to the guards: They must not let anyone slip out of Ramoth Gilead to warn King Joram of the coup
  2) Jehu personally took a regiment of commandos & set out for Jezreel to arrest King Joram
     • The tower lookout spotted the approaching troops & warned the king
     • The king sent out a horseman to investigate & to make sure the troops were coming in peace

     • The horseman confronted Jehu & was threatened, so he joined Jehu's forces

     • The lookout reported that the horseman was not returning
     • The king sent a second horseman with the same result

- The lookout again reported that the second rider was not returning & that the chariot appeared to be Jehu's

- The king ordered his chariot prepared & both he & King Ahaziah of Judah—each in his own chariot—rode out to meet Jehu: They met at Naboth's vineyard, the land stolen by Ahab, 1 Ki.21:1-29
- The king asked Jehu if he had come in peace

3) Jehu spelled out the charges against Joram
  - The king had misled Israel in the idolatry & witchcraft of Jezebel
  - The king, realizing his life was in danger, turned & fled

4) Jehu executed King Joram
  - He drew his bow & pierced the heart of the king

  - He instructed his chariot driver Bidkar to throw the body on the field that had belonged to Naboth

  - He reminded the driver of Elijah's prophecy 10 years earlier

b. Jehu executed justice upon Ahaziah, Judah's evil king
1) Ahaziah also fled from Jehu
  - He was shot but only wounded
  - He escaped to Megiddo where he died

2) Ahaziah was taken to Jerusalem where he was buried in the royal tombs

---

to do with peace? turn thee behind me.

20 And the watchman told, saying, He came even unto them, and cometh not again: and the driving is like the driving of Jehu the son of Nimshi; for he driveth furiously.

21 And Joram said, Make ready. And his chariot was made ready. And Joram king of Israel and Ahaziah king of Judah went out, each in his chariot, and they went out against Jehu, and met him in the portion of Naboth the Jezreelite.

22 And it came to pass, when Joram saw Jehu, that he said, Is it peace, Jehu? And he answered, What peace, so long as the whoredoms of thy mother Jezebel and her witchcrafts are so many?

23 And Joram turned his hands, and fled, and said to Ahaziah, There is treachery, O Ahaziah.

24 And Jehu drew a bow with his full strength, and smote Jehoram between his arms, and the arrow went out at his heart, and he sunk down in his chariot.

25 Then said Jehu to Bidkar his captain, Take up, and cast him in the portion of the field of Naboth the Jezreelite: for remember how that, when I and thou rode together after Ahab his father, the LORD laid this burden upon him;

26 Surely I have seen yesterday the blood of Naboth, and the blood of his sons, saith the LORD; and I will requite thee in this plat, saith the LORD. Now therefore take and cast him into the plat of ground, according to the word of the LORD.

27 But when Ahaziah the king of Judah saw this, he fled by the way of the garden house. And Jehu followed after him, and said, Smite him also in the chariot. And they did so at the going up to Gur, which is by Ibleam. And he fled to Megiddo, and died there.

28 And his servants carried him in a chariot to Jerusalem, and buried him in his sepulchre with his fathers in the city of David.

29 And in the eleventh year of Joram the son of Ahab began Ahaziah to reign over Judah.

30 And when Jehu was come to Jezreel, Jezebel heard of it; and she painted her face, and tired her head, and looked out at a window.

31 And as Jehu entered in at the gate, she said, Had Zimri peace, who slew his master?

32 And he lifted up his face to the window, and said, Who is on my side? who? And there looked out to him two or three eunuchs.

33 And he said, Throw her down. So they threw her down: and some of her blood was sprinkled on the wall, and on the horses: and he trode her under foot.

34 And when he was come in, he did eat and drink, and said, Go, see now this cursed woman, and bury her: for she is a king's daughter.

35 And they went to bury her: but they found no more of her than the skull, and the feet, and the palms of her hands.

36 Wherefore they came again, and told him. And he said, This is the word of the LORD, which he spake by his servant Elijah the Tishbite, saying, In the portion of Jezreel shall dogs eat the flesh of Jezebel:

37 And the carcase of Jezebel shall be as dung upon the face of the field in the portion of Jezreel; so that they shall not say, This is Jezebel.

CHAPTER 10

And Ahab had seventy sons in Samaria. And Jehu wrote letters, and sent to Samaria, unto the rulers of Jezreel, to the elders, and to them that brought up Ahab's children, saying,

2 Now as soon as this letter cometh to you, seeing your master's sons are with you, and there are with you chariots and horses, a fenced city also, and armour;

3 Look even out the best and meetest of your master's sons, and set him on his father's throne, and fight for your master's house.

4 But they were exceedingly

---

3) Ahaziah reigned only one year

c. Jehu executed justice upon Jezebel, wicked wife Ahab's
1) Jezebel had heard of Jehu's coup, prepared herself to die as a queen, & defiantly waited for him by the window: She shouted sarcastic insults as he entered the city
2) Jehu looked up & ordered some servants to throw her down

  - Her blood splattered everywhere
  - Her body was trampled under the horses
  - She died a gruesome death

3) Jehu entered the palace & ate
4) Jehu later ordered the cursed Jezebel to be buried

  - The servants found only her skull, hands, & feet

  - They reported the fact to Jehu
5) Jehu recalled the prophecy of Elijah, that Jezebel's body would suffer a grisly end
  - Dogs would devour her flesh
  - Her body would be like refuse, meaning there would be no marker & no one mourning for her

d. Jehu executed justice upon the seventy sons of Ahab who were in Samaria
1) Jehu wrote a letter to the city officials of Samaria & to Jezreel (who had fled to the capital for safety)
  - He warned them to mobilize their forces

  - He challenged them to select Ahab's most capable son as their king & to prepare to fight for Ahab's dynasty & family
2) The city officials were

terrified by Jehu's threat & knew resistance was futile: They sent a letter of surrender to him

- They switched their allegiance to him
- They stated that they would do anything he asked

3) Jehu sent a second letter demanding that the heads of Ahab's seventy sons be brought to Jezreel the next day & presented to him

4) The city officials carried out the executive order
- They executed Ahab's sons & sent their heads to Jehu in Jezreel

- Jehu ordered the heads to be placed in two piles at the city gate until morning: An object lesson to show subjection & to discourage rebellion

5) Jehu assembled & addressed the people the next morning, declaring his divine mission
- He declared the innocence of the people in the coup
- He declared that he had the support & help of the city officials
- He claimed that he was acting as the agent of God in executing justice in the land & against the house of Ahab

e. Jehu unjustly & sinfully executed others who were not wicked relatives of Ahab, 9:7; Ho.1:4-5

f. Jehu executed questionable justice upon some relatives of King Ahaziah of Judah
1) Jehu set out for Samaria & met forty-two men at Beth Eked of the Shepherds

afraid, and said, Behold, two kings stood not before him: how then shall we stand?
5 And he that *was* over the house, and he that *was* over the city, the elders also, and the bringers up *of the children,* sent to Jehu, saying, We are thy servants, and will do all that thou shalt bid us; we will not make any king: do thou *that which is* good in thine eyes.
6 Then he wrote a letter the second time to them, saying, If ye *be* mine, and *if* ye will hearken unto my voice, take ye the heads of the men your master's sons, and come to me to Jezreel by tomorrow this time. Now the king's sons, *being* seventy persons, *were* with the great men of the city, which brought them up.
7 And it came to pass, when the letter came to them, that they took the king's sons, and slew seventy persons, and put their heads in baskets, and sent him *them* to Jezreel.
8 And there came a messenger, and told him, saying, They have brought the heads of the king's sons. And he said, Lay ye them in two heaps at the entering in of the gate until the morning.
9 And it came to pass in the morning, that he went out, and stood, and said to all the people, Ye *be* righteous: behold, I conspired against my master, and slew him: but who slew all these?
10 Know now that there shall fall unto the earth nothing of the word of the LORD, which the LORD spake concerning the house of Ahab: for the LORD hath done *that* which he spake by his servant Elijah.
11 So Jehu slew all that remained of the house of Ahab in Jezreel, and all his great men, and his kinsfolks, and his priests, until he left him none remaining.
12 And he arose and departed, and came to Samaria. *And* as he *was* at the shearing house in the way,
13 Jehu met with the brethren of Ahaziah king of Judah, and said, Who *are* ye? And they answered, We *are* the

brethren of Ahaziah; and we go down to salute the children of the king and the children of the queen.
14 And he said, Take them alive. And they took them alive, and slew them at the pit of the shearing house, *even* two and forty men; neither left he any of them.
15 And when he was departed thence, he lighted on Jehonadab the son of Rechab *coming* to meet him: and he saluted him, and said to him, Is thine heart right, as my heart *is* with thy heart? And Jehonadab answered, It is. If it be, give *me* thine hand. And he gave *him* his hand; and he took him up to him into the chariot.
16 And he said, Come with me, and see my zeal for the LORD. So they made him ride in his chariot.
17 And when he came to Samaria, he slew all that remained unto Ahab in Samaria, till he had destroyed him, according to the saying of the LORD, which he spake to Elijah.
18 And Jehu gathered all the people together, and said unto them, Ahab served Baal a little; *but* Jehu shall serve him much.
19 Now therefore call unto me all the prophets of Baal, all his servants, and all his priests; let none be wanting: for I have a great sacrifice *to do* to Baal; whosoever shall be wanting, he shall not live. But Jehu did *it* in subtilty, to the intent that he might destroy the worshippers of Baal.
20 And Jehu said, Proclaim a solemn assembly for Baal. And they proclaimed *it.*
21 And Jehu sent through all Israel: and all the worshippers of Baal came, so that there was not a man left that came not. And they came into the house of Baal; and the house of Baal was full from one end to another.
22 And he said unto him that *was* over the vestry, Bring forth vestments for all the worshippers of Baal. And he brought them forth vestments.
23 And Jehu went, and Jehonadab the son of Rechab,

- They claimed to be relatives of King Ahaziah
- They were traveling to visit the royal family

2) Jehu ordered their arrest & executions

g. Jehu executed justice upon the rest of Ahab's relatives who were in Samaria
1) Jehu continued his trip & was soon met by Jehonadab: The prominent founder of the Rechabites who was a strong follower of the LORD & of the law, Je.35:1-16
- Jehu asked Jehonadab for his loyalty & he received it
- Jehu invited Jehonadab to travel along & witness his zeal for the LORD

2) Jehu soon arrived in Samaria & zealously executed justice upon the rest of Ahab's family: The execution fulfilled Elijah's prophecy, 1 Ki.21:21

h. Jehu executed justice upon the prophets of Baal
1) Jehu deceptively declared his loyalty to Baal: Summoned all the prophets of Baal to a special worship service in Samaria
- He demanded attendance—under penalty of death

- He planned to destroy all the prophets

- He called the assembly in honor of the false god Baal
- He sent messengers throughout all Israel & they all came

2) Jehu had all the prophets meet in the temple of Baal

- He had them presented with special robes

- He, along with Jehonadab, personally joined

the prophets & charged them to make sure no minister of the LORD was present (could be identified by the robes) • He posted eighty guards outside to make sure no Baal prophet could leave the temple 3) Jehu remained in the service until the burnt sacrifice had been offered & then stepped outside: He gave the order for the guards to enter the temple & execute the prophets • They dragged the bodies outside • They went into the inner shrine & brought the sacred pillar out of the temple & destroyed it • They destroyed both the image & temple of Baal • They used the area as a refuse dump: To symbolize distastefulness, contempt 4) Jehu completely destroyed all Baal worship in Israel **3. Jehu's evil reign: A legacy of disobedience to God** a. The evaluation of his life 1) He failed to turn away	into the house of Baal, and said unto the worshippers of Baal, Search, and look that there be here with you none of the servants of the LORD, but the worshippers of Baal only. 24 And when they went in to offer sacrifices and burnt offerings, Jehu appointed fourscore men without, and said, *If* any of the men whom I have brought into your hands escape, *he that letteth him go,* his life *shall be* for the life of him. 25 And it came to pass, as soon as he had made an end of offering the burnt offering, that Jehu said to the guard and to the captains, Go in, *and* slay them; let none come forth. And they smote them with the edge of the sword; and the guard and the captains cast *them* out, and went to the city of the house of Baal. 26 And they brought forth the images out of the house of Baal, and burned them. 27 And they brake down the image of Baal, and brake down the house of Baal, and made it a draught house unto this day. 28 Thus Jehu destroyed Baal out of Israel. 29 Howbeit *from* the sins of Jeroboam the son of Nebat, who made Israel to sin, Jehu departed not from after them,	*to wit,* the golden calves that *were* in Bethel, and that *were* in Dan. 30 And the LORD said unto Jehu, Because thou hast done well in executing *that which is* right in mine eyes, *and* hast done unto the house of Ahab according to all that *was* in mine heart, thy children of the fourth *generation* shall sit on the throne of Israel. 31 But Jehu took no heed to walk in the law of the LORD God of Israel with all his heart: for he departed not from the sins of Jeroboam, which made Israel to sin. 32 In those days the LORD began to cut Israel short: and Hazael smote them in all the coasts of Israel; 33 From Jordan eastward, all the land of Gilead, the Gadites, and the Reubenites, and the Manassites, from Aroer, which is by the river Arnon, even Gilead and Bashan. 34 Now the rest of the acts of Jehu, and all that he did, and all his might, *are* they not written in the book of the chronicles of the kings of Israel? 35 And Jehu slept with his fathers: and they buried him in Samaria. And Jehoahaz his son reigned in his stead. 36 And the time that Jehu reigned over Israel in Samaria *was* twenty and eight years.	from the sins of Jeroboam, 1 Ki.12:25-33; 14:16 2) He was commended for eliminating Baal worship: As a gracious blessing from God, he was promised a dynasty that would last for four generations 3) He was guilty of disobedience, of partial, half-hearted commitment: He was gripped by an extreme execution of justice & by political self-interest, 9:7; Ho.1:4-5 b. The judgment of God against Jehu & Israel 1) The size of Israel was significantly reduced by Hazael of Syria 2) The king & nation lost all the territory of East Jordan c. The achievements & summary of Jehu's life 1) His reign: Recorded in the book, *The History of the Kings of Israel* 2) His death & burial: In the capital of Samaria 3) His successor: His son Jehoahaz 4) His years of rule: Twenty-eight

DIVISION II

THE MINISTRY AND MIRACLES AND OF ELISHA: A DRAMATIC DEMONSTRATION OF GOD'S POWER AND CARE FOR HIS PEOPLE, 4:1–13:25

F. The Secret Anointing of Jehu As King of Israel and His Bloody Purge: A Picture of Misguided Justice Due to Self-Interest, 9:1–10:36

(9:1–10:36) **Introduction**: justice is an absolute essential within society. Justice protects the life, rights and property of people. Within a just and equitable society, a person can expect his life and health to be protected. And he knows that his home and possessions, money and wealth will be protected. Also within a just society, a person knows that his family and friends and fellow workers, as well as their work, employment, schooling and recreation and all else will be protected. Within a just society, the dignity of human life and the value of property are respected, held in the highest esteem. And everyone works together to preserve life and protect the property. A just society eliminates lawlessness: there is no lying to one another, no stealing of each other's property, no cheating among the citizens, no abuse of wife, husband or children, no assaults and no murder. People are not allowed to live lawless, abusive lives. If they are lawless, they are arrested and brought to court where they face the verdict of *guilty*. And they pay the punishment for their guilt, whether by fine or imprisonment or both. In theological language, if they sin, they receive the wages for their sin. They reap what they sow.

This is the practical message of the present Scripture. The Scripture paints a picture of misguided justice due to self-interest. This is the story of the commander of Israel's army Jehu, who rose to the throne with lightning speed, but who became gripped with political self-interest. As a result, he set out on a bloody purge to consolidate power over Israel. This is, *The Secret Anointing of Jehu As King of Israel and His Bloody Purge: A Picture of Misguided Justice Due to Self-Interest, 9:1–10:36.*

1. Jehu's anointing as king of Israel: a picture of rulers being appointed as ministers of justice (9:1-13).
2. Jehu's bloody purge—executions that exceeded true justice and became atrocities (He.1:4-5): a picture of murder and of sin's wages (9:14–10:28).
3. Jehu's evil reign: a legacy, condemnation of a terrible evil (10:29-36).

---

1 **(9:1-13) Rulers, Duty—Justice, of Rulers, Duty—Appointment, of Rulers, Example of—Anointing, Example of—Jehu, King of Israel—Elisha, Ministry**: Jehu, the commander of Israel's army, was anointed to be king of Israel. Some years earlier, the LORD had instructed Elijah to anoint Jehu king over Israel and Hazael king over Syria or Aram (1 K.19:15-18). Right before Elisha was taken home to heaven, he instructed Elisha to carry out these instructions of the LORD. As seen in the former chapter, Elisha confronted Hazael and informed him that he was to be the king of Syria (8:7-15). Now it was time for Elisha to carry out the instructions of the LORD regarding Jehu. The anointing of Jehu is a dramatic picture of rulers being appointed as ministers of justice.

OUTLINE	SCRIPTURE	SCRIPTURE	OUTLINE
1. Jehu's anointing as king of Israel: A picture of rulers being appointed as ministers of justice	And Elisha the prophet called one of the children of the prophets, and said unto him, Gird up thy loins, and take this box of oil in thine hand, and go to Ramoth-gilead:	that I may avenge the blood of my servants the prophets, and the blood of all the servants of the LORD, at the hand of Jezebel.	spelled out: To execute justice upon the family of Ahab for their murder of God's prophets & people, 1 Ki.18:4; 21:13, 17-26
a. The anointing was executed by Elisha		8 For the whole house of Ahab shall perish: and I will cut off from Ahab him that pisseth against the wall, and him that is shut up and left in Israel:	1) The family members to be executed
1) He summoned one of the prophets to go quickly to Ramoth Gilead to find the army commander Jehu	2 And when thou comest thither, look out there Jehu the son of Jehoshaphat the son of Nimshi, and go in, and make him arise up from among his brethren, and carry him to an inner chamber;		• To execute all males
2) He instructed the prophet		9 And I will make the house of Ahab like the house of Jeroboam the son of Nebat, and like the house of Baasha the son of Ahijah:	
• To anoint Jehu in private			• To end the house, dynasty of Ahab just as the dynasties of Jeroboam & Ba-asha ended, 1 Ki.14:7-12; 15:27-30; 16:1-4, 8-122)
• To declare that God had appointed him king over Israel	3 Then take the box of oil, and pour *it* on his head, and say, Thus saith the LORD, I have anointed thee king over Israel. Then open the door, and flee, and tarry not.	10 And the dogs shall eat Jezebel in the portion of Jezreel, and *there shall be* none to bury *her.* And he opened the door, and fled.	2) The death & fate of Jezebel predicted
• To quickly flee the scene			3) The prophet immediately fled
b. The instructions of Elisha were obeyed	4 So the young man, *even* the young man the prophet, went to Ramoth-gilead.	11 Then Jehu came forth to the servants of his lord: and *one* said unto him, Is all well? wherefore came this mad *fellow* to thee? And he said unto them, Ye know the man, and his communication.	d. The commander cautiously, carefully revealed the anointing to his officers: Lest they oppose & arrest him for treason
1) The prophet traveled to Jehu's camp & found him in a council meeting with his commanders	5 And when he came, behold, the captains of the host *were* sitting; and he said, I have an errand to thee, O captain. And Jehu said, Unto which of all us? And he said, To thee, O captain.	12 And they said, *It is* false; tell us now. And he said, Thus and thus spake he to me, saying, Thus saith the LORD, I have anointed thee king over Israel.	1) They questioned him about the visit
• He asked to see Jehu alone			2) He dodged their questioning
			3) They pressed him for an explanation
• Jehu took him into the house	6 And he arose, and went into the house; and he poured the oil on his head, and said unto him, Thus saith the LORD God of Israel, I have anointed thee king over the people of the LORD, *even* over Israel.	13 Then they hasted, and took every man his garment, and put *it* under him on the top of the stairs, and blew with trumpets, saying, Jehu is king.	4) He sensed their support & loyalty: Revealed the anointing
2) The prophet anointed the commander, declaring that God had appointed him king over Israel			e. The army enthusiastically accepted & proclaimed Jehu as king
c. The purpose for Jehu's special appointment was then	7 And thou shalt smite the house of Ahab thy master,		

a. In obedience to the LORD Elisha carried out the anointing of the commander Jehu (vv.1-3). But either due to his age or to the fact that his presence would be too conspicuous, Elisha did not actually carry out the anointing himself. Rather he summoned one of the prophets to quickly travel to Ramoth-Gilead where he would find the army commander. Once locating the commander, the prophet was to do three things:

⇒ to take the commander into an inner room and privately anoint him out of sight of everyone.
⇒ to declare that God had appointed him king over Israel
⇒ to quickly flee the scene

Just why Elisha instructed the prophet to quickly flee is unknown. Most likely, Elisha feared there might be opposition to Jehu when he launched his uprising against King Joram who was wounded and recovering in Jezreel (14-15).

b. Following the instructions of Elisha, the prophet traveled to Jehu's camp located at Ramoth-Gilead. Arriving, he found Jehu conducting a counsel meeting with his commanders (vv.4-6). Asking to see Jehu alone, he took the commander inside a house where they could be private. Once inside, the prophet anointed the commander and declared that God had appointed him king over Israel.

c. Continuing his message to Jehu, the prophet said that the commander was being appointed for a special purpose: to execute justice upon the family of Ahab because of their murder of God's prophets and people (vv.7-10; also see 1 K.18:4; 21:13, 17-26). In carrying out the execution against the family members of Ahab, he was to execute all males in order to end the house and dynasty of Ahab. Ahab's dynasty was to be erased just as the dynasty's of Jeroboam and Baasha had been erased (1 K.14:7-12; 15:27-30; 16:1-4, 8-12). Finally the prophet shared the death and fate of Jezebel with the commander. He prophesied exactly how she would die just as Elijah had predicted some years before (v.10; 1 K.21:23).

Having finished his task, the prophet quickly turned and fled, literally running from the house. Standing there by himself—all alone—Jehu had been appointed to carry out justice against the evil and bloodthirsty family of Ahab and Jezebel.

d. Returning to his officers, the commander Jehu cautiously revealed the anointing to his officers. Caution was necessary lest they oppose and arrest him for treason. When he returned to the counsel meeting, they immediately question him about the visit of the prophet (vv.11-12). Note that they called the prophet a "madman." This was a term of contempt and exposes their wicked hearts, indicating just how far the society of that day had fallen from worshipping and serving the LORD. At first, Jehu dodged the questioning of his officers, but they continued to press him for an explanation. Sensing their support and loyalty, he revealed exactly what had happened: he had been anointed to be king over Israel.

e. This news struck a chord of hope within the officers' hearts, for they enthusiastically accepted and proclaimed Jehu as their king (v.13). As quickly as they could, they yanked their cloaks off and spread them under him on the bare steps of the house. Then they had the trumpet blown and shouted out their support for the new king: "Jehu is king."

Thought 1. Simply stated, Jehu was appointed to be a just ruler, a ruler who would execute justice within the nation of Israel. When a national ruler is appointed, he or she is to be a minister of justice. They are to see that justice is executed throughout the land. Whether local city official, or judge, or some law enforcement official, or a member of some legislative body, or prime minister, or president—whoever the ruler may be, he or she is primarily a minister of justice. The ruler is to make sure that the relationships and dealings among neighbors, workers and citizens are fair and equitable. No citizen is to be allowed to lie, steal, cheat, kill—no person is to be allowed to abuse and mistreat others. The responsibility for watching and guarding the behavior of citizens rests upon the rulers of a nation. And every ruler stands accountable to God.

God will hold every ruler accountable for executing justice. How a ruler ministers justice will determine how God will minister justice to that ruler. Whatever a ruler sows in justice, he will reap in God's justice. Whatever justice a ruler measures out to others, the ruler will have measured out to him by God Himself. Every ruler within a nation will reap the exact justice he has sown. For God will execute perfect justice upon every ruler, giving the ruler exactly what he or she deserves: good for good, and bad for bad. No ruler will ever be mistreated, judged more severely than what he deserves. And every ruler will receive from God all the good and blessings he deserves. Listen to what God's Holy Word says about rulers being the ministers of justice:

> "For with what judgment ye judge, ye shall be judged: and with what measure ye mete, it shall be measured to you again" (Mt.7:2).
>
> "Be not deceived; God is not mocked: for whatsoever a man soweth, that shall he also reap. For he that soweth to his flesh shall of the flesh reap corruption; but he that soweth to the Spirit shall of the Spirit reap life everlasting" (Ga.6:7-8).
>
> "Masters, give unto *your* servants that which is just and equal; knowing that ye also have a Master in heaven" (Co.4:1).
>
> "That which is altogether just shalt thou follow, that thou mayest live, and inherit the land which the LORD thy God giveth thee" (De.16:20).
>
> "Thou shalt not pervert the judgment of the stranger, *nor* of the fatherless; nor take a widow's raiment to pledge" (De.24:17).
>
> "Cursed *be* he that perverteth the judgment of the stranger, fatherless, and widow. And all the people shall say, Amen" (De.27:19).
>
> "The God of Israel said, the Rock of Israel spake to me, He that ruleth over men *must be* just, ruling in the fear of God" (2 S.23:3).
>
> "And said to the judges, Take heed what ye do: for ye judge not for man, but for the LORD, who is with you in the judgment" (2 Chr.19:6).
>
> "Then I consulted with myself, and I rebuked the nobles, and the rulers, and said unto them, Ye exact usury, every one of his brother. And I set a great assembly against them" (Ne.5:7).
>
> "Be wise now therefore, O ye kings: be instructed, ye judges of the earth. Serve the LORD with fear, and rejoice with trembling" (Ps.2:10-11).
>
> "*It is* an abomination to kings to commit wickedness: for the throne is established by righteousness" (Pr.16:12).
>
> "Mercy and truth preserve the king: and his throne is upholden by mercy" (Pr.20:28).
>
> "To do justice and judgment *is* more acceptable to the LORD than sacrifice" (Pr.21:3).
>
> "The king by judgment establisheth the land: but he that receiveth gifts overthroweth it" (Pr.29:4).
>
> "The king that faithfully judgeth the poor, his throne shall be established for ever" (Pr.29:14).

"*It is* not for kings, O Lemuel, *it is* not for kings to drink wine; nor for princes strong drink: Lest they drink, and forget the law, and pervert the judgment of any of the afflicted" (Pr.31:4-5).

"How long will ye judge unjustly, and accept the persons of the wicked? Selah. Defend the poor and fatherless: do justice to the afflicted and needy" (Ps.82:2-3).

"Righteousness exalteth a nation: but sin *is* a reproach to any people" (Pr.14:34).

"Thy princes *are* rebellious, and companions of thieves: every one loveth gifts, and followeth after rewards: they judge not the fatherless, neither doth the cause of the widow come unto them. Therefore saith the Lord, the LORD of hosts, the mighty One of Israel, Ah, I will ease me of mine adversaries, and avenge me of mine enemies" (Is.1:23-24).

"The LORD will enter into judgment with the ancients of his people, and the princes thereof: for ye have eaten up the vineyard; the spoil of the poor *is* in your houses" (Is.3:14).

"Woe unto them that decree unrighteous decrees, and that write grievousness *which* they have prescribed; To turn aside the needy from judgment, and to take away the right from the poor of my people, that widows may be their prey, and *that* they may rob the fatherless! And what will ye do in the day of visitation, and in the desolation *which* shall come from far? to whom will ye flee for help? and where will ye leave your glory" (Is.10:1-3).

"Thus saith the LORD, Keep ye judgment, and do justice: for my salvation *is* near to come, and my righteousness to be revealed" (Is.56:1).

"Her princes in the midst thereof *are* like wolves ravening the prey, to shed blood, *and* to destroy souls, to get dishonest gain. And her prophets have daubed them with untempered *morter,* seeing vanity, and divining lies unto them, saying, Thus saith the Lord GOD, when the LORD hath not spoken. The people of the land have used oppression, and exercised robbery, and have vexed the poor and needy: yea, they have oppressed the stranger wrongfully. And I sought for a man among them, that should make up the hedge, and stand in the gap before me for the land, that I should not destroy it: but I found none. Therefore have I poured out mine indignation upon them; I have consumed them with the fire of my wrath: their own way have I recompensed upon their heads, saith the Lord GOD" (Eze.22:27-31).

2 (9:14-10:28) **Murder, Example of—Sin, Penalty—Execution, Example of—Purge, Example of—Reform, Example of—Atrocity, Example of—Jehu, King of Israel, Reform of—Jehu, Bloody Purge of**: Jehu carried out a bloody purge throughout the nation of Israel. But his executions far exceeded reform, exceeded the execution of justice against the family of Ahab and Jezebel. In executing justice against Ahab and Jezebel's family, he was doing a service to the nation; but in the execution of many others, he committed atrocities that went well beyond justice. Once he launched the executions, he obviously became gripped with political self-interest and set out to eliminate anyone who could conceivably become a threat to his power. Scripture definitely says that Jehu's executions exceeded true justice and became atrocities, that his reform went well beyond the execution of justice (Ho.1:4-5). In fact, Jehu himself became very much like those he was executing, more focused upon political self-interest and survival than upon executing true justice in the land. He became more of a bloodthirsty tyrant than he did a reformer who had been appointed by God to execute justice in behalf of the people.

Jehu launched eight different executions, in some cases dealing with and executing one individual at a time, and in other cases executing whole groups of people simultaneously. The bloody purge of Jehu is lengthy, very lengthy, over 52 verses. Because of its length, it is best to place the Scripture and outline with the discussion of each of the sub-points.

a. Having just been anointed king by the prophet and receiving the support of the army, Jehu decided that now was the time to act and take over the throne of Israel (vv.14-26). Justice was now to be executed upon Joram, Israel's evil king. Note the Scripture and outline:

OUTLINE	SCRIPTURE	SCRIPTURE	OUTLINE
2. Jehu's bloody purge—executions that exceeded true justice & became atrocities (Ho.1:4-5): A picture of murder & of sin's wages, "the judgment of death"	14 So Jehu the son of Jehoshaphat the son of Nimshi conspired against Joram. (Now Joram had kept Ramoth-gilead, he and all Israel, because of Hazael king of Syria.	Joram lay there. And Ahaziah king of Judah was come down to see Joram.	set out for Jezreel to arrest King Joram
a. Jehu executed justice upon Joram, Israel's evil king	15 But king Joram was returned to be healed in Jezreel of the wounds which	17 And there stood a watchman on the tower in peace? And Jehu said, What	• The tower lookout spotted the approaching troops & warned the king
1) Jehu planned a conspiracy against King Joram	the Syrians had given him, when he fought with	hast thou to do with peace? turn thee behind me. And the	• The king sent out a horseman to investigate
• Joram was in Jezreel recovering from his wounds	Hazael king of Syria.) And Jehu said, If it be your	watchman told, saying, The messenger came to them, but	& to make sure the troops were coming in peace
• The wounded king had been defending Ramoth-Gilead	minds, *then* let none go	he cometh not again.	
• Jehu issued strict orders to the guards: They must not let anyone slip out of Ramoth Gilead to warn King Joram of the coup	forth *nor* escape out of the city to go to tell *it* in Jezreel.	18 So there went one on horseback to meet him, and said, Thus saith the king, *Is it* peace? And Jehu said, What hast thou to do with peace? turn thee behind me. And the	• The horseman confronted Jehu & was threatened, so he joined Jehu's forces
2) Jehu personally took a regiment of commandos &	16 So Jehu rode in a chariot, and went to Jezreel; for	watchman told, saying, The messenger came to them, but he cometh not again.	• The lookout reported that the horseman was not returning

OUTLINE	SCRIPTURE	SCRIPTURE	OUTLINE
• The king sent a second horseman with the same result	19 Then he sent out a second on horseback, which came to them, and said, Thus saith the king, Is it peace? And Jehu answered, What hast thou to do with peace? turn thee behind me.	witchcrafts are so many?	witchcraft of Jezebel
		23 And Joram turned his hands, and fled, and said to Ahaziah, There is treachery, O Ahaziah.	• The king, realizing his life was in danger, turned & fled
• The lookout again reported that the second rider was not returning & that the chariot appeared to be Jehu's	20 And the watchman told, saying, He came even unto them, and cometh not again:and the driving is like the driving of Jehu the son of Nimshi; for he driveth furiously.	24 And Jehu drew a bow with his full strength, and smote Jehoram between his arms, and the arrow went out at his heart, and he sunk down in his chariot.	4) Jehu executed King Joram • He drew his bow & pierced the heart of the king
• The king ordered his chariot prepared & both he & King Ahaziah of Judah—each in his own chariot—rode out to meet Jehu: They met at Naboth's vineyard, the land stolen by Ahab, 1 Ki.21:1-29	21 And Joram said, Make ready. And his chariot was made ready. And Joram king of Israel and Ahaziah king of Judah went out, each in his chariot, and they went out against Jehu, and met him in the portion of Naboth the Jezreelite.	25 Then said Jehu to Bidkar his captain, Take up, and cast him in the portion of the field of Naboth the Jezreelite: for remember how that, when I and thou rode together after Ahab his father, the LORD laid this burden upon him;	• He instructed his chariot driver Bidkar to throw the body on the field that had belonged to Naboth
• The king asked Jehu if he had come in peace	22 And it came to pass, when Joram saw Jehu, that he said, Is it peace, Jehu? And he answered, What peace, so long as the whoredoms of thy mother Jezebel and her	26 Surely I have seen yesterday the blood of Naboth, and the blood of his sons, saith the LORD; and I will requite thee in this plat, saith the LORD. Now therefore take and cast him into the plat of ground, according to the word of the LORD.	• He reminded the driver of Elijah's prophecy 10 years earlier
3) Jehu spelled out the charges against Joram • The king had misled Israel in the idolatry &			

1) Sitting down with his officers, Jehu planned a conspiracy against King Joram (v.15). Remember that Joram was in Jezreel recovering from battle wounds inflicted upon him by the Syrians or Arameans (8:28-29). Once the plans had been laid for capturing the throne, the commander instructed his officers to guard the gates of Ramoth-Gilead and not let anyone slip out to warn King Joram of the coup. For the success of the rebellion depended upon secrecy in catching King Joram by surprise.

2) Taking a small regiment of commandos, Jehu set out to arrest and execute King Joram in Jezreel, which was a journey of about 40 miles. As the commander approached the city, the tower lookouts spotted the approaching troops and sent word to warn the king (v.17). Immediately Joram ordered a horseman to investigate and make sure the troops were coming in peace. But in confronting Jehu, the horseman was threatened, so he quickly made the decision to join the commanders forces (v.18).

    Noticing that the first horseman was not returning, the lookout quickly sent another report to the king that something had happened, for the horseman was not returning (v.19). Once again the king sent a second horseman with the same result. And again the lookout reported that the second rider was not returning. Moreover he gave additional information in his report, that the chariot approaching seemed to be that of Jehu's. For he was driving just like Jehu always drove his horses, furiously and recklessly—like a madman (v.20).

    Hearing that it might by Jehu, Joram feared that the Syrian army had counter-attacked and broken through the defenses of Israel; thus Jehu and the survivors were fleeing the onrush of Syrian troops. Acting quickly, Joram and King Ahaziah ordered that their chariots be prepared so that they could ride out to meet Jehu (v.21). Note that they met at the very vineyard that had once belonged to Naboth but had been stolen by Ahab (1 K.21:1-29). Approaching the commander, King Joram asked if he had come in peace.

3) Wasting no time, Jehu spelled out the charges against Joram (vv.22-23). There could be no peace as long as he and his mother Jezebel continued to promote the whoredom or idolatry and witchcraft throughout the nation (De.13.1-18; 18:9-14; 28:25-26; 1 K.21:25-26). Realizing his life was in danger, King Joram quickly turned his chariot around and fled for his life.

4) But Jehu was determined to execute justice upon King Joram, just as he was planning to execute justice against his mother Jezebel (vv.24-26). Quickly drawing his bow, he shot and pierced the heart of the king as he was fleeing. Then turning to his chariot driver Bidkar, the commander instructed him to throw the body of the king on the field that had belonged to Naboth. Note why: years before when Jehu was just a young soldier serving as a chariot driver in Ahab's army, he had apparently overheard Elijah's prophecy against Ahab. Because Ahab had killed Naboth in order to secure his property, Ahab would suffer a judgment upon this very plot of ground. Reminding his chariot driver of Elijah's prophecy some ten years earlier, Jehu fulfilled the prophecy by ordering the body of King Joram, Ahab's son, thrown on the vineyard of Naboth (vv.25-26).

b. Now Jehu turned to executing justice upon Ahaziah, Judah's evil king (vv.27-28). Remember that Ahaziah had also ridden out with King Joram to meet the commander Jehu. But Ahaziah had driven his own chariot. Standing there in his chariot and seeing Jehu lay out the charges against Joram and begin his attack against Israel's king, Ahaziah quickly whipped his chariot around and began to flee while Jehu was occupied with assassinating King Joram. Seeing Ahaziah flee, Jehu barked out the order to kill him also. One of the arrows found its mark, but it only wounded the king. He escaped to Megiddo where he eventually died. Why would the commander and newly crowned king of the northern kingdom execute Ahaziah, the king of the southern kingdom of Judah? Keep in mind that Ahaziah was a blood relative of Ahab through his mother Athaliah who was the daughter of Ahab. Ahaziah had lived a wicked, evil life so justice was also to be executed upon him. Having reigned for only one year, his body was taken to Jerusalem where it was buried.

OUTLINE	SCRIPTURE	SCRIPTURE	OUTLINE
b. Jehu executed justice upon Ahaziah, Judah's evil king 1) Ahaziah also fled from Jehu • He was shot but only wounded	27 But when Ahaziah the king of Judah saw *this,* he fled by the way of the garden house. And Jehu followed after him, and said, Smite him also in the chariot. *And they did so* at the going up to Gur, which *is* by Ibleam. And he	fled to Megiddo, and died there. 28 And his servants carried him in a chariot to Jerusalem, and buried him in his sepulchre with his fathers in the city of David.	• He escaped to Megiddo where he died 2) Ahaziah was taken to Jerusalem where he was buried in the royal tombs

c. Next to be executed was Jezebel, the wicked wife of Ahab who had committed so many atrocities against the prophets and the citizens of the nation (vv.30-37). No doubt, Jezebel was quite elderly and had spent years launching persecution after persecution against the true believers of Israel. Somehow she had heard about the coup of Jehu knew she had no way to defend herself. Thus she began to prepare herself to die as a queen. Putting on makeup and fixing her hair, she defiantly waited for him by the window of her balcony. As Jehu entered the city in his triumphant march, she shouted out sarcastic insults (vv.30-31). As he passed by her window, he looked up and ordered some servants to throw her down (vv.32-33). Two or three of the servants grabbed her and cast her out the window. As her body hit the ground, blood splattered everywhere, and her body was trampled under the horses as they marched by. She died a gruesome death.

Once reaching the palace, Jehu went in and had a meal (v.34). No doubt, he sat there pondering what had taken place over the last few hours, for he was now the crown king of Israel. At some point, he ordered the cursed Jezebel's body to be buried, for after all, she was a king's daughter (vv.34-35). However, the servants were able to find only her skull, hands and feet. Reporting this fact to Jehu, the newly crowned king recalled the prophecy of Elijah, that Jezebel's body would suffer a grizzly end (vv.36-37). Elijah had prophesied that dogs would devour her flesh, and her body would be like refuge, meaning there would be no marker over her grave and no one mourning for her. Her body would totally disappear, be eaten by dogs and passed as refuge through the bodies of the dogs.

OUTLINE	SCRIPTURE	SCRIPTURE	OUTLINE
c. Jehu executed justice upon Jezebel, wicked wife Ahab's 1) Jezebel had heard of Jehu's coup, prepared herself to die as a queen, & defiantly waited for him by the window: She shouted sarcastic insults as he entered the city 2) Jehu looked up & ordered some servants to throw her down • Her blood splattered everywhere • Her body was trampled under the horses • She died a gruesome death 3) Jehu entered the palace & ate	30 And when Jehu was come to Jezreel, Jezebel heard *of it;* and she painted her face, and tired her head, and looked out at a window. 31 And as Jehu entered in at the gate, she said, *Had* Zimri peace, who slew his master? 32 And he lifted up his face to the window, and said, Who *is* on my side? who? And there looked out to him two *or* three eunuchs. 33 And he said, Throw her down. So they threw her down: and *some* of her blood was sprinkled on the wall, and on the horses: and he trode her under foot. 34 And when he was come in, he did eat and drink, and	said, Go, see now this cursed *woman,* and bury her: for she *is* a king's daughter. 35 And they went to bury her: but they found no more of her than the skull, and the feet, and the palms of *her* hands. 36 Wherefore they came again, and told him. And he said, This *is* the word of the LORD, which he spake by his servant Elijah the Tishbite, saying, In the portion of Jezreel shall dogs eat the flesh of Jezebel: 37 And the carcase of Jezebel shall be as dung upon the face of the field in the portion of Jezreel; *so* that they shall not say, This *is* Jezebel.	4) Jehu later ordered the cursed Jezebel to be buried • The servants found only her skull, hands, & feet • They reported the fact to Jehu 5) Jehu recalled the prophecy of Elijah, that Jezebel's body would suffer a grisly end • Dogs would devour her flesh • Her body would be like refuse, meaning there would be no marker & no one mourning for her

d. Next Jehu moved to execute justice upon the 70 sons of Ahab, which most likely included both grandsons and perhaps great-grandsons as well. Note that all the sons either lived in Samaria or else had fled into Samaria having heard about the coup of Jehu. Note also that some of the officials of Jezreel had escaped the purge of their city and had also fled to the capital Samaria for safety (10:1-3). In a bold move Jehu wrote a letter to the city officials of Samaria and to Jezreel, a letter that challenged them to mobilize their forces for war. He suggested they select Ahab's most capable son as their king and prepare to fight to protect Ahab's dynasty and family.

Receiving the letter, the city officials were terrified by the threat. For they knew that resistance against Jehu would be futile (vv.4-5). Sending a letter of surrender to him, they stated that they were switching their allegiance to support his rule, and they would do anything he asked.

In response to their surrender, Jehu sent a second letter demanding that the officials execute justice against the seventy sons of Ahab. They must be put to death. And their heads must be brought to Jezreel the very next day and presented to him, proving that the officials were giving their allegiance to him as the newly crowned king (v.6).

Just as Jehu ordered, the officials carried out the royal command (vv.7-8). They executed Ahab's sons and sent their heads to Jehu in Jezreel. Once presented to him, Jehu ordered that the heads be placed in two piles at the city gate and be left there until morning. They were to be an object lesson to show subjection and to discourage any uprising against his claim to the throne.

The next morning Jehu assembled and addressed the people, declaring that he had been sent on a divine mission, a very special mission by God Himself (vv.9-10). Simply stated, Jehu stood by the piled heads of Ahab's 70 sons and declared that his rise to power had been ordained by God. Apparently standing there looking at the 70 heads of Ahab's sons, some of the people were grieving over the bloody purge and massacre. Sensing their grief, Jehu declared that the people were innocent before God. If anyone was to be blamed it was to be he and the city officials, for he had launched rebellion and the city officials had actually executed the sons of Ahab. Thus whatever guilt was to be executed by God would be executed upon them.

Note what Jehu was doing: through this argument he was seeking to secure the sympathy and full support of the public, the citizens of Jezreel and Samaria. Continuing, he claimed that he was acting as the agent of God Himself in executing justice throughout the land and against the house of Ahab. By executing the sons of Ahab, he had done exactly what Elijah the prophet had promised would be done, that his house and dynasty would be completely cut off (see outline and note—1 K.21:20-29 for more discussion).

OUTLINE	SCRIPTURE	SCRIPTURE	OUTLINE
	CHAPTER 10	hearken unto my voice, take ye the heads of the men your master's sons, and come to me to Jezreel by tomorrow this time. Now the king's sons, *being* seventy persons, *were* with the great men of the city, which brought them up.	brought to Jezreel the next day & presented to him
d. Jehu executed justice upon the seventy sons of Ahab who were in Samaria	**A**nd Ahab had seventy sons in Samaria. And Jehu wrote letters, and sent to Samaria, unto the rulers of Jezreel, to the elders, and to them that brought up Ahab's *children,* saying,		
1) Jehu wrote a letter to the city officials of Samaria & to Jezreel (who had fled to the capital for safety)			
• He warned them to mobilize their forces	2 Now as soon as this letter cometh to you, seeing your master's sons *are* with you, and *there are* with you chariots and horses, a fenced city also, and armour;	7 And it came to pass, when the letter came to them, that they took the king's sons, and slew seventy persons, and put their heads in baskets, and sent him *them* to Jezreel.	4) The city officials carried out the executive order
			• They executed Ahab's sons & sent their heads to Jehu in Jezreel
• He challenged them to select Ahab's most capable son as their king & to prepare to fight for Ahab's dynasty & family	3 Look even out the best and meetest of your master's sons, and set *him* on his father's throne, and fight for your master's house.	8 And there came a messenger, and told him, saying, They have brought the heads of the king's sons. And he said, Lay ye them in two heaps at the entering in of the gate until the morning.	• Jehu ordered the heads to be placed in two piles at the city gate until morning: An object lesson to show subjection & to discourage rebellion
2) The city officials were terrified by Jehu's threat & knew resistance was futile: They sent a letter of surrender to him	4 But they were exceedingly afraid, and said, Behold, two kings stood not before him: how then shall we stand?	9 And it came to pass in the morning, that he went out, and stood, and said to all the people, Ye *be* righteous: behold, I conspired against my master, and slew him: but who slew all these?	5) Jehu assembled & addressed the people the next morning, declaring his divine mission
	5 And he that *was* over the house, and he that *was* over the city, the elders also, and the bringers up *of the children,* sent to Jehu, saying, We are thy servants, and will do all that thou shalt bid us; we will not make any king: do thou *that which is* good in thine eyes.	10 Know now that there shall fall unto the earth nothing of the word of the LORD, which the LORD spake concerning the house of Ahab: for the LORD hath done *that* which he spake by his servant Elijah.	• He declared the innocence of the people in the coup
• They switched their allegiance to him			• He declared that he had the support & help of the city officials
• They stated that they would do anything he asked			• He claimed that he was acting as the agent of God in executing justice in the land & against the house of Ahab
3) Jehu sent a second letter demanding that the heads of Ahab's seventy sons be	6 Then he wrote a letter the second time to them, saying, If ye *be* mine, and *if* ye will		

e. Jehu unjustly and sinfully executed others who were not of the family of Ahab, who were not wicked relatives of the evil king (v.11). Going well beyond the authority assigned him by God, Jehu executed all of Ahab's important officials, close friends and even the priests who had served him. Jehu left no survivor who had any contact with Ahab. Again, his bloody purge went well beyond the authority that had been assigned him (9:7-10; Ho.1:4-5).

OUTLINE	SCRIPTURE
e. Jehu unjustly & sinfully executed others who were not wicked relatives of Ahab, 9:7; Ho.1:4-5	11 So Jehu slew all that remained of the house of Ahab in Jezreel, and all his great men, and his kinsfolks, and his priests, until he left him none remaining.

f. Jehu even executed questionable justice upon some relatives of King Ahaziah of Judah (vv.12-14). Knowing that the ultimate success of his rebellion depended on his capturing the capitol of Samaria, Jehu set out for the city. Along the way, he met 42 relatives of King Ahaziah who were traveling to visit the royal family in Samaria. As soon as Jehu discovered that they were relatives of Judah's King Ahaziah, he ordered their arrest and execution, leaving no survivors.

OUTLINE	SCRIPTURE	SCRIPTURE	OUTLINE
f. Jehu executed questionable justice upon some relatives of King Ahaziah of Judah 1) Jehu set out for Samaria & met forty-two men at Beth Eked of the Shepherds • They claimed to be relatives of King Ahaziah	12 And he arose and departed, and came to Samaria. *And* as he *was* at the shearing house in the way, 13 Jehu met with the brethren of Ahaziah king of Judah, and said, Who *are* ye? And they answered, We *are* the brethren of Ahaziah; and we	go down to salute the children of the king and the children of the queen. 14 And he said, Take them alive. And they took them alive, and slew them at the pit of the shearing house, *even* two and forty men; neither left he any of them.	• They were traveling to visit the royal family 2) Jehu ordered their arrest & executions

g. Once arriving in Samaria, Jehu immediately executed justice upon the rest of Ahab's relatives (vv.15-17). But prior to this, while he was traveling toward Samaria, Jehu met Jehonadab who was the prominent founder of the Rechabites. The Rechabites were an ascetic movement that opposed the worship of Baal and strongly followed the LORD and His law (Je.35:1-16). In reaction to the carnal, lawless and corrupt society of the day, Jehonadab and his followers lived a nomadic life in the desert, living in tents. They abstained from drinking wine. Jeremiah held the Rechabites in the highest esteem, commending them for opposing the worship of Baal and committing themselves to follow the LORD and His law (Je.35:1-16).

OUTLINE	SCRIPTURE	SCRIPTURE	OUTLINE
g. Jehu executed justice upon the rest of Ahab's relatives who were in Samaria 1) Jehu continued his trip & was soon met by Jehonadab: The prominent founder of the Rechabites who was a strong follower of the LORD & of the law, Je.35:1-16 • Jehu asked Jehonadab for his loyalty & he	15 And when he was departed thence, he lighted on Jehonadab the son of Rechab *coming* to meet him: and he saluted him, and said to him, Is thine heart right, as my heart *is* with thy heart? And Jehonadab answered, It is. If it be, give *me* thine hand. And he gave *him* his hand; and he took him up to him into the	chariot. 16 And he said, Come with me, and see my zeal for the LORD. So they made him ride in his chariot. 17 And when he came to Samaria, he slew all that remained unto Ahab in Samaria, till he had destroyed him, according to the saying of the LORD, which he spake to Elijah.	received it • Jehu invited Jehonadab to travel along & witness his zeal for the LORD 2) Jehu soon arrived in Samaria & zealously executed justice upon the rest of Ahab's family: The execution fulfilled Elijah's prophecy, 1 Ki.21:21

Learning that Jehonadab was a staunch opponent to the worship of Baal, Jehu asked the ascetic leader for his support as he purged the land of idolatry and false worship. Taking the hand of Jehu, Jehonadab committed his allegiance to the newly appointed king. As a consequence, Jehu invited Jehonadab to travel along and witness his zeal for the LORD. Being spurred on by the committed loyalty of Jehonadab, Jehu rushed to Samaria and zealously executed justice upon the rest of Ahab's family (v.17). Note that the executions fulfilled the prophecy of Elijah (1 K.21:21).

h. Finally the entire family of Ahab was eliminated. Now Jehu could turn his attention to purging the land of the false prophets and therefore worship of Baal (vv.18-28). In executing justice against the prophets of Baal, Jehu had to make sure there were no survivors. For if some of the prophets survived, they could reinstitute the worship of Baal sometime in the future, in particular after Jehu's death. Thus he laid out a plan by which he could entrap all the false prophets in one place. Note how Scripture paints this dramatic scene:

OUTLINE	SCRIPTURE	SCRIPTURE	OUTLINE
h. Jehu executed justice upon the prophets of Baal 1) Jehu deceptively declared his loyalty to Baal: Summoned all the prophets of Baal to a special worship service in Samaria • He demanded attendance—under penalty of death • He planned to destroy all the prophets • He called the assembly in honor of the false god	18 And Jehu gathered all the people together, and said unto them, Ahab served Baal a little; *but* Jehu shall serve him much. 19 Now therefore call unto me all the prophets of Baal, all his servants, and all his priests; let none be wanting: for I have a great sacrifice *to do* to Baal; whosoever shall be wanting, he shall not live. But Jehu did *it* in subtilty, to the intent that he might destroy the worshippers of Baal. 20 And Jehu said, Proclaim a solemn assembly for Baal.	And they proclaimed *it*. 21 And Jehu sent through all Israel: and all the worshippers of Baal came, so that there was not a man left that came not. And they came into the house of Baal; and the house of Baal was full from one end to another. 22 And he said unto him that *was* over the vestry, Bring forth vestments for all the worshippers of Baal. And he brought them forth vestments. 23 And Jehu went, and Jehonadab the son of Rechab, into the house of Baal, and	Baal • He sent messengers throughout all Israel & they all came 2) Jehu had all the prophets meet in the temple of Baal • He had them presented with special robes • He, along with Jehonadab, personally joined the prophets & charged

OUTLINE	SCRIPTURE	SCRIPTURE	OUTLINE
them to make sure no minister of the LORD was present (could be identified by the robes) • He posted eighty guards outside to make sure no Baal prophet could leave the temple 3) Jehu remained in the service until the burnt sacrifice had been offered & then stepped outside: He	said unto the worshippers of Baal, Search, and look that there be here with you none of the servants of the LORD, but the worshippers of Baal only. 24 And when they went in to offer sacrifices and burnt offerings, Jehu appointed fourscore men without, and said, *If* any of the men whom I have brought into your hands escape, *he that letteth him go,* his life *shall be* for the life of him. 25 And it came to pass, as soon as he had made an end of offering the burnt offering, that Jehu said to the guard	and to the captains, Go in, *and* slay them; let none come forth. And they smote them with the edge of the sword; and the guard and the captains cast *them* out, and went to the city of the house of Baal. 26 And they brought forth the images out of the house of Baal, and burned them. 27 And they brake down the image of Baal, and brake down the house of Baal, and made it a draught house unto this day. 28 Thus Jehu destroyed Baal out of Israel.	gave the order for the guards to enter the temple & execute the prophets • They dragged the bodies outside • They went into the inner shrine & brought the sacred pillar out of the temple & destroyed it • They destroyed both the image & temple of Baal • They used the area as a refuse dump: To symbolize distastefulness, contempt 4) Jehu completely destroyed all Baal worship in Israel

1) Jehu's plan was a clever deception to entrap the prophets of Baal (vv.18-21). Using the guise of false loyalty, he declared his commitment to Baal by saying that Ahab's fervor for Baal would be small to Jehu's service for him. After making this declaration publicly to the people, Jehu summoned all the prophets of Baal to a worship service in Samaria. He demanded their attendance under the penalty of death (vv.19-21). But this was a deception, for Jehu planned to destroy all the prophets and ministers of Baal. After announcing the assembly in honor of the false god, he sent messengers throughout the nation to rally all the prophets and ministers to attend, upon penalty of death.

2) When the day for the assembly finally arrived, all the false prophets met in the temple of Baal (vv.21-24). As the ministers of Baal arrived, Jehu had them presented with special robes that would readily identify them as Baal worshipers. When it was time to begin the meeting, Jehu, along with Jehonadab, entered the temple and personally joined the prophets (v.23). Then to make sure that no one was present other than the Baal ministers, he charged everyone in the crowd to make sure no one was present other than Baal worshippers. This was a simple matter to determine, for all Baal worshippers could be identified by their robes. Once Jehu was sure that only Baal worshippers were present, he and the bad priests went in to make sacrifices and burnt offerings to the false god Baal. Note this fact: prior to entering the temple, Jehu had posted 80 guards outside to make sure no bad priest could leave the temple (v.24). And the guards were warned, it would be their life for any life they allowed to escape.

3) Jehu remained in the service until the burnt sacrifice had been offered to the false god Baal (vv.25-27). Once the sacrifice had been made, Jehu slipped outside and gave the order for the guards to enter the temple and execute the prophets. Once they were executed, they dragged the bodies outside and went into the inner shrine and brought the sacred pillar out of the temple and burned it. They then destroyed both the image of Baal and the temple of Baal (v.27). And note, they used the area for a toilet up until the very day that the book of Kings was written.

4) Jehu completely destroyed all Baal worship in Israel (v.28). During Jehu's reign, there was no false worship of Baal. The reform launched by Elijah was completed by Jehu.

Thought 1. Jehu's executions went beyond the realm of justice, slipping over into the realm of murder. His reform exceeded by far God's instructions to execute justice throughout the nation. As a result, innocent people were executed. And Jehu became as guilty of spilling blood as Ahab, Jezebel and their family had been.

Murder is a sin, a terrible sin. For it snatches the life of a person out of this world. And a dead person no longer has the privilege of experiencing love, joy and peace. Moreover, when the life of a person is gone, the hearts of many who are left behind suffer pain, and grief and in many cases hardship. For when the life of a parent is snatched away, one of the major sources of income is no longer available. As a result, the family suffers by not having the money to adequately provide for their livelihood. Think of the single mothers and fathers who struggle to provide an adequate living for their children, and of the widows and widowers who often struggle just as much.

No life is to ever be murdered. God warns the murderer: he will suffer the consequences of his terrible evil.

"For the wrath of God is revealed from heaven against all ungodliness and unrighteousness of men, who hold the truth in unrighteousness…Being filled with all unrighteousness, fornication, wickedness, covetousness, maliciousness; full of envy, murder, debate, deceit, malignity; whisperer…Who knowing the judgment of God, that they which commit such things are worthy of death, not only do the same, but have pleasure in them that do them" (Ro.1:18, 29, 32).

"Envyings, murders, drunkenness, revellings, and such like: of the which I tell you before, as I have also told *you* in time past, that they which do such things shall not inherit the kingdom of God" (Ga.5:21).

"Whosoever hateth his brother is a murderer: and ye know that no murderer hath eternal life abiding in him" (1 Jn.3:15).

"But the fearful, and unbelieving, and the abominable, and murderers, and whoremongers, and sorcerers, and idolaters, and all liars, shall have their part in the lake which burneth with fire and brimstone: which is the second death" (Re.21:8).

Thought 2: There is a second lesson for us in this point, the lesson of sin's wages. For the wages of sin is death. The execution of Jezebel and the wicked family of Ahab took place because of their terrible evil and the slaughter of God's prophets and people. They had sowed a life of wickedness and evil, therefore they suffered the judgment of God. The wages of their sin was death.

If we live a life of sin—wickedness and evil—then we will receive the wages of sin, which is death. We will reap what we sow. If we sow a life of unrighteousness, then we will stand before a Holy God and reap exactly what we have sown: an eternity of unrighteousness and judgment. The coming judgment of God upon all wickedness is the picture being painted in the execution of Ahab and Jezebel, and their wicked family. The hands of the family were bloody with the murder of innocent victims; consequently, they were doomed to suffer death in the bloody purge of Jehu. Listen to the warning of God's Holy Word:

> "For the Son of man shall come in the glory of his Father with his angels; and then he shall reward every man according to his works" (Mt.16:27).

> "For the wages of sin *is* death; but the gift of God *is* eternal life through Jesus Christ our Lord" (Ro.6:23).

> "For he that soweth to his flesh shall of the flesh reap corruption; but he that soweth to the Spirit shall of the Spirit reap life everlasting" (Ga.6:8).

> "For if the word spoken by angels was stedfast, and every transgression and disobedience received a just recompence of reward; How shall we escape, if we neglect so great salvation; which at the first began to be spoken by the Lord, and was confirmed unto us by them that heard *him*" (He.2:2-3).

> "And I saw a great white throne, and him that sat on it, from whose face the earth and the heaven fled away; and there was found no place for them. And I saw the dead, small and great, stand before God; and the books were opened: and another book was opened, which is *the book* of life: and the dead were judged out of those things which were written in the books, according to their works. And the sea gave up the dead which were in it; and death and hell delivered up the dead which were in them: and they were judged every man according to their works. And death and hell were cast into the lake of fire. This is the second death. And whosoever was not found written in the book of life was cast into the lake of fire" (Re.20:11-15).

> "And, behold, I come quickly; and my reward *is* with me, to give every man according as his work shall be" (Re.22:12).

> "Even as I have seen, they that plow iniquity, and sow wickedness, reap the same" (Jb.4:8).

> "Also unto thee, O Lord, *belongeth* mercy: for thou renderest to every man according to his work" (Ps.62:12).

> "He that soweth iniquity shall reap vanity: and the rod of his anger shall fail" (Pr.22:8).

> "I the LORD search the heart, *I* try the reins, even to give every man according to his ways, *and* according to the fruit of his doings" (Je.17:10).

3 (10:29-36) **Disobedience, Example of—Half-Heartedness, Example of—Law of God, Disobeying, Example of—Legacy, Evil, Example of—Kings, of Israel, Jehu**: in giving a summary of Jehu's reign, the author concludes that he was a sad, tragic disappointment to God. In summarizing his life, the author pulls no punches in describing how he failed God:

OUTLINE	SCRIPTURE	SCRIPTURE	OUTLINE

3. Jehu's evil reign: A legacy of disobedience to God
a. The evaluation of his life
  1) He failed to turn away from the sins of Jeroboam, 1 Ki.12:25-33; 14:16
	29 Howbeit *from* the sins of Jeroboam the son of Nebat, who made Israel to sin, Jehu departed not from after them, *to wit,* the golden calves that *were* in Bethel, and that *were* in Dan.	32 In those days the LORD began to cut Israel short: and Hazael smote them in all the coasts of Israel;	b. The judgment of God against Jehu & Israel
			
			  1) The size of Israel was significantly reduced by Hazael of Syria

2) He was commended for eliminating Baal worship: As a gracious blessing from God, he was promised a dynasty that would last for four generations	30 And the LORD said unto Jehu, Because thou hast done well in executing *that which is* right in mine eyes, *and* hast done unto the house of Ahab according to all that *was in* mine heart, thy children of the fourth *generation* shall sit on the throne of Israel.	33 From Jordan eastward, all the land of Gilead, the Gadites, and the Reubenites, and the Manassites, from Aroer, which is by the river Arnon, even Gilead and Bashan.	2) The king & nation lost all the territory of East Jordan c. The achievements & summary of Jehu's life 1) His reign: Recorded in the book, *The History of the Kings of Israel*
3) He was guilty of disobedience, of partial, half-hearted commitment: He was gripped by an extreme execution of justice & by political self-interest, 9:7; Ho.1:4-5	31 But Jehu took no heed to walk in the law of the LORD God of Israel with all his heart: for he departed not from the sins of Jeroboam, which made Israel to sin.	34 Now the rest of the acts of Jehu, and all that he did, and all his might, *are* they not written in the book of the chronicles of the kings of Israel? 35 And Jehu slept with his fathers: and they buried him in Samaria. And Jehoahaz his son reigned in his stead. 36 And the time that Jehu reigned over Israel in Samaria *was* twenty and eight years.	2) His death & burial: In the capital of Samaria 3) His successor: His son Jehoahaz 4) His years of rule: Twenty-eight

a. In the evaluation of Jehu's life, he tragically failed to turn away from the sins of Jeroboam (1 K.12:25-23; 14:16). Although he purged the land of the worship of Baal, he saw great benefit in keeping the false worship of the golden calves at Bethel and Dan, the worship instituted by Jeroboam. Remember that these had become a state religion, providing a substitute place in the northern kingdom where the people could worship instead of traveling to Jerusalem. Jehu feared, even as Jeroboam had feared, that if the people traveled to Jerusalem to worship, they might become attached to the southern kingdom. They might rebel against him wishing to reunite the nation under one king, the dynasty of David. For this reason, he refused to purge the land of the false worship of the golden calves instituted by Jeroboam.

However, the LORD did commend Jehu for eliminating Baal worship, and as a blessing for his faithfulness in this area, he was promised a dynasty that would last for four generations.

But tragically, Jehu was guilty of the most serious offence of all, that of disobedience. Despite his faithfulness in executing justice upon the wicked house of Ahab and their false Baal worship, his commitment was only partial and half-hearted (v.31). He was not careful to keep the Word of God. He allowed himself to become gripped by an extreme execution of justice due to political self-interest, an attempt to make sure that his throne was secure against any possible foe (9:7-10; Ho.1:4-5).

b. As a consequence, Jehu and Israel suffered the judgment of God. During his reign the size of Israel was significantly reduced. Syria, under the leadership of King Hazael, conquered all the territory of East Jordan. Throughout his reign, Syria dominated the northern kingdom, causing constant problems and consternation for Jehu.

c. Jehu's achievements and a summary of his reign are recorded in the book *The History of the Kings of Israel* (vv.34-36). After his death he was buried in the capital of Samaria and succeeded by his son Jehoahaz. His rule lasted for 28 years, but in the words of *The Expositor's Bible Commentary,* "Despite his comet-like beginning, spiritually speaking, Jehu was a falling star; so his reign is largely passed in silence."[1]

Thought 1. What a terrible legacy to leave this world: disobedient to God. Imagine a tombstone or a plaque hanging in a mausoleum with the words inscribed under a name, disobedient to God.

But what is even more tragic than imagining this scene is this fact: there are many people who are disobedient to God. For many of us live sinful lives, disobeying God's commandments. We live like we want, not like God says. We do our own thing in our own way when we want. What God says has little if any impact upon us. Far too often, we allow our hearts to rise up in rebellion against God. And we refuse to keep His commandments. Consequently the legacy being left by many of us is just this: disobedient to God. The inscription that God sees written across the tombstone of any person who has lived a sinful, wicked life is the most tragic words: he has been disobedient to God.

> **"For this ye know, that no whoremonger, nor unclean person, nor covetous man, who is an idolater, hath any inheritance in the kingdom of Christ and of God. Let no man deceive you with vain words: for because of these things cometh the wrath of God upon the children of disobedience"** (Ep.5:5-6).
>
> **"And to you who are troubled rest with us, when the Lord Jesus shall be revealed from heaven with his mighty angels, In flaming fire taking vengeance on them that know not God, and that obey not the gospel of our Lord Jesus Christ: Who shall be punished with everlasting destruction from the presence of the Lord, and from the glory of his power"** (2 Th.1:7-9).
>
> **"For if the word spoken by angels was stedfast, and every transgression and disobedience received a just recompence of reward; How shall we escape, if we neglect so great salvation; which at the first began to be spoken by the Lord, and was confirmed unto us by them that heard *him*"** (He.2:2-3).
>
> **"And a curse, if ye will not obey the commandments of the LORD your God, but turn aside out of the way which I command you this day, to go after other gods, which ye have not known"** (De.11:28).
>
> **"But if ye will not obey the voice of the LORD, but rebel against the commandment of the LORD, then shall the hand of the LORD be against you, as *it was* against your fathers"** (1 S.12:15).

---

[1] *Expositor's Bible Commentary*, p.212.

CHAPTER 11

G. The Evil Reign of Queen Athaliah in Judah: A Picture of the Desperate Need for a Just & Righteous Leader, 11:1-21

11:1-21; see 2 Chr.22:10–23:21

1. The murderous seizure of the throne by Athaliah: A picture of self-exaltation & murder
   a. Was Ahab & Jezebel's daughter
   b. Killed all the royal family
2. The rescue & secret rearing of David's descendant—the baby Joash—in the temple: A picture of godly training
   a. He was the only surviving descendant of David
   b. He was rescued by the godly woman Jehosheba, the wife of the High Priest Jehoiada, 2 Chr.22:11
   c. He was secretly hidden & reared in the temple during the entire six-year reign of Athaliah
3. The coup to overthrow Queen Athaliah & the crowning of the child Joash: A picture of renewal, of recommitment to the LORD
   a. The plot to secure the throne of David's heir was planned by the High Priest Jehoiada
      1) He secured the allegiance of the temple guards by showing them Joash
      2) He planned a brilliant strategy for the guards: To launch the coup during the changing of the guard—on the Sabbath when more people were present to witness the event
         • Those coming on duty were to guard the royal palace & the gates or entrances

         • Those going off duty were to guard the temple & the newly crowned king

         • Those guarding the boy king were to protect him with their lives, killing anyone who tried to approach him: He was the last surviving heir of David
   b. The overthrow of the throne was successful: The young boy Joash—David's only

And when Athaliah the mother of Ahaziah saw that her son was dead, she arose and destroyed all the seed royal.
2 But Jehosheba, the daughter of king Joram, sister of Ahaziah, took Joash the son of Ahaziah and stole him from among the king's sons *which were* slain; and they hid him, *even* him and his nurse, in the bedchamber from Athaliah, so that he was not slain.
3 And he was with her hid in the house of the LORD six years. And Athaliah did reign over the land.
4 And the seventh year Jehoiada sent and fetched the rulers over hundreds, with the captains and the guard, and brought them to him into the house of the LORD, and made a covenant with them, and took an oath of them in the house of the LORD, and showed them the king's son.
5 And he commanded them, saying, This is the thing that ye shall do; A third part of you that enter in on the sabbath shall even be keepers of the watch of the king's house;
6 And a third part *shall be* at the gate of Sur; and a third part at the gate behind the guard: so shall ye keep the watch of the house, that it be not broken down.
7 And two parts of all you that go forth on the sabbath, even they shall keep the watch of the house of the LORD about the king.
8 And ye shall compass the king round about, every man with his weapons in his hand: and he that cometh within the ranges, let him be slain: and be ye with the king as he goeth out and as he cometh in.
9 And the captains over the hundreds did according to all *things* that Jehoiada the priest

commanded: and they took every man his men that were to come in on the sabbath, with them that should go out on the sabbath, and came to Jehoiada the priest.
10 And to the captains over hundreds did the priest give king David's spears and shields, that *were* in the temple of the LORD.
11 And the guard stood, every man with his weapons in his hand, round about the king, from the right corner of the temple to the left corner of the temple, *along* by the altar and the temple.
12 And he brought forth the king's son, and put the crown upon him, and *gave him* the testimony; and they made him king, and anointed him; and they clapped their hands, and said, God save the king.
13 And when Athaliah heard the noise of the guard *and* of the people, she came to the people into the temple of the LORD.
14 And when she looked, behold, the king stood by a pillar, as the manner *was,* and the princes and the trumpeters by the king, and all the people of the land rejoiced, and blew with trumpets: and Athaliah rent her clothes, and cried, Treason, Treason.
15 But Jehoiada the priest commanded the captains of the hundreds, the officers of the host, and said unto them, Have her forth without the ranges: and him that followeth her kill with the sword. For the priest had said, Let her not be slain in the house of the LORD.
16 And they laid hands on her; and she went by the way by the which the horses came into the king's house: and there was she slain.
17 And Jehoiada made a covenant between the LORD and the king and the people that they should be the LORD'S people; between the king also and the people.
18 And all the people of the land went into the house of Baal, and brake it down; his altars and his images brake they in pieces thoroughly, and slew Mattan the priest of

surviving heir—was crowned king of Judah
      1) The temple guard did just as Jehoiada ordered

         • He equipped each commander with David's ceremonial spears & shields

         • He ordered each guard to rush to his station: To encircle the young king & form a line that stretched from the south to the north side of the temple
      2) The young boy Joash was then brought out & presented to all the worshippers
         • He was crowned & given a copy of God's law
         • He was anointed & proclaimed king

      3) The people celebrated the coronation
   c. The queen was executed
      1) She heard the noise of the celebration & went to the temple
      2) She saw the young boy king standing by a particular pillar—the place where kings stood
      3) She heard the enormously loud celebration
      4) She was gripped by despair & began to shout out, "Treason! Treason!"
      5) She was immediately arrested: Jehoiada ordered the commanders to seize & execute her outside the temple, along with anyone else who followed her

      6) She was executed

   d. The young king & the people were led by Jehoiada to make a spiritual renewal
      1) They made a covenant to obey God & made another covenant to support the king
      2) They destroyed the temple & worship of Baal (no doubt built by Athaliah): Smashed the altars & idols & executed Mattan, the priest of Baal

3) They posted guards at the temple of the LORD to protect against retaliation by Baal worshippers	Baal before the altars. And the priest appointed pointed officers over the house of the LORD.	gate of the guard to the king's house. And he sat on the throne of the kings.	officials took their places in ordered fashion?
4) They organized & conducted an exciting, dynamic procession to the royal palace	19 And he took the rulers over hundreds, and the captains, and the guard, and all the people of the land; and they brought down the king from the house of the LORD, and came by the way of the	20 And all the people of the land rejoiced, and the city was in quiet: and they slew Athaliah with the sword *beside* the king's house.	• The people followed 5) They placed the king on the royal throne 6) They were flooded with joy & rejoicing
• Jehoiada led the march			e. The city & land were blessed by God: Given peace
• The young king, his bodyguard, & the royal		21 Seven years old *was* Jehoash when he began to reign.	f. The young king was seven years old when crowned

DIVISION II

THE MINISTRY AND MIRACLES OF ELISHA: A DRAMATIC DEMONSTRATION OF GOD'S POWER AND CARE FOR HIS PEOPLE, 4:1–13:25

G. The Evil Reign of Queen Athaliah in Judah: A Picture of the Desperate Need for a Just and Righteous Leader, 11:1-21

(11:1-21) **Introduction—Society, Needs of, Just and Righteous Leaders—Leaders, Corrupt, Results—Society, Corrupt, Caused by**: one of the greatest needs within any society is for just and righteous leaders, men and women who will govern in fairness and honesty. For when leaders lie, steal, cheat, and deceive, when they are prideful, arrogant, selfish, and dictatorial—they fail their followers. A corrupt or unjust leader serves himself, not his people. His people suffer, never receiving what they should nor growing into what they could become. Whether a football team, a social club, a classroom of students, a business, or a nation—whatever the group or body of people—the body or group never achieves what it could under righteous leadership. A corrupt leader keeps a group from reaching its full potential and its highest achievement.

The need for a just and righteous leader is the lesson learned from this present Scripture. Remember that Israel's King Jehu had just carried out a bloody purge throughout the nation. In his purge of the Northern Kingdom, he also killed the king of Judah, Ahaziah (9:27-28). When Ahaziah was killed, a woman took the throne of Judah for the first and only time in the history of the Northern and Southern Kingdoms. This is the story of that woman, Queen Athaliah, the mother of Ahaziah. Her six-year reign demonstrated the desperate need of the nation for a just, righteous leader. This is: *The Evil Reign of Queen Athaliah in Judah: A Picture of the Desperate Need for a Just and Righteous Leader,* 11:1-21.

1. The murderous seizure of the throne by Athaliah: a picture of self-exaltation and murder (v.1).
2. The rescue and secret rearing of David's descendant—the baby Joash—in the temple: a picture of godly training (vv.2-3).
3. The coup to overthrow Queen Athaliah and the crowning of the child Joash: a picture of renewal, of recommitment to the LORD (vv.4-21).

1 (11:1) **Murder, Example of—Cruelty, Example of—Self-Exaltation, Example of—Athaliah, Queen of Judah—Queens, of Judah, Listed**: when Queen Mother Athaliah received the report that her son Ahaziah had been killed by Jehu, she immediately made her move to claim the kingdom of Israel for herself. Note how: without hesitation she killed all the heirs to the throne, the entire royal family, and assumed power. She actually murdered her own grandchildren. Filled with a spirit of worldly ambition, Athaliah hungered for the power to rule. In a murderous rampage, she eliminated all competitors to the throne.

Remember that Athaliah was the daughter of wicked Ahab and his wife, the infamous Jezebel. And remember the bloody history that surrounded the rule of her family. Her husband Jehoram had killed all of his brothers in order to consolidate his power upon the throne (2 Chr.21:4). Later Athaliah witnessed the Arabs killing all of her sons except Ahaziah (2 Chr.22:1). Then she witnessed Jehu killing not only Ahaziah, but all of his relatives (2 K.10:13; 2 Chr.22:8-9). Intrigue and murder had surrounded Queen Athaliah all of her life. Beginning when she was a small child living in the palace of Ahab and Jezebel and continuing on through the murder of her husband and sons. She had witnessed one murder after another. Seldom has so much royal blood been shed within one dynasty. As much as any royal dynasty that has ever ruled, the family of Ahab stands guilty of self-exaltation and murder.

OUTLINE	SCRIPTURE
1. The murderous seizure of the throne by Athaliah: A picture of self-exaltation & murder	And when Athaliah the mother of Ahaziah saw that her son was dead, she arose and destroyed all the seed royal.
a. Was Ahab & Jezebel's daughter	
b. Killed all the royal family	

Thought 1. There are two very distinct lessons for us in this point:

(1) Self-exaltation is a terrible evil, a destructive sin. When we exalt ourselves, we put others down. By elevating ourselves above others, we are declaring that we are better than they, more deserving of praise and honor and

attention, more deserving of this world's goods and wealth. We are saying that other people are less than we are—less educated, less wealthy, less intellectual, and so on—therefore we deserve far more than the inferior of this world. A person who exalts himself above others is puffed up with pride and a self-centeredness that expects the world to focus upon him.

It is often self-exaltation that leads to wickedness. After all, if I am above others, then I deserve more, and I can take more. It is self-exaltation that leads to the lust for power and often creates dictatorial leadership. Self-exaltation—a puffed up pride—can lead a person to lie, steal, cheat, murder, and commit a host of other terrible evils in order to secure positions of authority and power. In the workplace, if a person feels superior to those who work around him, he will sometimes do anything to secure a higher position or greater authority over them. He will lie, start rumors, steal, or finagle the books; he will do anything to get more money, a higher position, or greater authority.

Within society, we all see people who exalt themselves over others: within families and among relatives, within groups of friends and among acquaintances, at school, in the military, within the halls of government and among the leaders of the world—especially among the harsh dictators of the world. But God warns us: he who exalts himself will be abased, lowered, and face the judgment of God. Listen to what God's Holy Word says:

"And whosoever shall exalt himself shall be abased; and he that shall humble himself shall be exalted" (Mt.23:12).

"He loveth transgression that loveth strife: *and* **he that exalteth his gate seeketh destruction" (Pr.17:19).**

"For thou hast said in thine heart, I will ascend into heaven, I will exalt my throne above the stars of God: I will sit also upon the mount of the congregation, in the sides of the north: I will ascend above the heights of the clouds; I will be like the most High. Yet thou shalt be brought down to hell, to the sides of the pit" (Is.14:13-15).

"Because ye have said, We have made a covenant with death, and with hell are we at agreement; when the overflowing scourge shall pass through, it shall not come unto us: for we have made lies our refuge, and under falsehood have we hid ourselves... And your covenant with death shall be disannulled, and your agreement with hell shall not stand; when the overflowing scourge shall pass through, then ye shall be trodden down by it" (Is.28:15, 18).

"Therefore hear now this, *thou that art* **given to pleasures, that dwellest carelessly, that sayest in thine heart, I** *am,* **and none else beside me; I shall not sit** *as* **a widow, neither shall I know the loss of children: But these two** *things* **shall come to thee in a moment in one day, the loss of children, and widowhood: they shall come upon thee in their perfection for the multitude of thy sorceries,** *and* **for the great abundance of thine enchantments. For thou hast trusted in thy wickedness: thou hast said, None seeth me. Thy wisdom and thy knowledge, it hath perverted thee; and thou hast said in thine heart, I** *am,* **and none else beside me. Therefore shall evil come upon thee; thou shalt not know from whence it riseth: and mischief shall fall upon thee; thou shalt not be able to put if off: and desolation shall come upon thee suddenly,** *which* **thou shalt not know" (Is.47:8-11).**

"Son of man, say unto the prince of Tyrus, Thus saith the Lord GOD; Because thine heart *is* **lifted up, and thou hast said, I** *am* **a God, I sit** *in* **the seat of God, in the midst of the seas; yet thou** *art* **a man, and not God, though thou set thine heart as the heart of God...Therefore thus saith the Lord GOD; Because thou hast set thine heart as the heart of God; Behold, therefore I will bring strangers upon thee, the terrible of the nations: and they shall draw their swords against the beauty of thy wisdom, and they shall defile thy brightness. They shall bring thee down to the pit, and thou shalt die the deaths of** *them that are* **slain in the midst of the seas" (Eze.28:2, 6-8).**

"The pride of thine heart hath deceived thee, thou that dwellest in the clefts of the rock, whose habitation *is* **high; that saith in his heart, Who shall bring me down to the ground? Though thou exalt** *thyself* **as the eagle, and though thou set thy nest among the stars, thence will I bring thee down, saith the LORD" (Ob.3-4).**

(2) Murder is the ultimate evil against a person, for it steals his life away—and the victim *is* no more. Never again will the victim be upon this earth among us. Never again will the victim's family or friends know the presence, the warmth, the love, the care, nor any other experience of the person whose life has been brutally snatched away. God warns the murderer: he will face the severe condemnation of God.

"For the wrath of God is revealed from heaven against all ungodliness and unrighteousness of men, who hold the truth in unrighteousness...Being filled with all unrighteousness, fornication, wickedness, covetousness, maliciousness; full of envy, murder, debate, deceit, malignity; whisperers...Who knowing the judgment of God, that they which commit such things are worthy of death, not only do the same, but have pleasure in them that do them" (Ro.1:18, 29, 32).

"Envyings, murders, drunkenness, revellings, and such like: of the which I tell you before, as I have also told *you* **in time past, that they which do such things shall not inherit the kingdom of God" (Ga.5:21).**

"Whosoever hateth his brother is a murderer: and ye know that no murderer hath eternal life abiding in him" (1 Jn.3:15).

"But the fearful, and unbelieving, and the abominable, and murderers, and whoremongers, and sorcerers, and idolaters, and all liars, shall have their part in the lake which burneth with fire and brimstone: which is the second death" (Re.21:8).

2 (11:2-3) **Training, Godly—Teaching, Duty—Joash, Childhood of—Jehosheba, Rescued and Hid Joash**: one son of the royal family—the baby Joash—did escape the murderous rampage of Queen Athaliah. As this dramatic story unfolds, keep in mind that the child Joash is the only surviving descendant of David. In saving his life, God's power is seen moving events in order to fulfill His promise to David, that his family would rule over God's people forever. Of course, this was a promise that was ultimately fulfilled in the Son of God Himself, the Lord Jesus Christ.

Rescuing the child Joash was a godly woman named Jehosheba, who was the wife of the High Priest Jehoiada (2 Chr.22:11). Note that she was the daughter of King Jehoram and the sister of King Ahaziah. Being a princess of royal blood, she knew from the very beginning about Queen Athaliah's murderous rampage. She also had immediate access to the royal palace and was able to secretly grab the baby Joash to save his life. Knowing her godly heart, God used her to save the royal line of David, that the promise of the coming Savior and King might be fulfilled. Being the wife of the High Priest Jehoiada, she was able to secretly hide the child in the temple. Thus the baby Joash was reared in the temple during the entire six-year reign of Athaliah (v.3). For six years the secret of the child's survival was successfully guarded.

OUTLINE	SCRIPTURE	SCRIPTURE	OUTLINE
2. The rescue & secret rearing of David's descendant—the baby Joash—in the temple: A picture of godly training a. He was the only surviving descendant of David b. He was rescued by the godly	2 But Jehosheba, the daughter of king Joram, sister of Ahaziah, took Joash the son of Ahaziah and stole him from among the king's sons *which were* slain; and they hid him, *even* him and his	nurse, in the bedchamber from Athaliah, so that he was not slain. 3 And he was with her hid in the house of the LORD six years. And Athaliah did reign over the land.	woman Jehosheba, the wife of the High Priest Jehoiada, 2 Chr.22:11 c. He was secretly hidden & reared in the temple during the entire six-year reign of Athaliah

Thought 1. Just as the child Samuel had years earlier been reared in the temple by the priest Eli, so the child Joash was now being reared in the temple by the High Priest Jehoiada. A unique privilege was being given the young child, that of godly training. No training is more important than that of being instructed in godliness. For only a godly person will experience the fullness of life and inherit eternal life. In God is found perfection, the fullness of every good quality and experience of life. Therefore, the human heart must seek godliness, to be like God, perfect in everything we do. In seeking love, we want the fullness and perfection of love. We want to experience as much love as we can. So it is with joy and peace. We want to experience the fullness and perfection of joy and peace. In seeking inner strength and power—the strength and power to conquer all the struggles and trials of this life—we want to experience as much of God's perfect strength and power as we can.

Therefore, any of us would be foolish—very foolish—not to seek after godliness. For the most important training in all the world is godly training. We must train our children to walk after the LORD, seeking to be conformed to His godly image. For only God can fill the human heart with the fullness of life and give the assurance of living eternally with Him. Listen to what God's Holy Word says about godly teaching and training.

"So when they had dined, Jesus saith to Simon Peter, Simon, *son* of Jonas, lovest thou me more than these? He saith unto him, Yea, Lord; thou knowest that I love thee. He saith unto him, Feed my lambs" (Jn.21:15).

"Having therefore these promises, dearly beloved, let us cleanse ourselves from all filthiness of the flesh and spirit, perfecting holiness in the fear of God" (2 Co.7:1).

"For bodily exercise profiteth little: but godliness is profitable unto all things, having promise of the life that now is, and of that which is to come" (1 Ti.4:8).

"But godliness with contentment is great gain" (1 Ti.6:6).

"But thou, O man of God, flee these things; and follow after righteousness, godliness, faith, love, patience, meekness. Fight the good fight of faith, lay hold on eternal life, whereunto thou art also called, and hast professed a good profession before many witnesses" (1 Ti.6:11-12).

"Study to show thyself approved unto God, a workman that needeth not to be ashamed, rightly dividing the word of truth" (2 Ti.2:15).

"Teaching us that, denying ungodliness and worldly lusts, we should live soberly, righteously, and godly, in this present world; Looking for that blessed hope, and the glorious appearing of the great God and our Saviour Jesus Christ" (Tit.2:12-13).

"*This is* a faithful saying, and these things I will that thou affirm constantly, that they which have believed in God might be careful to maintain good works. These things are good and profitable unto men" (Tit.3:8).

"Follow peace with all *men*, and holiness, without which no man shall see the Lord" (He.12:14).

"And that ye may teach the children of Israel all the statutes which the LORD hath spoken unto them by the hand of Moses" (Le.10:11).

"Only take heed to thyself, and keep thy soul diligently, lest thou forget the things which thine eyes have seen, and lest they depart from thy heart all the days of thy life: but teach them thy sons, and thy sons' sons" (De.4:9).

"Thou shalt keep therefore his statutes, and his commandments, which I command thee this day, that it may go well with thee, and with thy children after thee, and that thou mayest prolong *thy* days upon the earth, which the LORD thy God giveth thee, for ever" (De.4:40).

"And these words, which I command thee this day, shall be in thine heart: And thou shalt teach them diligently unto thy children, and shalt talk of them when thou sittest in thine house, and when thou walkest by the way, and when thou liest down, and when thou risest up" (De.6:6-7).

"For he established a testimony in Jacob, and appointed a law in Israel, which he commanded our fathers, that they should make them known to their children: That the generation to come might know *them, even* the children *which* should be born; *who* should arise and declare *them* to their children: That they might set their hope in God, and not forget the works of God, but keep his commandments" (Ps.78:5-7).

"Train up a child in the way he should go: and when he is old, he will not depart from it" (Pr.22:6).

"Say ye to the righteous, that *it shall be* well *with him:* for they shall eat the fruit of their doings" (Is.3:10).

"Whom shall he teach knowledge? and whom shall he make to understand doctrine? *them that are* weaned from the milk, *and* drawn from the breasts" (Is.28:9).

"And they shall teach my people *the difference* between the holy and profane, and cause them to discern between the unclean and the clean" (Eze.44:23).

3 (11:4-21) **Recommitment, Example of—Renewal, Example of—Rededication, Example of—Covenant, Renewed, by Jehoiada and Joash—Joash, Crowned King of Judah—Judah, Kings of, Listed—Athaliah, Queen, Overthrown—Queen, of Judah, Athaliah**: in the seventh year of Queen Athaliah's reign she was overthrown, and the child Joash was crowned king. He was about eight years old when he was placed upon the throne. The insurrection launched against the murderous queen is a dramatic, suspenseful picture:

OUTLINE	SCRIPTURE	SCRIPTURE	OUTLINE
3. **The coup to overthrow Queen Athaliah & the crowning of the child Joash: A picture of renewal, of recommitment to the LORD**	4 And the seventh year Jehoiada sent and fetched the rulers over hundreds, with the captains and the guard, and brought them to him into the house of the LORD, and made a covenant with them, and took an oath of them in the house of the LORD, and showed them the king's son.	hundreds did the priest give king David's spears and shields, that *were* in the temple of the LORD.	commander with David's ceremonial spears & shields
a. The plot to secure the throne of David's heir was planned by the High Priest Jehoiada		11 And the guard stood, every man with his weapons in his hand, round about the king, from the right corner of the temple to the left corner of the temple, *along* by the altar and the temple.	• He ordered each guard to rush to his station: To encircle the young king & form a line that stretched from the south to the north side of the temple
1) He secured the allegiance of the temple guards by showing them Joash			
2) He planned a brilliant strategy for the guards: To launch the coup during the changing of the guard—on the Sabbath when more people were present to witness the event	5 And he commanded them, saying, This is the thing that ye shall do; A third part of you that enter in on the sabbath shall even be keepers of the watch of the king's house;	12 And he brought forth the king's son, and put the crown upon him, and *gave him* the testimony; and they made him king, and anointed him; and they clapped their hands, and said, God save the king.	2) The young boy Joash was then brought out & presented to all the worshippers • He was crowned & given a copy of God's law • He was anointed & proclaimed king
• Those coming on duty were to guard the royal palace & the gates or entrances	6 And a third part *shall be* at the gate of Sur; and a third part at the gate behind the guard: so shall ye keep the watch of the house, that it be not broken down.	13 And when Athaliah heard the noise of the guard *and* of the people, she came to the people into the temple of the LORD.	3) The people celebrated the coronation c. The queen was executed 1) She heard the noise of the celebration & went to the temple
• Those going off duty were to guard the temple & the newly crowned king	7 And two parts of all you that go forth on the sabbath, even they shall keep the watch of the house of the LORD about the king.	14 And when she looked, behold, the king stood by a pillar, as the manner *was,* and the princes and the trumpeters by the king, and all the people of the land rejoiced,	2) She saw the young boy king standing by a particular pillar—the place where kings stood
• Those guarding the boy king were to protect him with their lives, killing anyone who tried to approach him: He was the last surviving heir of David	8 And ye shall compass the king round about, every man with his weapons in his hand: and he that cometh within the ranges, let him be slain: and be ye with the king as he goeth out and as he cometh in.	and blew with trumpets: and Athaliah rent her clothes, and cried, Treason, Treason.	3) She heard the enormously loud celebration 4) She was gripped by despair & began to shout out, "Treason! Treason!"
b. The overthrow of the throne was successful: The young boy Joash—David's only surviving heir—was crowned king of Judah	9 And the captains over the hundreds did according to all *things* that Jehoiada the priest commanded: and they took every man his men that were to come in on the sabbath, with them that should go out on the sabbath, and came to Jehoiada the priest.	15 But Jehoiada the priest commanded the captains of the hundreds, the officers of the host, and said unto them, Have her forth without the ranges: and him that followeth her kill with the sword. For the priest had said, Let her not be slain in the house of the LORD.	5) She was immediately arrested: Jehoiada ordered the commanders to seize & execute her outside the temple, along with anyone else who followed her
1) The temple guard did just as Jehoiada ordered			
• He equipped each	10 And to the captains over	16 And they laid hands on her; and she went by the way by the which the horses came	6) She was executed

OUTLINE	SCRIPTURE	SCRIPTURE	OUTLINE
d. The young king & the people were led by Jehoiada to make a spiritual renewal 1) They made a covenant to obey God & made another covenant to support the king 2) They destroyed the temple & worship of Baal (no doubt built by Athaliah): Smashed the altars & idols & executed Mattan, the priest of Baal 3) They posted guards at the temple of the LORD to protect against retaliation by Baal worshippers	into the king's house: and there was she slain. 17 And Jehoiada made a covenant between the LORD and the king and the people that they should be the LORD'S people; between the king also and the people. 18 And all the people of the land went into the house of Baal, and brake it down; his altars and his images brake they in pieces thoroughly, and slew Mattan the priest of Baal before the altars. And the priest appointed pointed officers over the house of the LORD.	19 And he took the rulers over hundreds, and the captains, and the guard, and all the people of the land; and they brought down the king from the house of the LORD, and came by the way of the gate of the guard to the king's house. And he sat on the throne of the kings. 20 And all the people of the land rejoiced, and the city was in quiet: and they slew Athaliah with the sword be-side the king's house. 21 Seven years old was Jehoash when he began to reign.	4) They organized & conducted an exciting, dynamic procession to the royal palace • Jehoiada led the march • The young king, his bodyguard, & the royal officials took their places in ordered fashion? • The people followed 5) They placed the king on the royal throne 6) They were flooded with joy & rejoicing e. The city & land were blessed by God: Given peace f. The young king was seven years old when crowned

a. The plot to secure the throne for David's only surviving heir was planned by the High Priest Jehoiada (vv.4-8). First, he secured the allegiance of the temple guards by making them swear an oath of loyalty to the dynasty. Actually, he made them swear the oath in the temple itself, which gave it even more sacred meaning. Once they had sworn their allegiance, Jehoiada showed them the young descendant of David, the true heir to the throne.

Second, Jehoiada planned a brilliant strategy for the guards to overthrow Queen Athaliah and to place the young boy Joash upon the throne (vv.5-8). The coup was to be launched during the changing of the guard on the Sabbath. This meant that the maximum number of soldiers would be available to carry out the revolution. In addition, more people would be gathered in the temple for worship who would witness the event and rally their support behind the young prince Joash. Note the strategy laid out by the High Priest:

⇒ The soldiers coming on duty were to guard the royal palace and the gates or entrances into the palace and temple (v.6).

⇒ The soldiers going off duty were to guard the temple and the newly crowned king (v.7).

⇒ The soldiers guarding the boy king were to protect him with their lives, killing anyone who threatened or tried to approach him.

b. The revolution was successful: the young boy Joash, David's only surviving heir, was crowned king of Judah (vv.9-12). The temple guards did just as the High Priest Jehoiada had ordered. For he had equipped each guard with David's ceremonial spears and shields that had been stored in the temple of the LORD, and he had ordered each guard to rush to his station. They immediately encircled the young king and formed a line that stretched from the south to the north side of the temple, guarding all the entrances. All the guards standing in formation with the ceremonial shields and spears naturally attracted the attention of the gathered crowd.

Suddenly the young boy Joash was brought out and presented to all the worshippers, with the announcement that he was a true descendant of David, the rightful heir to the throne of Judah (v.12). Once the announcement had been made, the High Priest turned to the young prince and laid the crown upon his head. Then he presented the young king with a copy of God's law and anointed him. After the anointing, Jehoiada turned to the throng of people who had gathered in the temple and proclaimed young Joash as the rightful king of the nation. Celebrating the coronation, the people clapped their hands and shouted out, "God save the king!" or "Long live the king!"

c. Only one step was left to secure the throne: the execution of Queen Athaliah (vv.13-16). Hearing the noise of the loud celebration, the queen rushed to the temple. As she entered the temple, she saw the young boy king standing by the particular pillar where the kings always stood. This was the place of authority that was reserved for the rulers of the nation. She further saw the officers and trumpeters surrounding the boy king and heard the trumpets blaring above the shouts of the people. No doubt stunned by the sight and gripped with terror, she tore her robes in an act of despair and began shouting, "Treason! Treason!"

In reality, it was not the High Priest or the young boy who were committing treason. Rather, it was Athaliah who had committed treason when she slaughtered her own grandsons, all the descendants of David who were the rightful heirs to the throne. Remember, she had killed all of them except the young child king who now stood before her.

Arresting Athaliah immediately, the High Priest Jehoiada ordered commanders to execute her outside the temple, along with anyone else who followed her. Obeying the orders, some of the guards seized and led her out the back gate of the temple courtyard, the one used for horses led to the royal stables.

d. The High Priest Jehoiada, having successfully placed the young king upon the throne, immediately began to lay a solid foundation for the new government. He knew that only one foundation could secure the government and assure its survival: the foundation of God Himself. A recommitment was needed, a recommitment of the people to God and a recommitment of the king and the people to one another. Thus, the High Priest Jehoiada led the young king and the people of the nation to make a spiritual renewal to the LORD and to one another (vv.17-20). First, the young king and the people made a covenant to obey God, to worship and serve Him alone and to keep all His commandments (Ex.19:5-6; 24:3-8; De.4:1-20; 27:9-10; Jos.24:1-27; also see 2 Chr.15:12).

Second, the young king and people made a covenant to support one another (v.17). No doubt, this covenant included God's promises to David, that his dynasty would be established forever. A recommitment of the people to support the descendants and dynasty of David was desperately needed at this time. For Queen Athaliah had attempted to wipe out the line of David, rejecting the LORD and His promises given to the nation through David's descendants. But the covenant between king and people included far more than just the Davidic promises: it also included the responsibilities spelled out by God's Word given through Moses (De.17:14-20; 1 K.2:1-4). In summary, the king was to rule in justice, governing by the law and protecting the people and their property. In return, the people were to obey the laws of the land and give their allegiance to the king.

After the covenant ceremony had been conducted, the people marched to the temple of Baal, which had probably been built by Athaliah. Once there, they smashed the altars and idols and executed Mattan, the priest of Baal. Then they posted guards at the temple of the LORD to protect against retaliation by Baal worshippers (v.18).

After carrying out this purge of false worship, the priest Jehoiada conducted an enthusiastic processional and marched to the royal palace (v.19). Jehoiada led the march, with the young king, his royal bodyguard, and the royal officials taking their place in ordered fashion behind him. The joyous people followed after. On reaching the palace, the king took his place upon the royal throne. It was a great day of joy and rejoicing for the people throughout the land (v.20).

e. The city and land were blessed by God for some time. God brought a very special peace to the land. Note why: because the murderous Queen Athaliah had been removed from power.

f. The young boy Joash was seven years old, almost eight, when he was crowned (v.21).

Thought 1. This is a much-needed lesson: we must constantly renew, recommit ourselves to the LORD and to the support of one another. Rulers must have support to survive. And people within a community must support one another in order to keep peace within their community. If we are divided and struggling against each other, the community collapses into lawlessness and abuse of neighbor against neighbor. Making a constant renewal to support one another is the only way to keep peace among us and among the nations of the world.

But just as important is making a renewal, a recommitment to God. If we are not committed to the LORD, our hearts are uneasy, lacking a deep sense of purpose, meaning, and significance. Without God, the depth and fullness of life are missing; there is a lack of satisfaction and fulfillment in life. Why? Because the human heart was made for God, to know and fellowship and share with Him day by day. If we are not maintaining a relationship with God, there is no victory, no conquering power to overcome the trials and temptations of life. In order to experience the fullness of joy and the power to conquer the difficult hardships and tragic trials of life, a close relationship with the LORD must be maintained. For this reason we must constantly renew and recommit our lives to God. Listen to the challenge of God's Holy Word:

"And he said to *them* all, If any *man* will come after me, let him deny himself, and take up his cross daily, and follow me" (Lu.9:23).

"The thief cometh not, but for to steal, and to kill, and to destroy: I am come that they might have life, and that they might have *it* more abundantly" (Jn.10:10).

"I beseech you therefore, brethren, by the mercies of God, that ye present your bodies a living sacrifice, holy, acceptable unto God, *which is* your reasonable service. And be not conformed to this world: but be ye transformed by the renewing of your mind, that ye may prove what is that good, and acceptable, and perfect, will of God" (Ro.12:1-2).

"There hath no temptation taken you but such as is common to man: but God *is* faithful, who will not suffer you to be tempted above that ye are able; but will with the temptation also make a way to escape, that ye may be able to bear *it*" (1 Co.10:13).

"For which cause we faint not; but though our outward man perish, yet the inward *man* is renewed day by day. For our light affliction, which is but for a moment, worketh for us a far more exceeding *and* eternal weight of glory; While we look not at the things which are seen, but at the things which are not seen: for the things which are seen *are* temporal; but the things which are not seen *are* eternal" (2 Co.4:16-18).

"I am crucified with Christ: nevertheless I live; yet not I, but Christ liveth in me: and the life which I now live in the flesh I live by the faith of the Son of God, who loved me, and gave himself for me" (Ga.2:20).

"Now unto him that is able to do exceeding abundantly above all that we ask or think, according to the power that worketh in us" (Ep.3:20).

"That ye put off concerning the former conversation [behavior, conduct] the old man, which is corrupt according to the deceitful lusts; And be renewed in the spirit of your mind; And that ye put on the new man, which after God is created in righteousness and true holiness" (Ep.4:22-24).

"And have put on the new *man,* which is renewed in knowledge after the image of him that created him" (Co.3:10).

"If my people, which are called by my name, shall humble themselves, and pray, and seek my face, and turn from their wicked ways; then will I hear from heaven, and will forgive their sin, and will heal their land" (2 Chr.7:14).

"Create in me a clean heart, O God; and renew a right spirit within me" (Ps.51:10).

"Blessed *are* they that keep his testimonies, *and that* seek him with the whole heart" (Ps.119:2).

"Trust in the LORD with all thine heart; and lean not unto thine own understanding. In all thy ways acknowledge him, and he shall direct thy paths" (Pr.3:5-6).

"My son, give me thine heart, and let thine eyes observe my ways" (Pr.23:26).

"But they that wait upon the LORD shall renew *their* strength; they shall mount up with wings as eagles; they shall run, and not be weary; *and* they shall walk, and not faint" (Is.40:31).

CHAPTER 12

H. The Good Reign of Jehoash (Joash) in Judah: A Strong & Righteous Beginning but a Weak & Sinful Ending, 12:1-21

12:1-21; see 2 Chr.14:1-14; 23-27

1. The strong & righteous beginning of Joash's reign: Following a godly example
a. His reign: Lasted 40 years
b. His mother: Was Zibiah

c. His strength & righteousness: Lasted as long as he had the example & counsel of Jehoiada the priest

d. His one serious flaw, a half-hearted commitment: Did not destroy the high places

e. His most important act as king: The restoration of Solomon's temple (was now 140 years old & had even been vandalized, 2 Chr.24:7)
   1) Joash ordered that certain monies be collected for the repairs

   2) Joash placed the priests in charge of the offerings & the building project

   3) Joash waited years for them to complete the project: They disappointedly failed
      • He summoned Jehoiada & the other priests to the royal court—during the 23rd year of his reign when he was about 30 years old, 11:21
      • He questioned their irresponsible failure

   4) Joash dismissed them from the project & personally took over the fund-raising
   5) Joash ordered Jehoiada to set a chest at the entrance of the temple where the people could give their offerings for the temple repairs
      • The collection box was protected by guards

In the seventh year of Jehu Jehoash began to reign; and forty years reigned he in Jerusalem. And his mother's name *was* Zibiah of Beer-sheba.
2 And Jehoash did *that which was* right in the sight of the LORD all his days wherein Jehoiada the priest instructed him.
3 But the high places were not taken away: the people still sacrificed and burnt incense in the high places.
4 And Jehoash said to the priests, All the money of the dedicated things that is brought into the house of the LORD, *even* the money of every one that passeth *the account,* the money that every man is set at, *and* all the money that cometh into any man's heart to bring into the house of the LORD,
5 Let the priests take *it* to them, every man of his acquaintance: and let them repair the breaches of the house, wheresoever any breach shall be found.
6 But it was *so, that* in the three and twentieth year of king Jehoash the priests had not repaired the breaches of the house.
7 Then king Jehoash called for Jehoiada the priest, and the *other* priests, and said unto them, Why repair ye not the breaches of the house? now therefore receive no *more* money of your acquaintance, but deliver it for the breaches of the house.
8 And the priests consented to receive no *more* money of the people, neither to repair the breaches of the house.
9 But Jehoiada the priest took a chest, and bored a hole in the lid of it, and set it beside the altar, on the right side as one cometh into the house of the LORD: and the priests that kept the door put therein all the money *that was* brought into the house of the

LORD.
10 And it was *so,* when they saw that *there was* much money in the chest, that the king's scribe and the High Priest came up, and they put up in bags, and told the money that was found in the house of the LORD.
11 And they gave the money, being told, into the hands of them that did the work, that had the oversight of the house of the LORD: and they laid it out to the carpenters and builders, that wrought upon the house of the LORD,
12 And to masons, and hewers of stone, and to buy timber and hewed stone to repair the breaches of the house of the LORD, and for all that was laid out for the house to repair *it.*
13 Howbeit there were not made for the house of the LORD bowls of silver, snuffers, basons, trumpets, any vessels of gold, or vessels of silver, of the money *that was* brought into the house of the LORD:
14 But they gave that to the workmen, and repaired therewith the house of the LORD.
15 Moreover they reckoned not with the men, into whose hand they delivered the money to be bestowed on workmen: for they dealt faithfully.
16 The trespass money and sin money was not brought into the house of the LORD: it was the priests'.
17 Then Hazael king of Syria went up, and fought against Gath, and took it: and Hazael set his face to go up to Jerusalem.
18 And Jehoash king of Judah took all the hallowed things that Jehoshaphat, and Jehoram, and Ahaziah, his fathers, kings of Judah, had dedicated, and his own hallowed things, and all the gold *that was* found in the treasures of the house of the LORD, and in the king's house, and sent *it* to Hazael king of Syria: and he went away from Jerusalem.
19 And the rest of the acts of Joash, and all that he did, *are* they not written in the book of the chronicles of the kings

• The money was counted by two people—the royal secretary & the High Priest—each time the box was filled

6) Joash appointed building supervisors & had the money given to them
   • They paid all labor costs

   • They purchased all building materials
   • They met all other costs involved in restoring the temple

   • They were to focus upon repairs on the temple itself, not on the furnishings or sacred utensils: These were to be replaced only after the temple structure had been repaired, 2 Chr.24:14
   • They were first to use the money to pay labor costs & to repair the temple

   • They proved so honest & trustworthy that an accounting of the money was not even required

7) Joash decreed that all money from the guilt offerings & sin offerings be given to support the priests, not the restoration project
2. The weak, sinful ending of Joash's reign: Backsliding
a. His war with Syria

b. His backslidden state: He turned away from his dedication
   1) He used the temple treasures to pay the ransom demanded by Syria, treasures that he had earlier dedicated to the LORD, 12:4-16
   2) He engaged in false worship & killed the prophet who warned him, 2 Chr. 24:17-25
c. His achievements & the summary of his life: Recorded in the book *The History of the Kings of Judah*

d. His assassination by his own officials: Due to his murder of Zechariah, son of Jehoiada, 2 Chr.24:25	of Judah? 20 And his servants arose, and made a conspiracy, and slew Joash in the house of Millo, which goeth down to Silla. 21 For Jozachar the son of	of Shimeath, and Jehozabad the son of Shomer, his servants, smote him, and he died; and they buried him with his fathers in the city of David: and Amaziah his son reigned in his stead.	e. His burial: In Jerusalem, but not in the royal tomb, 2 Chr.24:25 f. His successor: His son Amaziah

DIVISION II

THE MINISTRY AND MIRACLES OF ELISHA: A DRAMATIC DEMONSTRATION OF GOD'S POWER AND CARE FOR HIS PEOPLE, 4:1–13:25

H. The Good Reign of Jehoash (Joash) in Judah: A Strong and Righteous Beginning but a Weak and Sinful Ending, 12:1-21

(12:1-21) **Introduction—Beginning, New, Need for—Ending, of Life, Tragic and Terrible Ending—Church, Condition of—Perseverance, Duty—Beginning, Need, Endurance**: How many people have a wonderful beginning in life but a terrible ending? All of us know such people. Perhaps some of us even had a great start in life, but today we are engaged in wicked behavior that will lead us to a tragic and terrible end. Far too many people who begin with Christ eventually turn away, backsliding and forsaking Him. Think of those who profess to believe in Christ, are baptized, and join the church; still they eventually slip away from the church, seldom returning to become regular worshippers. Many churches have people on their roles who never attend regular services. On any given Sunday, there are far more church members who are absent than are present. Yet years before, many of those absentees had a marvelous beginning; but they have failed to persevere to the end. They have turned away from Christ and His church, living in a backslidden state of apostasy and denial. Having a wonderful beginning but a terrible ending is the important subject of the present Scripture: *The Good Reign of Jehoash (Joash) in Judah: A Strong and Righteous Beginning but a Weak and Sinful Ending,* 12:1-21.

1. The strong and righteous beginning of Joash's reign: following a godly example (vv.1-16).
2. The weak, sinful ending of Joash's reign: backsliding (vv.17-21).

[1] (12:1-16) **Godliness, Example, Duty—Walk, Spiritual, Duty—Life, Duty—Temple, Restoration of—Joash, King, Reign of—Kings, of Judah, Listed**: Joash had a strong and righteous beginning as king because he had a godly example to follow, the example of the High Priest Jehoiada. Although Joash begins well, he will be seen in the next point slipping back like so many others before and after him. He failed to persevere during the waning years of his life. But for now, his strong and righteous beginning is discussed. One achievement in particular is stressed, that of the temple restoration. Note the Scripture and outline:

OUTLINE	SCRIPTURE	SCRIPTURE	OUTLINE
1. The strong & righteous beginning of Joash's reign: Following a godly example a. His reign: Lasted 40 years b. His mother: Was Zibiah c. His strength & righteousness: Lasted as long as he had the example & counsel of Jehoiada the priest d. His one serious flaw, a half-hearted commitment: Did not destroy the high places e. His most important act as king: The restoration of Solomon's temple (was now 140 years old & had even been vandalized, 2 Chr.24:7) 1) Joash ordered that certain monies be collected for the repairs	In the seventh year of Jehu Jehoash began to reign; and forty years reigned he in Jerusalem. And his mother's name *was* Zibiah of Beersheba. 2 And Jehoash did *that which was* right in the sight of the LORD all his days wherein Jehoiada the priest instructed him. 3 But the high places were not taken away: the people still sacrificed and burnt incense in the high places. 4 And Jehoash said to the priests, All the money of the dedicated things that is brought into the house of the LORD, *even* the money of every one that passeth *the account,* the money that every man is set at, *and* all the money that cometh into any man's heart to bring into the house of the LORD,	5 Let the priests take *it* to them, every man of his acquaintance: and let them repair the breaches of the house, wheresoever any breach shall be found. 6 But it was *so, that* in the three and twentieth year of king Jehoash the priests had not repaired the breaches of the house. 7 Then king Jehoash called for Jehoiada the priest, and the *other* priests, and said unto them, Why repair ye not the breaches of the house? now therefore receive no *more* money of your acquaintance, but deliver it for the breaches of the house. 8 And the priests consented to receive no *more* money of the people, neither to repair the breaches of the house. 9 But Jehoiada the priest took a chest, and bored a hole in	2) Joash placed the priests in charge of the offerings & the building project 3) Joash waited years for them to complete the project: They disappointedly failed • He summoned Jehoiada & the other priests to the royal court—during the 23rd year of his reign when he was about 30 years old, 11:21 • He questioned their irresponsible failure 4) Joash dismissed them from the project & personally took over the fund-raising 5) Joash ordered Jehoiada to set a chest at the entrance

OUTLINE	SCRIPTURE	SCRIPTURE	OUTLINE
of the temple where the people could give their offerings for the temple repairs • The collection box was protected by guards • The money was counted by two people—the royal secretary & the High Priest—each time the box was filled 6) Joash appointed building supervisors & had the money given to them • They paid all labor costs • They purchased all building materials • • They met all other costs involved in restoring the temple	the lid of it, and set it beside the altar, on the right side as one cometh into the house of the LORD: and the priests that kept the door put therein all the money *that was* brought into the house of the LORD. 10 And it was *so,* when they saw that *there was* much money in the chest, that the king's scribe and the High Priest came up, and they put up in bags, and told the money that was found in the house of the LORD. 11 And they gave the money, being told, into the hands of them that did the work, that had the oversight of the house of the LORD: and they laid it out to the carpenters and builders, that wrought upon the house of the LORD, 12 And to masons, and hewers of stone, and to buy timber and hewed stone to repair	the breaches of the house of the LORD, and for all that was laid out for the house to repair *it.* 13 Howbeit there were not made for the house of the LORD bowls of silver, snuffers, basons, trumpets, any vessels of gold, or vessels of silver, of the money *that was* brought into the house of the LORD: 14 But they gave that to the workmen, and repaired therewith the house of the LORD. 15 Moreover they reckoned not with the men, into whose hand they delivered the money to be bestowed on workmen: for they dealt faithfully. 16 The trespass money and sin money was not brought into the house of the LORD: it was the priests'.	• They were to focus upon repairs on the temple itself, not on the furnishings or sacred utensils: These were to be replaced only after the temple structure had been repaired, 2 Chr.24:14 • They were first to use the money to pay labor costs & to repair the temple • They proved so honest & trustworthy that an accounting of the money was not even required 7) Joash decreed that all money from the guilt offerings & sin offerings be given to support the priests, not the restoration project

a. Remember that Joash's reign began when he was only a young child, seven years old (11:21). He was crowned king in the seventh year of Jehu, the ruler of the Northern Kingdom. Joash went on to rule the Southern Kingdom for a period of 40 years.

b. Joash's mother was Zibiah, who was from Beersheba. Surprisingly, his mother was not mentioned during his narrow escape from the massacre of Queen Athaliah (11:1-3). Just why is not stated, but it was probably because she had died either giving birth to Joash or soon thereafter.

c. Joash had a strong and righteous beginning, pleasing the LORD and doing what was right in the eyes of the LORD (v.2). As long as he had the example and counsel of Jehoiada the priest, he lived a righteous life before the LORD.

d. But he had one serious flaw, a half-hearted commitment to the LORD. He did not destroy the high places throughout the nation. As a result, the people continued to worship at the sites that had formerly been the worship centers of pagan shrines and false gods. When the Israelites first entered the promised land of Canaan, the LORD had instructed them to destroy the high places with their pagan altars and idols. They were not to use the high places for their own worship of the LORD (Nu.33:52; De.7:5; 12:3). There was good reason for this prohibition: by using the former worship sites of false gods, the people would more easily be influenced to compromise with the former false worship and be led away from the LORD. They would more easily slip into apostasy and a religion of syncretism, that is, a combination of different forms of religion or practice. Their religion would include some truth and some falsehood, some true worship and some false worship. The people's commitment to the LORD would be weakened and eventually destroyed. They would become worshippers of false gods. For this reason, the LORD commanded the people to destroy the false worship sites and to have nothing to do with them as worship centers.

It was this that Joash failed to do. He failed to destroy the high places and to prohibit the people from worshipping at the sites. This was his one serious flaw, a flaw that exposed a half-hearted commitment to the LORD.

e. Joash did, however, accomplish one great feat, that of restoring Solomon's temple. Beyond question, this was his most important achievement for the nation (vv.4-7). Solomon's temple was now about 140 years old, and for many years it had been neglected and allowed to deteriorate. During these years of apostasy, the people had been engaged in worshipping Baal and other false gods. They had little interest in the LORD and His temple, little interest in the true worship of the only living and true God. As a result, the temple was in bad need of repairs. In fact, it needed a complete restoration.

Under the influence and counsel of the High Priest Jehoiada, Joash ordered that certain monies be collected for the repairs (v.4). Three sources for raising money were instituted:

⇒ the *annual census tax* that was collected from every Israelite 20 years old or older (Ex.30:13)
⇒ the *special tax* or *assessment money* that a person had to pay to the temple when he made a vow to the LORD (Le.17:1-25)
⇒ *freewill offerings* or *voluntary gifts* given for the building project (Le.22:18-23; De.16:10)

Once the method for collecting funds for the restoration had been determined, Joash placed the priests in charge of the offerings and the building project (v.5). But note what happened: many years later the project had not been completed. Unfortunately, the priests had failed in their assignment (v.6). Just what year the restoration project had been assigned by the king is not known. However, it must have been in the early years of his reign, for restoring the temple would have been one of the first acts encouraged by the High Priest Jehoiada.

Now Joash has been on the throne for 23 years and the project has not yet been completed. Being 30 years old, Joash was at this time mature enough to take action himself. Consequently, he summoned Jehoiada and the other priests to the royal court (vv.7-8). Questioning their irresponsible failure, he dismissed them from the project and personally took over the fund-raising himself. He then forcefully charged his aged counselor Jehoiada to set a chest at the entrance of the temple where the people could give their offerings as they entered for worship (v.9). As the people entered the temple, they handed their money to the temple guards and the guards were actually the ones who put the money into the chest and guarded the contributions. Each time the box was filled with offerings, the gifts were taken and counted by two people, the royal secretary and the High Priest himself (v.10).

When the money for the repairs had been collected, Joash then appointed some building supervisors and had the money given to them (vv.11-15). Note that the supervisors paid all labor costs, purchased all building materials, and met all other costs in restoring the temple (vv.11-12). The contractors were to focus solely upon repairing the temple itself, spending none of the money on the furnishings or sacred utensils (v.13).

All labor and material costs to repair the temple were to be met first. Then money could be used for furnishings and utensils (2 Chr.24:14). In constructing the temple, the contractors proved so honest and trustworthy that the king did not demand an accounting. What a dynamic example for contractors today!

In repairing and restoring the temple, another important fact needs to be noted: the support of the priests was not neglected. By the king's decree, all money from guilt offerings and sin offerings was to continue to be given for the priests' support and livelihood (v.16).

Thought 1. As a child, from age one up until at least age thirty, Joash had a godly example to follow. And he followed that example. He made a deliberate choice and decision to follow the steps of a godly man. As a result, Joash was a righteous man. He lived a good, honest, and moral life. He had a sterling character and was trustworthy and dependable. What he said, he meant; and what he set his mind to do, he followed through with. Joash's life sets a dynamic example for us, in particular for children and young people.

As we walk through life, we must look around for godly examples. And we must follow those godly examples. If we follow in the steps of godly people, we will live righteous lives, lives that are good, honest, noble, upright, and pure. We will have strong, moral characters. We will be trustworthy and dependable in all our dealings with people. And by living such upright lives and having such strong characters, people will respect us and hold us in the highest esteem. For these reasons and so many more, we must look for and follow godly examples. Listen to what God says about how we should walk through life:

"Then said Jesus unto his disciples, If any *man* will come after me, let him deny himself, and take up his cross, and follow me" (Mt.16:24).

"Then spake Jesus again unto them, saying, I am the light of the world: he that followeth me shall not walk in darkness, but shall have the light of life" (Jn.8:12).

"My sheep hear my voice, and I know them, and they follow me" (Jn.10:27).

"If any man serve me, let him follow me; and where I am, there shall also my servant be: if any man serve me, him will *my* Father honour" (Jn.12:26).

"Therefore we are buried with him by baptism into death: that like as Christ was raised up from the dead by the glory of the Father, even so we also should walk in newness of life" (Ro.6:4).

"(For we walk by faith, not by sight)" (2 Co.5:7).

"*This* I say then, Walk in the Spirit, and ye shall not fulfil the lust of the flesh" (Ga.5:16).

"I therefore, the prisoner of the Lord, beseech you that ye walk worthy of the vocation wherewith ye are called" (Ep.4:1).

"And walk in love, as Christ also hath loved us, and hath given himself for us an offering and a sacrifice to God for a sweetsmelling savour" (Ep.5:2).

"See then that ye walk circumspectly, not as fools, but as wise" (Ep.5:15).

"As ye have therefore received Christ Jesus the Lord, *so* walk ye in him" (Co.2:6).

"For even hereunto were ye called: because Christ also suffered for us, leaving us an example, that ye should follow his steps" (1 Pe.2:21).

"But if we walk in the light, as he is in the light, we have fellowship one with another, and the blood of Jesus Christ his Son cleanseth us from all sin" (1 Jn.1:7).

"He that saith he abideth in him ought himself also so to walk, even as he walked" (1 Jn.2:6).

2 (12:17-21) **Backsliding, Example of—Life, Ending of, Backsliding—Slipping Away, When, End of Life—Apostasy, When Committed, End of Life—Joash, Backsliding of**: despite a strong beginning, Joash ended his life in a weak and sinful state. He backslid, turned away from his dedication to the LORD. Scripture briefly, but graphically describes what happened and then gives a summary of Joash's life.

OUTLINE	SCRIPTURE	SCRIPTURE	OUTLINE
2. The weak, sinful ending of Joash's reign: Backsliding a. His war with Syria	17 Then Hazael king of Syria went up, and fought against Gath, and took it: and Hazael set his face to go up to Jerusalem.	things that Jehoshaphat, and Jehoram, and Ahaziah, his fathers, kings of Judah, had dedicated, and his own hallowed things, and all the gold *that was* found in the treasures of the house of the	dedication 1) He used the temple treasures to pay the ransom demanded by Syria, treasures that he had earlier dedicated to the LORD, 12:4-16
b. His backslidden state: He turned away from his	18 And Jehoash king of Judah took all the hallowed		

OUTLINE	SCRIPTURE	SCRIPTURE	OUTLINE
2) He engaged in false worship & killed the prophet who warned him, 2 Chr. 24:17-25 c. His achievements & the summary of his life: Recorded in the book *The History of the Kings of Judah* d. His assassination by his own officials: Due to his murder	LORD, and in the king's house, and sent *it* to Hazael king of Syria: and he went away from Jerusalem. 19 And the rest of the acts of Joash, and all that he did, *are* they not written in the book of the chronicles of the kings of Judah? 20 And his servants arose, and made a conspiracy, and	slew Joash in the house of Millo, which goeth down to Silla. 21 For Jozachar the son of Shimeath, and Jehozabad the son of Shomer, his servants, smote him, and he died; and they buried him with his fathers in the city of David: and Amaziah his son reigned in his stead.	of Zechariah, son of Jehoiada, 2 Chr.24:25 e. His burial: In Jerusalem, but not in the royal tomb, 2 Chr.24:25 f. His successor: His son Amaziah

After Jehoiada's death, Syria invaded the Northern Kingdom of Israel and conquered a significant part of that nation. Sometime later, Syria began to push down along the Mediterranean Coast and conquered the Philistine city of Gath. They then turned to invade Judah and attack Jerusalem. According to *Second Chronicles*, they eventually defeated the far superior army of Joash (2 Chr.24:23-24). But as this passage tells us, Joash paid a huge ransom to keep Syria from occupying the city and exiling the citizens. To pay the ransom, he raided the palace and temple treasuries, using all the gifts he had earlier dedicated to the LORD (12:4-16). On receiving the ransom, King Hazael of Syria withdrew his forces from Jerusalem and Judah.

According to *Second Chronicles*, the LORD used the attack of Syria as a chastisement, a judgment against Joash and the people of Judah because of their terrible apostasy (2 Chr.24:24).When the High Priest Jehoiada died, Joash and the people turned away from the LORD. They began to engage in false worship, and abandon the temple of the LORD. Instead of worshipping the only living and true God, they began to worship the false gods of this world. Although the LORD sent prophets to warn the people, they rejected the prophets and refused to repent.

But in mercy, the LORD sent warning after warning, testifying against the people. Still they would not listen, shutting their ears and rejecting the message of God's mercy and forgiveness. Then the people committed the final act of rebellion: the LORD raised up Zechariah, the son of Jehoiada the priest, to testify against them. Zechariah proclaimed the final warning to the people: they were disobeying God's holy commandments and had forsaken Him, the only living LORD. Consequently, He had forsaken them. When Joash heard this strong message from the prophet Zechariah, he reacted with violent rage. He and some of his officials laid plans to assassinate the prophet, the very son of Jehoiada who had been such a wise and godly counselor to the king. Surprisingly, Joash himself gave the order for the prophet Zechariah to be killed (2 Chr.24:17-22).

This is the background to the apostasy of Joash. Slipping away from the LORD, he raided the treasury of the temple and engaged in false worship, even killing the prophet whom God had sent with a special warning for the king and his people.

In concluding the reign of Joash, the author simply says that his achievements and a summary of his life were recorded in the book of *The History of the Kings of Judah* (v.19). After Joash's murder of Zechariah, some of the royal officials conspired to assassinate Joash on a trip he was taking outside the city (v.20). The assassins who took his life were Jozabad and Jehozabad. Nothing is known about these two murderers. Note that Joash was buried in Jerusalem, but he was not given an honorable burial in the royal tomb—all because he had turned so violently away from the LORD (2 Chr.24:25). He was succeeded by his son Amaziah (v.21).

Thought 1. How many people have a wonderful beginning in life, but a terrible ending? Think of elderly, retired people. How many have walked through life with the most upright character, living honest, moral, and just lives. But in the latter years of their lives their character has declined, deteriorated. They have become immoral and dishonest, even cheating other people. They are no longer kind and gracious but, rather, unkind and mean-spirited, cantankerous and easily angered, reactionary and verbally abusive, cursing and using profanity, sometimes even assaulting those who love and care for them. Whereas they used to live righteous lives and profess to be followers of the LORD, they are now backsliding, moving away from the LORD, living carnal, fleshly lives, reacting with a mean spirit toward others.

However, it is not only the elderly who backslide and turn away from the LORD, committing apostasy. Many of us who have had wonderful beginnings in life are now engaging in behavior that will lead us to a terrible end. Many used to live righteous and moral lives, just and honest lives, loving and caring lives, kind and helpful lives that encouraged and built up people. But no longer. They have backslidden, fallen away from the LORD. And some are not only ignoring the LORD but also denying Him. They are cursing His name, using profanity, and telling off-colored jokes. They no longer worship the LORD, being faithful in church attendance and setting an example that we must hear and listen to the Word of God being taught. In addition, many have slipped into immorality, tearing the hearts out of wives, husbands, and children.

Far too many who began with Christ have now turned away from Him. They stand guilty of backsliding, slipping away, and committing terrible apostasy against Him. Listen to what God's Holy Word says about backsliding and slipping away:

"And because iniquity shall abound, the love of many shall wax cold" (Mt.24:12).
"They on the rock *are they*, which, when they hear, receive the word with joy; and these have no root, which for a while believe, and in time of temptation fall away" (Lu.8:13).
"And Jesus said unto him, No man, having put his hand to the plough, and looking back, is fit for the kingdom of God" (Lu.9:62).

"When the unclean spirit is gone out of a man, he walketh through dry places, seeking rest; and finding none, he saith, I will return unto my house whence I came out. And when he cometh, he findeth *it* swept and garnished. Then goeth he, and taketh *to him* seven other spirits more wicked than himself; and they enter in, and dwell there: and the last *state* of that man is worse than the first" (Lu.11:24-26).

"It is the spirit that quickeneth; the flesh profiteth nothing: the words that I speak unto you, *they* are spirit, and *they* are life. But there are some of you that believe not. For Jesus knew from the beginning who they were that believed not, and who should betray him. And he said, Therefore said I unto you, that no man can come unto me, except it were given unto him of my Father. From that *time* many of his disciples went back, and walked no more with him" (Jn.6:63-66).

"I marvel that ye are so soon removed from him that called you into the grace of Christ unto another gospel: Which is not another; but there be some that trouble you, and would pervert the gospel of Christ. But though we, or an angel from heaven, preach any other gospel unto you than that which we have preached unto you, let him be accursed. As we said before, so say I now again, If any *man* preach any other gospel unto you than that ye have received, let him be accursed" (Ga.1:6-9).

"But now, after that ye have known God, or rather are known of God, how turn ye again to the weak and beggarly elements, whereunto ye desire again to be in bondage" (Ga.4:9).

"This charge I commit unto thee, son Timothy, according to the prophecies which went before on thee, that thou by them mightest war a good warfare; Holding faith, and a good conscience; which some having put away concerning faith have made shipwreck: Of whom is Hymenaeus and Alexander; whom I have delivered unto Satan, that they may learn not to blaspheme" (1 Ti.1:18-20).

"Now the Spirit speaketh expressly, that in the latter times some shall depart from the faith, giving heed to seducing spirits, and doctrines of devils; Speaking lies in hypocrisy; having their conscience seared with a hot iron; Forbidding to marry, *and commanding* to abstain from meats, which God hath created to be received with thanksgiving of them which believe and know the truth. For every creature of God *is* good, and nothing to be refused, if it be received with thanksgiving" (1 Ti.4:1-4).

"For Demas hath forsaken me, having loved this present world, and is departed unto Thessalonica; Crescens to Galatia, Titus unto Dalmatia" (2 Ti.4:10).

"Harden not your hearts, as in the provocation, in the day of temptation in the wilderness: When your fathers tempted me, proved me, and saw my works forty years. Wherefore I was grieved with that generation, and said, They do alway err in *their* heart; and they have not known my ways. So I sware in my wrath, They shall not enter into my rest.) Take heed, brethren, lest there be in any of you an evil heart of unbelief, in departing from the living God" (He.3:8-12).

"Now the just shall live by faith: but if *any man* draw back, my soul shall have no pleasure in him" (He.10:38).

"For if after they have escaped the pollutions of the world through the knowledge of the Lord and Saviour Jesus Christ, they are again entangled therein, and overcome, the latter end is worse with them than the beginning. For it had been better for them not to have known the way of righteousness, than, after they have known *it,* to turn from the holy commandment delivered unto them" (2 Pe.2:20-21).

"Ye therefore, beloved, seeing ye know *these things* before, beware lest ye also, being led away with the error of the wicked, fall from your own stedfastness" (2 Pe.3:17).

"They went out from us, but they were not of us; for if they had been of us, they would *no doubt* have continued with us: but *they went out,* that they might be made manifest that they were not all of us" (1 Jn.2:19).

"Nevertheless I have *somewhat* against thee, because thou hast left thy first love" (Re.2:4).

"For it came to pass, when Solomon was old, *that* his wives turned away his heart after other gods: and his heart was not perfect with the LORD his God, as *was* the heart of David his father" (1 K.11:4).

"The backslider in heart shall be filled with his own ways: and a good man *shall be satisfied* from himself" (Pr.14:14). end with his own ways

"Ah sinful nation, a people laden with iniquity, a seed of evildoers, children that are corrupters: they have forsaken the LORD, they have provoked the Holy One of Israel unto anger, they are gone away backward" (Is.1:4).

"And my people are bent to backsliding from me: though they called them to the most High, none at all would exalt *him*" (Ho.11:7).

CHAPTER 13

I. The Evil Reigns of Jehoahaz & Jehoash in Israel & the Final Days of Elisha: A Contrast Between Weak & Strong Character, 13:1-25

1. The evil reign of Jehoahaz in Israel: A weak character who seeks the LORD but fails to repent

a. His reign: Lasted 17 years

b. His failure & sin: He followed the sins of Jeroboam
   1) He engaged in idolatry
   2) He was a stumbling block, leading Israel into false worship, 1 K.12:25-33

c. His discipline & chastisement from the LORD: The LORD subjected Israel to Syrian oppression

d. His seeking of & deliverance by the LORD
   1) The king sought the LORD
   2) The LORD heard the king's cry
   • He provided a deliverer, saved them from the Syrian oppression
   • He gave a period of peace & security to the people

e. His & Israel's refusal to repent
   • They continued in sin, especially the sins of idolatry & false worship
   • They did not destroy the Asherah pole in Samaria: Symbolized a false goddess

f. His judgment from the LORD renewed: Syria destroyed most of Israel's army

g. His achievements & the summary of his life
   1) His reign: Recorded in the book *The History of the Kings of Israel*
   2) His death & burial: In Samaria
   3) His successor: Jehoash, his son, a weak character who built & left a legacy of evil

2. The evil reign of Jehoash in

In the three and twentieth year of Joash the son of Ahaziah king of Judah Jehoahaz the son of Jehu began to reign over Israel in Samaria, *and reigned* seventeen years.
2 And he did *that which was* evil in the sight of the LORD, and followed the sins of Jeroboam the son of Nebat, which made Israel to sin; he departed not therefrom.
3 And the anger of the LORD was kindled against Israel, and he delivered them into the hand of Hazael king of Syria, and into the hand of Ben-hadad the son of Hazael, all *their* days.
4 And Jehoahaz besought the LORD, and the LORD hearkened unto him: for he saw the oppression of Israel, because the king of Syria oppressed them.
5 (And the LORD gave Israel a saviour, so that they went out from under the hand of the Syrians: and the children of Israel dwelt in their tents, as beforetime.
6 Nevertheless they departed not from the sins of the house of Jeroboam, who made Israel sin, *but* walked therein: and there remained the grove also in Samaria.)
7 Neither did he leave of the people to Jehoahaz but fifty horsemen, and ten chariots, and ten thousand footmen; for the king of Syria had destroyed them, and had made them like the dust by threshing.
8 Now the rest of the acts of Jehoahaz, and all that he did, and his might, *are* they not written in the book of the chronicles of the kings of Israel?
9 And Jehoahaz slept with his fathers; and they buried him in Samaria: and Joash his son reigned in his stead.
10 In the thirty and seventh

year of Joash king of Judah began Jehoash the son of Jehoahaz to reign over Israel in Samaria, *and reigned* sixteen years.
11 And he did *that which was* evil in the sight of the LORD; he departed not from all the sins of Jeroboam the son of Nebat, who made Israel sin: *but* he walked therein.
12 And the rest of the acts of Joash, and all that he did, and his might wherewith he fought against Amaziah king of Judah, *are* they not written in the book of the chronicles of the kings of Israel?
13 And Joash slept with his fathers; and Jeroboam sat upon his throne: and Joash was buried in Samaria with the kings of Israel.
14 Now Elisha was fallen sick of his sickness whereof he died. And Joash the king of Israel came down unto him, and wept over his face, and said, O my father, my father, the chariot of Israel, and the horsemen thereof.
15 And Elisha said unto him, Take bow and arrows. And he took unto him bow and arrows.
16 And he said to the king of Israel, Put thine hand upon the bow. And he put his hand *upon it:* and Elisha put his hands upon the king's hands.
17 And he said, Open the window eastward. And he opened *it.* Then Elisha said, Shoot. And he shot. And he said, The arrow of the LORD'S deliverance, and the arrow of deliverance from Syria: for thou shalt smite the Syrians in Aphek, till thou have consumed *them.*
18 And he said, Take the arrows. And he took *them.* And he said unto the king of Israel, Smite upon the ground. And he smote thrice, and stayed.
19 And the man of God was wroth with him, and said, Thou shouldest have smitten five or six times; then hadst thou smitten Syria till thou hadst consumed *it:* whereas now thou shalt smite Syria *but* thrice.
20 And Elisha died, and they buried him. And the bands of the Moabites invaded the

Israel

a. His reign: Lasted 16 years

b. His failure & sin: Continued in the sins of Jeroboam; did not turn away from a single sin, 1 K.12:25-33

c. His achievements & the summary of his life
   1) His reign & his war against Judah: Recorded in the book *The History of the Kings of Israel*
   2) His death & burial: In Samaria
   3) His successor: Jeroboam (named after the evil Jeroboam, 1 K.12:25-33)

3. The prophecy of Elisha & his death: A strong character of iron determination

a. The emotional visit of King Jehoash at Elisha's deathbed: Acknowledged Elisha as Israel's defense against all enemies

b. The symbolic picture of Israel's victory over Syria at Aphek
   1) Elisha instructed the king to take a bow & some arrows in his hands
   • Elisha placed his hands on the king's hands
   • Elisha told him to open the east window & to shoot
   2) Elisha shouted out that the arrow symbolized the LORD's victory over Syria: Israel would defeat the Syrians at the battle of Aphek

c. The symbolic picture of Israel's continued victory over Syria
   1) Elisha instructed the king to continue shooting
   2) The king shot three times & stopped
   3) Elisha rebuked the king
   • He should have shot all the arrows
   • He would thereby have assured the complete destruction of Syria
   • He would now defeat Syria only three times

d. The death of Elisha

e. The miraculous power of God to raise the dead

OUTLINE	SCRIPTURE	SCRIPTURE	OUTLINE
symbolized in Elisha's body	land at the coming in of the year.	respect unto them, because of his covenant with Abraham, Isaac, and Jacob, and would not destroy them, neither cast he them from his presence as yet.	cause of His covenant with the forefathers of Israel
1) Some Israelites were burying a man when a band of Moabite raiders suddenly attacked: The dead body was quickly thrown into Elisha's tomb	21 And it came to pass, as they were burying a man, that, behold, they spied a band *of men;* and they cast the man into the sepulchre of Elisha: and when the man was let down, and touched the bones of Elisha, he revived, and stood up on his feet.	24 So Hazael king of Syria died; and Ben-hadad his son reigned in his stead.	2) God was not willing to totally destroy or banish Israel from His presence
2) The dead man's body immediately came to life when it touched Elisha's bones	22 But Hazael king of Syria oppressed Israel all the days of Jehoahaz.	25 And Jehoash the son of Jehoahaz took again out of the hand of Ben-hadad the son of Hazael the cities, which he had taken out of the hand of Jehoahaz his father by war. Three times did Joash beat him, and recovered the cities of Israel.	g. The prophecy of Elisha fulfilled
f. The continued oppression of Israel by Syria during Jehoahaz's reign: God's discipline	23 And the LORD was gracious unto them, and had compassion on them, and had		1) The king of Syria died
1) God nevertheless demonstrated compassion: Be-			2) The 25 cities earlier conquered by Syria were recaptured by King Jehoash in three battles—just as Elisha predicted, 19

DIVISION II

THE MINISTRY AND MIRACLES OF ELISHA: A DRAMATIC DEMONSTRATION OF GOD'S POWER AND CARE FOR HIS PEOPLE, 4:1–13:25

I. The Evil Reigns of Jehoahaz and Jehoash in Israel and the Final Days of Elisha: A Contrast Between Weak and Strong Character, 13:1-25

(13:1-25) **Introduction—Character, Need, Strong—Integrity, Need for—Leadership, Needs, Strong Character—Society, Hope for, Leaders of Integrity**: the contrast between weak and strong character is a much-needed topic of discussion today. Men and women with strong *character* and *integrity* are desperately needed at every level of society. But what is too often found are men and women who are insincere, deceptive, impure, dishonest, corrupt, wicked, and evil. They should instead be living lives of honor, goodness, purity, morality, and sincerity. We too must become men and women of integrity and uprightness, holding ever so high the principles of common decency, righteousness, and justice for all people everywhere.

The only hope for society—the only hope for handling the lawlessness and violence of this world—is for us to become men and women of strong character. We must *develop* characters of...

- truth and integrity
- righteousness and justice
- kindness and goodness
- compassion and care
- faith and trust

This is the practical subject of the present Scripture. Shifting to the Northern Kingdom, the author gives a brief summary of two kings with weak character. He then covers the final days of the great prophet Elisha, contrasting his strong character with the weak character of the two evil kings. This is: *The Evil Reigns of Jehoahaz and Jehoash in Israel and the Final Days of Elisha: A Contrast Between Weak and Strong Character,* 13:1-25.

1. The evil reign of Jehoahaz in Israel: a weak character who seeks the LORD but fails to repent (vv.1-9).
2. The evil reign of Jehoash in Israel, (vv.10-13).
3. The prophecy of Elisha and his death: a strong character of iron determination (vv.14-25).

1 (13:1-9) **Character, Weak—Repentance, Failure to—Deliverance, of God, Example of—Idolatry, Example of—Cult, of Jeroboam, Followed—Jeroboam, False Worship of, Followed—Worship, False, of Jeroboam, Followed—Kings, of Israel, Jehoahaz—Israel, Northern Kingdom, Kings of**: there was the evil reign of Jehoahaz in Israel. In looking at the brief description of Jehoahaz's reign, Israel's faith in and worship of the LORD are seen cast upon the ground, trampled upon and shamed. Just how far away from the LORD the people had turned is graphically described by Scripture. And the newly crowned King Jehoahaz did little if anything to lead the people back to the LORD. He was a man of weak character who occasionally sought the LORD, especially during moments of crisis, but he failed to repent of his evil.

OUTLINE	SCRIPTURE	SCRIPTURE	OUTLINE
1. The evil reign of Jehoahaz in Israel: A weak character who seeks the LORD but fails to repent	In the three and twentieth year of Joash the son of Ahaziah king of Judah Jehoahaz the son of Jehu began to reign over Israel in Samaria, *and reigned* seventeen	years. 2 And he did *that which was* evil in the sight of the LORD, and followed the sins of Jeroboam the son of Nebat, which made Israel to sin; he	b. His failure & sin: He followed the sins of Jeroboam
a. His reign: Lasted 17 years			1) He engaged in idolatry
			2) He was a stumbling block, leading Israel into false

103

OUTLINE	SCRIPTURE	SCRIPTURE	OUTLINE
worship, 1 K.12:25-33	departed not there from.	who made Israel sin, *but*	try & false worship
c. His discipline & chastisement from the LORD: The LORD subjected Israel to Syrian oppression	3 And the anger of the LORD was kindled against Israel, and he delivered them into the hand of Hazael king of Syria, and into the hand of Ben-hadad the son of Hazael, all *their* days.	walked therein: and there remained the grove also in Samaria.)	• They did not destroy the Asherah pole in Samaria: Symbolized a false goddess
		7 Neither did he leave of the people to Jehoahaz but fifty horsemen, and ten chariots, and ten thousand footmen; for the king of Syria had destroyed them, and had made them like the dust by threshing.	f. His judgment from the LORD renewed: Syria destroyed most of Israel's army
d. His seeking of & deliverance by the LORD	4 And Jehoahaz besought the LORD, and the LORD hearkened unto him: for he saw the oppression of Israel, because the king of Syria oppressed them.		
1) The king sought the LORD			
2) The LORD heard the king's cry		8 Now the rest of the acts of Jehoahaz, and all that he did, and his might, *are* they not written in the book of the chronicles of the kings of Israel?	g. His achievements & the summary of his life
• He provided a deliverer, saved them from the Syrian oppression	5 (And the LORD gave Israel a saviour, so that they went out from under the hand of the Syrians: and the children of Israel dwelt in their tents, as beforetime.		1) His reign: Recorded in the book *The History of the Kings of Israel*
• He gave a period of peace & security to the people		9 And Jehoahaz slept with his fathers; and they buried him in Samaria: and Joash his son reigned in his stead.	2) His death & burial: In Samaria
e. His & Israel's refusal to repent	6 Nevertheless they departed not from the sins of the house of Jeroboam,		3) His successor: Jehoash, his son, a weak character who built & left a legacy of evil
• They continued in sin, especially the sins of idola-			

a. Jehoahaz was crowned king of the Northern Kingdom in the twenty-third year of Joash, the king of Judah. This was the very year that Joash began to repair the temple. Apparently, Jehoahaz's father Jehu had great hopes that his son would live a righteous life, worshipping and serving the LORD. For Jehu had named his son Jehoahaz, which means "the LORD (Yahweh, Jehovah) has grasped." But, tragically, the hope of his father was to be dashed upon the rocks of disappointment. During his seventeen years of rule, Jehoahaz failed to worship the LORD, instead living a wicked life.

b. Jehoahaz did evil in the sight of the LORD, following the sins of Jeroboam (v.2). Remember what these sins were: in an attempt to solidify the power of the Northern Kingdom and to keep the people loyal, Jeroboam had instituted a new *state religion*. If the people were allowed to worship in the temple at Jerusalem, there was the danger they would become attached to the Southern Kingdom and seek reunification with them. Therefore, to combat this problem, Jeroboam had two golden calves erected as idols claiming that they were a representation of the LORD's strength and power. They were images to help the worshipper focus upon the LORD. Setting up one calf image in the north at Dan and the other calf image in the south at Bethel, Jeroboam had proclaimed that these would be the temple sites, the worship centers for the citizens of the Northern Kingdom. He further claimed that the LORD would accept the worship at these two sites just as much as He would accept the worship at the temple in Jerusalem. Thus, throughout the years the citizens of the Northern Kingdom became attached to the worship of the golden calves, engaging in idolatry and false worship.

The terrible sin of Jehoahaz was that he followed in the steps of Jeroboam, encouraging the people to worship the LORD at these false worship sites. As leader of the nation he should have encouraged the people to worship the LORD, the only living and true God. But instead he was a stumbling block and led his people into false worship (see outline and note—1 K.12:25-33 for more discussion). Throughout the history of the Northern Kingdom, every king used the *state religion* instituted by Jeroboam in order to secure the loyalty of the people.

c. As a result, the LORD's anger was aroused against Israel and He began to discipline and chastise them. His chastisement had already begun during the reign of Jehu when he allowed Syria to conquer *some* of the territory of the Northern Kingdom (10:32-33). Now the LORD actually allowed Syria to conquer *all* of the Northern Kingdom under the leadership of King Hazael and his son Ben-Hadad. Of course, this meant that a heavy tribute was imposed upon the Israelites, a tax that usually drained a nation's wealth and forced most of its citizens to live in poverty.

d. Suffering under the weight of the Syrian oppression, King Jehoahaz became desperate and began to seek the LORD for deliverance (vv.4-5). Demonstrating His patience with the sins of the people, the LORD heard the king's cry and provided a deliverer to save them from the Syrians. Just who this deliverer was is not known, though various opinions have been suggested. One such idea is that another nation attacked Syria, forcing Syria to turn its attention away from Israel to protect its own borders. Others suggest that the deliverer was Elisha himself, who begged the LORD for mercy and deliverance. Still others suggest that a courageous commander of Israel was raised up to deliver the people. Whatever the case, the LORD gave an extended period of peace and security to the people.

e. But despite God's wonderful deliverance, the king and people of Israel still refused to repent (v.6). Continuing on in their sins, especially idolatry and false worship, they refused to destroy the false worship centers established by Jeroboam at Dan and Bethel. They also refused to destroy the image or pole of the false goddess Asherah which was located in Samaria.

f. Thus, in time, God's judgment once again began to fall upon the people (v.7). Syria was again allowed to conquer the Northern Kingdom, and this time the enemy was allowed to destroy most of Israel's army. Only 50 horsemen, 10 chariots, and 10,000 foot soldiers survived the invasion and conquest by Syria.

g. Jehoahaz's achievements and a summary of his life are recorded in the book *The History of the Kings of Israel*. After his death, he was buried in Samaria and succeeded by his son Jehoash (vv.8-9).

Thought 1. When caught in a desperate situation Jehoahaz sought the LORD—but he failed to repent. He did what so many people do: when they face a crisis, they become desperate and cry out to the LORD for deliverance. But they never truly repent, never turn away from their sins. They never turn back to the LORD, worshipping Him and living righteous lives.

Likewise, when we cry out in desperation, the LORD often acts in compassion and mercy, delivering us and meeting our need. But, tragically and shamefully, we too continue on in our sinful lifestyles, committing sins of...

- immorality
- impurity
- vulgarity
- cursing or swearing
- blasphemy
- corruption
- false worship
- witchcraft or sorcery

- hatred
- discord
- jealousy
- selfish ambition
- dissension
- greed
- drunkenness
- drug or substance abuse

But God's patience and longsuffering—His dealing with us in mercy and compassion—have a limit. Eventually, He has to execute justice upon us. He has to chastise and discipline us. But even in His discipline and chastisement, God is seeking to correct us by arousing us to turn to Him. God's chastisement and justice are always for the purpose of driving us to moments of desperation, so we will realize that we need His help. But once God has heard our prayers and cries, we must repent and turn to Him.

(1) We must never have an impenitent heart, a heart that is self-willed, stubborn, inflexible, callous, unyielding, and closed to God.

> **"Then began he to upbraid the cities wherein most of his mighty works were done, because they repented not" (Mt.11:20).**
>
> **"And he said unto him, If they hear not Moses and the prophets, neither will they be persuaded, though one rose from the dead" (Lu.16:31).**
>
> **"Ye stiffnecked and uncircumcised in heart and ears, ye do always resist the Holy Ghost: as your fathers** *did,* **so** *do* **ye" (Ac.7:51).**
>
> **"Neither repented they of their murders, nor of their sorceries, nor of their fornication, nor of their thefts" (Re.9:21).**
>
> **"And the LORD said unto Moses, I have seen this people, and, behold, it** *is* **a stiffnecked people" (Ex.32:9).**
>
> **"So I spake unto you; and ye would not hear, but rebelled against the commandment of the LORD, and went presumptuously up into the hill" (De.1:43).**
>
> **"Notwithstanding they would not hear, but hardened their necks, like to the neck of their fathers, that did not believe in the LORD their God" (2 K.17:14).**
>
> **"Yet he sent prophets to them, to bring them again unto the LORD; and they testified against them: but they would not give ear" (2 Chr.24:19).**
>
> **"And in the time of his distress did he trespass yet more against the LORD: this** *is that* **king Ahaz" (2 Chr.28:22).**
>
> **"And testifiedst against them, that thou mightest bring them again unto thy law: yet they dealt proudly, and hearkened not unto thy commandments, but sinned against thy judgments, (which if a man do, he shall live in them;) and withdrew the shoulder, and hardened their neck, and would not hear" (Ne.9:29).**
>
> **"Be ye not as the horse,** *or* **as the mule,** *which* **have no understanding: whose mouth must be held in with bit and bridle, lest they come near unto thee. Many sorrows** *shall be* **to the wicked: but he that trusteth in the LORD, mercy shall compass him about" (Ps.32:9-10).**
>
> **"Because sentence against an evil work is not executed speedily, therefore the heart of the sons of men is fully set in them to do evil" (Ec.8:11).**
>
> **"To whom he said, This** *is* **the rest** *wherewith* **ye may cause the weary to rest; and this** *is* **the refreshing: yet they would not hear" (Is.28:12).**
>
> **"For thus saith the Lord GOD, the Holy One of Israel; In returning and rest shall ye be saved; in quietness and in confidence shall be your strength: and ye would not" (Is.30:15).**
>
> **"Hearken unto me, ye stouthearted, that** *are* **far from righteousness" (Is.46:12).**
>
> **"Because I knew that thou** *art* **obstinate, and thy neck** *is* **an iron sinew, and thy brow brass...** *There is* **no peace, saith the LORD, unto the wicked" (Is.48:4, 22).**
>
> **"Were they ashamed when they had committed abomination? nay, they were not at all ashamed, neither could they blush: therefore they shall fall among them that fall: at the time** *that* **I visit them they shall be cast down, saith the LORD" (Je.6:15).**
>
> **"And now, because ye have done all these works, saith the LORD, and I spake unto you, rising up early and speaking, but ye heard not; and I called you, but ye answered not; Therefore will I do unto** *this* **house, which is called by my name, wherein ye trust, and unto the place which I gave to you and to your fathers, as I have done to Shiloh. And I will cast you out of my sight, as I have cast out all your brethren,** *even* **the whole seed of Ephraim. Therefore pray not thou for this people, neither lift up cry nor prayer for them, neither make intercession to me: for I will not hear thee" (Je.7:13-16).**
>
> **"And when this people, or the prophet, or a priest, shall ask thee, saying, What** *is* **the burden of the LORD? thou shalt then say unto them, What burden? I will even forsake you, saith the LORD" (Je.23:33).**

"As *it is* written in the law of Moses, all this evil is come upon us: yet made we not our prayer before the LORD our God, that we might turn from our iniquities, and understand thy truth" (Da.9:13).

"And I also have given you cleanness of teeth in all your cities, and want of bread in all your places: yet have ye not returned unto me, saith the LORD" (Am.4:6).

"I smote you with blasting and with mildew and with hail in all the labours of your hands; yet ye *turned* not to me, saith the LORD" (Hag.2:17).

"But they refused to hearken, and pulled away the shoulder, and stopped their ears, that they should not hear" (Zec.7:11).

"If ye will not hear, and if ye will not lay *it* to heart, to give glory unto my name, saith the LORD of hosts, I will even send a curse upon you, and I will curse your blessings: yea, I have cursed them already, because ye do not lay *it* to heart" (Mal.2:2).

(2) We must repent and turn to the LORD in order to be saved and delivered from the enemies of this life. Repentance is an absolute essential in order to receive the fullness of life and the promise of eternal life that can come from God alone.

"And saying, Repent ye: for the kingdom of heaven is at hand" (Mt.3:2).

"Blessed *are* they that mourn: for they shall be comforted" (Mt.5:4).

"I tell you, Nay: but, except ye repent, ye shall all likewise perish" (Lu.13:3).

"Repent ye therefore, and be converted, that your sins may be blotted out, when the times of refreshing shall come from the presence of the Lord" (Ac.3:19).

"Repent therefore of this thy wickedness, and pray God, if perhaps the thought of thine heart may be forgiven thee" (Ac.8:22).

"And the times of this ignorance God winked at; but now commandeth all men every where to repent" (Ac.17:30).

"If my people, which are called by my name, shall humble themselves, and pray, and seek my face, and turn from their wicked ways; then will I hear from heaven, and will forgive their sin, and will heal their land" (2 Chr.7:14).

"Let the wicked forsake his way, and the unrighteous man his thoughts: and let him return unto the LORD, and he will have mercy upon him; and to our God, for he will abundantly pardon" (Is.55:7).

"But if the wicked will turn from all his sins that he hath committed, and keep all my statutes, and do that which is lawful and right, he shall surely live, he shall not die" (Eze.8:21).

"Cast away from you all your transgressions, whereby ye have transgressed; and make you a new heart and a new spirit: for why will ye die, O house of Israel" (Eze.18:31).

"Therefore also now, saith the LORD, turn ye *even* to me with all your heart, and with fasting, and with weeping, and with mourning" (Joel 2:12).

2 (13:10-13) **Legacy, of Evil—Character, Weak, Example of—Jehoash, King of Israel, Reign of—King, of Israel, Listed—Northern Kingdom, Kings of, Jehoash:** there was the evil reign of Jehoash in Israel. Only a brief summary is given of Jehoash's reign; although he plays a significant part in the death of Elisha (vv.14-25), and in the reign of King Amaziah (due to a war he launched against Judah, 14:8-16).

Jehoash took the throne in the thirty-seventh year of Joash, king of Judah, and he reigned for a period of 16 years (v.10). Note that his father Jehoahaz had begun his reign in the twenty-third year of Joash and had reigned for seventeen years (v.1), a difference of only 14 years. Most likely, this means that Jehoash ruled in a co-regency with his father for a period of 3 years.

Just like his father, Jehoash failed the LORD and continued on in the sins of Jeroboam (v.11). Sadly, he became even more entrenched in idolatry and false worship than his father had, refusing to turn away from any of the sins of Jeroboam. Note that Scripture states this very fact. A summary of his achievements and life, including his war against Amaziah king of Judah, are recorded in the book *The History of the Kings of Israel* (v.12). After Jehoash's death he was buried in Samaria, the capital of the Northern Kingdom. He was succeeded by his son Jeroboam. Note that Jehoash even named his son after the evil Jeroboam, the very king who had instituted the false *state religion* that had so corrupted the Northern Kingdom (see outline and notes—1 K.12:25-33; 2 K.13:1-9 for more discussion).

OUTLINE	SCRIPTURE	SCRIPTURE	OUTLINE
2. The evil reign of Jehoash in Israel a. His reign: Lasted 16 years b. His failure & sin: Continued in the sins of Jeroboam; did not turn away from a single sin, 1 K.12:25-33	10 In the thirty and seventh year of Joash king of Judah began Jehoash the son of Jehoahaz to reign over Israel in Samaria, and reigned sixteen years. 11 And he did *that which was* evil in the sight of the LORD; he departed not from all the sins of Jeroboam the son of Nebat, who made Israel sin: *but* he walked therein.	12 And the rest of the acts of Joash, and all that he did, and his might wherewith he fought against Amaziah king of Judah, *are* they not written in the book of the chronicles of the kings of Israel? 13 And Joash slept with his fathers; and Jeroboam sat upon his throne: and Joash was buried in Samaria with the kings of Israel.	c. His achievements & the summary of his life 1) His reign & his war against Judah: Recorded in the book *The History of the Kings of Israel* 2) His death & burial: In Samaria 3) His successor: Jeroboam (named after the evil Jeroboam, 1 K.12:25-33)

Thought 1. What a legacy to leave to the world, that of naming one's son after a famous leader who had lived an evil, wicked life. Yet this is exactly what Jehoash did.

Every one of us needs to ask him- or herself: What kind of life am I building and what kind of legacy am I leaving for my family and for the world? A legacy of sin, evil, and wickedness? Or a legacy of faith in the LORD, of righteousness and service to others?

Am I living a righteous life, trusting the LORD for my salvation and worshipping Him consistently? Am I living a moral, clean, and upright life, being kind and gracious to other people in both my speech and behavior? Am I walking humbly before others and respecting them?

Or am I living a life of sin and wickedness, cursing and using profanity? Am I engaging in immorality and lawlessness; lying, stealing, and cheating; getting drunk and participating in wild, vulgar parties? Am I being unkind and mean-spirited, mistreating people and acting selfishly toward others.

Again, what kind of life am I building and what kind of legacy am I leaving behind for the world? A legacy of faith in God, and of consistent worship, righteousness, and service to others? Or a legacy of sin, wickedness, and evil?

(1) Listen to what God's Word says about living a life of sin and leaving behind a legacy of disobedience and rebelliousness.

"For the wrath of God is revealed from heaven against all ungodliness and unrighteousness of men, who hold the truth in unrighteousness...Being filled with all unrighteousness, fornication, wickedness, covetousness, maliciousness; full of envy, murder, debate, deceit, malignity; whisperers, Backbiters, haters of God, despiteful, proud, boasters, inventors of evil things, disobedient to parents, Without understanding, covenantbreakers, without natural affection, implacable, unmerciful: Who knowing the judgment of God, that they which commit such things are worthy of death, not only do the same, but have pleasure in them that do them" (Ro.1:18, 29-32).

"Know ye not that the unrighteous shall not inherit the kingdom of God? Be not deceived: neither fornicators, nor idolaters, nor adulterers, nor effeminate, nor abusers of themselves with mankind, Nor thieves, nor covetous, nor drunkards, nor revilers, nor extortioners, shall inherit the kingdom of God" (1 Co.6:9-10).

"But fornication, and all uncleanness, or covetousness, let it not be once named among you, as becometh saints; Neither filthiness, nor foolish talking, nor jesting, which are not convenient: but rather giving of thanks. For this ye know, that no whoremonger, nor unclean person, nor covetous man, who is an idolater, hath any inheritance in the kingdom of Christ and of God" (Ep.5:3-5).

"But the fearful, and unbelieving, and the abominable, and murderers, and whoremongers, and sorcerers, and idolaters, and all liars, shall have their part in the lake which burneth with fire and brimstone: which is the second death" (Re.21:8).

(2) Listen to what God's Word says about living a life of righteousness and service and leaving behind a legacy of faith in the LORD.

"But seek ye first the kingdom of God, and his righteousness; and all these things shall be added unto you" (Mt.6:33).

"And whosoever shall give to drink unto one of these little ones a cup of cold *water* only in the name of a disciple, verily I say unto you, he shall in no wise lose his reward" (Mt.10:42).

"Then shall the righteous shine forth as the sun in the kingdom of their Father. Who hath ears to hear, let him hear" (Mt.13:43).

"But glory, honour, and peace, to every man that worketh good, to the Jew first, and also to the Gentile" (Ro.2:10).

"Awake to righteousness, and sin not; for some have not the knowledge of God: I speak *this* to your shame" (1 Co.15:34).

"Knowing that whatsoever good thing any man doeth, the same shall he receive of the Lord, whether *he be* bond or free" (Ep.6:8).

"But thou, O man of God, flee these things; and follow after righteousness, godliness, faith, love, patience, meekness. Fight the good fight of faith, lay hold on eternal life, whereunto thou art also called, and hast professed a good profession before many witnesses" (1 Ti.6:11-12).

"Teaching us that, denying ungodliness and worldly lusts, we should live soberly, righteously, and godly, in this present world; Looking for that blessed hope, and the glorious appearing of the great God and our Saviour Jesus Christ" (Tit.2:12-13).

"And ye shall serve the LORD your God, and he shall bless thy bread, and thy water; and I will take sickness away from the midst of thee" (Ex.23:25).

"He withdraweth not his eyes from the righteous: but with kings *are they* on the throne; yea, he doth establish them for ever, and they are exalted" (Jb.36:7).

"The eyes of the LORD *are* upon the righteous, and his ears *are open* unto their cry" (Ps.34:15).

"I have been young, and *now* am old; yet have I not seen the righteous forsaken, nor his seed begging bread" (Ps.37:25).

"The righteous shall flourish like the palm tree: he shall grow like a cedar in Lebanon" (Ps.92:12).

"Say ye to the righteous, that *it shall be* well *with him:* for they shall eat the fruit of their doings" (Is.3:10).

"Sow to yourselves in righteousness, reap in mercy; break up your fallow ground: for *it is* time to seek the LORD, till he come and rain righteousness upon you" (Ho.10:12).

3 (13:14-25) **Perseverance, Example of—Steadfastness, Example of—Determination, Strong, Example of—Elisha, Death of—Elisha, Title of—Jehoash, Prophecies Concerning—Elisha, Prophecies of**: there was the prophecy of Elisha given to King Jehoash and Elisha's death. About 50 years have passed since the last event of Elisha's ministry was mentioned (2 K.9:1-3). Throughout his long life, Elisha had seen corruption and wickedness eat away progressively at the fiber of the Northern Kingdom. Now, as he lay upon his deathbed, the nation had deteriorated into a torrid cesspool of sin and false worship. Although he had faithfully proclaimed the Word of God, warning the people and nation, his message for the most part had fallen upon deaf ears. Nevertheless, up until the last day of his life, he continued to bear strong witness for the LORD. As Scripture closes out his life, it is his strong witness that is emphasized:

OUTLINE	SCRIPTURE	SCRIPTURE	OUTLINE
3. The prophecy of Elisha & his death: A strong character of iron determination	14 Now Elisha was fallen sick of his sickness whereof he died. And Joash the king of Israel came down unto him, and wept over his face, and said, O my father, my father, the chariot of Israel, and the horsemen thereof.	*but* thrice. 20 And Elisha died, and they buried him. And the bands of the Moabites invaded the land at the coming in of the year.	Syria only three times d. The death of Elisha e. The miraculous power of God to raise the dead symbolized in Elisha's body
a. The emotional visit of King Jehoash at Elisha's deathbed: Acknowledged Elisha as Israel's defense against all enemies			
b. The symbolic picture of Israel's victory over Syria at Aphek	15 And Elisha said unto him, Take bow and arrows. And he took unto him bow and arrows.	21 And it came to pass, as they were burying a man, that, behold, they spied a band *of men;* and they cast the man into the sepulchre of Elisha: and when the man was let down, and touched the bones of Elisha, he revived, and stood up on his feet.	1) Some Israelites were burying a man when a band of Moabite raiders suddenly attacked: The dead body was quickly thrown into Elisha's tomb
1) Elisha instructed the king to take a bow & some arrows in his hands	16 And he said to the king of Israel, Put thine hand upon the bow. And he put his hand *upon it:* and Elisha put his hands upon the king's hands.		2) The dead man's body immediately came to life when it touched Elisha's bones
• Elisha placed his hands on the king's hands			
• Elisha told him to open the east window & to shoot	17 And he said, Open the window eastward. And he opened *it.* Then Elisha said, Shoot. And he shot. And he said, The arrow of the LORD'S deliverance, and the arrow of deliverance from Syria: for thou shalt smite the Syrians in Aphek, till thou have consumed *them.*	22 But Hazael king of Syria oppressed Israel all the days of Jehoahaz. 23 And the LORD was gracious unto them, and had compassion on them, and had respect unto them, because of his covenant with Abraham, Isaac, and Jacob, and would not destroy them, neither cast he them from his presence as yet.	f. The continued oppression of Israel by Syria during Jehoahaz's reign: God's discipline
2) Elisha shouted out that the arrow symbolized the LORD's victory over Syria: Israel would defeat the Syrians at the battle of Aphek			1) God nevertheless demonstrated compassion: Because of His covenant with the forefathers of Israel
c. The symbolic picture of Israel's continued victory over Syria	18 And he said, Take the arrows. And he took *them.* And he said unto the king of Israel, Smite upon the ground. And he smote thrice, and stayed.	24 So Hazael king of Syria died; and Ben-hadad his son reigned in his stead.	2) God was not willing to totally destroy or banish Israel from His presence
1) Elisha instructed the king to continue shooting			g. The prophecy of Elisha fulfilled
2) The king shot three times & stopped		25 And Jehoash the son of Jehoahaz took again out of the hand of Ben-hadad the son of Hazael the cities, which he had taken out of the hand of Jehoahaz his father by war. Three times did Joash beat him, and recovered the cities of Israel.	1) The king of Syria died
3) Elisha rebuked the king	19 And the man of God was wroth with him, and said, Thou shouldest have smitten five or six times; then hadst thou smitten Syria till thou hadst consumed *it:* whereas now thou shalt smite Syria		2) The 25 cities earlier conquered by Syria were recaptured by King Jehoash in three battles—just as Elisha predicted, 19
• He should have shot all the arrows He would thereby have assured the complete destruction of Syria			
• He would now defeat			

a. Out of respect for Elisha, the aged man of God now lying upon his deathbed, King Jehoash paid him a visit. The prophet had stood staunchly for the LORD during the days of terrible apostasy. As soon as the king entered Elisha's room, he knew the prophet was at the point of death. Jehoash, weeping, finally acknowledged that Elisha had been Israel's true defense against the enemies invading the land (v.14). By this confession, the king was demonstrating some faith in the LORD and His prophet. Addressing Elisha as "the chariots and horsemen of Israel" simply meant that Elisha was Israel's true protector. The nation's true defense and protection were in the prayers of Elisha and in the LORD who answered his prayers. Throughout his life Elisha had been the true strength of the nation, the true defender and protector against its enemies. Note that "the chariots and horsemen of Israel" was the same title Elisha himself had given to Elijah at the prophet's ascension some years earlier (2 K.2:12).

Because Jehoash had expressed *some faith* in the LORD, Elisha sought to arouse a complete faith within the king. For if he could arouse a complete faith within Jehoash, the king could launch a reform throughout the nation, turning the people back to the LORD.

b. Thus, lying upon his deathbed, Elisha gave the king one last prediction and a wonderful promise, a symbolic picture of Israel's coming victory over Syria (vv.15-17). Instructing the king to take a bow and arrows in his hands, Elisha then placed his hands on the king's hand and told him to open the east window and shoot the arrow as far as he could. As the king shot the arrow, the dying prophet shouted out that the arrow symbolized the LORD's victory over Syria. Israel would defeat the Syrians at the battle of Aphek.

c. But this promise was not the only message Elisha used to arouse a *complete faith* within the king. Elisha gave the king an opportunity to completely destroy Syria. This he did by instructing the king to continue shooting arrows (vv.18-19). But note what happened: Jehoash shot only three times and stopped. Becoming angry, the prophet Elisha strongly rebuked the king. He should have completed the task, shooting all the arrows in his possession. If he had, he would have completely destroyed the Syrians. But now he would defeat them only the number of times he had shot the arrows, that is, three times.

In contrast to the strong character of the dying prophet Elisha, a godly man of iron determination and perseverance, the king had failed to persevere to the end. Full, *complete faith* was simply not in the heart of the king. For too long he had lived in unbelief and wickedness. What little faith arose in his heart was just not enough to continue to follow the instructions of God's messenger, the prophet Elisha. Consequently, although he would be blessed with a few victories over Syria, he would also suffer oppression from the enemy.

d. Having completed his task upon this earth, the great prophet Elisha died. Scripture simply says that he was buried. Russell Dilday has an excellent statement on the death of Elisha that is well worth quoting:

> "Here Elisha is an old man, sick and at the point of death. Unlike the flamboyant Elijah, whose life ended in a dramatic whirlwind exit in a fiery chariot, Elisha died from a wasting illness. But God was just as near to him as he passed through the shadows of the valley of death as He had been to Elijah as he passed through the skies on his fiery chariots."[1]

e. Although Elisha had just died, his ministry was not finished. For God used even his dead body to symbolize the coming *resurrection of the dead* by the power of God (vv.20-21). A spectacular miracle took place. Some Israelites were burying a man when a band of Moabite raiders suddenly attacked. Being forced to flee for their lives, the burial party quickly threw the dead body into the first available tomb, which was Elisha's. When the lifeless body touched Elisha's bones, the dead man was immediately revived and stood on his feet. In the word's of *The Expositor's Bible Commentary*:

> Herein was another...sign for Jehoash and Israel: God was the God of the living, not the dead (cf. Lu.20:38), not only for Elisha and the man who had been restored to life, but for Israel as well. Israel could yet "live" if she would but appropriate the eternally living God as her own.[2]

f. Just as Elisha had prophesied, Syria continued to oppress the Northern Kingdom during the reign of Jehoahaz. In love and compassion, God continued to discipline the nation. But God did not allow the Syrians to utterly destroy the Northern Kingdom, for God still had the hope that the people would turn back to Him. He wanted to give them every opportunity possible, until their hearts became so hardened that He knew they would never again repent. Because of His covenant with Abraham, Isaac, and Jacob, God was just not willing to cast them off, not willing to banish them from His presence—not yet (vv.22-23).

g. Note that the prophecy of Elisha was fulfilled exactly as he had predicted (vv.24-25). The king of Syria soon died, and his son Ben-Hadad succeeded him as king. During Ben-Hadad's reign, King Jehoash was able to recapture 25 Israelite cities from the Syrians. In fulfillment of the prophecy, he defeated the Syrians three times and recovered the 25 cities (v.19).

Thought 1. In contrast to the weak character of Jehoash, Elisha demonstrated a character of iron determination in following the LORD and in living a righteous life. Persevering to the end, he was saved and given his eternal reward by the power of God.

So it is with us. If we have a strong, iron determination in trusting the Lord Jesus Christ and live righteous lives—if we persevere to the very end—God's power will work in our lives. When facing death, God will save us from the experience of death itself, transferring us directly into His presence to live with Him eternally. We will never taste death, never suffer any of the torments of hell. Quicker than the eye can blink, we will be transferred from this life right into the perfection, glory, and joy of heaven itself.

But note this fact: we must believe in the Lord Jesus Christ and commit our lives to His righteousness. Simply stated, we must believe Christ and live for Him. Once we profess to believe and to be a follower of the Lord, we must do just what we say: believe and follow Him. We must persevere, be steadfast in our faith.

Another way to say the same thing is this: once we profess Christ, we must continue to profess and follow after Him. *Continuing on* is the evidence of our faith. When people see us *continuing* to follow Christ, they know that our profession is true. On the other hand, if we profess to be followers of the Lord and then refuse to live as He says, people know that we are making a *false* profession. They know that we are hypocrites. But continuing on, being steadfast, enduring, persevering in following Christ—this assures our salvation, that our profession is true, that we mean what we say. Listen to what the Word of God says about perseverance and steadfastness:

> **"And ye shall be hated of all *men* for my name's sake: but he that endureth to the end shall be saved" (Mt.10:22).**
> **"As the Father hath loved me, so have I loved you: continue ye in my love" (Jn.15:9).**
> **"Therefore, my beloved brethren, be ye stedfast, unmovable, always abounding in the work of the Lord, forasmuch as ye know that your labour is not in vain in the Lord" (1 Co.15:58).**
> **"Stand fast therefore in the liberty wherewith Christ hath made us free, and be not entangled again with the yoke of bondage" (Ga.5:1).**

---

[1] Russell Dilday. *1, 2 Kings*, p.384.
[2] Richard D. Patterson and Hermann J. Austel. *1, 2 Kings*, p.226.

"And let us not be weary in well doing: for in due season we shall reap, if we faint not" (Ga.6:9).

"Only let your conversation [conduct, behavior] be as it becometh the gospel of Christ: that whether I come and see you, or else be absent, I may hear of your affairs, that ye stand fast in one spirit, with one mind striving together for the faith of the gospel" (Ph.1:27).

"Wherefore seeing we also are compassed about with so great a cloud of witnesses, let us lay aside every weight, and the sin which doth so easily beset us, and let us run with patience the race that is set before us" (He.12:1).

"Wherefore gird up the loins of your mind, be sober, and hope to the end for the grace that is to be brought unto you at the revelation of Jesus Christ" (1 Pe.1:13).

"Be sober, be vigilant; because your adversary the devil, as a roaring lion, walketh about, seeking whom he may devour: Whom resist stedfast in the faith, knowing that the same afflictions are accomplished in your brethren that are in the world" (1 Pe.5:8-9).

"Ye therefore, beloved, seeing ye know *these things* before, beware lest ye also, being led away with the error of the wicked, fall from your own stedfastness. But grow in grace, and *in* the knowledge of our Lord and Saviour Jesus Christ. To him *be* glory both now and for ever. Amen" (2 Pe.3:17-18).

"Behold, I come quickly: hold that fast which thou hast, that no man take thy crown" (Re.3:11).

"But cleave unto the LORD your God, as ye have done unto this day" (Jos.23:8).

"The righteous also shall hold on his way, and he that hath clean hands shall be stronger and stronger" (Jb.17:9).

THE UTTER DISINTEGRATION AND FALL OF ISRAEL, THE NORTHERN KINGDOM: A TRAGIC END DUE TO AN UNBROKEN STREAM OF WICKEDNESS AND LAWLESSNESS, 14:1–17:41

(14:1–17:41) **DIVISION OVERVIEW**: For over 150 years, since the division of the kingdom, the Israelites had lived wicked, lawless lives and engaged in false worship, rejecting the LORD. As a result, both the Northern and Southern Kingdoms had deteriorated and were now weak politically, economically, militarily, socially, and spiritually. Because of their divisive spirit and weakened condition, both nations were in constant turmoil. They were in conflict with each other and with the surrounding nations. In addition, both were suffering under the continued oppression of the Syrian Empire. There was little hope for a bright future among the people. Because of their self-centered, indulgent and sinful lifestyles, there was little chance their society and nation could ever again become strong and prosperous. Based upon God's warnings, the future could only be the inevitable hand of utter destruction. For God's patience with the Israelites and their leaders was bound to be running out.

However, in the present division of Scripture the reader witnesses an amazing event. The LORD had mercy upon the Israelites, both the Northern and Southern Kingdoms. Note what the author of *Second Kings* has just said in the former chapter:

> **"And the Lord was gracious unto them, and had compassion on them, and had respect unto them, because of his covenant with Abraham, Isaac, and Jacob, and would not destroy them, neither cast he them from his presence as yet" (2 K.13:23).**

Although the leaders and people of Israel had given no indication of interest in the LORD, the LORD took the initiative and gave them one *last chance* to repent. The Northern Kingdom of Israel received one *final opportunity* to turn to the LORD, to turn from their wicked, lawless and unjust ways.

Once again the LORD poured out His blessings of success and prosperity upon the people. By giving them an era of success and prosperity, the LORD longed for the people to realize their blessings had come from Him. And in their realization, there was the hope that they would turn from their unrighteous ways back to Him. This period of success and prosperity came during the reigns of Jeroboam II in Israel and Amaziah, who was also known as Uzziah, in Judah (14:23–15:7). But as the prophets Amos and Hosea pointed out, instead of arousing the people to turn to the LORD, the enormous success and prosperity caused the leaders and people to become proud, boastful, and self-sufficient. They gloried in their own abilities and achievements, ignoring, denying, and rejecting the LORD. The kings and people continued their downward spiral into utter corruption and decadence. Thus the inevitable hand of judgment fell upon the Northern Kingdom of Israel, and they entered a period of severe political disorder soon thereafter (15:8-31). The nation was conquered by the Assyrians, who had some years earlier defeated and replaced the Syrians as the dominant world power.

Samaria, the capital of Israel, was destroyed and the people exiled by the Assyrian King Shalmaneser V in 722 B.C. (17:1-6). In discussing why God executed judgment against the Northern Kingdom, it is interesting to note that God gives an astounding twenty-two reasons for the judgment in Scripture (17:7-23).

Judah lasted longer than Israel because of the good, righteous kings who occasionally ruled the nation. For this reason the LORD delayed their judgment, hoping that the leaders and people would make a permanent commitment to Him. Every generation of Judeans needed to be taught to live consistent, righteous lives and to acknowledge the LORD alone as the only living and true God.

But as has been seen since David, the rulers and generations refused to heed the Word of God and the warnings of the prophets. Thus one of the primary causes for the coming judgment upon Judah is that of *inconsistency*. The generations of Judean people had the major flaw of being half-hearted, double-minded, indecisive, indifferent, neglectful—just *inconsistent*. Consequently, as will be seen in the next division, the inevitable hand of judgment against an immoral, unrighteous nation will also fall upon Judah.

**THE UTTER DISINTEGRATION AND
FALL OF ISRAEL, THE NORTHERN
KINGDOM: A TRAGIC END DUE TO AN
UNBROKEN STREAM OF WICKEDNESS
AND LAWLESSNESS, 14:1–17:41**

A. The Reign of Amaziah in Judah and His Provoking War with Israel: Losing One's Opportunity to Serve, 14:1-22

B. The Long Reigns of Jeroboam II in Israel and Azariah (Uzziah) in Judah: God's Blessing the People and Giving Them One Last Chance to Repent, 14:23–15:7

C. The Reigns of Five Kings in Israel, Four of Whom Were Assassinated: Political Disorder Due to the People's Continued Wickedness and Rejection of God, 15:8-31

D. The Reigns of Two Kings in Judah, Jotham and Ahaz: A Sharp Contrast Between Righteousness and Wickedness, 15:32–16:20

E. The Tragic Fall of Israel, Its Conquest and Deportation of the People by the Assyrians (722 BC): The End of God's Long-Suffering and the Execution of His Judgment, 17:1-41

1. The summary of Amaziah's reign: A partial, halfhearted commitment
a. His background
1) His father: King Joash of Judah, 12:1-21
2) His term: 29 years (796-767 B.C.)
3) His mother: Jehoaddan

b. His spiritual commitment
1) He did what was right, but not as David had done
2) He followed his father's example
• Failed to remove the high places of worship
• Was not wholeheartedly committed, 2 Chr.25:2

c. His execution of justice
1) He put to death the officials who had assassinated his father, 12:20-21

2) He did not murder the sons of the assassins as was the custom of Near Eastern rulers: He spared their lives as the Law of God dictates, De.24:16

d. His major military victory: Conquered Edom
1) He killed 10,000 soldiers
2) He captured Sela, an impregnable fortress
2. The unwise declaration of war by Amaziah against the Northern Kingdom of Israel: A picture of boastful pride & arrogance

---

CHAPTER 14

III. THE UTTER DISINTEGRATION & FALL OF ISRAEL, THE NORTHERN KINGDOM: A TRAGIC END DUE TO AN UNBROKEN STREAM OF WICKEDNESS & LAWLESSNESS, 14:1–17:41

A. The Reign of Amaziah in Judah & His Provoking War with Israel: A Picture of Losing One's Opportunity to Serve, 14:1-22

14:1-6; see 2 Chr.25:1-4
14:7; see 2 Chr.25:11-12
14:8-22; see 2 Chr.25:17–26:2

In the second year of Joash son of Jehoahaz king of Israel reigned Amaziah the son of Joash king of Judah.
2 He was twenty and five years old when he began to reign, and reigned twenty and nine years in Jerusalem. And his mother's name *was* Jehoaddan of Jerusalem.
3 And he did *that which was* right in the sight of the LORD, yet not like David his father: he did according to all things as Joash his father did.
4 Howbeit the high places were not taken away: as yet the people did sacrifice and burnt incense on the high places.
5 And it came to pass, as soon as the kingdom was confirmed in his hand, that he slew his servants which had slain the king his father.
6 But the children of the murderers he slew not: according unto that which is written in the book of the law of Moses, wherein the LORD commanded, saying, The fathers shall not be put to death for the children, nor the children be put to death for the fathers; but every man shall be put to death for his own sin.
7 He slew of Edom in the valley of salt ten thousand, and took Selah by war, and called the name of it Joktheel unto this day.
8 Then Amaziah sent messengers to Jehoash, the son of Jehoahaz son of Jehu, king of Israel, saying, Come, let us look one another in the face.

9 And Jehoash the king of Israel sent to Amaziah king of Judah, saying, The thistle that *was* in Lebanon sent to the cedar that *was* in Lebanon, saying, Give thy daughter to my son to wife: and there passed by a wild beast that *was* in Lebanon, and trode down the thistle.
10 Thou hast indeed smitten Edom, and thine heart hath lifted thee up: glory *of this,* and tarry at home: for why shouldest thou meddle to *thy* hurt, that thou shouldest fall, *even* thou, and Judah with thee?
11 But Amaziah would not hear. Therefore Jehoash king of Israel went up; and he and Amaziah king of Judah looked one another in the face at Beth-shemesh, which *belongeth* to Judah.
12 And Judah was put to the worse before Israel; and they fled every man to their tents.
13 And Jehoash king of Israel took Amaziah king of Judah, the son of Jehoash the son of Ahaziah, at Beth-shemesh, and came to Jerusalem, and brake down the wall of Jerusalem from the gate of Ephraim unto the corner gate, four hundred cubits.
14 And he took all the gold and silver, and all the vessels that were found in the house of the LORD, and in the treasures of the king's house, and hostages, and returned to Samaria.
15 Now the rest of the acts of Jehoash which he did, and his might, and how he fought with Amaziah king of Judah, *are* they not written in the book of the chronicles of the kings of Israel?
16 And Jehoash slept with his fathers, and was buried in Samaria with the kings of Israel; and Jeroboam his son reigned in his stead.
17 And Amaziah the son of Joash king of Judah lived after the death of Jehoash son of Jehoahaz king of Israel fifteen years.
18 And the rest of the acts of Amaziah, *are* they not written in the book of the chronicles of the kings of Judah?

a. The declaration of war sent to King Jehoash, 2 Chr.25:6-24
b. The warning sent back to Amaziah of Judah
1) Jehoash warned that Israel was like a strong cedar & Judah nothing more than a thistle that could easily be trampled underfoot

2) Jehoash stated that Amaziah was filled with pride & arrogance due to his victory over Edom: He was only asking for trouble & certain defeat in attacking Israel

3) Amaziah rejected Jehoash's warning
c. The initiative seized & a quick strike launched by Jehoash at Beth Shemesh (only about 15 miles west of Jerusalem)

1) He routed the troops of Judah & sent them fleeing

2) He captured King Amaziah of Judah

3) He conquered Jerusalem, breaking down a section of the wall about 600 feet long

4) He looted the temple & palace of their treasures & furnishings
5) He took hostages (including the king) & returned to Samaria

d. The summary of Jehoash's reign repeated (13:12-13): To mark the end of his life & the release of Amaziah to return as king of Judah
1) His reign recorded in the book *The History of the Kings of Israel*
2) His death & burial in Samaria
3) His successor: His son Jeroboam II
3. The fifteen remaining years of Amaziah's life & his death: A lost opportunity to serve

a. His achievements & the summary of his life:
1) His reign: Recorded in the book *The History of the Kings of Judah*

113

| 2) His death: Was assassinated
• Fled a conspiracy
• Was killed in Lachish

3) His burial: In the royal tomb in Jerusalem | 19 Now they made a conspiracy against him in Jerusalem: and he fled to Lachish; but they sent after him to Lachish, and slew him there.
20 And they brought him on horses: and he was buried at Jerusalem with his fathers in the city of David. | 21 And all the people of Judah took Azariah, which *was* sixteen years old, and made him king instead of his father Amaziah.
22 He built Elath, and restored it to Judah, after that the king slept with his fathers. | b. His successor: His son Azariah or Uzziah
1) He was 16 years old

2) He secured control over Elath, a seaport on the Gulf of Aqaba, 1 K.9:26 |

DIVISION III

THE UTTER DISINTEGRATION AND FALL OF ISRAEL, THE NORTHERN KINGDOM: A TRAGIC END DUE TO AN UNBROKEN STREAM OF WICKEDNESS AND LAWLESSNESS, 14:1–17:22

A. The Reign of Amaziah in Judah and His Provoking War with Israel: A Picture of Losing One's Opportunity to Serve, 14:1-22

(14:1-22) **Introduction—Opportunity, Lost, Caused by—Lost, Opportunity, Results of—Humankind, Lost Opportunity, Caused by**: when an opportunity arises, we must grab it or else lose the opportunity. The words *LOST OPPORTUNITY* could be written across the faces or the tombstones of many of us. For one opportunity after another has been made available to us; yet we failed to grab hold and take the chance. In many cases, fear kept us from seizing the opportunity: the fear of insecurity, of losing money, of taking the risk, or of the time demanded. In other cases, opportunity was lost because we were not willing to discipline ourselves. The personal discipline and sacrifice required were just too much.

Think of the people who have not secured education or developed their skills because they were simply not willing to commit themselves to the discipline required to study or attend classes or training sessions. In dealing with sinful, wicked behavior, how many have lost the opportunity to be a good example, to be a role model to others, to say "No!"? They failed to reject the offer to take the first drug, the first drink, the first smoke, or the first look at pornographic literature or film? How many lost the opportunity to say "No!" to illicit sex? Again, the words "LOST OPPORTUNITY" could be written across the faces or tombstones of many of us. *Lost opportunity* is the practical subject of this present Scripture.

As a background to this chapter, Syria had become a weakened nation; as a result, both the Northern Kingdom and Judah were able to gain some freedom from the tyranny of Syria. But instead of using the opportunity to strengthen their nations economically, militarily, and spiritually, the two kings waged war against one another. Squandering the years of peace, they etched into the history of their nations these tragic words: *lost opportunity*. As a result, they continued the downward spiral of wicked behavior, madly rushing to the day when God could take no more and was forced to execute His final judgment. This is: *The Reign of Amaziah in Judah and & His Provoking War with Israel: A Picture of Losing One's Opportunity to Serve,* 14:1-22.

1. The summary of Amaziah's reign: a partial, halfhearted commitment (vv.1-7).
2. The unwise declaration of war by Amaziah against the Northern Kingdom of Israel: a picture of boastful pride and arrogance (vv.8-16).
3. The fifteen remaining years of Amaziah's life and his death: a lost opportunity to serve (vv.17-22).

1 (14:1-7) **Commitment, Halfhearted, Example of—Dedication, Halfhearted, Example of—Kings, of Judah, Amaziah—Justice, Execution, Example of**: Amaziah's father was King Joash, who had been assassinated by two of his own royal officials (12:20). Shortly after his father's assassination, Amaziah was crowned king at the rather young age of twenty-five (vv.1-2). He began his rule in the second year of King Jehoash of Israel and ruled for twenty-nine years (796-767 B.C.). His mother's name was Jehoaddan. She had been born and reared in Jerusalem, the capital of the Southern Kingdom.

At some point during his early life, King Amaziah had obviously made a spiritual commitment to the LORD. Scripture says that he was righteous. He did what was right in the eyes of the LORD, following the example of his father Joash. But sadly, he did not follow the LORD with his whole heart, not like his ancestor King David had done (v.3). Tragically, he failed to remove the high places of worship (v.4). Just like so many Judean kings before him, he allowed the people to continue building worship centers on the former pagan sites where false worship had been conducted. By continuing to worship at the high places—even though the people were worshipping the LORD—there was a tendency for the people to allow some practices of false worship to seep into their true worship. The result was catastrophic, for this small compromise eventually led to a full-fledged compromise. Everything from mixed religion to outright worship of idols and false gods eventually seeped into the worship centers located at the high places.

Regrettably, worship at the high places would continue for many years yet to come, until the great reformation launched by the godly King Josiah (see outline and note—23:4-25 for more discussion). But until the days of Josiah, the high places would remain, indicating that the kings of Judah were not wholeheartedly committed to the LORD. They were only partially committed, being unwilling to remove the high places that had formerly been used for false worship. Obviously, the kings of Judah feared a reaction from the people if they destroyed their worship centers built at the high places. Rather than risk losing the people's favor and loyalty, the kings took the easy route and compromised. They allowed the people to continue slipping into false worship. A total, heartfelt commitment to the LORD was sadly lacking in the leaders (2 Chr.25:2). In evaluating the life of King Amaziah, he did step forth to take a stand for the execution of justice (vv.5-6). This is seen in his putting to death the royal officials who had assassinated his father (12:20-21). After killing them, however, he did not murder the sons of the assassins as was the custom of Near Eastern rulers. But, rather, he spared their lives as the law of God dictates, declaring that a father or child must not be punished for the other. Each was individually, personally responsible for his own act of wickedness (De.24:16).

Amaziah's major military victory was achieved against the nation of Edom (v.7). Remember that the Edomites were descendants of Esau, the brother of Jacob. Down through the centuries there had always been conflict between the descendants of the two brothers, that is, between the Israelites who descended from Jacob and the Edomites who descended from Esau. As pointed out by Russell Dilday, from Genesis 25:30 to Malachi 1:5, the two peoples are seen holding a bitter hatred and hostility for each other and are engaged in constant battle. In fact, it was the continued conflict between the two peoples that aroused the prophet Obadiah to sit down and write the great book of *Obadiah,* which is a strong condemnation of the Edomites.[1]

For years Edom had been under the domination of Israel and had been forced to pay a heavy taxation, but the nation was able to gain its independence from the Southern Kingdom during the reign of Jehoram (8:20-22). Sensing the need to bolster his nation's economy, King Amaziah made the decision to once again subject the Edomites in order to collect taxes from them. Declaring war against the descendants of Esau, he attacked the Edomites in the Valley of Salt and killed 10,000 of their soldiers (v.7). He was also able to conquer the fortified city of Selah. The name *"Selah"* means rock, which accurately described this city, for it sat on top of a high range of formidable, unapproachable cliffs. Conquering the impregnable fortress was a significant feat for King Amaziah. News of the feat no doubt spread far and wide throughout the known world of that time.

OUTLINE	SCRIPTURE	SCRIPTURE	OUTLINE

1. **The summary of Amaziah's reign: A partial, halfhearted commitment**
a. His background
  1) His father: King Joash of Judah, 12:1-21
  2) His term: 29 years (796-767 B.C.)
  3) His mother: Jehoaddan
 	
b. His spiritual commitment
  1) He did what was right, but not as David had done
  2) He followed his father's example
  • Failed to remove the high places of worship
  • Was not wholeheartedly committed, 2 Chr.25:2
 	
c. His execution of justice
	In the second year of Joash son of Jehoahaz king of Israel reigned Amaziah the son of Joash king of Judah.
	2 He was twenty and five years old when he began to reign, and reigned twenty and nine years in Jerusalem. And his mother's name *was* Jehoaddan of Jerusalem.
	3 And he did *that which was* right in the sight of the LORD, yet not like David his father: he did according to all things as Joash his father did.
	4 Howbeit the high places were not taken away: as yet the people did sacrifice and burnt incense on the high places.
	5 And it came to pass, as
		soon as the kingdom was confirmed in his hand, that he slew his servants which had slain the king his father.
		6 But the children of the murderers he slew not: according unto that which is written in the book of the law of Moses, wherein the LORD commanded, saying, The fathers shall not be put to death for the children, nor the children be put to death for the fathers; but every man shall be put to death for his own sin.
		7 He slew of Edom in the valley of salt ten thousand, and took Selah by war, and called the name of it Joktheel unto this day.
			1) He put to death the officials who had assassinated his father, 12:20-21
			
			2) He did not murder the sons of the assassins as was the custom of Near Eastern rulers: He spared their lives as the Law of God dictates, De.24:16
			
			d. His major military victory: Conquered Edom
			1) He killed 10,000 soldiers
			2) He captured Sela, an impregnable fortress

Thought 1. Sadly, Amaziah's life is a picture of partial, halfhearted commitment. Although he lived a somewhat righteous life and pleased the LORD in some of the decisions he made, he was not totally committed. He refused to destroy the high places, the worship centers that had been built on sites where the people had formerly engaged in false worship. Being willing to compromise with some forms of false worship, Amaziah stood condemned, accused of having only a partial, halfhearted commitment.

What an indictment against many of us: to be only partially, halfheartedly committed to the LORD. How many of us engage in false worship occasionally or even regularly? How many of us attend and participate in church services where Jesus Christ is not honored and the Word of God is not truly preached and taught? How many of us belong to churches that are nothing more than worldly social organizations? That allow worldly activities to take place within their walls, such as immodest dances or parties that sometimes allow drinking and can lead to immorality or drunkenness or other tragedies? What do such functions have to do with the church, God's institution established for...

• worship, praise, and thanksgiving?
• preaching and teaching God's Holy Word?
• bearing a strong testimony to the salvation of God?
• reaching out in service to meet the needs of the community?

How many of us have only a partial, halfhearted commitment to the LORD and His church? Our hearts belong to God, and we are to commit them to God. Listen to what God says about a halfhearted commitment:

"And every one that heareth these sayings of mine, and doeth them not, shall be likened unto a foolish man, which built his house upon the sand: And the rain descended, and the floods came, and the winds blew, and beat upon that house; and it fell: and great was the fall of it" (Mt.7:26-27).

"And that servant, which knew his lord's will, and prepared not *himself,* neither did according to his will, shall be beaten with many *stripes*" (Lu.12:47).

---

[1] Russell Dilday. *1, 2 Kings*, p.392.

"No servant can serve two masters: for either he will hate the one, and love the other; or else he will hold to the one, and despise the other. Ye cannot serve God and mammon" (Lu.16:13).

"Ye cannot drink the cup of the Lord, and the cup of devils: ye cannot be partakers of the Lord's table, and of the table of devils" (1 Co.10:21).

"A double minded man *is* unstable in all his ways" (Js.1:8).

"What *doth it* profit, my brethren, though a man say he hath faith, and have not works? can faith save him?" (Js.2:14).

"Draw nigh to God, and he will draw nigh to you. Cleanse *your* hands, *ye* sinners; and purify *your* hearts, *ye* double minded" (Js.4:8).

"Therefore to him that knoweth to do good, and doeth *it* not, to him it is sin" (Js.4:17).

"I know thy works, that thou art neither cold nor hot: I would thou wert cold or hot. So then because thou art lukewarm, and neither cold nor hot, I will spue thee out of my mouth" (Re.3:15-16).

"Because thou sayest, I am rich, and increased with goods, and have need of nothing; and knowest not that thou art wretched, and miserable, and poor, and blind, and naked" (Re.3:17).

"But Jehu took no heed to walk in the law of the LORD God of Israel with all his heart: for he departed not from the sins of Jeroboam [false worship], which made Israel to sin" (2 K.10:31).

"And he [Amaziah] did *that which was* right in the sight of the LORD, but not with a perfect heart" (2 Chr.25:2).

"Their heart is divided; now shall they be found faulty: he shall break down their altars, he shall spoil their images" (Ho.10:2).

---

2 (14:8-16) **Arrogance, Example of—Pride, Example of—Boasting, Example of—Self-exaltation, Example of—Amaziah, Wars of—Northern Kingdom of Israel, Wars of—Judah, Wars of**: King Amaziah made a very unwise declaration of war against the Northern Kingdom of Israel. What caused Amaziah to launch a war against his northern neighbor, fellow Israelites? Scripture does not specifically say. However, it may be due to the angered reaction of 100,000 mercenary troops from Israel he had hired to help in the Edomite campaign. Although the author of Kings does not mention this fact, the author of *Second Chronicles* does. When King Amaziah had earlier secured the services of 100,000 Israelite soldiers, a prophet had confronted and warned Amaziah against the unholy alliance. Heeding the prophet's warning, Amaziah had discharged the mercenary troops from Israel. They left, but they were furious, filled with rage. Consequently, on their way back home and acting out of frustration, they raided several Judean towns, killing over 3,000 people and carrying off a huge amount of plunder (see outline and note—2 Chr.25:5-13 for more discussion). While the author of *Kings* does not share this fact about the mercenary soldiers, he does give a graphic description of the conflict between the Northern and Southern Kingdoms.

OUTLINE	SCRIPTURE	SCRIPTURE	OUTLINE
2. The unwise declaration of war by Amaziah against the Northern Kingdom of Israel: A picture of boastful pride & arrogance	8 Then Amaziah sent messengers to Jehoash, the son of Jehoahaz son of Jehu, king of Israel, saying, Come, let us look one another in the face.	worse before Israel; and they fled every man to their tents.	Judah & sent them fleeing
a. The declaration of war sent to King Jehoash, 2 Chr.25:6-24	9 And Jehoash the king of Israel sent to Amaziah king of Judah, saying, The thistle that was in Lebanon sent to the cedar that was in Lebanon, saying, Give thy daughter to my son to wife: and there passed by a wild beast that was in Lebanon, and trode down the thistle.	13 And Jehoash king of Israel took Amaziah king of Judah, the son of Jehoash the son of Ahaziah, at Bethshemesh, and came to Jerusalem, and brake down the wall of Jerusalem from the gate of Ephraim unto the corner gate, four hundred cubits.	2) He captured King Amaziah of Judah
b. The warning sent back to Amaziah of Judah 1) Jehoash warned that Israel was like a strong cedar & Judah nothing more than a thistle that could easily be trampled underfoot			3) He conquered Jerusalem, breaking down a section of the wall about 600 feet long
2) Jehoash stated that Amaziah was filled with pride & arrogance due to his victory over Edom: He was only asking for trouble & certain defeat in attacking Israel	10 Thou hast indeed smitten Edom, and thine heart hath lifted thee up: glory *of this*, and tarry at home: for why shouldest thou meddle to *thy* hurt, that thou shouldest fall, *even* thou, and Judah with thee?	14 And he took all the gold and silver, and all the vessels that were found in the house of the LORD, and in the treasures of the king's house, and hostages, and returned to Samaria.	4) He looted the temple & palace of their treasures & furnishings
3) Amaziah rejected Jehoash's warning	11 But Amaziah would not hear. Therefore Jehoash king of Israel went up; and he and Amaziah king of Judah looked one another in the face at Beth-shemesh, which *belongeth* to Judah.	15 Now the rest of the acts of Jehoash which he did, and his might, and how he fought with Amaziah king of Judah, *are* they not written in the book of the chronicles of the kings of Israel?	5) He took hostages (including the king) & returned to Samaria d. The summary of Jehoash's reign repeated (13:12-13): To mark the end of his life & the release of Amaziah to return as king of Judah
c. The initiative seized & a quick strike launched by Jehoash at Beth Shemesh (only about 15 miles west of Jerusalem)		16 And Jehoash slept with his fathers, and was buried in Samaria with the kings of Israel; and Jeroboam his son reigned in his stead.	1) His reign recorded in the book *The History of the Kings of Israel* 2) His death & burial in Samaria
1) He routed the troops of	12 And Judah was put to the		3) His successor: His son Jeroboam II

a. King Amaziah was puffed up with boastful pride and arrogance due to his great military victory over the Edomites. Unwisely, he sent a declaration of war to King Jehoash of the Northern Kingdom (v.8). Brimming with over-confidence, Amaziah felt undefeatable. He was sure he could crush the Northern Kingdom in battle; he could gain far more plunder than his own people had lost to the mercenary soldiers. Apparently, he felt that King Jehoash and the Israelites would be stricken with terror by his threat of invasion. For after all, he had achieved a monumental victory over Edom and the capture of the impregnable fortress of Selah.

b. But far from cowering under the threat of Amaziah, Jehoash fired a warning back to the threatening king (vv.9-11). The truth was that Israel was like a strong cedar and Judah was nothing more than a thistle that could easily be trampled under the foot of the Israelites. Continuing his warning, Jehoash stated that Amaziah had indeed defeated Edom, but he had allowed his victory to fill him with an empty pride and arrogance. If he attacked the Northern Kingdom, he was only asking for trouble and certain defeat (v.10). But Jehoash's warning failed to deflate the arrogance that Amaziah was feeling due to his victory over Edom. He rejected Jehoash's warning.

c. Learning of Amaziah's rejection, Jehoash quickly seized the initiative and launched a strike at Beth-Shemesh which was only about 15 miles west of Jerusalem (vv.11-14). He immediately routed the troops of Judah and sent them scurrying for their lives (v.12). In his pursuit of the fleeing troops, Jehoash was able to capture Amaziah the king of Judah (v.13). After capturing the king, Jehoash continued his march to Jerusalem and conquered the city by breaking down a section of the wall, a section about 600 feet long. After capturing the capital Jerusalem, Jehoash looted the temple and the royal palace, taking all the silver and gold and all other articles found in the temple and palace treasuries (v.14). Then he took both the king and the remaining citizens as hostages and returned back home to Samaria.

d. Although a summary of Jehoash's reign was given earlier (13:12-13), it is repeated here for two reasons: to mark the end of his life and the release of Amaziah to return as king of Judah (vv.15-16). As Scripture indicates, after Jehoash's death Amaziah was released and allowed to return as ruler of the Southern Kingdom.

In summarizing the reign of Israel's King Jehoash, the author says that his achievements were recorded in the book of *The History of the Kings of Israel*. After his death, Jehoash was buried in Samaria, the capital of the Northern Kingdom, and succeeded by his son Jeroboam II (v.16).

Thought 1. Amaziah became boastful and arrogant. Due to his achievement, he allowed himself to become *puffed up*, to have an inflated sense of self-worth. How many of us have become *puffed up* with pride and arrogance? How many of us have become inflated with a sense of *self-importance*?

We should take pride in our skills and achievements; but we must never become *puffed up*, thinking too highly of ourselves, as though we were better and superior to everyone around us. We must never look at other people as though they were inferior, less than we are, of less value and worth than we are. When pride in oneself becomes inflated, egotistical, or super-spiritual, then pride becomes evil, sinful, and wicked. It is a *puffed up* pride that leads a person to be mean-spirited and to mistreat people. A *puffed up* pride causes conflict at work, school, home, church, social activities, or wherever else we may be.

Being *puffed up* with pride, feeling that one is superior or of more value and worth than others, is what drives people to subject others under their control. A *puffed up* person seeks to impose his will upon others, other men, women, even children. On occasion it leads to the abuse of others—whether sexual, physical, verbal, or mental abuse—or even to enslavement. Listen to what God's Holy Word says about pride, boasting, arrogance, and self-exaltation over others:

> "And whosoever shall exalt himself shall be abased; and he that shall humble himself shall be exalted" (Mt.23:12).
> "*Be* of the same mind one toward another. Mind not high things, but condescend to men of low estate. Be not wise in your own conceits" (Ro.12:16).
> "But he giveth more grace. Wherefore he saith, God resisteth the proud, but giveth grace unto the humble" (Js.4:6).
> "Love not the world, neither the things *that are* in the world. If any man love the world, the love of the Father is not in him. For all that *is* in the world, the lust of the flesh, and the lust of the eyes, and the pride of life, is not of the Father, but is of the world" (1 Jn.2:15-16).
> "Talk no more so exceeding proudly; let *not* arrogancy come out of your mouth: for the LORD *is* a God of knowledge, and by him actions are weighed" (1 S.2:3).
> "The wicked in *his* pride doth persecute the poor: let them be taken in the devices that they have imagined" (Ps.10:2).
> "Who have said, With our tongue will we prevail; our lips *are* our own: who *is* lord over us?" (Ps.12:4).
> "They that trust in their wealth, and boast themselves in the multitude of their riches; None *of* them can by any means redeem his brother, nor give to God a ransom for him" (Ps.49:6-7).
> "Therefore pride compasseth them about as a chain; violence covereth them *as* a garment" (Ps.73:6).
> "*When* pride cometh, then cometh shame: but with the lowly *is* wisdom" (Pr.11:2).
> "Pride *goeth* before destruction, and an haughty spirit before a fall" (Pr.16:18).
> "He loveth transgression that loveth strife: *and* he that exalteth his gate seeketh destruction" (Pr.17:19).
> "An high look, and a proud heart, *and* the plowing of the wicked, *is* sin" (Pr.21:4).
> "Seest thou a man wise in his own conceit? *there is* more hope of a fool than of him" (Pr.26:12).
> "He that is of a proud heart stirreth up strife: but he that putteth his trust in the LORD shall be made fat" (Pr.28:25).
> "A man's pride shall bring him low: but honour shall uphold the humble in spirit" (Pr.29:23).

"Moreover the LORD saith, Because the daughters of Zion are haughty, and walk with stretched forth necks and wanton eyes, walking and mincing *as* they go, and making a tinkling with their feet: Therefore the LORD will smite with a scab the crown of the head of the daughters of Zion, and the LORD will discover their secret parts" (Is.3:16-17).

"Woe unto *them that are* wise in their own eyes, and prudent in their own sight!" (Is.5:21).

"And I will punish the world for *their* evil, and the wicked for their iniquity; and I will cause the arrogancy of the proud to cease, and will lay low the haughtiness of the terrible" (Is.13:11).

"For thou hast said in thine heart, I will ascend into heaven, I will exalt my throne above the stars of God: I will sit also upon the mount of the congregation, in the sides of the north: I will ascend above the heights of the clouds; I will be like the most High. Yet thou shalt be brought down to hell, to the sides of the pit" (Is.14:13-15).

"Though thou exalt *thyself* as the eagle, and though thou set thy nest among the stars, thence will I bring thee down, saith the LORD" (Obad.4).

3 (14:17-22) **Opportunity, Duty—Service, Duty—Opportunity, Lost—Loss of Opportunity, Example of— Amaziah, Reign of, Summary**: after his return from exile in Israel, King Amaziah ruled for fifteen more years. But note, no achievement whatsoever is recorded during these 15 years of his life. It is as though he accomplished nothing, absolutely nothing. The author simply mentions several facts about the end of his life.

His achievements and a summary of his life are recorded in the book *The History of the Kings of Judah* (v.18). Fifteen years after his release from exile, he somehow discovered a plot against his life and fled to Lachish. But the assassins pursued and killed him there (v.19). However, his body was escorted back to Jerusalem where he was buried (v.20). His son Azariah or Uzziah succeeded him as ruler of the Southern Kingdom (v.21).

Uzziah is the same king mentioned by the prophet Isaiah. It was in the days of Uzziah that Isaiah received his great vision concerning Judah and Jerusalem (Is.1:1). Although he was only 16 years old when crowned ruler over the Southern Kingdom, Uzziah obviously had widespread support. For Scripture says that all the people of Judah rallied behind the young boy in setting him upon the throne. He immediately set about to complete a project undertaken by his father, that of rebuilding the city of Elath, which was a seaport on the Gulf of Aqaba (1 K.9:26).

OUTLINE	SCRIPTURE	SCRIPTURE	OUTLINE
3. The fifteen remaining years of Amaziah's life & his death: A lost opportunity to serve	17 And Amaziah the son of Joash king of Judah lived after the death of Jehoash son of Jehoahaz king of Israel fifteen years.	horses: and he was buried at Jerusalem with his fathers in the city of David.	tomb in Jerusalem
a. His achievements & the summary of his life:	18 And the rest of the acts of Amaziah, *are* they not written in the book of the chronicles of the kings of Judah?	20 And they brought him on horses: and he was buried at Jerusalem with his fathers in the city of David.	
1) His reign: Recorded in the book *The History of the Kings of Judah*		21 And all the people of Judah took Azariah, which *was* sixteen years old, and made	b. His successor: His son Azariah or Uzziah
2) His death: Was assassinated	19 Now they made a conspiracy against him in Jerusalem: and he fled to Lachish;	him king instead of his father Amaziah.	1) He was 16 years old
• Fled a conspiracy	but they sent after him to	22 He built Elath, and restored it to Judah, after	
• Was killed in Lachish	Lachish, and slew him there.	that the king slept with his fathers.	2) He secured control over Elath, a seaport on the Gulf of Aqaba, 1 K.9:26
3) His burial: In the royal	20 And they brought him on		

Thought 1. How many of us, like Amaziah, have had opportunities laid before us—opportunities to grow, to accomplish something worthwhile, to help others—but we failed to take hold of the opportunity? We lost the chance, the opening, the break. How many opportunities have we had...

- to improve our skill or education?
- to enter business or secure a better job?
- to meet a wonderful lady or a prince of a man?
- to make more money or to secure more property?
- to become more financially secure and less indebted?
- to encourage or build up our wives, husbands, or children?
- to reconcile and make peace with someone?
- to bring joy or pleasure to someone?

- to help or minister to the needs of someone?
- to make a decision for Christ or join the church?
- to repent of our sins and change our lives?
- to begin anew and get a fresh start in life?
- to undertake a challenging task or make a significant contribution?
- to be charitable or compassionate?
- to help the suffering, diseased, weak, or dying?

When opportunities like these are offered to us and we fail to take hold of them, we lose the opportunity—sometimes forever. As a result, some of us are uneducated; others are living lives of drudgery, loathing their jobs or professions. Still others regret whom they have married or formed business partnerships with or taken on as close friends. Many regret that they did not further their education or develop their skills or work diligently at their jobs. Thus, they missed out on promotions or pay increases or even lost their jobs. While all of us have had the option to live honest and moral lives, many have chosen instead to cheat, steal, lie, behave immorally, or rebel against all authority. In addition, many had the opportunity—but failed to turn down—the first smoke or drink or drug or first act of illicit sex.

How many opportunities have we failed to grab, letting them slip from our grasp? Consequently, we lost the chance to develop and advance ourselves or to build our character by living more righteously. But in considering lost opportunities, this one truth is essential to know: we must forget those things that are past and reach forth to the future, to the things that lie before us. For God will still give us many opportunities to develop our character and skills and to live more fulfilling lives. God will empower us to be productive and victorious in life.

"And every one that heareth these sayings of mine, and doeth them not, shall be likened unto a foolish man, which built his house upon the sand: And the rain descended, and the floods came, and the winds blew, and beat upon that house; and it fell: and great was the fall of it" (Mt.7:26-27).

"Then shall the kingdom of heaven be likened unto ten virgins, which took their lamps, and went forth to meet the bridegroom. And five of them were wise, and five *were* foolish. They that *were* foolish took their lamps, and took no oil with them: But the wise took oil in their vessels with their lamps. While the bridegroom tarried, they all slumbered and slept. And at midnight there was a cry made, Behold, the bridegroom cometh; go ye out to meet him. Then all those virgins arose, and trimmed their lamps. And the foolish said unto the wise, Give us of your oil; for our lamps are gone out. But the wise answered, saying, *Not so;* lest there be not enough for us and you: but go ye rather to them that sell, and buy for yourselves. And while they went to buy, the bridegroom came; and they that were ready went in with him to the marriage: and the door was shut. Afterward came also the other virgins, saying, Lord, Lord, open to us. But he answered and said, Verily I say unto you, I know you not. Watch therefore, for ye know neither the day nor the hour wherein the Son of man cometh" (Mt.25:1-13).

"His lord answered and said unto him, *Thou* wicked and slothful servant, thou knewest that I reap where I sowed not, and gather where I have not strawed: Thou oughtest therefore to have put my money to the exchangers, and *then* at my coming I should have received mine own with usury" (Mt.25:26-27).

"Then shall they also answer him, saying, Lord, when saw we thee an hungred, or athirst, or a stranger, or naked, or sick, or in prison, and did not minister unto thee? Then shall he answer them, saying, Verily I say unto you, Inasmuch as ye did *it* not to one of the least of these, ye did *it* not to me" (Mt.25:44-45).

"And he cometh unto the disciples, and findeth them asleep, and saith unto Peter, What, could ye not watch with me one hour? Watch and pray, that ye enter not into temptation: the spirit indeed *is* willing, but the flesh *is* weak" (Mt.26:40-41).

"I must work the works of him that sent me, while it is day: the night cometh, when no man can work" (Jn.9:4).

"Not slothful in business; fervent in spirit; serving the Lord" (Ro.12:11).

"Let him that stole steal no more: but rather let him labour, working with *his* hands the thing which is good, that he may have to give to him that needeth" (Ep.4:28).

"Brethren, I count not myself to have apprehended: but *this* one thing *I do,* forgetting those things which are behind, and reaching forth unto those things which are before, I press toward the mark for the prize of the high calling of God in Christ Jesus" (Ph.3:13-14).

"Now them that are such we command and exhort by our Lord Jesus Christ, that with quietness they work, and eat their own bread" (2 Th.3:12).

"Therefore to him that knoweth to do good, and doeth *it* not, to him it is sin" (Js.4:17).

"Nevertheless we, according to his promise, look for new heavens and a new earth, wherein dwelleth righteousness. Wherefore, beloved, seeing that ye look for such things, be diligent that ye may be found of him in peace, without spot, and blameless" (2 Pe.3:13-14).

"Go to the ant, thou sluggard; consider her ways, and be wise" (Pr.6:6).

"He becometh poor that dealeth *with* a slack hand: but the hand of the diligent maketh rich. He that gathereth in summer *is* a wise son: *but* he that sleepeth in harvest *is* a son that causeth shame" (Pr.10:4-5).

"He that tilleth his land shall be satisfied with bread: but he that followeth vain *persons is* void of understanding" (Pr.12:11).

"The soul of the sluggard desireth, and *hath* nothing: but the soul of the diligent shall be made fat" (Pr.13:4).

"Wealth *gotten* by vanity shall be diminished: but he that gathereth by labour shall increase" (Pr.13:11).

"In all labour there is profit: but the talk of the lips *tendeth* only to penury" (Pr.14:23).

"Love not sleep, lest thou come to poverty; open thine eyes, *and* thou shalt be satisfied with bread" (Pr.20:13).

"Whatsoever thy hand findeth to do, do *it* with thy might; for *there is* no work, nor device, nor knowledge, nor wisdom, in the grave, whither thou goest" (Ec.9:10).

"The harvest is past, the summer is ended, and we are not saved" (Je.8:20).

	B. The Long Reigns of Jeroboam II in Israel & Azariah (Uzziah) in Judah: God's Blessing the People & Giving Them One Last Chance to Repent, 14:23–15:7 *15:1-7; see 2 Chr.26:3-4, 21-23*	had belonged to Yaudi, are they not written in the book of the annals of the kings of Israel? 29 Jeroboam rested with his fathers, the kings of Israel. And Zechariah his son succeeded him as king.	Hamath: Recorded in the book *The History of the Kings of Israel* 2) His death & burial in Samaria 3) His successor: His son Zechariah
1. The reign of Jeroboam II in Israel: A picture of God's mercy & patience despite Jeroboam's continued wickedness a. His reign: 41 years, the longest rule in Israel b. His evil, 1 K.12:25-33 1) He lived a wicked life 2) He refused to turn from the sins of Jeroboam I 3) He was a stumbling block, causing Israel to sin c. His being used to bless & give one last chance to Israel 1) God blessed Israel by restoring the nation's territory: From Hamath to the Dead Sea 2) God sent a prophet to Israel: Jonah (also Amos) 3) God had compassion upon Israel—one last time—despite their continued rejection & wickedness • He saw their bitter suffering • He delivered them: Because He had not yet decreed their final judgment • He used Jeroboam II to rescue them d. His achievements & the summary of his life 1) His deeds & his military accomplishments—including the recovery of both Damascus &	23 In the fifteenth year of Amaziah son of Joash king of Judah, Jeroboam son of Jehoash king of Israel became king in Samaria, and he reigned forty-one years. 24 He did evil in the eyes of the LORD and did not turn away from any of the sins of Jeroboam son of Nebat, which he had caused Israel to commit. 25 He was the one who restored the boundaries of Israel from Lebo Hamath to the Sea of the Arabah, in accordance with the word of the LORD, the God of Israel, spoken through his servant Jonah son of Amittai, the prophet from Gath Hepher. 26 The LORD had seen how bitterly everyone in Israel, whether slave or free, was suffering; there was no one to help them. 27 And since the LORD had not said he would blot out the name of Israel from under heaven, he saved them by the hand of Jeroboam son of Jehoash. 28 As for the other events of Jeroboam's reign, all he did, and his military achievements, including how he recovered for Israel both Damascus and Hamath, which	**CHAPTER 15** In the twenty-seventh year of Jeroboam king of Israel, Azariah son of Amaziah king of Judah began to reign. 2 He was sixteen years old when he became king, and he reigned in Jerusalem fifty-two years. His mother's name was Jecoliah; she was from Jerusalem. 3 He did what was right in the eyes of the LORD, just as his father Amaziah had done. 4 The high places, however, were not removed; the people continued to offer sacrifices and burn incense there. 5 The LORD afflicted the king with leprosy until the day he died, and he lived in a separate house. Jotham the king's son had charge of the palace and governed the people of the land. 6 As for the other events of Azariah's reign, and all he did, are they not written in the book of the annals of the kings of Judah? 7 Azariah rested with his fathers and was buried near them in the City of David. And Jotham his son succeeded him as king.	**2. The reign of Azariah (Uzziah) in Judah: A picture of God's blessing & His chastisement due to Uzziah's pride & arrogance** a. His reign 1) He began to reign at age 16 2) He ruled for 52 years b. His spiritual life 1) He lived righteously, pleasing the LORD 2) He compromised: Did not remove the high places (where false gods had formerly been worshipped) c. His chastisement, discipline by the LORD: Stricken with leprosy (due to his burning incense in the temple, usurping the role of the priest, 2 Chr.26:16-21) d. His joint rule with his son e. His achievements & the summary of his life 1) His reign: Recorded in the book *The History of the Kings of Judah* 2) His death & burial: In Jerusalem 3) His successor: His son Jotham

DIVISION III

THE UTTER DISINTEGRATION AND FALL OF ISRAEL, THE NORTHERN KINGDOM: A TRAGIC END DUE TO AN UNBROKEN STREAM OF WICKEDNESS AND LAWLESSNESS, 14:1–17:22

B. The Long Reigns of Jeroboam II in Israel and Azariah (Uzziah) in Judah: God Blessing the People and Giving Them One Last Chance to Repent, 14:23–15:7

(14:23–15:7) **Introduction—Chance, One Last, Experience of Many—Opportunity, Fact, Given One Last Chance**: Have you ever been given one last chance? At a job or promotion? At saving your marriage? One last chance to do a better job or else you would be fired? One last chance to take the test or try out for the team? One last chance to change your behavior or else?

Being given one last chance is the practical subject of the present Scripture. For over 150 years, since Solomon's apostasy, the Israelites had lived wicked lives and rejected the LORD. God's patience was dwindling, and His mercy was about to be withdrawn. But before the hand of God's judgment was to fall, the LORD longed to give the people one last chance to repent and turn from their wicked lives and rejection of Him. In order to give them one final opportunity, the LORD poured out His blessings of peace and prosperity upon both the Northern Kingdom of Israel and the Southern Kingdom of

Judah. Once again the people were to be blessed with unparalleled success and prosperity, all with the hope that they would realize their blessings had come from the LORD. And in their realization, they would turn from their wicked behavior back to the LORD. But instead of repenting, the people continued their downward spiral into utter corruption and decadence. This is: *The Long Reigns of Jeroboam II in Israel and Azariah (Uzziah) in Judah: God's Blessing the People and Giving Them One Last Chance to Repent,* 14:23–15:7.

1. The reign of Jeroboam II in Israel: a picture of God's mercy and patience despite Jeroboam's continued wickedness (14:23-29).
2. The reign of Azariah (Uzziah) in Judah: a picture of God's blessing and His chastisement due to Uzziah's pride and arrogance (15:1-7).

1 (14:23-29) **Longsuffering, of God, Example of—Rejection, of God, Example of—Wickedness, Example of— Jeroboam II, King of Israel, Reign of—Kings, of the Northern Kingdom of Israel, Listed—Blessings, of God, upon Israel—Chance, One Last, Given by God—Opportunity, One Last, Given by God**: the author switches back to the Northern Kingdom of Israel to cover the reign of Jeroboam II. Remember that his father Jehoash had followed the wicked example of Jeroboam I, who had been the first king to rule in the Northern Kingdom. Despite Jeroboam I's spiritual wickedness, Jehoash obviously respected the founder of the Northern Kingdom so much that he named his own son after him. Upon Jehoash's death from natural causes, his son Jeroboam II was crowned king of Israel.

OUTLINE	SCRIPTURE	SCRIPTURE	OUTLINE
1. The reign of Jeroboam II in Israel: A picture of God's mercy & patience despite Jeroboam's continued wickedness	23 In the fifteenth year of Amaziah son of Joash king of Judah, Jeroboam son of Jehoash king of Israel became	whether slave or free, was suffering; there was no one to help them.	despite their continued rejection & wickedness
a. His reign: 41 years, the longest rule in Israel	king in Samaria, and he reigned forty-one years.	27 And since the LORD had not said he would	• He saw their bitter suffering
b. His evil, 1 K.12:25-33	24 He did evil in the eyes of the LORD and did not turn	blot out the name of Israel from under heaven,	• He delivered them: Because He had not yet de-
1) He lived a wicked life	away from any of the sins of	he saved them by the hand	creed their final judgment
2) He refused to turn from the sins of Jeroboam I	Jeroboam son of Nebat, which he had caused Israel to	of Jeroboam son of Jehoash.	• He used Jeroboam II to
3) He was a stumbling block, causing Israel to sin	commit.	28 As for the other events of Jeroboam's reign, all he did,	rescue them
c. His being used to bless & give one last chance to Israel	25 He was the one who restored the boundaries of	and his military achievements, including how he re-	d. His achievements & the summary of his life
1) God blessed Israel by restoring the nation's territory: From Hamath to the Dead Sea	Israel from Lebo Hamath to the Sea of the Arabah, in accordance with the word	covered for Israel both Damascus and Hamath, which had belonged to Yaudi, are	1) His deeds & his military accomplishments— including the recovery of both Damascus & Ha-
2) God sent a prophet to Israel: Jonah (also Amos)	of the LORD, the God of Israel, spoken through his servant Jonah son of Amittai, the prophet from Gath Hepher.	they not written in the book of the annals of the kings of Israel?	math: Recorded in the book *The History of the Kings of Israel*
		29 Jeroboam rested with his	2) His death & burial in Sa-
3) God had compassion upon Israel—one last time—	26 The LORD had seen how bitterly everyone in Israel,	fathers, the kings of Israel. And Zechariah his son succeeded him as king.	maria 3) His successor: His son Zechariah

a. Jeroboam II had one of the most illustrious and prosperous reigns in the Northern Kingdom of Israel. He took the throne in the fifteenth year of King Amaziah's reign in Judah and he ruled for 41 years, the longest rule in the Northern Kingdom (793-753 B.C.).

b. Despite his lengthy and legendary reign, Jeroboam II committed terrible evil in the eyes of the LORD (v.24). Living a wicked life, he refused to turn from the sins of Jeroboam I.

⇒ Just as his name had been taken from the founder of the nation, so he patterned his life after Jeroboam I's wicked example.

⇒ Just as Jeroboam I had been a capable leader, so Jeroboam II achieved political, economic, and military prosperity and power.

But Jeroboam II had no concern for the worship of the LORD. He had no interest in turning the people to the truth, the truth that there is only one living and true God, the LORD Himself (Jehovah, Yahweh). His concern focused upon keeping the people loyal to the throne, so he continued to encourage the people to follow the *state religion* founded by Jeroboam I. (see outlines and notes—1 K.12:25-33 for more discussion).

c. Nevertheless, from a heart of pure grace and mercy, God chose the rule and reign of Jeroboam II to give one last chance to the people to repent (vv.25-27). Using the wicked ruler as his instrument, God poured out blessing after blessing upon the people—all with the hope that His goodness would arouse the people to turn from their wickedness and false worship, turn back to Him. Under Jeroboam II's leadership, the Northern Kingdom of Israel reached a summit of prosperity and power—political, economic, and military power—that had been unmatched since the days of Solomon. But note there was no spiritual prosperity. God maneuvered and worked world events to allow Jeroboam II to recover the territories of Israel that reached to the northern border of Lebo Hamath, a territory that equaled that ruled over by Solomon (1 K.8:65). In the south, Jeroboam II's kingdom extended to the Sea of the Arabah, which is the Dead Sea. The prophet Amos confirms this (Am.6:14).

Throughout the reign of Jeroboam II God sent prophets—Jonah, Amos, and Hosea—to warn the people. Jonah actually predicted the military victories and the recovering of the territory by Israel (v.25). The prophet Amos issued a strong warning to Jeroboam II, declaring that if they failed to repent and turn back to the LORD, they would lose the territory he had gained (Am.6:14). Under Jeroboam II's leadership the people had gained so much prosperity that it was corrupting their lives. They had become an overripe fruit that was doomed to utter decay (Am.8:1-2).

The prophet Hosea emphasized the compassion and mercy of God for the wicked, both for the unfaithful king and the people. Hosea's wife was an adulterous who refused to turn from her immoral ways despite Hosea's pleas and willingness to forgive her. Using the tragedy of his own personal marriage, the prophet declared that God loves the people who had turned away from Him, those who have committed adultery against Him. If they would just turn back to Him, He would forgive them.

Paul R. House, in *The New American Commentary,* has an excellent summary on the messages of Hosea and Amos to the King Jeroboam II and Israel, a summary that is well worth quoting:

> Hosea and Amos, both of whom minister during this time period (Hos 1:1; Amos 1:1), reflect the author's emphasis on the Lord's patience and kindness toward the covenant people. Hosea compares God's love for straying Israel to his own commitment to Gomer, his adulterous wife (cf. Hos 1–3). Amos notes that God has tried to turn Israel from sin (Amos 4:6-13) and has delayed judgment more than once (Amos 7:1-6). Still the people reject the Lord, which means they will face punishment, just as Moses promises in Leviticus 26 and Deuteronomy 27–28 (cf. Amos 7:7-9; 8:1–9:10).
>
> What sins do the people commit during these years? Hosea says they are spiritual adulterers (Hos 1:2; 4:1), thieves (4:2), and ungrateful children (11:1-7). In short, there is "no acknowledgement of God in the land" (Hos 4:1). God desires mercy (Hos 6:6) and monotheism (Hos 13:4) but receives only meaningless sacrifice and idolatry. Likewise, Amos finds oppression of the poor (Amos 2:6), injustice (2:7), and immorality (2:8). The people love wealth more than kindness (4:1-3), ease more than righteous character (6:1-7). How can the nation avoid divine wrath? God waits for change, then sends his prophets; yet he must still punish in the end.[1]

Despite the people's continued rejection and wickedness, God had compassion upon them. But this was the last time. No longer would He show compassion. If the people failed to repent this time, judgment would fall upon them. Yet for now, God saw their bitter suffering and He delivered them. Note why: because He had not yet decreed their final judgment (vv.26-27). He would not yet blot out their names from under heaven. Rather, He would use Jeroboam II to rescue them from their enemies, freeing the people throughout the entire territory that had been conquered by the Syrians and others since the days of Solomon.

d. Jeroboam II's achievements and a summary of his life are recorded in the book *The History of the Kings of Israel* (v.28). One of his significant achievements was his recovery of both Damascus and Hamath, which had once been ruled by David and Solomon (2 S.8:6; 2 Chr.8:3). After his death, Jeroboam II was buried in Samaria and succeeded by his son Zechariah (vv.28-29).

With the death of Jeroboam II, the final chance for the people to repent and turn back to God had passed. Instead of forsaking their wicked ways, they had continued to commit every form of evil imaginable. As a result, God was left with no choice, for the people had proven they would never repent, never live righteous lives nor build a peaceful, compassionate, and just society. Judgment was now to begin falling upon the nation. Using other nations as instruments of His judgment, God allowed the Assyrians to destroy the Northern Kingdom of Israel.

Thought 1. God's patience with Israel was amazing, incomprehensible. For over 150 years He had been longsuffering with them, tolerating their rejection of Him. But no more. Israel had gone too far for too long. God had given them their last chance, had shown them His final act of compassion. Judgment was to fall upon the people. And all this has been recorded for our benefit, to teach us how we should live (Ro.15:4; 1 Co.6, 11).

Think of how patient God is with our society, our nation, our world. Think of all the evil behavior and lawlessness within our own communities and throughout the world. Think of all the corruption and wickedness committed by people...

- the divisiveness and conflicts
- the anger and malice
- the assaults and brutality
- the abuse of little children and the elderly
- the lies and thefts
- the murder and war
- the immorality and depravity

God's patience with our sin and wickedness, our false worship and rejection of Him as the only living and true God is also astounding, unfathomable. Yet this is exactly what Scripture declares, that God is longsuffering with us, that He suffers a long time with our rejection of Him and His commandments.

But the day of a *final chance* will come. There will be *one final act* of patience with us; no longer will God tolerate our rejection and wickedness. But for now, the lesson stressed is God's patience, His compassion and mercy upon us. If we will turn back to Him, He will have mercy upon us and forgive our sin and wickedness.

"And his mercy *is* on them that fear him from generation to generation" (Lu.1:50).
"But God, who is rich in mercy, for his great love wherewith he loved us, Even when we were dead in sins, hath quickened us together with Christ, (by grace ye are saved;) And hath raised *us* up

1 Paul R. House. *1, 2 Kings,* pp.326-327.

together, and made *us* sit together in heavenly *places* in Christ Jesus: That in the ages to come he might show the exceeding riches of his grace in *his* kindness toward us through Christ Jesus. For by grace are ye saved through faith; and that not of yourselves: *it is* the gift of God" (Ep.2:4-8).

"Not by works of righteousness which we have done, but according to his mercy he saved us, by the washing of regeneration, and renewing of the Holy Ghost; Which he shed on us abundantly through Jesus Christ our Saviour; That being justified by his grace, we should be made heirs according to the hope of eternal life" (Tit.3:5-7).

"The Lord is not slack concerning his promise, as some men count slackness; but is longsuffering to us-ward, not willing that any should perish, but that all should come to repentance" (2 Pe.3:9).

"But he, *being* full of compassion, forgave *their* iniquity, and destroyed *them* not: yea, many a time turned he his anger away, and did not stir up all his wrath" (Ps.78:38).

"But thou, O Lord, *art* a God full of compassion, and gracious, longsuffering, and plenteous in mercy and truth" (Ps.86:15).

"But the mercy of the LORD *is* from everlasting to everlasting upon them that fear him, and his righteousness unto children's children" (Ps.103:17).

"For my name's sake will I defer mine anger, and for my praise will I refrain for thee, that I cut thee not off" (Is.48:9).

"*It is of* the LORD'S mercies that we are not consumed, because his compassions fail not. *They are* new every morning" (Lam.3:22-23).

"But though he cause grief, yet will he have compassion according to the multitude of his mercies" (Lam.3:32).

"And rend your heart, and not your garments, and turn unto the LORD your God: for he *is* gracious and merciful, slow to anger, and of great kindness, and repenteth him of the evil" (Joel 2:13).

"Who *is* a God like unto thee, that pardoneth iniquity, and passeth by the transgression of the remnant of his heritage? he retaineth not his anger for ever, because he delighteth *in* mercy. He will turn again, he will have compassion upon us; he will subdue our iniquities; and thou wilt cast all their sins into the depths of the sea" (Mi.7:18-19).

---

2 (15:1-7) **Commandments, Disobeying—Disobedience, Example of—Chastisement, of God, Example of—Discipline, of God, Example of—Judgment, Example of—Kings, of the Northern Kingdom of Israel, Azariah or Uzziah—Israel, Kings of**: switching back to the Southern Kingdom, the author of *Kings* discusses the tenth king of Judah, Azariah or Uzziah. Remember that Uzziah's father, King Amaziah, had left Jerusalem in utter ruins (14:8-14). In a war of Judah he had launched against Israel, he had been totally defeated, then captured and forced to surrender the capital city of Jerusalem. In attacking Jerusalem, the Northern forces had broken down a major section of the wall, looted the temple and palace wealth, and taken many of the skilled and wealthy of the land back to Samaria as hostages. Consequently, when Uzziah took the throne, he inherited a devastated nation economically, politically, and militarily. Only a short account is given of his reign in *Second Kings*; a much longer account is recorded in *Second Chronicles* (2 Chr.26:1-23).

OUTLINE	SCRIPTURE	SCRIPTURE	OUTLINE

2. The reign of Azariah (Uzziah) in Judah: A picture of God's blessing & His chastisement due to Uzziah's pride & arrogance
a. His reign
  1) He began to reign at age 16
  2) He ruled for 52 years
 	
b. His spiritual life
  1) He lived righteously, pleasing the LORD
 	
  2) He compromised: Did not remove the high places (where false gods had formerly been
	In the twenty-seventh year of Jeroboam king of Israel, Azariah son of Amaziah king of Judah began to reign.
	2 He was sixteen years old when he became king, and he reigned in Jerusalem fifty-two years. His mother's name was Jecoliah; she was from Jerusalem.
	3 He did what was right in the eyes of the LORD, just as his father Amaziah had done.
	4 The high places, however, were not removed; the people continued to offer sacrifices and burn incense
		there.
		5 The LORD afflicted the king with leprosy until the day he died, and he lived in a separate house. Jotham the king's son had charge of the palace and governed the people of the land.
		6 As for the other events of Azariah's reign, and all he did, are they not written in the book of the annals of the kings of Judah?
		7 Azariah rested with his fathers and was buried near them in the City of David. And Jotham his son succeeded him as king.
			worshipped)
			c. His chastisement, discipline by the LORD: Stricken with leprosy (due to his burning incense in the temple, usurping the role of the priest, 2 Chr.26:16-21)
			d. His joint rule with his son
			e. His achievements & the summary of his life
			  1) His reign: Recorded in the book *The History of the Kings of Judah*
			  2) His death & burial: In Jerusalem
			  3) His successor: His son Jotham

a. Uzziah was crowned king at the early age of 16, but he survived upon the throne for 52 years, one of the longest reigns among all the kings of both the Northern and Southern Kingdoms (v.2). By ruling so long, Uzziah had time to rebuild the nation. And, in fact, *Second Chronicles* says that he succeeded just as Jeroboam II had succeeded in the Northern Kingdom. He achieved enormous success in wars against the Philistines, Arabs, Menunites, and Ammonites. He became so powerful that his fame spread all the way down to Egypt (2 Chr.26:6-8). Economically, he rebuilt the nation through major construction projects and through agriculture and ranching (2 Chr.26:9-10). Militarily, he built one of the strongest armies of that day, an elite force of over 300,000 troops. He even developed some special machines that shot arrows and hurled stones like a catapult (2 Chr.26:11-15).

b. Spiritually, Uzziah lived a righteous life, doing what was right in the eyes and sight of the LORD (vv.3-4). But sadly and tragically, he compromised when it came to the worship of the LORD. He did not remove the high places where false gods had formerly been worshipped. He continued to follow a *state policy of noninterference* with the people's worship of false gods.[2] In addition to his compromise, *Second Chronicles* tells us that he became puffed up with pride and a sense of self-exaltation (2 Chr.26:16-19). Exalting himself as a God-appointed priest, he actually entered the temple and burned incense before the LORD—a function that was to be performed only by the priest, God's appointed intercessor. When confronted and rebuked by the High Priest and a committee of 80 other brave priests, Uzziah became furious and reacted in a verbal rage against the priests.

c. Because of his compromise, his *puffed up* pride, and his self-exaltation, God chastised and disciplined him. When he broke out in the verbal rage against the priests, he was immediately stricken with leprosy—even while he was standing there spouting out his rage.

d. Now, because of his affliction of leprosy, he was forced to live in isolation and to step aside from public ruling. Left with no choice, he put his son in charge of the government and they both ruled in a co-regency until his death (v.6).

e. A summary of his achievements and life are recorded in the book *The History of the Kings of Judah.* After his death and burial in Jerusalem, he was succeeded on the throne by his son Jotham.

With the death of Uzziah, the Southern Kingdom experienced one of its last peaceful and prosperous periods. Although the people were unaware of the fact, never again would they enjoy such success and prosperity as a nation. Other than for a few years during Josiah's reign (640-609 B.C.), they would always be suffering from the oppression of another nation or else facing the threat and pressure of being attacked. The Northern Kingdom would fall first, but shortly thereafter the Southern Kingdom would collapse. The patience of the LORD would soon run out. The day of His longsuffering and mercy would at long last be over. Judgment would finally come.

> **Thought 1**. The inescapable chastisement of God is the major warning for us to heed in Uzziah's reign. Uzziah was disciplined by God due to his compromise, his *puffed up* pride, and his self-exaltation.
>
> Likewise, if we compromise with the world, God will chastise us. By compromising with the world, we run the risk of damaging our bodies and our minds. Abusing drugs, alcohol, or any other substance can damage our bodies or cause us to become involved in an accident that injures or kills either us or someone else. Committing immorality damages through divorce, disease, and unbearable suffering and pain for children, spouses, and parents. Cursing the name of God and using profanity displeases both God and other people and brings the curse of God upon a person. Driving too fast in an automobile breaks the laws of society and threatens to damage the lives and property of others.
>
> All sinful and wicked behavior has some damaging effect. For this reason, God chastises us. He disciplines us in order to prevent us from harming ourselves or someone else or from damaging the environment or property. As difficult as it may be to bear, discipline is good for us. It corrects and teaches us, saving us and others from injury, sometimes even from death. Listen to what God's Holy Word says about chastisement or discipline:
>
> > **"Every branch in me that beareth not fruit he taketh away: and every *branch* that beareth fruit, he purgeth it, that it may bring forth more fruit" (Jn.15:2).**
> >
> > **"For this cause many *are* weak and sickly among you, and many sleep. For if we would judge ourselves, we should not be judged. But when we are judged, we are chastened of the Lord, that we should not be condemned with the world" (1 Co.11:30-32).**
> >
> > **"And ye have forgotten the exhortation which speaketh unto you as unto children, My son, despise not thou the chastening of the Lord, nor faint when thou art rebuked of him: For whom the Lord loveth he chasteneth, and scourgeth every son whom he receiveth" (He.12:5-6).**
> >
> > **"As many as I love, I rebuke and chasten: be zealous therefore, and repent" (Re.3:19).**
> >
> > **"Thou shalt also consider in thine heart, that, as a man chasteneth his son, *so* the LORD thy God chasteneth thee" (De.8:5).**
> >
> > **"Blessed *is* the man whom thou chastenest, O LORD, and teachest him out of thy law" (Ps.94:12).**
> >
> > **"My son, despise not the chastening of the LORD; neither be weary of his correction: For whom the LORD loveth he correcteth; even as a father the son *in whom* he delighteth" (Pr.3:11-12).**
> >
> > **"But he knoweth the way that I take: *when* he hath tried me, I shall come forth as gold" (Jb.23:10).**

---

2 Richard D. Patterson and Hermann J. Austel. *1, 2 Kings*, p.233.

C. The Reigns of Five Kings in Israel, Four of Whom Were Assassinated: A Downward Spiral into Political Disorder Due to Continued Wickedness, 15:8-31

1. The reign of Zechariah & his assassination: A picture of God's faithfulness in fulfilling His promises
a. His rule: Lasted only six months
b. His wicked life, 1 K.12:25-33
   1) Did evil—just as his father had done
   2) Did not turn away from Jeroboam I's sins
   3) Was a stumbling block, causing Israel to sin
c. His assassination by Shallum
   1) Was killed publicly: A sign of public apathy
   2) Was succeeded by Shallum
d. His reign: Recorded in the book *The History of the Kings of Israel*
e. His reign: A proof of God's faithfulness, of the fulfillment of His promises

2. The reign of Shallum & his assassination: A picture of God's judicial judgment—reaping what one sows
a. His rule: Only one month, the second shortest in Israel
b. His assassination
   1) Was killed in a vengeful raid by Menahem, Zechariah's commander
   2) Was succeeded by Menahem
c. His reign & the conspiracy he led against Zechariah: Recorded in the book *The History of the Kings of Israel*

3. The reign of Menahem & the Assyrian invasion: A picture of compromise—turning to the world for deliverance
a. His terrible atrocity & brutality against a city that rejected his kingship
b. His rule: Lasted 10 years

8 In the thirty and eighth year of Azariah king of Judah did Zachariah the son of Jeroboam reign over Israel in Samaria six months.
9 And he did *that which was* evil in the sight of the LORD, as his fathers had done: he departed not from the sins of Jeroboam the son of Nebat, who made Israel to sin.
10 And Shallum the son of Jabesh conspired against him, and smote him before the people, and slew him, and reigned in his stead.
11 And the rest of the acts of Zachariah, behold, they *are* written in the book of the chronicles of the kings of Israel.
12 This *was* the word of the LORD which he spake unto Jehu, saying, Thy sons shall sit on the throne of Israel unto the fourth *generation.* And so it came to pass.
13 Shallum the son of Jabesh began to reign in the nine and thirtieth year of Uzziah king of Judah; and he reigned a full month in Samaria.
14 For Menahem the son of Gadi went up from Tirzah, and came to Samaria, and smote Shallum the son of Jabesh in Samaria, and slew him, and reigned in his stead.
15 And the rest of the acts of Shallum, and his conspiracy which he made, behold, they *are* written in the book of the chronicles of the kings of Israel.
16 Then Menahem smote Tiphsah, and all that *were* therein, and the coasts thereof from Tirzah: because they opened not *to him,* therefore he smote *it; and* all the women therein that were with child he ripped up.
17 In the nine and thirtieth year of Azariah king of Judah began Menahem the son of Gadi to reign over Israel, *and* reigned ten years in Samaria.

18 And he did *that which was* evil in the sight of the LORD: he departed not all his days from the sins of Jeroboam the son of Nebat, who made Israel to sin.
19 *And* Pul the king of Assyria came against the land: and Menahem gave Pul a thousand talents of silver, that his hand might be with him to confirm the kingdom in his hand.
20 And Menahem exacted the money of Israel, *even* of all the mighty men of wealth, of each man fifty shekels of silver, to give to the king of Assyria. So the king of Assyria turned back, and stayed not there in the land.
21 And the rest of the acts of Menahem, and all that he did, *are* they not written in the book of the chronicles of the kings of Israel?
22 And Menahem slept with his fathers; and Pekahiah his son reigned in his stead.
23 In the fiftieth year of Azariah king of Judah Pekahiah the son of Menahem began to reign over Israel in Samaria, *and reigned* two years.
24 And he did *that which was* evil in the sight of the LORD: he departed not from the sins of Jeroboam the son of Nebat, who made Israel to sin.
25 But Pekah the son of Remaliah, a captain of his, conspired against him, and smote him in Samaria, in the palace of the king's house, with Argob and Arieh, and with him fifty men of the Gileadites: and he killed him, and reigned in his room.
26 And the rest of the acts of Pekahiah, and all that he did, behold, they *are* written in the book of the chronicles of the kings of Israel.
27 In the two and fiftieth year of Azariah king of Judah Pekah the son of Remaliah began to reign over Israel in Samaria, *and reigned* twenty years.
28 And he did *that which was* evil in the sight of the LORD: he departed not from the sins of Jeroboam the son of Nebat, who made Israel to sin.

c. His evil
   1) Lived a wicked life
   2) Did not turn away from the sins of Jeroboam I, 1 K.12:25-33

d. His compromise with the invading Assyrians
   1) He turned to the world, to King Pul (Tiglath-Pileser III), for deliverance, instead of turning to God: Paid 1000 talents of silver (37 tons) for Assyria to withdraw
   2) He sought to strengthen his control
   3) He raised the money by taxing the wealthy of Israel: 20 ounces of silver
   4) He compromised, & Assyria withdrew
e. His achievements & the summary of his life
   1) His reign: Recorded in the book *The History of the Kings of Israel*
   2) His death: In Samaria
   3) His successor: Pekahiah, his son

4. The reign of Pekahiah & his assassination: A picture of greed & covetousness, of grasping for power
a. His rule: Lasted 2 years

b. His evil
   1) Lived a wicked life
   2) Continued in the sins of Jeroboam I, 1 K.12:25-33
   3) Was a stumbling block, causing the people to sin
c. His assassination
   1) Was attacked by Pekah, an army commander, & 50 men from Gilead: Killed the king in the citadel of the royal palace along with two loyal supporters, Argob & Arieh
   2) Was succeeded by the commander Pekah
d. His achievements & the summary of his life: Recorded in the book *The History of the Kings of Israel*

5. The reign of Pekah & his assassination: A picture of the desperate need for God's saving power—found only in Christ
a. His rule: 20 years
b. His evil
   1) Lived a wicked life
   2) Followed the sins of Jeroboam I, 1 K.12:25-33
   3) Was a stumbling block, causing the people to sin

	29 In the days of Pekah king of Israel came Tiglath-pileser king of Assyria, and took Ijon, and Abel-beth-maachah, and Janoah, and Kedesh, and Hazor, and Gilead, and Galilee, all the land of Naphtali, and carried them captive to Assyria.	against Pekah the son of Remaliah, and smote him, and slew him, and reigned in his stead, in the twentieth year of Jotham the son of Uzziah.	
c. His war with Assyria: Facing God's impending judgment 1) He lost all Galilee—the land of Naphtali—& also Gilead, 1 Chr.5:25-26 2) He faced Assyrian troops all along Israel's western border, right across the Jordan River d. His assassination 1) Was conspired against &			murdered by Hoshea 2) Was succeeded by Hoshea
	30 And Hoshea the son of Elah made a conspiracy	31 And the rest of the acts of Pekah, and all that he did, behold, they *are* written in the book of the chronicles of the kings of Israel.	e. His achievements & the summary of his life: Recorded in the book *The History of the Kings of Israel*

DIVISION III

THE UTTER DISINTEGRATION AND FALL OF ISRAEL, THE NORTHERN KINGDOM: A TRAGIC END DUE TO AN UNBROKEN STREAM OF WICKEDNESS AND LAWLESSNESS, 14:1–17:22

C. The Reigns of Five Kings in Israel, Four of Whom Were Assassinated: A Downward Spiral into Political Disorder Due to Continued Wickedness, 15:8-31

(15:8-31) **Introduction—Politics, Disorder, Fact—Division, Caused by Disorder—Strife, Places Where Division Takes Place**: political disorder takes place all over the world. In fact, every generation witnesses upheavals in one form or another. History shows that no nation and no government escape political division and strife.

However governments are not the only institution to suffer disorder, division, and strife. Disorder can take place within any group or body of people. When two or more people are gathered together, any one of them can grasp for more power, authority, or control. And the grasp for power can easily cause disturbance and disorder. That disorder can take place in the workplace, schools, social clubs, civic organizations, churches, synagogues, temples, or even within the family.

Political disorder is the subject of this chapter of Scripture. Five kings quickly plunge the Northern Kingdom into a swift, downward spiral. Israel's continued wickedness drives the nation to a point of never returning to God. In introducing Israel's political upheaval, commentator Paul R. House says this:

> Events now move swiftly, and none of them are kind to Israel. At just the moment that Assyria becomes a belligerent, conquering nation, Israel suffers through a succession of weak kings who come to power usually through intrigue and assassination. Of course, the author does not view these events as simply bad luck and poor timing. God is at work, punishing the sins of a stubborn people. Two hundred years of rebellion will soon be judged.[1]

No better introduction could be given to this passage than what commentator Russell Dilday gives:

> Having stepped on the slippery slope of apostasy and disobedience, Israel was careening with accelerating speed toward an inevitable destiny of destruction and captivity. Within the next forth-three years half a dozen "pseudo-kings" would reign in rapid succession, one murderer replacing another on the throne, as the nation tottered on the brink of anarchy. Only one king, Menahem, died a natural death and was succeeded by his son on the throne of Samaria. The other five were violently dethroned by the rebels. Most of the rulers were not so much kings as robbers and tyrants, unworthy of the august name of "king."
>
> It did not require special insight for Hosea to conclude that such political bedlam signified the approaching doom of Israel. Sadly he declared to his countrymen the word of the Lord: "I will avenge the bloodshed of Jezreel on the house of Jehu, and bring an end to the kingdom of the house of Israel (Hos. 1:4). In a few short years, the Northern Kingdom would be no more.[2]

The people of the Northern Kingdom had become callous toward God, hard as granite, so hard that God knew they would never repent. Consequently, He was left with no choice. His patience with their terrible evil had run out and He soon would deliver them no more. Judgment would be executed. This is: *The Reigns of Five Kings in Israel, Four of Whom Were Assassinated: A Downward Spiral into Political Disorder Due to Continued Wickedness, 15:8-31.*

1. The reign of Zechariah and his assassination: A picture of God's faithfulness in fulfilling His promises, (vv.8-12).
2. The reign of Shallum and his assassination: God's judicial judgment—reaping what one sows (vv.13-15).
3. The reign of Menahem and the Assyrian invasion: compromise—turning to the world for deliverance (vv.16-22).
4. The reign of Pekahiah and his assassination: a picture of greed and covetousness, of grasping for power (vv.23-26).
5. The reign of Pekah and his assassination: facing the clouds of impending judgment (vv.27-31).

1 (15:8-12) **Faithfulness, of God, Fulfilling His Promises—Fulfillment, of God's Promises, Example of—Kings, of the Northern Kingdom of Israel, Zechariah—Assassination, Example of**: the downward spiral of the Northern

---

1 Paul R. House. *1, 2 Kings.* "The New American Commentary," Vol.8. (Nashville, TN: Broadman & Holman Publishers, 1995), pp.328-329.
2 Russell Dilday. *1, 2 Kings*, p.401.

Kingdom began with the reign of Zechariah and his assassination. Remember, the Northern Kingdom of Israel had reached a summit of peace and prosperity under Jeroboam II that had not been experienced since the days of Solomon (14:23-29). Assuming the throne after Jeroboam II's death was his son Zechariah (v.8). He took the throne in the thirty-eighth year of King Uzziah of Judah. But he was assassinated after only six months. Although he ruled for only six months, Scripture strongly indicts him. Throughout his life he had been wicked, committing evil in the eyes of the LORD—just as his father had done (v.9). He did not turn away from the sins of Jeroboam I but, rather, set a wicked example for the people to follow. His life was a stumbling block to them, encouraging them to sin (see outline and note—1 K.12:25-33 for more discussion).

Note the reference to Zechariah's being openly assassinated by Shallum (v.10). The very public murder points to two facts: that Shallum must have had a large following, and that the public was gripped by a spirit of apathy due to the evil that permeated every level of society.

Zechariah's brief reign was recorded in the book *The History of the Kings of Israel* (v.11). When he died, the promise given to the former King Jehu was fulfilled, the promise that his dynasty would continue for four generations (10:30).

OUTLINE	SCRIPTURE	SCRIPTURE	OUTLINE

1. The reign of Zechariah & his assassination: A picture of God's faithfulness in fulfilling His promises
a. His rule: Lasted only six months
b. His wicked life, 1 K.12:25-33
  1) Did evil—just as his father had done
  2) Did not turn away from Jeroboam I's sins
  3) Was a stumbling block, causing Israel to sin
c. His assassination by Shallum
  1) Was killed publicly: A
	8 In the thirty and eighth year of Azariah king of Judah did Zechariah the son of Jeroboam reign over Israel in Samaria six months.
	9 And he did *that which was* evil in the sight of the LORD, as his fathers had done: he departed not from the sins of Jeroboam the son of Nebat, who made Israel to sin.
	10 And Shallum the son of Jabesh conspired against him,
		and smote him before the people, and slew him, and reigned in his stead.
		11 And the rest of the acts of Zechariah, behold, they *are* written in the book of the chronicles of the kings of Israel.
		12 This *was* the word of the LORD which he spake unto Jehu, saying, Thy sons shall sit on the throne of Israel unto the fourth *generation.* And so it came to pass.
			sign of public apathy
			  2) Was succeeded by Shallum
			d. His reign: Recorded in the book *The History of the Kings of Israel*
			
			e. His reign: A proof of God's faithfulness, of the fulfillment of His promises

Thought 1. God is faithful, always fulfilling His promises. Once God has given a promise—whatever the promise may be—He fulfills it. And the Word of God overflows with promises:

⇒ promises of protection, provision, and guidance
⇒ promises of joy, happiness, and pleasure
⇒ promises of peace, security, and assurance
⇒ promises of salvation, rescue, and deliverance
⇒ promises of conquest, victory, and triumph
⇒ promises of heaven and life forever with God

All the wonderful things in life and in eternity are promised us by God. Scripture even declares that "All things are yours" (1 Co.3:21-22), and that "Every good gift and every perfect gift is from above, and comes down from the father of lights" (Jas.1:17). There is no end to the promises of God, nor to the wonderful life God promises us if we will only trust Him. Moreover, the proven fact is, no promise of God has ever failed. God fulfills His promises.

> "Jesus said unto him, If thou canst believe, all things *are* possible to him that believeth" (Mk.9:23).
> "He staggered not at the promise of God through unbelief; but was strong in faith, giving glory to God; And being fully persuaded that, what he had promised, he was able also to perform" (Ro.4:20-21).
> "For all the promises of God in him *are* yea, and in him Amen, unto the glory of God by us" (2 Co.1:20).
> "Having therefore these promises, dearly beloved, let us cleanse ourselves from all filthiness of the flesh and spirit, perfecting holiness in the fear of God" (2 Co.7:1).
> "Whereby are given unto us exceeding great and precious promises: that by these ye might be partakers of the divine nature, having escaped the corruption that is in the world through lust" (2 Pe.1:4).
> "And this is the promise that he hath promised us, *even* eternal life" (1 Jn.2:25).
> "Blessed *be* the LORD, that hath given rest unto his people Israel, according to all that he promised: there hath not failed one word of all his good promise, which he promised by the hand of Moses his servant" (1 K.8:56).

2 (15:13-15) **Reaping, What One Sows—Sowing, Results of—Judgment, Described As—Assassination, Example of—Shallum, King of Israel, Reign of—Judgment, Judicial, Example of**: the downward spiral of Israel continued under the reign of Shallum and his assassination by his successor. Having himself taken the throne by assassinating King Zechariah, Shallum was now to reap what he had sown and be slain as well. Assuming the throne in the thirty-ninth year of King Uzziah of Judah, he ruled for only one month, the second shortest reign in Israel (v.13). Menahem, the commander of the armed forces, sought to take revenge on Shallum for his assassination of Zechariah. He therefore marched up to Samaria where he killed the newly crowned king (v.14). The reign of Shallum and the conspiracy he led against Zechariah were recorded in the book *The History of the Kings of Israel* (v.15).

OUTLINE	SCRIPTURE	SCRIPTURE	OUTLINE
2. The reign of Shallum & his assassination: A picture of God's judicial judgment— reaping what one sows a. His rule: Only one month, the second shortest in Israel b. His assassination 1) Was killed in a vengeful raid by Menahem,	13 Shallum the son of Jabesh began to reign in the nine and thirtieth year of Uzziah king of Judah; and he reigned a full month in Samaria. 14 For Menahem the son of Gadi went up from Tirzah, and came to Samaria, and	smote Shallum the son of Jabesh in Samaria, and slew him, and reigned in his stead. 15 And the rest of the acts of Shallum, and his conspiracy which he made, behold, they *are* written in the book of the chronicles of the kings of Israel.	Zechariah's commander 2) Was succeeded by Menahem c. His reign & the conspiracy he led against Zechariah: Recorded in the book *The History of the Kings of Israel*

Thought 1. The lesson for us is that of sowing and reaping. Simply put, we reap what we sow. If we sow lives of joy and goodness, God promises that we will reap joy and goodness. When we are around others, if we control our emotions and act pleased, rejoicing in their presence, then most people will respond to us with happy, joyful spirits. But if we have sour spirits, grumbling all the time, then people will avoid us and not enjoy being in our presence. We will have reaped what we sowed.

If we work diligently at our jobs, then we will reap rewards by being recognized and usually compensated through raises or promotions. If husbands and wives are kind and loving to one another and correctly discipline their children, not indulging or neglecting them, then they will reap a loving and nurturing family.

If we obey the commandments of God, then we reap a conquering, victorious life over the trials and temptations that confront us, even death itself.

If we study the Holy Bible, pray, and worship God daily, then we reap a close fellowship with God. We reap a closeness that makes Him the most wonderful companion in life and that pours assurance of eternal life into our hearts.

But the opposite behavior is also true. If we commit sin, then we will reap a life of more and more sin and wickedness. We become conditioned, enslaved, and held in bondage by sin. We become *hooked* on or addicted to drugs, overeating, sex, money, possessions, pleasures, and a host of other activities that can prove harmful or even fatal. In addition, if we continue in the downward spiral of corruption, we reap eternal judgment and destruction. Listen to what God's Holy Word says about reaping what we sow:

> **"For the wages of sin *is* death; but the gift of God *is* eternal life through Jesus Christ our Lord" (Ro.6:23).**
> **"Be not deceived; God is not mocked: for whatsoever a man soweth, that shall he also reap. For he that soweth to his flesh shall of the flesh reap corruption; but he that soweth to the Spirit shall of the Spirit reap life everlasting" (Ga.6:7-8).**
> **"Even as I have seen, they that plow iniquity, and sow wickedness, reap the same" (Jb.4:8).**
> **"He that soweth iniquity shall reap vanity: and the rod of his anger shall fail" (Pr.22:8).**
> **"They have sown wheat, but shall reap thorns: they have put themselves to pain, *but* shall not profit: and they shall be ashamed of your revenues because of the fierce anger of the LORD" (Je.12:13).**
> **"For they have sown the wind, and they shall reap the whirlwind: it hath no stalk: the bud shall yield no meal: if so be it yield, the strangers shall swallow it up" (Ho.8:7).**

3 (15:16-22) **Compromise, Example of—Turning, to the World, Example of—Menahem, King of Israel, Reign of—Israel, the Northern Kingdom, Kings of**: the downward spiral of Israel continued in a whirlwind of corruption. In less than one year's time three men had been crowned king of the nation. And the man now crowned, King Menahem, was to pursue a compromise with the Assyrians that was to doom and bring disaster upon the nation.

According to the Jewish historian Josephus, Menahem was the commander of King Zechariah's army.[3] As noted in the former point, when King Zechariah was assassinated by Shallum, his commander Menahem sought revenge. Marching to Samaria, he killed Shallum. After assuming the throne for himself, Menahem marched against the city of Tiphsah, but the city refused his offer of surrender (v.16). As a result, Menahem attacked the city; and in a savage act of revenge, he killed all the citizens of the city and murdered all the pregnant women by ripping open their stomachs.

Menahem assumed the throne in the thirty-ninth year of King Azariah (Uzziah) of Judah. Although he was the third king to be crowned over Israel within one year's time, his reign did last ten years. But, sadly, just like the other kings of Israel preceding him, he lived a wicked life and committed evil in the eyes of the LORD (v.18). Spiritually, he failed to turn the people back to the LORD, failed to set a righteous example or take the lead in worshipping the LORD. Instead, he encouraged the people to continue worshipping the state religion established by Jeroboam I (see outline and note— 1 K.12:25-33 for more discussion).

Politically, King Menahem made a bad decision to compromise with the invading Assyrians, a compromise that would bring about constant oppression from the Assyrians. During his reign, Assyria invaded Israel and was threatening to capture the capital Samaria. To keep the capital from falling and to remain in power himself, Menahem made a deal with King Pul of Assyria, who is sometimes known as Tiglath-Pileser III. Menahem agreed to pay a huge ransom if the Assyrian forces would withdraw, a ransom of 1,000 talents of silver, which amounted to 37 tons. In paying such a large

---

3 Flavius Josephus. *Antiquities of the Jews*, Book 9, Ch.11, "Complete Works," (Grand Rapids, MI: Kregel Publications, 1981), pp.208-209.

amount, he was seeking to gain the support of Assyria to tighten his own grip on the throne. Note how he raised the money: by taxing the wealthy citizens of Israel, demanding that each man pay a tax of 50 shekels, which amounted to 20 ounces of silver.

Once the compromise with King Pul (Tiglath-Pileser III) was agreed to, the Assyrians withdrew their forces. But note this fact: Menahem should have turned to the LORD for deliverance instead of turning to the worldly Assyrians. For when Tiglath-Pileser III left, Menahem knew this:

> Israel has neither the power nor the will necessary to oppose [Tiglath-Pileser III]. Menahem merely whets Assyria's appetite for expansion and oppression. Further, Menahem's levying of taxes for this appeasement begins the ongoing policy of draining Israel's resources, sometimes to fight Assyria and at other times to buy their favor. From now on the Northern Kingdom will never be rid of Assyria...[Menahem] begins a tradition of unstable, ever-shifting foreign policy where Assyria is concerned. His religious policies do not help Israel heal it's breach with the LORD. Thus his reign is but a longer episode in the swift decline of the northern people.[4]

A summary of Menahem's achievements in life are recorded in the book *The History of the Kings of Israel* (vv.21-22). After his death, he was buried in the capital Samaria and succeeded by his son Pekahiah.

OUTLINE	SCRIPTURE	SCRIPTURE	OUTLINE

3. The reign of Menahem & the Assyrian invasion: A picture of compromise—turning to the world for deliverance
a. His terrible atrocity & brutality against a city that rejected his kingship
 	
b. His rule: Lasted 10 years
 	
c. His evil
  1) Lived a wicked life
  2) Did not turn away from the sins of Jeroboam I, 1 K.12:25-33
 	
d. His compromise with the invading Assyrians
	16 Then Menahem smote Tiphsah, and all that *were* therein, and the coasts thereof from Tirzah: because they opened not *to him,* therefore he smote *it; and* all the women therein that were with child he ripped up.
	17 In the nine and thirtieth year of Azariah king of Judah began Menahem the son of Gadi to reign over Israel, *and reigned* ten years in Samaria.
	18 And he did *that which was* evil in the sight of the LORD: he departed not all his days from the sins of Jeroboam the son of Nebat, who made Israel to sin.
	19 *And* Pul the king of Assyria came against the land:
		and Menahem gave Pul a thousand talents of silver, that his hand might be with him to confirm the kingdom in his hand.
		20 And Menahem exacted the money of Israel, *even* of all the mighty men of wealth, of each man fifty shekels of silver, to give to the king of Assyria. So the king of Assyria turned back, and stayed not there in the land.
		21 And the rest of the acts of Menahem, and all that he did, *are* they not written in the book of the chronicles of the kings of Israel?
		22 And Menahem slept with his fathers; and Pekahiah his son reigned in his stead.
			1) He turned to the world, to King Pul (Tiglath-Pileser III), for deliverance, instead of turning to God: Paid 1000 talents of silver (37 tons) for Assyria to withdraw
			2) He sought to strengthen his control
			3) He raised the money by taxing the wealthy of Israel: 20 ounces of silver
			4) He compromised, & Assyria withdrew
			e. His achievements & the summary of his life
			  1) His reign: Recorded in the book *The History of the Kings of Israel*
			  2) His death: In Samaria
			  3) His successor: Pekahiah, his son

Thought 1. How many of us have compromised with the world some time in the past? Instead of offending someone or risking the loss of friendship, we went along with and did whatever the person requested. We knew the behavior was wrong, sinful. Nevertheless we gave in and committed the wrong deed. Perhaps it was taking drugs, smoking, or giving in to illicit sex. Perhaps it was doing something illegal at work or participating in another lawless act. Or perhaps it was a seemingly innocent act of telling a lie.

Whatever we did, we compromised our values and standards. And by compromising, we violated God's Holy Word and commandments. God's Word is very straightforward: we are to reject worldliness, turn away from and have nothing to do with sin and evil. If a person is living a worldly and wicked life, we are to withdraw from the person's evil behavior. Of course, we are to be friendly and maintain a friendship with the individual, but we are to have nothing to do with the individual's wickedness. We are not to fellowship with the person when he or she is engaging in sinful behavior. Listen to what the Word of God says:

> **"And take heed to yourselves, lest at any time your hearts be overcharged with surfeiting, and drunkenness, and cares of this life, and so that day come upon you unawares" (Lu.21:34).**

> **"And be not conformed to this world: but be ye transformed by the renewing of your mind, that ye may prove what is that good, and acceptable, and perfect, will of God" (Ro.12:2).**

> **"Wherefore come out from among them, and be ye separate, saith the Lord, and touch not the unclean *thing;* and I will receive you, And will be a Father unto you, and ye shall be my sons and daughters, saith the Lord Almighty" (2 Co.6:17-18).**

> **"By faith Moses, when he was come to years, refused to be called the son of Pharaoh's daughter; Choosing rather to suffer affliction with the people of God, than to enjoy the pleasures of sin for a season" (He.11:24-25).**

> **"Love not the world, neither the things *that are* in the world. If any man love the world, the love of the Father is not in him. For all that *is* in the world, the lust of the flesh, and the lust of the eyes, and the pride of life, is not of the Father, but is of the world" (1 Jn.2:15-16).**

---

4 Paul R. House. *1, 2 Kings,* p.331.

"Thou shalt not follow a multitude to *do* evil; neither shalt thou speak in a cause to decline after many to wrest *judgment*" (Ex.23:2).

"Take heed to thyself that thou be not snared by following them, after that they be destroyed from before thee; and that thou enquire not after their gods, saying, How did these nations serve their gods? even so will I do likewise" (De.12:30).

"And they rejected his statutes, and his covenant that he made with their fathers, and his testimonies which he testified against them; and they followed vanity, and became vain, and went after the heathen that *were* round about them, *concerning* whom the LORD had charged them, that they should not do like them" (2 K.17:15).

4 (15:23-26) **Greed, Example, for Power—Coveting, Example, for Power—Power, Coveting, Example— Assassination, Example—Pekahiah, King of Israel, Reign of**: the downward spiral of Israel's decline is seen again in the reign of Pekahiah and his assassination by one of his chief officers. His murder exposes the true spirit of Israel's leaders, a spirit of greed and self-interest, of covetous men grabbing hold of all the power and wealth they could seize.

Pekahiah assumed the throne in the fiftieth year of King Azariah (Uzziah) of Judah, but he ruled for only 24 months (v.23). Just as the rulers before him had done, he lived a wicked life. Therefore, when he began his rule, he did nothing to establish a righteous kingdom. Rather, he continued to live an evil life before the LORD, leading the people further away from God and continuing on in the sins of Jeroboam I (see outline and note—1 K.12:25-33 for more discussion). In an aggressive move to seize power, Pekah, the commander of Pekahiah's army, led a conspiracy against him. Rallying the support of 50 men from Gilead, Pekah attacked the king in the royal palace and assassinated him. According to Josephus, the unsuspected attack took place while the king was holding a royal banquet for his friends.[5]

Note that two of the king's royal bodyguards or chief officials, Argob and Arieh, were killed along with him (v.25). Pekahiah's achievements and a summary of his life are recorded in the book *The History of the Kings of Israel* (v.26). In summarizing the reign of Pekahiah, the commentator Paul R. House says this:

"Nothing has changed for the better. Assyria continues to lurk in the shadows, waiting for a chance to extract more blood money; Israel's kings failed to lead the people in a positive spiritual direction; and grasping, greedy, power-hungry men kill monarchs and take their place. Nothing occurs to slow Israel's demise."[6]

OUTLINE	SCRIPTURE	SCRIPTURE	OUTLINE

4. The reign of Pekahiah & his assassination: A picture of greed & covetousness, of grasping for power
a. His rule: Lasted 2 years
 	
b. His evil
  1) Lived a wicked life
  2) Continued in the sins of Jeroboam I, 1 K.12:25-33
  3) Was a stumbling block, causing the people to sin
c. His assassination
	23 In the fiftieth year of Azariah king of Judah Pekahiah the son of Menahem began to reign over Israel in Samaria, *and reigned* two years.
	24 And he did *that which was* evil in the sight of the LORD: he departed not from the sins of Jeroboam the son of Nebat, who made Israel to sin.
	25 But Pekah the son of Re-
		maliah, a captain of his, conspired against him, and smote him in Samaria, in the palace of the king's house, with Argob and Arieh, and with him fifty men of the Gileadites: and he killed him, and reigned in his room.
		26 And the rest of the acts of Pekahiah, and all that he did, behold, they *are* written in the book of the chronicles of the kings of Israel.
			1) Was attacked by Pekah, an army commander, & 50 men from Gilead: Killed the king in the citadel of the royal palace along with two loyal supporters, Argob & Arieh
			2) Was succeeded by the commander Pekah
			d. His achievements & the summary of his life: Recorded in the book *The History of the Kings of Israel*

Thought 1. How many of us have become greedy in life, wanting more and more, never being satisfied? How many are consumed with the pleasures and possessions of this world, squandering our thoughts and energy, our work and time?

When a person becomes greedy or covetous, always seeking more, he will begin to neglect family and responsibilities in order to satisfy his lusts. He will neglect work, friends, and loved ones. Because of greed, he will lie, steal, and cheat. If he covets sex, he will feast his mind upon pornography. He might even abuse others—men, women, or children—in order to satisfy his depraved urges.

When it comes to money, greed will cause people to deceive others, to lie about the value of property, to hide defects in homes that are for sale, and to misrepresent the truth of what an item is worth. Coveting money will drive some people to assault or even kill others in order to secure their wealth or property. Our prisons are full of thieves and murderers who are driven by greed. And walking the streets are many more who are guilty of the same sins but who have not been caught. These who walk among us have so far been able to hide their hearts of covetousness and their crimes of thievery and murder. But God knows. He knows and pronounces His judgment against every heart gripped by covetousness and greed.

> "And he said unto them, Take heed, and beware of covetousness: for a man's life consisteth not in the abundance of the things which he possesseth. And he spake a parable unto them, saying, The ground of a certain rich man brought forth plentifully: And he thought within himself, saying, What shall I do, because I have no room where to bestow my fruits? And he said, This will I do: I will pull down my barns, and build greater; and there will I bestow all my fruits and my goods. And I will say to my soul, Soul, thou hast much goods laid up for many years; take thine ease, eat, drink, *and* be

---

5 Josephus. *Antiquities of the Jews*, Book 9, Ch.11, p.209.
6 Paul R. House. *1, 2 Kings, pp.*331-332.

merry. But God said unto him, *Thou* fool, this night thy soul shall be required of thee: then whose shall those things be, which thou hast provided? So *is* he that layeth up treasure for himself, and is not rich toward God" (Lu.12:15-21).

"For the wrath of God is revealed from heaven against all ungodliness and unrighteousness of men, who hold the truth in unrighteousness...Being filled with all unrighteousness, fornication, wickedness, covetousness, maliciousness; full of envy, murder, debate, deceit, malignity; whisperers...Who knowing the judgment of God, that they which commit such things are worthy of death, not only do the same, but have pleasure in them that do them" (Ro.1:18, 29, 32).

"Know ye not that the unrighteous shall not inherit the kingdom of God? Be not deceived: neither fornicators, nor idolaters, nor adulterers, nor effeminate, nor abusers of themselves with mankind, Nor thieves, nor covetous, nor drunkards, nor revilers, nor extortioners, shall inherit the kingdom of God" (1 Co.6:9-10).

"But fornication, and all uncleanness, or covetousness, let it not be once named among you, as becometh saints; Neither filthiness, nor foolish talking, nor jesting, which are not convenient: but rather giving of thanks. For this ye know, that no whoremonger, nor unclean person, nor covetous man, who is an idolater, hath any inheritance in the kingdom of Christ and of God. Let no man deceive you with vain words: for because of these things cometh the wrath of God upon the children of disobedience" (Ep.5:3-6).

"For the love of money is the root of all evil: which while some coveted after, they have erred from the faith, and pierced themselves through with many sorrows" (1 Ti.6:10).

"Thou shalt not covet thy neighbour's house, thou shalt not covet thy neighbour's wife, nor his manservant, nor his maidservant, nor his ox, nor his ass, nor any thing that *is* thy neighbour's" (Ex.20:17).

"And his sons walked not in his ways, but turned aside after lucre, and took bribes, and perverted judgment" (1 S.8:3).

"The desire of the slothful killeth him; for his hands refuse to labour. He coveteth greedily all the day long: but the righteous giveth and spareth not" (Pr.21:25-26).

"Yea, *they are* greedy dogs *which* can never have enough, and they *are* shepherds *that* cannot understand: they all look to their own way, every one for his gain, from his quarter" (Is.56:11).

"For from the least of them even unto the greatest of them every one *is* given to covetousness; and from the prophet even unto the priest every one dealeth falsely" (Je.6:13).

"He that loveth silver shall not be satisfied with silver; nor he that loveth abundance with increase: this *is* also vanity" (Ec.5:10).

"And they come unto thee as the people cometh, and they sit before thee as my people, and they hear thy words, but they will not do them: for with their mouth they show much love, *but* their heart goeth after their covetousness" (Eze.33:31).

"And they covet fields, and take *them* by violence; and houses, and take *them* away: so they oppress a man and his house, even a man and his heritage" (Mi.2:2).

"Woe to him that coveteth an evil covetousness to his house, that he may set his nest on high, that he may be delivered from the power of evil" (Hab.2:9).

---

5 (15:27-31) **Judgment, Example of—Northern Kingdom of Israel, Kings of—Assassination, Example of**: having just assassinated King Pekahiah, Pekah assumed the throne in the fifty-second year of King Azariah (Uzziah) of Judah. He ruled for 20 years (752–732 B.C.).[7] Apparently Pekah had rebelled against the rule of Menahem and organized a rival government. The years of his independent rule are included in the 20 years listed here.

Whatever the case, Pekah lived a wicked life, following in the footsteps of Jeroboam I and leading the people to sin (see outline and note—1 K.12:25-33 for more discussion). Because of the people's wicked behavior, God launched His judgment against the Northern Kingdom, using the Assyrians to instigate the beginning of the end for Israel. Assyria invaded the land and captured a number of towns: Ijon, Abel-Beth-Maachah, Janoah, Kedesh, and Hazor. They also conquered the districts of Gilead, Galilee, and all the land of Naphtali. But that was not all. Tiglath-Pileser deported the people of the Northern Kingdom, taking them all back to Assyria as captives. From this point on, Israel faced Assyrian troops all along the nation's eastern border, right across the Jordan River. The people were facing extinction.

Apparently, a number of the leaders within Israel became pro-Assyrian supporters. As a result, a conspiracy headed up by a man named Hoshea was plotted against King Pekah (v.30). Attacking Pekah, Hoshea assassinated him and then succeeded him as king.

A summary of King Pekah's achievements and life are recorded in the book *The History of the Kings of Israel* (v.31). In summarizing the Assyrian oppression and the reign of Pekah, the commentator Russell Dilday says this:

> Later, in 2 Kings 15:37, we are told about an alliance between Pekah and King Rezin of Syria. The two of them tried to enlist Ahaz of Judah to join an alliance with them, and when he refused, they attacked the Southern Kingdom in what is known as the Syrian-Ephraimite invasion.[8] It may have been this alliance with Rezin that caused Tiglath-Pileser III of Assyria to launch the attack against Israel (v.29), fearing that they might try to rebel with the help of their new friend.

---

7 For a detailed study on the problems with the dates of Pekah's reign see *1, 2 Kings,* "The Expositor's Bible Commentary," Vol.4, pp.238-239.

8 Robert C. Dentan. *Kings and Chronicles.* "Layman's Bible Commentary," Vol. 7. (Richmond, VA: John Knox Press, 1964), p.81.

Assyria's invasion of Israel is also referred to in several other inscriptions, including one in Tiglath-Pileser's royal annals. According to this account, he created three districts from the conquered territory: (1) Meggido, covering Galilee and the Northern Plains; (2) Dor, including the Plain of Sharon and extending to the Philistine border; and (3) Gilead, in the Transjordan area.[9] The inscription also says, "They overthrew their king Peqaha and I placed Ausi [Hoshea] as king over them." This indicates that Tiglath-Pileser III may have actually participated in Hoshea's conspiracy to kill King Pekah (v.30).[10] Archaeological evidence of the invasion has also been unearthed in the excavations of Hazor.[11] Together, all the cities mentioned in verse 29 make up "the land of Naphtali" (synonymous with Galilee). Igon is the most northerly of the cities listed and was therefore the first to fall before the Assyrian invaders, who came from that direction.

This oppression in 733 B.C., a precursor of the major captivity in 722 B.C., seems to be the first test of Assyria's strategy of reducing a conquered nation into an Assyrian province by deporting the upper classes to another part of the empire and replacing them with foreign immigrants.[12] For another graphic picture of this grim period in Israel's history read Hosea 13:11, 7:11, 4:17, 4:1-2, and 8:2.

These were dark days for Israel, her territory now reduced to a tiny kingdom only thirty miles wide by forty miles long. The Northern Kingdom was down to its last ruler. Hoshea would be the final king of this dying nation. No wonder these tragic events became the occasion for the "Immanuel" passages in Isaiah 7:1ff.[13]

OUTLINE	SCRIPTURE	SCRIPTURE	OUTLINE

5. The reign of Pekah & his assassination: A picture of the desperate need for God's saving power—found only in Christ
a. His rule: 20 years
b. His evil
  1) Lived a wicked life
  2) Followed the sins of Jeroboam I, 1 K.12:25-33
  3) Was a stumbling block, causing the people to sin
c. His war with Assyria: Facing God's impending judgment
  1) He lost all Galilee—the land of Naphtali—& also Gilead, 1 Chr.5:25-26
	27 In the two and fiftieth year of Azariah king of Judah Pekah the son of Remaliah began to reign over Israel in Samaria, *and reigned* twenty years.
	28 And he did *that which was* evil in the sight of the LORD: he departed not from the sins of Jeroboam the son of Nebat, who made Israel to sin.
	29 In the days of Pekah king of Israel came Tiglath-pileser king of Assyria, and took Ijon, and Abel-beth-maachah, and Janoah, and Kedesh, and
		Hazor, and Gilead, and Galilee, all the land of Naphtali, and carried them captive to Assyria.
		30 And Hoshea the son of Elah made a conspiracy against Pekah the son of Remaliah, and smote him, and slew him, and reigned in his stead, in the twentieth year of Jotham the son of Uzziah.
		31 And the rest of the acts of Pekah, and all that he did, behold, they *are* written in the book of the chronicles of the kings of Israel.
			2) He faced Assyrian troops all along Israel's western border, right across the Jordan River
			d. His assassination
			  1) Was conspired against & murdered by Hoshea
			  2) Was succeeded by Hoshea
			
			e. His achievements & the summary of his life: Recorded in the book *The History of the Kings of Israel*

Thought 1. This passage marks the beginning of the end for Israel. Judgment has begun to fall upon the sinful, wicked citizens of the Northern Kingdom. Very soon the nation would collapse and be exiled to the land of Assyria. And the Northern Kingdom would be no more.

When will the beginning of the end occur for us? The day is coming when we will face the judgment of God. And we cannot stop it. Judgment is inevitable for those who have never accepted Christ. But if we have accepted Christ as our Savior and LORD, judgment has been removed from us. For when Christ died upon the cross, He bore our sin and judgment in our place. The guilt of our sin was removed from us, taken by Him, freeing us from all accusation. All who have truly trusted Christ are freed from judgment. Judgment has been taken off of us and placed upon Christ. This is the reason Christ died, the meaning of the cross. He paid the penalty for our sin and judgment *once for all*.

God is pleased with what Christ has done. God approves, accepts the death of Christ on our behalf. God accepts His bearing our sin and judgment for us—in our stead, in our place of us. That is what is meant by the statement, "Christ died for us." Again, if we have truly accepted Christ, there is no judgment of sin for us. But if we have rejected Christ, living wicked lives and refusing to worship Him, then the hand of God's judgment will fall upon us. Listen to what the Word of God says:

> **"And then shall appear the sign of the Son of man in heaven: and then shall all the tribes of the earth mourn, and they shall see the Son of man coming in the clouds of heaven with power and great glory" (Mt.24:30).**

> **"Whosoever therefore shall be ashamed of me and of my words in this adulterous and sinful generation; of him also shall the Son of man be ashamed, when he cometh in the glory of his Father with the holy angels" (Mk.8:38).**

> **"And this is the condemnation, that light is come into the world, and men loved darkness rather than light, because their deeds were evil" (Jn.3:19).**

---

9 Gwilym H. Jones. *1 and 2 Kings.* "New Century Bible Commentary." Ronald E. Clements, Editor. (Grand Rapids, MI: Eerdmans Publishing Co., 1984), p.529

10 John Gray. *I and II Kings.* "Old Testament Library." (Philadelphia, PA: Westminster Press, 1963), p.569.

11 John Gray. *I and II Kings*, p.568.

12 Gwilym H. Jones. *1 and 2 Kings*, p.529.

13 Russell Dilday. *1, 2 Kings*, pp.406-407.

"Marvel not at this: for the hour is coming, in the which all that are in the graves shall hear his voice, And shall come forth; they that have done good, unto the resurrection of life; and they that have done evil, unto the resurrection of damnation" (Jn.5:28-29).

"And to you who are troubled rest with us, when the Lord Jesus shall be revealed from heaven with his mighty angels, In flaming fire taking vengeance on them that know not God, and that obey not the gospel of our Lord Jesus Christ" (2 Th.1:7-8).

"And as it is appointed unto men once to die, but after this the judgment" (He.9:27).

"The Lord knoweth how to deliver the godly out of temptations, and to reserve the unjust unto the day of judgment to be punished" (2 Pe.2:9).

"But the heavens and the earth, which are now, by the same word are kept in store, reserved unto fire against the day of judgment and perdition of ungodly men" (2 Pe.3:7).

"Herein is our love made perfect, that we may have boldness in the day of judgment: because as he is, so are we in this world" (1 Jn.4:17).

"And Enoch also, the seventh from Adam, prophesied of these, saying, Behold, the Lord cometh with ten thousands of his saints, To execute judgment upon all, and to convince all that are ungodly among them of all their ungodly deeds which they have ungodly committed, and of all their hard *speeches* which ungodly sinners have spoken against him" (Jude 14-15).

"Behold, he cometh with clouds; and every eye shall see him, and they *also* which pierced him: and all kindreds of the earth shall wail because of him. Even so, Amen" (Re.1:7).

"And I saw a great white throne, and him that sat on it, from whose face the earth and the heaven fled away; and there was found no place for them. And I saw the dead, small and great, stand before God; and the books were opened: and another book was opened, which is *the book* of life: and the dead were judged out of those things which were written in the books, according to their works. And the sea gave up the dead which were in it; and death and hell delivered up the dead which were in them: and they were judged every man according to their works. And death and hell were cast into the lake of fire. This is the second death. And whosoever was not found written in the book of life was cast into the lake of fire" (Re.20:11-15).

Thought 2. Russell Dilday gives an excellent application of this point that is well worth sharing:

Nowhere in the Word of God is there a clearer illustration of the consequences of sin. Israel was helpless to save herself. Even the powerful preaching of the prophets could not stem the tide. Destruction was inevitable. And it's still that way today. Sin still brings consequences so overpowering that even the strongest human efforts cannot withstand them.

The Bible makes it clear that in spite of our impressive technological sophistication, without Christ, our own generation, like Israel, is dead in trespasses and sins. Even our unprecedented scientific power cannot save us. Nothing short of a divine miracle can defeat Satan and redeem the sinner. That's why this passage in Kings points us so plainly to the cross of Calvary, God's ultimate solution to humankind's lostness. Over seven hundred years after Israel's captivity, on a cross just outside the walls of Jerusalem, another monarch, this time a perfect descendant of David—Jesus Christ, the King of kings—gave his life for the sins of the world, so that those who believe in Him might not perish, but have eternal life. No wonder the Bible calls that atoning event "the good news!"[14]

14 Russell Dilday. *1, 2 Kings,* p.407.

D. The Reigns of Two Kings in Judah: A Sharp Contrast Between Righteousness & Wickedness, 15:32–16:20

15:32-38; see 2 Chr.27:1-9
16:1-20; see 2 Chr.28:1-27

1. The reign of Jotham: A ruler who worshipped God as instructed
a. His background
   1) He was the son of Uzziah & Jerusha
   2) He was 25 years old when crowned
   3) He reigned 16 years

b. His spiritual life
   1) He was righteous & faithful in worship, 2 Chr.27:2

   2) He failed to remove the high places: Allowed the people to continue their worship there
c. His major building achievement: Rebuilt the Upper Gate of the temple, 2 Chr.27:3-4
d. His achievements & the summary of his life
   1) His reign: Recorded in the book *The History of the Kings of Judah*
   2) His military conflict with Syria & Israel: The beginning of God's final judgment against Judah
   3) His death & burial: In Jerusalem
   4) His successor: Ahaz, his son

2. The reign of Ahaz: A ruler who looked for a savior other than the LORD
a. His background
   1) His age: 20 years old
   2) His rule: Lasted 16 years
b. His terrible evil
   1) He lived a wicked life: Did not live righteously as David did

   2) He walked in the sinful ways of Israel's kings
   3) He offered his son as a human sacrifice to a false god, 17:17; 21:6; 23:10

32 In the second year of Pekah the son of Remaliah king of Israel began Jotham the son of Uzziah king of Judah to reign.
33 Five and twenty years old was he when he began to reign, and he reigned sixteen years in Jerusalem. And his mother's name *was* Jerusha, the daughter of Zadok.
34 And he did *that which was* right in the sight of the LORD: he did according to all that his father Uzziah had done.
35 Howbeit the high places were not removed: the people sacrificed and burned incense still in the high places. He built the higher gate of the house of the LORD.
36 Now the rest of the acts of Jotham, and all that he did, *are* they not written in the book of the chronicles of the kings of Judah?
37 In those days the LORD began to send against Judah Rezin the king of Syria, and Pekah the son of Remaliah.
38 And Jotham slept with his fathers, and was buried with his fathers in the city of David his father: and Ahaz his son reigned in his stead.

CHAPTER 16

In the seventeenth year of Pekah the son of Remaliah Ahaz the son of Jotham king of Judah began to reign.
2 Twenty years old *was* Ahaz when he began to reign, and reigned sixteen years in Jerusalem, and did not *that which was* right in the sight of the LORD his God, like David his father.
3 But he walked in the way of the kings of Israel, yea, and made his son to pass through the fire, according to the abominations of the heathen, whom the LORD cast out from before the children of Israel.
4 And he sacrificed and burnt incense in the high places, and on the hills, and under every green tree.
5 Then Rezin king of Syria and Pekah son of Remaliah king of Israel came up to Jerusalem to war: and they besieged Ahaz, but could not overcome *him.*
6 At that time Rezin king of Syria recovered Elath to Syria, and drave the Jews from Elath: and the Syrians came to Elath, and dwelt there unto this day.
7 So Ahaz sent messengers to Tiglath-pileser king of Assyria, saying, I *am* thy servant and thy son: come up, and save me out of the hand of the king of Syria, and out of the hand of the king of Israel, which rise up against me.
8 And Ahaz took the silver and gold that was found in the house of the LORD, and in the treasures of the king's house, and sent *it for* a present to the king of Assyria.
9 And the king of Assyria hearkened unto him: for the king of Assyria went up against Damascus, and took it, and carried *the people of* it captive to Kir, and slew Rezin.
10 And king Ahaz went to Damascus to meet Tiglath-pileser king of Assyria, and saw an altar that *was* at Damascus: and king Ahaz sent to Urijah the priest the fashion of the altar, and the pattern of it, according to all the workmanship thereof.
11 And Urijah the priest built an altar according to all that king Ahaz had sent from Damascus: so Urijah the priest made *it* against king Ahaz came from Damascus.
12 And when the king was come from Damascus, the king saw the altar: and the king approached to the altar, and offered thereon.
13 And he burnt his burnt offering and his meat offering, and poured his drink offering, and sprinkled the blood of his peace offerings, upon the altar.
14 And he brought also the brasen altar, which *was* be-

4) He worshipped false gods at the high places, 2 Chr.28:2-4

5) He turned to Tiglath-Pileser of Assyria—not to God—to save him from an attack by Israel & Syria
   • Israel & Syria were not able to conquer Jerusalem but did retake Elath for the Syrians
   • Israel & Syria sought to replace Ahaz with a ruler who would join them against Assyria, 15:29; Is.7:6
   • Ahaz appealed to Tiglath-Pileser—not to God—for help & deliverance, Is.7:3-25

6) He confiscated the wealth from the treasuries of the temple & palace to hire Assyria to save him

   • Assyria responded: Captured Damascus & deported its citizens to Kir
   • Assyria executed Rezin, the Syrian king

7) He was impressed with an Assyrian altar—an unholy altar—he saw in Damascus: Made a commitment to follow the false gods of Assyria
   • He made a sketch of the altar
   • He sent the sketch to Uriah the High Priest with orders to complete it before he returned from Damascus

8) He approached the unholy altar in worship & presented offerings to the Assyrian god(s)

   • The burnt offering
   • The grain offering
   • The drink offering
   • The sprinkled blood of the fellowship or peace offering
9) He moved the LORD'S bronze altar from the

central position in the temple & replaced it with the new altar, the unholy altar: Had the LORD's altar moved to the north side

10) He ordered all regular offerings thereafter to be made on his new (unholy) altar: A tragic worship of false gods

11) He practiced witchcraft in the temple itself by setting aside the LORD's bronze altar for his own personal use: For him to use when he needed to seek special guidance from his false gods of divination

12) He corrupted the High Priest: Forced him to en-

fore the LORD, from the forefront of the house, from between the altar and the house of the LORD, and put it on the north side of the altar. 15 And king Ahaz commanded Urijah the priest, saying, Upon the great altar burn the morning burnt offering, and the evening meat offering, and the king's burnt sacrifice, and his meat offering, with the burnt offering of all the people of the land, and their meat offering, and their drink offerings; and sprinkle upon it all the blood of the burnt offering, and all the blood of the sacrifice: and the brasen altar shall be for me to enquire *by*. 16 Thus did Urijah the priest, according to all that

king Ahaz commanded. 17 And king Ahaz cut off the borders of the bases, and removed the laver from off them; and took down the sea from off the brasen oxen that *were* under it, and put it upon a pavement of stones. 18 And the covert for the sabbath that they had built in the house, and the king's entry without, turned he from the house of the LORD for the king of Assyria. 19 Now the rest of the acts of Ahaz which he did, *are* they not written in the book of the chronicles of the kings of Judah? 20 And Ahaz slept with his fathers, and was buried with his fathers in the city of David: and Hezekiah his son reigned in his stead.

gage in the false worship

13) He confiscated the brass from the furnishings

14) He removed the Sabbath canopy & the royal entryway to the temple: In order to show deference to the Assyrian ruler, not offending, but pleasing, him

c. His achievements & the summary of his life

1) His reign: Recorded in the book *The History of the Kings of Judah*

2) His death & burial: In Jerusalem

3) His successor: Hezekiah, his son

DIVISION III

THE UTTER DISINTEGRATION AND FALL OF ISRAEL, THE NORTHERN KINGDOM: A TRAGIC END DUE TO AN UNBROKEN STREAM OF WICKEDNESS AND LAWLESSNESS, 14:1–17:22

D. The Reigns of Two Kings in Judah: A Sharp Contrast Between Righteousness and Wickedness, 15:32–16:20

(15:32–16:20) **Introduction—Righteousness, Contrasted with Wickedness—Wickedness, Contrasted with Righteousness—Society, Building, Source—Behavior, Righteous vs. Wicked—Righteousness, Duty**: there is a sharp contrast between the qualities of righteousness and wickedness. So much contrast exists between the two that both have been symbolized within the language of men. Picture the difference between...

- light and darkness
- white and black
- sight and blindness

- hearing and deafness
- life and death
- heaven and hell

When it comes to human behavior, the contrast between righteousness and wickedness is every bit as sharp. Consider the difference in such behaviors as...

- love and hate
- faithfulness and unfaithfulness
- generosity and stinginess
- telling the truth and lying
- kindness and meanness

- sobriety and drunkenness
- humility and boasting
- equality and discrimination
- godly speech and profanity
- morality and immorality

A righteous person builds up society, whereas a wicked person tears down society. Building up lives should be our focus, not tearing them down. Righteousness, not wickedness, should dominate our lives. Wickedness and all its lawless and depraved behavior is eating away at society—so much so that it dominates the news of our communities and our nation. Somehow, in some way, we as individuals must take hold of our lives and change our behavior. We must become men and women of integrity and uprightness, not treachery and wickedness.

This is the important message to be learned from the present passage of Scripture. It is a contrast between two kings of Judah, one righteous and one wicked. In looking at their lives and reigns, the reader can see that the downfall of Judah was bound to come. A stream of wickedness had begun, one that was bound to gain momentum before its inevitable end: catastrophic destruction. The hand of God's judgment was bound to fall upon the Southern Kingdom because of the people's wicked lives. This is: *The Reigns of Two Kings in Judah: A Sharp Contrast Between Righteousness and Wickedness,* 15:32–16:20.

1. The reign of Jotham: a ruler who worshipped God as instructed (15:32-38).
2. The reign of Ahaz: a ruler who looked for a savior other than the LORD (16:1-20).

[1] (15:32-38) **Worship, Faithful—Righteousness, Example of—Jotham, King of Judah, Reign of—Southern Kingdom, Kings of, Jotham—Faithfulness, in Worship, Example of**: there was the reign in Judah of Jotham, a

righteous ruler who was strong and faithful in worship. He was only 25 years old when he was crowned king, in the second year of King Pekah of Israel (vv.32-33). Jotham reigned for 16 years, 10 of which were apparently spent as co-regent with his father Uzziah (15:5). Remember, his father had been stricken with leprosy because he failed to worship God as instructed. Because a person with leprosy was isolated, not able to carry on public functions, Jotham had to step in to rule right beside his father. He managed the government with his father serving behind the scenes. Note that his mother was the daughter of the priest Zadok, both of whom obviously had a godly influence upon him throughout his life.

OUTLINE	SCRIPTURE	SCRIPTURE	OUTLINE

1. The reign of Jotham: A ruler who worshipped God as instructed
a. His background
  1) He was the son of Uzziah & Jerusha
  2) He was 25 years old when crowned
  3) He reigned 16 years
 	
b. His spiritual life
  1) He was righteous & faithful in worship, 2 Chr.27:2
 	
  2) He failed to remove the high places: Allowed the people to continue their
	32 In the second year of Pekah the son of Remaliah king of Israel began Jotham the son of Uzziah king of Judah to reign.
	33 Five and twenty years old was he when he began to reign, and he reigned sixteen years in Jerusalem. And his mother's name *was* Jerusha, the daughter of Zadok.
	34 And he did *that which was* right in the sight of the LORD: he did according to all that his father Uzziah had done.
	35 Howbeit the high places were not removed: the people sacrificed and burned
		incense still in the high places. He built the higher gate of the house of the LORD.
		36 Now the rest of the acts of Jotham, and all that he did, *are* they not written in the book of the chronicles of the kings of Judah?
		37 In those days the LORD began to send against Judah Rezin the king of Syria, and Pekah the son of Remaliah.
		38 And Jotham slept with his fathers, and was buried with his fathers in the city of David his father: and Ahaz his son reigned in his stead.
			worship there
			c. His major building achievement: Rebuilt the Upper Gate of the temple, 2 Chr.27:3-4
			d. His achievements & the summary of his life
			  1) His reign: Recorded in the book *The History of the Kings of Judah*
			  2) His military conflict with Syria & Israel: The beginning of God's final judgment against Judah
			  3) His death & burial: In Jerusalem
			  4) His successor: Ahaz, his son

Just as his godly father Uzziah had done, Jotham lived a righteous life in the eyes of the LORD. He proved to be even more faithful to the LORD than his father had, always worshipping and approaching the LORD just as the LORD instructed. However, like so many of the kings before him, he failed in one very serious area: he did not remove the high places (v.35). By not removing them, he became a stumbling block to the people, permitting them to continue to worship at the very sites where false gods had formerly been worshipped. Through the years, many of the people had allowed false worship to seep back into their lives. As a result, the people's worship was now totally corrupted. Allowing the people to continue their false worship at the high places cut the heart of God. In this area, King Jotham failed and stood guilty before the LORD.

By having served ten years as co-regent with his father Uzziah, Jotham continued the work begun by him, strengthening the economy through the public works projects he had launched. His major building achievement was the repairing of the Upper Gate of the temple. This particular gate stood near the palace and was the major gate used by the king and his royal officials. Other Scripture tells us that he also repaired part of the wall of Jerusalem, and built towns, forts, and military lookout towers (2 Chr.27:3-4).

But, sadly, Jotham and the people allowed their prosperity to make them comfortable, so comfortable that they eventually became complacent and ignored the LORD and His commandments. Soon forgetting and neglecting the LORD, they set the stage for a king who would be utterly wicked and totally depraved. This man was to be the very next king, King Ahaz the son of Jotham. Just how complacent and wicked the people became is vividly described by the prophet Isaiah (see Isaiah, chapters 1-5).

A summary of Jotham's achievements and life are recorded in *The History of the Kings of Judah* (v.36). A significant fact needs to be noted about his reign: because of the people's sinful and wicked lives, the beginning of God's final judgment upon Judah was launched (v.37). God used a coalition of Syria and Israel as his instruments of judgment, arousing the coalition to begin making incursions or hostile entrances into Judah. No doubt, the LORD'S hope was that the people would turn to Him in repentance and cry out for His help. But such was not to be the case. Stubbornly, the people continued in their wickedness and false worship.[1]

After his death, Jotham was buried in the royal tombs in Jerusalem (v.38). He was succeeded by his son Ahaz, who was to be one of the most wicked kings to rule in either the Northern or Southern Kingdoms.

Thought 1. During Jotham's reign some of the people had turned to false worship and were living sinful, wicked lives. Because of this, Jotham should have launched a nationwide reform to turn people back to the LORD and back to true worship. This he did not do. But despite his failure, he did live a righteous life and he personally worshipped the LORD. In fact, he was far more faithful in worship than his father Uzziah had been. His father had attempted to approach and worship God in his own way, rejecting God's clear instructions about how he is to be approached and worshipped.

So it is with many of us. We seek to approach God as we wish and the way we think He should be approached. We reject God's clear instructions, that we are to approach Him only through Jesus Christ. God teaches us there is only one Mediator between Him and us, only one Intercessor who is acceptable to Him, only one Advocate who has the right to stand in the holy, perfect court of heaven. That Mediator, that Intercessor, and that Advocate is the Lord Jesus Christ. Teaching us this great truth, God proclaims loudly and clearly that there is no other acceptable

---

1 Richard D. Patterson and Hermann J. Austel. *1, 2 Kings*, p.241.

approach for worship. He receives no person and no worship of any *imperfect* being. All approaches and worship must come through the *holy perfection* of Jesus Christ.

When we who are sinners wish to approach God and offer Him our worship, we must go to the *Perfect Intercessor* who is Christ and offer Him our worship. He in all His perfection then offers us and our worship to the Father. And God the Father accepts us and our worship because God the Son—in all of His *holy perfection*—is the One who presents us and our worship to Him.

Just as Jotham approached and worshipped God exactly as God instructed, so we must approach God just as God's Holy Word says, through the Lord Jesus Christ. This is the only acceptable approach and worship of the LORD.

> "I said therefore unto you, that ye shall die in your sins: for if ye believe not that I am *he,* ye shall die in your sins" (Jn.8:24).

> "Neither is there salvation in any other: for there is none other name under heaven given among men, whereby we must be saved" (Ac.4:12).

> "Who *is* he that condemneth? *It is* Christ that died, yea rather, that is risen again, who is even at the right hand of God, who also maketh intercession for us" (Ro.8:34).

> "For other foundation can no man lay than that is laid, which is Jesus Christ" (1 Co.3:11).

> "For this *is* good and acceptable in the sight of God our Saviour; Who will have all men to be saved, and to come unto the knowledge of the truth. For *there is* one God, and one mediator between God and men, the man Christ Jesus" (1 Ti.2:3-5).

> "Wherefore in all things it behooved him to be made like unto *his* brethren, that he might be a merciful and faithful -high priest in things *pertaining* to God, to make reconciliation for the sins of the people" (He.2:17).

> "Wherefore he is able also to save them to the uttermost that come unto God by him, seeing he ever liveth to make intercession for them. For such an high priest became us, *who is* holy, harmless, undefiled, separate from sinners, and made higher than the heavens; Who needeth not daily, as those high priests, to offer up sacrifice, first for his own sins, and then for the people's: for this he did once, when he offered up himself" (He.7:25-27).

> "Neither by the blood of goats and calves, but by his own blood he entered in once into the holy place, having obtained eternal redemption *for us.* For if the blood of bulls and of goats, and the ashes of an heifer sprinkling the unclean, sanctifieth to the purifying of the flesh: How much more shall the blood of Christ, who through the eternal Spirit offered himself without spot to God, purge your conscience from dead works to serve the living God? And for this cause he is the mediator of the new testament, that by means of death, for the redemption of the transgressions *that were* under the first testament, they which are called might receive the promise of eternal inheritance" (He.9:12-15).

> "For Christ is not entered into the holy places made with hands, *which are* the figures of the true; but into heaven itself, now to appear in the presence of God for us" (He.9:24).

> "My little children, these things write I unto you, that ye sin not. And if any man sin, we have an advocate with the Father, Jesus Christ the righteous" (1 Jn.2:1).

---

2 (16:1-20) **Depravity, Example of—Wickedness, Example of—Worship, False, Sacrificing Children—Molech, False God, Worship of, Sacrificing Children—Ahaz, King of Judah, Reign of—Kings, of Judah—Judah, Kings of**: now begins the evil reign of King Ahaz of Judah, a reign that can be matched only by that of Jeroboam I in the Northern Kingdom (1 K.12:25–13:34). Among all the kings of Judah, no reign plunged the nation into the depths of utter wickedness and total depravity as much as the reign of Ahaz did. He unleashed a flood of wickedness that ultimately doomed the nation to total destruction under the hand of God's judgment. Glance quickly at the outline, noting how the author of *Kings* simply introduces Ahaz and then immediately launches into the torrent of evil he set in motion within the nation. Focusing upon his sinful life and reign, the author lists 14 acts of wickedness that characterized his life (vv.2-18).

OUTLINE	SCRIPTURE	SCRIPTURE	OUTLINE
2. The reign of Ahaz: A ruler who looked for a savior other than the LORD	In the seventeenth year of Pekah the son of Remaliah Ahaz the son of Jotham king of Judah began to reign.	then, whom the LORD cast out from before the children of Israel.	
a. His background			
1) His age: 20 years old	2 Twenty years old *was* Ahaz when he began to reign,	4 And he sacrificed and burnt incense in the high places, and on the hills, and under every green tree.	4) He worshipped false gods at the high places, 2 Chr.28:2-4
2) His rule: Lasted 16 years	and reigned sixteen years in Jerusalem, and did not *that*		
b. His terrible evil			
1) He lived a wicked life: Did not live righteously as David did	*which was* right in the sight of the LORD his God, like David his father.	5 Then Rezin king of Syria and Pekah son of Remaliah king of Israel came up to Jerusalem to war: and they besieged Ahaz, but could not overcome *him.*	5) He turned to Tiglath-Pileser of Assyria—not to God—to save him from an attack by Israel & Syria
2) He walked in the sinful ways of Israel's kings	3 But he walked in the way of the kings of Israel, yea,		• Israel & Syria were not able to conquer Jerusalem but did retake Elath for the Syrians
3) He offered his son as a human sacrifice to a false god, 17:17; 21:6; 23:10	and made his son to pass through the fire, according to the abominations of the hea-	6 At that time Rezin king of Syria recovered Elath to Syria, and drave the Jews from	

OUTLINE	SCRIPTURE	SCRIPTURE	OUTLINE
• Israel & Syria sought to replace Ahaz with a ruler who would join them against Assyria, 15:29; Is.7:6 • Ahaz appealed to Tiglath-Pileser—not to God—for help & deliverance, Is.7:3-25	Elath: and the Syrians came to Elath, and dwelt there unto this day. 7 So Ahaz sent messengers to Tiglath-pileser king of Assyria, saying, I *am* thy servant and thy son: come up, and save me out of the hand of the king of Syria, and out of the hand of the king of Israel, which rise up against me.	upon the altar. 14 And he brought also the brasen altar, which *was* before the LORD, from the forefront of the house, from between the altar and the house of the LORD, and put it on the north side of the altar. 15 And king Ahaz commanded Urijah the priest, saying, Upon the great altar	offering 9) He moved the LORD'S bronze altar from the central position in the temple & replaced it with the new altar, the unholy altar: Had the LORD'S altar moved to the north side
6) He confiscated the wealth from the treasuries of the temple & palace to hire Assyria to save him	8 And Ahaz took the silver and gold that was found in the house of the LORD, and in the treasures of the king's house, and sent *it for* a present to the king of Assyria.	burn the morning burnt offering, and the evening meat offering, and the king's burnt sacrifice, and his meat offering, with the burnt offering of all the people of the land, and their meat offering, and their drink of-	10) He ordered all regular offerings thereafter to be made on his new (unholy) altar: A tragic worship of false gods
• Assyria responded: Captured Damascus & deported its citizens to Kir • Assyria executed Rezin, the Syrian king	9 And the king of Assyria hearkened unto him: for the king of Assyria went up against Damascus, and took it, and carried *the people of* it captive to Kir, and slew Rezin.	ferings; and sprinkle upon it all the blood of the burnt offering, and all the blood of the sacrifice: and the brasen altar shall be for me to enquire *by.*	11) He practiced witchcraft in the temple itself by setting aside the LORD'S bronze altar for his own personal use: For him to use when he needed to seek special guidance from his false gods of divination
7) He was impressed with an Assyrian altar—an unholy altar—he saw in Damascus: Made a commitment to follow the false gods of Assyria • He made a sketch of the altar • He sent the sketch to Uriah the High Priest with orders to complete it before he returned from Damascus	10 And king Ahaz went to Damascus to meet Tiglath-pileser king of Assyria, and saw an altar that *was* at Damascus: and king Ahaz sent to Urijah the priest the fashion of the altar, and the pattern of it, according to all the workmanship thereof. 11 And Urijah the priest built an altar according to all that king Ahaz had sent from Damascus: so Urijah the priest made *it* against king Ahaz came from Damascus.	16 Thus did Urijah the priest, according to all that king Ahaz commanded. 17 And king Ahaz cut off the borders of the bases, and removed the laver from off them; and took down the sea from off the brasen oxen that *were* under it, and put it upon a pavement of stones.	12) He corrupted the High Priest: Forced him to engage in the false worship 13) He confiscated the brass from the furnishings
8) He approached the unholy altar in worship & presented offerings to the Assyrian god(s) • The burnt offering • The grain offering • The drink offering • The sprinkled blood of the fellowship or peace	12 And when the king was come from Damascus, the king saw the altar: and the king approached to the altar, and offered thereon. 13 And he burnt his burnt offering and his meat offering, and poured his drink offering, and sprinkled the blood of his peace offerings,	18 And the covert for the sabbath that they had built in the house, and the king's entry without, turned he from the house of the LORD for the king of Assyria. 19 Now the rest of the acts of Ahaz which he did, *are* they not written in the book of the chronicles of the kings of Judah? 20 And Ahaz slept with his fathers, and was buried with his fathers in the city of David: and Hezekiah his son reigned in his stead.	14) He removed the Sabbath canopy & the royal entryway to the temple: In order to show deference to the Assyrian ruler, not offending, but pleasing, him c. His achievements & the summary of his life 1) His reign: Recorded in the book *The History of the Kings of Judah* 2) His death & burial: In Jerusalem 3) His successor: Hezekiah, his son

a. Ahaz began to rule in the seventeenth year of King Pekah of Israel. Taking the throne at the age of 20, he ruled for 16 years (vv.1-2). Based upon his age and the years of his rule, he must have served as co-regent with his father Jotham for some years.

In stark contrast to the righteous lives of his father and grandfather, Ahaz lived a shockingly evil life. When studying about Ahaz, a person's mind just staggers under the weight of evil that characterized his life. Note the list of 14 evils pointed out by the author of *Kings.*

    1) Ahaz lived a wicked life, rejecting the righteous example of his father Jotham and his grandfather Uzziah. He failed to walk in the righteous steps of his ancestor King David (v.2). Remember that David was held up as the *ideal righteous king* whose example was to be followed by all who succeeded him. For David was a man after God's own heart (1 S.13:14).

    2) Ahaz walked in the sinful ways of Israel's kings instead of following the righteous examples set by Judah's kings (v.3).

    3) Ahaz offered his son as a human sacrifice to a false god, either the god Molech or another god associated with Baal worship (v.3). Ahaz was even guilty of leading his people in the terrible evil of human sacrifice as a form of worship (2 Chr.28:2-4).

4) Ahaz worshipped false gods at various high places throughout the nation (v.4). Note how Scripture describes his participation in false worship: as though he rushed from high place to high place, on the hilltops and under every tree where an altar or worship center had been built. He was totally dedicated and sold out to the worship of false gods.

5) Ahaz turned to Tiglath-Pileser of Assyria—not to God—to save him from an attack by Israel and Syria (vv.5-7). Remember he had served a few years in a co-regency with his father Jotham; therefore, he was ruling when Israel and Syria had begun to launch military raids against Judah (15:37). This coalition force launched an invasion of Judah, but they were unable to conquer Jerusalem. However, they did retake Elath for the Syrians (v.6). Their purpose for invading Judah had been to replace Ahaz with a ruler who would join and support them against Assyria. Remember, Assyria had earlier conquered and subjected a large part of the Northern Kingdom under its rule, even exiling a large number of its population (15:29; Is.7:6). Thus, Israel and Syria's purpose was to mobilize an insurrection and throw off the yoke of Assyrian oppression and taxation. To do this they needed the army and wealth of Judah to help them.

But, sadly, when Syria and Israel attacked Ahaz, he did not turn to God for help and deliverance. Instead he turned to Tiglath-Pileser (v.7; Is.7:3-25). In explaining what happened, *The Expositor's Bible Commentary* gives an excellent background to the complex international situation that was taking place in that day and time:

> *The causes of Ahaz's war with Israel and Syria were at least fourfold.*
> *1. On the human level, Rezin of Syria and Pekah of Israel were doubtless desirous of Judah's support in their planed insurrection against Tiglath-pileser III of Assyria.*
> *2. As Edersheim (History, 7:96ff.) notes, the two leaders may have had a personal dislike for Ahaz.*
> *3. On the spiritual plain, the whole affair seems to be a concentrated satanic effort to put an end to the Davidic line on the throne in Jerusalem (cf. Isa 7:5-7).*
> *4. God was superintending the whole complex undertaking. He would deal with an apostate Israel (cf. 17:5-18; 18-11-12), thwart the satanically inspired plans against the house of Israel by bringing defeat to Rezin and Pekah (Isa 7:5-16), and bring chastisement to a spiritually bankrupt Ahaz (2 Chron 28:5, 19).*
>
> *The full details of the complex international situation must be gleaned not only from chapter 16 but also from 15:37; 2 Chronicles 28; and Isaiah 7:1-16. These sources show that the Syro-Israelite alliance had been operative against Judah already in Jotham's day (15:37). The allied attack against Judah was two-pronged. Rezin came along the eastern portion of Judah, driving down to the key seaport of Elath and taking it (v.6; 2 Chron 28:5). Pekah launched an effective general campaign against northern Judah that resulted in the death of thousands of Judeans and the capture of hundreds of others (though the captives were later granted their freedom and returned to Jericho through the intercession of the prophet Obed; cf. 2 Chron 28:6-15). Moreover the newly liberated Edom took the opportunity to strike back, carrying away some Judeans into captivity (2 Chron 28:17). As well the Philistines found the time ripe to make renewed incursions into the western Shephelah and take captive certain cities in southern Judah.*
>
> *Then a new attack, aimed at taking Jerusalem itself and installing a client king on the throne, took place (Isa 7:2-6). Surrounded by hostile enemies on all sides, Ahaz received God's prophet Isaiah. He assured Ahaz that the enemy would fail; God himself would see to that. Ahaz could ask any confirmatory sign that he wished, and it would be granted (Isa 7:7-11). Ahaz, with a flare of piety, refused Isaiah's words (Isa 7:12), preferring to rely on his own resourcefulness. (Notice that God did nevertheless give Ahaz a sign, the prophecy associated with the virgin birth of the Messiah, Isa 7:13-16; cf. Matt. 1:22-23).*[2]

6) Ahaz confiscated the wealth from the treasuries of the temple and palace in order to hire Assyria to save him (vv.8-9). He then sent the gold and silver to the Assyrian king. Upon receiving the gift, Tiglath-Pileser marched his forces against Damascus, capturing the city and deporting its citizens to Kir. He then executed the Syrian king, Rezin. It should be noted that the Northern Kingdom of Israel was spared only because Hoshea had assassinated Pekah and quickly surrendered the nation to Assyria (15:29-30).

This fact should also be noted: by turning to Assyria to save himself, Ahaz was subjecting Judah to Assyria, making it a vassal or subservient state to the great empire of that day. As the leader of the vassal state, Ahaz was allowed to remain on the throne to govern the nation. The people were also allowed to keep their property, but they had to pay a huge annual tribute or tax to Assyria.

7) Apparently, Tiglath-Pileser summoned all the rulers from his new vassal states to meet him in Damascus. While there, Ahaz became impressed with an Assyrian altar and subsequently made a commitment to follow the false gods of Assyria (vv.10-11). Note that he made a sketch of the altar and sent the sketch back to Jerusalem ahead of him, issuing orders for the High Priest to build the altar. He wanted it completed *before* he returned from Damascus. Keep in mind that this was an unholy altar used in the worship of false gods.

8) After returning home from Damascus, Ahaz approached the unholy altar in worship and presented offerings to the false Assyrian god(s) (vv.12-13). Since Assyria had just rescued him from the attack by Israel and Syria, most likely he was offering thanks to the false gods for the deliverance. Note that the offerings he presented to the false gods seemed to be the very offerings presented by true believers.

9) Shockingly, Ahaz actually moved the LORD's bronze altar from the central position in the temple and replaced it with the unholy altar (v.14). By placing the unholy altar in the central position within the temple, he had made a total commitment to forsake the true worship of the LORD. He was now totally committed to serving false gods and to destroying the true worship of the LORD.

---

2 Richard D. Patterson and Hermann J. Austel. *1, 2 Kings*, pp.243-244.

10) Turning to the High Priest Uriah, King Ahaz gave orders for all regular offerings thereafter to be made on his new altar (v.15). Tragically, he was instituting a false worship within the very temple of God.

11) But even more shockingly, Ahaz practiced witchcraft in the temple by setting aside the LORD's bronze altar for his own personal use (v.15). He wanted to use it when he felt the need to seek special guidance from his false gods of divination. The word "inquire" (*baqar*) means to search or seek out, which often refers to seeking the counsel from the world of the occult.

12) By forcing the High Priest to engage in false worship, Ahaz corrupted the High Priest (v.16).

13) Ahaz even stole the brass from the furnishings of the temple (v.17).

14) Finally, in order to please the Assyrian ruler, Ahaz removed the Sabbath canopy in the royal entryway to the temple (v.18). By doing this he was showing deference to the Assyrian king, seeking not to offend but rather please him.

According to *Second Chronicles*, Ahaz went far beyond what is described here in *Second Kings*. He even closed the temple, plundering and destroying its furnishings and barricading the doors. Furthermore, he set up false altars at every street corner of Jerusalem and built false worship centers in every town of Judah (2 Chr.28:24-25).

In evaluating his life and reign, few men or rulers have lived such a wicked life and brought so much evil upon a nation and its people as Ahaz did. In the excellent summary of *The Expositor's Bible Commentary*:

> *All this not only speaks of Ahaz's depraved spiritual condition but was probably carried out as an expression of his good will toward Tiglath-pileser. Officially nothing offensive to the Assyrian king would henceforth be practiced. Thus did Ahaz go to his reward, clothed, spiritually speaking, in an Assyrian mantle (cf. Josh 7:21).*[3]

Ahaz's savior had become Tiglath-Pileser of Assyria. His confidence was placed in a man, no longer in the LORD.

c. A summary of Ahaz's achievements and life are recorded in the book *The History of the Kings of Judah*. After his death, he was buried in Jerusalem; but he was dishonored by the public who refused to bury him in the royal cemetery of the kings (vv.19-20; 2 Chr.28:27). Hezekiah, his son, succeeded him upon the throne of Judah.

Thought 1. Ahaz was a man who looked for a savior other than the LORD. In seeking deliverance from trouble, he turned to a man, to Tiglath-Pileser, not to God. But there is only one true Savior, the LORD Himself. And the LORD has proven His power to deliver His people down through the centuries. Still, Ahaz rejected the lessons of history and sought salvation in a man instead of turning to the LORD.

Yet Ahaz is not the only person to make this mistake. How many of us seek salvation in someone other than the Lord Jesus Christ? Only the Lord can save us. Only He has the power to deliver us from the sin and bondages of this life. When trials and temptations, hardships and misfortunes, or some other bitter enemy confronts us—there is only one living Savior who can deliver us. That Savior is the Lord Jesus Christ Himself. He is the only Savior who has the power to deliver us victoriously through this life right into the eternity of heaven. Listen to what God's Holy Word says:

> "For God so loved the world, that he gave his only begotten Son, that whosoever believeth in him should not perish, but have everlasting life" (Jn.3:16).

> "For the Son of man is come to seek and to save that which was lost" (Lu.19:10).

> "Him hath God exalted with his right hand *to be* a Prince and a Saviour, for to give repentance to Israel, and forgiveness of sins" (Ac.5:31).

> "There hath no temptation taken you but such as is common to man: but God *is* faithful, who will not suffer you to be tempted above that ye are able; but will with the temptation also make a way to escape, that ye may be able to bear *it*" (1 Co.10:13).

> "Now unto him that is able to do exceeding abundantly above all that we ask or think, according to the power that worketh in us" (Ep.3:20).

> "And the Lord shall deliver me from every evil work, and will preserve *me* unto his heavenly kingdom: to whom *be* glory for ever and ever. Amen" (2 Ti.4:18).

> "Forasmuch then as the children are partakers of flesh and blood, he also himself likewise took part of the same; that through death he might destroy him that had the power of death, that is, the devil; And deliver them who through fear of death were all their lifetime subject to bondage" (He.2:14-15).

> "For Christ also hath once suffered for sins, the just for the unjust, that he might bring us to God, being put to death in the flesh, but quickened by the Spirit" (1 Pe.3:18).

> "The Lord knoweth how to deliver the godly out of temptations, and to reserve the unjust unto the day of judgment to be punished" (2 Pe.2:9).

> "Be not afraid of their faces: for I *am* with thee to deliver thee, saith the LORD" (Je.1:8).

---

3 Richard D. Patterson and Hermann J. Austel. *1, 2 Kings*, p.245.

CHAPTER 17

E. The Tragic Fall of Israel, Its Conquest & Deportation of the People by the Assyrians (721 or 722 B.C.): The End of God's Patience & the Execution of His Judgment, 17:1-41

17:3-23; see 2 K.18:9-12

1. The reign of Hoshea, the last king of Israel: A picture of reaping what one sows

a. His reign: Lasted 9 years

b. His evil: Lived a wicked life, but not as evil as the kings before him

c. His treachery

1) He had surrendered Israel to Assyria when he took the throne, 15:30

2) He later committed treason against Assyria
   • Sought an alliance with Egypt against Assyria
   • Refused to pay tribute or taxes to Assyria

3) He was immediately seized & imprisoned

2. The climactic fall of Israel: The end of God's patience & His final judgment

a. Assyria's invasion of the entire land

b. Assyria's three-year siege & capture of the capital Samaria & their exile of the Israelites to Assyria

1) To Halah

2) To Gozan

3) To the towns of the Medes

3. The terrible sins that caused Israel's fall: A tragic picture of sin's consequences

a. The sins listed

1) Failed to remember the Exodus—God's salvation

2) Feared & worshipped false gods

3) Walked in the wicked ways of the world & their own wicked leaders

4) Tried to hide & keep secret their unrighteous behavior

5) Built false worship centers & constructed idols & images everywhere (sacred

In the twelfth year of Ahaz king of Judah began Hoshea the son of Elah to reign in Samaria over Israel nine years.
2 And he did *that which was* evil in the sight of the LORD, but not as the kings of Israel that were before him.
3 Against him came up Shalmaneser king of Assyria; and Hoshea became his servant, and gave him presents.
4 And the king of Assyria found conspiracy in Hoshea: for he had sent messengers to So king of Egypt, and brought no present to the king of Assyria, as *he had done* year by year: therefore the king of Assyria shut him up, and bound him in prison.
5 Then the king of Assyria came up throughout all the land, and went up to Samaria, and besieged it three years.
6 In the ninth year of Hoshea the king of Assyria took Samaria, and carried Israel away into Assyria, and placed them in Halah and in Habor *by* the river of Gozan, and in the cities of the Medes.
7 For *so* it was, that the children of Israel had sinned against the LORD their God, which had brought them up out of the land of Egypt, from under the hand of Pharaoh king of Egypt, and had feared other gods,
8 And walked in the statutes of the heathen, whom the LORD cast out from before the children of Israel, and of the kings of Israel, which they had made.
9 And the children of Israel did secretly *those* things that *were* not right against the LORD their God, and they built them high places in all their cities, from the tower of

the watchmen to the fenced city.
10 And they set them up images and groves in every high hill, and under every green tree:
11 And there they burnt incense in all the high places, as *did* the heathen whom the LORD carried away before them; and wrought wicked things to provoke the LORD to anger:
12 For they served idols, whereof the LORD had said unto them, Ye shall not do this thing.
13 Yet the LORD testified against Israel, and against Judah, by all the prophets, *and by* all the seers, saying, Turn ye from your evil ways, and keep my commandments *and* my statutes, according to all the law which I commanded your fathers, and which I sent to you by my servants the prophets.
14 Notwithstanding they would not hear, but hardened their necks, like to the neck of their fathers, that did not believe in the LORD their God.
15 And they rejected his statutes, and his covenant that he made with their fathers, and his testimonies which he testified against them; and they followed vanity, and became vain, and went after the heathen that *were* round about them, *concerning* whom the LORD had charged them, that they should not do like them.
16 And they left all the commandments of the LORD their God, and made them molten images, *even* two calves, and made a grove, and worshipped all the host of heaven, and served Baal.
17 And they caused their sons and their daughters to pass through the fire, and used divination and enchantments, and sold themselves to do evil in the sight of the LORD, to provoke him to anger.
18 Therefore the LORD was very angry with Israel, and removed them out of his sight: there was none left but

stone altars & Asherah poles)

6) Set up sacred stones & wooden poles or images of the goddess Asherah

7) Burned incense—offered up prayers & worship—to false gods

8) Did many wicked things that angered, provoked the LORD

9) Worshipped false gods; violated God's Holy Word, His clear command

10) Rejected God's warnings proclaimed by His prophets
   • The warning to repent
   • The warning to obey His commandments & statutes, the entire Law

11) Refused to listen to God's prophets: Became stubborn & rebellious

12) Failed to believe & trust the LORD

13) Rejected God's Word, His laws, His covenant, & His warnings

14) Worshipped empty, worthless gods & became empty & worthless themselves

15) Followed the sinful behavior of the worldly nations & people, violating the Word of God

16) Disobeyed all the commandments of God

17) Made & worshipped two calf idols, 1 K.12:25-33

18) Made a wooden image (Asherah pole) & worshipped all the starry host: Sun, moon, & stars

19) Worshipped Baal, 16

20) Offered human sacrifices

21) Practiced the occult: Divination, witchcraft, fortune-telling & sorcery

22) Sold themselves to sin: Became slaves to do evil

b. The consequences of their sins

1) They aroused God's anger & judgment: Were removed from His presence—

only Judah's tribe was left

2) They became stumbling blocks to others: Influenced Judah to follow their wickedness (Judah fell in 586 or 587 B.C.)

3) They stirred God's discipline against them: Were afflicted by plunderers & enemy invaders until they were finally cast out of God's presence

c. The major blame for Israel's fall: The evil of Jeroboam I
1) His evil
   • Split the nation; led the 10 northern tribes away
   • Instituted a new religion

   • Set a pattern of wicked behavior that was followed by the Israelites

2) God's judgment: He removed them forever from His presence—after warning them for over 200 years

3) Israel's fall: Taken from the promised land & exiled to Assyria

4. The settlement of foreign refugees in the land of Israel: A clear warning to the reader

a. The foreigners resettled in Israel to replace the Israelites: From Babylon, Cuthah, Avva, Hamath, & Sepharvaim

b. The immediate problem faced by the settlers
1) Their ignorance of the LORD: Lions killed people due to God's judgment

2) Their appeal to the king
   • Stated that they were foreigners who did not know how to worship the god of that land

   • Felt that the god was displeased & had sent lions to punish & kill them off

c. The settlers' request for help granted by the Assyrian king: He sent a priest to help them
   • The priest was an Israelite who had been taken from Samaria to Assyria during the exile

   • The priest settled in Bethel & taught the people

the tribe of Judah only.
19 Also Judah kept not the commandments of the LORD their God, but walked in the statutes of Israel which they made.
20 And the LORD rejected all the seed of Israel, and afflicted them, and delivered them into the hand of spoilers, until he had cast them out of his sight.
21 For he rent Israel from the house of David; and they made Jeroboam the son of Nebat king: and Jeroboam drave Israel from following the LORD, and made them sin a great sin.
22 For the children of Israel walked in all the sins of Jeroboam which he did; they departed not from them;
23 Until the LORD removed Israel out of his sight, as he had said by all his servants the prophets. So was Israel carried away out of their own land to Assyria unto this day.
24 And the king of Assyria brought *men* from Babylon, and from Cuthah, and from Ava, and from Hamath, and from Sepharvaim, and placed *them* in the cities of Samaria instead of the children of Israel: and they possessed Samaria, and dwelt in the cities thereof.
25 And *so* it was at the beginning of their dwelling there, *that* they feared not the LORD: therefore the LORD sent lions among them, which slew *some* of them.
26 Wherefore they spake to the king of Assyria, saying, The nations which thou hast removed, and placed in the cities of Samaria, know not the manner of the God of the land: therefore he hath sent lions among them, and, behold, they slay them, because they know not the manner of the God of the land.
27 Then the king of Assyria commanded, saying, Carry thither one of the priests whom ye brought from thence; and let them go and dwell there, and let him teach them the manner of the God of the land.
28 Then one of the priests whom they had carried away

from Samaria came and dwelt in Bethel, and taught them how they should fear the LORD.
29 Howbeit every nation made gods of their own, and put *them* in the houses of the high places which the Samaritans had made, every nation in their cities wherein they dwelt.
30 And the men of Babylon made Succoth-benoth, and the men of Cuth made Nergal, and the men of Hamath made Ashima,
31 And the Avites made Nibhaz and Tartak, and the Sepharvites burnt their children in fire to Adrammelech and Anammelech, the gods of Sepharvaim.
32 So they feared the LORD, and made unto themselves of the lowest of them priests of the high places, which sacrificed for them in the houses of the high places.
33 They feared the LORD, and served their own gods, after the manner of the nations whom they carried away from thence.
34 Unto this day they do after the former manners: they fear not the LORD, neither do they after their statutes, or after their ordinances, or after the law and commandment which the LORD commanded the children of Jacob, whom he named Israel;
35 With whom the LORD had made a covenant, and charged them saying, Ye shall not fear other gods, nor bow yourselves to them, nor serve them, nor sacrifice to them:
36 But the LORD, who brought you up out of the land of Egypt with great power and a stretched out arm, him shall ye fear, and him shall ye worship, and to him shall ye do sacrifice.
37 And the statutes, and the ordinances, and the law, and the commandment, which he wrote for you, ye shall observe to do for evermore; and ye shall not fear other gods.
38 And the covenant that I have made with you ye shall not forget; neither shall ye

how to worship the LORD—the only living & true God

d. The settlers' corruption of the true worship of the LORD
1) They—each national group of foreigners— continued to worship their own gods & shrines

   • Babylonians worshipped Succoth Benoth
   • Cuthahians worshipped Nergal
   • Hamath citizens worshipped Ashima
   • Avvites worshipped Nibhaz & Tartak
   • Sepharvites offered human sacrifices to the false gods Adrammelech & Anammelech

2) They worshipped the LORD but were led by false priests appointed by men instead of by God

3) They combined the worship of the LORD with the worship of their own false gods (a religion of syncretism): They compromised & accepted all views

4) They continued living sinful, wicked lives
   • Did not fear nor worship the LORD
   • Did not obey God, His Word & commandments
   • Ignored the fact that God had given His Word to the world through Israel

e. The warning to the reader
1) The reader must remember God's covenant, His basic commandment
   • Must not worship false gods

   • Must remember that it is the LORD alone who saves & delivers His people from Egypt (the world)
   • Must worship the LORD alone

2) The reader must always obey God's Word
   • Must keep all His Word
   • Must heed this command above all: Must not worship false gods

3) The reader must heed & never forget God's covenant
   • Must not worship false

gods • Must worship the LORD God & Him alone • Must know that the LORD alone saves 4) The reader must remember Israel's failure: They	fear other gods. 39 But the LORD your God ye shall fear; and he shall deliver you out of the hand of all your enemies. 40 Howbeit they did not hearken, but they did after	their former manner. 41 So these nations feared the LORD, and served their graven images, both their children, and their children's children: as did their fathers, so do they unto this day.	would not listen • They worshipped the LORD but also their false gods • Their descendants have continued to follow this false, empty religion of syncretism to this day

DIVISION III

THE UTTER DISINTEGRATION AND FALL OF ISRAEL, THE NORTHERN KINGDOM: A TRAGIC END DUE TO AN UNBROKEN STREAM OF WICKEDNESS AND LAWLESSNESS, 14:1–17:22

E. The Tragic Fall of Israel, Its Conquest and Deportation of the People by the Assyrians (721 or 722 B.C.): The End of God's Patience and the Execution of His Judgment, 17:1-41

(17:1-41) **Introduction—Patience, Traits of—Patience, Difficulty—God, Patience, Ends—Northern Kingdom of Israel, God's Patience with**: patience is one of the most important qualities a person can possess. Bear in mind that a patient person is slow to speak, not easily angered, not prone to overreact. A patient person is more likely to understand, to be merciful and compassionate; more likely to be gentle and kind, a better listener. A patient person is also more open to receive others, even when a mistake is made. But, in reality, it is sometimes very difficult to be patient. A family member or fellow worker aggravates us or moves too slowly or fails to do what he or she promised. A parent becomes impatient with a child or a child with a parent. In the workplace, a supervisor or employee becomes impatient with others. The list of scenarios is endless.

The great subject of this passage is the patience of God and the end of His patience with the Northern Kingdom of Israel. The day came when God's patience finally ended and His hand of judgment struck. For over 200 years God's patience had endured Israel's sin. He had been longsuffering with their wicked behavior, their turning to false gods and worship, and their rejection of Him. Imagine the patience and forbearing needed to put up with the sinful, rebellious Israelites of the Northern Kingdom for over 200 long years.

Because of Israel's wickedness and their rejection of Him, God had no choice. The people had reached a point of no return, a day when their hearts would never repent nor turn back to Him. Consequently, there would be nothing but evil and wickedness flowing out of their lives. This, God could not allow. If there was no hope of the Israelites' ever repenting and living righteous lives as a testimony to the only living and true God, it was time for them to face the judgment of God.

Sadly and tragically, the Northern Kingdom of Israel fell under the assault of the Assyrians and the people were transplanted into other conquered nations. This is: *The Tragic Fall of Israel, Its Conquest and Deportation of the People by the Assyrians (721 or 722 B.C.): The End of God's Patience and the Execution of His Judgment,* 17:1-41.

1. The reign of Hoshea, the last king of Israel: a picture of reaping what one sows (vv.1-4).
2. The climactic fall of Israel: the end of God's patience and His final judgment (vv.5-6).
3. The terrible sins that caused Israel's fall: a tragic picture of sin's consequences (vv.7-23).
4. The settlement of foreign refugees in the land of Israel: a clear warning to the reader (vv.24-41).

1 (17:1-4) **Reaping, What One Sows, Example—Sowing, Principle of—Evil, Results of—Northern Kingdom of Israel, Kings of**: Hoshea, the last ruler of the Northern Kingdom, had assassinated his predecessor Pekah. He had led an uprising of pro-Assyrian supporters. Because of Pekah's opposition and war against Assyria, much of the territory of Israel had been lost to the Assyrians. Now the Assyrian troops were stationed all along Israel's eastern border, right across the Jordan River (see outline and note—2 K.15:27-31 for more discussion). Israel was facing annihilation, extinction. A cloud of hopelessness swept the nation. Because of this, Hoshea and his pro-Assyrian supporters made a secret agreement to become a vassal state of Assyria, that is, to pay an annual tax if Assyria would allow them to keep their land. Agreeing with the proposal made by Hoshea and the pro-Assyrian supporters, Tiglath-Pileser apparently backed or at least encouraged the uprising against King Pekah (see outline and note—2 K.15:27-31 for more discussion). Once the secret agreement had been settled upon, Hoshea assassinated the Israelite king and assumed the throne for himself.

OUTLINE	SCRIPTURE	SCRIPTURE	OUTLINE

1. The reign of Hoshea, the last king of Israel: A picture of reaping what one sows
a. His reign: Lasted 9 years
 	
b. His evil: Lived a wicked life, but not as evil as the kings before him
 	
c. His treachery
   1) He had surrendered Israel
	In the twelfth year of Ahaz king of Judah began Hoshea the son of Elah to reign in Samaria over Israel nine years.
	2 And he did *that which was* evil in the sight of the LORD, but not as the kings of Israel that were before him.
	3 Against him came up Shalmaneser king of Assyria;
		and Hoshea became his servant, and gave him presents.
		4 And the king of Assyria found conspiracy in Hoshea: for he had sent messengers to So king of Egypt, and brought no present to the king of Assyria, as *he had done* year by year: therefore the king of Assyria shut him up, and bound him in prison.
			to Assyria when he took the throne, 15:30
			2) He later committed treason against Assyria
			   • Sought an alliance with Egypt against Assyria
			   • Refused to pay tribute or taxes to Assyria
			3) He was immediately seized & imprisoned

Hoshea took the throne in the twelfth year of King Ahaz of Judah, and he reigned nine years (vv.1-2). Throughout his life, Hoshea had lived wickedly and, as ruler of Israel, he continued to do evil in the eyes of the LORD (v.2). But note what Scripture says: he did not do as much evil as the kings who had ruled before him had done. Nevertheless, he stood guilty before God because of his wicked life and because he did not lead the people to repentance. He failed to encourage them to turn away from their false worship back to the LORD.

The downward spiral into more and more wickedness continued; consequently, the whirlwind of God's judgment became a force that was unstoppable. The citizens of the Northern Kingdom would now reap the consequences of their sins, and Hoshea would be the king sitting upon the throne when the tragic fall of Israel took place.

At some point in his reign, Hoshea made the decision to break the yoke of Assyrian bondage (vv.3-4). Forming an alliance with Egypt against Assyria, he refused to pay the tribute or taxes to the Assyrian king. Note this fact: by this time, Tiglath-Pileser III had died and his son Shalmaneser had become king of the foreign power. As soon as Shalmaneser heard of the revolt, he immediately arrested and imprisoned Hoshea.

> **Thought 1**. Hoshea lived a life of wickedness that climaxed in a plot of intrigue and murder. Then, after securing the throne, he quickly launched a foolish plan of conspiracy against the king of Assyria, the greatest power of that day. Throughout his adult life, Hoshea sowed one wicked seed after another—deception, intrigue, conspiracy, and murder. In the end, the law of sowing and reaping struck a heavy blow. He sowed corruption and reaped arrest and imprisonment.
>
> If there is any lesson God's Holy Word teaches, it is this: we reap what we sow. It is a law that has been established by God Himself, established throughout the whole universe. If a certain condition exists, there will be a particular result. In the area of human behavior, if we sow righteousness, we will reap good and fruitful lives and build up society. We will set examples of righteousness, justice, compassion, kindness, and love for all with whom we come in contact. But if we sow lives of sin and wickedness, we will ultimately reap lives that suffer catastrophic consequences. Sinful, wicked lives tear down society, promoting immorality, injustice, lawlessness, violence, murder, abuse, assault, rape, profanity, unbelief, idol worship, and a host of other evils. But of even more significance, wicked lives will eventually suffer the doom of God's eternal judgment, being separated from His presence forever and ever.
>
> Anything a man does—good or bad—has consequences. God has established certain principles or laws throughout the universe that always take place:
>
> (1) There is the law of sowing and reaping. If a man sows wickedness, he reaps corruption.
>
> > **"Bear ye one another's burdens, and so fulfil the law of Christ" (Ga.6:2).**
>
> (2) There is the law of measure. If a man measures, doles out, distributes wickedness, he will be measured by wickedness. Whatever a man measures, he receives.
>
> > **"For with what judgment ye judge, ye shall be judged: and with what measure ye mete, it shall be measured to you again" (Mt.7:2).**
>
> (3) There is the law of seeking. If a man seeks, he finds. The harder he seeks, the more he finds.
>
> > **"Ask, and it shall be given you; seek, and ye shall find; knock, and it shall be opened unto you" (Mt.7:7).**
>
> (4) There is the law of willful hardness and impenitence. The more a man hardens himself and refuses to repent, the harder and more impenitent he becomes. In fact, a man can become so hardened that he never repents, never even thinks about repentance. Such a man stores up wrath against himself.
>
> > **"But after thy hardness and impenitent heart treasurest up unto thyself wrath against the day of wrath and revelation of the righteous judgment of God; Who will render to every man according to his deeds" (Ro.2:5-6).**
>
> (5) There is the law of being *fitted* for destruction. The more a man refuses to believe the LORD, the more he is *fitted* and conditioned for destruction. In other words, a man prepares and conditions himself for destruction through unbelief.
>
> > **"*What* if God, willing to show *his* wrath, and to make his power known, endured with much longsuffering the vessels of wrath fitted to destruction" (Ro.9:22).**
>
> (6) There is the law of God's patience. God is "not willing that any should perish, but that all should come to repentance." Therefore, God allows the world to continue to exist, allowing more and more people to be saved. He endures with patience the unbelievers who harden themselves and store up wrath against themselves in order that *some* might be saved and given the privilege of knowing the riches of His grace (Ro.2:5; see Ro.2:22-23)
>
> > **"Knowing this first, that there shall come in the last days scoffers, walking after their own lusts, And saying, Where is the promise of his coming? for since the fathers fell asleep, all things continue as *they were* from the beginning of the creation....But, beloved, be not ignorant of this one thing, that one day *is* with the Lord as a thousand years, and a thousand years as one day. The Lord is not slack concerning his promise, as some men count slackness; but is longsuffering to us-ward, not willing that any should perish, but that all should come to repentance" (2 Pe.3:3-4, 8-9).**

(7) There is the law of God's supreme purpose. God's supreme purpose is that His Son "be the first among many brothers" (Ro.8:29). God wants Jesus Christ to have many brothers and sisters who will be conformed to His image and count Christ as the One who is to be worshipped and served eternally.

In order for Christ to gain more and more brothers who will honor Him, God is willing for unbelievers to continue on in their unbelief, ever hardening themselves under the just and judicial laws He has established. Men are allowed to go on in their unbelief, condemning themselves under the just and judicial laws of the universe.

"And we know that all things work together for good to them that love God, to them who are the called according to *his* purpose. For whom he did foreknow, he also did predestinate *to be* conformed to the image of his Son, that he might be the firstborn among many brethren. Moreover whom he did predestinate, them he also called: and whom he called, them he also justified: and whom he justified, them he also glorified" (Ro.8:28-30).

2 (17:5-6) **Longsuffering, of God—Judgment, of God—Northern Kingdom of Israel, Fall of—Assyria, Conquered Israel—Samaria, Fall of**: the tragic and climactic fall of Israel was now about to take place. God's patience ended and His final judgment fell upon the sinful, evil people of the Northern Kingdom. Note that King Hoshea of Israel seems to have been seized and imprisoned prior to the invasion of Assyria (v.5; cp. v.4). Whatever the case, immediately after Hoshea's foolish rebellion, Shalmaneser quickly marched in and conquered the entire land of the Northern Kingdom except for the capital Samaria. Once he had the Northern Kingdom under his control, he turned against the capital and laid siege to it. But it took three years to conquer Samaria, for the city was like an impregnable fortress. During the three-year siege, King Shalmaneser of Assyria died and his brother Sargon II succeeded him. Thus, Samaria finally fell after three long years (725-722 B.C.) during the reign of Sargon II.

Once the Assyrians had captured Samaria, they deported or exiled many of the Israelites to various parts of Assyria: Halah, Gozan, and the towns of the Medes (v.6). Later the Assyrians would resettle the Northern Kingdom with foreign refugees from other lands they had conquered (v.24).

About 200 years earlier, right after Jeroboam I had led a rebellion that split Israel into the Northern and Southern Kingdoms, the LORD had sent a prophet to pronounce the future prophetic judgment upon Israel. The LORD was going to strike Israel, uproot the nation, and scatter the people in exile beyond the Euphrates River. Why? Because of their wickedness and their rejection of Him. They had turned to false gods and engaged in false worship (14:15-16). The shocking prophecy regarding Israel was now fulfilled. What God had predicted had happened. The Northern Kingdom of Israel fell, with many of its people being deported, exiled into the cities of Assyria beyond the Euphrates River.

OUTLINE	SCRIPTURE	SCRIPTURE	OUTLINE
2. The climactic fall of Israel: The end of God's patience & His final judgment	5 Then the king of Assyria came up throughout all the land, and went up to Samaria, and besieged it three years.	shea the king of Assyria took Samaria, and carried Israel away into Assyria, and placed them in Halah and in Habor *by* the river of Gozan, and in the	capture of the capital Samaria & their exile of the Israelites to Assyria
a. Assyria's invasion of the entire land			1) To Halah
b. Assyria's three-year siege &	6 In the ninth year of Ho-	cities of the Medes.	2) To Gozan
			3) To the towns of the Medes

Thought 1. God's patience had run its course. He had given the people of Israel countless opportunities to repent over a period of 200 years. But the people refused to turn away from their wickedness, refused to give up their false gods and false worship. They rejected the LORD for so long that they became obstinate in their unbelief. They were a stubborn, stiff-necked people who stood against the LORD God Himself. Allowing their hearts to become hardened by their sinful, evil behavior, they reached a point of no return, a point when they would never repent and turn back to God.

Only God knows when a person reaches the point of no return, the point when he has sinned so much he will never repent. No man can ever know when that point arrives in another person's life. But God knows. And He knew when the Israelites reached this point. Consequently, His patience had reached its end. No longer would God be longsuffering with them. For they would no longer respond to His love and appeal to return to Him. Consequently, it was time for judgment to fall. And judgment did fall.

So it is with us. There is a limit to God's patience and longsuffering. Any one of us can sin so much that we become enslaved by sin. We can reach the point of no return, the point when we will never repent or turn back to God. But again note this fact: only God knows when a person has become so steeped in sin, wickedness, and evil. No other person can ever know when any of us has reached that point. But God does know.

However, this one fact must be heeded. Right now God is patient with us, appealing and calling us to repentance, to turn to Him, worshipping and serving Him. But if we come to the end of life and have never trusted Christ as our Savior, we will slip out into eternity without God. We will face the terrifying judgment of God. Therefore, today is the day of salvation! Today is the day to receive Christ!

(1) Listen to what the Word of God says about the patience, the longsuffering of the LORD.

"Then said he unto the dresser of his vineyard, Behold, these three years I come seeking fruit on this fig tree, and find none: cut it down; why cumbereth it the ground? And he answering said unto him, Lord, let it alone this year also, till I shall dig about it, and dung *it*: And if it bear fruit, *well*: and if not, *then* after that thou shalt cut it down" (Lu.13:7-9).

"Him hath God exalted with his right hand *to be* a Prince and a Saviour, for to give repentance to Israel, and forgiveness of sins" (Ac.5:31).

"*What* if God, willing to show *his* wrath, and to make his power known, endured with much long-suffering the vessels of wrath fitted to destruction" (Ro.9:22).

"In whom we have redemption through his blood, the forgiveness of sins, according to the riches of his grace" (Ep.1:7).

"Not by works of righteousness which we have done, but according to his mercy he saved us, by the washing of regeneration, and renewing of the Holy Ghost; Which he shed on us abundantly through Jesus Christ our Saviour; That being justified by his grace, we should be made heirs according to the hope of eternal life" (Tit.3:5-7).

"But, beloved, be not ignorant of this one thing, that one day *is* with the Lord as a thousand years, and a thousand years as one day. The Lord is not slack concerning his promise, as some men count slackness; but is longsuffering to us-ward, not willing that any should perish, but that all should come to repentance" (2 Pe.3:8-9).

"If we confess our sins, he is faithful and just to forgive us *our* sins, and to cleanse us from all unrighteousness" (1 Jn.1:9).

"But *there is* forgiveness with thee, that thou mayest be feared" (Ps.130:4).

"For my name's sake will I defer mine anger, and for my praise will I refrain for thee, that I cut thee not off" (Is.48:9).

"*It is of* the LORD'S mercies that we are not consumed, because his compassions fail not. *They are* new every morning: great *is* thy faithfulness" (La.3:22-23).

"And rend your heart, and not your garments, and turn unto the LORD your God: for he *is* gracious and merciful, slow to anger, and of great kindness, and repenteth him of the evil" (Joel 2:13).

(2) Listen to what God says about the coming final judgment.

"When the Son of man shall come in his glory, and all the holy angels with him, then shall he sit upon the throne of his glory: And before him shall be gathered all nations: and he shall separate them one from another, as a shepherd divideth *his* sheep from the goats: And he shall set the sheep on his right hand, but the goats on the left" (Mt.25:31-33).

"Marvel not at this: for the hour is coming, in the which all that are in the graves shall hear his voice, And shall come forth; they that have done good, unto the resurrection of life; and they that have done evil, unto the resurrection of damnation" (Jn.5:28-29).

"And to you who are troubled rest with us, when the Lord Jesus shall be revealed from heaven with his mighty angels, In flaming fire taking vengeance on them that know not God, and that obey not the gospel of our Lord Jesus Christ" (2 Th.1:7-8).

"And as it is appointed unto men once to die, but after this the judgment" (He.9:27).

"And if ye call on the Father, who without respect of persons judgeth according to every man's work, pass the time of your sojourning *here* in fear" (1 Pe.1:17).

"The Lord knoweth how to deliver the godly out of temptations, and to reserve the unjust unto the day of judgment to be punished" (2 Pe.2:9).

"But the heavens and the earth, which are now, by the same word are kept in store, reserved unto fire against the day of judgment and perdition of ungodly men" (2 Pe.3:7).

"And Enoch also, the seventh from Adam, prophesied of these, saying, Behold, the Lord cometh with ten thousands of his saints, To execute judgment upon all, and to convince all that are ungodly among them of all their ungodly deeds which they have ungodly committed, and of all their hard *speeches* which ungodly sinners have spoken against him" (Jude 1:14-15).

"And I saw a great white throne, and him that sat on it, from whose face the earth and the heaven fled away; and there was found no place for them. And I saw the dead, small and great, stand before God; and the books were opened: and another book was opened, which is *the book* of life: and the dead were judged out of those things which were written in the books, according to their works. And the sea gave up the dead which were in it; and death and hell delivered up the dead which were in them: and they were judged every man according to their works. And death and hell were cast into the lake of fire. This is the second death. And whosoever was not found written in the book of life was cast into the lake of fire" (Re.20:11-15).

"Also unto thee, O Lord, *belongeth* mercy: for thou renderest to every man according to his work" (Ps.62:12).

Thought 2. Paul R. House gives an excellent application that speaks to the heart of the reader:

A long time has passed since the prophet Ahijah told the wife of Jeroboam I that idolatry would lead to Israel's exile (1 Kgs 14:14-16). Over these two hundred years Israel has seemed determined to make this prophecy come to pass. No reform occurs. No real repentance emerges. No leader calls a halt to pagan worship. No prophet is taken seriously. Thus the spare, unadorned description of Samaria's fall is dramatic only in the sense that it is Israel's final scene. God's grace alone has delayed the fall this long.[1]

---

[1] Paul R. House. *1, 2 Kings*, p.340.

3 (17:7-23) **Sin, of Israel—Wickedness, of Israel—Evil, of Israel—Israel, Sins of—Northern Kingdom of Israel, Fall of, Reasons—Sin, Consequences of, Threefold—Israel, Fall of, Caused by—Northern Kingdom, Fall of, Caused by**: simply stated, Israel fell because of its terrible sin, its evil and wickedness. A graphic description is given of the failure:

OUTLINE	SCRIPTURE	SCRIPTURE	OUTLINE
3. The terrible sins that caused Israel's fall: A tragic picture of sin's consequences a. The sins listed 1) Failed to remember the Exodus—God's salvation	7 For *so* it was, that the children of Israel had sinned against the LORD their God, which had brought them up out of the land of Egypt, from under the hand of Pharaoh king of Egypt, and had feared other gods,	testified against them; and they followed vanity, and became vain, and went after the heathen that *were* round about them, *concerning* whom the LORD had charged them, that they should not do like them.	worthless gods & became empty & worthless themselves 15) Followed the sinful behavior of the worldly nations & people, violating the Word of God
2) Feared & worshipped false gods 3) Walked in the wicked ways of the world & their own wicked leaders	8 And walked in the statutes of the heathen, whom the LORD cast out from before the children of Israel, and of the kings of Israel, which they had made.	16 And they left all the commandments of the LORD their God, and made them molten images, *even* two calves, and made a grove, and worshipped all the host of heaven, and served Baal.	16) Disobeyed all the commandments of God 17) Made & worshipped two calf idols, 1 K.12:25-33 18) Made a wooden image (Asherah pole) & worshipped all the starry host: Sun, moon, & stars
4) Tried to hide & keep secret their unrighteous behavior 5) Built false worship centers & constructed idols & images everywhere (sacred stone altars & Asherah poles)	9 And the children of Israel did secretly *those* things that *were* not right against the LORD their God, and they built them high places in all their cities, from the tower of the watchmen to the fenced city.	17 And they caused their sons and their daughters to pass through the fire, and used divination and enchantments, and sold themselves to do evil in the sight of the LORD, to provoke him	19) Worshipped Baal, 16 20) Offered human sacrifices 21) Practiced the occult: Divination, witchcraft, fortune-telling & sorcery
6) Set up sacred stones & wooden poles or images of the goddess Asherah	10 And they set them up images and groves in every high hill, and under every green tree:	to anger.	22) Sold themselves to sin: Became slaves to do evil
7) Burned incense—offered up prayers & worship—to false gods	11 And there they burnt incense in all the high places, as *did* the heathen whom the LORD carried away before them; and wrought wicked things to provoke the LORD to anger:	18 Therefore the LORD was very angry with Israel, and removed them out of his sight: there was none left but the tribe of Judah only.	b. The consequences of their sins 1) They aroused God's anger & judgment: Were removed from His presence—only Judah's tribe was left
8) Did many wicked things that angered, provoked the LORD		19 Also Judah kept not the commandments of the LORD their God, but walked in the statutes of Israel which they made.	2) They became stumbling blocks to others: Influenced Judah to follow their wickedness (Judah fell in 586 or 587 B.C.)
9) Worshipped false gods; violated God's Holy Word, His clear command	12 For they served idols, whereof the LORD had said unto them, Ye shall not do this thing.	20 And the LORD rejected all the seed of Israel, and afflicted them, and delivered them into the hand of spoil ers, until he had cast them out of his sight.	3) They stirred God's discipline against them: Were afflicted by plunderers & enemy invaders until they were finally cast out of God's presence
10) Rejected God's warnings proclaimed by His prophets • The warning to repent • The warning to obey His commandments & statutes, the entire Law	13 Yet the LORD testified against Israel, and against Judah, by all the prophets, *and by* all the seers, saying, Turn ye from your evil ways, and keep my commandments *and* my statutes, according to all the law which I commanded your fathers, and which I sent to you by my servants the prophets.	21 For he rent Israel from the house of David; and they made Jeroboam the son of Nebat king: and Jeroboam drave Israel from following the LORD, and made them sin a great sin.	c. The major blame for Israel's fall: The evil of Jeroboam I 1) His evil • Split the nation; led the 10 northern tribes away • Instituted a new religion
11) Refused to listen to God's prophets: Became stubborn & rebellious 12) Failed to believe & trust the LORD	14 Notwithstanding they would not hear, but hardened their necks, like to the neck of their fathers, that did not believe in the LORD their God.	22 For the children of Israel walked in all the sins of Jeroboam which he did; they departed not from them;	• Set a pattern of wicked behavior that was followed by the Israelites
13) Rejected God's Word, His laws, His covenant, & His warnings 14) Worshipped empty,	15 And they rejected his statutes, and his covenant that he made with their fathers, and his testimonies which he	23 Until the LORD removed Israel out of his sight, as he had said by all his servants the prophets. So was Israel carried away out of their own land to Assyria unto this day.	2) God's judgment: He removed them forever from His presence—after warning them for over 200 years 3) Israel's fall: Taken from the promised land & exiled to Assyria

a. What an indictment, a condemnation against any people! Yet this is just what this list of sins is: God's indictment against the Israelites of the Northern Kingdom. Charge after charge of sin and evil—at least 22 charges—are leveled against them. Glancing back at the list of sins, note how serious, how grievous they are. How they must have broken and cut the heart of God time and again. And note when their sin and rebellion against God began: right after He had freed them from Egyptian slavery under the leadership of Moses (v.7). From the earliest days of their deliverance from Egyptian bondage, there was a tendency to forget God and His wonderful salvation. From the very first, they began to turn away from the only living and true God to false gods and false worship, living lives of sin, wickedness, and evil. Sadly, despite God's obvious leading in their lives and His miraculous deliverance from oppression, the Israelites continued to reject the LORD and His Holy Word. They chose instead to follow the immoral, lawless, and violent ways of their neighbors, disobeying the LORD and His commandments.

b. As a result, the Israelites suffered the consequences of their sins, evil, and wickedness (vv.18-20). Three very specific consequences are covered, and these three always follow upon the heels of sin. Whether committed by the ancient Israelites or by us today, three very specific consequences take place.

1) In their sin, the Israelites aroused God's anger and judgment against them. *Judgment* is always the inevitable result of sin. Therefore if any person sins—unless he repents and turns to God—the judgment of God will eventually fall upon him (v.18). Because of the Israelites' sin—their evil and wickedness—Israel was removed from God's presence. As a nation with a separate identity, they were erased from the face of the earth—never again to exist as the Northern Kingdom of Israel. Only the kingdom of Judah, the Southern Kingdom was left. Going too far in their sin—beyond the point of repentance—the citizens of the Northern Kingdom aroused God's anger and judgment. They chose to live apart from God while on this earth, so they were given their desire. God removed them from His presence forever.

2) In their sins, the ancient Israelites became *stumbling blocks* to others (v.19). They set a bad and sinful example, influencing the people of Judah to follow their wickedness. Sadly and tragically, the people of Judah chose to follow in their footsteps, committing the very same sins as the Israelites. Consequently, the inevitable result of sin would take effect in their lives and upon their nation. Judah itself would collapse and the Judeans would be taken into captivity by the Babylonian empire in 587-586 B.C. (See outline and notes—2 K.25:1-30 for more discussion.)

3) A third consequence of sin is that of *chastisement*, God's discipline against the sinner (v.20). The ancient Israelites were not exempt from God's chastisement. During the 200 years of their rebellion against God, the LORD had disciplined them by sending plunderers and enemy invaders against them. In mercy, God used enemy nations to attack them, attempting to arouse the Israelites to turn to God for help, to cry out for deliverance. If they had just turned to Him and cried out, He would have delivered and saved them from any and all enemies. But after 200 years of rejecting His discipline, God was left with no choice. Finally, He cast them out and thrust them from His presence (v.20).

Note this fact: the major blame for Israel's fall lay upon the shoulders of Jeroboam I (vv.21-23). He committed three terrible evils that were bound to have catastrophic results:

⇒ He split the nation by leading the ten northern tribes away from the tribe of Judah (the Southern Kingdom).

⇒ He instituted a new religion for the people of the Northern Kingdom and led them away from the LORD (see outline and note—1 K.12:25-33 for more discussion).

⇒ He set a pattern, an example of wicked behavior that was followed by the Israelites down through the 200 years of their history.

Hence, God's judgment fell upon the nation Israel. God removed the Northern Kingdom from His presence, but only after warning them for over 200 long years. Because of their sin—their evil and wickedness—Israel fell. The people were taken from the promised land and scattered as exiles throughout the land of Assyria. And to this day, the Northern Kingdom of Israel has not stood as a separate nation. Furthermore the Northern Kingdom never will. The people had been displaced, scattered all over, never again to be united as the Northern Kingdom of Israel (vv.18, 20, 23).

Thought 1. Sin has its consequences. When we break God's commandments, we will suffer the penalty. And Scripture is clear: there is a penalty for sin, for living wicked lives and walking in the wicked ways of unbelievers. If we follow in the footsteps of unbelievers—committing immorality, lawlessness, and violence—we will suffer the penalty for our sinful behavior. Listen to what God's Holy Word says about the penalty of sin:

"**Wherefore, as by one man sin entered into the world, and death by sin; and so death passed upon all men, for that all have sinned**" (Ro.5:12).

"**For the wages of sin *is* death; but the gift of God *is* eternal life through Jesus Christ our Lord**" (Ro.6:23).

"**For to be carnally minded *is* death; but to be spiritually minded *is* life and peace**" (Ro.8:6).

"**Know ye not that the unrighteous shall not inherit the kingdom of God? Be not deceived: neither fornicators, nor idolaters, nor adulterers, nor effeminate, nor abusers of themselves with mankind, Nor thieves, nor covetous, nor drunkards, nor revilers, nor extortioners, shall inherit the kingdom of God**" (1 Co.6:9-10).

"**Then when lust hath conceived, it bringeth forth sin: and sin, when it is finished, bringeth forth death**" (Js.1:15).

"**Let him know, that he which converteth the sinner from the error of his way shall save a soul from death, and shall hide a multitude of sins**" (Js.5:20).

"**But the fearful, and unbelieving, and the abominable, and murderers, and whoremongers, and sorcerers, and idolaters, and all liars, shall have their part in the lake which burneth with fire and brimstone: which is the second death**" (Re.21:8).

148

"So Saul died for his transgression which he committed against the LORD, *even* against the word of the LORD, which he kept not, and also for asking *counsel* of *one that had* a familiar spirit, to enquire *of it*" (1 Chr.10:13).

"As righteousness *tendeth* to life: so he that pursueth evil *pursueth it* to his own death" (Pr.11:19).

"He, that being often reproved hardeneth *his* neck, shall suddenly be destroyed, and that without remedy" (Pr.29:1).

"But your iniquities have separated between you and your God, and your sins have hid *his* face from you, that he will not hear" (Is.59:2).

"And *there is* none that calleth upon thy name, that stirreth up himself to take hold of thee: for thou hast hid thy face from us, and hast consumed us, because of our iniquities" (Is.64:7).

"Behold, all souls are mine; as the soul of the father, so also the soul of the son is mine: the soul that sinneth, it shall die" (Eze.18:4).

Thought 2. Russell Dilday makes an excellent application that is worth quoting in full:

The ten tribes of the North disappeared after this, never to be heard from again. These ten lost tribes of Israel have been a mystery through the years. People have tried to find them in the Jewish communities of southern Arabia, in various tribes in India, in China, in Turkey, in Cashmir, in Afghanistan, in the American Indians; but not a trace remains. Verse 23 says, "the Lord removed Israel out of His sight."

Only Judah remained, and in verse 19 the writer inserts a parenthetical reminder that within 160 years, Judah also would follow in the same tragic pattern.

Unlike technical secular historians, the purpose of the Old Testament historians was not to catalogue various events in chronological order, nor to analyze the various movements in history, but to declare God's righteous dealings with His people. Therefore, great events like the fall of a kingdom were of little significance to them unless they revealed the righteous purpose of God. The main thing about this passage then is not the details of the siege, nor the names of the Assyrian kings, nor the military strategies, nor the political maneuvering—items which secular historians would have emphasized. The main thing for the biblical historian is the long list of the reasons for God's judgment on Israel.

Here, the important message is the postmortem inquiry into the spiritual diseases that killed the kingdom, because that message becomes a warning for nations of all ages. In this passage are warnings against the danger of ingratitude, the danger of stiff-necked resistance to the word of God, the danger of yielding to the unhealthy influences of godless people around us, the folly of secret transgressions, the impotence of cheap, convenient religion, the danger of pride, the peril of provoking God to anger, the hazards of idolatry (which is still practiced in many diverse forms today), the warning of inevitable judgment.

But one of the most vivid lessons in this passage is in verse 15. The New King James Version translates the phrase, "They followed idols, became idolaters." The original is more accurate at this point: "They worshiped emptiness and became empty." The word here is hebel meaning "air," "delusion," or "vanity."[2] The idea is that they became like the gods they worshiped. They bowed down to nothingness and became nothing."[3]

4 (17:24-41) **Warning, to Whom, the Reader of Scripture—Warning, to Whom, the Believer—Promised Land, the, After Israel's Fall—Land, the Promised, After Israel's Fall—Believers, Warning to—Foreigners, in the Promised Land**: sometime after Israel's fall, the Assyrians repopulated the land with foreign refugees from other conquered nations. A close study of this point needs to be made, for the point closes with a striking warning to the reader (see vv.35-41). Under the Assyrian king Tiglath-Pileser III, a policy was begun of transferring or transplanting the populace of conquered nations into foreign nations. By switching the inhabitants, the king hoped to break the loyalty of the people to their own land and to transfer their allegiance to Assyria. Moreover, the *transfer or transplantation policy* helped eliminate the possibility of any major uprisings. It also assured intermarriage between various nations and the elimination of distinctive nationalities, which helped weaken the allegiance of people to their homeland. With this as background, note the Scripture and outline:

OUTLINE	SCRIPTURE	SCRIPTURE	OUTLINE
4. The settlement of foreign refugees in the land of Israel: A clear warning to the reader	24 And the king of Assyria brought *men* from Babylon, and from Cuthah, and from Ava, and from Hamath, and from Sepharvaim, and placed *them* in the cities of Samaria instead of the children of Israel: and they possessed Samaria, and dwelt in the cities thereof.	LORD: therefore the LORD sent lions among them, which slew *some* of them.	LORD: Lions killed people due to God's judgment
a. The foreigners resettled in Israel to replace the Israelites: From Babylon, Cuthah, Avva, Hamath, & Sepharvaim		26 Wherefore they spake to the king of Assyria, saying, The nations which thou hast removed, and placed in the cities of Samaria, know not the manner of the God of the land: therefore he hath sent lions among them, and, behold, they slay them, because they know not the manner of	2) Their appeal to the king • Stated that they were foreigners who did not know how to worship the god of that land

• Felt that the god was displeased & had sent lions to punish & kill them off |
| b. The immediate problem faced by the settlers 1) Their ignorance of the | 25 And *so* it was at the beginning of their dwelling there, *that* they feared not the | | |

---

2 Gwilym H. Jones. *1 and 2 Kings*, p.549.
3 Russell Dilday. *1, 2 Kings*, pp.418-419.

OUTLINE	SCRIPTURE	SCRIPTURE	OUTLINE
c. The settlers' request for help granted by the Assyrian king: He sent a priest to help them • The priest was an Israelite who had been taken from Samaria to Assyria during the exile • The priest settled in Bethel & taught the people how to worship the LORD—the only living & true God d. The settlers' corruption of the true worship of the LORD 1) They—each national group of foreigners—continued to worship their own gods & shrines • Babylonians worshipped Succoth Benoth • Cuthahians worshipped Nergal • Hamath citizens worshipped Ashima • Avvites worshipped Nibhaz & Tartak • Sepharvites offered human sacrifices to the false gods Adrammelech & Anammelech 2) They worshipped the LORD but were led by false priests appointed by men instead of by God 3) They combined the worship of the LORD with the worship of their own false gods (a religion of syncretism): They compromised & accepted all views 4) They continued living sinful, wicked lives	the God of the land. 27 Then the king of Assyria commanded, saying, Carry thither one of the priests whom ye brought from thence; and let them go and dwell there, and let him teach them the manner of the God of the land. 28 Then one of the priests whom they had carried away from Samaria came and dwelt in Bethel, and taught them how they should fear the LORD. 29 Howbeit every nation made gods of their own, and put *them* in the houses of the high places which the Samaritans had made, every nation in their cities wherein they dwelt. 30 And the men of Babylon made Succoth-benoth, and the men of Cuth made Nergal, and the men of Hamath made Ashima, 31 And the Avites made Nibhaz and Tartak, and the Sepharvites burnt their children in fire to Adrammelech and Anammelech, the gods of Sepharvaim. 32 So they feared the LORD, and made unto themselves of the lowest of them priests of the high places, which sacrificed for them in the houses of the high places. 33 They feared the LORD, and served their own gods, after the manner of the nations whom they carried away from thence. 34 Unto this day they do after the former manners:	they fear not the LORD, neither do they after their statutes, or after their ordinances, or after the law and commandment which the LORD commanded the children of Jacob, whom he named Israel; 35 With whom the LORD had made a covenant, and charged them saying, Ye shall not fear other gods, nor bow yourselves to them, nor serve them, nor sacrifice to them: 36 But the LORD, who brought you up out of the land of Egypt with great power and a stretched out arm, him shall ye fear, and him shall ye worship, and to him shall ye do sacrifice. 37 And the statutes, and the ordinances, and the law, and the commandment, which he wrote for you, ye shall observe to do for evermore; and ye shall not fear other gods. 38 And the covenant that I have made with you ye shall not forget; neither shall ye fear other gods. 39 But the LORD your God ye shall fear; and he shall deliver you out of the hand of all your enemies. 40 Howbeit they did not hearken, but they did after their former manner. 41 So these nations feared the LORD, and served their graven images, both their children, and their children's children: as did their fathers, so do they unto this day.	Did not fear nor worship the LORD • Did not obey God, His Word & commandments • Ignored the fact that God had given His Word to the world through Israel e. The warning to the reader 1) The reader must remember God's covenant, His basic commandment • Must not worship false gods • Must remember that it is the LORD alone who saves & delivers His people from Egypt (the world) • Must worship the LORD alone 2) The reader must always obey God's Word • Must keep all His Word • Must heed this command above all: Must not worship false gods 3) The reader must heed & never forget God's covenant • Must not worship false gods • Must worship the LORD God & Him alone • Must know that the LORD alone saves 4) The reader must remember Israel's failure: They would not listen • They worshipped the LORD but also their false gods • Their descendants have continued to follow this false, empty religion of syncretism to this day

a. In resettling the land of Israel, the Assyrians chose foreign refugees from five conquered nations to populate the territory (v.24). Coming from the regions of Babylon and Syria, the refugees were scattered throughout the towns of Samaria, that is, the Northern Kingdom of Israel. Through the following generations, the mixing of these races with the few Israelites who had been left behind became known as the Samaritans, especially during the times of the New Testament.

b. When the settlers arrived in the land of Israel, they faced an immediate problem (vv.25-26). Lions were roaming all over the land since the Assyrians had depopulated it. As a result, some of the new settlers were being attacked and others killed. Scripture says this was a direct judgment of God, a judgment being executed due to the settlers' false worship. No doubt, the LORD was attempting to arouse them to turn to Him, the only true and living God.

In their desperation, the new settlers appealed to the king for help. Being polytheistic—worshippers of many gods—the settlers felt that the god of this particular land was displeased with their worship. So they shared this fact with the Assyrian king, apparently requesting the return of a priest from Israel who could instruct them in how to worship the God of Israel (v.26). Note how little help the Israelites were who had been left behind, how ignorant they were of the LORD. Obviously, they knew so little about the LORD and His Word that they were unable to instruct or point the new settlers to Him.

c. Granting the request of the settlers, the Assyrian king sent a priest back to help them (vv.27-28). Although unnamed, the priest was an Israelite who had been taken from Samaria to Babylon during the exile. The priest, settling in Bethel, began to teach the people how to worship the LORD, the only living and true God.

d. Sadly, however, the settlers corrupted the true worship of the LORD (vv.29-34). They committed four serious errors:

1) Each national group of foreigners continued to worship their own false gods and shrines (vv.29-31). None of them worshipped the LORD, not as the LORD instructed and demanded. Rather, the settlers worshipped as they had always worshipped:

⇒ The Babylonians worshipped Succoth Benoth.
⇒ The Cuthahians worshipped Nergal.
⇒ The Hamath citizens worshipped Ashima.
⇒ The Avvites worshipped Nibhaz and Tartak.
⇒ The Sepharvites offered human sacrifices to the false gods Adrammelech and Anammelech.

Knowing any details about these false gods with any accuracy or certainty is simply impossible.

2) Being polytheistic (believing in or worshipping more than one god), the settlers had no problem adding another god to their agenda. They worshipped the LORD and even appointed their own priests to lead them in worship (v.32).

3) Of course, their own priests combined the worship of the true LORD with the worship of their own false gods (v.33). This led to a *religion of syncretism*—a religion of compromise, of accommodation—a religion that accepted the viewpoints of all religions.[4]

4) The settlers continued living sinful, wicked lives (v.34). They had no fear of the LORD; consequently they did not worship Him nor obey His Word and commandments. They ignored the fact that God had given His Holy Word to the world through Israel.

e. With this verse, the author gives a strong warning to *the reader* (vv.35-41). Four specific warnings are issued.

1) The reader must remember God's covenant, His basic commandment (vv.35-36). What is the basic—the foundational, primary—commandment? You must not fear or worship other gods: neither bow down to them nor serve them nor sacrifice to them.

You must remember that the LORD alone saved and delivered His people from Egypt (a symbol of the world). Therefore, you must worship the LORD alone, bowing down and offering sacrifices to Him alone.

2) The reader must always obey God's Word (v.37). You must keep all of God's Word, heeding this commandment in particular: you must not fear, worship false gods.

3) The reader must heed and never forget God's covenant (vv.38-39). You must not worship false gods, but must worship the LORD and Him alone. You must know that the LORD alone saves you from the hand of all your enemies.

4) The reader must remember Israel's failure: they would not listen, but continued to walk in their wicked ways (vv.40-41). They worshipped the LORD, but they also worshipped false gods. And sadly, to this very day, they have continued to follow this false and empty religion of syncretism (mixing the worship of the LORD with false gods.)

Thought 1. Note how all four of the warnings given to the reader focus upon the first of God's Ten Commandments. The first commandment says this: thou shalt have no other gods before me (Ex.20:3).

In this commandment, God is making a forceful declaration and demand: people are to know and acknowledge the only living and true God, the LORD God Himself.

(1) God declares that people who think there is no God are wrong (atheists). I AM the LORD God, the true and living God. *Atheists* may deny God, and *agnostics* may question if God really exists, but God is forceful in His declaration.

⇒ "I AM—I AM the LORD your God" (v.2).

"The fool hath said in his heart, There is no God" (Ps.14:1).

(2) No other object and no other being are ever to be set up as a so-called 'god.' Taking ideas or objects and beings and calling them God is forbidden, absolutely forbidden.

⇒ The LORD Himself (Jehovah, Yahweh) emphatically declares:

"I am the LORD: that is my name: and my glory will I not give to another, neither my praise to graven images" (Is.42:8).

⇒ The great apostle Paul declared:

"For though there be [many] that are called gods, whether in heaven or in earth, (as there be gods many, and lords many,) But to us there is but one God, the Father, of whom are all things" (1 Co.8:5-6).

We make a god out of anything that we esteem or love, fear or serve more than God. Again, whatever the heart clings to, that is a person's god. It may be oneself. Frankly, many people focus upon pleasing and satisfying themselves. They live by their own values and are concerned primarily with their own feelings, comfort, desires, and pleasures. They simply live like they want and do their own thing. They have exalted themselves to be their own god. Other people make gods out of...

• heavenly bodies	• images	• recognition	• family	• the latest fashions
• science	• money	• fame	• sex	• cars, trucks
• force, energy	• property	• a career	• food	• sports
• animals	• position	• power	• pleasure	• recreation

---

4 Russell Dilday. *1, 2 Kings*, p.423.

A god can be anything or any person. Man's first allegiance, first loyalty, first devotion is to be to the LORD God. The LORD God is to be first in a man's life; He is to be enthroned in the heart of man. Man is to know and acknowledge that there is one God and one God alone. The first commandment of the LORD is to be obeyed:

"You shall have no other gods before me" (v.3)

Note several points.

⇒ The so called gods of heaven and earth are nothing more than the creation of man's imagination and hands.

"Professing themselves to be wise, they became fools, And changed the glory of the uncorruptible God into an image made like to corruptible man, and to birds, and fourfooted beasts, and creeping things" (Ro.1:22-23).

"Ye know that ye were Gentiles, carried away unto these dumb idols, even as ye were led" (1 Co.12:2).

"Their idols are silver and gold, the work of men's hands. They have mouths, but they speak not: eyes have they, but they see not: They have ears, but they hear not: noses have they, but they smell not: They have hands, but they handle not: feet have they, but they walk not: neither speak they through their throat. They that make them are like unto them; so is every one that trusteth in them" (Ps.115:4-8).

"To whom then will ye liken God? or what likeness will ye compare unto him? The workman melteth a graven image, and the goldsmith spreadeth it over with gold, and casteth silver chains. He that is so impoverished that he hath no oblation chooseth a tree that will not rot; he seeketh unto him a cunning workman to prepare a graven image, that shall not be moved" (Is.40:18-20).

"Assemble yourselves and come; draw near together, ye that are escaped of the nations: they have no knowledge that set up the wood of their graven image, and pray unto a god that cannot save" (Is.45:20).

"Thus saith the LORD, Learn not the way of the heathen, and be not dismayed at the signs of heaven; for the heathen are dismayed at them. For the customs of the people are vain: for one cutteth a tree out of the forest, the work of the hands of the workman, with the axe. They deck it with silver and with gold; they fasten it with nails and with hammers, that it move not. They are upright as the palm tree, but speak not: they must needs be borne, because they cannot go. Be not afraid of them; for they cannot do evil, neither also is it in them to do good" (Je.10:2-5).

⇒ There is only one true and living God, the LORD Himself (Jehovah, Yahweh).

"And the scribe said unto him, Well, Master, thou hast said the truth: for there is one God; and there is none other but he" (Mk.12:32).

"And Jesus answered him, The first of all the commandments [is], Hear, O Israel; The Lord our God is one Lord" (Mk.12:29).

"As concerning therefore the eating of those things that are offered in sacrifice unto idols, we know that an idol is nothing in the world, and that there is none other God but one. For though there be that are called gods, whether in heaven or in earth, (as there be gods many, and lords many,) But to us there is but one God, the Father, of whom are all things, and we in him; and one Lord Jesus Christ, by whom are all things, and we by him" (1 Co.8:4-6).

"One God and Father of all, who is above all, and through all, and in you all" (Ep.4:6).

"For there is one God, and one mediator between God and men, the man Christ Jesus" (1 Ti.2:5).

"Unto thee it was showed, that thou mightest know that the LORD he is God; there is none else beside him" (De.4:35).

"Hear, O Israel: The LORD our God is one LORD: And thou shalt love the LORD thy God with all thine heart, and with all thy soul, and with all thy might" (De.6:4-5).

"Wherefore thou art great, O LORD God: for there is none like thee, neither is there any God beside thee, according to all that we have heard with our ears" (2 S.7:22).

"O LORD, there is none like thee, neither is there any God beside thee, according to all that we have heard with our ears" (1 Chr.17:20).

"That men may know that thou, whose name alone is JEHOVAH, art the most high over all the earth" (Ps.83:18).

"For thou art great, and doest wondrous things: thou art God alone" (Ps.86:10).

"Ye are my witnesses, saith the LORD, and my servant whom I have chosen: that ye may know and believe me, and understand that I am he: before me there was no God formed, neither shall there be after me. I, even I, am the LORD; and beside me there is no saviour" (Is.43:10-11).

"Thus saith the LORD the King of Israel, and his redeemer the LORD of hosts; I am the first, and I am the last; and beside me there is no God" (Is.44:6).

"For thus saith the LORD that created the heavens; God himself that formed the earth and made it; he hath established it, he created it not in vain, he formed it to be inhabited: I am the LORD; and there is none else" (Is.45:18).

"Look unto me, and be ye saved, all the ends of the earth: for I am God, and there is none else" (Is.45:22).

⇒   There is only one sovereign Creator who meets the needs of man.

"For as I passed by, and beheld your devotions, I found an altar with this inscription, TO THE UNKNOWN GOD. Whom therefore ye ignorantly worship, him declare I unto you. God that made the world and all things therein, seeing that he is Lord of heaven and earth, dwelleth not in temples made with hands; Neither is worshipped with men's hands, as though he needed any thing, seeing he giveth to all life, and breath, and all things; And hath made of one blood all nations of men for to dwell on all the face of the earth, and hath determined the times before appointed, and the bounds of their habitation; That they should seek the Lord, if haply they might feel after him, and find him, though he be not far from every one of us: For in him we live, and move, and have our being; as certain also of your own poets have said, For we are also his offspring. Forasmuch then as we are the offspring of God, we ought not to think that the Godhead is like unto gold, or silver, or stone, graven by art and man's device. And the times of this ignorance God winked at; but now commandeth all men every where to repent: Because he hath appointed a day, in the which he will judge the world in righteousness by that man whom he hath ordained; whereof he hath given assurance unto all men, in that he hath raised him from the dead" (Ac.17:23-31).

"Through faith we understand that the worlds were framed by the word of God, so that things which are seen were not made of things which do appear" (He.11:3).

"In the beginning God created the heaven and the earth" (Ge.1:1).

"Thou, even thou, art LORD alone; thou hast made heaven, the heaven of heavens, with all their host, the earth, and all things that are therein, the seas, and all that is therein, and thou preservest them all; and the host of heaven worshippeth thee" (Ne.9:6).

"He stretcheth out the north over the empty place, and hangeth the earth upon nothing" (Jb.26:7).

"By the word of the LORD were the heavens made; and all the host of them by the breath of his mouth" (Ps.33:6).

"Of old hast thou laid the foundation of the earth: and the heavens are the work of thy hands" (Ps.102:25).

DIVISION IV

THE UTTER DISINTEGRATION AND FALL OF JUDAH, THE SOUTHERN KINGDOM: AN APPALLING DESTRUCTION DUE TO INCONSISTENCY, DISLOYALTY, AND EVER-GROWING WICKEDNESS, 18:1–25:30

(18:1–25:30) **DIVISION OVERVIEW**: When the Northern Kingdom of Israel fell to the Assyrians, a strong and godly king named Hezekiah was on the throne in Judah. And he was experienced, for he had already been ruling for about seven years. He was perhaps the strongest king to ever rule the Southern Kingdom of Judah. Once again, the LORD had looked after the Judean people. He had provided a strong, godly and experienced ruler to guide them through the frightening days of upheaval within the Northern Kingdom, which was obviously a threat to their own survival. For Hezekiah and his people were bound to be gripped by fear, the fear that Assyria might attack Judah next. And just as feared, Assyria did invade Judah about seven years later. But Hezekiah led the people to seek the LORD in prayer, and the LORD miraculously delivered Judah from the terrorizing enemy (18:13–19:37).

However, even Hezekiah slipped into sin by giving in to a spirit of pride and boasting. Although he repented, God sent the prophet Isaiah to pronounce the inevitable judgment and utter destruction of Jerusalem that was coming—all due to the sins of the rulers and people down through the centuries.

After the fall of Samaria in 722, Judah was to survive for an additional 135 years. But eventually the trait of being *inconsistent, double-minded*—sometimes hot and sometimes cold to the LORD—was to lead to the fall of Jerusalem.

Because of some serious illness, Hezekiah had to rule as co-regent with his son Manasseh for a decade. After Hezekiah's death, Manasseh rejected the godly example of his father and turned completely away from the LORD. Among all the kings of Judah, Manasseh and his grandfather Ahaz were the most wicked and brutal and did more to bring about the downfall of Judah than any other king. This persecution and slaughter of true believers had been horrifying. (See outline and notes—2 K.16:1-20 for more discussion). Although Manasseh surprisingly repented and turned back to the LORD in the latter years of his life, the damage to the nation had already been done. And the downward spiral into utter destruction had picked up speed.

Upon the death of Manasseh, his evil son Amon succeeded him. However, he ruled for only two years before he was assassinated. But the verdict upon his reign was clearly pronounced by the LORD and the author. Amon was guilty of an evil life and rule. He failed to use the two years of his reign to turn the people back to God. Thus the downward spiral to destruction only picked up more steam.

However, God was not yet done with Judah. One more chance would be given to the people and nation, one more opportunity for them to turn back to the LORD permanently and to pass the torch of righteousness down to succeeding generations. This last chance was given in the ruler of Josiah, the great-grandson of Hezekiah. Of all the kings of Judah, he was apparently the most godly. But keep in mind this surprising, even shocking fact: during the entire 344 years of the divided kingdom—among all the kings of Israel and Judah—there were only four good and godly kings. And all four were from Judah. The Northern Kingdom of Israel never produced a good and righteous king. The four righteous kings in Judah were:

⇒ Asa
⇒ Jehoshaphat
⇒ Hezekiah
⇒ Josiah

Among these four, Hezekiah and Josiah are considered to have been the most godly because of the major reforms they carried out. However, the righteous and just reforms of one generation are often not passed down nor carried over into the next generation. And the LORD knew this fact. For the very trait that had so characterized Judah's history had been that of *inconsistency*, being double-minded.

Consequently, the hand of God's judgment fell. The people of Judah had been warned—warned time and again by the prophets—but they were stiff-necked, refusing to heed God's Word. The result: four successive evil kings took the throne of Judah, and each was either conquered or appointed by Egypt or Babylon.

All hope for the rulers and people of Judah was now gone. During the reign of the last ruler, Zedekiah, the final invasion of Judah by Babylon was launched. Soon thereafter the siege of Jerusalem began. After living under the siege for two years and reaching the point of starvation and insanity, the city collapsed. Because of the people's inconsistent lives—their unrighteous and unjust ways and their false worship—Jerusalem fell to the Babylonian army in 586 B.C. and the people were enslaved and exiled to Babylon.

After centuries of possessing the promised land, God's people now live either outside the land as exiles, or as tenants on their own ground. Only one bright spot remains for the author to report. Jehoiachin, exiled in 597 B.C., is elevated to favored status ca. 560 B.C. David's lineage still exists, albeit in Babylonian exile. Hope does remain. Whenever God chooses, the people can return. However he chooses, the Davidic promise and kingdom can emerge. God is not weak, powerless, or in exile. Therefore, all who turn to this sovereign LORD may also look forward to strength, victory, and a home going.[1]

THE UTTER DISINTEGRATION AND FALL OF JUDAH, THE SOUTHERN KINGDOM: AN APPALLING DESTRUCTION DUE TO INCONSISTENCY, DISLOYALTY, AND EVER-GROWING WICKEDNESS, 18:1–25:30

A. The Righteous Reign of Hezekiah (Part 1)—Assyria's Invasion of Judah: A Man Who Trusted and Held Fast to the LORD, 18:1-37

B. The Righteous Reign of Hezekiah (Part 2)—Judah's Deliverance from Assyria: God's Power to Rescue His People, 19:1-37

C. The Righteous Reign of Hezekiah (Part 3)—His Terminal Illness and Miraculous Healing: The Power of Prayer and the Danger of Pride, 20:11-21

D. The Evil Reigns of Manasseh and Amon: A Look at the Horrible Depths of Wicked Behavior, 21:1-26

E. The Godly Reign of Josiah (Part 1)—His Temple Restoration and Discovery of God's Word: Two Major Concerns of the Believer, 22:1-20

F. The Godly Reign of Josiah (Part 2)—His Spiritual Renewal and Reform: A Need for Conversion, for Trusting the Only Living and True God, 23:1-30

G. The Reigns Controlled by Egypt and Babylon: A Look at Four Critical Failures, 23:31–24:20

H. The Final Siege and Fall of Jerusalem: The Surety of God's Predicted Judgment, 25:1-30

---

[1] Paul R. House. *1, 2 Kings*, p.351.

CHAPTER 18

IV. THE UTTER DISINTEGRATION & FALL OF JUDAH, THE SOUTHERN KINGDOM: AN APPALLING DESTRUCTION DUE TO INCONSISTENCY, DISLOYALTY, & EVER-GROWING WICKEDNESS, 18:1–25:30

A. The Righteous Reign of Hezekiah (Part 1)—Assyria's Invasion of Judah: A Man Who Trusted & Held Fast to the LORD, 18:1-37

18:2-4; see 2 Chr.29:1-2
18:5-7; see 2 Chr.31:20-21; 31:1
18:9-12; see 2 K.17:3-23
18:17-35; see 2 Chr.32:9-19; Is.36:1-22

1. The righteous life of Hezekiah: The picture of a man totally devoted & committed to the LORD

a. His background
  1) He was 25 years old
  2) He reigned 29 years
  3) He was the son of King Ahaz & Abijah

b. His spiritual commitment
  1) He lived a righteous life—just as David had

  2) He removed the high places (false worship sites)
    • Destroyed the altars & images of the false gods Baal & Asherah
    • Destroyed the bronze snake made by Moses (Nu.21:4-9): Had become an idol
  3) He trusted in the LORD: More than all the kings of the Southern Kingdom before or after him

  4) He held fast to the LORD: Was faithful all his life
  5) He obeyed the commandments of God

c. His blessings from God
  1) Given God's presence
  2) Given success in all he did
  3) Given inner strength & courage to resist Assyrian oppression
  4) Given military victory over the Philistines

d. His major crisis: The fall of

Now it came to pass in the third year of Hoshea son of Elah king of Israel, *that* Hezekiah the son of Ahaz king of Judah began to reign.
2 Twenty and five years old was he when he began to reign; and he reigned twenty and nine years in Jerusalem. His mother's name also *was* Abi, the daughter of Zachariah.
3 And he did *that which was* right in the sight of the LORD, according to all that David his father did.
4 He removed the high places, and brake the images, and cut down the groves, and brake in pieces the brasen serpent that Moses had made: for unto those days the children of Israel did burn incense to it: and he called it Nehushtan.
5 He trusted in the LORD God of Israel; so that after him was none like him among all the kings of Judah, nor *any* that were before him.
6 For he clave to the LORD, *and* departed not from following him, but kept his commandments, which the LORD commanded Moses.
7 And the LORD was with him; *and* he prospered whithersoever he went forth: and he rebelled against the king of Assyria, and served him not.
8 He smote the Philistines, *even* unto Gaza, and the borders thereof, from the tower of the watchmen to the fenced city.
9 And it came to pass in the fourth year of king Hezekiah, which *was* the seventh year of Hoshea son of Elah king of Israel, *that* Shalmaneser king of Assyria came up against Samaria, and besieged it.
10 And at the end of three years they took it: *even* in the sixth year of Hezekiah, that *is* the ninth year of Hoshea king of Israel, Samaria was taken.
11 And the king of Assyria did carry away Israel unto Assyria, and put them in Halah and in Habor *by* the river of Gozan, and in the cities of the Medes:
12 Because they obeyed not the voice of the LORD their God, but transgressed his covenant, *and* all that Moses the servant of the LORD commanded, and would not hear *them,* nor do *them.*
13 Now in the fourteenth year of king Hezekiah did Sennacherib king of Assyria come up against all the fenced cities of Judah, and took them.
14 And Hezekiah king of Judah sent to the king of Assyria to Lachish, saying, I have offended; return from me: that which thou puttest on me will I bear. And the king of Assyria appointed unto Hezekiah king of Judah three hundred talents of silver and thirty talents of gold.
15 And Hezekiah gave *him* all the silver that was found in the house of the LORD, and in the treasures of the king's house.
16 At that time did Hezekiah cut off *the gold from* the doors of the temple of the LORD, and *from* the pillars which Hezekiah king of Judah had overlaid, and gave it to the king of Assyria.
17 And the king of Assyria sent Tartan and Rabsaris and Rab-shakeh from Lachish to king Hezekiah with a great host against Jerusalem. And they went up and came to Jerusalem. And when they were come up, they came and stood by the conduit of the upper pool, which is in the highway of the fuller's field.
18 And when they had called to the king, there came out to

Israel, the Northern Kingdom
  1) The Assyrians invaded &laid siege to Samaria in the fourth year of Hezekiah's reign: A serious threat to Judah
  2) The capital Samaria collapsed & fell three years later: In the sixth year of Hezekiah's reign

  3) The Assyrian king exiled the Israelites & resettled them in Assyria

  4) The reason for Israel's fall was the disobedience of the people, failing to obey God's commandments: A warning to Hezekiah & his people

2. The invasion of Judah by the Assyrian king Sennacherib: A decision demanded—trust the power of man or of God

a. The easy conquest by Assyria of all the fortified cities
b. The desperate attempt by Hezekiah to buy off the Assyrians
  1) Hezekiah sent an envoy to the Assyrian king: Offered to surrender & pay whatever ransom was demanded for peace
  2) The Assyrian king demanded 300 talents of silver (11 tons) & 30 talents of gold (1 ton)
  3) Hezekiah emptied the treasuries of the temple & palace to pay the ransom

  4) Hezekiah even stripped the temple of its gold ornaments & added this wealth to the demanded ransom: Probably in an effort to show good will

c. The intimidating threat by the Assyrian king & his demand for Hezekiah to surrender
  1) The Assyrian king sent an envoy & several regiments of troops to Jerusalem: To intimidate, threaten, & demand Hezekiah's surrender
    • They camped at the city's water source
    • They summoned Hezekiah for negotiations,

but he sent three court officials instead

2) The Assyrian field commander—as spokesman for the "great king" of Assyria—questioned the tactics of Hezekiah & why he was confident
- Questioned Hezekiah's claim of military strength: His claim was empty, his army weak

- Questioned Hezekiah's dependence on Egypt: In war, Egypt would splinter like a reed & cause the destruction of any ally leaning upon it

- Questioned Hezekiah's dependence on the LORD: Because Hezekiah must have displeased the LORD by destroying the high places & altars of worship (a misunderstanding of God & idolatry)

3) The field commander demanded Hezekiah's surrender
- Because of the weakness of Judah's army: Had few horses & horsemen
- Because the whole army of Judah could not stand against one officer's regiment of Assyrian troops
- Because Judah could not depend upon Egypt
- Because even the LORD Himself was now against Judah: The LORD had instructed Assyria's king to attack & destroy the nation

d. The Judean official's request for the Assyrian envoys to speak in Aramaic, not Hebrew: Feared that despair would grip the heart of the crowd standing on the wall & listening to the negotiations

1) The commander refused: Realized the importance of propaganda in destroying the people's confidence
2) The commander stated that his message was for all the people, not just the leaders:

them Eliakim the son of Hilkiah, which *was* over the household, and Shebna the scribe, and Joah the son of Asaph the recorder.
19 And Rab-shakeh said unto them, Speak ye now to Hezekiah, Thus saith the great king, the king of Assyria, What confidence is this wherein thou trustest?
20 Thou sayest, (but *they are but* vain words,) *I have* counsel and strength for the war. Now on whom dost thou trust, that thou rebellest against me?
21 Now, behold, thou trustest upon the staff of this bruised reed, *even* upon Egypt, on which if a man lean, it will go into his hand, and pierce it: so is Pharaoh king of Egypt unto all that trust on him.
22 But if ye say unto me, We trust in the LORD our God: *is* not that he, whose high places and whose altars Hezekiah hath taken away, and hath said to Judah and Jerusalem, Ye shall worship before this altar in Jerusalem?
23 Now therefore, I pray thee, give pledges to my lord the king of Assyria, and I will deliver thee two thousand horses, if thou be able on thy part to set riders upon them.
24 How then wilt thou turn away the face of one captain of the least of my master's servants, and put thy trust on Egypt for chariots and for horsemen?
25 Am I now come up without the LORD against this place to destroy it? The LORD said to me, Go up against this land, and destroy it.
26 Then said Eliakim the son of Hilkiah, and Shebna, and Joah, unto Rab-shakeh, Speak, I pray thee, to thy servants in the Syrian language; for we understand *it:* and talk not with us in the Jews' language in the ears of the people that *are* on the wall.
27 But Rab-shakeh said unto them, Hath my master sent me to thy master, and to thee, to speak these words? *hath he* not *sent me* to the men which sit on the wall, that they may eat their own

dung, and drink their own piss with you.
28 Then Rab-shakeh stood and cried with a loud voice in the Jews' language, and spake, saying, Hear the word of the great king, the king of Assyria:
29 Thus saith the king, Let not Hezekiah deceive you: for he shall not be able to deliver you out of his hand:
30 Neither let Hezekiah make you trust in the LORD, saying, The LORD will surely deliver us, and this city shall not be delivered into the hand of the king of Assyria.
31 Hearken not to Hezekiah: for thus saith the king of Assyria, Make *an agreement* with me by a present, and come out to me, and *then* eat ye every man of his own vine, and every one of his fig tree, and drink ye every one the waters of his cistern:
32 Until I come and take you away to a land like your own land, a land of corn and wine, a land of bread and vineyards, a land of oil olive and of honey, that ye may live, and not die: and hearken not unto Hezekiah, when he persuadeth you, saying, The LORD will deliver us.
33 Hath any of the gods of the nations delivered at all his land out of the hand of the king of Assyria?
34 Where *are* the gods of Hamath, and of Arpad? where *are* the gods of Sepharvaim, Hena, and Ivah? have they delivered Samaria out of mine hand?
35 Who *are* they among all the gods of the countries, that have delivered their country out of mine hand, that the LORD should deliver Jerusalem out of mine hand?
36 But the people held their peace, and answered him not a word: for the king's commandment was, saying, Answer him not.
37 Then came Eliakim the son of Hilkiah, which *was* over the household, and Shebna the scribe, and Joah the son of Asaph the recorder, to Hezekiah with *their* clothes rent, and told him the words of Rab-shakeh.

The people would suffer the most if Assyria attacked
e. The commander's second speech: Addressed more to the crowd standing nearby
1) He appealed for them to hear the "great king"
2) He encouraged them to oppose Hezekiah
- Hezekiah could not deliver them
- Hezekiah was only deceiving them by persuading them to trust the LORD: The LORD *would not* deliver them

3) He challenged them to surrender & to make a peace treaty: Because life would be far better under Assyrian rule
- They would have plenty to eat & drink (not dung & urine as they would under a siege, 27)
- They would be transported to a fruitful land just like their own
4) He challenged them to make a decision: Choose life, not death
- They must not listen to Hezekiah
- They were being misled by his promise of the LORD's deliverance
5) He threatened the people with the power of Assyria
- No nation had ever been delivered from Assyria, not by any god

- No god was able to deliver Samaria (or Israel)
- Not even the LORD would be able to deliver Jerusalem (or Judah) from an Assyrian attack

f. The response to the Assyrian threats
1) The people kept silent

2) The royal officials carried their report to Hezekiah: Approached him with torn clothes, a sign of distress & grief

DIVISION IV

THE UTTER DISINTEGRATION AND FALL OF JUDAH, THE SOUTHERN KINGDOM: AN APPALLING DESTRUCTION DUE TO INCONSISTENCY, DISLOYALTY, AND EVER-GROWING WICKEDNESS, 18:1–25:30

A. The Righteous Reign of Hezekiah (Part 1)—Assyria's Invasion of Judah: A Man Who Trusted and Held Fast to the LORD, 18:1-37

(18:1-37) **Introduction—Hold Fast, Failure to—Steadfast, Failure to Be—Trials, Results of—Temptations, Results of—Discouragement, Caused by—Fear, Caused by—Despair, Caused by**: When facing a serious trial, how often has fear gripped your heart, your knees buckled, and your courage disappeared? How often have you been gripped with despair or felt utter discouragement? And when facing a temptation, has your will to withstand ever collapsed? Did you give in to the seduction when the appeal was just too enticing? Did you allow your flesh to be aroused, your passion to run wild to the point that you could no longer resist or refuse?

Standing tall and holding fast for the LORD—being a real man or woman—is the great practical lesson of this Scripture. This is the story of Hezekiah, perhaps the greatest king who ever ruled the Southern Kingdom of Judah. In God's sovereignty, He knew that a strong, righteous king would need to be upon the throne of Judah right after the fall of Israel, right after the Northern Kingdom collapsed under the assault of Assyria. Thus, God moved to turn the heart of a young man to the LORD, a young man who was reared in one of the most ungodly environments imaginable. Although the godly reign of Hezekiah would not stop the tide of wickedness from flowing throughout Judah, it would significantly delay the hand of God's judgment from falling upon the Southern Kingdom. Judah would not fall to Babylon for over 100 years. Note this fact: after the fall of the Northern Kingdom, the Southern Kingdom of Judah is often given the ancient name of Israel. This fact needs to be kept in mind as the remaining kings are studied. This is: *The Righteous Reign of Hezekiah (Part 1)—Assyria's Invasion of Judah: A Man Who Trusted and Held Fast to the LORD,* 18:1-37.

1. The righteous life of Hezekiah: the picture of a man totally devoted and committed to the LORD (vv.1-12).
2. The invasion of Judah by the Assyrian king Sennacherib: a decision demanded to trust the power of man or of God (vv.13-37).

---

1 (18:1-12) **Commitment, Example of—Dedication, Example of—Devotion, to the LORD, Example of—Righteousness, Example of—Hezekiah, King of Judah—Israel, Fall of—Northern Kingdom of Israel, Fall of**: the major feature of Hezekiah's reign was his righteous life before the LORD. He was totally devoted and committed to the LORD.

OUTLINE	SCRIPTURE	SCRIPTURE	OUTLINE
1. The righteous life of Hezekiah: The picture of a man totally devoted & committed to the LORD	Now it came to pass in the third year of Hoshea son of Elah king of Israel, *that* Hezekiah the son of Ahaz king of Judah began to reign.	*and* departed not from following him, but kept his commandments, which the LORD commanded Moses.	Was faithful all his life 5) He obeyed the commandments of God
a. His background 1) He was 25 years old 2) He reigned 29 years 3) He was the son of King Ahaz & Abijah	2 Twenty and five years old was he when he began to reign; and he reigned twenty and nine years in Jerusalem. His mother's name also *was* Abi, the daughter of Zachariah.	7 And the LORD was with him; *and* he prospered whithersoever he went forth: and he rebelled against the king of Assyria, and served him not.	c. His blessings from God 1) Given God's presence 2) Given success in all he did 3) Given inner strength & courage to resist Assyrian oppression 4) Given military victory over the Philistines
b. His spiritual commitment 1) He lived a righteous life—just as David had	3 And he did *that which was* right in the sight of the LORD, according to all that David his father did.	8 He smote the Philistines, *even* unto Gaza, and the borders thereof, from the tower of the watchmen to the fenced city.	
2) He removed the high places (false worship sites) • Destroyed the altars & images of the false gods Baal & Asherah • Destroyed the bronze snake made by Moses (Nu.21:4-9): Had become an idol	4 He removed the high places, and brake the images, and cut down the groves, and brake in pieces the brasen serpent that Moses had made: for unto those days the children of Israel did burn incense to it: and he called it Nehushtan.	9 And it came to pass in the fourth year of king Hezekiah, which *was* the seventh year of Hoshea son of Elah king of Israel, *that* Shalmaneser king of Assyria came up against Samaria, and besieged it. 10 And at the end of three years they took it: *even* in the sixth year of Hezekiah,	d. His major crisis: The fall of Israel, the Northern Kingdom 1) The Assyrians invaded & laid siege to Samaria in the fourth year of Hezekiah's reign: A serious threat to Judah 2) The capital Samaria collapsed & fell three years later: In the sixth year of Hezekiah's reign
3) He trusted in the LORD: More than all the kings of the Southern Kingdom before or after him	5 He trusted in the LORD God of Israel; so that after him was none like him among all the kings of Judah, nor *any* that were before him.	that *is* the ninth year of Hoshea king of Israel, Samaria was taken.	
4) He held fast to the LORD:	6 For he clave to the LORD,	11 And the king of Assyria did carry away Israel unto	3) The Assyrian king exiled the Israelites & resettled

THE
PREACHER'S
OUTLINE & SERMON
BIBLE®

OUTLINE	SCRIPTURE	SCRIPTURE	OUTLINE
them in Assyria	Assyria, and put them in Halah and in Habor *by* the river of Gozan, and in the cities of the Medes:	their God, but transgressed his covenant, *and* all that Moses the servant of the LORD commanded, and would not hear *them,* nor do *them.*	the people, failing to obey God's commandments: A warning to Hezekiah & his people
4) The reason for Israel's fall was the disobedience of	12 Because they obeyed not the voice of the LORD		

a. Hezekiah assumed the throne in the third year of King Hoshea of Israel. Beginning his reign at just 25 years of age, he reigned a total of 29 years (715-686 B.C.). Apparently, he spent 14 years of his reign as co-regent with his father Ahaz, then 18 years alone and another 11 years as co-regent with his son Manasseh.[1] Considering that his father Ahaz was wicked, it is surprising that Hezekiah made a deep, genuine commitment to the LORD; but he did. He also had one of the most successful reigns among all the kings.

His mother was Abijah, the daughter of a man named Zechariah. Perhaps Zechariah was the godly man who had advised King Uzziah (2 Chr.26:5) and served as a witness for the prophet Isaiah (Is.8:2). If so, then Hezekiah's mother was probably a genuine believer who had a righteous influence upon him.

b. Whatever the case, at some point in his life Hezekiah made a deep spiritual commitment to the LORD and lived a righteous life (vv.3-6). Only four kings are said to have followed the godly example of David: Asa (1 K.15:11), Jehoshaphat (1 K.22:43), Josiah (2 K.22:2), and Hezekiah (18:3).

Hezekiah launched a reformation throughout the nation that had been unmatched since the days of David and Solomon. Significantly, he took action that had never before been taken by any king: he aroused the courage to remove the high places, the false worship sites throughout the nation (vv.4-5). Although he knew the worshippers of false gods would be disturbed and might react, for their own spiritual welfare he destroyed the altars and images of the false gods. And note, he also destroyed the bronze snake that had been made by Moses and preserved down through the years (see outline and notes— Nu.21:1-35 for more discussion). Obviously the bronze serpent had become such an object of reverence that it was eventually looked upon as a symbol or image of some god or idol, perhaps even of the LORD. Whatever the case, so many people worshipped the bronze serpent that it was given a popular name, Nehushtan, which simply means "bronze thing."[2]

In addition to destroying the worship centers of idols and false gods, Hezekiah carried out several other major reforms that are recorded in *Second Chronicles*, chapters 29–30. These reforms included:
⇒ immediately opening and repairing the doors of the temple (2 Chr.29:3)
⇒ immediately cleansing the temple: 1) encouraging the priests to sanctify and set themselves apart to the LORD in a rededication of their lives, and 2) removing all rubbish and every defiling thing from the temple (2 Chr.29:4-19)
⇒ rededicating the temple, reinstituting the regular services (2 Chr.29:20-36)
⇒ reinstituting the Passover and the Festival or Feast of Unleavened Bread (2 Chr.30:1-20)
⇒ reaching out to the entire nation—including the people of the Northern Kingdom who had not been transplanted— challenging everyone to return to the LORD and to join in the great celebration of the Passover (2 Chr.30:5-12)
⇒ launching a genuine revival among the entire nation (2 Chr.30:13-27)

Hezekiah had a great and most unusual trust in the LORD (v.5). Scripture actually says that he trusted the LORD more than all the kings of the Southern Kingdom. No king before or after him ever trusted the LORD as much as he did. And unlike some of the other good kings who slipped back into sin or failure, Hezekiah held fast to the LORD and persevered to the very end (v.6). He was faithful all his life, always seeking to obey the commandments of God.

c. Because of Hezekiah's strong trust and faithfulness to the LORD, the LORD poured out His blessings upon him (vv.7-8). Above all else, the LORD was with Hezekiah. The LORD granted His presence as the king walked about serving day by day. Furthermore, the LORD granted success and prosperity in everything Hezekiah undertook. Filling him with inner strength, the LORD even gave Hezekiah the courage to resist the oppression of the Assyrians. And keep in mind that the Assyrians were the superpower of that day and that his father Ahaz had willingly subjected the nation of Judah to Assyria, which meant that they were paying an annual tribute or tax. Thus, rebelling against the king of Assyria and refusing to pay the tax took enormous courage on Hezekiah's part, an inner strength seldom seen in rulers. But not only this, Hezekiah began to march against the Philistines, who were also one of the vassal states of Assyria. In battle after battle, he defeated the Philistines as far as Gaza and its territory (v.8). Demonstrating an enormous courage that could only arise from an infilling of God's strength, Hezekiah stood in stark contrast to the spiritually weak and fearful leaders of the past.[3]

d. When the Northern Kingdom of Israel fell under the Assyrian invasion, Hezekiah faced a dangerous crisis (vv.9-12). Once the Assyrians conquered Samaria, they would then pose a very serious threat to Hezekiah and Judah. For this reason, the king and the people must remember what happened to the Northern Kingdom. The capital Samaria collapsed and fell three years after the siege of Assyria began (v.10). Then the Assyrian king exiled the Israelites, scattering and transplanting them throughout Assyria (v.11). This happened to the Northern Kingdom because of their disobedience to the LORD. They violated their covenant or promise to the LORD that they would keep His commandments. They refused to listen to God's commandments, and they refused to obey them. Note how Scripture clearly states that the cause of Israel's collapse was their disobedience to the LORD. These facts were being repeated by the author of *Kings* as a reminder to the readers of his day and future generations: a refusal to keep God's commandments will bring judgment.

---

1   John F. Walvoord and Roy B. Zuck, Editors. *The Bible Knowledge Commentary, Old Testament.* (Colorado Springs, CO: Chariot Victor Publishing, 1985), p.572.

2   Russell Dilday. *1, 2 Kings,* p.430.

3   Richard D. Patterson and Hermann J. Austel. *1, 2 Kings,* pp.254-255.

Thought 1. Hezekiah's commitment to the LORD is a dynamic example for us. Always remember where he came from, his roots: the most wicked family imaginable. His father Ahaz was probably the most wicked ruler who ever ruled in the Southern Kingdom. Furthermore, his mother was the daughter of a wicked king who ruled in Israel. His family was literally steeped in sinful, wicked behavior. Yet despite being surrounded by a world of evil, Hezekiah rejected the sinful lifestyle of his parents and surroundings. When he came of age he turned to the LORD, making a deliberate decision to follow the LORD. Furthermore, throughout the years he grew even closer to the LORD, so close that he is said to have trusted the LORD more than any other ruler of the Southern Kingdom. He trusted, loved, and was totally devoted to serving the LORD. What a tremendous example to the people of his generation and to all generations down through history.

Hezekiah's life stands as a challenges to us today to trust the LORD and to give our hearts to Him. We should believe the Lord, have faith in Him as our Savior and Master, the One to whom we owe our total allegiance and loyalty. Our hearts and lives should be devoted to the Lord, totally committed to Him. Listen to what God's Holy Word demands of us:

"And he said to *them* all, If any *man* will come after me, let him deny himself, and take up his cross daily, and follow me" (Lu.9:23).

"If any *man* come to me, and hate not his father, and mother, and wife, and children, and brethren, and sisters, yea, and his own life also, he cannot be my disciple. And whosoever doth not bear his cross, and come after me, cannot be my disciple" (Lu.14:26-27).

"And Philip said, If thou believest with all thine heart, thou mayest [be baptized]. And he answered and said, I believe that Jesus Christ is the Son of God" (Ac.8:37).

"But God be thanked, that ye were the servants of sin, but ye have obeyed from the heart that form of doctrine which was delivered you. Being then made free from sin, ye became the servants of righteousness" (Ro.6:17-18).

"I beseech you therefore, brethren, by the mercies of God, that ye present your bodies a living sacrifice, holy, acceptable unto God, *which is* your reasonable service. And be not conformed to this world: but be ye transformed by the renewing of your mind, that ye may prove what is that good, and acceptable, and perfect, will of God" (Ro.12:1-2).

"I am crucified with Christ: nevertheless I live; yet not I, but Christ liveth in me: and the life which I now live in the flesh I live by the faith of the Son of God, who loved me, and gave himself for me" (Ga.2:20).

"But what things were gain to me, those I counted loss for Christ. Yea doubtless, and I count all things *but* loss for the excellency of the knowledge of Christ Jesus my Lord: for whom I have suffered the loss of all things, and do count them *but* dung, that I may win Christ" (Ph.3:7-8).

"And the very God of peace sanctify you wholly; and *I pray God* your whole spirit and soul and body be preserved blameless unto the coming of our Lord Jesus Christ" (1 Th.5:23).

"Nevertheless the foundation of God standeth sure, having this seal, The Lord knoweth them that are his. And, Let every one that nameth the name of Christ depart from iniquity. But in a great house there are not only vessels of gold and of silver, but also of wood and of earth; and some to honour, and some to dishonour. If a man therefore purge himself from these, he shall be a vessel unto honour, sanctified, and meet for the master's use, *and* prepared unto every good work" (2 Ti.2:19-21).

"For Moses had said, Consecrate yourselves to day to the LORD, even every man upon his son, and upon his brother; that he may bestow upon you a blessing this day" (Ex.32:29).

"And thou shalt love the LORD thy God with all thine heart, and with all thy soul, and with all thy might" (De.6:5).

"Blessed *are* they that keep his testimonies, *and that* seek him with the whole heart" (Ps.119:2).

"Give me understanding, and I shall keep thy law; yea, I shall observe it with *my* whole heart" (Ps.119:34).

"Trust in the LORD with all thine heart; and lean not unto thine own understanding" (Pr.3:5).

"My son, give me thine heart, and let thine eyes observe my ways" (Pr.23:26).

"And ye shall seek me, and find *me,* when ye shall search for me with all your heart" (Je.29:13).

"Therefore also now, saith the LORD, turn ye *even* to me with all your heart, and with fasting, and with weeping, and with mourning" (Joel 2:12).

---

2 (18:13-37) **Persecution, by Whom, Enemies—Oppression, by Whom, Spiritual Enemies—Enemies, Works of, Threats and Oppression—Judah, Wars of, Against Assyria—Assyria, Invasion of Judah**: because of Hezekiah's rebellion against Assyria and his military moves against the Philistines, the Assyrians eventually turned their attention to Hezekiah. Having conquered all of the Northern Kingdom, they now invaded Judah. The invasion took place in the fourteenth year of King Hezekiah's reign, but note: Hezekiah had expected the invasion by the Assyrians. He had prepared Jerusalem by fortifying the capital, by making more weapons for the army, and by organizing the citizen's army. He went so far as to stop up the springs outside the city in order to block or conceal the water supply from the Assyrians (2 Chr.32:1-6). A dramatic, suspenseful account of Assyria's invasion and threats against Judah is pictured:

OUTLINE	SCRIPTURE	SCRIPTURE	OUTLINE

2. The invasion of Judah by the Assyrian king Sennacherib: A decision demanded—trust the power of man or of God
a. The easy conquest by Assyria of all the fortified cities
b. The desperate attempt by Hezekiah to buy off the Assyrians
  1) Hezekiah sent an envoy to the Assyrian king: Offered to surrender & pay whatever ransom was demanded for peace
  2) The Assyrian king demanded 300 talents of silver (11 tons) & 30 talents of gold (1 ton)
  3) Hezekiah emptied the treasuries of the temple & palace to pay the ransom
 	
  4) Hezekiah even stripped the temple of its gold ornaments & added this wealth to the demanded ransom: Probably in an effort to show good will
 	
c. The intimidating threat by the Assyrian king & his demand for Hezekiah to surrender
  1) The Assyrian king sent an envoy & several regiments of troops to Jerusalem: To intimidate, threaten, & demand Hezekiah's surrender
   • They camped at the city's water source
   • They summoned Hezekiah for negotiations, but he sent three court officials instead
 	
  2) The Assyrian field commander—as spokesman for the "great king" of Assyria— questioned the tactics of Hezekiah & why he was confident
   • Questioned Hezekiah's claim of military strength: His claim was empty, his army weak
 	
   • Questioned Hezekiah's dependence on Egypt: In war, Egypt would splinter like a reed & cause the destruction of any ally leaning upon it
	13 Now in the fourteenth year of king Hezekiah did Sennacherib king of Assyria come up against all the fenced cities of Judah, and took them. 14 And Hezekiah king of Judah sent to the king of Assyria to Lachish, saying, I have offended; return from me: that which thou puttest on me will I bear. And the king of Assyria appointed unto Hezekiah king of Judah three hundred talents of silver and thirty talents of gold. 15 And Hezekiah gave *him* all the silver that was found in the house of the LORD, and in the treasures of the king's house. 16 At that time did Hezekiah cut off *the gold from* the doors of the temple of the LORD, and *from* the pillars which Hezekiah king of Judah had overlaid, and gave it to the king of Assyria. 17 And the king of Assyria sent Tartan and Rabsaris and Rab-shakeh from Lachish to king Hezekiah with a great host against Jerusalem. And they went up and came to Jerusalem. And when they were come up, they came and stood by the conduit of the upper pool, which is in the highway of the fuller's field. 18 And when they had called to the king, there came out to them Eliakim the son of Hilkiah, which *was* over the household, and Shebna the scribe, and Joah the son of Asaph the recorder. 19 And Rab-shakeh said unto them, Speak ye now to Hezekiah, Thus saith the great king, the king of Assyria, What confidence is this wherein thou trustest? 20 Thou sayest, (but *they are but* vain words,) *I have* counsel and strength for the war. Now on whom dost thou trust, that thou rebellest against me? 21 Now, behold, thou trustest upon the staff of this bruised reed, *even* upon Egypt, on which if a man lean, it will go into his hand, and pierce it: so is Pharaoh king of Egypt unto all that	trust on him. 22 But if ye say unto me, We trust in the LORD our God: *is* not that he, whose high places and whose altars Hezekiah hath taken away, and hath said to Judah and Jerusalem, Ye shall worship before this altar in Jerusalem? 23 Now therefore, I pray thee, give pledges to my lord the king of Assyria, and I will deliver thee two thousand horses, if thou be able on thy part to set riders upon them. 24 How then wilt thou turn away the face of one captain of the least of my master's servants, and put thy trust on Egypt for chariots and for horsemen? 25 Am I now come up without the LORD against this place to destroy it? The LORD said to me, Go up against this land, and destroy it. 26 Then said Eliakim the son of Hilkiah, and Shebna, and Joah, unto Rab-shakeh, Speak, I pray thee, to thy servants in the Syrian language; for we understand *it:* and talk not with us in the Jews' language in the ears of the people that *are* on the wall. 27 But Rab-shakeh said unto them, Hath my master sent me to thy master, and to thee, to speak these words? *hath he* not *sent me* to the men which sit on the wall, that they may eat their own dung, and drink their own piss with you? 28 Then Rab-shakeh stood and cried with a loud voice in the Jews' language, and spake, saying, Hear the word of the great king, the king of Assyria: 29 Thus saith the king, Let not Hezekiah deceive you: for he shall not be able to deliver you out of his hand: 30 Neither let Hezekiah make you trust in the LORD, saying, The LORD will surely deliver us, and this city shall not be delivered into the hand of the king of Assyria. 31 Hearken not to Hezekiah: for thus saith the king of	• Questioned Hezekiah's dependence on the LORD: Because Hezekiah must have displeased the LORD by destroying the high places & altars of worship (a misunderstanding of God & idolatry)
			  3) The field commander demanded Hezekiah's surrender
			   • Because of the weakness of Judah's army: Had few horses & horsemen
			   • Because the whole army of Judah could not stand against one officer's regiment of Assyrian troops
			   • Because Judah could not depend upon Egypt
			   • Because even the LORD Himself was now against Judah: The LORD had instructed Assyria's king to attack & destroy the nation
			d. The Judean official's request for the Assyrian envoys to speak in Aramaic, not Hebrew: Feared that despair would grip the heart of the crowd standing on the wall & listening to the negotiations
			
			  1) The commander refused: Realized the importance of propaganda in destroying the people's confidence
			  2) The commander stated that his message was for all the people, not just the leaders: The people would suffer the most if Assyria attacked
			e. The commander's second speech: Addressed more to the crowd standing nearby
			  1) He appealed for them to hear the "great king"
			  2) He encouraged them to oppose Hezekiah
			   • Hezekiah could not deliver them
			   • Hezekiah was only deceiving them by persuading them to trust the LORD: The LORD *would not* deliver them
			  3) He challenged them to surrender & to make a

OUTLINE	SCRIPTURE	SCRIPTURE	OUTLINE
peace treaty: Because life would be far better under Assyrian rule • They would have plenty to eat & drink (not dung & urine as they would under a siege, 27) • They would be transported to a fruitful land just like their own 4) He challenged them to make a decision: Choose life, not death • They must not listen to Hezekiah • They were being misled by his promise of the LORD's deliverance 5) He threatened the people with the power of Assyria • No nation had ever been delivered from Assyria, not by any god	Assyria, Make *an agreement* with me by a present, and come out to me, and *then* eat ye every man of his own vine, and every one of his fig tree, and drink ye every one the waters of his cistern: 32 Until I come and take you away to a land like your own land, a land of corn and wine, a land of bread and vineyards, a land of oil olive and of honey, that ye may live, and not die: and hearken not unto Hezekiah, when he persuadeth you, saying, The LORD will deliver us. 33 Hath any of the gods of the nations delivered at all his land out of the hand of the king of Assyria? 34 Where *are* the gods of Hamath, and of Arpad?	where *are* the gods of Sepharvaim, Hena, and Ivah? have they delivered Samaria out of mine hand? 35 Who *are* they among all the gods of the countries, that have delivered their country out of mine hand, that the LORD should deliver Jerusalem out of mine hand? 36 But the people held their peace, and answered him not a word: for the king's commandment was, saying, Answer him not. 37 Then came Eliakim the son of Hilkiah, which *was* over the household, and Shebna the scribe, and Joah the son of Asaph the recorder, to Hezekiah with *their* clothes rent, and told him the words of Rab-shakeh.	• No god was able to deliver Samaria (or Israel) • Not even the LORD would be able to deliver Jerusalem (or Judah) from an Assyrian attack f. The response to the Assyrian threats 1) The people kept silent 2) The royal officials carried their report to Hezekiah: Approached him with torn clothes, a sign of distress & grief

a. The large military campaign was launched by Assyria against the western world of that time, so they easily conquered all the fortified cities of Judah. According to the historical records of Sennacherib, he captured 46 fortified cities, numerous small towns or villages; captured over 200,000 people; and, through their siege, trapped Hezekiah in Jerusalem just "like a caged bird."[4]

b. Standing all alone against the mighty Assyrians, Hezekiah was desperate to make peace and to prevent the Assyrians from attacking Jerusalem (vv.14-16). He therefore sent an envoy to the Assyrian king Sennacherib who was camped at the Judean city Lachish, which he had just captured. If the Assyrian king would withdraw, Hezekiah offered to surrender and to pay whatever ransom was demanded for peace. Seeing an opportunity to gain a huge amount of money, Sennacherib demanded 300 talents of silver (11 tons) and 30 talents of gold (1 ton). To meet this enormous demand, Hezekiah emptied the treasuries of the temple and palace (vv.14-15). In a further effort to show goodwill and just how hopeful he was for peace, Hezekiah even stripped the temple of its gold ornaments and added this wealth to the demanded ransom (v.16).

But the Assyrian king had deceived Hezekiah. He had no intention of withdrawing his forces, for Hezekiah had been a thorn in his side through his rebellious actions. To teach this Judean king a lesson on subjection, Sennacherib was determined to conquer Jerusalem, strip the city of all its wealth, and reinstate the annual tribute or tax that Hezekiah had stopped paying. In addition, he was probably planning to replace Hezekiah with an Assyrian governor who would enforce loyalty and allegiance to the Assyrian ruler.

c. Remaining behind at Lachish with the main army, Sennacherib sent an envoy with a large number of troops to position a blockade around Jerusalem (vv.17-25). With this action, the Assyrian king was launching a propaganda war of intimidation, threatening and demanding that Hezekiah surrender Jerusalem to the Assyrians (vv.17-18). After setting up the siege around the capital, the three officials sent by Sennacherib approached the city and stopped at the aqueduct of the upper pool (vv.17-18). Note that the location of the canal or aqueduct was called the Washerman's Field, which means that the spot was a popular place where some of the city residents washed their clothes. Obviously, this spot was within earshot of the city walls, for the Assyrian officials called out and summoned Hezekiah to join them in negotiations for surrender. But instead of joining the negotiations himself, Hezekiah sent three royal officials whose positions would match those of the Assyrian officials. By this action, Hezekiah was insistent on being treated as an equal to the Assyrian king. Had the king of Assyria himself come for negotiations, Hezekiah no doubt would have carried out the negotiations personally, king to king.

Standing face-to-face with the Judean negotiators, the Assyrian commander questioned the tactics of Hezekiah and why he was confident (vv.19-22). Claiming that he was the personal spokesman for the "great king" of Assyria, he questioned three of Hezekiah's actions:

⇒ He questioned Hezekiah's claim of military strength, alleging that Hezekiah's words were empty and the Judean army was weak (v.20).

⇒ He also questioned Hezekiah's dependence upon Egypt, claiming that in an actual war Egypt would splinter like a reed and cause the defeat of any ally who was leaning upon it (v.21; Is.42:3).

⇒ Continuing to belittle Hezekiah, the Assyrian spokesman questioned Hezekiah's dependence on the LORD (v.22). But note that he showed a complete misunderstanding of God and of idolatry, for he claimed that Hezekiah had displeased the LORD by destroying the high places and altars of worship throughout Judah and Jerusalem.

Having questioned Hezekiah's military strength, his alliance with Egypt, and his dependence on the LORD, the Assyrian commander then demanded that Hezekiah surrender (vv.23-25). Obviously a skilled negotiator, the commander gave four strong reasons why Hezekiah should surrender:

---

4 Daniel David Luckenbill. *Ancient Records of Assyria and Babylonia,* Vol.2. (London, ENG: Histories & Mysteries of Man Ltd., 1989), p.120.

⇒ Hezekiah should surrender because of the weakness of Judah's army. Ridiculing the fact that Judah had few horses and horsemen, the commander declared that he would give 2,000 horses to Judah if they could put riders on them.

⇒ Hezekiah should surrender because the whole army of Judah could not defend against one officer's regiment of Assyrian troops (v.24).

⇒ Hezekiah should surrender because Judah could not depend upon Egypt.

⇒ Hezekiah should surrender because even the LORD Himself was now against Judah (v.25).

Note that the commander declared that the LORD had actually instructed Assyria's king to attack Judah and destroy the nation. No doubt this struck fear in those who overheard the claim. Keep in mind that the Northern Kingdom of Israel had already fallen to Assyria. The question must have been in the minds of the hearers: Could God actually be behind the Assyrian invasion, using the Assyrians as an instrument of His judgment?

d. When it was time for the Judean officials to speak, they surprisingly requested that the Assyrian envoy speak in Aramic not in Hebrew (vv.26-27). There was a twofold reason for this: because Aramaic was the international language for diplomacy and commercial transaction throughout western Asia and because the Judean people standing on the wall could overhear the negotiations.[5] By overhearing the threats of the Assyrian envoys spoken in their own Hebrew language, there was the danger that the crowd would be gripped with fear and despair.

But the Assyrian commander refused, for he realized the importance of propaganda, of destroying the people's confidence. Even in responding to the Judean official he sought to turn the hearts of people on the wall by stating that his message was for all the people and not just for leaders because the people themselves would suffer the most if Assyria attacked. What a skillful negotiator the Assyrians had!

e. Still the commander was not through with his propaganda: launching a second major speech, he addressed his words more to the crowd standing nearby than to the Judean officials (vv.28-35). Shouting an appeal for them to hear the "great king," he encouraged the people to oppose Hezekiah, to actually launch a revolt against him. He declared that Hezekiah could not deliver them from the Assyrian forces, that the king was only deceiving them by persuading them to trust the LORD, for the LORD would not deliver them (vv.28-30).

Still shouting out to the crowd on the wall, he challenged them to surrender and make a peace treaty. He claimed life would be far better for them under Assyrian rule (vv.31-32). Under the Assyrians they would have plenty to eat and drink; whereas if they continued their opposition, they would end up eating their own filth and drinking their own urine (v.27). If they surrendered, though, they would be transplanted to another fruitful land, a land just like their own there in Judah.

Finally, the commander challenged the people to make a decision: to choose life not death (v.32). To choose life, they must not listen to Hezekiah, for he was misleading them by his promise of the LORD's deliverance.

In closing his second speech he threatened the people with the power of Assyria (vv.33-35). He bombarded the people with question after question, laying out three provoking thoughts:

⇒ No nation had ever been delivered from Assyria, not by any god.

⇒ No god was able to deliver Samaria, that is, the Northern Kingdom of Israel.

⇒ How, then, could the LORD deliver Jerusalem from the hand of the Assyrians?

f. Note the response of the people to the Assyrian threats: they kept silent (vv.36-37). Concluding the negotiations, the royal officials of Judah carried their report to Hezekiah. But note how they approached him: with torn clothes, a sign of distress and grief.

Thought 1. Hezekiah stood fast for the LORD, stood fast against a brutal and murderous enemy. And just think: the enemy was the superpower of that day with a far superior military force. Sweeping all across much of the known world, the Assyrians had already conquered and subjected nation after nation under their rule. Their conquest had even included the Northern Kingdom of Israel and all the cities of Judah except Jerusalem itself. Now the Assyrians were standing at the gates of Jerusalem, threatening to totally destroy the capital and exile all its citizens, scattering them all over the world. But even with the enemy at the gate threatening utter destruction, Hezekiah held fast to his faith in the LORD and stood strongly against the enemies of God and of His people.

What a living, dynamic example for us! No matter how terrible the trial or temptation, pressure or distress, threat or ridicule, persecution or abuse—no matter what may confront us—we must stand fast for the LORD. Standing up, standing tall, being a real man or woman for the LORD is one of the great needs of our day. We are not to be weaklings. Our knees are not to buckle. Our courage is not to collapse. Our hearts are not to shrink back. We are to persevere, endure, stand fast for the LORD, trusting His Spirit to empower us.

"And ye shall be hated of all _men_ for my name's sake: but he that endureth to the end shall be saved" (Mt.10:22).

"Therefore, my beloved brethren, be ye stedfast, unmovable, always abounding in the work of the Lord, forasmuch as ye know that your labour is not in vain in the Lord" (1 Co.15:58).

"Stand fast therefore in the liberty wherewith Christ hath made us free, and be not entangled again with the yoke of bondage" (Ga.5:1).

"And let us not be weary in well doing: for in due season we shall reap, if we faint not" (Ga.6:9).

"Only let your conversation [behavior, conduct] be as it becometh the gospel of Christ: that whether I come and see you, or else be absent, I may hear of your affairs, that ye stand fast in one spirit, with one mind striving together for the faith of the gospel" (Ph.1:27).

"Prove all things; hold fast that which is good. Abstain from all appearance of evil. And the very God of peace sanctify you wholly; and _I pray God_ your whole spirit and soul and body be preserved blameless unto the coming of our Lord Jesus Christ" (1 Th.5:21-23).

---

5 Russell Dilday. _1, 2 Kings_, p.437.

"Seeing then that we have a great high priest, that is passed into the heavens, Jesus the Son of God, let us hold fast *our* profession" (He.4:14).

"Let us hold fast the profession of *our* faith without wavering; (for he *is* faithful that promised;)" (He.10:23).

"Wherefore seeing we also are compassed about with so great a cloud of witnesses, let us lay aside every weight, and the sin which doth so easily beset *us*, and let us run with patience the race that is set before us" (He.12:1).

"Wherefore gird up the loins of your mind, be sober, and hope to the end for the grace that is to be brought unto you at the revelation of Jesus Christ" (1 Pe.1:13).

"Be sober, be vigilant; because your adversary the devil, as a roaring lion, walketh about, seeking whom he may devour: Whom resist stedfast in the faith, knowing that the same afflictions are accomplished in your brethren that are in the world" (1 Pe.5:8-9).

"Ye therefore, beloved, seeing ye know *these things* before, beware lest ye also, being led away with the error of the wicked, fall from your own stedfastness. But grow in grace, and *in* the knowledge of our Lord and Saviour Jesus Christ. To him *be* glory both now and for ever. Amen" (2 Pe.3:17-18).

"Remember therefore how thou hast received and heard, and hold fast, and repent. If therefore thou shalt not watch, I will come on thee as a thief, and thou shalt not know what hour I will come upon thee" (Re.3:3).

"Behold, I come quickly: hold that fast which thou hast, that no man take thy crown" (Re.3:11).

"But cleave unto the LORD your God, as ye have done unto this day" (Jos.23:8).

"If iniquity *be* in thine hand, put it far away, and let not wickedness dwell in thy tabernacles. For then shalt thou lift up thy face without spot; yea, thou shalt be stedfast, and shalt not fear" (Jb.11:14-15).

CHAPTER 19

B. The Righteous Reign of Hezekiah (Part 2)— Judah's Deliverance from Assyria: God's Power to Rescue His People, 19:1-37

19:1-37; see Is.37:1-38

19:35-37; see 2 Chr.32:20-21

1. The LORD's assurance of deliverance—given through Isaiah: God's assurance to the believer
   a. The distress of Hezekiah over the report, 18:37
   b. The appeal of Hezekiah to the prophet Isaiah
      1) He sent a delegation to Isaiah, seeking prayer & some word from the LORD

      2) He sent this message
         • That this was a black day of trouble, rebuke, & disgrace for Judah (due to their sins)

         • That perhaps the LORD had heard the Assyrian king ridicule & defy the name of the living God

         • That Isaiah needed to pray for those still surviving

   c. The concise & comforting prediction of Isaiah: Proclaimed the promise of God, a message of hope
      1) The people & Hezekiah were not to fear the threats & blasphemous words of Assyria's king

      2) The LORD would cause Sennacherib to return home: Once there, he would face a violent death by being cut down with a sword
   d. The beginning of Isaiah's prophecy: Began to take shape
      1) The Assyrian commander withdrew to help his king fight against Libnah
      2) The Assyrian king had received a report that Egypt was rapidly marching to fight against him
   e. The Assyrian king's second message sent to Hezekiah

And it came to pass, when king Hezekiah heard *it*, that he rent his clothes, and covered himself with sackcloth, and went into the house of the LORD.
2 And he sent Eliakim, which *was* over the household, and Shebna the scribe, and the elders of the priests, covered with sackcloth, to Isaiah the prophet the son of Amoz.
3 And they said unto him, Thus saith Hezekiah, This day *is* a day of trouble, and of rebuke, and blasphemy: for the children are come to the birth, and *there is* not strength to bring forth.
4 It may be the LORD thy God will hear all the words of Rab-shakeh, whom the king of Assyria his mas-ter hath sent to reproach the living God; and will reprove the words which the LORD thy God hath heard: wherefore lift up *thy* prayer for the remnant that are left.
5 So the servants of king Hezekiah came to Isaiah.
6 And Isaiah said unto them, Thus shall ye say to your master, Thus saith the LORD, Be not afraid of the words which thou hast heard, with which the servants of the king of Assyria have blasphemed me.
7 Behold, I will send a blast upon him, and he shall hear a rumour, and shall return to his own land; and I will cause him to fall by the sword in his own land.
8 So Rab-shakeh returned, and found the king of Assyria warring against Libnah: for he had heard that he was departed from Lachish.
9 And when he heard say of Tirhakah king of Ethiopia, Behold, he is come out to fight against thee: he sent messengers again unto Hezekiah, saying,

10 Thus shall ye speak to Hezekiah king of Judah, saying, Let not thy God in whom thou trustest deceive thee, saying, Jerusalem shall not be delivered into the hand of the king of Assyria.
11 Behold, thou hast heard what the kings of Assyria have done to all lands, by destroying them utterly: and shalt thou be delivered?
12 Have the gods of the nations delivered them which my fathers have destroyed; *as* Gozan, and Haran, and Rezeph, and the children of Eden which *were* in Thelasar?
13 Where *is* the king of Hamath, and the king of Arpad, and the king of the city of Sepharvaim, of Hena, and Ivah?
14 And Hezekiah received the letter of the hand of the messengers, and read it: and Hezekiah went up into the house of the LORD, and spread it before the LORD.
15 And Hezekiah prayed before the LORD, and said, O LORD God of Israel, which dwellest *between* the cherubims, thou art the God, *even* thou alone, of all the kingdoms of the earth: thou hast made heaven and earth.
16 LORD, bow down thine ear, and hear: open, LORD, thine eyes, and see: and hear the words of Sennacherib, which hath sent him to reproach the living God.
17 Of a truth, LORD, the kings of Assyria have destroyed the nations and their lands,
18 And have cast their gods into the fire: for they *were* no gods, but the work of men's hands, wood and stone: therefore they have destroyed them.
19 Now therefore, O LORD our God, I beseech thee, save thou us out of his hand, that all the kingdoms of the earth may know that thou *art* the LORD God, *even* thou only.
20 Then Isaiah the son of Amoz sent to Hezekiah, saying, Thus saith the LORD God of Israel, *That* which thou hast prayed to me against Sennacherib king of Assyria I have heard.

1) He stressed the absurdity of Hezekiah's trusting his God to deliver Jerusalem

2) He threatened Hezekiah
   • Reminded him what Assyria had done to all the countries they had attacked
   • Asked why Judah was different: Declared no god had delivered any nation from the power of Assyria

3) He threatened Hezekiah personally: Asked where the kings of the conquered nations were

2. The desperate prayer for deliverance—offered by Hezekiah: Seeking the LORD for help
   a. He spread the letter out before the LORD in the temple: A threefold prayer
   b. He declared God's greatness
      1) He is the LORD, the God of Israel
      2) He alone is God over all kingdoms
      3) He is the Creator

   c. He explained the problem
      1) He pleaded for the LORD to notice how Sennacherib had insulted the living God

      2) He acknowledged the power & conquests of Assyria

      3) He declared that the false gods of the conquered nations could not have saved them: They were only lifeless & powerless idols made by men's hands
   d. He cried for deliverance & expressed his major concern: That all nations know that the LORD alone is God

3. The deliverance promised by God—through His prophet Isaiah: God's wonderful deliverance

a. The message of judgment against King Sennacherib
 1) He would flee Jerusalem, 9the Virgin Daughter (not violate, rape the city)
 2) He would be mocked by the Virgin Daughter (the people, Jerusalem) as he fled
b. The reason for the judgment upon Sennacherib
 1) He had ridiculed & blasphemed the Holy One of Israel
 2) He had heaped insults on the LORD
 3) He thought himself above all men & gods, boasting in his military power
 • To conquer all mountains: Nations
 • To cut down the tallest trees: Leaders
 • To reach the farthest parts of the earth
 • To dig wells & drink fresh water of foreign lands
 • To dry up the rivers of Egypt when he set foot in the country
c. The basic truth not yet learned by the Assyrian king: God is sovereign over men & nations
 1) God Himself had ordained Assyria's conquests & rise to superpower status
 2) God had weakened the people conquered by Assyria: Used Assyria to judge—discipline & correct—Israel & other nations
 3) God knew every movement of Sennacherib & his rage against the LORD
d. The LORD's judgment pronounced upon Sennacherib & Assyria
 1) He would be defeated, subdued like an animal, & returned to his own land

21 This *is* the word that the LORD hath spoken concerning him; The virgin the daughter of Zion hath despised thee, *and* laughed thee to scorn; the daughter of Jerusalem hath shaken her head at thee.
22 Whom hast thou reproached and blasphemed? and against whom hast thou exalted *thy* voice, and lifted up thine eyes on high? *even* against the Holy *One* of Israel.
23 By the messengers thou hast reproached the Lord, and hast said, With the multitude of my chariots I am come up to the height of the mountains, to the sides of Lebanon, and will cut down the tall cedar trees thereof, *and* the choice fir trees thereof: and I will enter into the lodgings of his borders, *and into* the forest of his Carmel.
24 I have digged and drunk strange waters, and with the sole of my feet have I dried up all the rivers of besieged places.
25 Hast thou not heard long ago *how* I have done it, *and* of ancient times that I have formed it? now have I brought it to pass, that thou shouldest be to lay waste fenced cities *into* ruinous heaps.
26 Therefore their inhabitants were of small power, they were dismayed and confounded; they were *as* the grass of the field, and *as* the green herb, *as* the grass on the house tops, and *as* corn blasted before it be grown up.
27 But I know thy abode, and thy going out, and thy coming in, and thy rage against me.
28 Because thy rage against me and thy tumult is come up into mine ears, therefore I will put my hook in thy nose, and my bridle in thy lips, and I will turn thee back

by the way by which thou camest.
29 And this *shall be* a sign unto thee, Ye shall eat this year such things as grow of themselves, and in the second year that which springeth of the same; and in the third year sow ye, and reap, and plant vineyards, and eat the fruits thereof.
30 And the remnant that is escaped of the house of Judah shall yet again take root downward, and bear fruit upward.
31 For out of Jerusalem shall go forth a remnant, and they that escape out of mount Zion: the zeal of the LORD *of hosts* shall do this.
32 Therefore thus saith the LORD concerning the king of Assyria, He shall not come into this city, nor shoot an arrow there, nor come before it with shield, nor cast a bank against it.
33 By the way that he came, by the same shall he return, and shall not come into this city, saith the LORD.
34 For I will defend this city, to save it, for mine own sake, and for my servant David's sake.
35 And it came to pass that night, that the angel of the LORD went out, and smote in the camp of the Assyrians an hundred fourscore and five thousand: and when they arose early in the morning, behold, they *were* all dead corpses.
36 So Sennacherib king of Assyria departed, and went and returned, and dwelt at Nineveh.
37 And it came to pass, as he was worshipping in the house of Nisroch his god, that Adrammelech and Sharezer his sons smote him with the sword: and they escaped into the land of Armenia. And Esar-haddon his son reigned in his stead.

2) The reason: His rage & arrogance toward God
e. The LORD's sign of assurance given to Hezekiah
 1) Judah would recover from the invasion after two years: Would sow & reap in the third year
 2) Judah would be left with a remnant, survivors who would experience a miraculous growth in population
 • God would give a remnant out of Jerusalem, Is.10:20-23 (refers both to that day & to the day of the Messiah, Ro.11:5)
 • God's zeal would do this
f. The clear, unmistakable declaration of God: The Assyrian king would not conquer Jerusalem
 1) Would not enter the city, attack, shoot an arrow, nor lay a siege ramp
 2) Would return to his own land
 3) Would not enter Jerusalem: A strong reemphasis
 4) The reason: The city would be defended by God Himself—for His own honor & for the sake of David
g. The judgment of God against Assyria & Sennacherib: The prophecy of Isaiah fulfilled
 1) The angel of the LORD went into the Assyrian camp & executed 185,000 soldiers during the night
 2) The Assyrian survivors—stunned, perplexed—broke camp & withdrew, then returned to Nineveh & stayed there
 3) The Assyrian king Sennacherib was later assassinated while worshipping his false god
 • Was killed by his two sons, Adrammelech & Sharezer
 • Was succeeded by his son Esarhaddon

DIVISION IV

THE UTTER DISINTEGRATION AND FALL OF JUDAH, THE SOUTHERN KINGDOM: AN APPALLING DESTRUCTION DUE TO INCONSISTENCY, DISLOYALTY, AND EVER-GROWING WICKEDNESS, 18:1–25:30

B. The Righteous Reign of Hezekiah (Part 2)—Judah's Deliverance from Assyria: God's Power to Rescue His People, 19:1-37

(19:1-37) **Introduction—Deliverance, from What—Rescued, from What—Circumstances, Severe, Caused by—Crises, Caused by—Hardships, Caused by—God, Power of, to Deliver**: How often do we need to be rescued or delivered from a crisis? How many people suffer oppression by others: domination, verbal abuse, assault, enslavement, heavy and abusive taxation, exorbitant payments and interest? How many of us suffer physical ailments, disease, or accidents? How many of us have had to face financial difficulty, extreme worry, or pressure within the home or workplace or school?

God's power to rescue His people—those who genuinely trust Him—is the lesson to be learned from this chapter of Holy Scripture. King Hezekiah of Judah was facing the crisis of his life, the intimidating threat of total destruction by the Assyrian army. Surrounding the capital Jerusalem, the Assyrians were poised to conquer the city and unmercifully slaughter Hezekiah and many of his people. For Hezekiah, his small army, and the citizens of Jerusalem who had taken refuge behind the city walls, it was humanly impossible to escape the vengeful wrath of the massive Assyrian army. But there was a divine way of escape, the LORD God Himself. This is the story of God's wonderful deliverance of his dear, righteous servant Hezekiah and the citizens of Jerusalem. This is: *The Righteous Reign of Hezekiah (Part 2)—Judah's Deliverance from Assyria: God's Power to Rescue His People*, 19:1-37.

1. The LORD's assurance of deliverance—given through Isaiah: God's assurance to the believer (vv.1-13).
2. The desperate prayer for deliverance—offered by Hezekiah: Seeking the Lord for help (vv.14-19).
3. The deliverance promised by God—through His prophet Isaiah: God's wonderful deliverance (vv.20-37).

1 (19:1-13) **Assurance, of Deliverance, Example of—Promises, of God, Deliverance, Example of—God, Deliverance of—Hezekiah, Deliverance from Assyria, Promised**: the LORD gave a wonderful assurance to Hezekiah, the assurance that the king and his people would be delivered from the invading Assyrians. Remember what had happened years earlier: Hezekiah's father Ahaz had surrendered to Assyria, subjecting the nation as a *vassal state* under the Assyrian government. This meant that Ahaz was able to remain as king of Judah and that the people were allowed to keep their property, but they were forced to pay a large tribute or tax to Assyria (see outline and note—16:1-20 for more discussion). Once Hezekiah had become king, and because of his commitment to the LORD, he revolted against the oppressive domination of the Assyrians. It was this that had aroused King Sennacherib of Assyria to invade Judah and to lay siege to the capital Jerusalem (18:1-37). Envoys from the Assyrian king had just confronted representatives sent by Hezekiah, demanding that Hezekiah unconditionally surrender to the Assyrian forces. Using every intimidating threat known to negotiators, the Assyrian envoy demanded that Hezekiah either choose death or surrender (18:13-37). While his own royal officials were carrying on the negotiations, King Hezekiah anxiously waited back in the palace for their return. With this background, note what happened:

OUTLINE	SCRIPTURE	SCRIPTURE	OUTLINE
1. The LORD's assurance of deliverance—given through Isaiah: God's assurance to the believer	And it came to pass, when king Hezekiah heard *it,* that he rent his clothes, and covered himself with sackcloth, and went into the house of the LORD.	for the remnant that are left.	• pray for those still surviving
a. The distress of Hezekiah over the report, 18:37	2 And he sent Eliakim, which *was* over the household, and Shebna the scribe, and the elders of the priests, covered with sackcloth, to Isaiah the prophet the son of Amoz.	5 So the servants of king Hezekiah came to Isaiah. 6 And Isaiah said unto them, Thus shall ye say to your master, Thus saith the LORD, Be not afraid of the words which thou hast heard, with which the servants of the king of Assyria have blasphemed me.	c. The concise & comforting prediction of Isaiah: Proclaimed the promise of God, a message of hope
b. The appeal of Hezekiah to the prophet Isaiah			1) The people & Hezekiah were not to fear the threats & blasphemous words of Assyria's king
1) He sent a delegation to Isaiah, seeking prayer & some word from the LORD			
2) He sent this message	3 And they said unto him, Thus saith Hezekiah, This day *is* a day of trouble, and of rebuke, and blasphemy: for the children are come to the birth, and *there is* not strength to bring forth.	7 Behold, I will send a blast upon him, and he shall hear a rumour, and shall return to his own land; and I will cause him to fall by the sword in his own land.	2) The LORD would cause Sennacherib to return home: Once there, he would face a violent death by being cut down with a sword
• That this was a black day of trouble, rebuke, & disgrace for Judah (due to their sins)			
• That perhaps the LORD had heard the Assyrian king ridicule & defy the name of the living God	4 It may be the LORD thy God will hear all the words of Rab-shakeh, whom the king of Assyria his master hath sent to reproach the living God; and will reprove the words which the LORD thy God hath heard:	8 So Rab-shakeh returned, and found the king of Assyria warring against Libnah: for he had heard that he was departed from Lachish. 9 And when he heard say of Tirhakah king of Ethiopia, Behold, he is come out to fight against thee: he sent messengers again unto Hezekiah, saying,	d. The beginning of Isaiah's prophecy: Began to take shape 1) The Assyrian commander withdrew to help his king fight against Libnah 2) The Assyrian king had received a report that Egypt was rapidly marching to fight against him
• That Isaiah needed to	wherefore lift up *thy* prayer		e. The Assyrian king's second message sent to Hezekiah

OUTLINE	SCRIPTURE	SCRIPTURE	OUTLINE
1) He stressed the absurdity of Hezekiah's trusting his God to deliver Jerusalem	10 Thus shall ye speak to Hezekiah king of Judah, saying, Let not thy God in whom thou trustest deceive thee, saying, Jerusalem shall not be delivered into the hand of the king of Assyria.	12 Have the gods of the nations delivered them which my fathers have destroyed; *as* Gozan, and Haran, and Rezeph, and the children of Eden which *were* in Thelasar?	• Asked why Judah was different: Declared no god had delivered any nation from the power of Assyria
2) He threatened Hezekiah • Reminded him what Assyria had done to all the countries they had attacked	11 Behold, thou hast heard what the kings of Assyria have done to all lands, by destroying them utterly: and shalt thou be delivered?	13 Where *is* the king of Hamath, and the king of Arpad, and the king of the city of Sepharvaim, of Hena, and Ivah?	3) He threatened Hezekiah personally: Asked where the kings of the conquered nations were

a. When Hezekiah's negotiators returned and gave their report on the Assyrian threats and their ridicule of the LORD, Hezekiah was filled with deep distress. Tearing his clothes and putting on sackcloth as a symbol of his repentance and grief, he went into the temple to seek the face of the LORD. Knowing that the troops within Jerusalem could not stand against the mighty army of Assyria, he recognized there was nothing in his power he could do to save the people. Thus, he took the only step that could save them: he turned to the LORD for help.

b. But before entering the temple, Hezekiah sent a delegation to make an appeal to the prophet Isaiah, seeking prayer and some word from the LORD (vv.2-4). Three points were included in the message sent by the king to the prophet:

⇒ He stated that this was a black day for Judah, a day of trouble, rebuke, and disgrace. The LORD was obviously chastising and correcting them for their sins (v.3; He.5:9-15). Note the illustration used by Hezekiah to describe his inability to deliver the people: just as a mother sometimes does not have the power to deliver a child, so he and Jerusalem did not have the power to deliver themselves from Assyria.

⇒ He said that perhaps the LORD had heard the Assyrian king ridicule and defy the name of the living God (v.4).

⇒ He appealed to Isaiah for prayer, prayer for all of them who still survived.

c. Responding to the king's appeal, Isaiah sent back a concise and comforting prediction from God, a wonderful promise and message of hope (vv.5-7). The people and Hezekiah were not to fear the threats and blasphemous words of Assyria's king. For the LORD Himself had indeed heard the commander's threats against Jerusalem and his blasphemy against the name of the LORD. Thus the LORD would call Sennacherib to return home to his own country, and once there he would face a violent death by being cut down with a sword (v.7).

d. Immediately after the prediction by Isaiah, God's promise to His people began to take shape (vv.8-9). The Assyrian commander, hearing that Sennacherib had left Lachish to join the fighting against Libnah, left Jerusalem to give his report. When he reached Sennacherib, he discovered that the king had received a report that Egypt was rapidly marching up the Philistine coast to join in the fight against the Assyrians.

e. To prevent Judah from joining the forces that were mobilizing against him, the Assyrian king quickly sent a second message to Hezekiah (vv.9-13). His message stressed the absurdity of Hezekiah's trusting his God to deliver Jerusalem. Again threatening Hezekiah, he reminded the king what Assyria had done to all the countries they had attacked. Then he asked why Hezekiah thought Judah would be any different, declaring that no god had delivered any nation from the power of Assyria (vv.11-12). Finally, he threatened Hezekiah personally, asking where all the kings of the conquered nations were (v.13). The implication was clear: all of the kings who had opposed Assyria had died violent deaths.

Thought 1. Think of the wonderful assurance of God given to Hezekiah. Facing impossible odds and a hopeless situation, he was utterly helpless to deliver himself and his people. But God stepped forth in the person of His prophet Isaiah and gave Hezekiah the assurance of deliverance.

Nothing compares to the assurance that God gives us—His people—in times of need. Above all else, when the crises of life confront us, the one thing needed is God's assurance. God's assurance builds confidence, courage, and security within us. And when God assures us of His presence and promises, our hearts are encouraged, inspired, persuaded, and fulfilled. Listen to some of the great assurances of God:

"Being confident of this very thing, that he which hath begun a good work in you will perform *it* until the day of Jesus Christ" (Ph.1:6).

"That their hearts might be comforted, being knit together in love, and unto all riches of the full assurance of understanding, to the acknowledgement of the mystery of God, and of the Father, and of Christ" (Co.2:2).

"For our gospel came not unto you in word only, but also in power, and in the Holy Ghost, and in much assurance; as ye know what manner of men we were among you for your sake" (1 Th.1:5).

"For the which cause I also suffer these things: nevertheless I am not ashamed: for I know whom I have believed, and am persuaded that he is able to keep that which I have committed unto him against that day" (2 Ti.1:12).

"And the Lord shall deliver me from every evil work, and will preserve *me* unto his heavenly kingdom: to whom *be* glory for ever and ever. Amen" (2 Ti.4:18).

"Let us draw near with a true heart in full assurance of faith, having our hearts sprinkled from an evil conscience, and our bodies washed with pure water" (He.10:22).

"And hereby we do know that we know him, if we keep his commandments" (1 Jn.2:3).

"And hereby we know that we are of the truth, and shall assure our hearts before him" (1 Jn.3:19).

"Hereby know we that we dwell in him, and he in us, because he hath given us of his Spirit" (1 Jn.4:13).

"And this is the record, that God hath given to us eternal life, and this life is in his Son. He that hath the Son hath life; *and* he that hath not the Son of God hath not life. These things have I written unto you that believe on the name of the Son of God; that ye may know that ye have eternal life, and that ye may believe on the name of the Son of God" (1 Jn.5:11-13).

"Now unto him that is able to keep you from falling, and to present *you* faultless before the presence of his glory with exceeding joy, To the only wise God our Saviour, *be* glory and majesty, dominion and power, both now and ever. Amen" (Jude 24-25).

2   (19:14-19) **Seeking, for Deliverance—Deliverance, Seeking, Example of—Prayer, for Deliverance, Example of—Desperation, Answer to, Prayer, Example of—Distress, Answer to, Prayer—Grief, Answer to, Prayer—Hezekiah, Prayer of, for Deliverance**: in response to the second message from the Assyrian king, Hezekiah again took his desperate situation to the LORD in prayer. But this time he did not seek the LORD's word through Isaiah the prophet. Under intense pressure and strain, he personally went directly to the LORD in prayer.

OUTLINE	SCRIPTURE	SCRIPTURE	OUTLINE
2. The desperate prayer for deliverance—offered by Hezekiah: **Seeking the LORD for help**	14 And Hezekiah received the letter of the hand of the messengers, and read it: and Hezekiah went up into the	which hath sent him to reproach the living God. 17 Of a truth, LORD, the kings of Assyria have de-	
a. He spread the letter out before the LORD in the temple: A threefold prayer	house of the LORD, and spread it before the LORD.	stroyed the nations and their lands,	2) He acknowledged the power & conquests of Assyria
b. He declared God's greatness	15 And Hezekiah prayed before the LORD, and said, O	18 And have cast their gods into the fire: for they *were* no	
1) He is the LORD, the God of Israel	LORD God of Israel, which dwellest *between* the cheru-	gods, but the work of men's hands, wood and stone:	3) He declared that the false gods of the conquered nations could not have saved
2) He alone is God over all kingdoms	bims, thou art the God, *even* thou alone, of all the king-	therefore they have destroyed them.	them: They were only lifeless & powerless idols
3) He is the Creator	doms of the earth: thou hast made heaven and earth.	19 Now therefore, O LORD our God, I beseech thee, save	made by men's hands
	16 LORD, bow down thine	thou us out of his hand, that	d. He cried for deliverance & expressed his major concern:
c. He explained the problem	ear, and hear: open, LORD,	all the kingdoms of the earth	That all nations know that
1) He pleaded for the LORD to notice how Sennacherib had insulted the living God	thine eyes, and see: and hear the words of Sennacherib,	may know that thou *art* the LORD God, *even* thou only.	the LORD alone is God

a. Once again, Hezekiah went up to the temple and humbled himself as a child before the LORD (v.14). Spreading out the letter from the Assyrian king, he laid it before the LORD and began to pour out his soul, crying for deliverance. Note that he offered up a threefold prayer.

b. First, Hezekiah declared God's greatness (v.15). Addressing the LORD as the God of Israel who is enthroned between the cherubim of the Ark, Hezekiah acknowledged that the LORD alone is God over all the kingdoms of the earth. He alone is the Supreme Creator who has made heaven and earth.

c. Second, Hezekiah explained the problem confronting him and the Judeans (vv.16-18). Yet note Hezekiah's major concern, what he stressed first: the insults launched against the LORD by the Assyrians. He pleaded for the LORD to open His eyes and notice how the Assyrian king Sennacherib had insulted the living God. He then acknowledged the power and conquests of Assyria, how they had destroyed nation after nation. Then Hezekiah declared a significant truth: the false gods of the conquered nations could not have saved them, for they were only lifeless and powerless idols made by men's hands (v.18).

d. Third, Hezekiah cried out for the LORD God to deliver him and his people from the hand of the Assyrians. But note why: that all the kingdoms of the earth may know that the LORD alone is God (v.19).

Thought 1. When crises—desperate, hopeless, and helpless situations—confront us, we have at our disposal one great resource: prayer. We have access into the very presence of the living God Himself. The door into God's presence is always open, and God is always available to help us. Whether by miraculous deliverance or by infusing us with the strength to walk through the crisis, God will help us. He will help us through any difficult problem, even through the crisis of death itself. Prayer, seeking and calling upon the name of the LORD, is always available to us. This is the reason the LORD has established prayer as the most powerful law throughout the universe. Through the *law of prayer*, God operates and moves to meet the needs of His people. Listen to what the Word of God says about prayer and seeking His face for help:

"Therefore I say unto you, What things soever ye desire, when ye pray, believe that ye receive *them*, and ye shall have *them*" (Mk.11:24).

"For every one that asketh receiveth; and he that seeketh findeth; and to him that knocketh it shall be opened" (Lu.11:10).

"If ye abide in me, and my words abide in you, ye shall ask what ye will, and it shall be done unto you" (Jn.15:7).

"Hitherto have ye asked nothing in my name: ask, and ye shall receive, that your joy may be full" (Jn.16:24).

"Is any among you afflicted? let him pray. Is any merry? let him sing psalms. Is any sick among you? let him call for the elders of the church; and let them pray over him, anointing him with oil in the name of the Lord" (Js.5:13-14).

"And whatsoever we ask, we receive of him, because we keep his commandments, and do those things that are pleasing in his sight" (1 Jn.3:22).

"But if from thence thou shalt seek the LORD thy God, thou shalt find *him,* if thou seek him with all thy heart and with all thy soul" (De.4:29).

"Seek the LORD and his strength, seek his face continually" (1 Chr.16:11).

"If my people, which are called by my name, shall humble themselves, and pray, and seek my face, and turn from their wicked ways; then will I hear from heaven, and will forgive their sin, and will heal their land" (2 Chr.7:14).

"Thou shalt not be afraid for the terror by night; *nor* for the arrow *that* flieth by day" (Ps.91:5).

"Seek the LORD, and his strength: seek his face evermore" (Ps.105:4).

"Seek ye the LORD while he may be found, call ye upon him while he is near" (Is.55:6).

"And it shall come to pass, that before they call, I will answer; and while they are yet speaking, I will hear" (Is.65:24).

"And ye shall seek me, and find *me,* when ye shall search for me with all your heart" (Je.29:13).

"For thus saith the LORD unto the house of Israel, Seek ye me, and ye shall live" (Am.5:4).

"Seek ye the LORD, all ye meek of the earth, which have wrought his judgment; seek righteousness, seek meekness: it may be ye shall be hid in the day of the LORD'S anger" (Zep.2:3).

3 (19:20-37) **Deliverance, Promised, Example of—Promise, of Deliverance, Example of—Deliverance, of Judah, from the Assyrians—Hezekiah, Deliverance from, the Assyrians—Prayer, Answered, Example**: the LORD reinforced His wonderful promise given earlier to Hezekiah. The king and his people would be delivered from the Assyrian threat. Even while Hezekiah was in the temple praying, the LORD was giving a message to Isaiah to deliver to the king. Isaiah delivers God's message—14 verses long—in the form of a poem or song, a *song of judgment* against the Assyrian king Sennacherib (vv.20-34). Then in the final three verses of the chapter, the judgment of God against King Sennacherib is seen taking place just as the prophet Isaiah predicted (vv.35-37).

OUTLINE	SCRIPTURE	SCRIPTURE	OUTLINE
3. The deliverance promised by God—through His prophet Isaiah: God's wonderful deliverance	20 Then Isaiah the son of Amoz sent to Hezekiah, saying, Thus saith the LORD God of Israel, *That* which thou hast prayed to me against Sennacherib king of Assyria I have heard.	sole of my feet have I dried up all the rivers of besieged places.	• To dry up the rivers of Egypt when he set foot in the country
a. The message of judgment against King Sennacherib	21 This *is* the word that the LORD hath spoken concerning him; The virgin the daughter of Zion hath despised thee, *and* laughed thee	25 Hast thou not heard long ago *how* I have done it, *and* of ancient times that I have formed it? now have I brought it to pass, that thou	c. The basic truth not yet learned by the Assyrian king: God is sovereign over men & nations
1) He would flee Jerusalem, 9the Virgin Daughter (not violate, rape the city)		shouldest be to lay waste fenced cities *into* ruinous heaps.	1) God Himself had ordained Assyria's conquests & rise to superpower status
2) He would be mocked by the Virgin Daughter (the people, Jerusalem) as he fled	to scorn; the daughter of Jerusalem hath shaken her head at thee.	26 Therefore their inhabitants were of small power, they were dismayed and	
b. The reason for the judgment upon Sennacherib	22 Whom hast thou reproached and blasphemed? and against whom hast thou	confounded; they were *as* the grass of the field, and *as* the green herb, *as* the grass	2) God had weakened the people conquered by Assyria: Used Assyria to judge—discipline & correct—Israel & other nations
1) He had ridiculed & blasphemed the Holy One of Israel	exalted *thy* voice, and lifted up thine eyes on high? *even* against the Holy *One* of Israel.	on the house tops, and *as* corn blasted before it be grown up.	
2) He had heaped insults on the LORD	23 By the messengers thou hast reproached the Lord,	27 But I know thy abode, and thy going out, and thy coming in, and thy rage against me.	3) God knew every movement of Sennacherib & his rage against the LORD
3) He thought himself above all men & gods, boasting in his military power	and hast said, With the multitude of my chariots I am come up to the height of the mountains, to the sides	28 Because thy rage against me and thy tumult is come up into mine ears, therefore	d. The LORD's judgment pronounced upon Sennacherib & Assyria
• To conquer all mountains: Nations	of Lebanon, and will cut down the tall cedar trees	I will put my hook in thy nose, and my bridle in thy lips, and I will turn thee back	1) He would be defeated, subdued like an animal, & returned to his own land
• To cut down the tallest trees: Leaders	thereof, *and* the choice fir trees thereof: and I will enter	by the way by which thou camest.	2) The reason: His rage & arrogance toward God
• To reach the farthest parts of the earth	into the lodgings of his borders, *and into* the forest of his Carmel.	29 And this *shall be* a sign unto thee, Ye shall eat this year such things as grow of	e. The LORD's sign of assurance given to Hezekiah
• To dig wells & drink fresh water of foreign lands	24 I have digged and drunk strange waters, and with the	themselves, and in the second year that which springeth of	1) Judah would recover from the invasion after two years: Would sow & reap

OUTLINE	SCRIPTURE	SCRIPTURE	OUTLINE
in the third year	the same; and in the third year sow ye, and reap, and plant vineyards, and eat the fruits thereof.	34 For I will defend this city, to save it, for mine own sake, and for my servant David's sake.	4) The reason: The city would be defended by God Himself—for His own honor & for the sake of David
2) Judah would be left with a remnant, survivors who would experience a miraculous growth in population	30 And the remnant that is escaped of the house of Judah shall yet again take root downward, and bear fruit upward.	35 And it came to pass that night, that the angel of the LORD went out, and smote in the camp of the Assyrians an hundred fourscore and five thousand: and when they arose early in the morning, behold, they *were* all dead corpses.	g. The judgment of God against Assyria & Sennacherib: The prophecy of Isaiah fulfilled
• God would give a remnant out of Jerusalem, Is.10:20-23 (refers both to that day & to the day of the Messiah, Ro.11:5)	31 For out of Jerusalem shall go forth a remnant, and they that escape out of mount Zion: the zeal of the LORD *of hosts* shall do this.		1) The angel of the LORD went into the Assyrian camp & executed 185,000 soldiers during the night
• God's zeal would do this	32 Therefore thus saith the LORD concerning the king of Assyria, He shall not come into this city, nor shoot an arrow there, nor come before it with shield, nor cast a bank against it.	36 So Sennacherib king of Assyria departed, and went and returned, and dwelt at Nineveh.	2) The Assyrian survivors—stunned, perplexed—broke camp & withdrew, then returned to Nineveh & stayed there
f. The clear, unmistakable declaration of God: The Assyrian king would not conquer Jerusalem			
1) Would not enter the city, attack, shoot an arrow, nor lay a siege ramp		37 And it came to pass, as he was worshipping in the house of Nisroch his god, that Adrammelech and Sharezer his sons smote him with the sword: and they escaped into the land of Armenia. And Esar-haddon his son reigned in his stead.	3) The Assyrian king Sennacherib was later assassinated while worshipping his false god
2) Would return to his own land	33 By the way that he came, by the same shall he return, and shall not come into this city, saith the LORD.		• Was killed by his two sons, Adrammelech & Sharezer
3) Would not enter Jerusalem: A strong reemphasis			• Was succeeded by his son Esarhaddon

a. Delivering the message of God to Hezekiah, Isaiah declared the judgment of God against King Sennacherib (vv.20-21). The Assyrian king would flee Jerusalem, and as he fled, he would be mocked by the people. Note that Jerusalem is referred to as "The Virgin Daughter of Zion," which simply means that no enemy had ever conquered or defiled the city, not since it had been made the capital of Israel by King David.

b. After stating the fact of the judgment, Isaiah gave the reasons for the judgment that were to come upon the Assyrian king (vv.22-24). First, he had ridiculed and blasphemed the Holy One of Israel, the LORD God of the universe Himself. Second, he had heaped insults on the LORD, on the God who would not tolerate insults or rejection. Third, the king considered himself above all men and gods, boasting in his military power (vv.23-24). He was taking great pride in himself and bragging…

- that he could conquer all mountains or nations
- that he could cut down the tallest trees, that is, leaders
- that he could reach the farthest parts of the earth
- that he could dig wells and drink the fresh water of foreign lands
- that he had the power to dry up the rivers of Egypt, that is, their defenses

c. God then charged the Assyrian king with being ignorant, ignorant of a very basic truth that he had never learned. What was this basic truth? That the LORD Himself was sovereign over all men and nations (vv.25-27). It was God Himself who had ordained the rise and superpower status of Assyria. The LORD had used Assyria as an instrument to weaken, discipline, and correct the other nations. Therefore, it was only because of God and for this reason that Assyria had been raised up by the LORD to become a world power. Judgment, discipline, and correction had to be carried out upon the nations of the world to stir them to turn and cry out to the LORD.

But God was not only sovereign over Assyria and the other nations of the world, He also knew every movement of the Assyrian king and his rage against the LORD (v.27).

d. After pronouncing the LORD's judgment upon King Sennacherib and Assyria, Isaiah declared that the king would be defeated, subdued like an animal, and returned to his own land (v.28). Sennacherib's rage and arrogance against the LORD were the reason he was to suffer the LORD's judgment. Note the reference to a hook being put in the king's nose and a bit in his mouth. The hook and bit were generally used to control animals, but it was the practice of the Assyrians to use hooks and bits to control their prisoners.

e. Turning to Hezekiah, Isaiah gave him a sign that assured the king of God's wonderful provision (vv.29-30). Judah would recover from the invasion after two years. The people would be able to sow and reap in the third year. Note how this wonderful promise is broken down year by year. In the first year, the year of the invasion, the people had not been able to plant their crops. But there would be enough food growing in the fields naturally to feed the population that had survived. During the second year there would still be enough food growing naturally from what had spilled upon the ground to feed the people. In the third year, the people would be able to cultivate the land and reap the harvest.

Yet the wonderful assurance of food was not all that God was promising. Judah would also be left with a remnant, survivors who would experience a miraculous growth in population (also see Is.10:20-23). In His zeal, the LORD of Hosts would fulfill this promise. Note how this reference to the remnant being left refers both to that day and the day of the Messiah (Ro.11:5).

f. In closing, Isaiah shared the clear, unmistakable assurance of God: the Assyrian king would not conquer Jerusalem (vv.32-34).

⇒ The Assyrian king would not enter the city, attack, shoot an arrow, nor lay a siege ramp against Jerusalem.

⇒ The Assyrian king would return to his own land, and he would return by the quickest route he knew.

⇒ The Assyrian king would definitely not enter the city of Jerusalem.

⇒ Note the reason why: the city would be defended by God Himself, defended for God's own honor and for the sake of David.

g. That very night the judgment of God against Assyria and King Sennacherib fell. The prophecy of Isaiah came true, and the promise of God was fulfilled (vv.35-37). Sometime during the night, the angel of the LORD went into the Assyrian camp and executed 185,000 soldiers. Utterly shocked and not understanding what had happened, the Assyrian survivors broke camp and withdrew, returning to Nineveh. And note, the Assyrian army remained in Ninevah and lived there. Sometime after returning, King Sennacherib was assassinated while worshipping in the temple of his false god Nishroch (v.37). He was killed by two of his sons, Adrammelech and Sharezer. Right after his death he was succeeded by another son Esarhaddon.

Thought 1. *Deliverance* is one of the great promises of God. When we call upon God for deliverance, one of two things happens: God either miraculously delivers us or else He gives us the power to walk through the obstacle standing in our way. Even in facing the obstacle of death, power is available to the believer. Quicker than the eye can blink, the power of God transfers the believer from this physical earth into the spiritual world. Death is conquered, triumphed over. And the believer lives forever in God's presence.

No matter what confronts us—disease, accident, financial difficulty, divorce, or any other trial or hardship—God promises to deliver us. If we will turn to the LORD for deliverance, cry out to Him in prayer, genuinely trust Him to deliver, He will give us the power to overcome the obstacle or to walk through it victoriously. Listen to the wonderful promises of God's deliverance:

"Who shall separate us from the love of Christ? *shall* tribulation, or distress, or persecution, or famine, or nakedness, or peril, or sword....Nay, in all these things we are more than conquerors through him that loved us. For I am persuaded, that neither death, nor life, nor angels, nor principalities, nor powers, nor things present, nor things to come, Nor height, nor depth, nor any other creature, shall be able to separate us from the love of God, which is in Christ Jesus our Lord" (Ro.8:35, 37-39).

"Now unto him that is able to do exceeding abundantly above all that we ask or think, according to the power that worketh in us" (Ep.3:20).

"There hath no temptation taken you but such as is common to man: but God *is* faithful, who will not suffer you to be tempted above that ye are able; but will with the temptation also make a way to escape, that ye may be able to bear *it*" (1 Co.10:13).

"For we would not, brethren, have you ignorant of our trouble which came to us in Asia, that we were pressed out of measure, above strength, insomuch that we despaired even of life: But we had the sentence of death in ourselves, that we should not trust in ourselves, but in God which raiseth the dead: Who delivered us from so great a death, and doth deliver: in whom we trust that he will yet deliver *us*" (2 Co.1:8-10).

"And the Lord shall deliver me from every evil work, and will preserve *me* unto his heavenly kingdom: to whom *be* glory for ever and ever. Amen" (2 Ti.4:18).

"Forasmuch then as the children are partakers of flesh and blood, he also himself likewise took part of the same; that through death he might destroy him that had the power of death, that is, the devil; And deliver them who through fear of death were all their lifetime subject to bondage" (He.2:14-15).

"The Lord knoweth how to deliver the godly out of temptations, and to reserve the unjust unto the day of judgment to be punished" (2 Pe.2:9).

"For whatsoever is born of God overcometh the world: and this is the victory that overcometh the world, *even* our faith. Who is he that overcometh the world, but he that believeth that Jesus is the Son of God" (1 Jn.5:4-5).

"He shall deliver thee in six troubles: yea, in seven [the full number of trials] there shall no evil touch thee" (Jb.5:19).

"Through thee will we push down our enemies: through thy name will we tread them under that rise up against us" (Ps.44:5).

"And *even* to *your* old age I *am* he; and *even* to hoar [gray] hairs will I carry *you*: I have made, and I will bear; even I will carry, and will deliver *you*" (Is.46:4).

"Be not afraid of their faces: for I *am* with thee to deliver thee, saith the LORD" (Je.1:8).

"He delivereth and rescueth, and he worketh signs and wonders in heaven and in earth, who hath delivered Daniel from the power of the lions" (Da.6:27).

CHAPTER 20

C. The Righteous Reign of Hezekiah (Part 3)—His Terminal Illness & Miraculous Healing: The Power of Prayer & the Danger of Pride, 20:1-21

20:1-11; see 2 Chr.32:24-26; Is.38:1-8

20:12-19; see Is.39:1-8

20:20-21; see 2 Chr.32:32-33

1. Hezekiah's terminal illness & healing: The power of prayer

a. Hezekiah's visit by Isaiah & the LORD's message
1) He was to put his affairs in order
2) He was to die, not recover

b. Hezekiah's earnest prayer
1) He turned his face to the wall & prayed
2) He reminded God of three facts
   • His faithful walk
   • His loyal heart
   • His righteous behavior
3) He wept bitterly: Submitted his life to God's will

c. Hezekiah's prayer immediately answered by God: Before Isaiah left the palace courtyard
1) The LORD sent Isaiah back to Hezekiah with a second message
   • God would heal him: He would arise on the third day, go up to the temple, & worship
   • God would add 15 years to his life

   • God would deliver him & Jerusalem from Assyria: For God's honor & for David's sake

2) The prophet had a treatment prepared: An ointment of fig leaves
3) The king recovered

d. Hezekiah's request for a sign from Isaiah: To assure that he would be healed, would worship in the temple

1) The LORD granted the request to prove His promise: Gave the king a choice that involved moving the sun's shadow on a sundial ten degrees backward or ten degrees forward

In those days was Hezekiah sick unto death. And the prophet Isaiah the son of Amoz came to him, and said unto him, Thus saith the LORD, Set thine house in order; for thou shalt die, and not live.
2 Then he turned his face to the wall, and prayed unto the LORD, saying,
3 I beseech thee, O LORD, remember now how I have walked before thee in truth and with a perfect heart, and have done *that which is* good in thy sight. And Hezekiah wept sore.
4 And it came to pass, afore Isaiah was gone out into the middle court, that the word of the LORD came to him, saying,
5 Turn again, and tell Hezekiah the captain of my people, Thus saith the LORD, the God of David thy father, I have heard thy prayer, I have seen thy tears: behold, I will heal thee: on the third day thou shalt go up unto the house of the LORD.
6 And I will add unto thy days fifteen years; and I will deliver thee and this city out of the hand of the king of Assyria; and I will defend this city for mine own sake, and for my servant David's sake.
7 And Isaiah said, Take a lump of figs. And they took and laid *it* on the boil, and he recovered.
8 And Hezekiah said unto Isaiah, What *shall be* the sign that the LORD will heal me, and that I shall go up into the house of the LORD the third day?
9 And Isaiah said, This sign shalt thou have of the LORD, that the LORD will do the thing that he hath spoken: shall the shadow go forward ten degrees, or go back ten degrees?

10 And Hezekiah answered, It is a light thing for the shadow to go down ten degrees: nay, but let the shadow return backward ten degrees.
11 And Isaiah the prophet cried unto the LORD: and he brought the shadow ten degrees backward, by which it had gone down in the dial of Ahaz.
12 At that time Berodachbaladan, the son of Baladan, king of Babylon, sent letters and a present unto Hezekiah: for he had heard that Hezekiah had been sick.
13 And Hezekiah hearkened unto them, and showed them all the house of his precious things, the silver, and the gold, and the spices, and the precious ointment, and *all* the house of his armour, and all that was found in his treasures: there was nothing in his house, nor in all his dominion, that Hezekiah showed them not.
14 Then came Isaiah the prophet unto king Hezekiah, and said unto him, What said these men? and from whence came they unto thee? And Hezekiah said, They are come from a far country, *even* from Babylon.
15 And he said, What have they seen in thine house? And Hezekiah answered, All *the things* that *are* in mine house have they seen: there is nothing among my treasures that I have not showed them.
16 And Isaiah said unto Hezekiah, Hear the word of the LORD.
17 Behold, the days come, that all that *is* in thine house, and that which thy fathers have laid up in store unto this day, shall be carried into Babylon: nothing shall be left, saith the LORD.
18 And of thy sons that shall issue from thee, which thou shalt beget, shall they take away; and they shall be eunuchs in the palace of the king of Babylon.
19 Then said Hezekiah unto Isaiah, Good is the word of the LORD which thou hast spoken. And he said, *Is it* not *good*, if peace and truth be in my days?

2) The king chose for the shadow to move backward ten degrees

3) The prophet called upon the LORD & the miracle occurred: The shadow of the sundial actually moved back ten degrees

2. Hezekiah's unwise entertainment of ambassadors from Babylon: A picture of pride, 2 Chr.32:25

a. The concern of Babylon's crown prince over Hezekiah's illness
b. The warm reception of Hezekiah & his foolish, prideful entertainment of the Babylonian representatives
1) He obviously shared the story of his healing
2) He foolishly, pridefully showed them his vast wealth in the palace treasury & throughout the kingdom

c. The rebuke of the LORD through His prophet Isaiah
1) Isaiah confronted & questioned Hezekiah about his unwise entertainment of the ambassadors

2) Hezekiah made no attempt to hide his actions, but freely shared what he had done: He had shown them the wealth, the treasuries of the nation

d. The judgment of God pronounced upon Hezekiah & Judah due to Hezekiah's pride & the sins of the nation down through the centuries
1) Some day Babylon would conquer Judah & carry off all the wealth of the nation

2) Some of Hezekiah's descendants would be exiled to Babylon

e. The repentance of Hezekiah
1) He humbly accepted God's Judgment
2) He privately questioned if he would finish his days in peace & security

f. The achievements & summary of Hezekiah's life 1) His reign & his major building project (constructing a water tunnel for Jerusalem): Recorded	20 And the rest of the acts of Hezekiah, and all his might, and how he made a pool, and a conduit, and brought water into the city, *are* they not written in the book of the	chronicles of the kings of Judah? 21 And Hezekiah slept with his fathers: and Manasseh his son reigned in his stead.	in the book *The History of the Kings of Judah* 2) His death, 2 Chr.32:33 3) His successor: Manasseh, his son

DIVISION IV

THE UTTER DISINTEGRATION AND FALL OF JUDAH, THE SOUTHERN KINGDOM: AN APPALLING DESTRUCTION DUE TO INCONSISTENCY, DISLOYALTY, AND EVER-GROWING WICKEDNESS, 18:1–25:30

C. The Righteous Reign of Hezekiah (Part 3)—His Terminal Illness and Miraculous Healing: The Power of Prayer and the Danger of Pride, 20:1-21

(20:1-21) **Introduction—Flesh, Fact, Is Corruptible and Decaying—Flesh, Needs of, Deliverance from Corruption—Prayer, Results, Deliverance—Pride, Results, Condemnation and Judgment**: in looking at ourselves as human beings, we realize that we are mere creatures of flesh and bone, made of decaying matter. In addition, our flesh is subject to numerous illnesses and injuries, many of which can severely cripple or shorten our lives. When we consider that we live in bodies of flesh and also in a corruptible world, a great need is immediately apparent. What is this need? The need to be delivered from this corruptible flesh and from all the diseases and accidents that happen to us in life. When disease strikes or an accident happens that severely injure us, we need a deliverer, a rescuer, a savior.

In such times, God's Holy Word gives us wonderful news: the LORD is available to help us. The LORD will rescue and deliver us from this corruptible flesh and through all the diseases and injuries that happen to us. *Through* our prayers—our calling out to God for help—and *because* of our prayers, God says He will deliver us. The importance of prayer is one of the great lessons taught in this present passage of Scripture.

But there is also another great lesson: the danger of pride. Nothing will condemn our souls before God quicker than the sin of pride. These two great lessons are clearly demonstrated in the life of King Hezekiah, the subject of the present Scripture. This is: *The Righteous Reign of Hezekiah (Part 3)—His Terminal Illness and Miraculous Healing: The Power of Prayer and the Danger of Pride, 20:1-21.*

1. Hezekiah's terminal illness and healing: the power of prayer (vv.1-11).
2. Hezekiah's unwise entertainment of ambassadors from Babylon: a picture of pride, 2 Chr.32:25 (vv.12-21).

1 (20:1-11) **Prayer, Power of—Sickness, Healed by—Illness, Healed by—Disease, Healed by—Healing, Source of, Prayer—Hezekiah, Terminal Illness of**: shockingly, right after the deliverance of Jerusalem from the Assyrian threat, Hezekiah became deathly sick and as soon to die. The actual date of Hezekiah's death was in 686 B.C., which means that his illness took place somewhere around 701 B.C., in the very year of Assyria's invasion (see Is.38).[1] In facing his illness, Hezekiah shows us the power of prayer:

OUTLINE	SCRIPTURE	SCRIPTURE	OUTLINE
1. Hezekiah's terminal illness & healing: The power of prayer	In those days was Hezekiah sick unto death. And the	the LORD came to him, saying,	courtyard
a. Hezekiah's visit by Isaiah & the LORD's message	prophet Isaiah the son of Amoz came to him, and said	5 Turn again, and tell Hezekiah the captain of my people, Thus saith the LORD, the	1) The LORD sent Isaiah back to Hezekiah with a second message
1) He was to put his affairs in order	unto him, Thus saith the LORD, Set thine house in order; for thou shalt die, and	God of David thy father, I have heard thy	• God would heal him: He would arise on the third day, go up to the temple,
2) He was to die, not recover	not live.	prayer, I have seen thy tears: behold, I will heal thee: on	& worship
b. Hezekiah's earnest prayer	2 Then he turned his face to the wall, and prayed unto the	the third day thou shalt go up unto the house of the	• God would add 15 years to his life
1) He turned his face to the wall & prayed	LORD, saying,	LORD.	
2) He reminded God of three facts	3 I beseech thee, O LORD, remember now how I have	6 And I will add unto thy days fifteen years; and I will	• God would deliver him & Jerusalem from As-
• His faithful walk	walked before thee in truth	deliver thee and this city out	syria: For God's honor
• His loyal heart	and with a perfect heart, and	of the hand of the king of As-	& for David's sake
• His righteous behavior	have done *that which is* good	syria; and I will defend this	
3) He wept bitterly: Submitted his life to God's will	in thy sight. And Hezekiah wept sore.	city for mine own sake, and for my servant David's sake.	
c. Hezekiah's prayer immediately answered by God: Before Isaiah left the palace	4 And it came to pass, afore Isaiah was gone out into the middle court, that the word of	7 And Isaiah said, Take a lump of figs. And they took	2) The prophet had a treatment prepared: An

---
1 John F. Walvoord and Roy B. Zuck, Editors. *The Bible Knowledge Commentary, Old Testament*, p.578.

OUTLINE	SCRIPTURE	SCRIPTURE	OUTLINE
ointment of fig leaves 3) The king recovered d. Hezekiah's request for a sign from Isaiah: To assure that he would be healed, would worship in the temple 1) The LORD granted the request to prove His promise: Gave the king a choice that involved moving the sun's shadow on a sundial	and laid *it* on the boil, and he recovered. 8 And Hezekiah said unto Isaiah, What *shall be* the sign that the LORD will heal me, and that I shall go up into the house of the LORD the third day? 9 And Isaiah said, This sign shalt thou have of the LORD, that the LORD will do the thing that he hath spoken: shall the shadow go forward	ten degrees, or go back ten degrees? 10 And Hezekiah answered, It is a light thing for the shadow to go down ten degrees: nay, but let the shadow return backward ten degrees. 11 And Isaiah the prophet cried unto the LORD: and he brought the shadow ten degrees backward, by which it had gone down in the dial of Ahaz.	ten degrees backward or ten degrees forward 2) The king chose for the shadow to move backward ten degrees 3) The prophet called upon the LORD & the miracle occurred: The shadow of the sundial actually moved back ten degrees

a. Right before Hezekiah's death, the LORD sent Isaiah to the king with the message that he was to put his affairs in order. For he was soon to die (v.1).

b. But note how Hezekiah received the fatal news: he immediately turned his face to the wall away from Isaiah and began to pray to the LORD (vv.2-3). He reminded the LORD of three facts:

⇒ He was faithful in following the LORD.
⇒ He was loyal and wholly devoted to the LORD.
⇒ He had behaved righteously before the LORD.

Then Hezekiah began to weep bitterly (v.3). By weeping, he was indicating that his heart was broken, that he was submitting his life to the LORD's will.

c. In compassion, the LORD immediately answered the prayer of King Hezekiah (vv.4-7). Obviously, Isaiah had already left the room heading for home when the king began to pray. For before Isaiah had left the palace courtyard, a message came to him from the LORD (vv.4-7). Isaiah was to return immediately to Hezekiah with a second message. God had heard his prayer and seen his brokenness; therefore the LORD would heal him. On the third day he would arise, go up to the temple, and worship the LORD. In fact, the LORD would add 15 years to his life and would deliver him and Jerusalem from Assyria (v.6). For God's honor and for David's sake, the LORD would defend the capital and not allow it to fall to the Assyrians. Note how this promise points toward the terminal illness' striking Hezekiah during the actual siege of Jerusalem by the Assyrians.

Turning to the servants, Isaiah instructed them to prepare an ointment of fig leaves to place upon the king. In obedience to the prophet, they nursed the king and he soon recovered.

d. Hezekiah, needing assurance from the LORD, requested a sign from Isaiah that he would recover and worship in the temple on the third day (vv.8-11). The LORD proved His promise and granted the request of the sick king. He gave Hezekiah a choice that involved moving the sun's shadow on the king's sundial either 10 degrees backward or 10 degrees forward. Choosing the more difficult miracle, Hezekiah asked for the shadow to move backward 10 degrees (v.10). As requested, the prophet Isaiah called upon the LORD and the miracle occurred (v.11). The shadow of the sundial actually moved back 10 degrees.

Thought 1. There is no limit to the power of prayer, for there is no limit to God's power. God is omnipotent, all-powerful, possessing perfect and unlimited power to do anything He desires. But God is not only omnipotent, He is omniscient, knowing all things. Nothing is hidden from God, out of His sight. God sees and knows all things.

In this message of God's omnipotence and omniscience is the most wonderful news. For God knows when serious illnesses strikes us or crises confront us. And God has the power to handle our serious illnesses and the severe crises. When we face these mammoth problems, our responsibility is to pray, turning our face toward the LORD and crying out to Him. If we are sincere and willing to turn our lives totally over to Him, God will hear and answer our prayer. In some cases, He will miraculously heal us. In other cases, He will give us the strength to walk through the illness or crisis victoriously. Through prayer there is nothing—absolutely nothing—that can defeat or overcome us, not even death itself. God knows the very number of hairs upon our head—everything about us—and God has the power to help us. Listen to what God's Word says about the *power of prayer*.

"**Ask, and it shall be given you; seek, and ye shall find; knock, and it shall be opened unto you**" (**Mt.7:7**).

"**Therefore I say unto you, What things soever ye desire, when ye pray, believe that ye receive *them*, and ye shall have *them*" (**Mk.11:24**).

"**If ye abide in me, and my words abide in you, ye shall ask what ye will, and it shall be done unto you**" (**Jn.15:7**).

"**Hitherto have ye asked nothing in my name: ask, and ye shall receive, that your joy may be full**" (**Jn.16:24**).

"**For this thing I besought the Lord thrice, that it might depart from me. And he said unto me, My grace is sufficient for thee: for my strength is made perfect in weakness. Most gladly therefore will I rather glory in my infirmities, that the power of Christ may rest upon me. Therefore I take pleasure in infirmities, in reproaches, in necessities, in persecutions, in distresses for Christ's sake: for when I am weak, then am I strong**" (**2 Co.12:8-10**).

"**Now unto him that is able to do exceeding abundantly above all that we ask or think, according to the power that worketh in us**" (**Ep.3:20**).

"And the prayer of faith shall save the sick, and the Lord shall raise him up; and if he have committed sins, they shall be forgiven him. Confess *your* faults one to another, and pray one for another, that ye may be healed. The effectual fervent prayer of a righteous man availeth much. Elias was a man subject to like passions as we are, and he prayed earnestly that it might not rain: and it rained not on the earth by the space of three years and six months. And he prayed again, and the heaven gave rain, and the earth brought forth her fruit" (Js.5:15-18).

"And whatsoever we ask, we receive of him, because we keep his commandments, and do those things that are pleasing in his sight" (1 Jn.3:22).

"Call unto me, and I will answer thee, and show thee great and mighty things, which thou knowest not" (Je.33:3).

2 (20:12-21) **Pride, Example of—Arrogance, Example of—Self-Exaltation, Example of—Hezekiah, Pride of**: although Hezekiah was righteous and totally committed to the LORD, he was not perfect. Soon after his illness, he unwisely entertained some ambassadors from Babylon, and in his entertaining he exposed a heart of pride and self-exaltation. Because of his pride, the judgment of God was pronounced upon him and a prediction made concerning the future destiny of the nation. In a very straightforward manner, Scripture shares the story of the king's pride.

OUTLINE	SCRIPTURE	SCRIPTURE	OUTLINE

2. Hezekiah's unwise entertainment of ambassadors from Babylon: A picture of pride, 2 Chr.32:25
a. The concern of Babylon's crown prince over Hezekiah's illness
b. The warm reception of Hezekiah & his foolish, prideful entertainment of the Babylonian representatives
  1) He obviously shared the story of his healing
  2) He foolishly, pridefully showed them his vast wealth in the palace treasury & throughout the kingdom
 	
c. The rebuke of the LORD through His prophet Isaiah
  1) Isaiah confronted & questioned Hezekiah about his unwise entertainment of the ambassadors
 	
  2) Hezekiah made no attempt to hide his actions, but freely shared what he had done: He had shown them the wealth, the treasuries of the nation
	12 At that time Berodach-baladan, the son of Baladan, king of Babylon, sent letters and a present unto Hezekiah: for he had heard that Hezekiah had been sick. 13 And Hezekiah hearkened unto them, and showed them all the house of his precious things, the silver, and the gold, and the spices, and the precious ointment, and *all* the house of his armour, and all that was found in his treasures: there was nothing in his house, nor in all his dominion, that Hezekiah showed them not. 14 Then came Isaiah the prophet unto king Hezekiah, and said unto him, What said these men? and from whence came they unto thee? And Hezekiah said, They are come from a far country, *even* from Babylon. 15 And he said, What have they seen in thine house? And Hezekiah answered, All *the things* that *are* in mine house have they seen: there is nothing among my treasures that I have not showed them.	16 And Isaiah said unto Hezekiah, Hear the word of the LORD. 17 Behold, the days come, that all that *is* in thine house, and that which thy fathers have laid up in store unto this day, shall be carried into Babylon: nothing shall be left, saith the LORD. 18 And of thy sons that shall issue from thee, which thou shalt beget, shall they take away; and they shall be eunuchs in the palace of the king of Babylon. 19 Then said Hezekiah unto Isaiah, Good is the word of the LORD which thou hast spoken. And he said, *Is it* not *good*, if peace and truth be in my days? 20 And the rest of the acts of Hezekiah, and all his might, and how he made a pool, and a conduit, and brought water into the city, *are* they not written in the book of the chronicles of the kings of Judah? 21 And Hezekiah slept with his fathers: and Manasseh his son reigned in his stead.	d. The judgment of God pronounced upon Hezekiah & Judah due to Hezekiah's pride & the sins of the nation down through the centuries
			  1) Some day Babylon would conquer Judah & carry off all the wealth of the nation
			
			  2) Some of Hezekiah's descendants would be exiled to Babylon
			
			e. The repentance of Hezekiah
			  1) He humbly accepted God's Judgment
			  2) He privately questioned if he would finish his days in peace & security
			f. The achievements & summary of Hezekiah's life
			  1) His reign & his major building project (constructing a water tunnel for Jerusalem): Recorded in the book *The History of the Kings of Judah*
			  2) His death, 2 Chr.32:33
			  3) His successor: Manasseh, his son

a. Hearing about Hezekiah's deathly illness, the crown prince of Babylon, Berodach-Baladan, sent a letter and some gifts to Hezekiah as an expression of his concern (v.12). Why would the crown prince of Babylon, the soon to be superpower of the world, want to express his concern for Hezekiah? *Second Chronicles* tells us that his curiosity was aroused when he heard about the miraculous healing of Hezekiah and the movement of the sundial (2 Chr.32:31). But additional information is supplied by the Jewish historian Josephus. He says that the king of Babylon sought Hezekiah as a friend and ally.[2]

b. Whatever Berodach-Baladan's purpose, Hezekiah gave the ambassadors a warm reception (v.13). With pride swelling up in his heart, Hezekiah entertained the envoys by sharing the story of his healing and then foolishly, pridefully showed them his vast wealth. There was nothing in his palace or throughout the kingdom that he failed to show them. Obviously, this included the strength of his military as well as the wealth found in the palace and temple treasuries.

c. As would be expected, the LORD immediately rebuked Hezekiah through the prophet Isaiah (vv.14-15). Isaiah confronted the king and questioned him about his entertainment of the ambassadors. Making no attempt to hide his actions, Hezekiah freely shared what he had done. He had shown them the wealth, the treasuries of the nation.

---

2 Flavius Josephus. *Antiquities of the Jews*. "Complete Works." Book 10, Ch.2, p.214.

d. Sadly, but with the authority of God Himself, the prophet Isaiah pronounced God's judgment upon Hezekiah and Judah. Due to Hezekiah's pride and the sins of the nation down through the centuries, Judah would face condemnation of God (vv.16-18). Some day in the near future, Babylon would conquer Judah and carry off all the wealth of the nation. What the Babylonian ambassadors had seen—all the wealth of the nation—would not be forgotten. Future leaders of Babylon would covet the wealth shown by Hezekiah in his moment of self-exaltation and pride. Moreover, some of Hezekiah's descendents would be exiled to Babylon and be forced to serve as eunuchs (devoted slaves) in the palace of Babylon's king.

e. In a spirit of repentance, Hezekiah humbly accepted God's judgment (v.19). But in his private thoughts, he was wondering and asking himself if he would finish out his days in peace and security.

f. His achievements in life are recorded in the book *The History of the Kings of Judah* (vv.20-21). Also recorded in the book is his major building project, that of constructing a water tunnel for Jerusalem. After his death, he was succeeded by his son Manasseh (v.21).

Thought 1. Pride is a terrible evil. When a person begins to look upon himself as being superior to or better than other people, he…
- exalts himself over others, applauding his own efforts
- feels that he should be preferred over others
- considers himself to be more valuable than others

A person who is full of pride and self-exaltation is often arrogant, overbearing, and disrespectful. He frequently puts other people down, degrades, shames, embarrasses, stifles, harms, subjects, and in some cases even enslaves others. For this reason, God strongly condemns pride and the exalting of ourselves above others:

"And whosoever shall exalt himself shall be abased; and he that shall humble himself shall be exalted" (Mt.23:12).

"*Be* of the same mind one toward another. Mind not high things, but condescend to men of low estate. Be not wise in your own conceits" (Ro.12:16).

"And if any man think that he knoweth any thing, he knoweth nothing yet as he ought to know" (1 Co.8:2).

"For if a man think himself to be something, when he is nothing, he deceiveth himself" (Ga.6:3).

"But he giveth more grace. Wherefore he saith, God resisteth the proud, but giveth grace unto the humble" (Js.4:6).

"For all that *is* in the world, the lust of the flesh, and the lust of the eyes, and the pride of life, is not of the Father, but is of the world" (1 Jn.2:16).

"The wicked in *his* pride doth persecute the poor: let them be taken in the devices that they have imagined" (Ps.10:2).

"They that trust in their wealth, and boast themselves in the multitude of their riches; None *of them* can by any means redeem his brother, nor give to God a ransom for him" (Ps.49:6-7).

"Thou hast rebuked the proud *that are* cursed, which do err from thy commandments" (Ps.119:21).

"Be not wise in thine own eyes: fear the LORD, and depart from evil" (Pr.3:7).

"These six *things* doth the LORD hate: yea, seven *are* an abomination unto him: A proud look, a lying tongue, and hands that shed innocent blood, An heart that deviseth wicked imaginations, feet that be swift in running to mischief, A false witness *that* speaketh lies, and he that soweth discord among brethren" (Pr.6:16-19).

"An heart that deviseth wicked imaginations, feet that be swift in running to mischief" (Pr.6:18).

"*When* pride cometh, then cometh shame: but with the lowly *is* wisdom" (Pr.11:2).

"An high look, and a proud heart, *and* the plowing of the wicked, *is* sin" (Pr.21:4).

"Seest thou a man wise in his own conceit? *there is* more hope of a fool than of him" (Pr.26:12).

"A man's pride shall bring him low: but honour shall uphold the humble in spirit" (Pr.29:23).

"He that is of a proud heart stirreth up strife: but he that putteth his trust in the LORD shall be made fat" (Pr.28:25).

"Woe unto *them that are* wise in their own eyes, and prudent in their own sight" (Is.5:21).

"For thou hast said in thine heart, I will ascend into heaven, I will exalt my throne above the stars of God: I will sit also upon the mount of the congregation, in the sides of the north: I will ascend above the heights of the clouds; I will be like the most High. Yet thou shalt be brought down to hell, to the sides of the pit" (Is.14:13-15).

"Son of man, say unto the prince of Tyrus, Thus saith the Lord GOD; Because thine heart *is* lifted up, and thou hast said, I *am* a God, I sit *in* the seat of God, in the midst of the seas; yet thou *art* a man, and not God, though thou set thine heart as the heart of God: Behold, thou *art* wiser than Daniel; there is no secret that they can hide from thee: With thy wisdom and with thine understanding thou hast gotten thee riches, and hast gotten gold and silver into thy treasures: By thy great wisdom *and* by thy traffic hast thou increased thy riches, and thine heart is lifted up because of thy riches: Therefore thus saith the Lord GOD; Because thou hast set thine heart as the heart of God; Behold, therefore I will bring strangers upon thee, the terrible of the nations: and they shall draw their swords against the beauty of thy wisdom, and they shall defile thy brightness. They shall bring thee down to the pit, and thou shalt die the deaths of *them that are* slain in the midst of the seas" (Eze.28:2-8).

"Though thou exalt *thyself* as the eagle, and though thou set thy nest among the stars, thence will I bring thee down, saith the LORD" (Obad.4).

CHAPTER 21

D. The Evil Reigns of Manasseh & Amon: A Look at the Terrible Depths of Wicked Behavior, 21:1-26

21:1-9; see 2 Chr.33:1-16
21:17-24; see 2 Chr.33:18-25

1. The evil reign of Manasseh: Rejecting the godly example of parents
  a. His background
    1) His age: Only 12 years old
    2) His term: 55 years
  b. His wicked perversions toward God
    1) He lived a wicked life
    2) He followed the detestable practices of the worldly nations
    3) He rebuilt the high places (pagan worship sites)
    4) He constructed altars to Baal & images (poles) of Asherah
    5) He introduced the Assyrian worship of the sun, moon, & stars, the Astral deities
    6) He actually built altars to the heavenly bodies & placed them in the temple of the LORD, the very sanctuary built to honor God's name alone

    7) He practiced human sacrifice, offering his own son
    8) He lived in the world of the occult: Practiced sorcery & divination (witchcraft); consulted mediums & spiritists (psychics)

    9) He set a carved pole—an image symbolizing the goddess Asherah—in the temple: Showed utter contempt for God's name & His temple

    10) He completely disregarded God's promises, law, & commandments: Rejected the Mosaic covenant

    11) He was a stumbling block, led the people astray
      • They refused to listen to

Manasseh *was* twelve years old when he began to reign, and reigned fifty and five years in Jerusalem. And his mother's name *was* Hephzibah.
2 And he did *that which was* evil in the sight of the LORD, after the abominations of the heathen, whom the LORD cast out before the children of Israel.
3 For he built up again the high places which Hezekiah his father had destroyed; and he reared up altars for Baal, and made a grove, as did Ahab king of Israel; and worshipped all the host of heaven, and served them.
4 And he built altars in the house of the LORD, of which the LORD said, In Jerusalem will I put my name.
5 And he built altars for all the host of heaven in the two courts of the house of the LORD.
6 And he made his son pass through the fire, and observed times, and used enchantments, and dealt with familiar spirits and wizards: he wrought much wickedness in the sight of the LORD, to provoke *him* to anger.
7 And he set a graven image of the grove that he had made in the house, of which the LORD said to David, and to Solomon his son, In this house, and in Jerusalem, which I have chosen out of all tribes of Israel, will I put my name for ever:
8 Neither will I make the feet of Israel move any more out of the land which I gave their fathers; only if they will observe to do according to all that I have commanded them, and according to all the law that my servant Moses commanded them.
9 But they hearkened not: and Manasseh seduced them to do more evil than did the

nations whom the LORD destroyed before the children of Israel.
10 And the LORD spake by his servants the prophets, saying,
11 Because Manasseh king of Judah hath done these abominations, *and* hath done wickedly above all that the Amorites did, which *were* before him, and hath made Judah also to sin with his idols:
12 Therefore thus saith the LORD God of Israel, Behold, I *am* bringing *such* evil upon Jerusalem and Judah, that whosoever heareth of it, both his ears shall tingle.
13 And I will stretch over Jerusalem the line of Samaria, and the plummet of the house of Ahab: and I will wipe Jerusalem as *a man* wipeth a dish, wiping *it,* and turning *it* upside down.
14 And I will forsake the remnant of mine inheritance, and deliver them into the hand of their enemies; and they shall become a prey and a spoil to all their enemies;
15 Because they have done *that which was* evil in my sight, and have provoked me to anger, since the day their fathers came forth out of Egypt, even unto this day.
16 Moreover Manasseh shed innocent blood very much, till he had filled Jerusalem from one end to another; beside his sin wherewith he made Judah to sin, in doing *that which was* evil in the sight of the LORD.
17 Now the rest of the acts of Manasseh, and all that he did, and his sin that he sinned, *are* they not written in the book of the chronicles of the kings of Judah?
18 And Manasseh slept with his fathers, and was buried in the garden of his own house, in the garden of Uzza: and Amon his son reigned in his stead.
19 Amon *was* twenty and two years old when he began to reign, and he reigned two years in Jerusalem. And his mother's name *was* Meshullemeth, the daughter of Haruz of Jotbah.
20 And he did *that which*

God's Word
    • They did even more evil than other nations
  c. His & Judah's judgment pronounced by God

    1) God had warned the people through the prophets about following Manasseh, Je.2:9-13; Am.9:7; Hab.1:5
      • His detestable sins
      • His wickedness
      • His idolatry
    2) God was going to bring disaster upon them, a disaster that would shock people, make their ears tingle with horror

    3) God was going to use His measuring (plumb) line of judgment to totally wipe them out, Am.7:7-9
      • Just like Samaria (Israel) & Ahab's dynasty
      • Just like a person wipes all dirt from a dish
    4) God was going to reject wicked Judah, the last remnant (survivors) of His inheritance: To be handed over as plunder to their enemies
      • Because of their unbelief & evil—all the wickedness committed since their deliverance from Egypt

      • Because Manasseh shed *so much* innocent blood, 9:7, 26
      • Because Manasseh led the people so far astray
      • Because the people did so much evil

  d. His achievements & the summary of his life, including his terrible sins
    1) His reign: Recorded in the book *The History of the Kings of Judah*
    2) His death: Buried in the palace garden of Uzza
    3) His successor: Amon, his son

2. The evil reign of Amon: Following the evil example of parents
  a. His background
    1) His age: 22
    2) His term: Only 2 years (642–640 B.C.)
  b. His evil reign

1) Lived a wicked life	*was* evil in the sight of the LORD, as his father Manasseh did.	24 And the people of the land slew all them that had conspired against king Amon; and the people of the land made Josiah his son king in his stead.	2) The assassins were caught & executed by a popular uprising of the people
2) Walked in the evil ways of his father	21 And he walked in all the way that his father walked in, and served the idols that his father served, and worshipped them:		3) The people made his son Josiah king
3) Worshipped the false gods his father had worshipped			
4) Forsook the LORD	22 And he forsook the LORD God of his fathers, and walked not in the way of the LORD.	25 Now the rest of the acts of Amon which he did, *are* they not written in the book of the chronicles of the kings of Judah?	d. His achievements & the summary of his life
5) Refused to follow the way of the LORD			1) His reign: Recorded in the book *The History of the Kings of Judah*
c. His assassination	23 And the servants of Amon conspired against him, and slew the king in his own house.	26 And he was buried in his sepulchre in the garden of Uzza: and Josiah his son reigned in his stead.	2) His burial: In the garden of Uzza
1) The plot was carried out by his own officials in the palace			3) His successor: Josiah, his son

DIVISION IV

THE UTTER DISINTEGRATION AND FALL OF JUDAH, THE SOUTHERN KINGDOM: AN APPALLING DESTRUCTION DUE TO INCONSISTENCY, DISLOYALTY, AND EVER-GROWING WICKEDNESS, 18:1–25:30

D. The Evil Reigns of Manasseh and Amon: A Look at the Terrible Depths of Wicked Behavior, 21:1-26

(21:1-26) **Introduction—Evil, Acts of, Listed—Sin, Acts of, Listed—World, Fallen, Proof—Man, Fallen, Proof—Depravity, Proof**: throughout the world today, how many people are filled with hostility and are seeking revenge? How many are terrorists or warmongers? How many wars are being fought? How many murders were committed this past week in our nation? In your state? City? Community? In addition to murder, think of all the rapes, assaults, and abuse of children, women, and men. Think of all the robberies and other acts of violence and lawlessness committed. How many people lied, stole, or cheated? How many committed adultery or some other illicit sexual act? How often this past week has God's name been used in vain, cursed, or other words of profanity uttered? How many people have worshipped a false god—or no god at all—instead of worshipping the LORD God Himself (Jehovah, Yahweh)?

When we think of all the acts of evil that occur within the world on any given day, we can come to only one conclusion: we live in a world that has fallen to the very depths of depravity. We live in a world where lawlessness and violence are commonplace, and immorality and the worship of false gods are merely alternative life choices.

The present Scripture covers the reigns of two evil kings—Manasseh and his son Amon—who ruled in the Southern Kingdom of Judah. In looking at the reigns of these two evil kings, we also see the terrible depths of wicked behavior.

As this passage is studied, keep in mind that the Assyrian empire dominated much of the world of that day. It was Assyria that had conquered the Northern Kingdom of Israel, deporting and scattering the Israelites throughout the empire of Assyria. Now to the present Scripture. This is: *The Evil Reigns of Manasseh and Amon: A Look at the Terrible Depths of Wicked Behavior, 21:1-26.*

1. The evil reign of Manasseh: rejecting the godly example of parents (vv.1-18).
2. The evil reign of Amon: following the evil example of parents (vv.19-26).

1 (21:1-18) **Example, Godly, Rejecting—Parents, Godly, Rejected by, Children—Children, Rejecting, Godly Parents—Manasseh, King of Judah, Evil Reign of—Kings, of Judah, Manasseh—Southern Kingdom of Judah**: the evil reign of Manasseh dramatically shows how a child can reject the godly example of parents. His father Hezekiah had lived a strong, righteous life and had done more for the people of Judah than any king had before or after him, except perhaps for David (18:3). But not Manasseh. Instead of following in the righteous steps of his father, he chose to follow the wicked steps of his grandfather Ahaz. Among all the kings of Judah, Manasseh and his grandfather Ahaz were the most wicked and did more to bring about the downfall of Judah than any other kings (see outline and note—2 K.16:1-20 for more discussion). Just how evil Manasseh was can be gleaned from three descriptive statements made about him: first, he reestablished false worship in Judah just as wicked Ahab had done in the Northern Kingdom of Israel (v.3). Second, he did *much* that was evil, wicked in the sight of God (v.6). Third, even the prophets charged him with committing *more evil* than the wicked, immoral Amorites or Canaanites who had lived in the land before Israel (v.11).

Glance down through the eighteen verses that record his life and note how no achievement is mentioned: no political, military, or public works project, not a single one. Although Manasseh had the longest reign of any king in Judah, the only facts recorded about him are his wicked perversions toward God. What a terrible legacy to leave to the world.

OUTLINE	SCRIPTURE	SCRIPTURE	OUTLINE
1. The evil reign of Manasseh: Rejecting the godly example of parents	Manasseh *was* twelve years old when he began to reign, and reigned fifty and five years in Jerusalem. And his mother's name *was* Hephzi-bah.	nations whom the LORD destroyed before the children of Israel.	God's Word • They did even more evil than other nations
a. His background	2 And he did *that which was* evil in the sight of the LORD, after the abominations of the heathen, whom the LORD cast out before the children of Israel.	10 And the LORD spake by his servants the prophets, saying,	c. His & Judah's judgment pronounced by God
1) His age: Only 12 years old		11 Because Manasseh king of Judah hath done these abominations, *and* hath done wickedly above all that the Amorites did, which *were* before him, and hath made Judah also to sin with his idols:	1) God had warned the people through the prophets about following Manasseh, Je.2:9-13; Am.9:7; Hab.1:5
2) His term: 55 years			• His detestable sins
b. His wicked perversions toward God			• His wickedness
1) He lived a wicked life			• His idolatry
2) He followed the detestable practices of the worldly nations	3 For he built up again the high places which Hezekiah his father had destroyed; and he reared up altars for Baal, and made a grove, as did Ahab king of Israel; and worshipped all the host of heaven, and served them.	12 Therefore thus saith the LORD God of Israel, Behold, I *am* bringing *such* evil upon Jerusalem and Judah, that whosoever heareth of it, both his ears shall tingle.	2) God was going to bring disaster upon them, a disaster that would shock people, make their ears tingle with horror
3) He rebuilt the high places (pagan worship sites)			
4) He constructed altars to Baal & images (poles) of Asherah		13 And I will stretch over Jerusalem the line of Samaria, and the plummet of the house of Ahab: and I will wipe Jerusalem as *a man* wipeth a dish, wiping *it,* and turning *it* upside down.	3) God was going to use His measuring (plumb) line of judgment to totally wipe them out, Am.7:7-9
5) He introduced the Assyrian worship of the sun, moon, & stars, the Astral deities	4 And he built altars in the house of the LORD, of which the LORD said, In Jerusalem will I put my name.		• Just like Samaria (Israel) & Ahab's dynasty
6) He actually built altars to the heavenly bodies & placed them in the temple of the LORD, the very sanctuary built to honor God's name alone	5 And he built altars for all the host of heaven in the two courts of the house of the LORD.		• Just like a person wipes all dirt from a dish
		14 And I will forsake the remnant of mine inheritance, and deliver them into the hand of their enemies; and they shall become a prey and a spoil to all their enemies;	4) God was going to reject wicked Judah, the last remnant (survivors) of His inheritance: To be handed over as plunder to their enemies
7) He practiced human sacrifice, offering his own son	6 And he made his son pass through the fire, and observed times, and used enchantments, and dealt with familiar spirits and wizards: he wrought much wickedness in the sight of the LORD, to provoke *him* to anger.	15 Because they have done *that which was* evil in my sight, and have provoked me to anger, since the day their fathers came forth out of Egypt, even unto this day.	• Because of their unbelief & evil—all the wickedness committed since their deliverance from Egypt
8) He lived in the world of the occult: Practiced sorcery & divination (witchcraft); consulted mediums & spiritists (psychics)			
9) He set a carved pole—an image symbolizing the goddess Asherah—in the temple: Showed utter contempt for God's name & His temple	7 And he set a graven image of the grove that he had made in the house, of which the LORD said to David, and to Solomon his son, In this house, and in Jerusalem, which I have chosen out of all tribes of Israel, will I put my name for ever:	16 Moreover Manasseh shed innocent blood very much, till he had filled Jerusalem from one end to another; beside his sin wherewith he made Judah to sin, in doing *that which was* evil in the sight of the LORD.	• Because Manasseh shed *so much* innocent blood, 9:7, 26 • Because Manasseh led the people so far astray • Because the people did so much evil
10) He completely disregarded God's promises, law, & commandments: Rejected the Mosaic covenant	8 Neither will I make the feet of Israel move any more out of the land which I gave their fathers; only if they will observe to do according to all that I have commanded them, and according to all the law that my servant Moses commanded them.	17 Now the rest of the acts of Manasseh, and all that he did, and his sin that he sinned, *are* they not written in the book of the chronicles of the kings of Judah?	d. His achievements & the summary of his life, including his terrible sins 1) His reign: Recorded in the book *The History of the Kings of Judah*
11) He was a stumbling block, led the people astray	9 But they hearkened not: and Manasseh seduced them to do more evil than did the	18 And Manasseh slept with his fathers, and was buried in the garden of his own house, in the garden of Uzza: and Amon his son reigned in his stead.	2) His death: Buried in the palace garden of Uzza 3) His successor: Amon, his son
• They refused to listen to			

a. When only 12 years old, Manasseh began ruling as a co-regent with his father Hezekiah. Apparently, the co-reign with his father was for about 10 years. In all, Manasseh had the longest reign of any king in Judah, 55 years (about 696–642 B.C.). His mother's name was Hephzibah, which means "my delight is in her." During Manasseh's reign, Isaiah the prophet used Hephzibah's name in one of his predictions, prophesying that Jerusalem would some day no longer be called forsaken or desolate but, rather, Hephzibah, "My delight is in her" (Is.62:4).[1]

---

[1] Russell Dilday. *1, 2 Kings*, p.458.

b. A long list of Manasseh's shameful, wicked perversions is now recorded for human history. They stand as a stern warning: wicked behavior—whether by a nation, a government or any individual—will not be tolerated by the LORD. Every person must guard against the seduction of immoral and wicked behavior. At least 11 perversions are listed:

1) Manasseh lived a wicked life, committing evil in the sight of the LORD. Despite having all the privileges of being reared in a godly home, he rejected the righteous example of his parents and pursued the immoral behavior and the false gods of the world (v.2).

2) Manasseh followed the sinful, detestable practices of worldly unbelievers (v.2). As disgusting as the wickedness of the Canaanite nations had been, Manasseh still chose to follow their worldly lifestyles.

3) Manasseh rebuilt the high places, the false worship sites his father Hezekiah had destroyed (v.3).

4) Manasseh constructed altars to the false god Baal and images of the false goddess Asherah. By doing this, he followed in the evil footsteps of Ahab, an earlier king of Israel (1 K.16:33). However, note the next point where Manasseh went far beyond the wicked behavior of Ahab.

5) Manasseh introduced into Judah the Assyrian worship of the sun, moon, and stars, the worship of the Astral deities (v.3). Looking to the heavenly bodies for one's future and destiny was a popular practice in the ancient world just as it has been down through the generations (in such practices as astrology and reading the signs of the zodiac to determine one's future).

6) Manasseh actually built altars to the heavenly bodies and placed them in the temple of the LORD, the very sanctuary built for God's Name and His Name alone (v.4-5). But he not only built these altars in the temple itself, he also built them in the courtyards of the temple, both the outer court used by the people and the inner court used by the priests.

7) Sadly, Manasseh also practiced human sacrifice, offering his very own son as a sacrifice to a false god (v.6). No doubt, he also encouraged human sacrifice throughout the nation in an attempt to appease and secure the favor of the god Molech.

8) Not surprisingly, Manasseh lived in the world of the occult, practicing sorcery and divination (witchcraft), and consulting mediums and spiritists or psychics (v.6).

9) Again showing utter contempt for God's Name and His temple, Manasseh set a carved pole, an image symbolizing the goddess Asherah, in the temple (v.7). Note what Scripture says about this particular act of wickedness: it violated the promise God had given through David and his son Solomon. What was the promise? In this temple—the very temple Manasseh defiled—God had promised to dwell among His people in a very special way and to put His Name upon the temple forever (2 S.7:13; 1 K.8:27).

10) Rejecting the Mosaic covenant, Manasseh completely disregarded God's promises, law, and commandments (v.8). This too was a very serious offense, for the LORD had promised to keep His people in the promised land as long as they obeyed and kept His commandments.

11) Manasseh led the people astray, becoming a stumbling block that was sure to doom them both individually and corporately as a nation (v.9). Refusing to listen to God's Word and to the warnings given to them by the prophets, the people unfortunately did more evil than the unbelieving nations who had earlier lived in Canaan.

c. During such wicked perversions, God cannot sit still doing nothing and taking no action. Once a person or people continue day after day in their sin and wickedness, the LORD is left with no choice. Just as God had warned both the kings and the people down through the years, He now pronounced His judgment upon Manasseh and Judah (vv.10-16).

1) Note that God had not left His people without a witness or warning. Time and again He had sent prophets to give strong warning to the people about following the wicked behavior of King Manasseh (Je.2:9-13; Am.9:7; Hab.1:5). Warnings were necessary because of Manasseh's detestable sins and wicked life. He was committing more evil than the immoral and wicked Amorites who had earlier lived in Canaan.

2) But as noted earlier, the people would not listen to the prophets. They refused to heed their warnings. Consequently, this is what the LORD, the God of Israel, said: He was going to bring disaster upon the people, a disaster that would utterly shock anyone who ever heard about the destruction of Judah. The very ears of the hearers would tingle with horror over the devastation brought about by the hand of God's judgment.

3) In executing the judgment, God would use His measuring line (plumb line) of judgment, totally wiping the people away just as a person cleans a dish by wiping away the dirt and grime. He would wipe them away just as He did Samaria or the Northern Kingdom of Israel and the dynasty of Ahab.

4) Although the people of Judah never expected God to judge them, He was going to reject them. Despite the fact that they were the last remnant or survivors of His inheritance, they were to be handed over as plunder to their enemies (vv.14-16). Note the four reasons for the coming judgment upon the people of Judah:

⇒ Because of their unbelief and evil, all the wickedness they had committed since their deliverance from Egypt (v.15).

⇒ Because Manasseh had shed so much innocent blood, so much that the blood ran from one end of Jerusalem to the other (v.16; 9:7, 26). Who were these murdered victims? Children sacrificed to the false god Molech? Prophets? Genuine believers who remained loyal to the LORD and were therefore persecuted by Manasseh? Nothing is known other than what is recorded here.

⇒ Because Manasseh had been a terrible stumbling block, leading the people far away from the LORD (v.16).

⇒ Because the people themselves had committed so much evil in the sight of the LORD (v.16).

d. Manasseh's achievements and a summary of his life, including his terrible sins, are recorded in the book *The History of the Kings of Judah* (vv.17-18). After his death, he was buried in the palace garden known as the garden of Uzza. He was succeeded by his son Amon (v.18).

Thought 1. Among all the lessons that can be learned from Manasseh's wicked reign, one lesson stands above all the others. He rejected the godly example of his parents. Just think of all the opportunities Manasseh had growing up in the palace. He always had the very best of everything: clothing, food, drink, housing, transportation, schooling, recreation, friends, and godly parents who loved and cared for him, no doubt rearing him in the ways of the LORD. But despite all these advantages, he never gave thanks or praise to God for the good gifts he had received and enjoyed. He never looked upon the advantages as being blessings from the LORD. Obviously his heart was cold, insensitive, and hard toward the LORD, his parents, and people in general. Rejecting the godly example set before him by his parents, he lived one of the most wicked lives imaginable. What a terrible legacy to leave the world!

In looking at Manasseh's life, the question we need to ask ourselves is this: have we rejected the godly examples set before us. Most of us have either known godly examples or at least observed godly people walking among us. In some case, the godly example was our parents; in other cases it was a relative, neighbor, co-worker, or friend. Whoever it was, have we followed in the person's godly footsteps? Or are we living sinful, wicked lives? Have we rejected the life of righteousness demanded by the LORD? Listen to what God's Holy Word says:

"And be not conformed to this world: but be ye transformed by the renewing of your mind, that ye may prove what *is* that good, and acceptable, and perfect, will of God" (Ro.12:2).

"Ye adulterers and adulteresses, know ye not that the friendship of the world is enmity with God? whosoever therefore will be a friend of the world is the enemy of God" (Js.4:4).

"Having eyes full of adultery, and that cannot cease from sin; beguiling unstable souls: an heart they have exercised with covetous practices; cursed children: Which have forsaken the right way, and are gone astray, following the way of Balaam *the son* of Bosor, who loved the wages of unrighteousness; But was rebuked for his iniquity: the dumb ass speaking with man's voice forbad the madness of the prophet. These are wells without water, clouds that are carried with a tempest; to whom the mist of darkness is reserved for ever" (2 Pe.2:14-17).

"Love not the world, neither the things *that are* in the world. If any man love the world, the love of the Father is not in him. For all that *is* in the world, the lust of the flesh, and the lust of the eyes, and the pride of life, is not of the Father, but is of the world" (1 Jn.2:15-16).

"And ye shall not walk in the manners of the nation, which I cast out before you: for they committed all these things, and therefore I abhorred them" (Le.20:23).

"Only take heed to thyself, and keep thy soul diligently, lest thou forget the things which thine eyes have seen, and lest they depart from thy heart all the days of thy life: but teach them thy sons, and thy sons' sons" (De.4:9).

"Take heed to thyself that thou be not snared by following them, after that they be destroyed from before thee; and that thou enquire not after their gods, saying, How did these nations serve their gods? even so will I do likewise" (De.12:30).

"But they mocked the messengers of God, and despised his words, and misused his prophets, until the wrath of the LORD arose against his people, till *there was* no remedy" (2 Chr.36:16).

"But unto the wicked God saith, What hast thou to do to declare my statutes, or *that* thou shouldest take my covenant in thy mouth? Seeing thou hatest instruction, and castest my words behind thee. When thou sawest a thief, then thou consentedst with him, and hast been partaker with adulterers. Thou givest thy mouth to evil, and thy tongue frameth deceit. Thou sittest *and* speakest against thy brother; thou slanderest thine own mother's son. These *things* hast thou done, and I kept silence; thou thoughtest that I was altogether *such an one* as thyself: *but* I will reprove thee, and set *them* in order before thine eyes. Now consider this, ye that forget God, lest I tear *you* in pieces, and *there be* none to deliver. Whoso offereth praise glorifieth me: and to him that ordereth *his* conversation *aright* will I show the salvation of God" (Ps.50:16-23).

"The fear of the LORD *is* the beginning of knowledge: *but* fools despise wisdom and instruction" (Pr.1:7).

"That thou mayest walk in the way of good *men,* and keep the paths of the righteous" (Pr.2:20).

"Hear me now therefore, O ye children, and depart not from the words of my mouth....And say, How have I hated instruction, and my heart despised reproof; And have not obeyed the voice of my teachers, nor inclined mine ear to them that instructed me!" (Pr.5:7, 12-13).

"He that walketh with wise *men* shall be wise: but a companion of fools shall be destroyed" (Pr.13:20).

"That this *is* a rebellious people, lying children, children *that* will not hear the law of the LORD" (Is.30:9).

2 (21:19-26) **Evil, Duty, Not to Follow—Children, Duty—Parents, Evil, Children of—Amon, King of Judah, Reign of—King, of Judah**: considering the long and evil reign of Manasseh, his son Amon stood little chance of escaping the wicked environment and lifestyle in which he was reared. Growing up as a child and then into manhood, the pleasures of sin undoubtedly flourished all around him. In all probability he never knew any other lifestyle. Thus, when he took the throne he simply continued on with the wickedness and the evil policies established by his father. Note the brief description of his evil reign:

OUTLINE	SCRIPTURE	SCRIPTURE	OUTLINE
2. The evil reign of Amon: Following the evil example of parents a. His background 　1) His age: 22 　2) His term: Only 2 years (642–640 B.C.) b. His evil reign 　1) Lived a wicked life 　2) Walked in the evil ways of his father 　3) Worshipped the false gods his father had worshipped 　4) Forsook the LORD 　5) Refused to follow the way of the LORD	19 Amon *was* twenty and two years old when he began to reign, and he reigned two years in Jerusalem. And his mother's name *was* Meshullemeth, the daughter of Haruz of Jotbah. 20 And he did *that which was* evil in the sight of the LORD, as his father Manasseh did. 21 And he walked in all the way that his father walked in, and served the idols that his father served, and worshipped them: 22 And he forsook the LORD God of his fathers, and walked not in the way of the LORD.	23 And the servants of Amon conspired against him, and slew the king in his own house. 24 And the people of the land slew all them that had conspired against king Amon; and the people of the land made Josiah his son king in his stead. 25 Now the rest of the acts of Amon which he did, *are* they not written in the book of the chronicles of the kings of Judah? 26 And he was buried in his sepulchre in the garden of Uzza: and Josiah his son reigned in his stead.	c. His assassination 　1) The plot was carried out by his own officials in the palace 　2) The assassins were caught & executed by a popular uprising of the people 　3) The people made his son Josiah king d. His achievements & the summary of his life 　1) His reign: Recorded in the book *The History of the Kings of Judah* 　2) His burial: In the garden of Uzza 　3) His successor: Josiah, his son

a. Assuming the throne at age 22, Amon ruled only two years (642–640 B.C.). Just as his father's wickedness had overshadowed Amon's life, so the 55-year rule of his father overshadowed his brief two-year reign. Seldom has a son stood so little opportunity to succeed before the Lord and the public as did Amon. Amon's mother was Meshullemeth and her father was Haruz. Both names seem to be of Arabian origin, which would mean that Amon was most likely reared by a pagan, unbelieving mother as well as a wicked father.

b. Amon lived a wicked life just as his father did. Scripture says that he did as much evil as his father, walking in all the evil ways of Manasseh. That is, he continued the evil lifestyle and policies of his father, even worshipping the false gods his father had worshipped (v.21). Amon completely forsook the LORD, the God of his fathers, refusing to walk in His righteous ways (v.22).

c. Within 24 months of being crowned king—even before he had time to consolidate his power—Amon was assassinated by his own royal officials (vv.23-24). Just who these officials were is not recorded, but note what happened to them: there was a popular uprising against the assassins, and they were executed by the people of the land. The people then set Amon's son Josiah upon the throne.

At this time, Judah was a vassal state under the control of the Assyrians. Because of the wicked reigns of Manasseh and Amon, it is conceivable that a *priestly party* assassinated Amon with the hope that they could place a righteous ruler upon the throne. If this was the case, then perhaps the popular uprising against the assassins was provoked by an *Assyrian party* who wanted to make sure that an Assyrian supporter took the throne.

d. Amon's achievements and a summary of his life are recorded in the book *The History of the Kings of Judah* (vv.25-26). After his assassination, he was buried in the garden of Uzza, the same garden where his father Manasseh had been buried. He was succeeded by Josiah, his son.

Thought 1. Tragically, Amon followed the evil example of his parents. But remember this fact: whereas his father Manasseh had had the example of godly parents, Amon had only the evil example of Manasseh. Nevertheless, Amon stood guilty for his own wicked behavior. The blame did not lie with his father but rather with Amon himself.

So it is with us. If we follow the wicked example of parents or of anyone else, the blame lies with us, not with them. For we are responsible for our own behavior. If we follow the evil example of others, committing wickedness, we are the ones who are doing the choosing and making the decision to walk in their steps. Consequently, we personally stand guilty and condemned before God. Listen to what God's Holy Word says about following the evil example of parents or of anyone else:

"**But now I have written unto you not to keep company, if any man that is called a brother be a fornicator, or covetous, or an idolater, or a railer, or a drunkard, or an extortioner; with such an one no not to eat**" (1 Co.5:11).

"**Be ye not unequally yoked together with unbelievers: for what fellowship hath righteousness with unrighteousness? and what communion hath light with darkness? And what concord hath Christ with Belial? or what part hath he that believeth with an infidel? And what agreement hath the temple of God with idols? for ye are the temple of the living God; as God hath said, I will dwell in them, and walk in *them;* and I will be their God, and they shall be my people**" (2 Co.6:14-16).

"**Thou shalt not follow a multitude to *do* evil; neither shalt thou speak in a cause to decline after many to wrest *judgment*"** (Ex.23:2).

"**Take heed to thyself that thou be not snared by following them, after that they be destroyed from before thee; and that thou enquire not after their gods, saying, How did these nations serve their gods? even so will I do likewise**" (De.12:30).

"**Blessed *is* the man that walketh not in the counsel of the ungodly, nor standeth in the way of sinners, nor sitteth in the seat of the scornful**" (Ps.1:1).

"**Enter not into the path of the wicked, and go not in the way of evil *men***" (Pr.4:14).

"**But I said unto their children in the wilderness, Walk ye not in the statutes of your fathers, neither observe their judgments, nor defile yourselves with their idols**" (Eze.20:18).

CHAPTER 22

E. The Godly Reign of Josiah (Part 1)—His Temple Restoration & Discovery of God's Word: Two Major Concerns of the Believer, 22:1-20

22:1-20; see 2 Chr.34:1-2; 8-28

1. The godliness of Josiah & his restoration of the temple: A concern for righteousness & for true worship
   a. His background
      1) His age: 8 years old
      2) His reign: 31 years
   b. His godly life & rule, 2 Chr.34:3-7
      1) He lived a righteous life
      2) He followed the example of David
      3) He never deviated from righteousness
   c. His major concerns: The restoration of the temple & of the true worship of the LORD
      1) Josiah ordered his secretary (of state), Shaphan, to manage the restoration project

      • To assign the fundraising for the project to the High Priest Hilkiah
      • To use the voluntary gifts from the worshippers to repair the temple
      • To give the money to the construction supervisors

      • To have the supervisors pay the workers & purchase the materials

      2) Josiah ordered that the supervisors be trusted with the money, for they had proven trustworthy

2. The discovery of God's Word, the Book of the Law: A concern for God's Word
   a. The priest discovered the book during construction: Gave it to Shaphan, who read it

   b. The secretary of state took the book to King Josiah
      1) He first gave the king a progress report on the

Josiah *was* eight years old when he began to reign, and he reigned thirty and one years in Jerusalem. And his mother's name *was* Jedidah, the daughter of Adaiah of Boscath.
2 And he did *that which was* right in the sight of the LORD, and walked in all the way of David his father, and turned not aside to the right hand or to the left.
3 And it came to pass in the eighteenth year of king Josiah, *that* the king sent Shaphan the son of Azaliah, the son of Meshullam, the scribe, to the house of the LORD, saying,
4 Go up to Hilkiah the high priest, that he may sum the silver which is brought into the house of the LORD, which the keepers of the door have gathered of the people:
5 And let them deliver it into the hand of the doers of the work, that have the oversight of the house of the LORD: and let them give it to the doers of the work which *is* in the house of the LORD, to repair the breaches of the house,
6 Unto carpenters, and builders, and masons, and to buy timber and hewn stone to repair the house.
7 Howbeit there was no reckoning made with them of the money that was delivered into their hand, because they dealt faithfully.
8 And Hilkiah the high priest said unto Shaphan the scribe, I have found the book of the law in the house of the LORD. And Hilkiah gave the book to Shaphan, and he read it.
9 And Shaphan the scribe came to the king, and brought the king word again, and said, Thy servants have

gathered the money that was found in the house, and have delivered it into the hand of them that do the work, that have the oversight of the house of the LORD.
10 And Shaphan the scribe showed the king, saying, Hilkiah the priest hath delivered me a book. And Shaphan read it before the king.
11 And it came to pass, when the king had heard the words of the book of the law, that he rent his clothes.
12 And the king commanded Hilkiah the priest, and Ahikam the son of Shaphan, and Achbor the son of Michaiah, and Shaphan the scribe, and Asahiah a servant of the king's, saying,
13 Go ye, enquire of the LORD for me, and for the people, and for all Judah, concerning the words of this book that is found: for great is the wrath of the LORD that is kindled against us, because our fathers have not hearkened unto the words of this book, to do according unto all that which is written concerning us.
14 So Hilkiah the priest, and Ahikam, and Achbor, and Shaphan, and Asahiah, went unto Huldah the prophetess, the wife of Shallum the son of Tikvah, the son of Harhas, keeper of the wardrobe; (now she dwelt in Jerusalem in the college;) and they communed with her.
15 And she said unto them, Thus saith the LORD God of Israel, Tell the man that sent you to me,
16 Thus saith the LORD, Behold, I will bring evil upon this place, and upon the inhabitants thereof, *even* all the words of the book which the king of Judah hath read:
17 Because they have forsaken me, and have burned incense unto other gods, that they might provoke me to anger with all the works of their hands; therefore my wrath shall be kindled against this place, and shall not be quenched.
18 But to the king of Judah

construction project

2) He then informed the king about the book
3) He read certain portions of the book to the king

c. The king reacted: Was convicted of sin & feared God's judgment—he wept, 19

d. The king appointed a delegation to seek the LORD for a full explanation of the book's message
   1) The delegation

   2) The charge: To learn what was written in the book
      • Because the LORD's anger burned against them in judgment?
      • Because they & their ancestors had sinned, disobeyed the LORD—not kept the commandments written in the book

e. The delegation consulted the prophetess Huldah
   1) Her background
      • Was the wife of Shallum, the keeper of the royal wardrobe
      • Lived in Jerusalem

   2) Her authority: Was commissioned by God to share His Word

f. The prophecy of Huldah foretold
   1) God will judge, destroy this city & people: Execute everything written in the book

      • Because the people had forsaken the LORD & worshipped false gods
      • Because the people had provoked the LORD to anger

   2) God had heard Josiah's

prayer • Because his heart was tender, responsive to the Word of God he had heard • Because he grieved, showed deep concern over the people's sin & the coming judgment upon them • Because he had humbled himself & wept	which sent you to enquire of the LORD, thus shall ye say to him, Thus saith the LORD God of Israel, *As touching* the words which thou hast heard; 19 Because thine heart was tender, and thou hast humbled thyself before the LORD, when thou heardest what I spake against this place, and against the inhabitants thereof, that they should be	come a desolation and a curse, and hast rent thy clothes, and wept before me; I also have heard *thee,* saith the LORD. 20 Behold therefore, I will gather thee unto thy fathers, and thou shalt be gathered into thy grave in peace; and thine eyes shall not see all the evil which I will bring upon this place. And they brought the king word again.	before the LORD in personal repentance 3) God would show mercy to Josiah • He would die in peace, knowing the peace of God in his heart • He would escape God's judgment, be spared the sight of it

DIVISION IV

THE UTTER DISINTEGRATION AND FALL OF JUDAH, THE SOUTHERN KINGDOM: AN APPALLING DESTRUCTION DUE TO INCONSISTENCY, DISLOYALTY, AND EVER-GROWING WICKEDNESS, 18:1–25:30

E. The Godly Reign of Josiah (Part 1)—His Temple Restoration and Discovery of God's Word: Two Major Concerns of the Believer, 22:1-20

(22:1-20) Introduction—World, Beautiful and Good, Evidence—Goodness, Nature, of World, Evidence—Mankind, Goodness of, Evidence—Righteousness, Acts of, Listed—World History, Power Shift, from Assyria to Babylon: when we look around at the world—thoughtfully and honestly—we see beauty within nature and in the attractiveness of people and their behavior. An honest evaluation also reveals people who are loving, kind, honest, just, caring, and helpful in ministry. People are seen encouraging one another and doing good deeds. They are also seen worshipping the true and living God, as God has instructed, loving one another and spreading the message of righteousness and love across the world. These two matters, righteousness and the worship of the true and living God, are the concerns to be dealt with in this passage of Holy Scripture.

This is the story of Josiah, the great-grandson of Hezekiah, the most godly king who had ever ruled over the Southern Kingdom of Judah. But when Josiah came upon the scene, his righteousness exceeded even that of Hezekiah. Among all the kings of Judah and Israel, there were only four reformers: Asa, Jehoshaphat, Hezekiah, and Josiah. Commentators considered Hezekiah and Josiah the most important because of the major reforms they carried out during their administrations.

In looking at the politics of Josiah's day, one sees a major shift in power that needs to be noted. Russell Dilday gives an excellent summary of the power shift:

> *Momentous events were erupting around the biblical world in 638 B.C. when Josiah came to the throne in Jerusalem in 638 B.C. As the powerful influence of Assyria was waning, the savage invasion of the Scythians emerged on the horizon and lasted until 624 B.C. Finally, in 612 B.C. the capital of Assyria fell before a combined army of Scythians, Medes, and Babylonians. That paved the way for the ominous rise to world power of Babylon, whose "innocent" envoys had visited the court of Josiah's great-grandfather (2 Kings 20:12). In 627 B.C. the articulate voice of Jeremiah, reinforced by the preaching of Zephaniah and Nahum, began to be heard in Judah. While not one of these events is mentioned in this historical account of Josiah's reign, they must have had an enormous impact on the king, both during his formative years and during the active years of his national reforms.*[1]

In covering the life and reforms instituted by Josiah, five major events are discussed, two of which are in chapter 22 and three in chapter 23. Each of these events paints the picture of a deep concern that should fill the heart of every person. This is: *The Godly Reign of Josiah (Part 1)—His Temple Restoration and Discovery of God's Word: Two Major Concerns of the Believer,* 22:1-20.

1. The godliness of Josiah and his restoration of the temple: a concern for righteousness and for true worship (vv.1-7).
2. The discovery of God's Word, the Book of the Law: a concern for God's Word (vv.8-20).

1 **(22:1-7) Righteousness, Concern for—Godliness, Example of—Testimony, of Godliness—Temple, Restoration of—Josiah, King of Judah, Reign of—Southern Kingdom of Judah, Kings of**: in beginning the story of Josiah, two facts are immediately emphasized: his godliness and his restoration of the temple. Remember that his father Amon had been assassinated by his own royal officials, most likely a priestly party (21:23-26). Afterward, the people had reacted in a popular uprising and executed the king's assassins, placing Josiah upon the throne to succeed his father. Most likely the assassins had been anti-Assyrians, and the group who reacted against them and placed Josiah on the throne were pro-Assyrians who had

---

[1] Russell Dilday. *1, 2 Kings*, pp.468-469.

feared retaliation from Assyria. Whatever the political reasons for the assassination, there was a deep concern by the godly leaders that the Davidic line, a true descendent of David, continue upon the throne. Thus, the story of Josiah begins:

OUTLINE	SCRIPTURE	SCRIPTURE	OUTLINE

1. The godliness of Josiah & his restoration of the temple: A concern for righteousness & for true worship
a. His background
  1) His age: 8 years old
  2) His reign: 31 years
b. His godly life & rule, 2 Chr.34:3-7
  1) He lived a righteous life
  2) He followed the example of David
  3) He never deviated from righteousness
c. His major concerns: The restoration of the temple & of the true worship of the LORD
  1) Josiah ordered his secretary (of state), Shaphan, to manage the restoration project
    • To assign the fundraising for the project to
	Josiah *was* eight years old when he began to reign, and he reigned thirty and one years in Jerusalem. And his mother's name *was* Jedidah, the daughter of Adaiah of Boscath.
	2 And he did *that which was* right in the sight of the LORD, and walked in all the way of David his father, and turned not aside to the right hand or to the left.
	3 And it came to pass in the eighteenth year of king Josiah, *that* the king sent Shaphan the son of Azaliah, the son of Meshullam, the scribe, to the house of the LORD, saying,
	4 Go up to Hilkiah the high priest, that he may sum the
		silver which is brought into the house of the LORD, which the keepers of the door have gathered of the people:
		5 And let them deliver it into the hand of the doers of the work, that have the oversight of the house of the LORD: and let them give it to the doers of the work which *is* in the house of the LORD, to repair the breaches of the house,
		6 Unto carpenters, and builders, and masons, and to buy timber and hewn stone to repair the house.
		7 Howbeit there was no reckoning made with them of the money that was delivered into their hand, because they dealt faithfully.
			the High Priest Hilkiah
			• To use the voluntary gifts from the worshippers to repair the temple
			
			• To give the money to the construction supervisors
			
			• To have the supervisors pay the workers & purchase the materials
			
			  2) Josiah ordered that the supervisors be trusted with the money, for they had proven trustworthy

a. Josiah was just a young boy when he began to reign, only eight years old (v.1). This meant that he was under the control and guidance of others until he became old enough to govern the nation on his own. Including the years of his rule as a child, he governed the nation for 31 years. He was killed in a battle with Egypt, dying at the young age of 39. His mother was Jedidah, who was probably a godly woman who reared her son Josiah in the knowledge of the LORD and gave him strong spiritual counsel.

b. Someone definitely had a strong, spiritual influence upon young Josiah, for he lived a righteous life in the sight of the LORD (v.2). In fact, Scripture says that he followed the godly example of David, never deviating from the righteous example set by the ancient king.

c. During his reign, Josiah had two major concerns: the restoration of the temple and the true worship of the LORD, the only living and true God (vv.3-7). Because of his godly, righteous upbringing, a deep concern for worshipping the LORD was bound to grip the young king's heart. When he reached the age of 26—the eighteenth year of his reign—he made the critical decision to restore the temple and to reinstitute the true worship of the living LORD. Turning to his chief official, the secretary of state affairs, Shaphan, he directed him to manage the restoration project. Four clear instructions were given to the secretary of state:

⇒ to assign the fundraising for the project to the High Priest Hilkiah (v.4)
⇒ to use the voluntary gifts from the worshippers to repair the temple
⇒ to give the money to the construction supervisors (v.5)
⇒ to have the supervisors use the money to pay the workers and to purchase the materials for the restoration project (v.6)

Although the secretary of state was the general manager of the project, the supervisors were to be trusted with the money. Because of their honesty, there was no need to keep an account of the money. They were both responsible and faithful supervisors of the restoration project.

Thought 1. Josiah had a deep concern for righteousness and for true worship. The same concerns should grip our hearts. For righteousness and true worship determine our destiny, both individually and corporately, as a society and nation. Righteousness builds a character of integrity within people, and righteous individuals build up a nation. If a person is righteous, he is honest, just, true, moral, and law-abiding. He not only keeps the laws of the land but he also works diligently at his job in order to make a significant contribution to society. Righteousness builds the character of the individuals. And when there are enough of us with righteous characters, we build a nation of righteousness, a nation of enormous strength. As we will see, this was the experience of Josiah; and it can be the experience of any of us.

Josiah had another concern from which we can also learn, the concern for true worship. True worship also determines our destiny. Common sense tells us this. Think about this glorious truth: God exists; He is living and He is loving. Therefore, if we worship the true and living God, then He is bound to accept us. He is the LORD God of the universe who created the world and all that is in it. He even sent His very own Son to die for our sins because He loves us so much. For that reason, it is God and God alone—the only true and living God—who is to be worshipped. Listen to what God's Holy Word says about these two concerns, concerns that should grip every one of our hearts:

(1) The concern for righteousness must grip us.

"For I say unto you, That except your righteousness shall exceed *the righteousness* of the scribes and Pharisees, ye shall in no case enter into the kingdom of heaven" (Mt.5:20).

"Awake to righteousness, and sin not; for some have not the knowledge of God: I speak *this* to your shame" (1 Co.15:34).

"Wherefore take unto you the whole armour of God, that ye may be able to withstand in the evil day, and having done all, to stand. Stand therefore, having your loins girt about with truth, and having on the breastplate of righteousness" (Ep.6:13-14).

"Being filled with the fruits of righteousness, which are by Jesus Christ, unto the glory and praise of God" (Ph.1:11).

"But thou, O man of God, flee these things; and follow after righteousness, godliness, faith, love, patience, meekness. Fight the good fight of faith, lay hold on eternal life, whereunto thou art also called, and hast professed a good profession before many witnesses" (1 Ti.6:11-12).

"Teaching us that, denying ungodliness and worldly lusts, we should live soberly, righteously, and godly, in this present world; Looking for that blessed hope, and the glorious appearing of the great God and our Saviour Jesus Christ" (Tit.2:12-13).

"But the day of the Lord will come as a thief in the night; in the which the heavens shall pass away with a great noise, and the elements shall melt with fervent heat, the earth also and the works that are therein shall be burned up. *Seeing* then *that* all these things shall be dissolved, what manner *of persons* ought ye to be in *all* holy conversation and godliness, Looking for and hasting unto the coming of the day of God, wherein the heavens being on fire shall be dissolved, and the elements shall melt with fervent heat? Nevertheless we, according to his promise, look for new heavens and a new earth, wherein dwelleth righteousness. Wherefore, beloved, seeing that ye look for such things, be diligent that ye may be found of him in peace, without spot, and blameless" (2 Pe.3:10-14).

"Blessed *is* the nation whose God *is* the LORD: *and* the people *whom* he hath chosen for his own inheritance" (Ps.33:12).

"By the blessing of the upright the city is exalted: but it is overthrown by the mouth of the wicked" (Pr.11:11).

"Righteousness exalteth a nation: but sin *is* a reproach to any people" (Pr.14:34).

"Take away the wicked *from* before the king, and his throne shall be established in righteousness" (Pr.25:5).

"Sow to yourselves in righteousness, reap in mercy; break up your fallow ground: for *it is* time to seek the LORD, till he come and rain righteousness upon you" (Ho.10:12).

(2) The concern for consistent, faithful worship of the only living and true God must grip us.

"Then saith Jesus unto him, Get thee hence, Satan: for it is written, Thou shalt worship the Lord thy God, and him only shalt thou serve" (Mt.4:10).

"And he came to Nazareth, where he had been brought up: and, as his custom was, he went into the synagogue on the sabbath day, and stood up for to read" (Lu.4:16).

"And they worshipped him, and returned to Jerusalem with great joy: And were continually in the temple, praising and blessing God. Amen" (Lu.24:52-53).

"God *is* a Spirit: and they that worship him must worship *him* in spirit and in truth" (Jn.4:24).

"Not forsaking the assembling of ourselves together, as the manner of some *is;* but exhorting *one another:* and so much the more, as ye see the day approaching" (He.10:25).

"Saying with a loud voice, Fear God, and give glory to him; for the hour of his judgment is come: and worship him that made heaven, and earth, and the sea, and the fountains of waters" (Re.14:7).

"Give unto the LORD the glory *due* unto his name: bring an offering, and come before him: worship the LORD in the beauty of holiness" (1 Chr.16:29).

"LORD, I have loved the habitation of thy house, and the place where thine honour dwelleth" (Ps.26:8).

"One *thing* have I desired of the LORD, that will I seek after; that I may dwell in the house of the LORD all the days of my life, to behold the beauty of the LORD, and to enquire in his temple" (Ps.27:4).

"O come, let us worship and bow down: let us kneel before the LORD our maker" (Ps.95:6).

"O worship the LORD in the beauty of holiness: fear before him, all the earth" (Ps.96:9).

2 **(22:8-20) Word of God, Discovered by, Josiah—Word of God, Importance of—Law, Book of, Discovered—Bible, Importance of—Scriptures, Importance of—Josiah, Discovery of the Book of the Law—Hilkiah, Discovered God's Law—Huldah, a Prophetess, Predicted Judah's Fall—Judah, Fall of, Predicted**: while restoring the temple, a most amazing, exciting discovery was made. God's Holy Word, "The Book of the Law," was discovered in the temple. For decades God's Word had been lost, at least for 75 years. For when the 55 years of Manasseh's reign is added to the 2 years of his son Amon's reign and to the 18 years of Josiah's childhood, God's Word had not been available to the people for at least 75 years. The significance of finding the scroll of God's Holy Word cannot be overemphasized.

How much of the law was discovered? Was it just the Ten Commandments? Or the book of *Deuteronomy,* which was sometimes called "The Book of the Law"? Or was it the entire Pentateuch, the first five books of the Old Testament? Scripture does not say, but considering that all Scripture seems to have been lost prior to this discovery and that copies of the Pentateuch were later passed down through the centuries even up into the present time, what was found was most likely the entire Pentateuch. Whatever the case, an exciting account of the discovery and the significant impact it had upon the nation is dramatically described by Scripture:

OUTLINE	SCRIPTURE	SCRIPTURE	OUTLINE

2. The discovery of God's Word, the Book of the Law: A concern for God's Word
a. The priest discovered the book during construction: Gave it to Shaphan, who read it
b. The secretary of state took the book to King Josiah
  1) He first gave the king a progress report on the construction project
	8 And Hilkiah the high priest said unto Shaphan the scribe, I have found the book of the law in the house of the LORD. And Hilkiah gave the book to Shaphan, and he read it. 9 And Shaphan the scribe came to the king, and brought the king word again, and said, Thy servants have gathered the money that was found in the house, and have delivered it into the hand of them that do the work, that have the oversight of the house of the LORD.	keeper of the wardrobe; (now she dwelt in Jerusalem in the college;) and they communed with her. 15 And she said unto them, Thus saith the LORD God of Israel, Tell the man that sent you to me, 16 Thus saith the LORD, Behold, I will bring evil upon this place, and upon the inhabitants thereof, *even* all the words of the book which the king of Judah hath read:	the royal wardrobe
			• Lived in Jerusalem
			
			2) Her authority: Was commissioned by God to share His Word
			
			f. The prophecy of Huldah foretold
			  1) God will judge, destroy this city & people: Execute everything written in the book

2) He then informed the king about the book 3) He read certain portions of the book to the king	10 And Shaphan the scribe showed the king, saying, Hilkiah the priest hath delivered me a book. And Shaphan read it before the king.	17 Because they have forsaken me, and have burned incense unto other gods, that they might provoke me to anger with all the works of their hands; therefore my wrath shall be kindled against	• Because the people had forsaken the LORD & worshipped false gods • Because the people had provoked the LORD to anger
c. The king reacted: Was convicted of sin & feared God's judgment—he wept, 19 d. The king appointed a delegation to seek the LORD for a full explanation of the book's message 1) The delegation	11 And it came to pass, when the king had heard the words of the book of the law, that he rent his clothes. 12 And the king commanded Hilkiah the priest, and Ahikam the son of Shaphan, and Achbor the son of Michaiah, and Shaphan the scribe, and Asahiah a servant of the king's, saying,	this place, and shall not be quenched. 18 But to the king of Judah which sent you to enquire of the LORD, thus shall ye say to him, Thus saith the LORD God of Israel, *As touching* the words which thou hast heard; 19 Because thine heart was	2) God had heard Josiah's prayer • Because his heart was tender, responsive to the Word of God he had heard
2) The charge: To learn what was written in the book • Because the LORD's anger burned against them in judgment? • Because they & their ancestors had sinned, disobeyed the LORD—not kept the commandments written in the book	13 Go ye, enquire of the LORD for me, and for the people, and for all Judah, concerning the words of this book that is found: for great is the wrath of the LORD that is kindled against us, because our fathers have not hearkened unto the words of this book, to do according unto all that which is written concerning us.	tender, and thou hast humbled thyself before the LORD, when thou heardest what I spake against this place, and against the inhabitants thereof, that they should become a desolation and a curse, and hast rent thy clothes, and wept before me; I also have heard *thee*, saith the LORD.	• Because he grieved, showed deep concern over the people's sin & the coming judgment upon them • Because he had humbled himself & wept before the LORD in personal repentance
e. The delegation consulted the prophetess Huldah 1) Her background • Was the wife of Shallum, the keeper of	14 So Hilkiah the priest, and Ahikam, and Achbor, and Shaphan, and Asahiah, went unto Huldah the prophetess, the wife of Shallum the son of Tikvah, the son of Harhas,	20 Behold therefore, I will gather thee unto thy fathers, and thou shalt be gathered into thy grave in peace; and thine eyes shall not see all the evil which I will bring upon this place. And they brought the king word again.	3) God would show mercy to Josiah • He would die in peace, knowing the peace of God in his heart • He would escape God's judgment, be spared the sight of it

a. The High Priest himself was the person who discovered the Book of the Law in the temple (v.8). When the secretary of state Shaphan visited the construction site, the High Priest gave the Book of the Law to him. Note that the secretary of state read it.

b. Once Shaphan had read the book, he returned to King Josiah and gave the king a progress report on the construction project (vv.9-10). Once the business matters were out of the way, he informed the king that a book had been discovered by the High Priest in the temple. He then read portions of the book to the king.

c. Sitting there listening to God's Word being read, King Josiah suddenly came under conviction. The fear of God and His judgment struck the king's heart and he began to weep (v.19). He actually tore his robes in an act of mourning over his sins and repentance before the LORD (v.11, 19).

d. After gaining his composure, Josiah appointed a delegation to study the book and to seek the LORD for a full explanation of its message (vv.12-13). The delegation included the following persons:

⇒ Hilkiah, the High Priest

⇒ Ahikam, who was the son of the secretary of state Shaphan

⇒ Asaiah, who was one of the king's royal officials

Only one charge was given to the delegation: to study and learn the meaning of the message in the book (v.13). Under heavy conviction from the LORD, Josiah gave two reasons for giving this charge to the delegation:

⇒ because the LORD's anger burned against him and his people in judgment

⇒ because they and their ancestors had sinned and disobeyed the LORD, not keeping the commandments that were written in the book

Perhaps the covenant promises and curses of God are what was read (see outlines and notes—Le.26:1-46; De.27–28 for more discussion). Whatever the Scripture was, Josiah was under deep conviction and sensed a desperate need to know if the judgments read to him were to take effect upon Judah. He needed to know if God would have mercy upon him and his people. Sensing deep conviction before the LORD, Josiah was compelled to unravel the meaning of the Scripture.

e. In seeking the LORD for the meaning, the delegation consulted with the prophetess Huldah (vv.14-15). This prophetess was the wife of Shallum, who was the keeper of the royal wardrobe. She and her husband lived in Jerusalem, in a section known as the Second District. Jerusalem seems to have been divided into two districts or quarters (Ne.3:9-12; Zep.1:10).

Considering that this is the only time the prophetess Huldah is mentioned, it is interesting that the LORD would choose her for this most important task. For during these days, three well-known prophets were active throughout the nation of Judah: Nahum, Zephaniah, and Jeremiah. No reason is given by Scripture for God's choosing the prophetess Huldah over the three well-known prophets. Whatever reason we might give would be mere speculation. Regardless of the reason, the LORD honored this woman, the prophetess Huldah. The LORD gave her the important task of predicting the coming judgment of God's hand. She was commissioned by God to share the meaning of His Holy Word that had recently been discovered.

f. The prophetess declared that God was going to judge and destroy the city of Jerusalem and its people (vv.16-20). Everything the king had read written in the book was to be executed (vv.16-17):

⇒ because the people had forsaken the LORD and worshipped false gods

⇒ because the people had provoked the LORD to anger

But despite the terrifying message of judgment in the book, the LORD had a very special message for King Josiah himself. God had heard his prayer:

⇒ because his heart had been tender, responsive to the Word of God

⇒ because he had grieved, showing deep concern over the people's sin and the coming judgment upon them

⇒ because he had humbled himself and wept before the LORD in personal repentance (vv.18-19)

For these three reasons God would show mercy to Josiah by doing two wonderful things for him (v.20). First, when he died, he would experience the peace of God within his heart. Second, he would personally escape God's judgment upon Judah and Jerusalem, be spared the sight of the coming anguish and condemnation of the people because of their sins.

Thought 1. What a lesson for us! To Josiah and his people, the Word of God had been lost. To many of us, the Word of God has been lost. For years, we have neglected and ignored His Word, acting as though we do not believe the Bible is the written Word of God. But if we truly believe that the Bible is God's Word, we must feast upon it. We must learn what God has to say to us. For if the Bible truly is what it claims to be, God's Word, and we have ignored and neglected it, what will God say to us when we face Him?

Above all that is to be feared in this life is the neglect or denial of God and His Holy Word. Nothing on this earth is as important as doing exactly what God's Word says, obeying Him and keeping His commandments. But before we can keep His commandments, we must know what His commandments are. And there is only one way to learn God's commandments: by studying His Holy Word. Listen to what God says about His Holy Word:

"Search the scriptures; for in them ye think ye have eternal life: and they are they which testify of me" (Jn.5:39).

"Now ye are clean through the word which I have spoken unto you" (Jn.15:3).

"Sanctify them through thy truth: thy word is truth" (Jn.17:17).

"But these are written, that ye might believe that Jesus is the Christ, the Son of God; and that believing ye might have life through his name" (Jn.20:31).

"Men _and_ brethren, this scripture must needs have been fulfilled, which the Holy Ghost by the mouth of David spake before concerning Judas, which was guide to them that took Jesus" (Ac.1:16).

"These were more noble than those in Thessalonica, in that they received the word with all readiness of mind, and searched the scriptures daily, whether those things were so" (Ac.17:11).

"For I am not ashamed of the gospel of Christ: for it is the power of God unto salvation to every one that believeth; to the Jew first, and also to the Greek" (Ro.1:16).

"For whatsoever things were written aforetime were written for our learning, that we through patience and comfort of the scriptures might have hope" (Ro.15:4).

"Now all these things happened unto them for ensamples: and they are written for our admonition, upon whom the ends of the world are come" (1 Co.10:11).

"Let the word of Christ dwell in you richly in all wisdom; teaching and admonishing one another in psalms and hymns and spiritual songs, singing with grace in your hearts to the Lord" (Co.3:16).

"Study to show thyself approved unto God, a workman that needeth not to be ashamed, rightly dividing the word of truth" (2 Ti.2:15).

"All scripture *is* given by inspiration of God, and *is* profitable for doctrine, for reproof, for correction, for instruction in righteousness" (2 Ti.3:16).

"For the word of God *is* quick, and powerful, and sharper than any twoedged sword, piercing even to the dividing asunder of soul and spirit, and of the joints and marrow, and *is* a discerner of the thoughts and intents of the heart" (He.4:12).

"We have also a more sure word of prophecy; whereunto ye do well that ye take heed, as unto a light that shineth in a dark place, until the day dawn, and the day star arise in your hearts: Knowing this first, that no prophecy of the scripture is of any private interpretation. For the prophecy came not in old time by the will of man: but holy men of God spake *as they were* moved by the Holy Ghost" (2 Pe.1:19-21).

"These things have I written unto you that believe on the name of the Son of God; that ye may know that ye have eternal life, and that ye may believe on the name of the Son of God" (1 Jn.5:13).

"Wherewithal shall a young man cleanse his way? by taking heed *thereto* according to thy word" (Ps.119:9).

"Thy word have I hid in mine heart, that I might not sin against thee" (Ps.119:11).

"And I will delight myself in thy commandments, which I have loved" (Ps.119:47).

"The law of thy mouth *is* better unto me than thousands of gold and silver" (Ps.119:72).

"O how love I thy law! it *is* my meditation all the day" (Ps.119:97).

CHAPTER 23

F. The Godly Reign of Josiah (Part 2)—His Spiritual Renewal & Reform: A Need for Conversion, for Trusting the Only Living & True God, 23:1-30

23:1-27; see 2 Chr.34:29–36:1

1. The public reading of God's Word & the dedication of the people to the LORD: A concern for obedience

a. Josiah summoned all the leaders & citizens to a renewal service in the temple

b. Josiah read the entire Book of the Covenant to the people

  1) He personally renewed the covenant, dedicated himself to follow the LORD & to keep His commandments—with all his heart & soul

  2) The people then dedicated themselves to the LORD & His covenant (Word)

2. The reforms instituted by Josiah: A concern for true belief—trusting the only living & true God

a. He removed all the idols from the temple & burned them
  1) Removed Baal, Asherah, & the Astral idols & articles
  2) Burned the idols in the Kidron Valley: Took the ashes to Bethel to desecrate the false worship center, 1 K.12:25-33

b. He drove away the priests of the false gods
  1) Those who led worship at the high places
  2) Those who led in the worship of the false god Baal & of the heavenly bodies

c. He took the wooden image of Asherah from the temple & burned it: Scattered its ashes over the graves of its worshippers

And the king sent, and they gathered unto him all the elders of Judah and of Jerusalem.
2 And the king went up into the house of the LORD, and all the men of Judah and all the inhabitants of Jerusalem with him, and the priests, and the prophets, and all the people, both small and great: and he read in their ears all the words of the book of the covenant which was found in the house of the LORD.
3 And the king stood by a pillar, and made a covenant before the LORD, to walk after the LORD, and to keep his commandments and his testimonies and his statutes with all *their* heart and all *their* soul, to perform the words of this covenant that were written in this book. And all the people stood to the covenant.
4 And the king commanded Hilkiah the high priest, and the priests of the second order, and the keepers of the door, to bring forth out of the temple of the LORD all the vessels that were made for Baal, and for the grove, and for all the host of heaven: and he burned them without Jerusalem in the fields of Kidron, and carried the ashes of them unto Bethel.
5 And he put down the idolatrous priests, whom the kings of Judah had ordained to burn incense in the high places in the cities of Judah, and in the places round about Jerusalem; them also that burned incense unto Baal, to the sun, and to the moon, and to the planets, and to all the host of heaven.
6 And he brought out the grove from the house of the LORD, without Jerusalem, unto the brook Kidron, and burned it at the brook Kidron, and stamped *it* small to powder, and cast the powder

thereof upon the graves of the children of the people.
7 And he brake down the houses of the sodomites, that *were* by the house of the LORD, where the women wove hangings for the grove.
8 And he brought all the priests out of the cities of Judah, and defiled the high places where the priests had burned incense, from Geba to Beer-sheba, and brake down the high places of the gates that *were* in the entering in of the gate of Joshua the governor of the city, which *were* on a man's left hand at the gate of the city.
9 Nevertheless the priests of the high places came not up to the altar of the LORD in Jerusalem, but they did eat of the unleavened bread among their brethren.
10 And he defiled Topheth, which *is* in the valley of the children of Hinnom, that no man might make his son or his daughter to pass through the fire to Molech.
11 And he took away the horses that the kings of Judah had given to the sun, at the entering in of the house of the LORD, by the chamber of Nathan-melech the chamberlain, which *was* in the suburbs, and burned the chariots of the sun with fire.
12 And the altars that *were* on the top of the upper chamber of Ahaz, which the kings of Judah had made, and the altars which Manasseh had made in the two courts of the house of the LORD, did the king beat down, and brake *them* down from thence, and cast the dust of them into the brook Kidron.
13 And the high places that *were* before Jerusalem, which *were* on the right hand of the mount of corruption, which Solomon the king of Israel had builded for Ashtoreth the abomination of the Zidonians, and for Chemosh the abomination of the Moabites, and for Milcom the abomination of the children of Ammon, did the king defile.
14 And he brake in pieces the images, and cut down the groves, and filled their places with the bones of men.

d. He tore down the living quarters of shrine prostitutes (male & female) that were inside the temple

e. He desecrated all the high places throughout the nation & brought the true but backslidden priests back to Jerusalem
  1) Destroyed the shrines

  2) Restored the rightful yet wayward priests to the Levitical priesthood, but disqualified them from leading the temple services

f. He desecrated Topheth, the place where human sacrifices were offered up to Molech

g. He wiped out the false worship of heavenly bodies, the sun, moon, & stars
  1) Disposed of the horses dedicated to the sun god

  2) Burned the chariots

h. He destroyed the altars on the palace roof & the altars built by Manasseh in the two courts of the temple
  1) He smashed them
  2) He threw the debris in the Kidron Valley

i. He destroyed the high places east of Jerusalem—the ones built by Solomon
  1) He destroyed the altars built to worship three idols
   • Ashtoreth, the vile, detestable goddess of Sidon
   • Chemosh, the vile, detestable god of Moab
   • Molech, the vile, detestable god of Ammon

  2) He smashed the sacred stones & cut down the wooden images of Asherah
  3) He defiled the sites with human bones

j. He demolished the high places—altars & images—at Bethel

  1) He destroyed Jeroboam's worship site
- Destroyed the altar
- Burned the high place & Asherah pole or image

  2) He removed the bones from a priestly cemetery & burned them on the false altar to defile it: Was the fulfillment of prophecy from an unknown prophet, 1 K.13:1-13

  3) He honored the grave of the unknown prophet from Judah who had earlier been buried at Bethel

  4) He also honored the grave of a prophet from Samaria, 1 K.13:31-32

k. He demolished all the high places—worship centers & shrines—in the towns of Samaria

l. He executed all the false priests of Israel's high places: Burned human bones on the altars to defile them in the eyes of the people

m. He reinstituted the Passover: Symbolized God's deliverance of His people from Egyptian bondage

  1) Was to be done exactly as God's Word said

  2) Was the first Passover celebrated correctly—exactly as God's Word dictated—since the days of the judges

15 Moreover the altar that *was* at Bethel, *and* the high place which Jeroboam the son of Nebat, who made Israel to sin, had made, both that altar and the high place he brake down, and burned the high place, *and* stamped *it* small to powder, and burned the grove.
16 And as Josiah turned himself, he spied the sepulchres that *were* there in the mount, and sent, and took the bones out of the sepulchres, and burned *them* upon the altar, and polluted it, according to the word of the LORD which the man of God proclaimed, who proclaimed these words.
17 Then he said, What title *is* that that I see? And the men of the city told him, It *is* the sepulchre of the man of God, which came from Judah, and proclaimed these things that thou hast done against the altar of Bethel.
18 And he said, Let him alone; let no man move his bones. So they let his bones alone, with the bones of the prophet that came out of Samaria.
19 And all the houses also of the high places that *were* in the cities of Samaria, which the kings of Israel had made to provoke *the LORD* to anger, Josiah took away, and did to them according to all the acts that he had done in Bethel.
20 And he slew all the priests of the high places that *were* there upon the altars, and burned men's bones upon them, and returned to Jerusalem.
21 And the king commanded all the people, saying, Keep the passover unto the LORD your God, as *it is* written in the book of this covenant.
22 Surely there was not holden such a passover from the days of the judges that judged Israel, nor in all the days of the kings of Israel, nor of the kings of Judah;

23 But in the eighteenth year of king Josiah, *wherein* this passover was holden to the LORD in Jerusalem.
24 Moreover the *workers with* familiar spirits, and the wizards, and the images, and the idols, and all the abominations that were spied in the land of Judah and in Jerusalem, did Josiah put away, that he might perform the words of the law which were written in the book that Hilkiah the priest found in the house of the LORD.
25 And like unto him was there no king before him, that turned to the LORD with all his heart, and with all his soul, and with all his might, according to all the law of Moses; neither after him arose there *any* like him.
26 Notwithstanding the LORD turned not from the fierceness of his great wrath, wherewith his anger was kindled against Judah, because of all the provocations that Manasseh had provoked him withal.
27 And the LORD said, I will remove Judah also out of my sight, as I have removed Israel, and will cast off this city Jerusalem which I have chosen, and the house of which I said, My name shall be there.
28 Now the rest of the acts of Josiah, and all that he did, *are* they not written in the book of the chronicles of the kings of Judah?
29 In his days Pharaohnechoh king of Egypt went up against the king of Assyria to the river Euphrates: and king Josiah went against him; and he slew him at Megiddo, when he had seen him.
30 And his servants carried him in a chariot dead from Megiddo, and brought him to Jerusalem, and buried him in his own sepulchre. And the people of the land took Jehoahaz the son of Josiah, and anointed him, and made him king in his father's stead.

  3) Was celebrated in honor of the LORD: In the 18th year of Josiah's reign

n. He weeded out the mediums & spiritists & all other forms of household idols, & false worship in Judah & Jerusalem

  1) The reason: To obey the Word of God, His commandments

  2) The fact: His commitment to obeying God's Law, His Word, was unparalleled—was more zealous than any king who had ever lived

3. The fierce judgment of God against Judah: A much-needed concern over the picture of coming judgment

a. The reason: The wickedness of the people, especially under Manasseh, 21:1-18

b. The fatal judgment: To be removed from God's presence, from the promised land—rejected by God
  1) The city rejected
  2) The temple rejected

c. The achievements & the summary of Josiah's life
  1) His reign: Recorded in the book *The History of the Kings of Judah*
  2) His death
- Egypt marched through Israel to join Assyria against Babylon, the new world power
- Josiah marched out to stop Egypt: Was killed in battle

  3) His burial: His body was brought from Megiddo (the battle site) to Jerusalem, where he was buried in his own tomb
  4) His successor: Jehoahaz, his son

DIVISION IV

THE UTTER DISINTEGRATION AND FALL OF JUDAH, THE SOUTHERN KINGDOM: AN APPALLING DESTRUCTION DUE TO INCONSISTENCY, DISLOYALTY, AND EVER-GROWING WICKEDNESS, 18:1–25:30

F. The Godly Reign of Josiah (Part 2)—His Spiritual Renewal and Reform: A Need for Conversion, for Trusting the Only Living and True God, 23:1-30

(23:1-30) Introduction—Worship, False, Trait of People—Gods False, Worship of—God, Revelation of, Is a Fact—God, Revelation of, Proof That God Is Love, Not Hate—God, Proof of, Has Revealed Himself: in looking at various practices and forms of worship around the world, it is evident that few people genuinely worship the LORD, the only living and true God. Most people worship a god created by their own mind and imagination. For example, what are your thoughts about God, about who He is and what He is like? When you think of God, what images come to your mind? What is your picture of who God is? In all honesty, most of us worship what our image, our imagination of God is. But this is not the true and living God, no matter what our image or thoughts are.

The true and living God is the God of *revelation*, the God who loves this earth so much that He would never leave us in the dark about who He is. He would never let us walk in darkness, wondering about the truth and the meaning of life, about who we are, why we are here, and where we are going. Nor would He leave us in the dark about Himself, whether or not He truly exists and if it is possible to gain a personal relationship with Him.

Again, the true and living God is a God of *revelation*, a God who loves us so much that He *has* revealed the truth to us. How has He revealed it? By coming to this earth Himself in the person of Jesus Christ. In Jesus Christ, God has shown us Himself, who He is, what He is like, and how we are to live. Jesus Christ is the image of the only living and true God.

Believing in and worshipping the only living and true God is the central theme to be grasped in this chapter of God's Holy Word. This is the story of Josiah's spiritual reform in Judah, his attempt to convert the people to the one and only living God. Remember that Josiah had just received the prophetic message of God's judgment upon Judah. And the judgment was to be terrifying, equal to that of the Northern Kingdom. The picture is one of utter destruction by the invading Babylonians and the deportation of the people from the promised land. But because of Josiah's righteousness, the LORD had promised him he would not personally witness the terrible destruction coming. Broken over the message of judgment, Josiah reached out to convert or bring his people back to the LORD with the hope that they would respond positively. And hopefully, the LORD would have mercy and hold back His hand of coming judgment. This is the important message of the present Scripture: *The Godly Reign of Josiah (Part 2)—His Spiritual Renewal and Reform: A Need for Conversion, for Trusting the Only Living and True God, 23:1-30.*

1. The public reading of God's Word and the dedication of the people to the LORD: a concern for obedience (vv.1-3).
2. The reforms instituted by Josiah: a concern for true belief—trusting the only living and true God (vv.4-20).
3. The fierce judgment of God against Judah: a much-needed concern over the picture of coming judgment (vv.26-30).

1 **(23:1-3) Obedience, Concern for, Example—Word of God, Reading of, in Worship, by Josiah—Worship, Services of, Reading of God's Word—Rededication, Example of—Covenant, Renewal of, Example of—Josiah, King of Judah, Reign of—Kings, of Judah—Josiah, Concerns of, Obedience**: in launching his reformation throughout the nation, the first decision made by Josiah was to hold a public worship service, read God's Word, and then call upon the people to commit their lives to the LORD. Having heard the message of God's coming judgment, Josiah's hope was for God's mercy. If the people would respond positively and be genuinely converted to the LORD, perhaps the LORD would have mercy. Perhaps He would forgive their sins and turn His judgment away from Judah. To bring about this conversion to the LORD, Josiah summoned all the leaders and citizens of the nation to the renewal service in the temple. From the least to the greatest were summoned, including all the people, the royal officials, and the priests and prophets.

By calling all the prophets to the service, this meant that Jeremiah, Zephaniah, and Nahum—men who wrote prophetic books included in the Holy Scripture—were most likely there. With the mass of people in attendance, Josiah took God's Word that had recently been discovered—the Book of the Covenant—and read it to the people (v.2). For the first time in over 75 years, the people heard the Word of God read. They heard the commandments of God, how they were to worship Him and Him alone and how they were to treat one another with kindness and justice, respecting human life and property.

Once Josiah had finished reading the Word of God—the Book of the Covenant—He personally renewed the covenant himself. He dedicated himself to follow the LORD and to keep His commandments—with all his heart and soul (v.3). Then turning to the people, he called upon them to turn their lives over to the LORD. Responding to the challenge, the people dedicated themselves to the covenant of God's Holy Word. Hereafter, they would obey the LORD and keep His commandments.

OUTLINE	SCRIPTURE	SCRIPTURE	OUTLINE
1. The public reading of God's Word & the dedication of the people to the LORD: A concern for obedience	And the king sent, and they gathered unto him all the elders of Judah and of Jerusalem.	covenant which was found in the house of the LORD.	
	2 And the king went up into the house of the LORD, and	3 And the king stood by a pillar, and made a covenant before the LORD, to walk after	1) He personally renewed the covenant, dedicated himself to follow the LORD &
a. Josiah summoned all the leaders & citizens to a renewal service in the temple	all the men of Judah and all the inhabitants of Jerusalem with him, and the priests, and the prophets, and all the people, both small and great:	the LORD, and to keep his commandments and his testimonies and his statutes with all *their* heart and all *their* soul, to perform the words of this covenant that were written in this book. And all the	to keep His commandments—with all his heart & soul
b. Josiah read the entire Book of the Covenant to the people	and he read in their ears all the words of the book of the	people stood to the covenant.	2) The people then dedicated themselves to the LORD & His covenant (Word)

Thought 1. Imagine not having the Word of God, the Holy Bible, available in any form. Picture the Bible gone, lost, with only one copy left in existence; yet no one knows where it is. This is what happened during the days of the kings, in both the Northern and Southern Kingdoms. The people had become so wicked and evil that they had forgotten the Word of God.

A world without God's Holy Word would be a world of darkness, a world void of morality and justice. Think back through history, from the present to the past. Think of the societies that do not honor the Word of God, the Holy Bible—the societies that ignore, neglect, or deny God's Word. Look at the false worship, the confusion of worship, and the immorality, lawlessness, and violence that have swept—and are still sweeping—through societies that fail to honor God's Holy Word. It is God's Word that gives us light, that gives us God's commandments telling us how to live. His commandments tell us that we must love God first and then love our neighbors as we love ourselves. In addition, they tell us that we must keep the Sabbath Day holy, worshipping God and taking care of our bodies. This means that we must take one day a week to rest and to worship Him.

In loving our neighbors, we must treat one another just as we want to be treated. We must not dishonor our fathers and mothers, nor kill one another, nor commit adultery, nor lie by bearing false witness against others, nor gossip about each other, nor covet each other's property.

It does no good to have God's Holy Word unless we obey it. Of what value is it to know something if we do not act upon it or follow through with it? Of what value is it to have the Word of God if we are going to neglect it or even deny that it is the Word of God? We must remember one important fact: denying a fact does not make the fact untrue. If a piece of information is true, it remains true whether or not we accept it. And above all other truths is this one truth: God exists and God is love. Therefore, God would never leave us in darkness, unable to know the truth. For this reason, God has given us His Holy Word so that we may know the truth. God is love; therefore God has revealed the truth to us, both in Christ and in His Holy Word.

Consequently, our duty is to obey His truth, the Holy Word of God. Listen to what God says about obedience:

> "Not every one that saith unto me, Lord, Lord, shall enter into the kingdom of heaven; but he that doeth the will of my Father which is in heaven. Many will say to me in that day, Lord, Lord, have we not prophesied in thy name? and in thy name have cast out devils? and in thy name done many wonderful works? And then will I profess unto them, I never knew you: depart from me, ye that work iniquity" (Mt.7:21-23).

> "And he said unto him, Why callest thou me good? *there is* none good but one, *that is,* God: but if thou wilt enter into life, keep the commandments" (Mt.19:17).

> "If ye keep my commandments, ye shall abide in my love; even as I have kept my Father's commandments, and abide in his love" (Jn.15:10).

> "All scripture *is* given by inspiration of God, and *is* profitable for doctrine, for reproof, for correction, for instruction in righteousness" (2 Ti.3:16).

> "But whoso looketh into the perfect law of liberty, and continueth *therein,* he being not a forgetful hearer, but a doer of the work, this man shall be blessed in his deed" (Js.1:25).

> "We have also a more sure word of prophecy; whereunto ye do well that ye take heed, as unto a light that shineth in a dark place, until the day dawn, and the day star arise in your hearts: Knowing this first, that no prophecy of the scripture is of any private interpretation. For the prophecy came not in old time by the will of man: but holy men of God spake *as they were* moved by the Holy Ghost" (2 Pe.1:19-21).

> "For this is the love of God, that we keep his commandments: and his commandments are not grievous" (1 Jn.5:3).

> "Here is the patience of the saints: here *are* they that keep the commandments of God, and the faith of Jesus" (Re.14:12).

> "Blessed *are* they that do his commandments, that they may have right to the tree of life, and may enter in through the gates into the city" (Re.22:14).

> "Now therefore, if ye will obey my voice indeed, and keep my covenant, then ye shall be a peculiar treasure unto me above all people: for all the earth *is* mine" (Ex.19:5).

> "And showing mercy unto thousands of them that love me, and keep my commandments" (Ex.20:6).

> "O that there were such an heart in them, that they would fear me, and keep all my commandments always, that it might be well with them, and with their children for ever!" (De.5:29).

> "This day the LORD thy God hath commanded thee to do these statutes and judgments: thou shalt therefore keep and do them with all thine heart, and with all thy soul" (De.26:16).

> "This book of the law shall not depart out of thy mouth; but thou shalt meditate therein day and night, that thou mayest observe to do according to all that is written therein: for then thou shalt make thy way prosperous, and then thou shalt have good success" (Jos.1:8).

> "And keep the charge of the LORD thy God, to walk in his ways, to keep his statutes, and his commandments, and his judgments, and his testimonies, as it is written in the law of Moses, that thou mayest prosper in all that thou doest, and whithersoever thou turnest thyself" (1 K.2:3).

> "That they might set their hope in God, and not forget the works of God, but keep his commandments" (Ps.78:7).

2 (23:4-25) **Belief, Concern for, Example—Faith, Concern for, Example—Trust, in the LORD, Concern for—Josiah, Concern of, True Belief—Reforms, Example of—Reformation, Example of—Renewal, Example of—Josiah, King of Judah, Reign of**: after committing their lives to the LORD, Josiah and the people immediately launched a major reform throughout the nation. Seldom in history has a reformation of such magnitude been witnessed. Not only was Judah affected, but the reformation also swept throughout the land of the old Northern Kingdom of Israel. At least 14 specific reforms are mentioned by Scripture:

OUTLINE	SCRIPTURE	SCRIPTURE	OUTLINE

2. The reforms instituted by Josiah: A concern for true belief—trusting the only living & true God
a. He removed all the idols from the temple & burned them
  1) Removed Baal, Asherah, & the Astral idols & articles
  2) Burned the idols in the Kidron Valley: Took the ashes to Bethel to desecrate the false worship center, 1 K.12:25-33
b. He drove away the priests of the false gods
  1) Those who led worship at the high places
  2) Those who led in the worship of the false god Baal & of the heavenly bodies
	4 And the king commanded Hilkiah the high priest, and the priests of the second order, and the keepers of the door, to bring forth out of the temple of the LORD all the vessels that were made for Baal, and for the grove, and for all the host of heaven: and he burned them without Jerusalem in the fields of Kidron, and carried the ashes of them unto Bethel.
	5 And he put down the idolatrous priests, whom the kings of Judah had ordained to burn incense in the high places in the cities of Judah, and in the places round about Jerusalem; them also that burned incense unto Baal, to the sun, and to the moon, and to the planets, and to all the host of heaven.
		horses that the kings of Judah had given to the sun, at the entering in of the house of the LORD, by the chamber of Nathan-melech the chamberlain, which was in the suburbs, and burned the chariots of the sun with fire.
		12 And the altars that were on the top of the upper chamber of Ahaz, which the kings of Judah had made, and the altars which Manasseh had made in the two courts of the house of the LORD, did the king beat down, and brake them down from thence, and cast the dust of them into the brook Kidron.
			worship of heavenly bodies, the sun, moon, & stars
			  1) Disposed of the horses dedicated to the sun god
			
			  2) Burned the chariots
			
			h. He destroyed the altars on the palace roof & the altars built by Manasseh in the two courts of the temple
			  1) He smashed them
			  2) He threw the debris in the Kidron Valley

c. He took the wooden image of Asherah from the temple & burned it: Scattered its ashes over the graves of its worshippers	6 And he brought out the grove from the house of the LORD, without Jerusalem, unto the brook Kidron, and burned it at the brook Kidron, and stamped it small to powder, and cast the powder thereof upon the graves of the children of the people.	13 And the high places that were before Jerusalem, which were on the right hand of the mount of corruption, which Solomon the king of Israel had builded for Ashtoreth the abomination of the Zidonians, and for Chemosh the abomination of the Moabites, and for Milcom the abomination of the children of Ammon, did the king defile.	i. He destroyed the high places east of Jerusalem—the ones built by Solomon
			  1) He destroyed the altars built to worship three idols
			  • Ashtoreth, the vile, detestable goddess of Sidon
			  • Chemosh, the vile, detestable god of Moab
			  • Molech, the vile, detestable god of Ammon

d. He tore down the living quarters of shrine prostitutes (male & female) that were inside the temple	7 And he brake down the houses of the sodomites, that were by the house of the LORD, where the women wove hangings for the grove.	14 And he brake in pieces the images, and cut down the groves, and filled their places with the bones of men.	2) He smashed the sacred stones & cut down the wooden images of Asherah 3) He defiled the sites with human bones

e. He desecrated all the high places throughout the nation & brought the true but backslidden priests back to Jerusalem
  1) Destroyed the shrines
	8 And he brought all the priests out of the cities of Judah, and defiled the high places where the priests had burned incense, from Geba to Beer-sheba, and brake down the high places of the gates that were in the entering in of the gate of Joshua the governor of the city, which were on a man's left hand at the gate of the city.	15 Moreover the altar that was at Bethel, and the high place which Jeroboam the son of Nebat, who made Israel to sin, had made, both that altar and the high place he brake down, and burned the high place, and stamped it small to powder, and burned the grove.	j. He demolished the high places—altars & images—at Bethel
			  1) He destroyed Jeroboam's worship site
			  • Destroyed the altar
			  • Burned the high place & Asherah pole or image

2) Restored the rightful yet wayward priests to the Levitical priesthood, but disqualified them from leading the temple services	9 Nevertheless the priests of the high places came not up to the altar of the LORD in Jerusalem, but they did eat of the unleavened bread among their brethren.	16 And as Josiah turned himself, he spied the sepulchres that were there in the mount, and sent, and took the bones out of the sepulchres, and burned them upon the altar, and polluted it, according to the word of the LORD which the man of God proclaimed, who proclaimed these words.	2) He removed the bones from a priestly cemetery & burned them on the false altar to defile it: Was the fulfillment of prophecy from an unknown prophet, 1 K.13:1-13
f. He desecrated Topheth, the place where human sacrifices were offered up to Molech	10 And he defiled Topheth, which is in the valley of the children of Hinnom, that no man might make his son or his daughter to pass through the fire to Molech.	17 Then he said, What title is that that I see? And the men of the city told him, It is the sepulchre of the man of God, which came from Judah, and proclaimed these	3) He honored the grave of the unknown prophet from Judah who had earlier been buried at Bethel
g. He wiped out the false	11 And he took away the	words.	

195

OUTLINE	SCRIPTURE	SCRIPTURE	OUTLINE
4) He also honored the grave of a prophet from Samaria, 1 K.13:31-32	things that thou hast done against the altar of Bethel. 18 And he said, Let him alone; let no man move his bones. So they let his bones alone, with the bones of the prophet that came out of Samaria.	holden such a passover from the days of the judges that judged Israel, nor in all the days of the kings of Israel, nor of the kings of Judah; 23 But in the eighteenth year of king Josiah, *wherein* this passover was holden to the LORD in Jerusalem.	celebrated correctly—exactly as God's Word dictated—since the days of the judges 3) Was celebrated in honor of the LORD: In the 18th year of Josiah's reign
k. He demolished all the high places—worship centers & shrines—in the towns of Samaria	19 And all the houses also of the high places that *were* in the cities of Samaria, which the kings of Israel had made to provoke *the LORD* to anger, Josiah took away, and did to them according to all the acts that he had done in Bethel.	24 Moreover the *workers with* familiar spirits, and the wizards, and the images, and the idols, and all the abominations that were spied in the land of Judah and in Jerusalem, did Josiah put away, that he might perform the words of the law which were written in the book that Hilkiah the priest found in the house of the LORD.	n. He weeded out the mediums & spiritists & all other forms of household idols, & false worship in Judah & Jerusalem 1) The reason: To obey the Word of God, His commandments
l. He executed all the false priests of Israel's high places: Burned human bones on the altars to defile them in the eyes of the people m. He reinstituted the Passover: Symbolized God's deliverance of His people from Egyptian bondage 1) Was to be done exactly as God's Word said 2) Was the first Passover	20 And he slew all the priests of the high places that *were* there upon the altars, and burned men's bones upon them, and returned to Jerusalem. 21 And the king commanded all the people, saying, Keep the passover unto the LORD your God, as *it is* written in the book of this covenant. 22 Surely there was not	25 And like unto him was there no king before him, that turned to the LORD with all his heart, and with all his soul, and with all his might, according to all the law of Moses; neither after him arose there *any* like him.	2) The fact: His commitment to obeying God's Law, His Word, was unparalleled—was more zealous than any king who had ever lived

a. Josiah instructed the priests to remove all the idols or false gods from the temple and burn them (v.4). Remember that Josiah's grandfather Manasseh had placed all kinds of idols in the temple, and Josiah's father Amon had continued the false worship of false gods. Thinking about the idols that filled the temple of the LORD must have sickened the heart of the true believer. There were images of the false gods Baal, Asherah, and the Astral gods of the sun, moon, and stars. In obedience to the king's command, the priests and doorkeepers removed the idols and various articles used in their worship. These were burned in the Kidron Valley, then the ashes taken to Bethel where they were scattered in order to desecrate the false worship site. Scattering the ashes was a symbol that the false worship center was being desecrated, rejected, and defiled because of its corruption of true worship.

b. Josiah also drove away the priests of the false gods throughout the nation (v.5). This included all the priests who served the false gods at the high places located within the countryside and the towns, including Jerusalem. Any priest who served the false god Baal or the Astral deities of the sun, moon, and stars was driven away.

c. Apparently, the wooden image of Asherah was a popular idol of worship, for Josiah gave it special attention. Removing the wooden image from the temple, he burned it and had its ashes scattered over the graves of its worshippers (v.6). No doubt, he was symbolizing that the idol had no more life than its worshippers who were lying in the grave dead.

d. Josiah then tore down the living quarters of shrine prostitutes—both male and female—who were living inside the temple (v.7). Nothing shows how false religion corrupts people any more than the practice of promiscuous sexual behavior within religion. The god and goddess of fertility were considered to be Baal and Asherah. In seeking fertility for their crops, the people worshipped and sought the favor of these two false gods by having sexual relations with their priests or priestesses. Sexual relations symbolized fertility through the blessing of children and a fruitful harvest.

e. When Josiah had desecrated all the high places throughout the nation, he brought the true but backslidden priests back to Jerusalem (vv.8-9). From Giba to Beersheba—the northern border to the southern border—Josiah destroyed all the shrines that had been built for false worship. This included all the shrines at the gates of the cities throughout the nation, including at the gate of Joshua in the city of Jerusalem. Once the backslidden, wayward priests had been returned to Jerusalem, they were restored to the Levitical priesthood, but disqualified from leading the temple worship services (v.9).

f. Note that special attention was given to the altar built at Topheth in the Valley of Ben Hinnom. For it was upon this altar that human sacrifice was made, being offered up to the false god Molech (v.10). By destroying this altar, the gruesome sacrifice of children was stopped, at least during the reign of Josiah.

g. Josiah literally wiped out the false worship of the heavenly bodies, the worship of the sun, moon, and stars (v.11). He did this by disposing of the sacred horses that were most likely used in the worship processionals to the sun. He also burned the chariots that had been dedicated and used in the processionals.

h. Josiah destroyed the false altars that had been built on the palace roof by various kings of Judah as well as the altars built by his grandfather Manasseh in the two courts of the temple (v.12). Smashing them, he had the debris thrown in the Kidron Valley where the trash dump of the city was located.

i. Special mention is given to Josiah's destruction of the high places east of Jerusalem, the ones that, sadly, had been built by Solomon (vv.13-14). In order to keep peaceful alliances with surrounding nations, Solomon had married the daughters of many royal houses. In order to maintain these alliances and to please his wives, he had built *worship altars* to the following false gods:

⇒ Ashtoreth, the vile and detestable goddess of Sidon
⇒ Chemosh, the vile and detestable god of Moab
⇒ Molech, the vile and detestable god of Amon

But thankfully, at long last, a righteous king was sitting upon the throne of Judah, a king who was attempting to turn the hearts of the people back to the LORD. In obedience to the LORD's commandments, Josiah destroyed all the altars to false gods that Solomon had built. In addition, he smashed the sacred stones and cut down the wooden images of Asherah, then defiled the worship sites with human bones, which would make them unsuitable for future worship.

j. Moving to Bethel, one of the two major worship sites in the Northern Kingdom, Josiah demolished the high place and its worship center (vv.15-18). In an attempt to build the loyalty of the people to the Northern Kingdom, Jeroboam I had chosen Bethel to be one of the two major sites of the new religion he instituted (see outline and note—1 K.12:25-33 for more discussion). Special attention was given to Bethel by Josiah. Four very special acts were taken:

⇒ He destroyed the altar and burned the high place and Asherah pole or image (v.15).
⇒ He removed the bones from a priestly cemetery and burned them on the false altar to defile it (v.16). This was the fulfillment of a prophecy from an unknown prophet (1 K.13:1-13).
⇒ He honored the grave of an unknown prophet from Judah who had earlier been buried at Bethel (v.17).
⇒ Josiah also honored the grave of a prophet from Samaria who had also been buried there (v.18; 1 K.13:31-32).

k. Continuing throughout the towns of Samaria, Josiah demolished all the high places with their worship centers and shrines (v.19).

l. When Josiah destroyed the high places, he executed all the false priests and burned human bones on the altars to defile the worship sites in the eyes of the people (v.20). By defiling the land, he made the sites unusable for future worship.

m. In carrying out his reforms, Josiah knew that positive action was just as necessary as purging the land of wickedness. Thus, he reinstituted the Passover, the celebration that symbolized God's deliverance of His people from Egyptian bondage (vv.21-23). For over 75 years the feast had been neglected, and no one had celebrated the Lord's wonderful deliverance. But now Josiah reinstituted the feast that God had commanded the people to celebrate annually in remembrance of their deliverance (see outline and notes—Ex.12:1-13; De.16:1-8).

Josiah gave only one very important instruction regarding the feast: the Passover was to be carried out exactly as God's Word said. And note the result of Josiah's charge: this was the first Passover celebrated correctly—exactly as God's Word dictated—since the days of the Judges (vv.21-22). This wonderful celebration of the Passover took place in the eighteenth year of Josiah's reign (v.23).

n. Josiah's reforms were so thorough that he actually weeded out the medians and spiritists and all other household idols in Judah and Jerusalem (vv.24-25). In his zeal for the LORD, he was determined to obey the Word of God and its commandments to the fullest. As a result, note what Scripture says about him: his commitment to obey God's Word was unparalleled (v.25). He sought to obey the LORD wholeheartedly, with more zeal than any other king who had ever lived.

Thought 1. Josiah had a concern for true belief, a concern that people would trust the only living and true God. When dealing with truth, there is only one living and true God—the LORD GOD Himself (Jehovah, Yahweh). All other so-called gods are false, only the creations of peoples' minds and imaginations. These imaginary gods are not living, are not able to help us nor respond to us. No other god can answer our prayers, except the LORD Himself. Only the LORD has loved the world so much that He sent His Son to take our sins upon Himself and to bear the punishment for those sins. Only the LORD has redeemed us, paid the ransom price to set us free from sin, death, and hell—through sending His Son to die in our place. Only the LORD has given His own Son to bear the punishment of our sin so that we might live with God and for Him eternally. No so-called god has ever demonstrated such an incomprehensible love for us. Only the LORD has demonstrated such love. And He did it to prove that He is the only living and true God. For this reason, no human being has an excuse for living in unbelief. If a person chooses to reject the LORD as the only living and true God, he will suffer the consequences of his decision, will bear the punishment for his own sin.

Listen to what God's Holy Word says about the LORD being the only living and true God:

"But Jesus held his peace. And the high priest answered and said unto him, I adjure thee by the living God, that thou tell us whether thou be the Christ, the Son of God. Jesus saith unto him, Thou hast said: nevertheless I say unto you, Hereafter shall ye see the Son of man sitting on the right hand of power, and coming in the clouds of heaven" (Mt.26:63-64).

"And saying, Sirs, why do ye these things? We also are men of like passions with you, and preach unto you that ye should turn from these vanities unto the living God, which made heaven, and earth, and the sea, and all things that are therein" (Ac.14:15).

"God that made the world and all things therein, seeing that he is Lord of heaven and earth, dwelleth not in temples made with hands; Neither is worshipped with men's hands, as though he needed any thing, seeing he giveth to all life, and breath, and all things; And hath made of one blood all nations of men for to dwell on all the face of the earth, and hath determined the times before appointed, and the bounds of their habitation; That they should seek the Lord, if haply they might feel after him, and find him, though he be not far from every one of us: For in him we live, and move, and have our being; as certain also of your own poets have said, For we are also his offspring. Forasmuch then as we are the offspring of God, we ought not to think that the Godhead is like unto gold, or silver, or stone, graven by art and man's device. And the times of this ignorance God winked at; but now commandeth all men every where to repent: Because he hath appointed a day, in the which he will judge the world in righteousness by *that* man whom he hath ordained; *whereof* he hath given assurance unto all *men*, in that he hath raised him from the dead" (Ac.17:24-31).

"For the wrath of God is revealed from heaven against all ungodliness and unrighteousness of men, who hold the truth in unrighteousness; Because that which may be known of God is manifest in them; for God hath showed *it* unto them. For the invisible things of him from the creation of the world are clearly seen, being understood by the things that are made, *even* his eternal power and Godhead; so that they are without excuse: Because that, when they knew God, they glorified *him* not as God, neither were thankful; but became vain in their imaginations, and their foolish heart was darkened. Professing themselves to be wise, they became fools, And changed the glory of the uncorruptible God into an image made like to corruptible man, and to birds, and fourfooted beasts, and creeping things. Wherefore God also gave them up to uncleanness through the lusts of their own hearts, to dishonour their own bodies between themselves: Who changed the truth of God into a lie, and worshipped and served the creature more than the Creator, who is blessed for ever. Amen" (Ro.1:18-25).

"As concerning therefore the eating of those things that are offered in sacrifice unto idols, we know that an idol *is* nothing in the world, and that *there is* none other God but one" (1 Co.8:4).

"One God and Father of all, who *is* above all, and through all, and in you all" (Ep.4:6).

"For they themselves show of us what manner of entering in we had unto you, and how ye turned to God from idols to serve the living and true God; And to wait for his Son from heaven, whom he raised from the dead, *even* Jesus, which delivered us from the wrath to come" (1 Th.1:9-10).

"For *there is* one God, and one mediator between God and men, the man Christ Jesus; Who gave himself a ransom for all, to be testified in due time" (1 Ti.2:5-6).

"He that despised Moses' law died without mercy under two or three witnesses: Of how much sorer punishment, suppose ye, shall he be thought worthy, who hath trodden under foot the Son of God, and hath counted the blood of the covenant, wherewith he was sanctified, an unholy thing, and hath done despite unto the Spirit of grace? For we know him that hath said, Vengeance *belongeth* unto me, I will recompense, saith the Lord. And again, The Lord shall judge his people. *It is* a fearful thing to fall into the hands of the living God" (He.10:28-31).

"Who *is* like unto thee, O LORD, among the gods? who *is* like thee, glorious in holiness, fearful *in* praises, doing wonders?" (Ex.15:11).

"Unto thee it was showed, that thou mightest know that the LORD he *is* God; *there is* none else beside him" (De.4:35).

"Hear, O Israel: The LORD our God *is* one LORD" (De.6:4).

"See now that I, *even* I, *am* he, and *there is* no god with me: I kill, and I make alive; I wound, and I heal: neither *is there any* that can deliver out of my hand" (De.32:39).

"Wherefore thou art great, O LORD God: for *there is* none like thee, neither *is there any* God beside thee, according to all that we have heard with our ears" (2 S.7:22).

"And he said, LORD God of Israel, *there is* no God like thee, in heaven above, or on earth beneath, who keepest covenant and mercy with thy servants that walk before thee with all their heart" (1 K.8:23).

"My soul thirsteth for God, for the living God: when shall I come and appear before God?" (Ps.42:2).

"That *men* may know that thou, whose name alone *is* JEHOVAH, *art* the most high over all the earth" (Ps.83:18).

"My soul longeth, yea, even fainteth for the courts of the LORD: my heart and my flesh crieth out for the living God" (Ps.84:2).

"For thou *art* great, and doest wondrous things: thou *art* God alone" (Ps.86:10).

"For who in the heaven can be compared unto the LORD? *who* among the sons of the mighty can be likened unto the LORD?" (Ps.89:6).

"Hast thou not known? hast thou not heard, *that* the everlasting God, the LORD, the Creator of the ends of the earth, fainteth not, neither is weary? *there is* no searching of his understanding. He giveth power to the faint; and to *them that have* no might he increaseth strength. Even the youths shall faint and be weary, and the young men shall utterly fall: But they that wait upon the LORD shall renew *their* strength; they shall mount up with wings as eagles; they shall run, and not be weary; *and* they shall walk, and not faint" (Is.40:28-31, cp. vv.18-27).

"Ye *are* my witnesses, saith the LORD, and my servant whom I have chosen: that ye may know and believe me, and understand that I *am* he: before me there was no God formed, neither shall there be after me" (Is.43:10).

"For thus saith the LORD that created the heavens; God himself that formed the earth and made it; he hath established it, he created it not in vain, he formed it to be inhabited: I *am* the LORD; and *there is* none else" (Is.45:18).

"Look unto me, and be ye saved, all the ends of the earth: for I *am* God, and *there is* none else. I have sworn by myself, the word is gone out of my mouth *in* righteousness, and shall not return, That unto me every knee shall bow, every tongue shall swear. Surely, shall *one* say, in the LORD have I righteousness and strength: *even* to him shall *men* come; and all that are incensed against him shall be ashamed" (Is.45:22-24).

"They *are* upright as the palm tree, but speak not: they must needs be borne, because they cannot go. Be not afraid of them; for they cannot do evil, neither also *is it* in them to do good" (Je.10:5).

3 (23:26-30) **Judgment, Predicted—Judah, Judgment of, Predicted—Prophecy, of Judah's Destruction—Josiah, Death of—Judah, Wars of**: despite Josiah's great reformation, the hand of God's judgment against Judah was to fall. For centuries, the wickedness of the people had accumulated to such a degree that they would never genuinely turn to the LORD, not consistently and not permanently. Because of all the wickedness down through the centuries and especially under Manasseh, the anger of the LORD had been aroused (21:1-18). As a result, the fatal judgment of God was to fall upon the nation. They were to be removed from God's presence, from the promised land, just as the Northern Kingdom of Israel had been removed. The city that God had chosen, Jerusalem, and the temple upon which God had said He would put His Name were both now rejected by the LORD and would be destroyed.

OUTLINE	SCRIPTURE	SCRIPTURE	OUTLINE
3. The fierce judgment of God against Judah: A much-needed concern over the picture of coming judgment a. The reason: The wickedness of the people, especially under Manasseh, 21:1-18 b. The fatal judgment: To be removed from God's presence, from the promised land—rejected by God 1) The city rejected 2) The temple rejected c. The achievements & the summary of Josiah's life 1) His reign: Recorded in the	26 Notwithstanding the LORD turned not from the fierceness of his great wrath, wherewith his anger was kindled against Judah, because of all the provocations that Manasseh had provoked him withal. 27 And the LORD said, I will remove Judah also out of my sight, as I have removed Israel, and will cast off this city Jerusalem which I have chosen, and the house of which I said, My name shall be there. 28 Now the rest of the acts of Josiah, and all that he did, *are* they not written in the	book of the chronicles of the kings of Judah? 29 In his days Pharaoh-nechoh king of Egypt went up against the king of Assyria to the river Euphrates: and king Josiah went against him; and he slew him at Megiddo, when he had seen him. 30 And his servants carried him in a chariot dead from Megiddo, and brought him to Jerusalem, and buried him in his own sepulchre. And the people of the land took Jehoahaz the son of Josiah, and anointed him, and made him king in his father's stead.	book *The History of the Kings of Judah* 2) His death • Egypt marched through Israel to join Assyria against Babylon, the new world power • Josiah marched out to stop Egypt: Was killed in battle 3) His burial: His body was brought from Megiddo (the battle site) to Jerusalem, where he was buried in his own tomb 4) His successor: Jehoahaz, his son

A summary of Josiah's achievements and life are recorded in the book *The History of the Kings of Judah* (v.28). At the early age of 39, Josiah was killed in a battle with King Neco II of Egypt (v.29). The Egyptians were marching to join forces with Assyria in a war against Babylon. Apparently, Josiah feared domination by Egypt if Egypt and Assyria were successful against the Babylonians. Thus, he marched out to face the Egyptians. *Second Chronicles* says that King Neco sought to avoid war with Josiah, but Josiah—in disobedience to the LORD—refused to heed Neco's appeal. As a result, he foolishly lost his life (see outline and note—2 Chr.35:20-27 for more discussion). *The Expositor's Bible Commentary* says this about the attempt of King Neco to join the Assyrian forces:

> By 625 the Chaldean king Nabopolassar had been able to achieve independence for Babylon. From that point onward throughout the course of the next two decades, the Assyrian territory was systematically reduced, especially as Nabopolassar found common cause against Assyria, first with the Medes (616) and later with the Ummanmande (possibly a designation for the Scythians). In 614 the time-honored capital of Assyria, Asshur, fell to the Medes. In 612 Nineveh itself fell to the coalition of Chaldeans, Medes, and Ummanmande, the surviving Assyrian forces under Ashur-u-ballit fleeing to Haran.
>
> In those critical times concerned with the rising power of the new Mesopotamian coalition, Egypt's Twenty-Sixth Dynasty Pharaoh, Neco, honored the previous diplomatic ties with Assyria. As Neco's predecessor, Psammetik I, had come to the aid of Assyria in 616 B.C., so Neco moved to join the surviving Assyrian forces under Ashur-u-ballit. It was to prevent this movement of Egyptian aid that Josiah deployed his forces in the Valley of Megiddo in 609. That action cost Josiah his life, though it did delay the Egyptian forces from linking with their Assyrian allies before Haran fell to the Chaldeans and Medes. A subsequent attempt to retake Haran failed completely; and the best Egypt could give the doomed Assyrians was a four-year standoff, the opposing armies facing each other at Carchemish, on the western Euphrates.[1]

After Josiah's death at the Battle of Megiddo, his body was brought back to Jerusalem where he was buried in his own tomb (v.30). He was succeeded by his son Jehoahaz.

Thought 1. Judgment was to fall upon Judah for one reason and one reason only: because of their sin, wickedness, and evil. They refused to be genuinely converted, refused to consistently and continually walk with the LORD. Disobeying the commandments of God, they lived lives of worldly pleasure, immorality, lawlessness, and violence. As a result, God had no choice but to bring His judgment upon them.

So it is with us if we continue in sin and wickedness. When we refuse to be genuinely converted, never turning to the LORD, we condemn ourselves. We choose the judgment of God instead of the mercy of God. God's mercy is available to us, but if we reject His mercy, justice has to be executed. We must face the hour of God's justice due to all the sin and wickedness of this earth committed by us—all the bitterness, anger, hatred, assaults, abuses, rapes, and murders. The day of judgment—that day when perfect justice will be executed—is coming. And the surety of its coming has been guaranteed by God. Listen to the clear, forceful statements of God's Holy Word, the straightforward statements that His judgment is coming.

---

1 Richard D. Patterson and Hermann J. Austel. *1, 2 Kings*, p.289.

"But I say unto you, It shall be more tolerable for Tyre and Sidon at the day of judgment, than for you. And thou, Capernaum, which art exalted unto heaven, shalt be brought down to hell: for if the mighty works, which have been done in thee, had been done in Sodom, it would have remained until this day. But I say unto you, That it shall be more tolerable for the land of Sodom in the day of judgment, than for thee" (Mt.11:22-24).

"For the Son of man shall come in the glory of his Father with his angels; and then he shall reward every man according to his works" (Mt.16:27).

"When the Son of man shall come in his glory, and all the holy angels with him, then shall he sit upon the throne of his glory: And before him shall be gathered all nations: and he shall separate them one from another, as a shepherd divideth *his* sheep from the goats: And he shall set the sheep on his right hand, but the goats on the left" (Mt.25:31-33).

"He that believeth on the Son hath everlasting life: and he that believeth not the Son shall not see life; but the wrath of God abideth on him" (Jn.3:36).

"For the wrath of God is revealed from heaven against all ungodliness and unrighteousness of men, who hold the truth in unrighteousness" (Ro.1:18).

"But unto them that are contentious, and do not obey the truth, but obey unrighteousness, indignation and wrath" (Ro.2:8).

"But fornication, and all uncleanness, or covetousness, let it not be once named among you, as becometh saints; Neither filthiness, nor foolish talking, nor jesting, which are not convenient: but rather giving of thanks. For this ye know, that no whoremonger, nor unclean person, nor covetous man, who is an idolater, hath any inheritance in the kingdom of Christ and of God. Let no man deceive you with vain words: for because of these things cometh the wrath of God upon the children of disobedience" (Ep.5:3-6).

"And to you who are troubled rest with us, when the Lord Jesus shall be revealed from heaven with his mighty angels" (2 Th.1:7).

"And Enoch also, the seventh from Adam, prophesied of these, saying, Behold, the LORD cometh with ten thousands of his saints, To execute judgment upon all, and to convince all that are ungodly among them of all their ungodly deeds which they have ungodly committed, and of all their hard *speeches* which ungodly sinners have spoken against him" (Jude 14-15).

"And I saw a great white throne, and him that sat on it, from whose face the earth and the heaven fled away; and there was found no place for them. And I saw the dead, small and great, stand before God; and the books were opened: and another book was opened, which is *the book* of life: and the dead were judged out of those things which were written in the books, according to their works. And the sea gave up the dead which were in it; and death and hell delivered up the dead which were in them: and they were judged every man according to their works. And death and hell were cast into the lake of fire. This is the second death. And whosoever was not found written in the book of life was cast into the lake of fire" (Re.20:11-15).

1. The reign of Jehoahaz (dethroned by Egypt): A failure to follow a godly father

a. His background
   1) His age: 23 years old
   2) His term: Only 3 months
   3) His mother: Hamutal
b. His wicked life: Ignored his father Josiah's righteousness & did evil

c. His immediate crisis: Pharaoh summoned him to Riblah, 29
   1) Neco arrested & imprisoned him
   2) Neco demanded a heavy tribute from Judah

2. The reign of Jehoiakim (appointed king by Egypt): A failure to heed the warning of God's prophets, 24:2; Je.27:9-11

a. His background
   1) His name changed by Egypt: To show subjection
   2) His father exiled by Egypt
   3) His program of heavy taxation: To pay tribute to Egypt

   4) His age: 25 years old

   5) His term: 11 years

   6) His mother: Zebidah

b. His wicked life: Did evil in the sight of the LORD

c. His major crisis: The invasion by King Nebuchadnezzar of Babylon
   1) He submitted & paid tribute for three years
   2) He then foolishly rebelled: Rejected the warning of Jeremiah, Je.27:9-11
d. He & his people's continued punishment by the LORD for their sins: Special forces

---

G. The Reigns Controlled by Egypt & Babylon: A Look at Four Critical Failures, 23:31–24:20

24:8-16; see 2 Chr.36:9-10
24:17-20; see 2 Chr.36:11-13; Je.52:1-3

31 Jehoahaz *was* twenty and three years old when he began to reign; and he reigned three months in Jerusalem. And his mother's name *was* Hamutal, the daughter of Jeremiah of Libnah.
32 And he did *that which was* evil in the sight of the LORD, according to all that his fathers had done.
33 And Pharaoh-nechoh put him in bands at Riblah in the land of Hamath, that he might not reign in Jerusalem; and put the land to a tribute of an hundred talents of silver, and a talent of gold.
34 And Pharaoh-nechoh made Eliakim the son of Josiah king in the room of Josiah his father, and turned his name to Jehoiakim, and took Jehoahaz away: and he came to Egypt, and died there.
35 And Jehoiakim gave the silver and the gold to Pharaoh; but he taxed the land to give the money according to the commandment of Pharaoh: he exacted the silver and the gold of the people of the land, of every one according to his taxation, to give *it* unto Pharaoh-nechoh.
36 Jehoiakim *was* twenty and five years old when he began to reign; and he reigned eleven years in Jerusalem. And his mother's name *was* Zebudah, the daughter of Pedaiah of Rumah.
37 And he did *that which was* evil in the sight of the LORD, according to all that his fathers had done.

CHAPTER 24

In his days Nebuchadnezzar king of Babylon came up, and Jehoiakim became his servant three years: then he turned and rebelled against him.
2 And the LORD sent against him bands of the Chaldees, and bands of the Syrians, and bands of the Moabites, and bands of the children of Ammon, and sent them against Judah to destroy it, according to the word of the LORD, which he spake by his servants the prophets.
3 Surely at the commandment of the LORD came *this* upon Judah, to remove *them* out of his sight, for the sins of Manasseh, according to all that he did;
4 And also for the innocent blood that he shed: for he filled Jerusalem with innocent blood; which the LORD would not pardon.
5 Now the rest of the acts of Jehoiakim, and all that he did, *are* they not written in the book of the chronicles of the kings of Judah?
6 So Jehoiakim slept with his fathers: and Jehoiachin his son reigned in his stead.
7 And the king of Egypt came not again any more out of his land: for the king of Babylon had taken from the river of Egypt unto the river Euphrates all that pertained to the king of Egypt.
8 Jehoiachin *was* eighteen years old when he began to reign, and he reigned in Jerusalem three months. And his mother's name *was* Nehushta, the daughter of Elnathan of Jerusalem.
9 And he did *that which was* evil in the sight of the LORD, according to all that his father had done.
10 At that time the servants of Nebuchadnezzar king of Babylon came up against Jerusalem, and the city was besieged.
11 And Nebuchadnezzar king of Babylon came against the city, and his servants did besiege it.
12 And Jehoiachin the king of Judah went out to the king of Babylon, he, and his mother, and his servants, and his princes, and his officers: and the king of Babylon took him in the eighth year of his reign.
13 And he carried out thence all the treasures of the house of the LORD, and the treasures of the king's house, and cut in pieces all the vessels of gold which Solomon king of Israel had made in the temple of the LORD, as the LORD had said.

---

were sent to weaken the nation for its destruction
   1) The LORD had warned the people through His prophets
      • He would remove them from His presence, from the promised land
      • He would judge them for their sins, especially for following the sins of Manasseh, 21:1-18
      • He would judge them for killing so many innocent people
   2) The reason: He was no longer willing to forgive
e. His achievements & the summary of his life
   1) His reign: Recorded in the book *The History of the Kings of Judah*
   2) His death: No burial, Je.22:18-19
   3) His successor: Jehoiachin, his son

3. The reign of Jehoiachin (forced to surrender to Babylon): A failure to shun evil examples

a. His background
   1) His loss of Egypt as an ally: Egypt had been defeated by Babylon, Je.46:2
   2) His age: 18 years old
   3) His term: 3 months
   4) His mother: Nehushta

b. His evil life: Lived a wicked life, following the example of his father

c. His immediate crisis: The retaliatory invasion & siege by Babylon

   1) Nebuchadnezzar himself decided to join his army to personally accept the surrender of Jerusalem & Judah
      • Jehoiachin & his mother, his servants, nobles, & royal officials—all went out to surrender to the Babylonian king
      • Jehoiachin was immediately taken prisoner
   2) Nebuchadnezzar raided the royal palace & temple, stripping the city of all wealth

3) Nebuchadnezzar deported all the people of Jerusalem
• Deported all who could instigate an uprising: The military, business, & government leaders; & the skilled & wealthy
• Left only the poorest
• Exiled Jehoiachin, his family, royal officials, & other leaders to Babylon
 	
• Deported the entire army of 7,000 soldiers & 1,000 skilled workers: Exiled 10,000 total people to Babylon, including the prophet Ezekiel, Eze.1:1-3
	14 And he carried away all Jerusalem, and all the princes, and all the mighty men of valour, *even* ten thousand captives, and all the craftsmen and smiths: none remained, save the poorest sort of the people of the land.
	15 And he carried away Jehoiachin to Babylon, and the king's mother, and the king's wives, and his officers, and the mighty of the land, *those* carried he into captivity from Jerusalem to Babylon.
	16 And all the men of might, *even* seven thousand, and craftsmen and smiths a thousand, all *that were* strong *and* apt for war, even them the king of Babylon brought captive to Babylon.
		17 And the king of Babylon made Mattaniah his father's brother king in his stead, and changed his name to Zedekiah.
		18 Zedekiah *was* twenty and one years old when he began to reign, and he reigned eleven years in Jerusalem. And his mother's name *was* Hamutal, the daughter of Jeremiah of Libnah.
		19 And he did *that which was* evil in the sight of the LORD, according to all that Jehoiakim had done.
		20 For through the anger of the LORD it came to pass in Jerusalem and Judah, until he had cast them out from his presence, that Zedekiah rebelled against the king of Babylon.
			4. The reign of Zedekiah, the last king (appointed by Babylon): A failure to escape condemnation, Je.38:5,19
			a. His name changed: To show subjection
			b. His background
			  1) His age: 21 years old
			  2) His rule: Lasted 11 years
			  3) His mother: Hamutal
			
			c. His evil: Lived a wicked life, following the example of Jehoiakim
			d. His & Judah's destiny: Judgment, 20
			  1) They were conquered, condemned due to their sin
			  2) They were to be thrust from God's presence, from the promised land
			e. His rebellion against Babylon

DIVISION IV

THE UTTER DISINTEGRATION AND FALL OF JUDAH, THE SOUTHERN KINGDOM: AN APPALLING DESTRUCTION DUE TO INCONSISTENCY, DISLOYALTY, AND EVER-GROWING WICKEDNESS, 18:1–25:30

G. The Reigns Controlled by Egypt and Babylon: A Look at Four Critical Failures, 23:31–24:20

(23:31–24:20) **Introduction—Failure, Feelings of, a Problem—Failure, Feelings of, Caused by—Failure, Caused by—Life, Failure in Life, Caused by—Failure, Four Examples of**: many people in our society today are plagued with feelings of inadequacy, feeling that they are failures in life. But they are not failures. Perhaps they have failed in one project or assignment or in one area of life or in a particular behavior. But failure is not a pattern in their lives. The totality of their lives is anything but a failure. They have been successful in much, controlling most of their behavior and being generally responsible in their work. Most areas of their lives are healthy, productive, and satisfying. But occasionally a person becomes discouraged or disappointed, depressed or emotionally unraveled. It is then that the person experiences a *false* sense of *failure*. Some event or physical problem or chemical imbalance has aroused a sense of inadequacy or low self-esteem in his life. While the individual may feel like a failure at the time, in reality he or she is not a failure at all. On the contrary, he or she has done well and to some degree has been useful and productive.

However, all feelings of failure are not false. Some persons are failures in life. A failure in life is a person who does little good, living a life that bears only a little fruit. For these persons, an unproductive, unfruitful life is a self-centered life, a life that is lived in sin, wickedness, and evil. When a person becomes engrossed in self—degrading, humiliating, and dominating other people—this person fails in life. No matter how much power, wealth, or fame he achieves, the person is a failure. For a person who fails to help other people—ministering to them, encouraging and upholding them, making sure their needs are met—is living a failed life. A person becomes a failure when he does not know or spread love, joy, peace, patience, kindness, goodness, faithfulness, humility, and self-control. A person who lacks this fruit of God's Spirit is a person who fails in life.

Four examples of failure are the subject of the present Scripture. Immediately after the death of the godly king Josiah, three of his sons and one grandson took the throne in rapid succession. The stream of wickedness that had earlier begun now gained enormous momentum. The raging flow of wickedness therefore continued until it became a mad rushing torrent of evil. A catastrophic judgment was to fall upon Jerusalem and Judah just as predicted by the LORD. The people were to be destroyed because of their terrible evil. This is the story of four kings who were utter failures in the eyes of the LORD: *The Reigns Controlled by Egypt and Babylon: A Look at Four Critical Failures,* 23:31–24:20.

1. The reign of Jehoahaz (dethroned by Egypt): a failure to follow a godly father (23:31-33).
2. The reign of Jehoiakim (appointed king by Egypt): a failure to heed the warning of God's prophets, 24:2; Je.27:9-11 (23:34–24:6).
3. The reign of Jehoiachin (forced to surrender to Babylon): a failure to shun evil examples (24:7-16).
4. The reign of Zedekiah, the last king (appointed by Babylon): a failure to escape condemnation, Je.38:5,19 (24:17-20).

1 (23:31-33) **Decision, for the LORD, Rejected—Parents, Godly Example, Rejected—Children, Rejection of Godly Example—Jehoahaz, King of Judah, Reign of—Judah, Conquest of, by Egypt—Egypt, Conquest of Judah**: the first son of Josiah to rule after his death was the middle son Jehoahaz, who was 23 years old. However, he reigned for only three months (in 609 B.C.). His mother Hamutal was from Libnah, a city with a strong anti-Egyptian political party. His mother was most likely a strong supporter of this faction; thus upon the death of her husband Josiah, Hamutal and the anti-Egyptian party moved swiftly to crown her son Jehoahaz king even though Eliakim was the oldest son of Josiah. Whatever the case, Pharaoh or King Neco arrested Jehoahaz shortly after he took the throne, placing him in chains and imprisoning him at Riblah. In addition, King Neco imposed a heavy tribute upon Judah, a tax that amounted to 7500 pounds of silver and 75 pounds of gold.

Note the reference to Jehoahaz's wicked life. Although he ruled for only three months, his earlier life as a child and young man was spent in the sins and pleasures of this world. Instead of making a decision for the LORD and living a righteous life, he lived a sinful and evil life, just as the wicked kings before him had done (v.32). Instead of following the godly example of his father Josiah, he chose to ignore the LORD. Failing to make a personal decision to accept the LORD, he walked through life in the fleshly pleasures and greed of this world.

OUTLINE	SCRIPTURE	SCRIPTURE	OUTLINE

1. The reign of Jehoahaz (dethroned by Egypt): A failure to follow a godly father
a. His background
  1) His age: 23 years old
  2) His term: Only 3 months
  3) His mother: Hamutal
b. His wicked life: Ignored his father Josiah's righteousness
	31 Jehoahaz *was* twenty and three years old when he began to reign; and he reigned three months in Jerusalem. And his mother's name *was* Hamutal, the daughter of Jeremiah of Libnah.
	32 And he did *that which was* evil in the sight of the
		LORD, according to all that his fathers had done.
		33 And Pharaoh-nechoh put him in bands at Riblah in the land of Hamath, that he might not reign in Jerusalem; and put the land to a tribute of an hundred talents of silver, and a talent of gold.
			& did evil
			
			c. His immediate crisis: Pharaoh summoned him to Riblah, 29
			  1) Neco arrested & imprisoned him
			  2) Neco demanded a heavy tribute from Judah

Thought 1. No matter how godly our parents may be, their godliness does not necessarily rub off on us. We are not accepted by God because of our parents' righteousness. Just because our parents may be genuinely committed to the LORD and His church does not mean that God will accept us. Our parents may go to heaven, but we may be barricaded, shut out from heaven. Our parents may receive eternal life, but we may receive eternal death, separated from God and our parents forever.

Following God is a personal decision. And it is an individual decision, one that must be made by each individual. No one can make the decision for us, not even a parent. No matter how much a parent may wish a child to be accepted by God, that child is accepted only when he or she makes a personal decision to follow the LORD. Every person is responsible to make his or her own decision. Listen to what the Word of God says:

"Go ye therefore into the highways, and as many as ye shall find, bid to the marriage" (Mt.22:9).

"In the last day, that great *day* of the feast, Jesus stood and cried, saying, If any man thirst, let him come unto me, and drink" (Jn.7:37).

"Then Peter said unto them, Repent, and be baptized every one of you in the name of Jesus Christ for the remission of sins, and ye shall receive the gift of the Holy Ghost" (Ac.2:38).

"For whosoever shall call upon the name of the Lord shall be saved" (Ro.10:13).

"(For he saith, I have heard thee in a time accepted, and in the day of salvation have I succoured thee: behold, now *is* the accepted time; behold, now *is* the day of salvation.)" (2 Co.6:2).

"Behold, I stand at the door, and knock: if any man hear my voice, and open the door, I will come in to him, and will sup with him, and he with me" (Re.3:20).

"And the Spirit and the bride say, Come. And let him that heareth say, Come. And let him that is athirst come. And whosoever will, let him take the water of life freely" (Re.22:17).

"Ho, every one that thirsteth, come ye to the waters, and he that hath no money; come ye, buy, and eat; yea, come, buy wine and milk without money and without price" (Is.55:1).

"Let the wicked forsake his way, and the unrighteous man his thoughts: and let him return unto the LORD, and he will have mercy upon him; and to our God, for he will abundantly pardon" (Is.55:7).

"But if the wicked will turn from all his sins that he hath committed, and keep all my statutes, and do that which is lawful and right, he shall surely live, he shall not die" (Eze.18:21).

2 (23:34—24:6) **Warning, of God, Rejected—Prophets, Warning of, Rejected—Jehoiakim, King of Judah—Egypt, Rule over Judah, Appointed Jehoiakim King**: in choosing a replacement for the throne of Judah, the Egyptian Pharaoh Neco chose the oldest son of Josiah, Eliakim, who was two years older than Jehoahaz. International turmoil was sweeping the world during these days, with world powers maneuvering for dominance. Right after the death of Josiah, the Egyptians subjected the nation of Judah. But three years later, the Egyptians were defeated at Carchemish by Babylon (in 605 B.C.). However, soon thereafter a far more fierce world power was to dominate the Southern Kingdom of Judah and eventually destroy the nation completely. That power was Babylon. But for now, Egypt is the nation dominating and oppressing the people of Judah. Note the Scripture and outline:

OUTLINE	SCRIPTURE	SCRIPTURE	OUTLINE
2. The reign of Jehoiakim (appointed king by Egypt): A failure to heed the warning of God's prophets, 24:2; Je.27:9-11	34 And Pharaoh-nechoh made Eliakim the son of Josiah king in the room of Josiah his father, and turned his name to Jehoiakim, and took Jehoahaz away: and he came to Egypt, and died there.	and Jehoiakim became his servant three years: then he turned and rebelled against him.	of Babylon
a. His background		2 And the LORD sent against him bands of the Chaldees, and bands of the Syrians, and bands of the Moabites, and bands of the children of Ammon, and sent them against Judah to destroy it, according to the word of the LORD, which he spake by his servants the prophets.	1) He submitted & paid tribute for three years
1) His name changed by Egypt: To show subjection			2) He then foolishly rebelled: Rejected the warning of Jeremiah, Je.27:9-11
2) His father exiled by Egypt			d. He & his people's continued punishment by the LORD for their sins: Special forces were sent to weaken the nation for its destruction
3) His program of heavy taxation: To pay tribute to Egypt	35 And Jehoiakim gave the silver and the gold to Pharaoh; but he taxed the land to give the money according to the commandment of Pharaoh: he exacted the silver and the gold of the people of the land, of every one according to his taxation, to give *it* unto Pharaoh-nechoh.	3 Surely at the commandment of the LORD came *this* upon Judah, to remove *them* out of his sight, for the sins of Manasseh, according to all that he did;	1) The LORD had warned the people through His prophets
			• He would remove them from His presence, from the promised land
4) His age: 25 years old	36 Jehoiakim *was* twenty and five years old when he began to reign; and he reigned eleven years in Jerusalem. And his mother's name *was* Zebudah, the daughter of Pedaiah of Rumah.	4 And also for the innocent blood that he shed: for he filled Jerusalem with innocent blood; which the LORD would not pardon.	• He would judge them for their sins, especially for following the sins of Manasseh, 21:1-18
5) His term: 11 years			• He would judge them for killing so many innocent people
6) His mother: Zebidah			2) The reason: He was no longer willing to forgive
b. His wicked life: Did evil in the sight of the LORD	37 And he did *that which was* evil in the sight of the LORD, according to all that his fathers had done. **CHAPTER 24**	5 Now the rest of the acts of Jehoiakim, and all that he did, *are* they not written in the book of the chronicles of the kings of Judah? 6 So Jehoiakim slept with his fathers: and Jehoiachin his son reigned in his stead.	e. His achievements & the summary of his life
			1) His reign: Recorded in the book *The History of the Kings of Judah*
			2) His death: No burial, Je.22:18-19
c. His major crisis: The invasion by King Nebuchadnezzar	In his days Nebuchadnezzar king of Babylon came up,		3) His successor: Jehoiachin, his son

a. In looking at the background of Jehoiakim, it is important to remember that he was placed on the throne by Egypt and that his name was changed by Pharaoh Neco, changed from Eliakim to Jehoiakim. By forcing a name change, Pharaoh Neco was indicating Egypt's dominance and Jehoiakim's subjection (v.35).

When Pharaoh Neco returned to Egypt, he took Jehoahaz back to Egypt with him in order to remove any threat he might be from the scene. But before Pharaoh left Judah, he demanded that the newly appointed king Jehoiakim pay the heavy tax he had earlier demanded (v.35; see also v.33). Since the treasuries of the palace and temple had already been used to pay tribute, Jehoiakim was forced to impose a heavy taxation upon the citizens of Judah (v.35).

Jehoiakim was 25 years old when he became king, and he reigned for a term of 11 years under the domination of Egypt (609-598 B.C.). Nothing is known about his mother Zebidah other than the fact that she was from Rumah (v.36).

b. Spiritually, Jehoiakim lived a wicked life. Instead of following in the godly steps of his father Josiah, he followed the example of the wicked kings who had ruled before him (v.37). In the words of *The Expositor's Bible*, "Jeremiah…represents him as a monster who (Je.22:17; 36:31)…

- "despoiled his own people (Je.22:13-14);
- "opposed the LORD's servants (Je.26:20-23; 36:21-23);
- "filled the land with violence, apostasy, and degradation (Je.18:18-20; cf.11:19; and
- "led his people into open apostasy and degradation (Je.8:4-12, 18–9:16; 10:1-9; 11:1-17; 12:10-12; 13:1-11; 17:21-23; 23:1-2, 9-40; 25:1-7)."[1]

c. In the early part of his reign, Jehoiakim and the nation of Judah faced a major crisis, that of being invaded by King Nebuchadnezzar of Babylon (24:1). Interestingly, Nebuchadnezzar had just succeeded his father Nabopolasser as king of Babylon (605 B.C.). And earlier that year he had commanded the Babylonian army when it defeated the coalition of Egyptian and Assyrian forces at Carchemish. Thus, all three major events took place in the same year of Nebuchadnezzar's life: the conquest of Egypt and Assyria, being crowned king of Babylon, and the conquest of Judah.

When Jehoiakim surrendered to Nebuchadnezzar, Judah became a *vassal state* to Babylon. But because of his surrender, Nebuchadnezzar allowed him to remain in power as a puppet king. For three years, Jehoiakim willingly subjected himself and paid the annual tribute to Nebuchadnezzar. But then he foolishly rebelled, for Egypt had launched a surprise attack against the army of Babylon and defeated them in a major battle. Sensing that he could now throw off the yoke of Babylon, Jehoiakim turned to the Egyptians to form an alliance. Nebuchadnezzar, needing to rebuild his army, had to wait some time to put down the uprising.

---

[1] Richard D. Patterson and Hermann J. Austel. *1, 2 Kings*, p.291. Statement outlined by us for clarity.

d. However, the LORD did not allow Judah a period of peace and rest from attack. Because of their sin, the LORD continued to execute judgment against the people. In His sovereign power, He aroused Nebuchadnezzar to form a regiment of special forces to harass Judah and launch raids against strategic sites. The purpose was to weaken Judah for the day when Babylon would return to retaliate against Jehoiakim's rebellion. Note that the special forces included a small number of soldiers from Nebuchadnezzar's own army as well as mercenary soldiers he had hired from Syria, Moab, and Ammon.

For over 200 years the LORD had warned His people through His prophets. In compassion He had sent prophet after prophet to them declaring the mercy of God, but also warning them. During the days of these latter kings, God was intensifying His warning through the prophet Jeremiah. But the people never listened to the prophets, not permanently nor consistently. They refused to heed God's warning, the warning that…

- He would remove them from His presence, from the promised land (v.3).
- He would judge them for their sins, especially for following the sins of Manasseh (21:1-18).
- He would judge them for killing so many innocent people (v.4; see 21:16).

As a result of their terrible evil, the LORD was no longer willing to forgive. The people had lived sinful and wicked lives and had committed a vast amount of evil against God and humanity. Consequently, justice had to be executed. Wrongs had to be dealt with. It was now time for judgment to fall.

e. A summary of Jehoiakim's achievements and life are recorded in *The History of the Kings of Judah* (v.5-6). Before Babylon could avenge Jehoiakim's uprising, he died and was succeeded by his son Jehoiachin.

Thought 1. Jehoiakim failed to heed God's warnings. He rejected the prophets of God and God's Holy Word. These we must guard against, never do. For God has given us warning after warning. From the beginning to the ending of His Holy Word, God pleads with us in mercy to accept Him. But he also warns us: if we reject Him, we will pay the consequence. Judgment will fall upon us. If we sin and live in wicked pleasure, judgment is inevitable. There is no escape. As Scripture says, we may enjoy the pleasures of sin for a season, but the enjoyment will be only for a season. Soon there will come a day of judgment, a day when justice will be executed upon this earth. Then all the wrongs that have been done will be avenged. All the oppressed and persecuted believers of this earth will be delivered from the attacks of evil men. All the injustices committed against any of us will be avenged, corrected. Justice will be executed upon those who have oppressed and persecuted others, who have lived in wicked pleasure and sin.

This is the warning of God's Holy Word, the warning that we must heed. Listen to some of God's warnings:

"And Jesus answered and said unto them, Take heed that no man deceive you" (Mt.24:4).

"And he said unto them, Take heed, and beware of covetousness: for a man's life consisteth not in the abundance of the things which he possesseth" (Lu.12:15).

"And that servant, which knew his lord's will, and prepared not *himself*, neither did according to his will, shall be beaten with many *stripes*" (Lu.12:47).

"And he said, Take heed that ye be not deceived: for many shall come in my name, saying, I am *Christ*; and the time draweth near: go ye not therefore after them" (Lu.21:8).

"But unto them that are contentious, and do not obey the truth, but obey unrighteousness, indignation and wrath" (Ro.2:8).

"Wherefore let him that thinketh he standeth take heed lest he fall" (1 Co.10:12).

"For this ye know, that no whoremonger, nor unclean person, nor covetous man, who is an idolater, hath any inheritance in the kingdom of Christ and of God. Let no man deceive you with vain words: for because of these things cometh the wrath of God upon the children of disobedience" (Ep.5:5-6).

"Beware lest any man spoil you through philosophy and vain deceit, after the tradition of men, after the rudiments of the world, and not after Christ" (Col.2:8).

"And to you who are troubled rest with us, when the Lord Jesus shall be revealed from heaven with his mighty angels, In flaming fire taking vengeance on them that know not God, and that obey not the gospel of our Lord Jesus Christ: Who shall be punished with everlasting destruction from the presence of the Lord, and from the glory of his power" (2 Th.1:7-9).

"The Lord knoweth how to deliver the godly out of temptations, and to reserve the unjust unto the day of judgment to be punished" (2 Pe.2:9).

"Ye therefore, beloved, seeing ye know *these things* before, beware lest ye also, being led away with the error of the wicked, fall from your own stedfastness" (2 Pe.3:17).

"Little children, let no man deceive you: he that doeth righteousness is righteous, even as he is righteous" (1 Jn.3:7).

"And whosoever was not found written in the book of life was cast into the lake of fire" (Re.20:15).

"Upon the wicked he shall rain snares, fire and brimstone, and an horrible tempest: *this shall be* the portion of their cup" (Ps.11:6).

"And I will punish the world for *their* evil, and the wicked for their iniquity; and I will cause the arrogancy of the proud to cease, and will lay low the haughtiness of the terrible" (Is.13:11).

"For, behold, the LORD cometh out of his place to punish the inhabitants of the earth for their iniquity: the earth also shall disclose her blood, and shall no more cover her slain" (Is.26:21).

"But I will punish you according to the fruit of your doings, saith the LORD: and I will kindle a fire in the forest thereof, and it shall devour all things round about it" (Je.21:14).

"When I say unto the wicked, Thou shalt surely die; and thou givest him not warning, nor speakest to warn the wicked from his wicked way, to save his life; the same wicked *man* shall die in his iniquity; but his blood will I require at thine hand" (Eze.3:18).

"Nevertheless, if thou warn the wicked of his way to turn from it; if he do not turn from his way, he shall die in his iniquity; but thou hast delivered thy soul" (Eze.33:9).

3 (24:7-16) **Evil, Example of—Shun, Duty—Jehoiachin, King of Judah, Reign of—Judah, Conquest, by Babylon—Babylon, Conquest of Judah—Judah, Invasion of, by Babylon**: with the passing of his father, Jehoiachin took the throne of Judah. Immediately, he faced the terrifying threat of Babylon's advancing army. For even before his father had died, Nebuchadnezzar had mobilized his massive army and begun the march to take vengeance upon Jehoiakim for rebelling against Babylon. In addition, help from Egypt would not be forthcoming, for Egypt had been defeated by Babylon at Carchemish. Now Babylon occupied the entire area formerly claimed by Egypt, ranging from the Brook of Egypt over to the Euphrates River (v.7). Furthermore, Jehoiachin was only 18 years old, far too inexperienced to be a competent ruler, especially against the invasion of a massive army. In fact, his reign was to last only three months, the time it took Babylon to reach and lay siege to Jerusalem.

Nothing is known about Jehoiachin's mother Nehushta other than the fact that she was a native of Jerusalem. Just as his father had lived a wicked life, so did Jehoiachin. He had never turned to the LORD, but rather from his earliest days of decision-making he had chosen to follow in the sinful, wicked lifestyle of his father.

Soon after taking the throne, Jehoiachin was faced with the retaliatory invasion and siege by Babylon (v.10). No doubt when the lookouts on the wall of Jerusalem first saw the massive army of Babylon approaching in the far distance, they sounded the trumpet alarm. Immediately rushing to the wall would have been not only Jehoiachin and his royal officials, but as many of the population as could stand on the walls. Spread out across the horizon as far as the eye could see was the awesome sight of hundreds of thousands of soldiers marching in their battle formations. This sight must have stricken an overwhelming fear in the hearts of the young king and his people. Reaching a safe distance from the wall, the army then laid siege to the great city of Jerusalem.

Sometime after the army had left Babylon, Nebuchadnezzar decided to join his army to accept the surrender of the rebellious Jehoiakim who had caused so much trouble for him (vv.11-12). But right after he reached the city, he no doubt learned that Jehoiakim had passed away and that his son Jehoiachin was now ruling in his place.

Being helpless against such a massive army, Jehoiachin and his mother, his servants, nobles, and royal officials all went out to surrender personally to King Nebuchadnezzar. In the eighth year of King Nebuchadnezzar, he conquered Jerusalem and took Jehoiachin prisoner (v.12). The year was 598 B.C. Note that Jehoiachin was also known as Jeconiah and Coniah (Je.22:24, 28).

Just as the LORD had earlier predicted (20:16-18), Nebuchadnezzar conquered the city of Jerusalem and raided the royal palace and temple, stripping the city of all its wealth (v.13). He then began deporting the citizens of Jerusalem and Judah back to Babylon. Hereafter they would be exiles scattered throughout the nation of Babylon, many of whom would never return to the promised land. Note the people who were deported: the military, the business and government leaders, and the skilled and wealthy—all who could instigate an uprising. Only the poorest and weakest people of the land were left.

Also included in the Babylonian exile was King Jehoiachin, his family, and the royal officials (v.15). In totaling up the number of people who were deported during the captivity of Jerusalem, the figures were as follows: 7,000 soldiers; 1,000 skilled workers; 2,000 common people—a total of 10,000 people, including the prophet Ezekiel (v.16; see also v.14; Eze.1:1-3).

OUTLINE	SCRIPTURE	SCRIPTURE	OUTLINE
3. The reign of Jehoiachin (forced to surrender to Babylon): A failure to shun evil examples	7 And the king of Egypt came not again any more out of his land: for the king of Babylon had taken from the river of Egypt unto the river Euphrates all that pertained to the king of Egypt.	city, and his servants did besiege it.	personally accept the surrender of Jerusalem & Judah
a. His background		12 And Jehoiachin the king of Judah went out to the king of Babylon, he, and his mother, and his servants, and his princes, and his officers: and the king of Babylon took him in the eighth year of his reign.	• Jehoiachin & his mother, his servants, nobles, & royal officials—all went out to surrender to the Babylonian king
1) His loss of Egypt as an ally: Egypt had been defeated by Babylon, Je.46:2			• Jehoiachin was immediately taken prisoner
2) His age: 18 years old	8 Jehoiachin *was* eighteen years old when he began to reign, and he reigned in Jerusalem three months. And his mother's name *was* Nehushta, the daughter of Elnathan of Jerusalem.		
3) His term: 3 months		13 And he carried out thence all the treasures of the house of the LORD, and the treasures of the king's house, and cut in pieces all the vessels of gold which Solomon king of Israel had made in the temple of the LORD, as the LORD had said.	2) Nebuchadnezzar raided the royal palace & temple, stripping the city of all wealth
4) His mother: Nehushta			
b. His evil life: Lived a wicked life, following the example of his father	9 And he did *that which was* evil in the sight of the LORD, according to all that his father had done.		
c. His immediate crisis: The retaliatory invasion & siege by Babylon	10 At that time the servants of Nebuchadnezzar king of Babylon came up against Jerusalem, and the city was besieged.	14 And he carried away all Jerusalem, and all the princes, and all the mighty men of valour, *even* ten thousand captives, and all the craftsmen and smiths: none remained, save the poorest sort	3) Nebuchadnezzar deported all the people of Jerusalem • Deported all who could instigate an uprising: The military, business, & government leaders, & the skilled & wealthy
1) Nebuchadnezzar himself decided to join his army to	11 And Nebuchadnezzar king of Babylon came against the		

OUTLINE	SCRIPTURE	SCRIPTURE	OUTLINE
• Left only the poorest • Exiled Jehoiachin, his family, royal officials, & other leaders to Babylon	of the people of the land. 15 And he carried away Jehoiachin to Babylon, and the king's mother, and the king's wives, and his officers, and the mighty of the land, *those* carried he into captivity from Jerusalem to	Babylon. 16 And all the men of might, *even* seven thousand, and craftsmen and smiths a thousand, all *that were* strong *and* apt for war, even them the king of Babylon brought captive to Babylon.	• Deported the entire army of 7,000 soldiers & 1,000 skilled workers: Exiled 10,000 total people to Babylon, including the prophet Ezekiel, Eze.1:1-3

Thought 1. Jehoiachin was nothing more than a pawn in the hands of fate, for catastrophic events had already been set in motion before he assumed the throne. But even prior to these days he had chosen to follow the evil example of his father. He had made a deliberate decision to live a life of sinful pleasure and self-centered wickedness. It is this that speaks to our hearts.

We must shun evil examples. When we see people living sinful and wicked lives, we must not follow their lead—even if it is our parents. If a close friend is seducing us to engage in sinful behavior—no matter how close we are to that person—we must reject his or her enticement. The sinful example is clearly not to be followed. Even if the person is a boyfriend or girlfriend, we are not to give in to the seduction. Or if the person is a coworker, supervisor, business partner, neighbor, politician, physician, attorney, or religious worker—if that person is suggesting sinful behavior—he or she is not to be given in to nor obeyed. When an evil example confronts us, we are to shun the person, turn away, and flee from the suggested wicked behavior.

> **"And take heed to yourselves, lest at any time your hearts be overcharged with surfeiting, and drunkenness, and cares of this life, and *so* that day come upon you unawares" (Lu.21:34).**

> **"I beseech you therefore, brethren, by the mercies of God, that ye present your bodies a living sacrifice, holy, acceptable unto God, *which is* your reasonable service. And be not conformed to this world: but be ye transformed by the renewing of your mind, that ye may prove what *is* that good, and acceptable, and perfect, will of God" (Ro.12:1-2).**

> **"Wherefore come out from among them, and be ye separate, saith the Lord, and touch not the unclean *thing;* and I will receive you, And will be a Father unto you, and ye shall be my sons and daughters, saith the Lord Almighty" (2 Co.6:17-18).**

> **"Let us labour therefore to enter into that rest, lest any man fall after the same example of unbelief" (He.4:11).**

> **"Ye therefore, beloved, seeing ye know *these things* before, beware lest ye also, being led away with the error of the wicked, fall from your own stedfastness" (2 Pe.3:17).**

> **"And ye shall not walk in the manners of the nation, which I cast out before you: for they committed all these things, and therefore I abhorred them" (Le.20:23).**

> **"Take heed to yourselves, that your heart be not deceived, and ye turn aside, and serve other gods, and worship them" (De.11:16).**

> **"Make no friendship with an angry man; and with a furious man thou shalt not go: Lest thou learn his ways, and get a snare to thy soul" (Pr.22:24-25).**

> **"But I said unto their children in the wilderness, Walk ye not in the statutes of your fathers, neither observe their judgments, nor defile yourselves with their idols" (Eze.20:18).**

4 (24:17-20) **Condemnation, Example of—Leader, Evil, Example of—Anger of the LORD, Caused By—Judgment, Caused By—Wrath of God, Caused By—Zedekiah, King of Judah**: when King Nebuchadnezzar of Babylon withdrew his army to return home, he left Jerusalem standing and appointed Mattaniah king. Mattaniah was Jehoiachin's uncle and the third son of Josiah to be placed upon the throne. Nebuchadnezzar changed the name of Mattaniah to Zedekiah in order to show his subjection to the throne of Babylon.

OUTLINE	SCRIPTURE	SCRIPTURE	OUTLINE

4. The reign of Zedekiah, the last king (appointed by Babylon): A failure to escape condemnation, Je.38:5,19
a. His name changed: To show subjection
b. His background
  1) His age: 21 years old
  2) His rule: Lasted 11 years
  3) His mother: Hamutal
	17 And the king of Babylon made Mattaniah his father's brother king in his stead, and changed his name to Zedekiah.
	18 Zedekiah *was* twenty and one years old when he began to reign, and he reigned eleven years in Jerusalem. And his mother's name *was* Hamutal, the daughter of Jeremiah of Libnah.
		19 And he did *that* which *was* evil in the sight of the LORD, according to all that Jehoiakim had done.
		20 For through the anger of the LORD it came to pass in Jerusalem and Judah, until he had cast them out from his presence, that Zedekiah rebelled against the king of Babylon.
			c. His evil: Lived a wicked life, following the example of Jehoiakim
			
			d. His & Judah's destiny: Judgment
			  1) They were conquered, condemned due to their sin
			  2) They were to be thrust from God's presence, from the promised land
			e. His rebellion against Babylon

Zedekiah assumed the throne when he was 21 years old and managed to rule for 11 years (v.18). He was the second son of Hamutal (his mother) to reign, Jehoahaz being the other son. Sadly, just as so many others before him, he chose to live a sinful and wicked life. Patterning his life after the evil example of his older brother Jehoiakim, he rejected the LORD and refused to follow the LORD's Holy Word. Consequently, his and Judah's destiny were already set, irrevocably set: judgment was to fall upon them. They were to be conquered, condemned before the LORD because of their continued sin and refusal to repent. They were to be thrust from God's presence, from the promised land. In the words of Paul R. House:

> Jer 21:1-2 indicates that he [Zedekiah] wants God to save Jerusalem even though he does not worship the Lord, while Jer 34:1-22 presents him as a man who hears and understands the prophet's warnings yet does not heed them. And he is presented as a king who first helps, then oppresses the poor in order to please the power brokers of Judah. Clearly, he lacks the moral fiber to be more than what he is, a man who gauges each situation by how long its results can keep him in power.
>
> Eventually Zedekiah's indecisiveness and self-interest prove a deadly combination, for they lead him to rebel against Babylon. There are two probable causes for this ill-fated rebellion. First, after more than one aborted attempt, Egypt persuades Judah, Tyre, and possibly Ammon to join a revolt against Babylon about 589-588 B.C. Jeremiah 27:1-11 indicates that Zedekiah has to be convinced of the "wisdom" of rebelling and that this counsel flies in the face of the prophet's. Thus, when he does finally rebel out of his inability to make and adhere to sound decisions, it is only with divided enthusiasm and divided loyalties.
>
> Second, Zedekiah's own people are divided over whether to trust Egypt or obey Babylon. But his self-interest eventually leads him to give in to adventurous army officers spoiling for a fight and false prophets who implant "in the people the confidence that the God of Israel would not desert his people nor allow the destruction of the temple (Jer 5:12; 14:13)." Zedekiah tries to please those who want to revolt, yet he also senses trouble. When the end comes, he is incapable of surrendering or standing up to his people (cf. Jer 38:14-28). So he considers his own situation so long that his future is decided for him.
>
> Of course, these reasons for Jerusalem's fall are not as significant to the author as the nation's unrepentant rebellion against the Lord. It is God who destroys Judah in his anger (v.20; cf. 2 Chr 36:15-16). Babylon only acts as the Lord's agent of justice....According to Jer 38:14-38, God's final act of mercy is to instruct Jeremiah to inform Zedekiah that surrender will avoid a bloodbath. But the king simply hopes the bearer of God's word is mistaken about the future.[2]

Russell Dilday also has an excellent comment on the character of Zedekiah that is worth quoting for the reader:

> According to Jeremiah, he was weak and vacillating in character and even though most of the talented people had been taken to Babylon he was completely dominated by stronger men in the kingdom. He had no courage nor power to offer resistance and be his own man. It appears that those who manipulated the young king represented the pro-Egyptian party. They encouraged him to rebel against Babylon and to appeal to Egypt for a military alliance. Jeremiah warned him of the folly of this tactic, but Zedekiah did not obey the words of the Lord that came through Jeremiah (Jer.38).
>
> There is nothing more pitiful than a weak character who cannot resist the temptation to "go with the flow," follow the lines of least resistance, and cater to the majority....Zedekiah's vacillating capitulation to the influential crowd and his unwillingness to stand courageously for the word of the Lord led to his foolish decision to rebel. And that rebellion was the last straw that brought on the final destruction of Jerusalem.[3]

Another quote from Russell Dilday says this:

> The fall of Jerusalem didn't come about in one cataclysmic battle; it occurred in stages. First came Nebuchadnezzar's initial subjection of the city about 605 B.C. Next was the cumulative destruction caused by Nebuchadnezzar's marauding bands from about 601 to 598 B.C. Then, during Jehoiachin's reign, Nebuchadnezzar's main army besieged Jerusalem and it fell on 16 March 597 B.C. Most of the leading citizens were transported to Babylon. Finally, when the puppet king Zedekiah again rebelled against Babylon, Nebuchadnezzar returned to completely destroy and depopulate the city in the summer of 586 B.C.
>
> Nothing could now avert the inevitable judgment that had been building up against Judah through all the history of the kings. The final denouement was about to begin.[4]

Thought 1. Zedekiah stood condemned before God, condemned because of his sinful and wicked life. Any person who commits sin, who breaks the commandments of God, stands condemned before God. For God's Holy Word is the rule of the universe, the laws that are to be obeyed. As the Creator and Sovereign Ruler of the universe, the LORD has the right to decree the laws to govern the universe. When He issues a law, He expects that law to be obeyed just as a state government expects its laws to be obeyed Therefore, when a law is disobeyed, there is condemnation. Just as state government condemns the offender, so the LORD condemns any of us who break His laws. Listen to what God's Holy Word says about condemnation:

> **"And this is the condemnation, that light is come into the world, and men loved darkness rather than light, because their deeds were evil" (Jn.3:19).**
> **"Therefore as by the offence of one *judgment came* upon all men to condemnation; even so by the righteousness of one *the free gift came* upon all men unto justification of life" (Ro.5:18).**

---

2 Paul R. House. *1, 2 Kings*, pp.395-396.
3 Russell Dilday. *1, 2 Kings*, pp.499-500.
4 Ibid, p.496.

"For this ye know, that no whoremonger, nor unclean person, nor covetous man, who is an idolater, hath any inheritance in the kingdom of Christ and of God. Let no man deceive you with vain words: for because of these things cometh the wrath of God upon the children of disobedience" (Ep.5:5-6).

"And to you who are troubled rest with us, when the Lord Jesus shall be revealed from heaven with his mighty angels, In flaming fire taking vengeance on them that know not God, and that obey not the gospel of our Lord Jesus Christ: Who shall be punished with everlasting destruction from the presence of the Lord, and from the glory of his power" (2 Th.1:7-9).

"But if ye will not obey the voice of the LORD, but rebel against the commandment of the LORD, then shall the hand of the LORD be against you, as *it was* against your fathers" (1 S.12:15).

"And I will punish the world for *their* evil, and the wicked for their iniquity; and I will cause the arrogancy of the proud to cease, and will lay low the haughtiness of the terrible" (Is.13:11).

1. The total destruction of Jerusalem by Babylon: A picture of final judgment

a. The attack & siege of the city: Because Zedekiah had rebelled against Babylon, 24:20

1) The Babylonian army built siege ramps of dirt around the city walls: To attack

2) The siege lasted almost two years: From the 9th–11th year of Zedekiah's reign

3) The famine was severe: The people were starving & committing cannibalism, eating one another, Je.38:2-9; 52:6; Lam.4:3-10; Eze.5:10

b. The fall of the city

1) The battering rams broke through the wall

2) The king & the few remaining soldiers escaped & fled by night

c. The capture of the king

1) The Babylonian army pursued & captured Zedekiah in the plains of Jericho

• Discovered that his royal guard & soldiers had abandoned him

• Took him to Nebuchadnezzar's headquarters

2) He was tried & sentenced by King Nebuchadnezzar

• They killed Zedekiah's sons, forcing him to watch

• They then gouged out his eyes, shackled him, & took him to Babylon

d. The burning of the city

1) The commander of the royal guard, Nebuzaradan, was sent by the king to supervise the destruction of Jerusalem: About one month after the conquest

• He burned the temple, the symbol of God's presence

• He burned the palace, all the houses, & all the important buildings

CHAPTER 25

H. The Final Siege & Fall of Jerusalem: The Surety of God's Predicted Judgment, 25:1-30

25:1-21; see 2 Chr.36:14-21; Je.52:4-30
25:22-26; see Je.40:5–41:18
25:27-30; see Je.52:31-34

And it came to pass in the ninth year of his reign, in the tenth month, in the tenth *day* of the month, *that* Nebuchadnezzar king of Babylon came, he, and all his host, against Jerusalem, and pitched against it; and they built forts against it round about.

2 And the city was besieged unto the eleventh year of king Zedekiah.

3 And on the ninth *day* of the *fourth* month the famine prevailed in the city, and there was no bread for the people of the land.

4 And the city was broken up, and all the men of war *fled* by night by the way of the gate between two walls, which *is* by the king's garden: (now the Chaldees *were* against the city round about:) and *the king* went the way toward the plain.

5 And the army of the Chaldees pursued after the king, and overtook him in the plains of Jericho: and all his army were scattered from him.

6 So they took the king, and brought him up to the king of Babylon to Riblah; and they gave judgment upon him.

7 And they slew the sons of Zedekiah before his eyes, and put out the eyes of Zedekiah, and bound him with fetters of brass, and carried him to Babylon.

8 And in the fifth month, on the seventh *day* of the month, which *is* the nineteenth year of king Nebuchadnezzar king of Babylon, came Nebuzaradan, captain of the guard, a servant of the king of Babylon, unto Jerusalem:

9 And he burnt the house of the LORD, and the king's house, and all the houses of Jerusalem, and every great *man's* house burnt he with fire.

10 And all the army of the Chaldees, that *were with* the captain of the guard, brake down the walls of Jerusalem round about.

11 Now the rest of the people *that were* left in the city, and the fugitives that fell away to the king of Babylon, with the remnant of the multitude, did Nebuzaradan the captain of the guard carry away.

12 But the captain of the guard left of the poor of the land *to be* vinedressers and husbandmen.

13 And the pillars of brass that *were* in the house of the LORD, and the bases, and the brasen sea that *was* in the house of the LORD, did the Chaldees break in pieces, and carried the brass of them to Babylon.

14 And the pots, and the shovels, and the snuffers, and the spoons, and all the vessels of brass wherewith they ministered, took they away.

15 And the firepans, and the bowls, *and* such things as *were* of gold, *in* gold, and of silver, *in* silver, the captain of the guard took away.

16 The two pillars, one sea, and the bases which Solomon had made for the house of the LORD; the brass of all these vessels was without weight.

17 The height of the one pillar *was* eighteen cubits, and the chapiter upon it *was* brass: and the height of the chapiter three cubits; and the wreathen work, and pomegranates upon the chapiter round about, all of brass: and like unto these had the second pillar with wreathen work.

18 And the captain of the guard took Seraiah the chief priest, and Zephaniah the second priest, and the three keepers of the door:

19 And out of the city he took an officer that was set over the men of war, and five men of them that were in the king's presence, which were found in the city, and the principal scribe of the host, which mustered the people of the land, and threescore men of the people of the land *that were* found in the city:

20 And Nebuzaradan captain of the guard took

2) The commander of the royal guard then instructed the army to demolish the walls of the city

e. The exile of the people

1) Nebuzaradan deported the people: Those who lived in & out of the city, including those who had surrendered to Babylon (Jeremiah was not exiled, Je.40:1-6)

2) Nebuzaradan left some of the poor to cultivate the land for the benefit of the empire

f. The defiling of the temple

1) The army broke up the bronze pillars, bronze water carts, & the Bronze Sea or large water basin: To make the bronze easier to transport to Babylon

2) The army also packed & took all the bronze utensils & articles

3) The army packed & took all the items made of silver & gold

4) The army took so much bronze that it could not be weighed: It was incalculable, of extreme value

5) The two pillars had huge amounts of bronze in them

g. The execution of the leaders

1) The commander arrested the religious leaders

2) The commander then arrested the military & government leaders & sixty other leading citizens

3) The commander took all the prisoners to

Nebuchadnezzar at his field headquarters: To stand trial & be executed for treason	these, and brought them to the king of Babylon to Riblah:	the son of Nethaniah, the son of Elishama, of the seed royal, came, and ten men with	men assassinated the governor, his officials, & some Babylonian soldiers

Nebuchadnezzar at his field headquarters: To stand trial & be executed for treason

h. The tragic completion of Judah's captivity: The people were exiled from the promised land

2. The appointment of Gedaliah as governor over the newly formed district of Babylon (Judah): A picture of despair
a. His headquarters: Mizpah

b. His most serious problem
1) He was visited by some army officers:
• They had escaped Jerusalem with the king, 4-5
• Others had escaped from the outposts scattered throughout the land

2) He swore that the Babylonians would not harm them: Encouraged them to return home & to live under Babylonian rule

c. His assassination
1) The officer Ishmael & ten

these, and brought them to the king of Babylon to Riblah:
21 And the king of Babylon smote them, and slew them at Riblah in the land of Hamath. So Judah was carried away out of their land.
22 And *as for* the people that remained in the land of Judah, whom Nebuchadnezzar king of Babylon had left, even over them he made Gedaliah the son of Ahikam, the son of Shaphan, ruler.
23 And when all the captains of the armies, they and their men, heard that the king of Babylon had made Gedaliah governor, there came to Gedaliah to Mizpah, even Ishmael the son of Nethaniah, and Johanan the son of Careah, and Seraiah the son of Tanhumeth the Netophathite, and Jaazaniah the son of a Maachathite, they and their men.
24 And Gedaliah sware to them, and to their men, and said unto them, Fear not to be the servants of the Chaldees: dwell in the land, and serve the king of Babylon; and it shall be well with you.
25 But it came to pass in the seventh month, that Ishmael

the son of Nethaniah, the son of Elishama, of the seed royal, came, and ten men with him, and smote Gedaliah, that he died, and the Jews and the Chaldees that were with him at Mizpah.
26 And all the people, both small and great, and the captains of the armies, arose, and came to Egypt: for they were afraid of the Chaldees.
27 And it came to pass in the seven and thirtieth year of the captivity of Jehoiachin king of Judah, in the twelfth month, on the seven and twentieth *day* of the month, *that* Evil-merodach king of Babylon in the year that he began to reign did lift up the head of Jehoiachin king of Judah out of prison;
28 And he spake kindly to him, and set his throne above the throne of the kings that *were* with him in Babylon;
29 And changed his prison garments: and he did eat bread continually before him all the days of his life.
30 And his allowance *was* a continual allowance given him of the king, a daily rate for every day, all the days of his life.

men assassinated the governor, his officials, & some Babylonian soldiers
2) The plot was instigated by the king of Ammon, Je.40:7–41:3

3) The effect of Gedaliah's death was catastrophic: The remaining refugees in Judah were forced to flee to Egypt to escape retaliation

3. The release of Jehoiachin from prison: A picture of hope, of being freed from captivity
a. The release: Granted after 37 years in prison by Evil-Merodach, who succeeded his father as king of Babylon

b. The honored position of Jehoiachin
1) He was honored more than the other exiled kings
2) He was a regular guest at the king's table

3) He was given an allowance for the rest of his life

DIVISION IV

THE UTTER DISINTEGRATION AND FALL OF JUDAH, THE SOUTHERN KINGDOM: AN APPALLING DESTRUCTION DUE TO INCONSISTENCY, DISLOYALTY, AND EVER-GROWING WICKEDNESS, 18:1–25:30

H. The Final Siege and Fall of Jerusalem: The Surety of God's Predicted Judgment, 25:1-30

(25:1-30) **Introduction—Judgment, Surety of—Judgment, Fact, Will Be Just—Judgment, Judicial, Will Be Perfect Justice—Justice, God's, Fact, to Be Executed Perfectly**: the surety of God's judgment is guaranteed by God's Word. And God's Word is irrevocable. What God says is coming to pass. Therefore God's judgment is coming. It is inevitable. It is definite. The day has been set and no person will escape God's judgment. The day is coming when every one of us will stand face-to-face with God and have perfect justice executed upon us. No injustice will seep into God's judgment. Only what we have done wrong will be condemned, nothing more and nothing less. We can rest in the assurance that God will not charge us with anything we have not done. But whatever sin or wickedness we have committed, for that we will give an account. And God's judgment will fall upon us.

As we come to the tragic downfall of Jerusalem, the commentator Russell Dilday gives an excellent statement that is well worth our attention.

> The reader cannot help but be struck by the passionless tone of the narrative in this chapter. Not once does the author show his feelings, even though he is describing the tragic downfall of his country. We have to turn to the Book of Lamentations for weeping and groaning. That book describes the emotion of devout hearts who mourned over the desolation of the beautiful City of David, but here in Kings we have the calm historical record of God's judgment.
> In Hebrew, the first twelve verses of the chapter are one long sentence, each verse beginning with "and." Clause is heaped upon clause in a kind of cadence, as if each one were another tick of the clock counting down Jerusalem's final hours.

Nor can the reader help but be impressed with the revelation throughout these chapters of God's patience and His reluctance to punish. More than four hundred years had passed since Solomon first disobeyed God and introduced the children of Israel to pagan idolatry. Faithfully, through all those years, a steady stream of prophets clearly proclaimed the warnings of punishment. Varying disasters confirmed their messages, vividly previewing what was to come if the people did not repent and turn to God. With steadfast love, God tried again and again to seek and save His people, but they mocked His warnings, killed His prophets, and would not listen to His reproof. So finally the hour struck and the impending crash came. The harshness of the judgment is somehow softened by the recognition that the Lord is indeed long-suffering toward His people. But His patience and steadfast love are balanced with justice. The destruction is a reminder that we must not presume on His grace and mercy. [1]

The surety of God's coming judgment is the subject of this Scripture. This is: *The Final Siege and Fall of Jerusalem: The Surety of God's Predicted Judgment*, 25:1-30.

1. The total destruction of Jerusalem by Babylon: a picture of final judgment (vv.1-21).
2. The appointment of Gedaliah as governor over the land and the newly formed district of Babylon: a picture of despair (vv.22-26).
3. The release of Jehoiachin from prison: a picture of hope, of being freed from captivity (vv.27-30).

---

1 (25:1-21) **Judgment, Example of—Judgment, Fulfilled—Jerusalem, Fall of—Southern Kingdom of Judah, Fall of—Destruction, of Jerusalem—Babylon, Destruction of Jerusalem—Deportation, of Judah—Exiles, of Judah**: the total destruction of Jerusalem was now set to take place. Down through the centuries the LORD had warned that this day was coming. Now the final destruction was just over the horizon. Scripture gives a graphic description of the tragic and devastating event:

OUTLINE	SCRIPTURE	SCRIPTURE	OUTLINE
1. The total destruction of Jerusalem by Babylon: A picture of final judgment	And it came to pass in the ninth year of his reign, in the tenth month, in the tenth *day* of the month, *that* Nebuchadnezzar king of Babylon came, he, and all his host, against Jerusalem, and pitched against it; and they built forts against it round about.	brass, and carried him to Babylon.	• They then gouged out his eyes, shackled him, & took him to Babylon
a. The attack & siege of the city: Because Zedekiah had rebelled against Babylon, 24:20		8 And in the fifth month, on the seventh *day* of the month, which *is* the nineteenth year of king Nebuchadnezzar king of Babylon, came Nebuzar-adan, captain of the guard, a servant of the king of Babylon, unto Jerusalem:	d. The burning of the city
1) The Babylonian army built siege ramps of dirt around the city walls: To attack			1) The commander of the royal guard, Nebuzaradan, was sent by the king to supervise the destruction of Jerusalem: About one month after the conquest
2) The siege lasted almost two years: From the 9th—11th year of Zedekiah's reign	2 And the city was besieged unto the eleventh year of king Zedekiah.	9 And he burnt the house of the LORD, and the king's house, and all the houses of Jerusalem, and every great *man's* house burnt he with fire.	• He burned the temple, the symbol of God's presence
3) The famine was severe: The people were starving & committing cannibalism, eating one another, Je.38:2-9; 52:6; Lam.4:3-10; Eze.5:10	3 And on the ninth *day* of the *fourth* month the famine prevailed in the city, and there was no bread for the people of the land.		• He burned the palace, all the houses, & all the important buildings
b. The fall of the city	4 And the city was broken up, and all the men of war *fled* by night by the way of the gate between two walls, which *is* by the king's garden: (now the Chaldees *were* against the city round about:) and *the king* went the way toward the plain.	10 And all the army of the Chaldees, that *were with* the captain of the guard, brake down the walls of Jerusalem round about.	2) The commander of the royal guard then instructed the army to demolish the walls of the city
1) The battering rams broke through the wall			
2) The king & the few remaining soldiers escaped & fled by night		11 Now the rest of the people *that were* left in the city, and the fugitives that fell away to the king of Babylon, with the remnant of the multitude, did Nebuzaradan the captain of the guard carry away.	e. The exile of the people
c. The capture of the king	5 And the army of the Chaldees pursued after the king, and overtook him in the plains of Jericho: and all his army were scattered from him.		1) Nebuzaradan deported the people: Those who lived in & out of the city, including those who had surrendered to Babylon (Jeremiah was not exiled, Je.40:1-6)
1) The Babylonian army pursued & captured Zedekiah in the plains of Jericho		12 But the captain of the guard left of the poor of the land *to be* vinedressers and husbandmen.	
• Discovered that his royal guard & soldiers had abandoned him			2) Nebuzaradan left some of the poor to cultivate the land for the benefit of the empire
• Took him to Nebuchadnezzar's headquarters	6 So they took the king, and brought him up to the king of Babylon to Riblah; and they gave judgment upon him.	13 And the pillars of brass that *were* in the house of the LORD, and the bases, and the brasen sea that *was* in the house of the LORD, did the Chaldees break in pieces, and carried the brass of them to	f. The defiling of the temple
2) He was tried & sentenced by King Nebuchadnezzar	7 And they slew the sons of Zedekiah before his eyes, and put out the eyes of Zedekiah, and bound him with fetters of		1) The army broke up the bronze pillars, bronze water carts, & the Bronze Sea or large water basin: To make the bronze easier to transport to Babylon
• They killed Zedekiah's sons, forcing him to watch			

---

1 Russell Dilday. *1, 2 Kings*, pp.505-506.

OUTLINE	SCRIPTURE	SCRIPTURE	OUTLINE
2) The army also packed & took all the bronze utensils & articles	Babylon. 14 And the pots, and the shovels, and the snuffers, and the spoons, and all the vessels of brass wherewith they ministered, took they away.	work. 18 And the captain of the guard took Seraiah the chief priest, and Zephaniah the second priest, and the three keepers of the door:	g. The execution of the leaders 1) The commander arrested the religious leaders
3) The army packed & took all the items made of silver & gold	15 And the firepans, and the bowls, *and* such things as *were* of gold, *in* gold, and of silver, *in* silver, the captain of the guard took away.	19 And out of the city he took an officer that was set over the men of war, and five men of them that were in the king's presence, which were found in the city, and the	2) The commander then arrested the military & government leaders & sixty other leading citizens
4) The army took so much bronze that it could not be weighed: It was incalculable, of extreme value	16 The two pillars, one sea, and the bases which Solomon had made for the house of the LORD; the brass of all these vessels was without weight.	principal scribe of the host, which mustered the people of the land, and threescore men of the people of the land *that were* found in the city:	
5) The two pillars had huge amounts of bronze in them	17 The height of the one pillar *was* eighteen cubits, and the chapiter upon it *was* brass: and the height of the chapiter three cubits; and the wreathen work, and pomegranates upon the chapiter round about, all of brass: and like unto these had the second pillar with wreathen	20 And Nebuzar-adan captain of the guard took these, and brought them to the king of Babylon to Riblah: 21 And the king of Babylon smote them, and slew them at Riblah in the land of Hamath. So Judah was carried away out of their land.	3) The commander took all the prisoners to Nebuchadnezzar at his field headquarters: To stand trial & be executed for treason h. The tragic completion of Judah's captivity: The people were exiled from the promised land

a. In the tenth month (January) of 588 B.C., the final siege and attack against Jerusalem were launched. Because of Zedekiah's rebellion against Babylon, Nebuchadnezzar marched against Jerusalem with the full force of his entire army. Surrounding the city, the Babylonian army set up camp and began to build siege ramps of dirt all around the city. In seeking to understand siege warfare, Russell Dilday gives an excellent description of this effective military strategy. Although long, his description is well worth quoting in its entirety:

> Siege warfare was a cruel but effective military strategy of the ancient East. Rather than making a concentrated assault to break down fortifications and overwhelm the defenders of a city, siege warriors simply surrounded the city and cut off all access to food and in some cases water. Then they patiently waited until the inhabitants ran out of supplies, began to starve, and were ready to surrender. This tactic took longer, but it cost fewer lives on the part of the invaders. The "siege wall" in verse 1 was a mound of earth piled up by slave labor to a level somewhat higher than the city wall itself. From the siege wall, the attackers could shoot at the defenders on the walls of the city. If the siege wall was close enough, as it was in some cases, battering rams could be used to break down the defenses.
> A few years ago, standing on the hilltop fortress of Masada near the Dead Sea, I looked down on a siege wall that the Romans had built nearly two thousand years before in order to overwhelm that stubborn garrison. From the hilltop you can see ruins of the series of Roman garrisons that were set up in a ring around Masada to cut off its supplies. But the ingenious fortress built by Herod the Great held enough food and water to last for years. Furthermore, its elevated location and high wall made it practically unapproachable by enemy troops.
> The only way the superior Roman army could conquer Eleazor, the commander of Masada, and the heroic Jewish defenders was to build a dirt assault ramp that would allow the imperial troops to storm Masada's walls. Furthermore, that task would have been impossible if the Roman general, Silva, had not used thousands of Jewish slaves to build the ramp. For from their superior position on the fortifications high above the plain, Eleazor and his soldiers could have easily killed any workers who attempted to construct such a ram. But when they discovered that the ramp builders were Jewish slaves, they could not bring themselves to kill their own countrymen.
> So the defenders of Masada watched helplessly as the ramp grew longer and higher each day. Finally, one evening in the spring of A.D. 73, it became obvious that the next morning the Roman siege-machines and battering rams would be pushed up the ramp, and the fortress would be conquered. That night Eleazor and his brave zealots decided to take their own lives rather than let Rome kill them or enslave them. Each soldier killed his own family, and then ten were selected to kill the rest. One of the ten was picked to kill the nine others, and then, after setting fire to the fortress, to take his own life. When the invaders broke through the next morning they discovered 960 bodies of courageous people who chose death over slavery.
> The dirt ramp is still there, 200 feet high and 645 feet long. Nebuchadnezzar's siege wall at Jerusalem must have looked a lot like it (v.1).[2]

---

2 Russell Dilday. *1, 2 Kings*, pp.502-503.

The siege lasted for almost two years, from the ninth to the middle of the eleventh year of Zedekiah's reign (v.2). While the main army was laying siege to the city, Nebuchadnezzar took a strike force and systematically destroyed the military outposts and fortresses throughout the country (Je.21:3-7; 34:7; 39:1; 52:4; Eze.24:2). During this time the Egyptian army marched out of Egypt to come to the aid of Jerusalem; therefore Nebuchadnezzar had to deal with them as well (Je.37:5-10). Somehow receiving word that the Egyptians were marching to help them break the Babylonian siege, the citizens of Jerusalem began to take heart and experience hope. But the prophet Jeremiah warned the people, their hope and joy was baseless, false, and deceptive, for the Babylonians would send the Egyptian army scurrying for their lives. Eventually, the Babylonians would utterly destroy Jerusalem by burning it with fire.

Eventually the famine became so severe that the people were at the point of starvation. Other Scriptures tell us that the famine was so critical the people even resorted to cannibalism or eating one another (Je.38:2-9; 52:6; Lam.4:3-10; Eze.5:10. See 2 K.6:26-30.) Jeremiah the prophet even attempted to persuade King Zedekiah to surrender in order to save the people from starvation. But the king's heart was so hardened toward the LORD that he simply would not listen (Je.38:17).

b. Finally, just as the LORD had predicted, the fall of Jerusalem occurred (v.4). Eventually the battering rams broke through the wall, and the soldiers of Babylon—by the thousands—rushed into the city. Zedekiah, stricken with absolute fear and cowardice, took his army and escaped by night through a gate between the two walls that surrounded Jerusalem. Throughout the generations the Israelites never thought this day would come, never thought God would allow their great capital to fall into the hands of an enemy force. But just as the LORD had warned His people, the tragic fall of Jerusalem was now occurring (De.28:15-68; 2 K.21:10-15; 22:15-20; Je.19-20; 27-28; 37:8-10, 17; 38:17-23).

c. As Zedekiah was fleeing for his life, all of his men abandoned him. Soon thereafter the pursuing Babylonians captured him and his family in the plains of Jericho (vv.5-6). The soldiers then took Zedekiah and his family to Nebuchadnezzar's headquarters at Riblah where he and his sons were tried and sentenced by the military court. In an act of cruel and savage justice, the Judean king was forced to watch the execution of his sons. Then his own eyes were gouged out before he was shackled and taken as a prisoner to Babylon where he would later die (Eze.12:13).

d. About one month after the fall of the royal city, Nebuchadnezzar of Babylon made the decision to totally destroy Jerusalem, burning it to the ground (vv.8-10). Turning to his most trusted commander of the royal guard, Nebuzaradan, the king assigned the demolition project to him.

After arriving in the city, Nebuchadnezzar first set fire to the temple of the LORD (v.9). To the few genuine believers left among the Israelites, the sight of the temple burning must have been heartbreaking, for the temple was the symbol of God's very own presence. It was a very special place where the worshipper could seek the LORD in a special way to receive forgiveness for his sins through the sacrificial offerings.

After setting fire to the temple, the commander began moving systematically all through the city, burning the royal palace, all the houses, and all the other important buildings and structures in the capital. When nothing was left standing within the city itself, the commander turned to the army and instructed them to demolish the walls of the city (v.10).

e. Rounding up most of the citizens of Jerusalem and Judah, the commander organized them for deportation to Babylon (vv.11-12). Soon thereafter the prisoners began their long, terrifying march into Babylonian captivity and exile. Only a few of the poorest people were left behind to cultivate the land and to keep it from being taken over by weeds and wild animals. In addition, surplus crops could be used to provide food for certain areas of the Babylonian Empire.

f. Because of the significance of the temple, a detailed description is given of its defilement and destruction (vv.13-17). Of course when the Babylonians looked at the temple, they did not sense the religious significance that was felt by the Israelites and by genuine believers down through the centuries. On the contrary, what the Babylonians saw was plunder and the spoils of war that always goes to the victor. Four details in particular are given:

First, they broke up the massive bronze pillars or columns, the bronze water carts, and the Bronze Sea or large water basin used for the cleansing of the sacrifices at the large altar (v.13). These items were broken into pieces in order to make them easier to transport to Babylon.

Second, they also packed and took all the bronze utensils and articles that were used in the temple services (v.14).

Third, they packed and took all the items made of silver and gold (v.15).

Fourth, they took so much bronze that it could not be weighed (vv.16-17). The amount was just incalculable, of extreme value. For example, the two pillars had huge amounts of bronze in them, so much that it could not be weighed, not without being broken or melted down.

g. All the leadership of Jerusalem and Judah was executed (vv.18-21). The commander arrested the religious leaders, the military and government leaders, and 60 other outstanding citizens (vv.18-19). While the major portion of the population was taken to Babylon, these leaders were taken to Nebuchadnezzar at his field headquarters in Riblah. There the prisoners were placed on trial in a military court, sentenced, and executed for treason (vv.20-21).

h. Once the sad destruction of Jerusalem had been completed, the tragic story of the Babylonian captivity began. The people were exiled, taken into captivity, away from the promised land. They had continued on in their sin and wickedness, refusing to repent. Thus the hand of God's judgment finally fell. The beloved city of Jerusalem was completely destroyed and the people were carried into Babylonian captivity.

Thought 1. The fall of Jerusalem is a clear picture of God's final judgment. Just as predicted by God's Holy Word, the hand of His judgment fell and fell forcefully. The lesson for us is striking, for God warns that a day of *final judgment* is coming. Some day out in the future, the Lord Jesus Christ will return to this earth to execute perfect justice and judgment. And no human being will escape. Judgment is inevitable. Every person must stand before the Lord Jesus Christ to give an account for everything he or she has done. An account of all behavior is being kept by God. Whatever is done in our bodies is being recorded. Whatever we use our bodies to do—all the works or deeds we do—this too is being recorded. Every act, word, and thought is being recorded. Whether just or unjust, in love or in hate, everything we think or do is being recorded.

In facing the record against us, there is only one way to have it erased or wiped clean. This way is the Lord Jesus Christ. When He died upon the cross, He took our sins and paid the penalty for us. If we will surrender our lives to

Christ and ask Him to save us, God will erase all the charges against us. God will forgive our sins and accept us to live with Him eternally.

This glorious message of forgiveness through Christ must never be forgotten. But for now, in this present Scripture, the thrust of the message is the coming judgment of God. Listen to what God's Holy Word says about the final judgment that is approaching ever so rapidly:

"For the Son of man shall come in the glory of his Father with his angels; and then he shall reward every man according to his works" (Mt.16:27).

"When the Son of man shall come in his glory, and all the holy angels with him, then shall he sit upon the throne of his glory: And before him shall be gathered all nations: and he shall separate them one from another, as a shepherd divideth *his* sheep from the goats: And he shall set the sheep on his right hand, but the goats on the left" (Mt.25:31-33).

"Marvel not at this: for the hour is coming, in the which all that are in the graves shall hear his voice, And shall come forth; they that have done good, unto the resurrection of life; and they that have done evil, unto the resurrection of damnation" (Jn.5:28-29).

"And to you who are troubled rest with us, when the Lord Jesus shall be revealed from heaven with his mighty angels, In flaming fire taking vengeance on them that know not God, and that obey not the gospel of our Lord Jesus Christ" (2 Th.1:7-8).

"And as it is appointed unto men once to die, but after this the judgment" (He.9:27).

"And if ye call on the Father, who without respect of persons judgeth according to every man's work, pass the time of your sojourning *here* in fear" (1 Pe.1:17).

"The Lord knoweth how to deliver the godly out of temptations, and to reserve the unjust unto the day of judgment to be punished" (2 Pe.2:9).

"But the heavens and the earth, which are now, by the same word are kept in store, reserved unto fire against the day of judgment and perdition of ungodly men" (2 Pe.3:7).

"And Enoch also, the seventh from Adam, prophesied of these, saying, Behold, the Lord cometh with ten thousands of his saints, To execute judgment upon all, and to convince all that are ungodly among them of all their ungodly deeds which they have ungodly committed, and of all their hard *speeches* which ungodly sinners have spoken against him" (Jude 14-15).

"And I saw a great white throne, and him that sat on it, from whose face the earth and the heaven fled away; and there was found no place for them. And I saw the dead, small and great, stand before God; and the books were opened: and another book was opened, which is *the book* of life: and the dead were judged out of those things which were written in the books, according to their works. And the sea gave up the dead which were in it; and death and hell delivered up the dead which were in them: and they were judged every man according to their works. And death and hell were cast into the lake of fire. This is the second death. And whosoever was not found written in the book of life was cast into the lake of fire" (Re.20:11-15).

"And, behold, I come quickly; and my reward *is* with me, to give every man according as his work shall be" (Re.22:12).

"Also unto thee, O LORD, *belongeth* mercy: for thou renderest to every man according to his work" (Ps.62:12).

"I the LORD search the heart, *I* try the reins, even to give every man according to his ways, *and* according to the fruit of his doings" (Je.17:10).

---

2 (25:22-26) **Despair, Example of—Hopelessness, Example of—Fear, Example of—Despondency, Example of—Discouragement, Example of—Disheartened, Example of—Gedaliah, Governor over Judah—Judah, District of Babylon—Babylon, Appointed Gedaliah As Governor**: being conquered by Nebuchadnezzar, Judah became a district of the Babylonian empire. Hence a governor needed to be appointed, a person who would be loyal to the empire. In searching for such a person, Nebuchadnezzar appointed Gedaliah as governor over Judah, the newly formed district of Babylon. Note that Gedaliah was the grandson of Shaphan, who had been the secretary of state under the godly king Josiah (vv.22-23). Shaphan had also supervised the restoration of the temple under Josiah. The newly appointed governor Gedaliah was a very close friend of Jeremiah and depended heavily upon the prophet for counsel in dealing with Babylon (Je.39:14).

At one point during his governorship, Gedaliah was visited by some army officers of Judah who had escaped the destruction of Jerusalem, either with the king or from the outposts scattered throughout the land (vv.23-24; also see vv.4-5). They approached him at his residence in Mizpah (v.25), to seek his support in terrorist actions against Babylonian outposts or to seek his counsel about the possibility of safely settling down in the land. After discussing whatever questions and issues they had, the governor swore that the Babylonians would not harm them. Encouraging to return home, he suggested they surrender and live under Babylonian rule (v.24).

But soon thereafter, a conspiracy was formed by one of the officers and the Ammonite king Baalis (vv.25-26; Je.40:7–41:3). Taking ten men with him, the officer named Ishmael attacked the governor during a banquet and assassinated him along with his officials and some Babylonian soldiers (v.25; Je.41:1-3). The effect of Gedaliah's death was catastrophic, for the remaining refugees in Judah were forced to flee to Egypt in order to escape retaliation from Babylon (v.26).

OUTLINE	SCRIPTURE	SCRIPTURE	OUTLINE

2. The appointment of Gedaliah as governor over the newly formed district of Babylon (Judah): A picture of despair
a. His headquarters: Mizpah
 	
b. His most serious problem
  1) He was visited by some army officers:
    • They had escaped Jerusalem with the king, 4-5
    • Others had escaped from the outposts scattered throughout the land
	22 And *as for* the people that remained in the land of Judah, whom Nebuchadnezzar king of Babylon had left, even over them he made Gedaliah the son of Ahikam, the son of Shaphan, ruler.
	23 And when all the captains of the armies, they and their men, heard that the king of Babylon had made Gedaliah governor, there came to Gedaliah to Mizpah, even Ishmael the son of Nethaniah, and Johanan the son of Careah, and Seraiah the son of Tanhumeth the Netophathite, and Jaazaniah the son of a Maachathite, they and their men.
		24 And Gedaliah sware to them, and to their men, and said unto them, Fear not to be the servants of the Chaldees: dwell in the land, and serve the king of Babylon; and it shall be well with you.
		25 But it came to pass in the seventh month, that Ishmael the son of Nethaniah, the son of Elishama, of the seed royal, came, and ten men with him, and smote Gedaliah, that he died, and the Jews and the Chaldees that were with him at Mizpah.
		26 And all the people, both small and great, and the captains of the armies, arose, and came to Egypt: for they were afraid of the Chaldees.
			2) He swore that the Babylonians would not harm them: Encouraged them to return home & to live under Babylonian rule
			
			c. His assassination
			  1) The officer Ishmael & ten men assassinated the governor, his officials, & some Babylonian soldiers
			  2) The plot was instigated by the king of Ammon, Je.40:7–41:3
			
			  3) The effect of Gedaliah's death was catastrophic: The remaining refugees in Judah were forced to flee to Egypt to escape retaliation

Thought 1. What a picture of despair and hopelessness! Now even the few Israelites who had been left behind to maintain order and local government had to flee for their lives. Any hope or dream of the future, of reclaiming the promised land, was now lost. No one was left behind to repopulate the land, to govern it, or to keep it cultivated.

A spirit of fear, despair, and despondency flooded the hearts of all Judeans—plus whatever other emotions grip the heart of a person who has lost all his property, who is being forced to flee for his life with no hope of ever returning.

How many of us are gripped by despair, by a sense of hopelessness, despondency, or discouragement? There are many experiences in life that can cause despair to sweep across our souls.
(1) Being without Christ, refusing to accept Him can cause despair and hopelessness.

> **"That at that time ye were without Christ, being aliens from the commonwealth of Israel, and strangers from the covenants of promise, having no hope, and without God in the world" (Ep.2:12).**

(2) Questioning the death of a loved one and grieving over the loss can cause despair and hopelessness.

> **"But I would not have you to be ignorant, brethren, concerning them which are asleep, that ye sorrow not, even as others which have no hope" (1 Th.4:13).**

(3) Physical suffering such as Job experienced can cause despair and hopelessness.

> **"And where *is* now my hope? as for my hope, who shall see it?" (Jb.17:15).**

(4) Feeling that God does not answer prayer, that He has forsaken us can cause despair.

> **"But Zion said, The LORD hath forsaken me, and my Lord hath forgotten me" (Is.49:14).**

(5) Lacking purpose in life, a sense of being unfulfilled and dissatisfied, can cause despair and hopelessness.

> **"My soul is weary of my life; I will leave my complaint upon myself; I will speak in the bitterness of my soul" (Jb.10:1).**
> **"O my God, my soul is cast down within me: therefore will I remember thee from the land of Jordan, and of the Hermonites, from the hill Mizar" (Ps.42:6).**
> **"Therefore I hated life; because the work that is wrought under the sun *is* grievous unto me: for all *is* vanity and vexation of spirit" (Ec.2:17).**

(6) Thinking about all the bad news, lawlessness, violence, immorality, and oppressions of this earth can cause distress.

> **"So I returned, and considered all the oppressions that are done under the sun: and behold the tears of *such as were* oppressed, and they had no comforter; and on the side of their oppressors *there was* power; but they had no comforter. Wherefore I praised the dead which are already dead more than the living which are yet alive" (Ec.4:1-2).**

(7) Feeling lonely and friendless, as though there is no one to comfort us, can cause distress and hopelessness.

> **"They have heard that I sigh: *there is* none to comfort me: all mine enemies have heard of my trouble; they are glad that thou hast done *it:* thou wilt bring the day *that* thou hast called, and they shall be like unto me" (Lam.1:21).**

(8) Sensing the brevity of life and the mad rush of aging can cause despair and hopelessness.

> **"My days are swifter than a weaver's shuttle, and are spent without hope" (Jb.7:6).**
> **"And I said, My strength and my hope is perished from the LORD" (Lam.3:18).**

(9) Having any kind of emotional or mental problem can cause depression, despair, and hopelessness.

> **"Wherefore is light given to him that is in misery, and life unto the bitter *in* soul; Which long for death, but it *cometh* not; and dig for it more than for hid treasures; Which rejoice exceedingly, *and* are glad, when they can find the grave?" (Jb.3:20-22).**
> **"So that my soul chooseth strangling, *and* death rather than my life" (Jb.7:15).**

(10) Being disappointed over something God has done—or not done—can cause despair. One of the experiences of Jonah teaches this. When God reached out to save the Babylonians, the very people who had conquered Jerusalem, Jonah was gripped with despair. He disagreed with God's action, became discouraged because God blessed the very enemies who had conquered Palestine.

> **"Therefore now, O LORD, take, I beseech thee, my life from me; for *it is* better for me to die than to live" (Jona.4:3).**

(11) Being poor—lacking the basic necessities of life—and envying the prosperity of the wicked can cause distress, despondency, and hopelessness.

> **"But as for me, my feet were almost gone; my steps had well nigh slipped. For I was envious at the foolish, *when* I saw the prosperity of the wicked" (Ps.73:2-3).**

(12) Setting goals too high and never achieving what we hope for can cause distress, discouragement, and despondency.

> **"Hope deferred maketh the heart sick: but *when* the desire cometh, *it is* a tree of life" (Pr.13:12).**

3 (25:27-30) **Captivity, Freed from, Example of—Freedom, from Captivity, Example of—Hope, for What, Freedom-Liberty—Jehoiachin, Released from Prison—Prison, Released From, Example of**: after 37 years in prison, the former king of Judah, Jehoiachin, was released by the Babylonian king (2 K.24:7-16). After Nebuchadnezzar's death in 561 B.C., his son Evil-Merodach became king of Babylon. It was he who released Jehoiachin from prison. He had given the former king of Judah an honored position, esteeming him more highly than the other exiled kings. In fact, Jehoiachin was so honored that he was a regular guest at the king's table. Moreover, he was given an allowance of money to take care of his needs for the rest of his life.

OUTLINE	SCRIPTURE	SCRIPTURE	OUTLINE
3. The release of Jehoiachin from prison: A picture of hope, of being freed from captivity a. The release: Granted after 37 years in prison by Evil-Merodach, who succeeded his father as king of Babylon b. The honored position of	27 And it came to pass in the seven and thirtieth year of the captivity of Jehoiachin king of Judah, in the twelfth month, on the seven and twentieth *day* of the month, *that* Evil-merodach king of Babylon in the year that he began to reign did lift up the head of Jehoiachin king of Judah out of prison; 28 And he spake kindly to	him, and set his throne above the throne of the kings that *were* with him in Babylon; 29 And changed his prison garments: and he did eat bread continually before him all the days of his life. 30 And his allowance *was* a continual allowance given him of the king, a daily rate for every day, all the days of his life.	Jehoiachin 1) He was honored more than the other exiled kings 2) He was a regular guest at the king's table 3) He was given an allowance for the rest of his life

Note how the last scene in the great book of *Kings* is a picture of hope, the hope of being freed from captivity. But because the Israelites from the Northern and Southern Kingdoms had been scattered throughout Assyria, Babylon, and Egypt, the reader is left with an unanswered question: How will God fulfill His promise to David? For God had promised David an eternal kingdom, that his own descendants would sit upon the throne ruling over God's people forever (2 S.7:1-17). In addition, other Scriptures had given the promise that the exiles, the enslaved would be returned to the promised land if they repented. If they would turn back to the LORD, they would be delivered and freed from their captivity (De.30:1-10; 1 K.8:46-53; Je.31:18; Lam.5:21).

With the Israelites scattered all over the known world, how could God conceivably fulfill His promise? As the reader proceeds through the Holy Bible, he discovers that the promise of God was ultimately fulfilled in the Lord Jesus Christ, who was a descendant in the line of David. Jesus Christ is both the son of David and the Son of God, the Savior and Messiah who was sent into the world to set mankind free from the captivity of sin and its penalty. Jesus Christ saves people from sin and death and from the coming judgment of hell and eternal separation from God. Thus, in the release of Jehoiachin from prison, a picture of great hope is given to the reader of every generation, the great hope of being freed from the most horrible enslavements of human life: the enslavement to sin, death, and hell.

"For God so loved the world, that he gave his only begotten Son, that whosoever believeth in him should not perish, but have everlasting life. For God sent not his Son into the world to condemn the world; but that the world through him might be saved" (Jn.3:16-17).

"Him hath God exalted with his right hand *to be* a Prince and a Saviour, for to give repentance to Israel, and forgiveness of sins" (Ac.5:31).

"Paul, a servant of Jesus Christ, called *to be* an apostle, separated unto the gospel of God, (Which he had promised afore by his prophets in the holy scriptures,) Concerning his Son Jesus Christ our Lord, which was made of the seed of David according to the flesh; And declared *to be* the Son of God with power, according to the spirit of holiness, by the resurrection from the dead" (Ro.1:1-4).

"For when we were yet without strength, in due time Christ died for the ungodly" (Ro.5:6).

"Know ye not, that to whom ye yield yourselves servants to obey, his servants ye are to whom ye obey; whether of sin unto death, or of obedience unto righteousness? But God be thanked, that ye were the servants of sin, but ye have obeyed from the heart that form of doctrine which was delivered you. Being then made free from sin, ye became the servants of righteousness" (Ro.6:16-18).

"But I see another law in my members, warring against the law of my mind, and bringing me into captivity to the law of sin which is in my members. O wretched man that I am! who shall deliver me from the body of this death? I thank God through Jesus Christ our Lord. So then with the mind I myself serve the law of God; but with the flesh the law of sin" (Ro.7:23-25).

"For I delivered unto you first of all that which I also received, how that Christ died for our sins according to the scriptures; And that he was buried, and that he rose again the third day according to the scriptures" (1 Co.15:3-4).

"Who gave himself for our sins, that he might deliver us from this present evil world, according to the will of God and our Father" (Ga.1:4).

"Remember that Jesus Christ of the seed of David was raised from the dead according to my gospel" (2 Ti.2:8).

"Henceforth there is laid up for me a crown of righteousness, which the Lord, the righteous judge, shall give me at that day: and not to me only, but unto all them also that love his appearing. Do thy diligence to come shortly unto me: For Demas hath forsaken me, having loved this present world, and is departed unto Thessalonica; Crescens to Galatia, Titus unto Dalmatia" (2 Ti.4:8-10).

"Who gave himself for us, that he might redeem us from all iniquity, and purify unto himself a peculiar people, zealous of good works" (Tit.2:14).

"Forasmuch then as the children are partakers of flesh and blood, he also himself likewise took part of the same; that through death he might destroy him that had the power of death, that is, the devil; And deliver them who through fear of death were all their lifetime subject to bondage" (He.2:14-15).

"For Christ also hath once suffered for sins, the just for the unjust, that he might bring us to God, being put to death in the flesh, but quickened by the Spirit" (1 Pe.3:18).

"And ye know that he was manifested to take away our sins; and in him is no sin" (1 Jn.3:5).

Thought 1. Several commentators give excellent statements in concluding the great book of *Kings*, statements that are well worth the attention of the reader.

(1) Russell Dilday in *Mastering the Old Testament* says this:

The Book of Kings, in its last four verses, ends on a bright note. The last surviving sovereign of Judah is set free from the rigors and humiliation of Babylonian prison. He is shown honor and good will. Here is a hopeful sign that a better future is in store for God's people. Someday the exile will end, and ultimately the Davidic monarchy will be restored.[3]

(2) Paul R. House in *The New American Commentary* says this:

These verses represent the unvarnished, clearheaded, realistic thinking the author exhibits throughout the history. The people are frail, sinful, and often unwilling to follow the Lord. But at their best they can do so. Hope for a better future still remains, then, because neither the Lord nor Israel's remnant are dead. God's word and God's promises to David remain in effect even if physical signs of the Yahweh-Israel relationship, such as the temple, no longer exist.

What does the writer tell the reader? Trust the Lord and find hope in him. If God can give the land once, God can give it again. If the Lord can raise up one David, another can come to take his ancestor's place. If people could be faithful in Hezekiah's and Josiah's reigns, then they can be obedient again. Even in exile the author believes in such possibilities. What he does not know, though, is when or if the potential will become reality. The decision, like the options, remains open.[4]

(3) *The Expositor's Bible Commentary* says this:

Thus the final curtain falls on the drama of the divided monarchy. What had been a note of dark despair is illuminated by the light of God's gracious concern for his own. Although God' people had been judged as they must,

3 Russell Dilday. *1, 2 Kings*, p.508.
4 Paul R. House. *1, 2 Kings*, pp.401-402.

yet God would be with them even in the midst of their sentence. Jehoiachin's release and renewed enjoyment of life thus stands as a harbinger [foreshadow] of the further release and return of all the nation, in accordance with God's promises (cf. Jer 31:18; Lam 5:21). The spiritually minded believers perhaps would see in this incident an assurance of God's greater redemption from bondage of those who looked forward to him who gives release and eternal refreshment to all who love his appearing. [5]

(4) *The Bible Knowledge Commentary* says this:

The positive note on which 2 Kings ends reveals again the Lord's mercy, which stands out repeatedly in 1 and 2 Kings. This notation also points to the continuation of the Davidic dynasty which God had promised would lead His people forever (2 Sam. 7:16). Evil-Merodach's attitude toward Jehoiachin was followed by policies that allowed the Israelites more freedom. When Cyrus overthrew Babylonia he allowed the Jews to return to their land (Ezra 1:1-4). [6]

(5) Matthew Henry closes his commentary with the simple statement:

To see their king thus advanced [released, freed] would be a comfortable earnest to them [the Israelites] of their own release in due time, in the set time. Unto the upright there thus ariseth light in the darkness, to encourage them to hope, even in the cloudy and dark day, that at evening time it shall be light; when therefore we are perplexed, let us not be in despair. [7]

(6) *The New International Study Bible* says this:

The book of Kings ends on a hopeful note. The judgment of exile will not destroy the people of Israel or the line of David. God's promise concerning David's house remains (see 2 Sa 7:14-16). [8]

(7) *The Nelson Study Bible* says this:

Evil-Merodach's kindness toward Jehoiachin brings the Book of Kings to an end—on a ray of hope. Exile is the end neither of Israel nor of the Davidic line. [9]

(8) *The Life Application Study Bible* says this:

The book of 2 Kings opens with Elijah being carried to heaven—the destination awaiting those who follow God. But the book ends with the people of Judah being carried off to foreign lands as humiliated slaves—the result of failing to follow God.
Second Kings is an illustration of what happens when we make anything more important than God, when we make ruinous alliances, when our consciences become desensitized to right and wrong, and when we are no longer able to discern God's purpose for our lives. We may fail, like the people of Judah and Israel, but God's promises do not. He is always there to help us straighten out our lives and start over. And that is just what would happen in the book of Ezra. When the people acknowledged their sins, God was ready and willing to help them return to their land and start again. [10]

5   Richard D. Patterson and Hermann J. Austel. *1, 2 Kings*, p.300.
6   John F. Walvoord, and Roy B. Zuck, Editors. *The Bible Knowledge Commentary, Old Testament*, p.588.
7   Matthew Henry, p.837.
8   *The NIV Study Bible*, 25:28.
9   *The Nelson Study Bible, New King James Version*. (Nashville, TN: Thomas Nelson Publishers, Inc., 1997), 25:28.
10 *Life Application® Bible*. (Wheaton, IL: Tyndale House Publishers, Inc., 1991), 25:30.

PRACTICAL BIBLE HELPS & RESOURCES

THE DIVIDED KINGDOM
OF
ISRAEL AND JUDAH

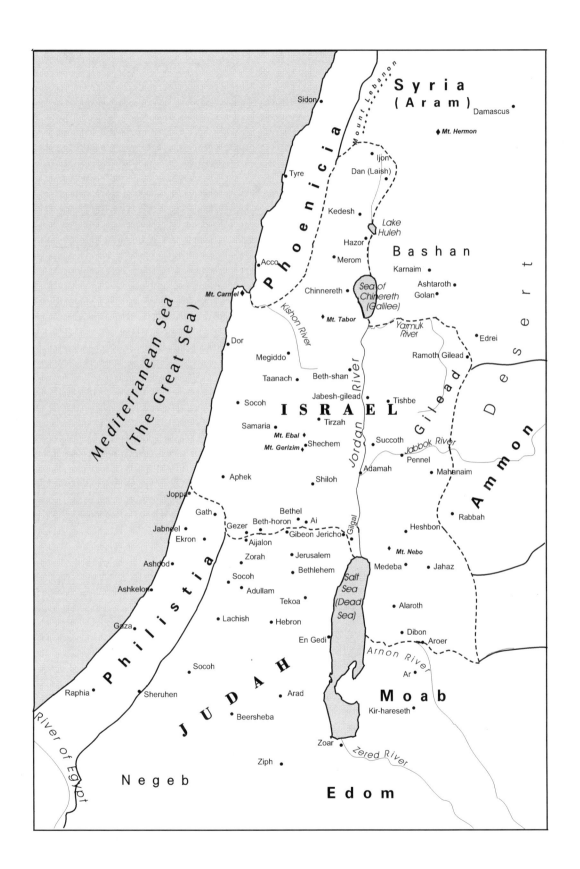

THE ASSYRIAN CONQUEST
OF THE
NORTHERN KINGDOM

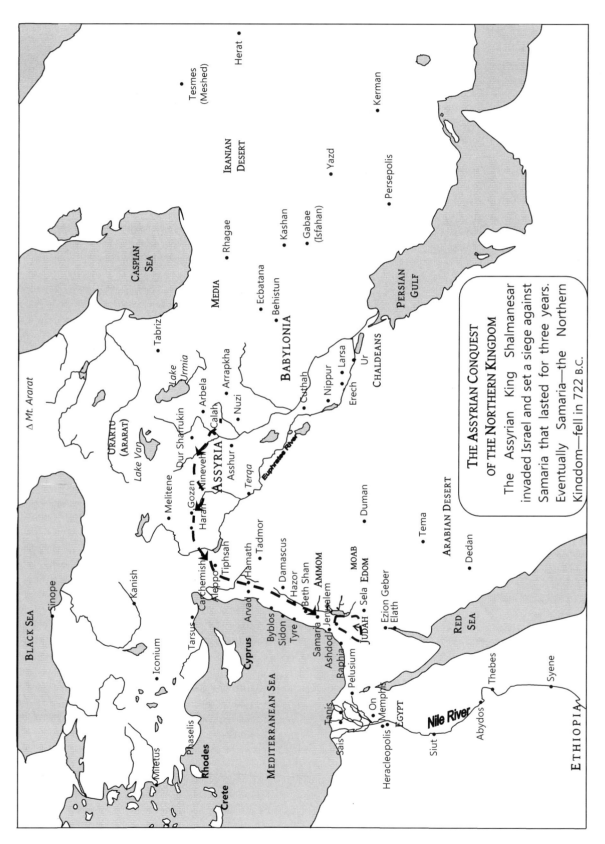

Herat

Tesmes
(Meshed)

Kerman

IRANIAN
DESERT

Yazd

CASPIAN
SEA

Rhagae

Kashan

Gabae
(Isfahan)

MEDIA

Persepolis

PERSIAN
GULF

Ecbatana

Behistun

BABYLONIA

Tabriz

Lake
Urmia

Arrapkha

Nuzi

Cuthah

Nippur

Larsa

Ur

Erech

CHALDEANS

Δ Mt. Ararat

URARTU
(ARARAT)

Lake Van

Arbela

Dur Sharrukin

Calah

Nineveh

ASSYRIA

Asshur

Terqa

Euphrates River

Melitene

Gozan

Haran

THE ASSYRIAN CONQUEST
OF THE NORTHERN KINGDOM

The Assyrian King Shalmanesar
invaded Israel and set a siege against
Samaria that lasted for three years.
Eventually Samaria—the Northern
Kingdom—fell in 722 B.C.

Tiphsah

Tadmor

Hamath

Damascus

Duman

Aleppo

Carchemish

Arvad

Hazor

Beth Shan

AMMOM

MOAB

Sela EDOM

Tema

ARABIAN DESERT

Dedan

Kanish

Sinope

BLACK SEA

Tarsus

Iconium

Cyprus

Byblos

Sidon

Tyre

Samaria

Ashdod

Jerusalem

JUDAH

Ezion Geber

Elath

RED
SEA

Phaselis

Miletus

Rhodes

Crete

MEDITERRANEAN SEA

Raphia

Pelusium

Tanis

Sais

On

Memphis

Heracleopolis

EGYPT

Siut

Nile River

Thebes

Abydos

Syene

ETHIOPIA

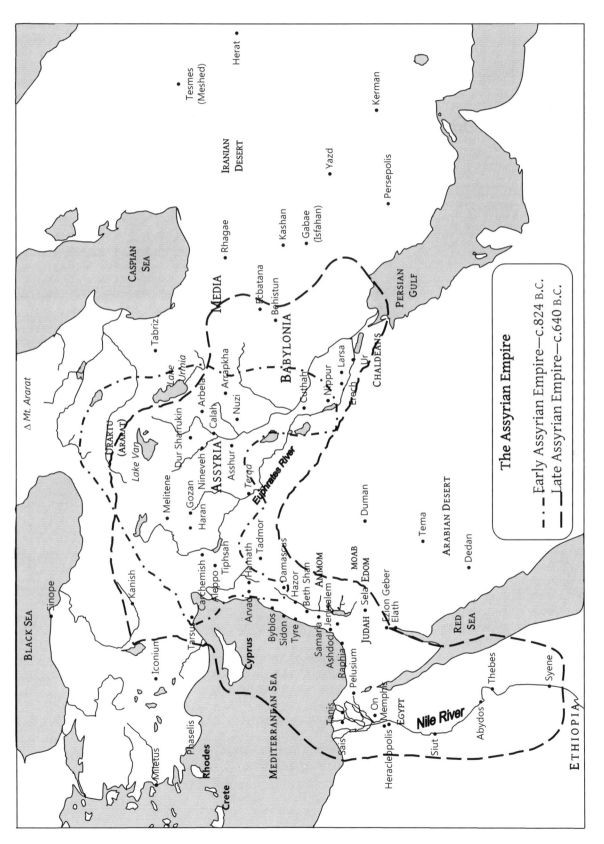

The Assyrian Empire

Early Assyrian Empire—c.824 B.C.
Late Assyrian Empire—c.640 B.C.

THE BABYLONIAN CONQUEST OF JUDAH

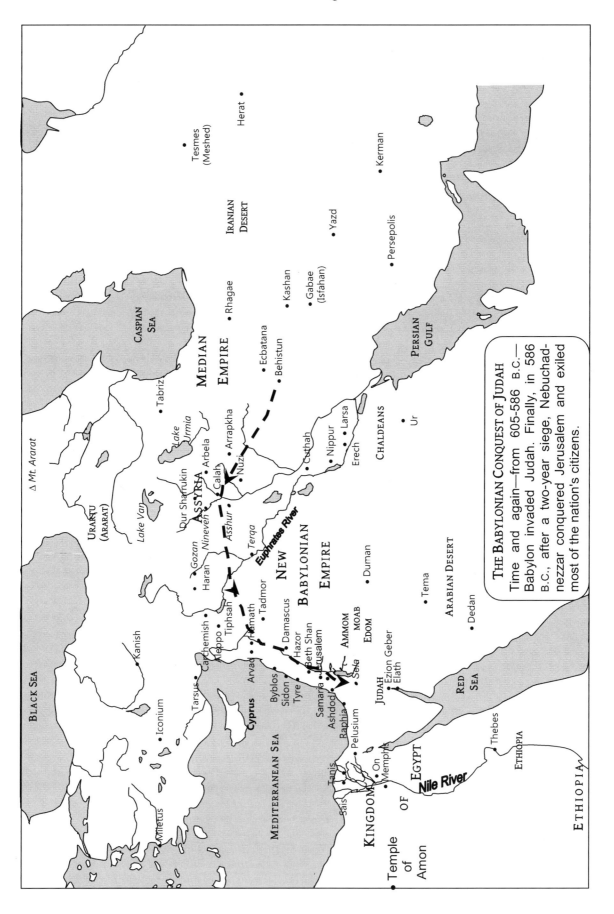

THE BABYLONIAN CONQUEST OF JUDAH
Time and again—from 605-586 B.C.—
Babylon invaded Judah. Finally, in 586
B.C., after a two-year siege, Nebuchad-
nezzar conquered Jerusalem and exiled
most of the nation's citizens.

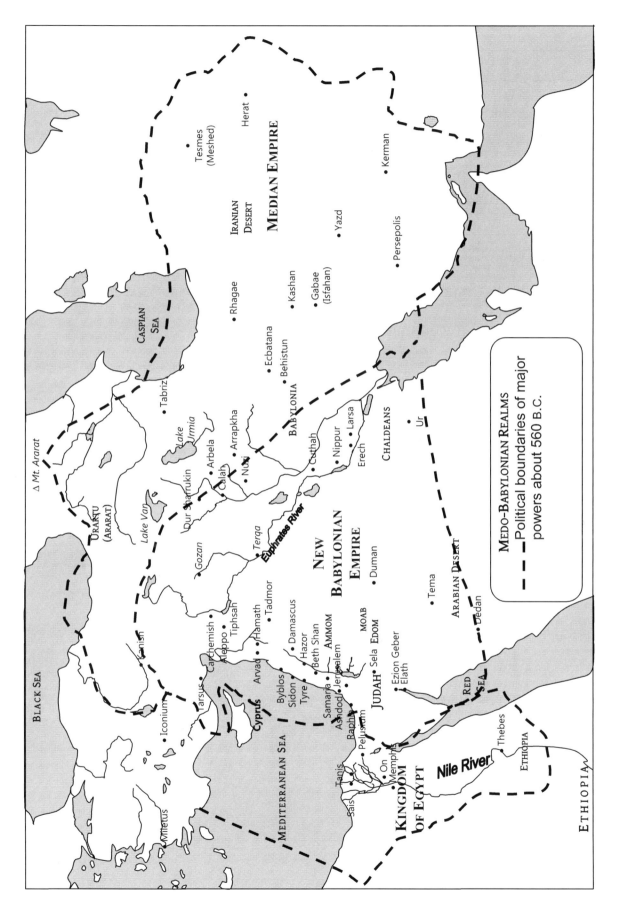

THE BABYLONIAN–MEDIAN EMPIRE

MEDIAN EMPIRE

Herat

Tesmes
(Meshed)

Kerman

IRANIAN
DESERT

Yazd

Persepolis

Kashan

Gabae
(Isfahan)

CASPIAN
SEA

Rhagae

Ecbatana
Behistun

BABYLONIA

Tabriz

Lake
Urmia

Arbela

Arrapkha

Larsa

Nuzi

Dur Sharrukin

Calah

Cuthah

Nippur

Erech

CHALDEANS

Ur

△ Mt. Ararat

Lake Van

URARTU
(ARARAT)

Terqa

Euphrates River

NEW
BABYLONIAN
EMPIRE

Duman

Gozan

ARABIAN DESERT

Tema

Tadmor

Carchemish
Aleppo
Tiphsah

Hamath

Damascus

Hazor
Beth Shan

AMMON

MOAB

Sela EDOM

Dedan

BLACK SEA

Canish

Tarsus

Iconium

Arvad

Cyprus

Byblos
Sidon
Tyre

Samaria
Ashdod Jerusalem

JUDAH

Raphia
Pelusium

Ezion Geber
Elath

RED SEA

Miletus

MEDITERRANEAN SEA

Tanis

On
Memphis

Sais

KINGDOM
OF EGYPT

Nile River

Thebes

ETHIOPIA

ETHIOPIA

MEDO-BABYLONIAN REALMS
— — Political boundaries of major
powers about 560 B.C.

TIMELINE OF KINGS, PROPHETS AND HISTORY*

HISTORY

DATE BC	FOREIGN KINGS	WORLD EVENTS
1000	Ashur-Rabi II (1010–970) (Assyria)	David captures Jerusalem (1004)
	Hiram (1003–966) (Tyre)	Foundation for the Temple (966)
950	Tiglath-Pileser II (960–935) (Assyria)	22nd Egyptian Dynasty (945)
930		Kingdom Divided (930)
	Shishak I (945–924) (Egypt)	
900	Ben-Hadad I (900) (Syria)	Assyria makes peace with Babylon (915); Jehoshaphat leads a revival (865)
	Eth-Baal (887–856) (Sidon)	Elijah's contest with prophets of Baal (857); Elijah's mantle passed to Elisha (845)
850	Hazael (840) (Syria)	
800	Ben-Hadad II (798) (Syria)	Carthage established (814); Joash repairs Temple (812); 23rd Egyptian dynasty (800)
	Ben-Hadad III (773) (Syria)	Olympic games begin (776); Rome founded (753)
750	Rezin (750) (Syria)	Babylonian and Chinese calendar (750)

THE UNITED KINGDOM

BIBLE REF.	KINGS (YEARS REIGNED)	PROPHETS
1 S.16:1–1 K.2:11; 1 Chr.11:1-30	David (40) (1011–971)	Samuel (1095–1015), Gad (1015–950), Asaph (1004), Nathan (1003–931), Heman (971)
1 K.2:12-11:43; 1 Chr.28:1–2 Chr.9:31	Solomon (40) (971–931)	

THE DIVIDED KINGDOM

NORTHERN KINGDOM OF ISRAEL

PROPHETS	KINGS (YEARS REIGNED)	BIBLE REF.
Ahijah (910–910), Man from Judah (930), Shemaiah (927)	Jeroboam I (22) (931–910)	1 K.12:1-24; 12:25-14:20; 2 Chr.1C:1-16
Jehu (886)	Nadab (2) (910–909)	1 K.15:25-31
	Baasha (24) (909–886)	1 K.15:16-16:7; 2 Chr.16:1-6
	Elah (2) (886–885)	1 K.16:6-14
Hanani (870)	Zimri (7 days) (885)	1 K.16:9-20
	Omri (12) (885–874)	1 K.16:21-28
Elijah (860–845)	Ahab (22) (874–853)	1 K.16:28-22:40; 2 Chr.18:1-34
Micaiah (853), Elisha (850–795), Eliezer (849–48)	Ahaziah (2) (853–852), Joram/Jehoram (12) (852–841)	1 K.22:49-51; 2 K.1:1-18; 2 Chr.20:35-37; 22:1-11
	Jehu (28) (841–814)	2 K.9:1-10:36; 2 Chr.22:7-9
	Jehoahaz (17) (814–798)	2 K.13:1-9
Zechariah (797)	Jehoash (16) (798–782)	2 K.13:9-25; 14:8-16
Jonah (780–765)	Jeroboam II (41) (793–753)	2 K.14:23-29
Amos (750)	Zechariah (6 mos) (753)	2 K.15:8-12
	Shallum (1 mo) (752)	2 K.15:13-15
	Menahem (10) (752–742)	2.K.15:16-22

SOUTHERN KINGDOM OF JUDAH

KINGS (YEARS REIGNED)	PROPHETS	BIBLE REF.
Rehoboam (17) (931–913)		1 K.12:1-24; 14:21-31; 2 Chr.9:31-12:16
Abijah (3) (913–911)		1 K.15:1-8; 2 Chr.12:16-14:1
Asa (3) (911–870)	Iddo (910), Azariah (896)	1 K.15:9-24; 2 Chr.14:1-16:14
Jehoshaphat (25) (873–848)		1 K.22:41-50; 2 K.3:6-14; 2 Chr.17:1-21:1
Jehoram (8) (853–841)		2 K.8:16-24; 2 Chr.21:1-20
Ahaziah (2) (841)		2 K.8:25-29; 9:27-29; 2 Chr.22:1-10
Athaliah (7) (841–835)		2 K.11:1-16; 2 Chr.22:10-23:21
Joash/Jehoash (40) (835–796)	Obadiah (845)	2 K.11:17-12:21; 2 Chr.22:11-12; 24:1-27
Amaziah (29) (796–767)	Joel (830)	2 K.14:1-20; 2 Chr.24:27-25:28
Azariah/Uzziah (52) (792–740)	Hosea (788–723), Jonah (780–765)	2 K.14:21-22; 15:1-7; 2 Chr.26:1-23
Jotham (16) (750–731)		2 K.15:32-38; 2 Chr.26:23-27:9

THE DIVIDED KINGDOM

SOUTHERN KINGDOM OF JUDAH			NORTHERN KINGDOM OF ISRAEL			DATE BC	FOREIGN KINGS	HISTORY — WORLD EVENTS
BIBLE REF.	KINGS (YEARS REIGNED)	PROPHETS	BIBLE REF.	KINGS (YEARS REIGNED)	PROPHETS			
			2 K.15:23-26	Pekahiah (2) (742-740)			Tiglath-Pil[n]eser III [or Pul] (745-727) (Assyria)	Assyria takes control of Northern Kingdom (745-627)
2 K.15:38-16:20; 2 Chr.27:9-27, Is.7:1-9:1	Ahaz (16) (735-715)	Isaiah (740-690)	2 K.15:27-31	Pekah (20) (752-732) (ruled only in Gilead) (752-740) · (740-732) (ruled in Samaria)			Shalmaneser V (727-722) (Assyria)	Assyria invades Northern Israel (732)
		Micah (735-725), Oded (733)	2 K.17:1-23	Hoshea (9) (732-722)			So (727-716) (Egypt); Sargon II (710-705) (Assyria)	Fall of Northern Kingdom (722)
2 K.18:1-20:21; 2 Chr.28:27-32:33; Pr.25:1, Is.36:1-39:8	Hezekiah (29) (729-686)						Sennacherib (705-681) (Assyria); Merodach-Baladan (721-710, 705-704) (Assyria)	Sennacherib defeats Egypt (701); Hezekiah's tunnel (701)
						700	Tirhakah (690-664) (Egypt)	185,000 Assyrians killed by God (701)
2 K.20:21-21:18; 2 Chr.32:33-33:20	Manasseh (55) (696-642)	Nahum (663-612)					Esarhaddon (681-669) (Assyria)	Sennacherib destroys Babylon (689)
2 K.21:18-26; 2 Chr.33:20-25	Amon (2) (642-640)					650	Nabopolassar (626-605) (Assyria)	Josiah's reform (621); Nineveh destroyed (612)
2 K.21:26-23:30; 2 Chr.33:25-35:27	Josiah (31) (640-609)	Zephaniah (640-609)					Neco (610-595) (Egypt)	Battle of Carchemish (605); 1st group of exiles from Judah taken to Babylon (605)
2 K.23:31-33; 2 Chr.36:1-4	Jehoaz/Jehoahaz (3 mos) (609)	Jeremiah (627-562)					Nebuchadnezzar II (605-562) (Babylon)	
2 K.23:34-24:7; 2 Chr.36:5-8	Jehoiakim (11) (608-598)	Habakkuk (615-598)				600		2nd group of exiles from Judah taken to Babylon (597)
2 K.24:8-17; 25:27-30; 2 Chr.36:8-10;	Jehoiachin (3 mos) (598-597)	Daniel (605-535)						Fall of Judah—Third group of exiles from Judah taken to Babylon (586)
2 K.24:18-25:21; 2 Chr.36:10-14; Je.21:1-52:11	Zedekiah/Mattaniah (11) (597-586)	Ezekiel (593-571)					Evil-Merodach (562-560) (Babylon)	Fall of Babylon to Medo-Persian Empire (539)
2 K.25:22-26; Je.40:5-41:18	Gedaliah (2 mos) (Appointed by Nebuchadnezzar) (586)					550	Cyrus II (559-530) (Medo-Persia); Belshazzar (552-539) (Babylon)	Cyrus II decrees that the Jews may return to the Holy Land (538); 1st exiles return to Holy Land with Zerubbabel (537)
		Haggai (520), Zechariah (520-518)						1st Temple foundation laid (536); 2nd Temple foundation laid (520)
						500	Darius I (521-486) (Medo-Persia)	Temple completed (516); Republic of Rome est. (509)
							Artaxerxes (465-425) (Persia)	2nd return under Ezra (458)
		Malachi (430)				450		3rd return under Nehemiah (445)

*Some dates are approximate.

The resources used for the Timeline in addition to the *Bible* are as follows:
1 Archer, Gleason L. *Encyclopedia of Bible Difficulties.* (Grand Rapids, Michigan: Zondervan Publishing House), 1982.
2 Freedman, David Noel, ed. et. al. *The Anchor Bible Dictionary.* (New York: Doubleday), 1992.
3 Grun, Bernard. *The Timetables of History.* 3rd ed. (New York: Simon & Schuster), 1991.
4 Kaiser, Walter C. *A History of Israel.* (Nashville, Tennessee: Broadman & Holman Publishers), 1998.
5 Silverman, David P., ed. *Ancient Egypt.* (New York: Oxford University Press), 1997.

SIGNIFICANT EVENTS IN THE HEBREW CALENDAR

Sacred Month	Secular Month	Hebrew Name	Modern Name	Feast or Event	Farm Seasons **	Bible Ref.	Old Testament Meaning	New Testament Meaning
1	7	Abib; Nisan	March-April	Passover	Harvesting barley & flax; Later Spring rains	Ex.12:2; 13:4; 23:15; 34:18; De.16:1; Ne.2:1; Est..3:7	Redemption from Egypt's bondage	Christ's Crucifixion
				Unleaven-ed Bread			Purging of all leaven (a symbol of sin)	Justification/ Sanctification
				Firstfruits		Le.23:10-12		Resurrection of Christ
2	8	Ziv or Zif Iyyar +	April-May	Second or "Little Passover"	Barley har-vest; Dry season begins	1K.6:1, 37	33rd day of the Omer (Sabbath), a minor holiday	
3	9	Sivan	May-June	Pentecost (Weeks)	Wheat harvest	Est.8:9	A Giving of Thanks for the First Harvest	The Coming of the Holy Spirit & The Birth of the Church
4	10	Tammuz+	June-July	Fast to re-member the breach in Jerusa-lem's wall	Tending the vines (grapes, olives, figs, pomegranates, etc.)	Je.52:5-6		
5	11	Ab +	July-August	Fast for the destruction of the Tem-ple (by Babylon OT & Rome-NT) (Mt.24:1-3)	Ripening of the vines			
6	12	Elul	August-September		Harvesting of the vines	Ne.6:15		

There were two other significant events in the Hebrew calendar: *The Sabbatical Year* and *The Year of Jubilee. The Sabbatical Year* was celebrated every seven years. During the seventh year the land was given rest from agricultural use and debts were forgiven (see Ex.23:10-11; Le.25:1-7; De.15:1 for more information). *The Year of Jubilee* was celebrated at the end of every forty-ninth year on the Day of Atonement. On this special day, the trumpet would sound out the message of freedom to all the inhabitants of the land who had been held in bondage. In addition, all property was to be returned to the original own-ers who had been forced to give it up because of poverty. This meant that all prices in the economy throughout the forty-nine years were to be fairly adjusted according to the closeness to The Year of Jubilee (see Le.25:8-17).

HEBREW CALENDAR

Sacred Month	Secular Month	Hebrew Name	Modern Name	Feast or Event	Farm Seasons **	Bible Ref.	Old Testament Meaning	New Testament Meaning
7	1 (Beginning of the civil year)	Ethanim Tishri +	September-October	Trumpets	Plowing of the fields: Early autumn rains	1K.8:2; Joel 2:23	A Somber Assembly in Preparation for the Day of Atonement	The Rapture of the Church & The Bodily Return of Christ
				Atonement (Yom Kippur)			A National Day of Repentance (yearly)	Forgiveness of Sins
				Tabernacles (Booths)			A Celebration for the Harvest	The Kingdom of God on Earth
				Branches or Palms				
8	2	Bul Marcheshvan +	October-November		Planting of the crops: Wheat & barley esp.	1K.6:38		
9	3	Kislev or Chislev or Chisleu	November-December	Hanukkah Feast of Dedication	Winter begins	Ne.1:1; Zec.7:1 (Extra-Biblical Source: 2 Macc.1:9)		
10	4	Tebeth	December-January	Fast remembering Nebuchadnezzar's siege of Jerusalem		Est.2:16 2 K.25:1		
11	5	Shebat or Sebat	January-February	Jewish Arbor Day	Blossoming of trees	Zec.1:7		
12	6	Adar *	February-March	Fast of Esther	Blooming of almond trees; Harvesting of citrus fruit	Ezr.6:15; Est.3:7,13 8:12;9:1, 15,17,19, 21,26-28		
				Purim			Israel was delivered from their enemies: a time to share with each other & with the poor	

* Note: An additional month (Second Adar or Adar Sheni or Veadar) was added to the Hebrew calendar about every three years. This was how the lunar calendar corresponded to the solar year.

+ Hebrew names of the month that are not in the Bible are marked with a plus sign (+). These are known as "Post-exilic" names, from the period of history known as "The Babylonian Exile."

** The idea for listing the Farm Seasons was stirred by the *NIV Study Bible*, Grand Rapids, MI: Zondervan Bible Publishers, 1985, pp.102-103.

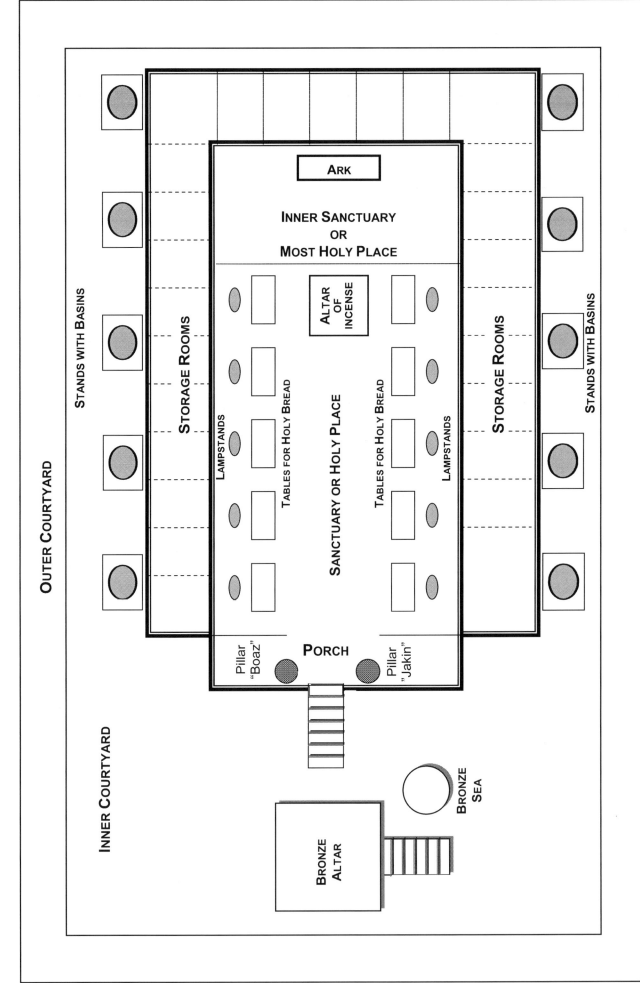

SOLOMON'S TEMPLE
(Inside)

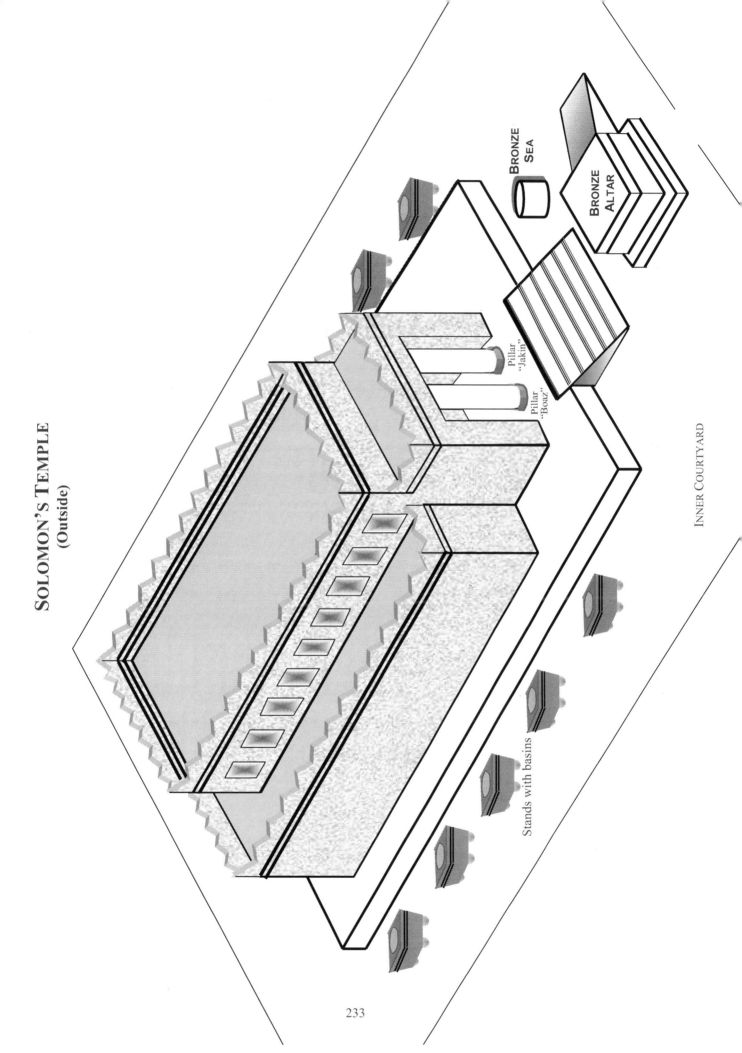

SOLOMON'S TEMPLE
(Outside)

Pillar "Jakin"

Pillar "Boaz"

BRONZE SEA

BRONZE ALTAR

Stands with basins

INNER COURTYARD

THE PROPHETS: THEIR MESSAGE—THEN AND NOW

The prophets were called and chosen by God to do two things:
> ➢ to proclaim God's salvation to man
> ➢ to prophesy and predict how God was going to save man

Both functions were necessary. The prophet had to proclaim salvation to the people of his own generation and to predict how God was going to save the people of all generations. But note: the predictions of the future salvation were not the prophet's own predictions. He had not been called to proclaim his own ideas or message; he had been called to proclaim the salvation of God Himself. He was a man given a very special call, a call to the most important task in all the world: the task of proclaiming the glory and wonder of God's salvation. God was making it possible for man to be saved and to live eternally.

The prophet conveyed the salvation of God…

- by pointing out the sins of the people
- by warning the people about the terrible and certain consequences of sin, the discipline and judgment of God
- by encouraging the people to repent by wholeheartedly turning back to God, worshipping Him and Him alone
- by proclaiming God's eternal plan of salvation and blessings to those who would believe

Speaking of the prophets, Peter Adams writes, "To respond to God's words is to respond to God."[1]

"But those things, which God before had showed by the mouth of all his prophets, that Christ should suffer, he hath so fulfilled. Repent ye therefore, and be converted, that your sins may be blotted out, when the times of refreshing shall come from the presence of the Lord; And he shall send Jesus Christ, which before was preached unto you: Whom the heaven must receive until the times of restitution of all things, which God hath spoken by the mouth of all his holy prophets since the world began. For Moses truly said unto the fathers, A prophet shall the Lord your God raise up unto you of your brethren, like unto me; him shall ye hear in all things whatsoever he shall say unto you. And it shall come to pass, that every soul, which will not hear that prophet, shall be destroyed from among the people. Yea, and all the prophets from Samuel and those that follow after, as many as have spoken, have likewise foretold of these days. Ye are the children of the prophets, and of the covenant which God made with our fathers, saying unto Abraham, And in thy seed shall all the kindreds of the earth be blessed. Unto you first God, having raised up his Son Jesus, sent him to bless you, in turning away every one of you from his iniquities" (Ac.3:18-26).

---

[1] Peter Adams. *Speaking God's Words.* (Downers Grove, IL: Inter-Varsity Press, 1996), pp.19-20.

ALPHABETICAL LISTING OF THE PROPHETS

NAME	DATE
Abel	Right after creation
Abraham	2000 B.C.
Agabus	A.D. 43
Ahijah	931–910 B.C.
Amos	750 B.C.
Anna	4 B.C.
Asaph	1004 B.C.
Azariah	896 B.C.
Daniel	605–535 B.C.
David	1029–971 B.C.
Deborah	1220 B.C.
Eliezer	849–848 B.C.
Elijah	860–845 B.C.
Elisha	850–795 B.C.
Ezekiel	593–571 B.C.
Gad	1015–950 B.C.
Habakkuk	615–598 B.C.
Haggai	520 B.C.
Hanani	870 B.C.
Heman	971 B.C.
Hosea	788–723 B.C.
Huldah	623 B.C.
Iddo	910 B.C.
Isaiah	740–690 B.C.
Jacob/Israel	1858 B.C.
Jehu	886 B.C.
Jeremiah	627–562 B.C.
Joel	830 B.C.
John the Apostle	A.D. 95
John the Baptist	A.D. 26
Jonah	780–765 B.C.
Joseph	1900–1885 B.C.
Malachi	430 B.C.
Micah	735–725 B.C.
Micaiah	853 B.C.
Moses	1405 B.C.

NAME	DATE
Nahum	663–612 B.C.
Nathan	1003–931 B.C.
Noah	At least seven generations after Adam
Obadiah	845 B.C.
Oded	733 B.C.
Paul	A.D. 35–64
Shemaiah	926 B.C.
Unnamed prophet Prophesied a total victory over the Syrians	855 B.C.
Unnamed prophet Prophesied a victory over the Syrians	856 B.C.
Unnamed prophet Rebuked Eli and his house for profaning the temple	1085 B.C.
Unnamed prophet Rebuked Israel for fearing idols	1210 B.C.
Unnamed prophet Rebuked King Ahab for sparing the evil Ben-Hadad	855 B.C.
Unnamed prophet Rebuked King Amaziah for his idolatry	767 B.C.
Unnamed prophet Rebuked King Jeroboam I for his idolatry	931 B.C.
Unnamed prophet Warned King Amaziah not to hire Israel's army	767 B.C.
Urijah	608 B.C.
Zechariah, son of Jehoiada	797 B.C.
Zephaniah	640–609 B.C.

THE PROPHETS

CHRONOLOGICAL LISTING OF THE PROPHETS[2]

NAME	DATE
Abel	Right after creation
Noah	At least seven generations after Adam
Abraham	2000 B.C.
Joseph	1900–1885 B.C.
Jacob/Israel	1858 B.C.
Moses	1405 B.C.
Deborah	1220 B.C.
Unnamed prophet Rebuked Israel for fearing idols	1210 B.C.
Samuel	1095–1015 B.C.
Unnamed prophet Rebuked Eli and his house for profaning the temple	1085 B.C.
David	1029–971 B.C.
Gad	1015–950 B.C.
Asaph	1004 B.C.
Nathan	1003-931 B.C.
Heman	971 B.C.
Unnamed prophet Rebuked King Jeroboam I for his idolatry	931 B.C.
Ahijah	931–910 B.C.
Shemaiah	926 B.C.
Iddo	910 B.C.
Azariah	896 B.C.
Jehu	886 B.C.
Hanani	870 B.C.
Elijah	860–845 B.C.
Unnamed prophet Prophesied a victory over the Syrians	856 B.C.
Unnamed prophet Prophesied total victory over the Syrians	855 B.C.
Unnamed prophet Rebuked King Ahab for sparing the evil Ben-Hadad	855 B.C.

NAME	DATE
Micaiah	853 B.C.
Elisha	850–795 B.C.
Eliezer	849–848 B.C.
Obadiah	845 B.C.
Joel	830 B.C.
Zechariah, son of Jehoiada	797 B.C.
Hosea	788–723 B.C.
Jonah	780–765 B.C.
Unnamed prophet Rebuked King Amaziah for his idolatry	767 B.C.
Unnamed prophet Warned King Amaziah not to hire Israel's army	767 B.C.
Amos	750 B.C.
Isaiah	740–690 B.C.
Micah	735–725 B.C.
Oded	733 B.C.
Nahum	663–612 B.C.
Zephaniah	640–609 B.C.
Jeremiah	627–562 B.C.
Huldah	623 B.C.
Habakkuk	615–598 B.C.
Urijah	608 B.C.
Daniel	605–535 B.C.
Ezekiel	593–571 B.C.
Haggai	520 B.C.
Zechariah, son of Berechiah	520–518 B.C.
Malachi	430 B.C.
Anna	4 B.C.
John the Baptist	A.D. 26
Paul	A.D. 35–64
Agabus	A.D. 43
John the Apostle	A.D. 95

---

2   The list above serves as a timeline for all the prophets discussed in the following chart. The unnamed prophets are listed according to their message. (Also see the *Timeline of Kings, Prophets, and History* chart, pp.392-393.)

PROPHET	TIME/PLACE GIVEN	MAIN MESSAGE	PRACTICAL APPLICATION
ABEL **(Breath)** **Known Facts** 1. Was the son of Adam (Ge.4:2). 2. Was called a prophet by Jesus Christ (Mt. 23:34-35; Lu. 11:50-51). 3. Kept the flocks of animals (Ge.4:2). 4. Brought an acceptable and pleasing sacrifice to God (Ge. 4:4). 5. Was murdered by his brother, Cain (Ge.4:8). 6. Was avenged by God (Ge.4:9-12). **Predictions and Messages** By example he taught that a person must approach God through the sacrifice of a substitute offering (Ge.4:4). **Scripture References** Ge.4:1-16; Mt.23:34-39; Lu.11:47-51; He.11:4; 12:24	**Time** *The first years after creation, when Adam was still alive.* **Place** *Outside the garden of Eden, where man first began to farm.*	Abel's message is seen in his worship. Note what Abel did: when he approached the LORD, he brought an animal, a blood sacrifice. Why? Because his father, Adam, had taught him to approach God through the sacrifice of an animal. God taught Adam… • that sin causes death • that an innocent substitute had to sacrificially die in order to clothe man's shame and guilt • that thereafter man could only approach God through the sacrificial death of an innocent substitute Thus Abel pointed forward to Christ, the perfect sacrifice. He may not have completely understood, but Abel did approach God through the blood sacrifice, just as his father had taught him. Abel had *faith*. He believed that God would forgive his sins and accept him through the sacrifice of an innocent life. And note the remarkable testimony Scripture gives about Abel's faith in the coming Savior: Abel even today, although dead, testifies of Christ (He.11:4). What a striking legacy Abel left to the world! **"And Abel, he also brought of the firstlings of his flock and of the fat thereof. And the LORD had respect unto Abel and to his offering" (Ge.4:4).** **"By faith Abel offered unto God a more excellent sacrifice than Cain, by which he obtained witness that he was righteous, God testifying of his gifts: and by it he being dead yet speaketh" (He.11:4).** **"And to Jesus the mediator of the new covenant, and to the blood of sprinkling, that speaketh better things than that of Abel" (He.12:24).**	No person can earn, win, or merit salvation. No person can approach God through his own works, energy, efforts, fruits, ways, religion, ceremony or ritual. The reason is clearly evident: no person is perfect. We have a sin problem and a death problem that has to be taken care of before we can ever become acceptable to God. God has taken care of this in the sacrifice of His Son for our sins. Jesus Christ took our sins upon Himself and died for them. This is what the sacrifice of the innocent life symbolized in the Old Testament. Just like Abel, we must believe God, believe that the death (the blood) of the sacrifice of Jesus Christ covers our sins. God accepts no person apart from Jesus Christ, the promised seed and Savior of the world. God has never accepted *any person* apart from the shedding of the blood of His dear Son. The blood of Christ had to be shed for all persons through all the generations of human history. Apart from Christ, apart from accepting His sacrifice, no person can be saved from sin. No person can escape the judgment of death and hell apart from Christ. **"Ye serpents, ye generation of vipers, how can ye escape the damnation of hell?" (Mt.23:33).** **"For when we were yet without strength, in due time Christ died for the ungodly" (Ro.5:6).** **"For I delivered unto you first of all that which I also received, how that Christ died for our sins according to the scriptures" (1 Co.15:3).** **"And walk in love, as Christ also hath loved us, and hath given himself for us an offering and a sacrifice to God for a sweetsmelling savour" (Ep.5:2).**

PROPHET	TIME/PLACE GIVEN	MAIN MESSAGE	PRACTICAL APPLICATION
AGABUS **(Locust)** **Known Facts** 1. Lived in Judea near Jerusalem (Ac.21:10). 2. Ministered among a company of prophets (Ac.11:27-28). 3. Prophesied with the words of the Holy Spirit (Ac.11:28; 21:11). 4. Spoke for the prophets (Ac.11:28). **Predictions and Messages** 1. A severe famine would come to the entire Roman world (Ac.11:28). 2. The Apostle Paul would be bound and taken prisoner, and eventually killed (Ac. 21:11-13). **Scripture References** Ac.11:27-30; 21:10-14	**Time** *A.D. 43, at the beginning of the terrible persecution of Agrippa.* **Place** *Antioch of Syria, where the followers of Jesus Christ were first called Christians.*	Agabus prophesied two future events by the Spirit of God. First, Agabus prophesied that a great famine would occur. The disciples accepted the message given and gathered funds and stores of food to be used for those in need. Note this fact: the disciples did not waste time questioning God; they simply acted immediately on the information given, doing what was necessary for the church to continue. Some time later, Agabus prophesied that the Gentiles (or Romans) would take the Apostle Paul prisoner. Despite the danger of suffering and persecution, and eventually death, Paul was unhindered in his mission to preach the gospel. Knowing the prophecy, the fire of devotion within Paul burned all the more. Why? Because Paul trusted God. He understood that nothing is out of God's control. He firmly believed that as long as he continued to do the will of the Lord, the Lord would richly bless his labor for the gospel. **"And in these days came prophets from Jerusalem unto Antioch. And there stood up one of them named Agabus, and signified by the Spirit that there should be great dearth throughout all the world" (Ac.11:27-28).** **"And as we tarried there many days, there came down from Judaea a certain prophet, named Agabus. And when he was come unto us, he took Paul's girdle, and bound his own hands and feet, and said, Thus saith the Holy Ghost, So shall the Jews at Jerusalem bind the man that owneth this girdle, and shall deliver him into the hands of the Gentiles" (Ac.21:10-11).**	1. Giving is essential. Believers must give to those in need. And they should practice regular giving, not waiting for some disaster to strike and then scrambling for a solution to the problem. Giving should be a regular habit of the believer so the mission of the church can be carried out, even in difficult times. 2. Believers will suffer. Believers suffer by: ➢ being ridiculed ➢ being mocked ➢ being assaulted ➢ being spoken evil of ➢ being gossiped about ➢ being slandered ➢ being reviled ➢ being insulted ➢ being scolded ➢ being falsely accused ➢ being put on trial ➢ even being murdered But suffering is necessary. First of all, believers must live out the calling given to them by the Lord no matter how unpleasant, no matter what the cost. Second, suffering prepares the believer to participate in the glory of Christ. It is the necessary condition for exaltation. Suffering and struggling are a refining process through which the believer must pass. It refines the believer by forcing him to expand his trust in God more and more. Suffering drives a believer to cast himself more and more upon the care of God; therefore, the believer moves closer and closer to the Lord praying, worshipping and fellowshipping with him more and more. God is in complete control of every situation. Sometimes He allows unpleasant trials to come our way, but this is all according to His will, according to His plan for our lives. We must trust God no matter what and do all we can to understand His will and to do it. **"Yea, and all that will live godly in Christ Jesus shall suffer persecution" (2 Ti.3:12).** **"For unto you it is given in the behalf of Christ, not only to believe on him, but also to suffer for his sake" (Ph.1:29).** **"Wherein ye greatly rejoice, though now for a season, if need be, ye are in heaviness through manifold temptations: That the trial of your faith, being much more precious than of gold that perisheth, though it be tried with fire, might be found unto praise and honour and glory at the appearing of Jesus Christ" (1 Pe.1:6-7).**

PROPHET	TIME/PLACE GIVEN	MAIN MESSAGE	PRACTICAL APPLICATION
AHIJAH (Brother in Jehovah/Yahweh) **THE SHILONITE** **Known Facts** 1. Lived in Shiloh (1 K. 11:29). 2. Called to minister during the time of Solomon and Jeroboam (1 K.11:28-29). 3. Became blind in his old age (1 K.14:4). **Predictions and Messages** 1. The division of the nation of Israel into two kingdoms—the Northern Kingdom of Israel and the Southern Kingdom of Judah (1 K.11:31). 2. The death of Abijah, the son of King Jeroboam (1 K.14:9-13). 3. The destruction of the entire family of King Jeroboam (1 K. 14:10-13). 4. The captivity and exile of Israel to a foreign land (1 K. 14:14-16). **Scripture References** 1 K.11:29-39; 12:15; 14:4-16; 2 Chr.9:29	**Time** *The end of Solomon's reign, just before 931 B.C. until 910 B.C., near the end of the reign of Jeroboam I.* **Place** *Ahijah's first prophecy was given in the countryside, just outside Jerusalem.* *Later, after the division of the kingdom, Ahijah ministered in his hometown of Shiloh, preaching mainly to the Northern Kingdom of Israel.*	Israel was divided because the king and people had forsaken God, engaged in false worship, disobeyed God's commandments and refused to walk in the ways of the LORD. Jeroboam, Solomon's very own trusted servant, became king over the Northern Kingdom just as Ahijah predicted. But when King Jeroboam displayed a life of wickedness and idolatry, judgment fell on him and on his entire household, beginning with the immediate death of his own son. Eventually, all Israel would go into captivity, because they would not repent of their wickedness, nor turn from the state religion of idolatry and false worship instituted by Jerusalem. **"And he said to Jeroboam, Take thee ten pieces: for thus saith the LORD, the God of Israel, Behold, I will rend the kingdom out of the hand of Solomon, and will give ten tribes to thee" (1 K. 11:31).** **"But [you] hast done evil above all that were before thee: for thou hast gone and made thee other gods, and molten images, to provoke me to anger, and hast cast me behind thy back: Therefore, behold, I will bring evil upon the house of Jeroboam,"...Arise thou therefore, get thee to thine own house:** *and* **when thy feet enter into the city, the child shall die. ...For the LORD shall smite Israel, as a reed is shaken in the water, and he shall root up Israel out of this good land, which he gave to their fathers, and shall scatter them beyond the river, because they have made their groves, provoking the LORD to anger" (1 K. 14:9-10, 12, 15).**	If we continue in sin and wickedness and become involved in false worship, we will face the judgment of God. God will chastise and discipline us in order to bring us back to Him. God is zealous for us and will not allow us to chase after worldly affections, not for long. If we refuse to repent, we will face the judgment of God's hand. Even future generations may suffer and bear the brunt of our sins, suffering the great and terrible consequences of God's wrath. **"The LORD knoweth how to deliver the godly out of temptations, and to reserve the unjust unto the day of judgment to be punished" (2 Pe.2:9).** **"Every branch in me that beareth not fruit he taketh away: and every branch that beareth fruit, he purgeth it, that it may bring forth more fruit" (Jn.15:2).** **"My son, despise not the chastening of the LORD; neither be weary of his correction: For whom the LORD loveth he correcteth; even as a father the son in whom he delighteth" (Pr. 3:11-12).** **"Thou shalt not bow down thyself to them, nor serve them: for I the LORD thy God am a jealous God, visiting the iniquity of the fathers upon the children unto the third and fourth generation of them that hate me; And showing mercy unto thousands of them that love me, and keep my commandments" (Ex.20:5-6).**

PROPHET	TIME/PLACE GIVEN	MAIN MESSAGE	PRACTICAL APPLICATION

AMOS
(Burden-bearer)
 	
Known Facts
1. Lived in Tekoa, on the edge of the Judean desert (Am.1:1).
2. Worked as a shepherd and as a farmer of sycamore trees (Am.1:1; 7:14).
3. Wrote the book of *Amos*.
4. Preached fiery sermons and saw startling visions.
 	
Predictions and Messages
1. A sermon about God's coming judgment on sinful nations, including Israel (Am.1:1-4:13).
2. A sermon about the need for seeking God with the whole heart (Am.5:1-27).
3. A sermon warning the people not to be greedy (Am.6:4-14).
4. The vision of locusts—a picture of the crops being destroyed by the ferocious insects, but Amos interceded and God had mercy (Am.7:1-3).
5. The vision of fire—a picture of the fields being destroyed, but Amos interceded and God had mercy (Am.7:4-5).
6. The vision of a plumb line—a picture of the crookedness of Israel (Am.7:7-9).
7. The vision of a basket of fruit—a picture of the rottenness of Israel's sin (Am.8:1-3).
8. A sermon warning that God will severely judge those who treat the poor unfairly (Am.8:4-14).
9. The vision of the LORD standing on the altar, striking His own temple (Am.9:1-10).
10. The prophecy about the captivity and return of Israel (Am.9:9-15).
 	
Scripture References
The book of *Amos*
	Time
	About 750 B.C., near the end of the rule of Jeroboam II in Israel and during the long reign of Uzziah in Judah.
	
	The time in which Amos preached was a very prosperous time economically and financially for the people of Israel, but not spiritually. Spiritually the hearts of the people were filled with greed, so much so that they oppressed the poor without mercy.
	
	Place
	Israel, the Northern Kingdom.
		God will judge sin wherever it is found. No sinner is exempt from judgment. Without genuine repentance, God's judgment will surely fall upon the sinner.
		
		Amos focused upon one theme, one subject: the coming judgment of God upon those who refused to turn from sin. Despite persecution and death threats, Amos faithfully continued to preach the messages given him by God, a series of blistering sermons against the sins of arrogance and pride.
		
		"Therefore thus will I do unto thee, O Israel: and because I will do this unto thee, prepare to meet thy God, O Israel" (Am. 4:12).
		
		"Then answered Amos, and said to Amaziah, I was no prophet, neither was I a prophet's son; but I was an herdman, and a gatherer of sycomore fruit: And the LORD took me as I followed the flock, and the LORD said unto me, Go, prophesy unto my people Israel" (Am.7:14-15).
			Worldly gain, such as riches, social position, heritage, even religion will not save a person. Such things can be good if they are used to help the poor or advance God's kingdom. But when a person uses worldly gain just for the purpose of more worldly gain, God's judgment is sure to fall upon that person.
			
			At least two major applications can be seen in the prophecies of Amos.
			1. Just think of the people gripped by greed who push aside the needs of others…
			  • to make themselves more comfortable
			  • to buy some luxury
			  • to enjoy more leisure time
			  • to hoard more riches
			
			Shockingly, some people are so gripped by greed, they even assault and murder in order to gain more and more. Unbelievably, they consider human life worthless if it stands in the way of their gaining more riches.
			2. The minister of God must boldly preach the Word of God. He must not form his sermon based on what people want to hear, nor avoid certain subjects because he will not be popular. The messenger of the LORD must be unashamed and unswerving in his calling to preach the whole counsel of God. Even persecution, no matter how serious, must not prevent the minister from proclaiming the Word of God, declaring what God has anointed him to say.
			
			"Charge them that are rich in this world, that they be not highminded, nor trust in uncertain riches, but in the living God, who giveth us richly all things to enjoy" (1 Ti.6:17).
			
			"I charge thee therefore before God, and the Lord Jesus Christ, who shall judge the quick [living] and the dead at his appearing and his kingdom; preach the word; be instant in season, out of season; reprove, rebuke, exhort with all longsuffering and doctrine" (2 Ti.1:3-4).

THE PROPHETS

PROPHET	TIME/PLACE GIVEN	MAIN MESSAGE	PRACTICAL APPLICATION
ANNA (Gracious) **Known Facts** 1. Served in the temple as a woman prophet (Lu.2:36). 2. Appeared as the first prophet since Malachi, a space of over 300 years. 3. Descended from the tribe of Asher (Lu. 2:36). 4. Widowed for many years (Lu.2:36). 5. Fasted and prayed continually (Lu.2:37). 6. Loved and hoped in God, therefore she was blessed (Lu.2:37). 7. Pointed out Christ to others (Lu.2:38). **Predictions and Messages** Jesus is the Christ, the Savior of the world (Lu.2:38). **Scripture References** Lu.2:36-38	**Time** *About 4 B.C., eight days after the birth of Jesus Christ.* **Place** *At the temple in Jerusalem.*	Anna's message was the greatest of all messages: Jesus Christ is the Redeemer, the promised Messiah Who brings redemption to all who ask for God's salvation. Anna shared this good news with anyone looking for redemption in Jerusalem. **"And she coming in that instant gave thanks likewise unto the Lord, and spake of him [the Christ child] to all them that looked for redemption in Jerusalem" (Lu.2:38).**	1. God will greatly bless the person who places his entire hope in Him. God will always bless the person who trusts in Him. We must rely on God for our salvation, rely on Him with our whole heart, holding nothing back, seeking Him continually. For there is no other person, no other place, no other source to whom we can turn for the salvation of our soul. Salvation is in Christ, and Christ alone. 2. Believers should be busy talking to everyone about Jesus Christ, for Jesus Christ came to earth to redeem us from our sins. And He will grant forgiveness to anyone who seeks for it, to anyone who will place his entire hope in the Lord. **"Behold the eye of the Lord is upon them that fear him, upon them that hope in his mercy" (Ps.33:18).** **"Being justified freely by his grace through the redemption that is in Christ Jesus" (Ro.3:24).**
ASAPH (Gathering) **Known Facts** 1. Was the son of Berechiah (1 Chr.6:39). 2. Descended from the tribe of Levi and the clan of Kohathites (1 Chr.6:33, 39). 3. Appointed by David as a musician, Asaph played the cymbals and sang (1 Chr. 6:31, 39). 4. Called a Seer (2 Chr. 29:30). 5. Wrote lyrics which were used many years after his death (2 Chr. 29:30). **Predictions and Messages** Sang and played music to praise and glorify the LORD. **Scripture References** 1 Chr.6:31-43; 15:17-19 2 Chr.29:30	**Time** *1004 B.C. Right after David was first crowned king in Hebron, he decided to bring the Ark of the Covenant from Kiriath-Jearim to Jerusalem. It was at this time that Asaph and the other musicians were appointed by King David to lead the people of Israel in worship, praising the LORD in songs of praise and celebration to the LORD.* **Place** *Jerusalem, the Holy City.*	Asaph was one of the leading musicians during the days of King David. Although there is not any specific message recorded by Asaph, he lived a life of praise and worship and greatly encouraged others to do so. Down through the years, Asaph's testimony was that of leading and encouraging the congregation in praising the LORD. **"So the Levites appointed Heman the son of Joel; and of his brethren, Asaph the son of Berechiah; and of the sons of Merari their brethren, Ethan the son of Kushaiah" (1 Chr.15:17).** **"Moreover Hezekiah the king and the princes commanded the Levites to sing praise unto the LORD with the words of David, and of Asaph the seer. And they sang praises with gladness, and they bowed their heads and worshipped" (2 Chr.29:30).**	The importance of praise and worship cannot be overstressed. As the Creator of the universe, the LORD expects us to praise and worship Him. It is the LORD Who has created life and Who sustains life. The air we breathe, the water we drink, the food we eat—every good and perfect gift we have comes from the hand of the LORD with Whom there is no changing. Because of all the richness and depth of all the blessings God pours out upon us—because of all the good and perfect gifts He so mercifully gives every day of our lives—the LORD expects, and rightly deserves, our worship and the praise of His holy name. **"Oh that men would praise the LORD for his goodness, and for his wonderful works to the children of men!" (Ps.107:8, 15, 21, 31).** **"Blessed be the Lord, who daily loadeth us with benefits, even the God of our salvation. Selah" (Ps.68:19).**

THE PROPHETS

PROPHET	TIME/PLACE GIVEN	MAIN MESSAGE	PRACTICAL APPLICATION
AZARIAH **(Jehovah/Yahweh is my Helper)** **Known Facts** 1. Was the son of Oded (2 Chr.15:1). 2. Ministered as the first of the prophets to the Southern Kingdom of Judah after the division of the nation of Israel. **Predictions and Messages** Azariah instructed King Asa to extend the revival which had begun in the land. Asa was not to lose courage, but to continue to serve God with fervor (2 Chr.15:2-7). **Scripture References** 2 Chr.15:1-12	**Time** 896 *B.C., during the reign of Asa, king of Judah, who stirred a great reformation and revival among the people.* **Place** *Jerusalem, the Holy City and capital of Judah.*	Revival was sweeping through the land of Judah resulting in changed lives and a reformation of worship. King Asa and his troops had just delivered a crushing defeat to the invading Ethiopians. But right afterward, Asa was tempted to rely on his own strength. So Azariah, the prophet, pressed the king and the people to seek the LORD more than ever before. He challenged them not to fall into a foolish and destructive attitude of pride and self-reliance. Azariah declared that the LORD wanted the people to be as strong spiritually as they had been in battle. King Asa responded to Azariah's message and continued to stir a strong reformation among the people. He removed the pagan images of idolatry as well as those in charge of their worship. Then, he made all false worship illegal, instituting the death penalty for all who practiced it. Committing himself totally to the LORD, he established the purity of true worship, the worship of the LORD God alone (Jehovah/Yahweh). **"Now the Spirit of God came on Azariah the son of Oded, and he went out to meet Asa and said to him, "Listen to me, Asa, and all Judah and Benjamin: the LORD is with you when you are with Him. And if you seek Him, He will let you find Him; but if you forsake Him, He will forsake you... be strong and do not lose courage, for there is reward for your work" (2 Chr.15:1-2, 7).**	Seeking the LORD is essential for every believer. We must seek Him with our whole heart, seek Him continually. Anything that could trap us in a deadly snare of sin must be removed. Placing God first in our lives, first in everything we do, must be our never-ending effort. We must draw close to the LORD, as close as we possibly can. We must continue to stoke the fire of revival in our hearts, to let it burn hotter and hotter. Why? Because we are always in need, in very desperate need, of God's help. Even when things seem to be going smoothly, we need God. We need Him... • for daily guidance • for spiritual strength • to escape temptation • for our daily food • to hold the world together • for our very next breath • for *all* our needs, *for every single need, every day of our lives* And remember this: God will *actively move in the behalf of the one who seeks Him.* Our labor is not in vain. There is a reward for serving God. God strongly supports those who wholeheartedly serve Him. **"And let us not be weary in well doing: for in due season we shall reap, if we faint not" (Ga.6:9).** **"But seek ye first the kingdom of God, and his righteousness; and all these things shall be added unto you" (Mt.6:33).** **"For the eyes of the Lord run to and fro throughout the whole earth to show himself strong in the behalf of them whose heart is perfect toward him" (2 Chr.16:9).**

PROPHET	TIME/PLACE GIVEN	MAIN MESSAGE	PRACTICAL APPLICATION
DANIEL **(God is my Judge)** **Known Facts** 1. Was taken captive by the Babylonians and forced to live in Babylon (Da.1:1-2). 2. Prophesied to three major world powers— Israel, Babylon and Medo-Persia (Da.1:1-2; 5:31). 3. Possessed tremendous integrity (Da.1:8-10; 6:4; Eze.14:1). 4. Was given a Babylonian name (Belteshazzar) because he was highly favored among the exiles, and because he needed to conduct business in Babylon (Da.1:7). 5. Was able to understand all kinds of mysteries (Da.7:15-28; 8:15-27; 9:24-27; 10:1-14; Eze.28:3). 6. Was delivered miraculously from the den of lions (Da.6:19-23). 7. Saw strange and vivid visions about Israel's future, about the coming dominant world powers of human history, and about a future period of history known as the *Great Tribulation* and the end of the world (Da.7:1–12:13). 8. Wrote the book of *Daniel*. **Predictions and Messages** 1. The interpretation of King Nebuchadnezzar's dream of a great statue, which symbolizes the coming great world powers (Da.2:17-19). 2. The interpretation of King Nebuchadnezzar's dream of a great tree which predicted the coming judgment against Nebuchadnezzar due to his pride (Da.4:19-27). (Cont. on next page)	**Time** *605–535 B.C., during the Babylonian captivity of Judah and on into the first years of the Medo-Persian Empire. Daniel was just a young man, only about thirty years old when he was taken captive. He lived the rest of his days in Babylon, ministering to his people, serving as a statesman for Babylon and recording history, writing down his visions and prophecies of the future.* **Place** *Near the Tigris River during the last years of the Babylonian Empire and the first few years of the Medo-Persian Empire.*	The book of *Daniel* has one unmistakable message: God sets up kings and puts down kings. The powers of the world will struggle and struggle to gain domination, wealth, and control; but God is in control and overrules everything they do, working all things out for the good of genuine believers and accomplishing His will for the world. Only He can exalt or humble; only He can deliver or destroy. God is sovereign over all. He lifts up those who acknowledge His sovereignty and puts down those who become filled with pride and self-sufficiency. After the end of the Assyrian Empire, control passed mainly to Babylon, which had been firmly established by Nabopolassar. Nabopolassar's son (Nebuchadnezzar II, the king we read about in the book of *Daniel*) then took over. The first thing Nebuchadnezzar did was to export most of the Judeans to Babylon. This included Daniel and his three friends. But despite their new pagan surroundings, Daniel and his three friends became very successful and were highly esteemed by the Babylonians. This was due to God's guidance, for they remained faithful to the LORD and to Him alone. Daniel became a close advisor and statesman for Nebuchadnezzar. Through the interpretation of dreams, which God inflicted upon the king, Daniel was lifted to a very high position in the Babylonian kingdom. Years later, Nebuchadnezzar's grandson Belshazzar became king. He was prideful like his grandfather before him. But there was a difference. Nebuchadnezzar repented and acknowledged God as the Sovereign over the earth, but Belshazzar refused to do so. The last straw came when Belshazzar defiled the articles of the temple of God by using them at a drunken feast in honor of a false god. At this, God literally wrote on the wall with His finger, burning a permanent message of immediate doom upon the king and the Babylonian empire. Belshazzar was slain that night as the Medo-Persian soldiers stormed the capital and the palace, and the new empire was put in place.	➢ All the world is to praise God for His holiness. ➢ All the world is to praise God for His sovereignty and omnipotence. ➢ All the world is to praise God for His eternal existence. What an indictment against man! How little we praise and worship God—truly praise and worship Him. Think for a moment and imagine in your mind the four beings who surround the throne of God. They were created to worship God, and they worship Him day and night, never ceasing from worshipping Him. They cry out day and night the glorious praise: "Holy, holy, holy, Lord God Almighty, which was, and is, and is to come" (Re. 4:8). The very thought of such a scene should bring us to our knees in repentance, humility and worship of God and His Son, Jesus Christ, the King of kings and Lord of lords. What a lesson the book of *Daniel* has for us! For the LORD God Almighty dwells in glory and majesty, dominion, and power. We owe Him our lives, all we are and have. **"Exalt the LORD our God, and worship at his holy hill; for the LORD our God is holy" (Ps.99:9).** **"And one cried unto another, and said, Holy, holy, holy, is the LORD of hosts: the whole earth is full of his glory" (Is.6:3).** **"Who shall not fear thee, O Lord, and glorify thy name? for thou only art holy: for all nations shall come and worship before thee; for thy judgments are made manifest" (Re.15:4).** **"For I am the LORD that bringeth you up out of the land of Egypt, to be your God: ye shall therefore be holy, for I am holy" (Lev.11:45).** **"I know that thou canst do every thing, and that no thought can be withholden from thee" (Jb.42:2).** **"But our God is in the heavens: he hath done whatsoever he hath pleased" (Ps.115:3).** **"Yea, before the day was I am he; and there is none that can deliver out of my hand: I will work, and who shall let [hinder] it?" (Is.43:13).**

PROPHET	TIME/PLACE GIVEN	MAIN MESSAGE	PRACTICAL APPLICATION
DANIEL (cont.) 3. The message that God gives political power to whomever He wishes (Da.4:25). 4. The interpretation of the handwriting on the wall written to King Belshazzar by the finger of God Himself—the prediction of the soon coming judgment against Belshazzar and the end of the Babylonian Empire (Da.5:10-28). 5. The vision of the four beasts arising from the sea—a prophecy of the coming dominant world powers (Da.7:1-8). 6. The vision of Jesus Christ, the Ancient of Days (Da.7:9-10; Re. 4:4; Mt.19:28; 1 Co.6:3). 7. The vision of the fourth beast being destroyed—the prophecy about the defeat of the antichrist (Da.7:11-12). 8. The vision of Jesus Christ—One like the Son of Man (Da. 7:13-14). 9. The vision of the ram and the two horns—a prophecy of the end of the Medo-Persian Empire and the rise of the Greek Empire (Da.8:1-14). 10. The message from Gabriel about Jeremiah's seventy weeks—the prediction that the Messiah, Jesus Christ, the Savior of the world, would be rejected 483 years in the future (Da.9:24-26). 11. The message from Gabriel about Jeremiah's seventieth week—the prediction of the coming Tribulation, the desecration of the temple by the antichrist and the end of the world (Da.9:26-27; Mt.24:15-25; Mk. 13:14-23). (Cont. on next page)		But Daniel, who continued to give God honor and to remain humble, was quickly lifted up to a high rank in the government of the Medes. Both before and after the change in power, Daniel saw amazing visions and received many startling messages from angels about the powers of the world, both present and future, and about the end times. Daniel wrote down many of these, but was instructed to withhold others. In all of his writings, Daniel continually proclaimed the great majesty of God and the need to honor Him. **"This is the dream; and we will tell the interpretation thereof before the king. Thou, O king, art a king of kings: for the God of heaven hath given thee a kingdom, power, and strength, and glory. And wheresoever the children of men dwell, the beasts of the field and the fowls of the heaven hath he given into thine hand, and hath made thee ruler over them all. Thou art this head of gold. And after thee shall arise another kingdom inferior to thee, and another third kingdom of brass, which shall bear rule over all the earth. And the fourth kingdom shall be strong as iron: forasmuch as iron breaketh in pieces and subdueth all things: and as iron that breaketh all these, shall it break in pieces and bruise. And whereas thou sawest the feet and toes, part of potters' clay, and part of iron, the kingdom shall be divided; but there shall be in it of the strength of the iron, forasmuch as thou sawest the iron mixed with miry clay. And as the toes of the feet were part of iron, and part of clay, so the kingdom shall be partly strong, and partly broken. And whereas thou sawest iron mixed with miry clay, they shall mingle themselves with the seed of men: but they shall not cleave one to another, even as iron is not mixed with clay. And in the days of these kings shall the God of heaven set up a kingdom, which shall never be destroyed: and the kingdom shall not be left to other people, but it shall break in pieces and consume all these kingdoms, and it shall stand for ever. Forasmuch as thou sawest that the stone was cut out of the**	**"But Jesus beheld them, and said unto them, With men this is impossible; but with God all things are possible" (Mt.19:26).** **"Now to him that is of power to stablish you according to my gospel, and the preaching of Jesus Christ, according to the revelation of the mystery, which was kept secret since the world began" (Ro.16:25).** **"For I lift up my hand to heaven, and say, I live for ever" (De.32:40).** **"The eternal God is thy refuge, and underneath are the everlasting arms" (De.33:27).** **"Thy name, O LORD, endureth for ever; and thy memorial, O Lord, throughout all generations" (Ps.135:13).** **"I am Alpha and Omega, the beginning and the ending, saith the Lord, which is, and which was, and which is to come, the Almighty" (Re.1:8).** **"Thine, O LORD, is the greatness, and the power, and the glory, and the victory, and the majesty: for all that is in the heaven and in the earth is thine; thine is the kingdom, O LORD, and thou art exalted as head above all" (1 Chr. 29:11).** **"The LORD reigneth, he is clothed with majesty; the LORD is clothed with strength, wherewith he hath girded himself: the world also is stablished, that it cannot be moved" (Ps.93:1).** **"I will speak of the glorious honour of thy majesty, and of thy wondrous works" (Ps.145:5).** **"And the seventh angel sounded; and there were great voices in heaven, saying, The kingdoms of this world are become the kingdoms of our Lord, and of his Christ; and he shall reign for ever and ever" (Re.11:15).**

PROPHET	TIME/PLACE GIVEN	MAIN MESSAGE	PRACTICAL APPLICATION

DANIEL (cont.)
12. The vision of the man dressed in linen standing by the Tigris River (Da.10:1-14).
13. The vision of the man who strengthened Daniel (Da.10:15-21).
14. The prophecy about the coming Greek Empire and Alexander the Great (Da.11:2-4).
15. The prophecies about the coming empires of Egypt and Syria and their struggle for world power (Da.11:5-35).
16. The prophecy of the distressing time at the end of the world—that those whose names are written in the Book of Life will be rescued (Da.12:1).
17. The prophecy of additional resurrections during the Tribulation (Da.12:2-3).
 	
Scripture References
The book of *Daniel*
		mountain without hands, and that it brake in pieces the iron, the brass, the clay, the silver, and the gold; the great God hath made known to the king what shall come to pass hereafter: and the dream is certain, and the interpretation thereof sure" (Da. 2:36-45).
		    "How great are his signs! and how mighty are his wonders! his kingdom is an everlasting kingdom, and his dominion is from generation to generation" (Da. 4:3).
		    "And at the end of the days I Nebuchadnezzar lifted up mine eyes unto heaven, and mine understanding returned unto me, and I blessed the most High, and I praised and honoured him that liveth for ever, whose dominion is an everlasting dominion, and his kingdom is from generation to generation: And all the inhabitants of the earth are reputed as nothing: and he doeth according to his will in the army of heaven, and among the inhabitants of the earth: and none can stay his hand, or say unto him, What doest thou?" (Da.4:34-35).
		    "And this is the writing that was written, MENE, MENE, TEKEL, UPHARSIN. This is the interpretation of the thing: MENE; God hath numbered thy kingdom, and finished it. TEKEL; Thou art weighed in the balances, and art found wanting. PERES; Thy kingdom is divided, and given to the Medes and Persians" (Da.5:25-28).	

PROPHET	TIME/PLACE GIVEN	MAIN MESSAGE	PRACTICAL APPLICATION
DAVID (Loved) **Known Facts** 1. Was the son of Jesse and the youngest of eight sons (1 S.16:11; 17:12). 2. Lived in Bethlehem (1 S.16:1; 17:12). 3. Descended from the tribe of Judah (Mt. 1:1-6). 4. Served the first king of Israel, King Saul, by playing music for him and by serving in Saul's army (1 S.16:23; 18:5). 5. Defeated the giant Goliath as a youth (1 S.17). 6. Was anointed king over all Israel and reigned forty years (1 S.16:1, 11-13; 2 S.5:5). 7. Was promised by God that the Savior would come through his lineage (Mt.1:1-17). 8. Wrote 73 Psalms (Ps. 22:1; 23:1; 41:1; 110:1). 9. Played musical instruments in praise to the LORD (2 S.23:2). 10. Was a brilliant military leader and strategist. Led great military campaigns (1 S. 18:5-7). 11. Had a heart that was like the heart of God (1 S.13:14; Ac.13:22). **Predictions and Messages** 1. The Messiah, the Savior of the world, would be a priest after the order of Melchizedek (Ps.110:4; Mt. 27:50-51; Mk. 15:37-38; Lu.23:44-46; He.6:20). 2. The Messiah would be betrayed by a friend (Ps.41:9; Mt. 26:20-25; Mk.14:10-11; Lu.22:2-6; Jn. 13:1-2; 1 Co.11:23). 3. The Messiah's betrayer would be removed from office and replaced (Ps. 109:7-8; Ac.1:18-20). (Cont. on next page)	**Time** *1029–971 B.C. All his life, King David sang and wrote psalms (songs) to the LORD. In his times of rejoicing and in his time of despair, David cried out to God in beautiful songs of poetry.* **Place** *Many places throughout Judea and Samaria as well as southern Jerusalem, the City of David.*	David was a shining example of trust in God, of placing his life in the palm of God's hand. Whenever David was in trouble, he turned to God as His Savior, trusting the LORD completely for deliverance. And the LORD always saved, delivered David because of the saving acts of God and in his behalf, David was able to write many heartfelt Psalms that are recorded in the Holy Scripture. And God was able to use David to predict many of the prophecies about Jesus Christ hundreds of years before the Savior was born. **"Now these are the last words of David. David the son of Jesse declares, The man who was raised on high declares, The anointed of the God of Jacob, And the sweet psalmist of Israel, 'The Spirit of the Lord spoke by me, And His word was on my tongue'" (2 S.23:1-2).**	David trusted fully that God would do exactly as He had promised, that He would send the promised King and Savior to establish His throne forever in the world. The confessions of David's heart were made in simple trust, arising from a heart that was truly convinced that God does exactly what He says He will do. David's trust is a dynamic example for us, for it is simple trust God desires from man—nothing more and nothing less. We simply must rely on God. We must lean on Him with our whole heart, put our complete trust in the LORD to do exactly as He says. The LORD will save those who trust in Him. **"The God of my rock; in him will I trust: he is my shield, and the horn of my salvation, my high tower, and my refuge, my saviour; thou savest me from violence" (2 S.22:3).** **"But let all those that put their trust in thee rejoice: let them ever shout for joy, because thou defendest them: let them also that love thy name be joyful in thee" (Ps.5:11).** **"O LORD my God, in thee do I put my trust: save me from all them that persecute me, and deliver me" (Ps.7:1).** **"The LORD redeemeth the soul of his servants: and none of them that trust in him shall be desolate" (Ps.34:22).** **"Cause me to hear thy lovingkindness in the morning; for in thee do I trust: cause me to know the way wherein I should walk; for I lift up my soul unto thee" (Ps.143:8).**

PROPHET	TIME/PLACE GIVEN	MAIN MESSAGE	PRACTICAL APPLICATION
DAVID (cont.) 4. The Messiah, the Savior of the world, would be falsely accused (Ps. 27:12; 35:11; Mt. 26:59-62; Mk. 14:55-59). 5. The Messiah would be hated for no reason (Ps.69:4; Jn.15:23-25). 6. The Messiah's hands and feet would be pierced (Ps.22:16; Jn. 20:25-27). 7. The Messiah would bear the sins of the world (Ps.22:1; Mt. 27:45-46; Mk.15:33-34). 8. The Messiah would be mocked (Ps.22:6-8; Mt.27:39-40; Mk. 15:29-32; Lu. 23:35-37). 9. The Messiah would be given gall and vinegar (Ps.69:21; Mt. 27:48; Mk.15:36; Jn. 19:28-29). 10. The Messiah would pray for His enemies (Ps.109:4; Lu.23:34). 11. The Messiah's garments would be gambled for (Ps.22:18; Mt.27:35; Mk.15:24; Lu.23:34; Jn.19:23-25). 12. The Messiah would not have any broken bones (Ps.34:20; see Ex. 12:46; Jn.19:31-37). 13. The Messiah would be resurrected (Ps. 16:10; Mt.12:39-41; 16:4; 28:1-7; Mk. 16:1-8; Lu.11:29-32; 24:1-8; Jn.20:1-8). 14. The Messiah would ascend to heaven (Ps. 68:18; Mk.16:19-20; Lu.24:50-51; Ac.1:6-9; Ep.4:8-10). **Scripture References** 1 S.16–1 K. 2; Ps.16, 22, 27, 34, 41, 68, 69, 109, 110			

DEBORAH
(Honey bee)

Known Facts
1. Was married to Lapidoth (Jud.4:4).
2. Judged Israel, deciding civil cases for the people according to God's Word (Jud. 4:4).
3. Wrote a song of deliverance after the defeat of Sisera and the Canaanite army (Jud.5).

Predictions and Messages
1. Barak was to gather ten thousand men from Naphtali and Zebulun, and God would deliver Sisera into his hand (Jud.4:4-8).
2. Sisera would be killed by a woman because Barak refused to go without Deborah (Jud.4:9).

Scripture References
Jud.4-5

Time
Approximately 1220 B.C., during a time of oppression by King Jabin of the Canaanites. It was about 200 plus years before King David and about 200 plus after the Exodus.

Place
Between Ramah and Bethel, in the hill country of Ephraim.

The LORD is a mighty Deliverer, Who will deliver Israel from the Canaanite enemies. Through Deborah, God instructed Barak to mobilize ten thousand troops and to meet the enemy commander Sisera, at the Kishon River. Gripped by fear and feeling inadequate for the task, Barak refused to go without Deborah's help. Granting his request, God used both Deborah and Barak to soundly defeat the oppressing Canaanites in a tremendous victory. But because Barak refused to obey God, he was denied the honor of capturing the enemy commander Sisera. Instead, the honor of killing the dreaded enemy commander was given to a woman name Jael.

"Now she sent and summoned Barak the son of Abinoam from Kedesh-naphtali, and said to him, 'Behold, the LORD, the God of Israel, has commanded, "Go and march to Mount Tabor, and take with you ten thousand men from the sons of Naphtali and from the sons of Zebulun. I will draw out to you Sisera, the commander of Jabin's army, with his chariots and his many troops to the river Kishon, and I will give him into your hand."' Then Barak said to her, 'If you will go with me, then I will go; but if you will not go with me, I will not go.' She said, 'I will surely go with you; nevertheless, the honor shall not be yours on the journey that you are about to take, for the LORD will sell Sisera into the hands of a woman.' Then Deborah arose and went with Barak to Kedesh" (Jud.4:6-9).

The courage of Deborah stands as a dynamic example for us all. Just imagine—facing a massive army unarmed! Deborah courageously accepted this challenge, but not Barak. He was reluctant, fainthearted, fearful, and unbelieving. From this experience of Deborah and Barak, we must learn one lesson: there is no room in the service of God for being fainthearted, fearful, or unbelieving. God commands us to be courageous, to step forth and face the enemy with courage and boldness, No matter what the enemy or its power, we are to be courageous in standing against it. God promises to help us and to deliver us if we will confront the enemy courageously in His name.

"Have I not commanded thee? Be strong and of a good courage; be not afraid, neither be thou dismayed: for the LORD thy God is with thee whithersoever thou goest" (Jos.1:9).

"The wicked flee when no man pursueth, But the righteous are bold as a lion" (Pr.28:1).

"Fear thou not; for I am with thee: be not dismayed; for I am thy God: I will strengthen thee; yea, I will help thee; yea, I will uphold thee with the right hand of my righteousness" (Is.41:10).

THE PROPHETS

PROPHET	TIME/PLACE GIVEN	MAIN MESSAGE	PRACTICAL APPLICATION
ELIEZER **(God is my Helper)** **Known Facts** 1. Was the son of Doda-vahu (2 Chr. 20:37). 2. Lived in Mareshah (2 Chr.20:37). **Predictions and Messages** Rebuked King Jehosha-phat for forming an alliance with an evil king, King Ahaziah of the Northern Kingdom of Israel (2 Chr.20:37). **Scripture References** 2 Chr.20:35-37	**Time** *849-48 B.C., at the end of the reign of Jehosha-phat, king of Ju-dah.* **Place** *Jerusalem, the capital of the Southern Kingdom of Judah.*	Eliezer rebuked King Jehosha-phat of Judah for making an agree-ment with the evil King Ahaziah of the Northern Kingdom of Israel. Eliezer declared that God had caused their gold-seeking ships to be destroyed because God was so displeased with Jehoshaphat's ac-tions. **"And after this did Jehosha-phat king of Judah join himself with Ahaziah king of Israel, who did very wickedly: And he joined himself with him to make ships to go to Tarshish: and they made the ships in Eziongeber. Then Eliezer the son of Dodavah of Mareshah prophesied against Jehoshaphat, saying, Because thou hast joined thyself with Aha-ziah, the LORD hath broken thy works. And the ships were broken, that they were not able to go to Tarshish" (2 Chr.20:35-37).**	God warns the believer against compromising and forming worldly alliances with the unbelievers and wicked people of this world. God demands spiritual separation. For if we fellowship, closely associate with the sinful and wicked of this earth, eventually we will be seduced to join in and participate in their sin. Com-promise is forbidden by God. We are to live lives of spiritual separation, not compromising our commitment to God, not engaging in the sinful and wicked behavior of unbelievers. **"And take heed to yourselves, lest at any time your hearts be overcharged with surfeiting, and drunkenness, and cares of this life, and so that day come upon you unawares" (Lu.21:34).** **"I beseech you therefore, breth-ren, by the mercies of God, that ye present your bodies a living sacri-fice, holy, acceptable unto God, which is your reasonable service. And be not conformed to this world: but be ye transformed by the renewing of your mind, that ye may prove what is that good, and acceptable, and perfect, will of God" (Ro.12:1-2).** **"But now I have written unto you not to keep company, if any man that is called a brother be a fornicator, or covetous, or an idol-ater, or a railer, or a drunkard, or an extortioner; with such an one no not to eat" (1 Co.5:11).**

PROPHET	TIME/PLACE GIVEN	MAIN MESSAGE	PRACTICAL APPLICATION
ELIJAH **(Yahweh is God)** **Known Facts** 1. Was from Tishbi (1 K.17:1). 2. Lived in Gilead (1 K.17:1). 3. Ministered to the Northern Kingdom of Israel (1 K.17:1). 4. Performed many miracles: ➤ Prevented rain for three years (1 K.17:1; Js.5:17). ➤ Multiplied flour and oil during the entire time of the drought (1 K.17:14). ➤ Raised a child from the dead (1 K.17:22). ➤ Called fire down from heaven (1 K.18:38; 2 K.1:10). ➤ Brought rain (1 K.18:41). ➤ Divided the Jordan River and crossed on dry ground (2 K.2:8). **Predictions and Messages** 1. A long, severe drought would come to Israel (1 K.17:1). 2. The flour and oil of the widow of Zarepath would multiply miraculously so that she would have an unending daily supply as long as the drought continued (1 K.17:14). 3. A torrential rain would come to end the long drought (1 K.18:41). 4. The blood of Ahab would be licked up by the dogs to avenge the blood of Naboth (1 K. 21:19; 2 K.9:24-26). 5. The household of Ahab would be destroyed and come to a complete end (1 K.21:21-24). **Scripture References** 1 K.17–2 K.2	**Time** *860-845 B.C., during the reigns of Ahab, Ahaziah, and Jehoram, kings of Northern Israel.* **Place** *The Northern Kingdom of Israel.*	For over three years, Elijah predicted that it would not rain. Through this terrible drought, Elijah was able to warn the people time and again against the false worship of Baal. Baal was thought to be the god of the weather and fertility, and the worship of this false god was strongly encouraged by King Ahab and Queen Jezebel. But with fervor and stunning miracles, God called people to repentance through Elijah's ministry. Finally, a showdown was held between Elijah and the false prophets of Baal, a confrontation that was to prove once and for all who the real God was. Perhaps no scene in the Old Testament is more dramatic than when Elijah called down fire from heaven upon his sacrifice on Mt. Carmel. The spectacular, miraculous event proved once for all that Jehovah/Yahweh is the One True God, the only real and living God. Sadly, despite this tremendous display of God's power, Ahab and the people still did not repent. **"And Elijah the Tishbite, who was of the inhabitants of Gilead, said unto Ahab, As the Lord God of Israel liveth, before whom I stand, there shall not be dew nor rain these years, but according to my word" (1 K.17:1).** **"For thus saith the Lord God of Israel, The barrel of meal shall not waste, neither shall the cruse of oil fail, until the day that the Lord sendeth rain upon the earth" (1 K.17:14).** **"And Elijah said unto Ahab, Get thee up, eat and drink; for there is a sound of abundance of rain" (1 K.18:41).** **"And will make thine house like the house of Jeroboam the son of Nebat, and like the house of Baasha the son of Ahijah, for the provocation wherewith thou hast provoked me to anger, and made Israel to sin" (1 K.21:22).**	1. The LORD (Jehovah, Yahweh) is the One and only living and true God: there is no other God. All false gods are just this: false. They are nonexistent, not really living, not possessing life. They are powerless, unable to respond. Being lifeless, they cannot hear prayers, nor reach out to help us in our desperate hours of need. False gods are totally incapable of being present with us as we walk day by day. They are unable to guide us or to fulfill any promise ever made by a false prophet. All other so-called gods are false. They exist only in a person's imagination. 2. If a person refuses to believe God's Word, he will not believe nor follow the Lord, even if he sees a dramatic sign from heaven. **"I am Alpha and Omega, the beginning and the ending, saith the Lord, which is, and which was, and which is to come, the Almighty" (Re.1:8).** **"Fear ye not, neither be afraid: have not I told thee from that time, and have declared it? ye are even my witnesses. Is there a God beside me? yea, there is no God; I know not any" (Is.44:8).** **"Then the steward said within himself, What shall I do? for my lord taketh away from me the stewardship: I cannot dig; to beg I am ashamed" (Lu.16:31).**

PROPHET	TIME/PLACE GIVEN	MAIN MESSAGE	PRACTICAL APPLICATION
ELISHA (God is the Savior) **Known Facts** 1. Was the son of Shaphat (1 K.19:16). 2. Lived in Abel-Meholah (1 K.19:16). 3. Was anointed by Elijah to take his place, as God instructed (1 K.19:16). 4. Performed many miracles: ➢ Parted the Jordan River (2 K.2:14). ➢ Made bitter water sweet (2 K.2:19-22). ➢ Saved an army by causing water to appear in ditches (2 K.3:13-20). ➢ Multiplied the widow's oil (2 K.4:1-7). ➢ Raised a child from the dead (2 K.4:32-37). ➢ Purified a pot of food from poison (2 K.4:38-41). ➢ Multiplied bread and grain to feed one hundred men (2 K.4:42-44). ➢ Healed a leper (2 K.5:1-14). ➢ Caused an ax head to float in the Jordan River (2 K.6:1-7). ➢ Raised a man from the dead, when the man came in contact with Elisha's bones (2 K.13:21). 5. Prophesied in the Northern Kingdom (2 K. 2:2). 6. Saw Elijah transported to heaven (2 K.2:9-13). 7. Was the model of a spiritual leader (1 K. 19:19-21; 2 K.5:16). (Cont. on next page)	**Time** *850–795 B.C., during the reigns of Jehoram, Jehu, Jehoahaz, and Jehoash, kings of Northern Israel.* **Place** *Israel, The Northern Kingdom of Israel.*	God will save those who have faith in Him. Time and time again, in both the words and deeds of Elisha, this message of salvation was demonstrated. Elisha had strong faith in God and faithfully followed God. But he not only followed, he demonstrated an iron determination in living a godly, righteous life. Elisha's life was a beacon, a bright example to everyone he met. Persevering to his very last day on earth, he repeatedly demonstrated the saving, miraculous power of God. **"And he went forth unto the spring of the waters, and cast the salt in there, and said, Thus saith the LORD, I have healed these waters; there shall not be from thence any more death or barren land" (2 K.2:21).** **"For thus saith the LORD, Ye shall not see wind, neither shall ye see rain; yet that valley shall be filled with water, that ye may drink, both ye, and your cattle, and your beasts" (2 K.3:17).** **"And his servitor said, What, should I set this before an hundred men? He said again, Give the people, that they may eat: for thus saith the LORD, They shall eat, and shall leave thereof" (2 K.4:43).** **"And he said unto him, Went not mine heart with thee, when the man turned again from his chariot to meet thee? Is it a time to receive money, and to receive garments, and oliveyards, and vineyards, and sheep, and oxen, and menservants, and maidservants? The leprosy therefore of Naaman shall cleave unto thee, and unto thy seed for ever. And he went out from his presence a leper as white as snow" (2 K.5:26-27).** **"Then Elisha said, Hear ye the word of the LORD; Thus saith the LORD, To morrow about this time shall a measure of fine flour be sold for a shekel, and two measures of barley for a shekel, in the gate of Samaria. Then a lord on whose hand the king leaned answered the man of God, and said, Behold, if the LORD would make windows in heaven, might this thing be? And**	Far too often men and women demonstrate traits of weak character, traits such as insincerity, deception, impurity, dishonesty, corruption and wickedness. Whereas they should be living lives of honor, goodness, purity, morality, & sincerity. This is not the way any of us should be living. We should be men and women of honor and uprightness, holding ever so high the principles of morality, righteousness and justice for all people everywhere. We should be followers of Christ, and we should persevere, be steadfast in our faith. Once we profess Christ, we must continue to profess and follow after Him. *Continuing on* is the evidence of our faith. When people see us continuing to follow Christ, they know that our profession is true. But if we profess to be a follower of the LORD and then refuse to live like He says, people know that we are making a false profession. We must *continue on,* being steadfast, enduring, persevering in following Christ—this assures our salvation, that our profession is true, that our life demonstrates what we say. **"Awake to righteousness, and sin not; for some have not the knowledge of God: I speak this to your shame" (1 Co.15:34).** **"Knowing that whatsoever good thing any man doeth, the same shall he receive of the Lord, whether he be bond or free" (Ep.6:8).** **"But thou, O man of God, flee these things; and follow after righteousness, godliness, faith, love, patience, meekness. Fight the good fight of faith, lay hold on eternal life, whereunto thou art also called, and hast professed a good profession before many witnesses" (1 Ti.6:11-12).** **"Teaching us that, denying ungodliness and worldly lusts, we should live soberly, righteously, and godly, in this present world; Looking for that blessed hope, and the glorious appearing of the great God and our Saviour Jesus Christ" (Tit.2:12-13).** **"And ye shall serve the Lord your God, and he shall bless thy bread, and thy water; and I will take sickness away from the midst of thee" (Ex.23:25).**

PROPHET	TIME/PLACE GIVEN	MAIN MESSAGE	PRACTICAL APPLICATION
ELISHA (cont.) **Predictions and Messages** 1. The water of a spring would be purified, will be sweet (2 K. 2:21). 2. Water would miraculously appear in some trenches especially prepared by faith to catch the water (2 K.3:17). 3. Food would be multiplied (2 K.4:43). 4. Gehazi and his descendants would be struck with leprosy (2 K.5:26-27). 5. A great famine would end in one day (2 K.7:1). 6. The king's attendant would see the end of the famine, but would not eat any of the food because he did not believe the Word of the LORD (2 K. 7:2). 7. Jehu would become king and kill the entire family of Ahab (2 K.9:6-8). 8. The prediction that Israel would have three victories over Syria (2 K.13:14-19). **Scripture References** 1 K.19:16-19; 2 K.2–13		he said, Behold, thou shalt see it with thine eyes, but shalt not eat thereof" (2 K.7:1-2). "And he arose, and went into the house; and he poured the oil on his head, and said unto him, Thus saith the LORD God of Israel, I have anointed thee king over the people of the Lord, even over Israel. And thou shalt smite the house of Ahab thy master, that I may avenge the blood of my servants the prophets, and the blood of all the servants of the LORD, at the hand of Jezebel. For the whole house of Ahab shall perish: and I will cut off from Ahab him that pisseth against the wall, and him that is shut up and left in Israel" (2 K.9:6-8).	"He withdraweth not his eyes from the righteous: but with kings are they on the throne; yea, he doth establish them for ever, and they are exalted" (Jb.36:7). "The eyes of the Lord are upon the righteous, and his ears are open unto their cry" (Ps.34:15). "I have been young, and now am old; yet have I not seen the righteous forsaken, nor his seed begging bread" (Ps.37:25).

PROPHET	TIME/PLACE GIVEN	MAIN MESSAGE	PRACTICAL APPLICATION
EZEKIEL **(God is strong)** **Known Facts** 1. Was the son of Buzi (Eze.1:3). 2. Served as a priest in the temple (Eze.1:3). 3. Wrote the book of *Ezekiel* (Eze.1:1-3). 4. Was taken captive into Babylon (Eze. 1:2; 2 K.24:11-16). 5. Called to be a watchman to the people of Israel (Eze. 3:17). 6. Called to be a sign or symbol to the people of Israel (Eze.12:6, 11; 24:21-27). **Predictions and Messages** 1. Visions of the glory of the LORD and Ezekiel's calling (Eze.1–3). 2. Prophecies concerning Judah and Jerusalem—that God would judge and send the people into captivity because they profaned the holy temple (Eze.4–24). 3. Prophecies concerning other nations—that God would judge their sin, especially Egypt, but Israel will be restored (Eze.25–32). 4. Prophecies concerning the restoring of Israel—that Israel would be restored when the people repented and turned back to the LORD (Eze.33–39). 5. A vision and a detailed description of the future temple and of heaven (Eze.40–48). **Scripture References** The book of *Ezekiel*	**Time** *593–571 B.C., before and during the final captivity and exile of Judah and Jerusalem in 586 B.C.* **Place** *Ezekiel first prophesied in Jerusalem, but later was taken captive into Babylon. In Babylon (or the land of the Chaldeans), Ezekiel was sitting next to the River Chebar when the Spirit of God revealed to him strange and wonderful visions of the glory of the LORD and of heaven (Eze.1:3).*	"Know that I am the LORD." This main message of Ezekiel occurs sixty-three times throughout the book of *Ezekiel*. Ezekiel's messages strongly emphasized the holiness of God, and the fact that God will judge sin. But the LORD will also forgive and restore those who repent and turn to Him. God is known by His judgment; but He is better known by His mercy. Throughout his ministry, Ezekiel was greatly persecuted and eventually killed for his straightforward preaching. But he stood fast, unswervingly preaching the messages the LORD laid upon his heart. **"For every one of the house of Israel, or of the stranger that sojourneth in Israel, which separateth himself from me, and setteth up his idols in his heart, and putteth the stumblingblock of his iniquity before his face, and cometh to a prophet to enquire of him concerning me; I the LORD will answer him by myself: And I will set my face against that man, and will make him a sign and a proverb, and I will cut him off from the midst of my people; and ye shall know that I am the LORD" (Eze.14:7-8).** **"And they shall know that I am the LORD, and that I have not said in vain that I would do this evil unto them" (Eze.6:10).** **"But if the wicked will turn from all his sins that he hath committed, and keep all my statutes, and do that which is lawful and right, he shall surely live, he shall not die" (Eze.18:21).** **"Say unto them, As I live, saith the Lord GOD, I have no pleasure in the death of the wicked; but that the wicked turn from his way and live: turn ye, turn ye from your evil ways; for why will ye die?" (Eze.33:11).**	Despite the love of God, people shockingly reject the LORD. This is why God judges and shows His wrath. Man is without excuse. Man has no defense, no answer, no reason that can justify his rebellion against God. Yet God is merciful to the person who repents. He gave His Son to die for us. We do not deserve it—we never have and we never will—but God loves us with an incomprehensible love. Therefore, He has given His Son to die *for* us, as our substitute, in our behalf. But a person must accept the gift of God's Son, accept Jesus Christ by true faith and repentance in order to receive God's mercy. **"Let the wicked forsake his way, and the unrighteous man his thoughts: and let him return unto the LORD, and he will have mercy upon him; and to our God, for he will abundantly pardon" (Is.55:7).** **"Therefore say thou unto them, Thus saith the LORD of hosts; Turn ye unto me, saith the LORD of hosts, and I will turn unto you, saith the LORD of hosts" (Zec. 1:3).**

PROPHET	TIME/PLACE GIVEN	MAIN MESSAGE	PRACTICAL APPLICATION
## GAD **(Fortunate)** **Known Facts** 1. Recorded some of the history of King David (1 Chr.29:29-30). 2. Ministered as a prophet for many years. 3. Served by the side of King David and King Solomon as the king's seer (2 Chr.29:25). **Predictions and Messages** 1. Warned David to flee from Judah whenever Saul was about to find him (1 S.22:5). 2. Announced God's judgment for David's sin of numbering the people (2 S.24:10-15; 1 Chr.21:9-13). 3. Gave instructions to David for ending the severe plague of judgment on the people (2 S. 24:18-19; 1 Chr. 21:18-19). **Scripture References** 1 S.22:4; 2 S.24:11-19; 1 Chr.9-19; 2 Chr.29:25	**Time** *1015–950 B.C., before the division of the nation of Israel.* **Place** *Jerusalem and certain areas to the south, while he served by the side of King David and King Solomon.*	Our strength and security is in the LORD. No amount of human ability or might can keep us safe—only God can. So as we face the trials, temptations and enemies of life, we must remain humble before the LORD, never allowing ourselves to become puffed up with pride, thinking that we have some great ability or resource to conquer the hardships and sufferings of life. It is never by our own strength, but God's that we triumph in life. **"They dwelt with him all the while that David was in the hold. And the prophet Gad said unto David, Abide not in the hold; depart, and get thee into the land of Judah. Then David departed, and came into the forest of Hareth" (1 S.22:4-5).** **"The word of the LORD came unto the prophet Gad, David's seer, saying, Go and say unto David, Thus saith the LORD, I offer thee three things; choose thee one of them, that I may do it unto thee. So Gad came to David, and told him, and said unto him, Shall seven years of famine come unto thee in thy land? or wilt thou flee three months before thine enemies, while they pursue thee? or that there be three days' pestilence in thy land?...advise, and see what answer I shall return to him that sent me" (2 S.24:11-13).** **"Then the angel of the LORD commanded Gad to say to David, that David should go up, and set up an altar unto the LORD in the threshingfloor of Ornan the Jebusite. And David went up at the saying of Gad, which he spake in the name of the LORD....Then David said to Ornan, Grant me...this threshingfloor, that I may build an altar...unto the LORD:...that the plague may be stayed from the people" And David built there an altar unto the LORD, and offered burnt offerings and peace offerings, and called upon the LORD; and he answered him from heaven by fire upon the altar of burnt offering. And the LORD commanded the angel; and he put up his sword again into the sheath thereof" (1 Chr.21:18-19, 22, 26-27).**	A spirit of pride, conceit, and haughtiness is a terrible evil. For when we exalt ourselves, we walk around acting as though we are better, more capable, more deserving, more moral, more righteous than someone else. But note this inescapable truth: we reap what we sow. If we sow prideful sin and evil, we reap the consequences. So it is with any act of wickedness. This is a spiritual law set up by God for the purpose of divine judgment. A person may repent, but the wickedness will result in some consequence of suffering. **"Pride goeth before destruction, and an haughty spirit before a fall" (Pr.16:18).** **"Be not deceived; God is not mocked: for whatsoever a man soweth, that shall he also reap" (Ga.6:7).** **"With him is an arm of flesh; but with us is the LORD our God to help us, and to fight our battles" (2 Chr.32:8).** **"He that trusteth in his own heart is a fool: but whoso walketh wisely, he shall be delivered" (Pr.28:26).**

PROPHET	TIME/PLACE GIVEN	MAIN MESSAGE	PRACTICAL APPLICATION

HABAKKUK
(Tightly embraced)
 	
Known Facts
1. Ministered to Judah, the Southern Kingdom.
2. Wrote the book of *Habakkuk* (Hab.1:1).
 	
Predictions and Messages
1. The oracle of the wickedness of the people (Hab.1:1-4).
2. The oracle of the shocking invasion of the Chaldeans (Hab. 1:5-17).
3. The answer of God to Habakkuk's plea—the wicked will be judged, but the righteous will live by faith (Hab.2:1-20).
4. The prayer of Habakkuk—the LORD is glorious and mighty (Hab.3:1-16).
5. The praise of Habakkuk—the LORD protects those who trust in Him even in the midst of trouble and distress (Hab.3:17-20).
 	
Scripture References
The book of *Habakkuk*; Ro.1:17; Ga.3:11-12; He.10:37-38
	Time
	615-598 B.C., during the reigns of Jehoahaz and Jehoiakim, about 20 years before the captivity of Judah and Jerusalem.
	
	Place
	Judah, the Southern Kingdom.
		The heart of Habakkuk ached to the point of breaking. The prophet was in anguish for three reasons. First, Habakkuk saw the horrible wickedness of Israel, the deep sin of his own people. Second, he knew that the terrible judgment of God's hand was coming because of Israel's sin. Third, and what weighed most heavily on his soul, Habakkuk longed to be acceptable before the holy God Whom he served.
		    In his book, Habakkuk recorded several question he asked of God and the LORD's answer to his questions. After humbly pleading and lamenting to the LORD, Habakkuk waited (for the prophet never presumed, not even for a moment, that God is unjust). He simply asked his questions and then waited for the LORD to change his heart, so that he could fully trust Him.
		    Among the LORD's answer to Habakkuk is the vital message found in Hab.2:4. This important verse teaches us that we must guard against pride and trust in God. Habakkuk faithfully preached this message, longing for his people to listen and repent.
		
		"Therefore the law is slacked, and judgment doth never go forth: for the wicked doth compass about the righteous; therefore wrong judgment proceedeth" (Hab.1:4).
		"For, lo, I raise up the Chaldeans, that bitter and hasty nation, which shall march through the breadth of the land, to possess the dwellingplaces that are not theirs"(Hab.1:6).
		"Behold, his soul which is lifted up is not upright in him: but the just shall live by his faith" (Hab.2:4).
		"God came from Teman, and the Holy One from mount Paran. Selah. His glory covered the heavens, and the earth was full of his praise" (Hab.3:3).
		"The LORD God is my strength, and he will make my feet like hinds' feet, and he will make me to walk upon mine high places" (Hab.3:19).
			God's chosen way for us to approach Him is that we "live by faith." After all, Scripture declares as clearly as it can: no man is justified by the law in the sight of God. God is perfect; He is perfectly righteous. No man can achieve perfection; therefore, no man can live in the presence of God. No matter how good he is or how much good he does, he cannot achieve perfection. The fact is evident, for if a man had achieved perfection, he would be perfect—living forever in a perfect state of being, even on this earth.
			    But note this: What God does is take a person's faith and count that faith as righteousness, as perfection. Therefore, a man is able to live in God's presence by faith or justification. The point is this: God's way for a man to approach Him is the way of faith: "The just shall live by faith."
			
			"But without faith it is impossible to please him: for he that cometh to God must believe that he is, and that he is a rewarder of them that diligently seek him" (He.11:6).
			"Let the heavens be glad, and let the earth rejoice: and let men say among the nations, The LORD reigneth" (1 Chr.16:31).
			"God reigneth over the heathen: God sitteth upon the throne of his holiness" (Ps.47:8).
			"Let not thine heart envy sinners: but be thou in the fear of the LORD all the day long" (Pr.23:17).
			"I know that, whatsoever God doeth, it shall be for ever: nothing can be put to it, nor any thing taken from it: and God doeth it, that men should fear before him" (Ec.3:14).

PROPHET	TIME/PLACE GIVEN	MAIN MESSAGE	PRACTICAL APPLICATION
HAGGAI (Feast of Yahweh) **Known Facts** 1. Ministered to Judah, the Southern Kingdom. 2. Wrote the book of *Haggai* (Hag.1:1). **Predictions and Messages** 1. The declaration that it is time to build the temple of the LORD (Hag.1:2). 2. A sermon about taking courage because the LORD is with you (Hag.2:4). 3. The foretelling of the future blessing of Israel by the LORD (Hag.2:19). 4. The prophecy that Zerubbabel will be lifted up as a leader (Hag.2:23). **Scripture References** The book of *Haggai*; Ezr.5:1; 6:14	**Time** *520 B.C., when the second foundation of the temple was to be laid.* **Place** *Jerusalem, the Holy City and place of the temple.*	Haggai's messages were given to encourage and strengthen the returned exiles of Jerusalem as they sought to rebuild their temple and nation. He taught that the Spirit of the LORD mightily dwells among those who reverence and honor Him. The citizens of Jerusalem at this time had just returned from captivity in Babylon. Although they were in their own land, it was new and unfamiliar because it was their ancestors, not them, who had been taken captive seventy years before. Naturally, the people were glad to be free. But they still felt somewhat discouraged, unsure of what to do next. They were a people without direction. Through the prophet Haggai, the LORD gave special direction and greatly encouraged the people. Haggai told of a bright future and promised a strong leader in Zerubbabel. Most of all, the Spirit of the LORD would be among the people if they would honor the LORD and give Him their true heartfelt worship. **"Thus speaketh the LORD of hosts, saying, This people say, The time is not come, the time that the LORD's house should be built" (Hag.1:2).** **"Yet now be strong, O Zerubbabel, saith the LORD; and be strong, O Joshua, son of Josedech, the high priest; and be strong, all ye people of the land, saith the LORD, and work: for I am with you, saith the LORD of hosts" (Hag.2:4).** **"Is the seed yet in the barn? yea, as yet the vine, and the fig tree, and the pomegranate, and the olive tree, hath not brought forth: from this day will I bless you" (Hag.2:19).** **"In that day, saith the LORD of hosts, will I take thee, O Zerubbabel, my servant, the son of Shealtiel, saith the LORD, and will make thee as a signet: for I have chosen thee, saith the LORD of hosts" (Hag.2:23).**	How many of us have little rituals, prayers, habits, ceremonies, and objects that we use to keep us religiously secure? So many of us seek religious security while at the same time we neglect the weightier matter of breaking God's Law. It is not the man-made place or the man-made ritual that saves a person. What saves a person is coming to God in true worship, bowing before Him, acknowledging Him as God, acknowledging that His Son, Jesus Christ, is the only way and the only hope of salvation. The place of worship is no longer the temple or any other particular location on earth. God's presence now dwells in the hearts and lives of His people. His people worship Him wherever they are, and they can worship Him every day all day long. True worship means that we focus on the object of worship, being sure that we are truly worshipping the Father, God Himself. A person may be in a fancy, expensive church or in a broom closet worshipping, and yet not be worshipping the Father. A man's whole being must be focused upon the only true and living God, worshipping Him and Him alone. God desires worship, for He created man to worship and fellowship with Him. Therefore, man needs to truly worship God. Man needs to worship God with the spiritual drive and ability of his soul, seeking the most intimate communion and fellowship with God. Man needs to worship God with the spiritual core of his life and being, trusting and resting in God's acceptance and love and care. **"Praise ye the LORD: for it is good to sing praises unto our God; for it is pleasant; and praise is comely" (Ps.147:1).** **"But thou art holy, O thou that inhabitest the praises of Israel" (Ps.22:3).** **"Let us be glad and rejoice, and give honour to him" (Re.19:7).** **"Praise ye the LORD. Sing unto the LORD a new song, and his praise in the congregation of saints" (Ps.149:1).** **"O magnify the LORD with me, and let us exalt his name together" (Ps.34:3).**

PROPHET	TIME/PLACE GIVEN	MAIN MESSAGE	PRACTICAL APPLICATION
HANANI **(Merciful)** **Known Facts** 1. Ministered to Judah, the Southern Kingdom (2 Chr.16:7). 2. Father of Jehu, the prophet (1 K.16:1-7). **Predictions and Messages** 1. The declaration that it was foolish for King Asa to rely on anyone other than the LORD (2 Chr.16:7-9). 2. The declaration that the LORD supports those who completely rely on Him (2 Chr. 16:9). **Scripture References** 2 Chr.16:7-10	**Time** *870 B.C., at the end of the reign of Asa, king of Judah, and just after King Asa made a treaty with the Arameans (Syrians).* **Place** *Jerusalem, in the palace of the king.*	We must rely totally on the LORD, and our dependence upon Him must not be passive. Rather, we must *actively seek* to trust the LORD more and more. For He searches the earth seeking people who are totally committed to Him. His eyes scan back and forth, looking for people who will place their lives fully into His hands. Furthermore, He longs to meet their needs and to strengthen and deliver them from all the hardships and temptations of life. But the people of Judah failed to actively trust and seek the Lord. Consequently, they were to suffer the judgment of God. **"And at that time Hanani the seer came to Asa king of Judah, and said unto him, Because thou hast relied on the king of Syria, and not relied on the LORD thy God, therefore is the host of the king of Syria escaped out of thine hand. Were not the Ethiopians and the Lubims a huge host, with very many chariots and horsemen? yet, because thou didst rely on the LORD, he delivered them into thine hand. For the eyes of the Lord run to and fro throughout the whole earth, to show himself strong in the behalf of them whose heart is perfect toward him. Herein thou hast done foolishly: therefore from henceforth thou shalt have wars" (2 Chr. 16:7-9).**	Note the wonderful promise of Scripture: God works through the events of this world to meet the needs of His dear people, those who are fully committed to Him. No matter how terrible the trial or temptation, God moves within the event for one purpose and one purpose only: to deliver and to strengthen those who are fully committed to Him. A person who is fully committed can rest assured in this promise of the Lord. For the Lord will provide, protect and guide His dear people. Even in the moment of death, the Lord will transfer us into His presence—quicker than the eye can blink (2 Ti.4:18). **"Wait on the LORD: be of good courage, and he shall strengthen thine heart: wait, I say, on the LORD" (Ps.27:4).** **"And the Lord shall deliver me from every evil work, and will preserve me unto his heavenly kingdom: to whom be glory for ever and ever. Amen" (2 Ti.4:18).** **"Fear thou not; for I am with thee: be not dismayed; for I am thy God: I will strengthen thee; yea, I will help thee; yea, I will uphold thee with the right hand of my righteousness" (Is.41:10).** **"But the God of all grace, who hath called us unto his eternal glory by Christ Jesus, after that ye have suffered a while, make you perfect, stablish, strengthen, settle you" (1 Pe.5:10).**

PROPHET	TIME/PLACE GIVEN	MAIN MESSAGE	PRACTICAL APPLICATION
HEMAN **(Faithful)** **Known Facts** 1. Was the son of Joel (1 Chr.15:17). 2. Served as the seer to King David (1 Chr. 25:5). 3. Appointed by David to lead the congregational music (1 Chr. 25:1). 4. Born into the tribe of Levi (1 Chr.24:31). 5. Prophesied along with his family through the music (1 Chr. 25:1-8). **Predictions and Messages** None recorded. Since he is called a *seer,* he must have sung some of the LORD's predictions through the music of worship, as well as advised David about the results of certain royal decisions. **Scripture References** 1 Chr.25:1-8	**Time** 971 B.C., *the last days of the life of King David. In these solemn times of final instructions from King David, Levites were assigned the task of making sure the worship of the LORD continued down through coming generations.* **Place** *Jerusalem, the Holy City.*	Heman praised the LORD with music and greatly encouraged the congregation of Israel in their worship of God. Leading music was his official position under King David. Heman prophesied while playing musical instruments. Just as Asaph, Heman's father, had faithfully served under King David, now Heman, Asaph's son, carried on the work. Heman carried on the legacy of his father, praising the LORD with music and spurring the people on in their devotion to the LORD. **"Moreover David and the captains of the host separated to the service of the sons of Asaph, and of Heman, and of Jeduthun, who should prophesy with harps, with psalteries, and with cymbals....Of Heman: the sons of Heman; Bukkiah, Mattaniah, Uzziel, Shebuel, and Jerimoth, Hananiah, Hanani, Eliathah, Giddalti, and Romamtiezer, Joshbekashah, Mallothi, Hothir, and Mahazioth: All these were the sons of Heman the king's seer in the words of God, to lift up the horn. And God gave to Heman fourteen sons and three daughters. All these were under the hands of their father for song in the house of the LORD, with cymbals, psalteries, and harps, for the service of the house of God, according to the king's order to Asaph, Jeduthun, and Heman" (1 Chr.25:1, 4-6).**	The importance of praise and worship cannot be overstressed. Because of all His good and perfect gifts—the LORD expects us to worship and praise His holy name. Music is one way, a very powerful way, to give praise to the Lord. We are to be talking about Christ, admonishing others in the Word of God and singing within our hearts the hymns of the church. We are to walk about rejoicing and praising the Lord within our hearts, being filled with the joy of the Lord and His Word, and bearing strong testimony for the Lord. **"Let the word of Christ dwell in you richly in all wisdom; teaching and admonishing one another in psalms and hymns and spiritual songs, singing with grace in your hearts to the Lord" (Col.3:16).**

PROPHET	TIME/PLACE GIVEN	MAIN MESSAGE	PRACTICAL APPLICATION
HOSEA **(Salvation)** **Known Facts** 1. Was the son of Beeri (Ho.1:1) 2. Prophesied for many years, his ministry extending through the reign of four kings (Ho.1:1). 3. Ministered to Israel, the Northern Kingdom (Ho.1:1). **Predictions and Messages** 1. The illustrated sermon about Hosea's unfaithful wife (Ho. 1:1–3:5). 2. The sermon about God's case against Israel, that they were full of sin and that they must repent (Ho.4:1–6:3). 3. The sermon about God's certain judgment of sin (Ho.6:4–10:15). 4. The sermon about God's love for Israel, even though they were rebellious (Ho. 11:1–13:16). 5. The prophecy that Christ would come out of Egypt (Ho. 11:1; Mt.2:15). 6. The sermon about God's call to repentance (Ho.14:1-3). 7. The promise of God's blessing coming upon the people (Ho.14:4-8). 8. The sermon about God's challenge to the wise listener (Ho.14:9). ***Scripture References*** The book of *Hosea*	**Time** *788–723 B.C., during the reigns of four Judean kings: Uzziah, Jotham, Ahaz, and Hezekiah. His ministry spawned the reigns of the last six kings of the Northern Kingdom, but he did not name these rulers. His ministry ended just before the fall of Samaria in 722 B.C.* **Place** *Judah, the Southern Kingdom of Israel.*	Hosea had a hard life. He was given a very unusual command from God: to marry a prostitute. Hosea's life was an illustrated sermon of the unfaithfulness of the people, and how they had turned away from God. During the course of their marriage, Gomer (Hosea's wife) bore three children to Hosea, two of them fathered by someone else. Once, Hosea had to go to the public auction and buy his wife back from slavery. The shame of the situation was unbearable, which was the very message preached to the people. Israel should have been… • ashamed at the way they had been acting • ashamed at the way they had run away from the LORD • ashamed at the way they had gone after the lust of their flesh • ashamed at the way they had failed to serve God, in particular after all He had done for them Hosea preached bold, straightforward messages to the people, warning them that they must repent from their sin and seek the LORD. The people had been committing spiritual adultery against the LORD, running after the pleasures and the false gods of the world, pleasing their carnal nature. They needed to allow the LORD to break through the callousness of their hearts, for their souls were as unyielding as dry ground that had not been plowed. Otherwise, the hand of God's judgment would chastise them. But even in chastisement, God's people must remember that God disciplines His people. **"Come, and let us return unto the Lord: for he hath torn, and he will heal us; he hath smitten, and he will bind us up. After two days will he revive us: in the third day he will raise us up, and we shall live in his sight. Then shall we know, if we follow on to know the LORD: his going forth is prepared as the morning; and he shall come unto us as the rain, as the latter and former rain unto the earth" (Ho.6:1-3).**	God disciplines believers. He chastens, corrects, and rebukes believers. Now God does not cause bad and evil in life. God loves man. Therefore, God's concern is not to cause problems and pain for us; His concern is to deliver us through all the trouble and pain on earth and to save us for heaven and eternity. How does God do this? By chastising us. When we think of chastisement, we usually think of discipline and correction and it does mean this. But it also means to train and teach and instruct a person. Every true child of God knows the discipline of God's hand. His discipline differs with each of us, but each of us can recognize His discipline nevertheless. God stirs, guides, directs, teaches, trains, and instructs us all along the way, making us stronger and stronger in life and drawing us closer and closer to Him. **"I will be as the dew unto Israel: he shall grow as the lily, and cast forth his roots as Lebanon. His branches shall spread, and his beauty shall be as the olive tree, and his smell as Lebanon" (Ho.14:5-6).** **"That ye may be blameless and harmless, the sons of God without rebuke, in the midst of a crooked and perverse nation, among whom ye shine as lights in the world" (Ph.2:15).** **"Acquaint now thyself with him, and be at peace: thereby good shall come unto thee" (Jb.22:21).** **"I am crucified with Christ: nevertheless I live; yet not I, but Christ liveth in me: and the life which I now live in the flesh I live by the faith of the Son of God, who loved me, and gave himself for me" (Ga.2:20).**

(Cont. on next page)

PROPHET	TIME/PLACE GIVEN	MAIN MESSAGE	PRACTICAL APPLICATION
HOSEA (cont.)		"It is in my desire that I should chastise them; and the people shall be gathered against them, when they shall bind themselves in their two furrows. And Ephraim is as an heifer that is taught, and loveth to tread out the corn; but I passed over upon her fair neck: I will make Ephraim to ride; Judah shall plow, and Jacob shall break his clods. Sow to yourselves in righteousness, reap in mercy; break up your fallow ground: for it is time to seek the LORD, till he come and rain righteousness upon you. Ye have plowed wickedness, ye have reaped iniquity; ye have eaten the fruit of lies: because thou didst trust in thy way, in the multitude of thy mighty men" (Ho.10:10-13).	

PROPHET	TIME/PLACE GIVEN	MAIN MESSAGE	PRACTICAL APPLICATION
### HULDAH **(Life)** **Known Facts** 1. Was the wife of Shallum, the keeper of the wardrobe (2 K. 22:14). 2. Lived in the Second Quarter of Jerusalem (2 K.22:14). **Predictions and Messages** 1. The prophecy that God would judge Jerusalem for idolatry, for ignoring God's Word (2 K.22:14-17; 2 Chr.34:22-25). 2. The prophecy that God would be kind to King Josiah, because Josiah had humbled himself, recognizing the sin of the people and the importance of heeding God's Word (2 K.22:18-20; 2 Chr. 34:26-28). **Scripture References** 2 K.22:14-20; 2 Chr. 34:22-28	**Time** *623 B.C., the eighteenth year of Josiah's reign, when King Josiah decided to repair the temple and a copy of the Law of Moses was found during the renovations.* **Place** *Jerusalem, the capital of Judah, the Southern Kingdom of Israel.*	King Josiah gave specific instructions to repair the temple of the LORD. While the repairs were being made, a copy of the Law was found in the temple. King Josiah read the Word of God and was aghast at what he read, because he realized that the people had grossly neglected the law and disobeyed the LORD's commandments. Earnestly wanting to understand what he had read, he commissioned a delegation of officials to seek a prophet who could explain God's Word to him. The delegation went to Huldah the prophetess who gave the following explanation: the penalties for disobeying the laws found written in the Book were to be executed, because the people had forsaken the LORD, worshipped false gods, and provoked the LORD to anger. God was going to judge and destroy the city of Jerusalem. But despite the terrifying message of judgment spoken by Huldah, the LORD had a very special message for King Josiah. Josiah had grieved over the people's sin, and he had humbled himself before the LORD in prayer and personal repentance. Because Josiah's heart was tender and responsive to the Word of God, Josiah would not personally experience the terrible judgment. It would come after Josiah's death. **"Thus saith the LORD God of Israel, Tell the man that sent you to me, Thus saith the LORD, Behold, I will bring evil upon this place, and upon the inhabitants thereof, even all the words of the book which the king of Judah hath read: Because they have forsaken me, and have burned incense unto other gods, that they might provoke me to anger with all the works of their hands; therefore my wrath shall be kindled against this place, and shall not be quenched. But...because thine heart was tender, and thou hast humbled thyself before the LORD, when thou heardest what I spake against this place, and against the inhabitants thereof, that they should become a desolation and a curse, and hast rent thy clothes, and wept before me; I also have heard thee, saith the LORD Behold therefore, I will gather thee unto thy fathers, and thou shalt be gathered into thy grave in peace; and thine eyes shall not see all the evil which I will bring upon this place" (2 K.22:15-20).**	What a lesson for us! To Josiah and his people, the Word of God had been lost. To many of us, the Word of God is neglected and ignored, even denied and rejected. Some of us act as though we do not believe the Bible is the written Word of God. After all, if we truly believed that the Bible is God's Word, we would read, study and feast upon it. The Bible truly is what it claims to be, God's Word; and if we ignore it and neglect it, what will God say to us when we face Him? Above all that is to be feared in this life is the neglect or denial of God and His Holy Word. Nothing on this earth is as important as doing exactly what God's Word says, obeying Him and keeping His commandments. But before we can keep His commandments, we must know what His commandments are. And there is only one way to learn God's commandments: study His Holy Word. **"Search the scriptures; for in them ye think ye have eternal life: and they are they which testify of me" (Jn.5:39).** **"These were more noble than those in Thessalonica, in that they received the word with all readiness of mind, and searched the scriptures daily, whether those things were so" (Ac.17:11).** **"Study to show thyself approved unto God, a workman that needeth not to be ashamed, rightly dividing the word of truth" (2 Ti.2:15).**

PROPHET	TIME/PLACE GIVEN	MAIN MESSAGE	PRACTICAL APPLICATION
IDDO **(Appointed)** **Known Facts** 1. Recorded some history about Solomon, Rehoboam, and Abijah (2 Chr.9:29). 2. Called a seer by the Scripture, a seer to whom God gave special vision against the wickedness and false worship of Jeroboam I (2 Chr.9:29). 3. Kept genealogical records (2 Chr.12:15). 4. Was not the "Iddo" who was the father of Zechariah the prophet. **Predictions and Messages** Wrote about the rebuke of Jeroboam given by the unnamed prophet at Bethel (1 K.13:1-5). **Scripture References** 2 Chr.9:29; 12:15; 13:22	**Time** *910 B.C., after the close of the ministry of Ahijah, the Shilonite, and after the reign of Jeroboam I, who put the idols of the golden calves at Dan and Bethel.* **Place** *Judah, the Southern Kingdom of Israel.*	Iddo was appointed by God to keep a record of Jeroboam's terrible wickedness and false worship and of the unknown prophets who rebuked the king. How did Iddo know about these events? The Scripture expressly states that Iddo was given special visions concerning Jeroboam (2 Chr.9:29). It should be noted that the unnamed prophet who gave the rebuke to Jeroboam did not remain faithful. He forgot God's Word and went off on his own, doing what he thought was right instead of following God's clear instructions. Apparently, because of the prophet's unfaithfulness, God later raised up Iddo to record the event so the world would have a permanent warning against the wickedness and the false worship of Jeroboam I. The unnamed prophet who cursed the altar at Bethel could not have been Iddo the seer because the unnamed prophet was killed before returning home (1 K.13:24). **"Now the rest of the acts of Solomon, first and last, are they not written in the book of Nathan the prophet, and in the prophecy of Ahijah the Shilonite, and in the visions of Iddo the seer against [about] Jeroboam the son of Nebat?" (2 Chr.9:29).** **"Now the acts of Rehoboam, first and last, are they not written in the book of Shemaiah the prophet, and of Iddo the seer concerning genealogies?" (2 Chr.12:15).** **"And the rest of the acts of Abijah, and his ways, and his sayings, are written in the story of the prophet Iddo" (2 Chr.13:22).**	Accountability is clearly taught in Scripture. The Lord is coming; and when He comes, He will judge the works of His servant and followers. All works of the believer will be inspected by the Lord so that each believer may be rewarded in perfect justice, receiving exactly what is due, whether good or bad (2 Co. 5:10). **"Therefore be ye also ready: for in such an hour as ye think not the Son of man cometh. Who then is a faithful and wise servant, whom his lord hath made ruler over his household, to give them meat in due season? Blessed is that servant whom his lord when he cometh shall find so doing" (Mt.24:44-46).** **"Moreover it is required in stewards, that a man be found faithful" (1 Co.4:2).** **"As every man hath received the gift, even so minister the same one to another, as good stewards of the manifold grace of God" (1 Pe. 4:10).** **"Therefore, my beloved brethren, be ye stedfast, unmoveable, always abounding in the work of the Lord, forasmuch as ye know that your labour is not in vain in the Lord" (1 Co.15:58).** **"Take heed unto thyself, and unto the doctrine; continue in them: for in doing this thou shalt both save thyself, and them that hear thee" (1 Ti.4:16).**

PROPHET	TIME/PLACE GIVEN	MAIN MESSAGE	PRACTICAL APPLICATION
### ISAIAH **(Salvation is from the LORD)** **Known Facts** 1. Was the son of Amoz (Is.1:1). 2. Ministered alongside Hosea the prophet. 3. Saw a tremendous vision of the LORD (Is.6). 4. Prophesied more about the Messiah than any other prophet. **Predictions and Messages** 1. A holy group of people will remain after the captivity (Is.6:11-13). 2. Christ, the Savior of the world, will live among men on the earth (Is.7:13-16). 3. Foreign armies will quickly invade and smash Samaria (Is. 8:1-4). 4. Christ will be the Wonderful Counselor (Is.9:1-7). 5. The Savior will come from the family of David (Is.11:1-6). 6. Judgment will come on wicked nations (Is.13:1–20:6). 7. The Servant of the LORD will come on a mission of mercy (Is.42:1-9). 8. A remnant of God's people will be gathered back to the promised land (Is. 43:1–45:25). 9. King Cyrus, who would help Israel many years later to return to the promised land, is called by name (Is. 45:1-13). 10. Yahweh is the only Savior (Is.45:18-25). 11. Babylon will fall (Is.47:1–48:15). 12. Christ will be the Suffering Servant and die an atoning death (Is.52:13–53:12). 13. An everlasting covenant will be given to Israel (Is.55:3-5). (cont. in col.3) **Scripture References** The book of *Isaiah*, 2 K.18–20	**Time** *740–690 B.C., during the reigns of Uzziah, Jotham, Ahaz, and Hezekiah.* **Place** *Jerusalem, the capital city of Judah.*	Isaiah's prophecies and sermons centered on the holiness of God and His desire to save mankind from his sin. Spurred on by his dramatic and unforgettable vision of God's holy throne, he warned people of coming disaster. But he also had many words of comfort to say from the LORD. Most importantly, Isaiah prophesied of the coming Savior, Who would bear the punishment for the sins of the world. But the main message of Isaiah is the same as the meaning of his name: "Salvation is from the LORD." It is essential to understand this biblical truth. For it is not just that salvation comes from the LORD (Jehovah/Yahweh) the One True God; but that salvation *only* comes from the LORD. It *only* comes through Jesus Christ, the Son of God, the Messiah whom the Father sent into the world to give His life as a ransom for the world. There is no other that can save. Only the LORD can rescue man from his desperately sinful situation. **"Behold, God is my salvation; I will trust, and not be afraid: for the LORD JEHOVAH is my strength and my song; he also is become my salvation" (Is.12:2).** **"And it shall be said in that day, Lo, this is our God; we have waited for him, and he will save us: this is the LORD; we have waited for him, we will be glad and rejoice in his salvation" (Is.25:9).** **"Tell ye, and bring them near; yea, let them take counsel together: who hath declared this from ancient time? who hath told it from that time? have not I the LORD? and there is no God else beside me; a just God and a Saviour; there is none beside me. Look unto me, and be ye saved, all the ends of the earth: for I am God, and there is none else" (Is.45:21-22).** **"But he was wounded for our transgressions, he was bruised for our iniquities: the chastisement of our peace was upon him; and with his stripes we are healed" (Is.53:5).** **Predictions and Messages** (cont. from col.1) 14. A Messiah will come to save (Is.61:1-11). 15. A description of the Millenium (Is.66:14-24).	The way to God is through Jesus Christ Himself. Jesus Christ alone saves, for there is no other exalted Lord. Therefore, no man can be saved by any other name other than the Lord's name. No teacher is capable enough, no prophet is noble enough, no minister is good enough to save himself, much less anyone else. Therefore, no matter the claim and no matter the strength of a person's name, no man has the name by which God can save people. All men are mortal. Therefore, no man can make another man immortal. But the Name which God uses to save men is eternal, the Name of the Lord Jesus Christ, the Son of God Himself. **"Jesus saith unto him, I am the way, the truth, and the life: no man cometh unto the Father, but by me." (Jn.14:6).** **"Neither is there salvation in any other: for there is none other name under heaven given among men, whereby we must be saved" (Ac.4:12).**

PROPHET	TIME/PLACE GIVEN	MAIN MESSAGE	PRACTICAL APPLICATION
JACOB/ISRAEL **(Deceiver/Contender with God)** **Known Facts** 1. Was the son of Isaac, son of Abraham (Ge. 25:19-26). 2. Fathered twelve sons, who became the heads of the twelve tribes of Israel (Ex.1:1-7). 3. Tricked his brother, Esau, into giving him the birthright; thus, the Messiah, the Savior of the world, came through Jacob's family (Ge.25:27-34). 4. Tricked his father, Isaac, into giving him the blessing of the firstborn, taking it from his brother, Esau (Ge.27:30-40). **Predictions and Messages** Jacob prophesied about the future of his twelve sons. The most important of all these prophetic utterances is that the Messiah, the Savior of the world, would come from the tribe of Judah. **Scripture References** Ge.48–49	**Time** *1858 B.C., after Jacob and his sons had sojourned in Egypt 17 years and more than 400 years before the Exodus.* **Place** *Goshen, a territory in the land of Egypt that was ruled by Pharaoh Sunusret III.*	In the later years of Jacob's life, he predicted the future of his twelve sons. His sons were to become the twelve tribes of Israel; consequently, Jacob was predicting the future of the nation of Israel and ultimately of the Savior to come, Jesus Christ. Although Jacob was not ordinarily a prophet, while on his deathbed, Jacob was anointed by God's Spirit to prophesy. The most important part of what Jacob predicted had to do with his son Judah. Judah would be the tribe from which the Messiah would arise. **"The sceptre shall not depart from Judah, nor a lawgiver from between his feet, until Shiloh come; and unto him shall the gathering of the people be" (Ge.49:10).**	Just think of this wonderful fact: God had a plan to save us before the world was ever made. How marvelous is God's love. And so that there would be no mistake, God revealed His plan in His Holy Word. God outlined very specific facts about Jesus Christ so that it would be clear that He is the Messiah, Son of God, and Savior of the world. Note just six of the essential facts, facts that clearly teach that Jesus Christ is the promised Seed, the Savior of the world: ➢ Jesus Christ is "the Lion of the tribe of Judah" (Re.5:5). ➢ Jesus Christ is the Prince of peace (Is.9:6). ➢ Jesus Christ gives rest to the human soul (Mt.11:29). ➢ Jesus Christ came to the earth so that we might have life, abundant life (Jn.10:10). ➢ Jesus Christ is the Savior and lord of the world and all owe their obedience to Him (Is.45:22-23; Ph.2:9-11). ➢ Jesus Christ came and gave His life on the cross for the redemption of humankind, and He will return again to gather His people unto Himself (Mk.13:27; Jn.14:1-3; 1 Th.4:16-18). **"And one of the elders saith unto me, Weep not: behold, the Lion of the tribe of Juda, the Root of David, hath prevailed to open the book, and to loose the seven seals thereof" (Re.5:5).** **"Wherefore God also hath highly exalted him, and given him a name which is above every name: That at the name of Jesus every knee should bow, of things in heaven, and things in earth, and things under the earth; And that every tongue should confess that Jesus Christ is Lord, to the glory of God the Father" (Ph.2:9-11).**

JAHAZIEL
(God sees me)

Known facts

1. Was a Levite (2 Chr. 20:14).
2. Was the son of Zechariah (not the prophet) (2 Chr.20:14).
3. Descended from the lineage of Asaph (2 Chr. 20:14).
4. Served during the reign of Jehoshaphat (2 Chr.20:15).

Predictions and Messages

Prophesied that the LORD Himself would defeat the foreign coalition that was coming to attack (2 Chr. 20:15-17).

Scripture References

2 Chr.20:14-18

Time

860 B.C., in the middle of the reign of Jehoshaphat and during the ministry of Elijah in the Northern Kingdom.

Place

Jerusalem, in the courtyard of the house of the LORD.

During the reign of King Jehoshaphat, a coalition of three nations joined together to attack Judah. Instead of turning to foreign alliances as he had done in the past, Jehoshaphat prayed to God for help. As he waited for an answer, the Spirit of the LORD came upon Jahaziel, a Levite standing in the courtyard. Jahaziel prophesied that the LORD Himself would defeat the enemy (2 Chr.20:15-17).

The next day when Judah went out to battle, they discovered the vast army of enemy soldiers lying dead all over the ground. During the night the LORD had apparently stirred the enemy soldiers to argue and fight among themselves. The result was catastrophic; and the enemy coalition, in a state of utter confusion, attacked and slaughtered each other. All Judah had to do was pick up the spoils. God had worked a wonderful miracle to rescue Judah and King Jehoshaphat (2 Chr.20:20-30).

"Then upon Jahaziel the son of Zechariah, the son of Benaiah, the son of Jeiel, the son of Mattaniah, a Levite of the sons of Asaph, came the Spirit of the Lord in the midst of the congregation; And he said, Hearken ye, all Judah, and ye inhabitants of Jerusalem, and thou king Jehoshaphat, Thus saith the Lord unto you, Be not afraid nor dismayed by reason of this great multitude; for the battle is not yours, but God's. To morrow go ye down against them: behold, they come up by the cliff of Ziz; and ye shall find them at the end of the brook, before the wilderness of Jeruel. Ye shall not need to fight in this battle: set yourselves, stand ye still, and see the salvation of the Lord with you, O Judah and Jerusalem: fear not, nor be dismayed; to morrow go out against them: for the Lord will be with you" (2 Chr.20:14-17).

The lesson for us is a much needed one on the importance of prayer and fasting. Jehoshaphat and his people faced an overwhelming crisis, a crisis that they stood no chance of getting through—at least not successfully. Within their own strength, they would have been crushed. Therefore, they did the only thing they could do: they turned to the LORD. In order to show the LORD how sincere and desperate they were, they set aside a full day for fasting and prayer. They showed the LORD the depth of their sincerity, that they were willing to repent, to turn away from their sins and recommit their lives to Him anew.

What a dynamic lesson for us! When we face a severe crisis, we too must seek to show the sincerity of our hearts and the depth of our need through fasting and prayer. We must commit ourselves to the LORD.

Simply stated, seeking God through prayer and fasting is the way to secure the presence and power of the LORD. When we face a crisis or are longing for more of God's blessings, we should fast and pray often, showing the depth of our sincerity.

"Watch and pray, that ye enter not into temptation: the spirit indeed is willing, but the flesh is weak" (Mt.26:41).

"But as for me, when they were sick, my clothing was sackcloth: I humbled my soul with fasting; and my prayer returned into mine own bosom" (Ps.35:13).

THE PROPHETS

PROPHET	TIME/PLACE GIVEN	MAIN MESSAGE	PRACTICAL APPLICATION
JEHU (Jehovah/Yahweh is He) **Known Facts** 1. Was the son of Hanani the seer (1 K.16:1). 2. Was not the king whom Elijah and Elisha anointed to be king of Israel and to execute the LORD's vengeance upon the household of Ahab. 3. Recorded history about some of the kings of Israel (2 Chr.20:34). **Predictions and Messages** 1. The family of King Baasha would be completely destroyed because of his terrible idolatry (1 K.16:1-3). 2. The wrath of the LORD would be upon Jehoshaphat because of the evil alliance he had made with King Ahab. However, because Jehoshaphat had removed the wicked idols of Ashtoreth, the LORD also saw the good in Jehoshaphat's heart (2 Chr.19:2-3). **Scripture References** 1 K.16:1-3, 12; 2 Chr. 19:1-3	**Time** *886 B.C., at the end of the reign of Baasha, king of Israel, to 853 B.C., during the reign of Jehoshaphat, king of Judah—the year Jehoshaphat made an alliance with the evil King Ahab of Israel.* **Place** *Samaria, the northern capital, in 886 B.C.; Jerusalem, the southern capital in 853 B.C.*	Before Israel conquered the land of Canaan, the LORD had strongly given them two warnings. First, they were to drive out the Canaanites completely and without mercy so that the evil of idolatry would not creep into the pure worship of the LORD. Second, they were not to intermarry with the heathen nations. The message of Jehu rekindled the fire of God's warning that had been given down through the centuries. But as before, His warnings through Jehu were not heeded. King Baasha followed after the false gods of idolatry. And King Jehoshaphat intermarried with the family of Ahab and Jezebel in order to form an alliance. God was angry because these kings, the leaders of His people, had rejected and disobeyed His Holy Word. They had ignored God's written message, so God raised up Jehu the prophet to once again warn the leaders and people: they must obey God's Word or face the judgment of God. **"Then the word of the LORD came to Jehu the son of Hanani against Baasha, saying, Forasmuch as I exalted thee out of the dust, and made thee prince over my people Israel; and thou hast walked in the way of Jeroboam, and hast made my people Israel to sin, to provoke me to anger with their sins; Behold, I will take away the posterity of Baasha, and the posterity of his house; and will make thy house like the house of Jeroboam the son of Nebat" (1 K.16:1-3).** **"And Jehu the son of Hanani the seer went out to meet him, and said to king Jehoshaphat, Shouldest thou help the ungodly, and love them that hate the LORD? therefore is wrath upon thee from before the LORD. Nevertheless there are good things found in thee, in that thou hast taken away the groves out of the land, and hast prepared thine heart to seek God" (2 Chr.19:2-3).**	God expects His followers to love everyone, even the wicked and those who hate God and His followers (Mt.5:44). But while loving and reaching out to the unbelievers of the world, the believer must never compromise his testimony for the LORD. He must never act against God's Word, disobeying the commandments of the LORD. He must always live a life of spiritual separation, a life that does not fellowship or form alliances with unbelievers. The believer must always take a stand for righteousness against wickedness. **"But now I have written unto you not to keep company, if any man that is called a brother be a fornicator, or covetous, or an idolater, or a railer, or a drunkard, or an extortioner; with such an one no not to eat" (1 Co.5:11).** **"If there come any unto you, and bring not this doctrine, receive him not into your house, neither bid him God speed: For he that biddeth him God speed is partaker of his evil deeds" (2 Jn.10-11).** **"Take heed to thyself, lest thou make a covenant with the inhabitants of the land whither thou goest, lest it be for a snare in the midst of thee" (Ex.34:12).** **"Blessed is the man that walketh not in the counsel of the ungodly, nor standeth in the way of sinners, nor sitteth in the seat of the scornful" (Ps.1:1).**

PROPHET	TIME/PLACE GIVEN	MAIN MESSAGE	PRACTICAL APPLICATION
JEREMIAH (Yahweh will rise up) **Known Facts** 1. Known as *the weeping prophet*. 2. Lived in Anathoth (Je.1:1; 29:27). 3. Was the son of Hilkiah (Je.1:1). 4. Served as a priest in the line of Abiathar. 5. Called as a youth. 6. Is thought to have written a large portion of the Bible: *1 & 2 Kings, Jeremiah, Lamentations*. **Predictions and Messages** 1. The vision of the almond branch (Je. 1:11-12). 2. The vision of the steaming pot (Je. 1:13-16). 3. The sermon about Israel's disobedience to God's Word and the coming judgment (Je. 2:1-6; 34:17; 35:17). 4. The sermon that Judah will be taken captive if they do not repent (Je.7:1-7; 26:1-7). 5. The prophecy that the house of the LORD will be made into a den of robbers (Je. 7:11; Mt.21:13). 6. The lesson of the linen waistband (Je. 13:1-10). 7. The prophecy of a great drought (Je.14:1-7). 8. The illustration of no comfort based upon the fact that Jeremiah remained unmarried (Je.16:1-6). 9. The sermon about observing the Sabbath (Je.17:20-27). 10. The illustration of the potter and the clay (Je.18:1-6). 11. The illustration of the broken jar (Je.19:1-6). 12. The sermon about administering righteous justice (Je.21:11-14). 13. The prophecy of the judgment against Jehoiachin (Je.22:29-30). (Cont. on next page)	**Time** *627–562 B.C., after the fall of Samaria until long after the final captivity of Judah, from King Josiah to King Gedaliah.* **Place** *Jerusalem until he was forced to go to Egypt.*	Many important prophecies and messages have been given to the world by the LORD through His prophet Jeremiah: Often the LORD aroused Jeremiah to use symbols or illustrated sermons to demonstrate the message of his prophecy. Of all his prophecies (some foretelling, but most preaching), one overall message comes through loud and clear: The LORD will rise up. Over and over Jeremiah's messages pointed out that God arises in favor of those who truly serve Him, and in judgment of those who refuse to hear His Word. God will arise and defend His faithful followers, delivering them from evil circumstances. God will even change His mind about judging a person if that person truly repents and then follows the LORD completely, trusting fully in His power to save. **"And the LORD hath sent unto you all his servants the prophets, rising early and sending them; but ye have not hearkened, nor inclined your ear to hear" (Je.25:4).** **"Behold, as the clay is in the potter's hand, so are ye in mine hand, O house of Israel. At what instant I shall speak concerning a nation, and concerning a kingdom, to pluck up, and to pull down, and to destroy it; If that nation, against whom I have pronounced, turn from their evil, I will repent of the evil that I thought to do unto them. And at what instant I shall speak concerning a nation, and concerning a kingdom, to build and to plant it; If it do evil in my sight, that it obey not my voice, then I will repent of the good, wherewith I said I would benefit them" (Je.18:6-10).** **"Therefore thus saith the LORD God of hosts, the God of Israel; Behold, I will bring upon Judah and upon all the inhabitants of Jerusalem all the evil that I have pronounced against them: because I have spoken unto them, but they have not heard; and I have called unto them, but they have not answered. And Jeremiah said unto the house of the Rechabites, Thus saith the LORD of hosts, the God of Israel; Because ye have obeyed the commandment of Jonadab your father, and kept**	God is not some far away Being Who has no interest in what happens in the world. The LORD is the Creator of the earth and everything and everyone in it. He created every person for the purpose of worshipping Him, that men and women might have communion, a personal relationship, with Him. He is zealous for the souls of people. He rises up, calling for people to turn from sin and follow Him. But God will not rise up in our behalf forever. Eventually the time of judgment comes. And when the instant comes for judgment, judgment will fall swiftly and justly. Every person will be placed on the scales of judgment. It is then that a person must be on the side of Jesus Christ, God's Son. Always remember this unchanging fact: Without being on Christ's side, the scales of judgment will never tip in our favor, no matter what: ➢ No matter how much money we have given to the church or charity. ➢ No matter how many people we have helped. ➢ No matter how *good* we have been. ➢ No matter how much we have sacrificed. ➢ No matter how we die, even if we paid the supreme sacrifice of dying as a martyr. The teaching of Scripture is definite. It is crystal clear. Even if a person were to give his life for another, it would not remove his sin nor make him acceptable to God. Christ is the only way to become acceptable to God. **"For I have no pleasure in the death of him that dieth, saith the Lord GOD: wherefore turn yourselves, and live ye" (Eze.18:32).** **"Neither is there salvation in any other: for there is none other name under heaven given among men, whereby we must be saved" (Ac.4:12).**

PROPHET	TIME/PLACE GIVEN	MAIN MESSAGE	PRACTICAL APPLICATION
JEREMIAH (cont.) 14. The prophecy that the righteous Messiah would be from the family line of King David (Je.23:5-6; 33:15). 15. The vision of the good and the bad figs (Je.24:1-10). 16. The prophecy that Judah will be taken to Babylon as captives (Je.25:8-9). 17. The sermon about the cup of God's wrath (Je.25:15-17). 18. The illustration of the yoke—a symbol of the power of Nebucadnazzar, king of Babylon, over other nations (Je.27:1-6). 19. The prediction that Hananiah, the false prophet, will die (Je.27:1-6). 20. The prediction of the public execution of the false prophets, Ahab and Zedekiah, by the hand of Nebuchadnezzar, the invading Babylonian king (Je.29:21-23). 21. The prediction of the destruction of the family of Shemaiah (Je.29:30). 22. The prophecy of promised restoration to Israel (Je.30:1-3; 31:10). 23. The prophecy of the slaughter of the infants in Bethlehem at the time of Christ (Je.31:15; Mt.2:17). 24. A prophecy of the new eternal covenant to be made with Israel (Je.31:31-34; He. 8:8-12). 25. The prediction that King Zedekiah will die in captivity (Je. 34:4-5). 26. The prediction that Jehoiakim's family will all die (Je.36:30). **Scripture References** The book of *Jeremiah*; 2 Chr.35:25; 36:12, 21-22		all his precepts, and done according unto all that he hath commanded you: Therefore thus saith the LORD of hosts, the God of Israel; Jonadab the son of Rechab shall not want a man to stand before me for ever" (Je. 35:17-19).	

PROPHET	TIME/PLACE GIVEN	MAIN MESSAGE	PRACTICAL APPLICATION
### JESUS CHRIST **(Jehovah is Salvation)** **Known Facts** 1. Is God's Son, the King of kings and LORD of lords, the Messiah, the Savior of the world (Mt.14:33; Mk.1:1; Lu. 1:35; 1 Ti.6:15; Re. 17:14; 19:16). 2. Is proclaimed by the Scriptures from Genesis to Revelation. 3. Stands forever as Prophet, Priest, and King (De.18:18; He. 5:6; Re.19:16). 4. Is the subject of endless facts too numerous to mention. **Predictions and Messages** 1. The proclamation that God wants to save every person ever born in the world (Jn.3:16). 2. The prophecy that the people would ask for Him to perform miracles of healing (Lu. 4:23). 3. The declaration that anyone who does not follow His teaching will be destroyed (Mt. 7:24-27). 4. The prophecy of the destruction of Jerusalem in A.D. 70 (Mt. 24:2; Mk.13:2). 5. The prophecy that the end of the world would come and terrible judgment would fall (Mt.24:1–25:46). 6. The prediction that Peter would deny the LORD three times in one night (Mt.26:34; Mk.14:30; Lu.22:34; Jn.13:38). 7. The prophecy that Christ would be killed and rise again on the third day (Mt.12:40; 17:22-23; 20:18-19; Mk.8:31; 9:31; 10:33-34; Lu.18:32-33). (cont. in col. 3) **Scripture References** De.18:15-18; Mt.21:11; Lu.24:19; Ac.7:37	**Time** *During the years of Roman Oppression* (A.D. 26-29) *the Preeminent Prophet, the Son of God Himself was sent into the world in human flesh to save and set free all people of all generations.* **Place** *The nation of Israel under Roman rule.*	No greater prophet than Christ has ever lived—or ever will live—for no one else is perfect; no other prophet is God in the flesh. No greater message has ever been proclaimed—or ever will be—than the great gospel message, the good news of salvation. The good news is that Jesus Christ has come so that we can escape death and hell and have eternal life through Christ's death upon the cross and His resurrection from the grave. Through Him we will live with God in perfection forever and ever. What more can be said? **"For God so loved the world, that he gave his only begotten Son, that whosoever believeth in him should not perish, but have everlasting life" (Jn.3:16).** **Predictions and Messages** (cont. from col. 1) 8. The prophecy that Christ would ascend to the right hand of the Father in heaven (Jn.6:62; 14:2-3; 16:10). 9. The prophecy that Christ would come again to judge the world, rewarding the faithful and punishing the wicked (Mt.10:42; 16:27; 22:13; 25:21; Re.22:12). 10. The prophecy that the end of this age and world was coming, coming suddenly and unexpectedly (Mt.24:1–25:46).	God loves every man, not just the religious and the good. He does not love only the people who love Him. He loves everyone, even the unlovely and the unloving, the unbelieving and the obstinate, the selfish and the greedy, the spiteful and the vengeful. God wants man to know His love. He wants to reach everyone in the world with His love. So God demonstrated His love in the most perfect way possible: He sent His Son into the world to reveal the truth of life to man and to pay the penalty of sin for man, in "behalf of man." Through the death of His Son upon the cross, God poured out the very life blood of His Son for man. No greater love could ever be expressed; no greater act could ever be carried out to show the depth of perfect love. **"Ho, every one that thirsteth, come ye to the waters, and he that hath no money; come ye, buy, and eat; yea, come, buy wine and milk without money and without price" (Is.55:1).** **"The Lord is not slack concerning his promise, as some men count slackness; but is longsuffering to us-ward, not willing that any should perish, but that all should come to repentance" (2 Pe.3:9).** **"But God commendeth his love toward us, in that, while we were yet sinners, Christ died for us" (Ro.5:8).** **"Who needeth not daily, as those high priests, to offer up sacrifice, first for his own sins, and then for the people's: for this he did once, when he offered up himself" (He.7:27).**

THE PROPHETS

PROPHET	TIME/PLACE GIVEN	MAIN MESSAGE	PRACTICAL APPLICATION
JOEL **(Yahweh is God)** **Known Facts** 1. Was the son of Pethuel (Joel 1:1). 2. Wrote the book of *Joel* (Joel 1:1). 3. Prophesied in Judah for a short time during the ministry of Elisha. **Predictions and Messages** 1. The prophecy of the coming devastating locust invasion (Joel 1:1–2:20). 2. The prophecy that restoration will come to Israel in abundance (Joel 2:21-27). 3. The prophecy of the Day of Pentecost (Joel 2:28-32; Ac.2:1-24). 4. The prophecy that a remnant will escape the coming judgment because they will call upon the LORD (Joel 2:32). 5. The prophecy of God's judgment against evil nations (Joel 3:1-19). 6. The prophecy of God's greatness and the truth that Jerusalem is protected by God (Joel 3:16-21). **Scripture References** The book of *Joel*; Ac.2:16	**Time** *830 B.C., during the ministry of Elisha and during the reign of Joash, king of Judah* **Place** *Jerusalem and Judah, the Southern Kingdom.*	Joel predicted several national disasters. In particular, Joel predicted that a locust invasion was going to wipe out the land, one that would be talked about for generations. The plague would be so terrible that no harvest would be left, none whatsoever. But Joel also prophesied that the Spirit of God would come in a special way and that there would be tremendous days of refreshing for those who stay true to the Lord. The message of Joel teaches that those who call upon the Lord will be saved. Judgment will come because of sin, but it will not last forever. Blessing and restoration will also be sent by God, but only for those who are called by God's name, only for those who truly acknowledge the Lord as the only true and living God. **"And it shall come to pass, *that* whosoever shall call on the name of the LORD shall be delivered: for in mount Zion and in Jerusalem shall be deliverance, as the LORD hath said, and in the remnant whom the LORD shall call" (Joel 2:32).**	Man is self-centered and rebellious toward God. He likes to feel independent. Consequently, man is dead to God and resistant to the pulling call and quickening power of God. Both God and man have a part in salvation. God calls. He attracts, draws, pulls, and tugs at the heart of man to come. But note: God will not call forever. When a man senses the call and pull of God, he must act then and there. He must believe and make the decision to follow Christ. **"I will take the cup of salvation, and call upon the name of the LORD" (Ps.116:13).** **"For whosoever shall call upon the name of the Lord shall be saved" (Ro.10:13).** **"This is the day which the LORD hath made; we will rejoice and be glad in it" (Ps.118:24).** **"For he saith, I have heard thee in a time accepted, and in the day of salvation have I succoured thee: behold, now is the accepted time; behold, now is the day of salvation" (2 Co.6:2).**

PROPHET	TIME/PLACE GIVEN	MAIN MESSAGE	PRACTICAL APPLICATION
JOHN THE APOSTLE (Jehovah/Yahweh has been gracious) **Known Facts** 1. Was the son of Zebedee, the brother of James (Mt.10:2). 2. Called away from the fishing trade to follow Christ (Mt.4:21). 3. Followed Christ closely. 4. Wrote the *Gospel of John*, the *Epistles of 1, 2, 3 John*, and the book of *Revelation*. 5. Was the only one of the twelve apostles not to be martyred, although an attempt was made against his life. **Predictions and Messages** The book of *Revelation* **Scripture References** The book of *John*, the *Epistles of 1, 2, 3 John*, and the book of *Revelation*	**Time** *A.D. 95, near the end of John's life.* **Place** *The island of Patmos, where John was exiled after a failed attempt to kill him by boiling him in oil.*	All prophecy points to this undeniable fact: Jesus Christ is the King of kings and LORD of lords. The book of *Revelation* shows Christ in all His glory and splendor. Christ is the Righteous Judge, the Righteous Lamb and the Righteous King. *Revelation* teaches us that to overcome the world, we must be fully committed to following Christ, the One Who has already overcome the world. 　God's purpose in revealing to John the great revelation of Christ is to focus attention upon the Lamb, the Lord Jesus Christ Himself, and His ultimate triumph over the world and its ungodliness and evil. 　God's purpose is to show the great redemption that He is preparing for all those who truly believe and follow His Son. God's purpose is to show man that he can be saved from the terrible things that are coming upon the earth. **"The Revelation of Jesus Christ, which God gave unto him, to show unto his servants things which must shortly come to pass; and he sent and signified it by his angel unto his servant John" (Re.1:1).** **"These things saith he that holdeth the seven stars in his right hand, who walketh in the midst of the seven golden candlesticks" (Re.2:1).** **"And every creature which is in heaven, and on the earth, and under the earth, and such as are in the sea, and all that are in them, heard I saying, Blessing, and honour, and glory, and power, be unto him that sitteth upon the throne, and unto the Lamb for ever and ever" (Re.5:13).** **"For the great day of his wrath is come; and who shall be able to stand?" (Re.6:17).** **"The testimony of Jesus is the spirit of prophecy" (Re.19:10).** **"And he hath on his vesture and on his thigh a name written, KING OF KINGS, AND LORD OF LORDS" (Re.19:16).**	God has appointed a day to judge the world. The day of judgment is set, already determined. God demands that all men repent now, repent of their sin and idolatry, from the vain imaginations of the world. Every man has a *concept*, a thought about God. But we should *seek* and find the only living and true God as revealed in the Holy Bible. This we do by reading and obeying His Word. Every person is personally responsible for forsaking the idols of this world and for finding God. Man is now to repent. 　God wants people to know that they can be saved while there is still time for them to repent. It is God's purpose to lead people to repentance and salvation, to lead them to the glorious inheritance of the great redemption that is to be given to all true followers of the Lord Jesus Christ. **"O Jerusalem, wash thine heart from wickedness, that thou mayest be saved. How long shall thy vain thoughts lodge within thee?" (Je.4:14).** **"And the times of this ignorance God winked at; but now commandeth all men every where to repent" (Ac.17:30).** **"But the heavens and the earth, which are now, by the same word are kept in store, reserved unto fire against the day of judgment and perdition of ungodly men" (2 Pe.3:7).** **"Knowing that of the Lord ye shall receive the reward of the inheritance: for ye serve the Lord Christ" (Col.3:24).**

PROPHET	TIME/PLACE GIVEN	MAIN MESSAGE	PRACTICAL APPLICATION
JOHN THE BAPTIST (Jehovah/Yahweh has been gracious) **Known Facts** 1. Was the son of Zacharias the priest and Elisabeth, and the first cousin of Jesus Christ (Lu.1:5-63). 2. Was the forerunner of Jesus Christ (Mal. 4:4-6; Mt.11:12-15; 17:10-13). 3. Lived and preached in the countryside and desert places of Palestine (Mt. 3:1-4). 3. Was jailed and beheaded by Herod (Mk.6:24-28). **Predictions and Messages** The unmistakable declaration that Jesus of Nazareth is the Christ, the sacrificial Lamb of God, Who would take away the sin of the world (Jn.1:29). **Scripture References** Mal.4:5; Mt.11:9; Mk.11:32; Lu.7:26; Jn.20:6	**Time** *A.D. 26, at the beginning of the earthly ministry of Jesus Christ.* **Place** *The Jordan River, about 20 miles east of Jerusalem.*	Jesus Christ is "the Lamb of God Who takes away the sin of the world" (Jn.1:29). Christ declared an astonishing thing: John the Baptist was the greatest man ever born of a woman. John was neither a prince nor a king. He was not a man of wealth, fame, or power. Who was he? Why would Christ make such a striking statement about him? He was simply a man who believed in the Messiah and who totally committed his life to that belief. But notice: John was chosen for this special task because he was so dedicated, so committed to God. John lived a life of total dedication to the Lord and of self-denial. He rejected the carnal, fleshly pleasures of this world and the coveting of its possessions. **"The next day John seeth Jesus coming unto him, and saith, Behold the Lamb of God, which taketh away the sin of the world" (Jn.1:29).**	God does not value a man by his social status nor by how far he gets in this world, but by his commitment to Jesus Christ. Christ declared John's eminence over all men; and in John, we have a blazing example of humility, of self-denial and commitment to God. And Christ declared that those who humble themselves will be greater still in the kingdom of God. It is an astonishing thought! But that is how much God values commitment and humility. **"Verily I say unto you, Among them that are born of women there hath not risen a greater than John the Baptist: notwithstanding he that is least in the kingdom of heaven is greater than he" (Mt.11:11).** **"For thus saith the high and lofty One that inhabiteth eternity, whose name is Holy; I dwell in the high and holy place, with him also that is of a contrite and humble spirit, to revive the spirit of the humble, and to revive the heart of the contrite ones" (Is.57:15).** **"And whosoever shall exalt himself shall be abased; and he that shall humble himself shall be exalted" (Mt.23:12).** **"Humble yourselves in the sight of the Lord, and he shall lift you up" (Js.4:10).**

THE PROPHETS

PROPHET	TIME/PLACE GIVEN	MAIN MESSAGE	PRACTICAL APPLICATION
JONAH **(Dove)** **Known Facts** 1. Was the son of Ammitai (2 K.14:25; Jona.1:1). 2. Wrote the book of *Jonah* (Jona.1:1). 3. Ministered to the Northern Kingdom of Israel (2 K.14:25). 4. Tried to resist obeying God's instructions to go to Nineveh (Jona.1:3). 5. Was called to a foreign nation (Jona.1:2). 6. Converted the entire city of Nineveh with his preaching (Jona. 3:5-10). 7. Lived in Gath-Hepher (2 K.14:25). 8. Quoted the Psalms repeatedly in his prayer for God to save him from the great fish (Jona.2:2-9) **Predictions and Messages** 1. Nineveh will be overthrown in forty days (Jona.3:4). 2. Israel's borders will be extended and restored to their original positions (2 K.14:25). **Scripture References** The book of *Jonah*; 2 K.14:25; Mt.12:39-41; 16:4	**Time** *780–765 B.C., during the reign of Jeroboam II, king of Israel.* **Place** *Nineveh, the capital of Assyria, about 500 miles east of Israel.*	Jonah was called by God to preach to Nineveh, the capital city of the Assyrians. But Jonah did not want to go. He had a simple reason: The Assyrians were known for their cruelty to his people. Their war strategy was not only designed to take control of lands, but to instill absolute terror in the people they were conquering. The Assyrians wanted to make sure that the people would be so afraid of them that they would not ever try to avoid paying the demanded tribute each year. So Jonah tried to run away from God. Jonah got on a ship sailing in the opposite direction. But God sent a storm. Jonah knew why the storm had come. At Jonah's request, the men of the ship threw him overboard. But God was gracious. He had a great fish prepared to swallow Jonah. When Jonah repented, the fish threw Jonah up onto the land. After recovering from his ordeal, the repentant prophet went to Nineveh and preached. The city repented too, and they were saved from judgment. The book of *Jonah* clearly teaches that no matter how evil a person is, God will forgive him if he truly repents. No place represented self-exaltation and opposition to God more than Nineveh. God was so angry with the Ninevites that their total destruction was only forty days away. Yet, when they repented, God relented, forgave Nineveh and spared the city. **"But I will sacrifice unto thee with the voice of thanksgiving; I will pay that that I have vowed. Salvation is of the LORD" (Jona.2:9).** **"But let man and beast be covered with sackcloth, and cry mightily unto God: yea, let them turn every one from his evil way, and from the violence that is in their hands. Who can tell if God will turn and repent, and turn away from his fierce anger, that we perish not? And God saw their works, that they turned from their evil way; and God repented of the evil, that he had said that he would do unto them; and he did it not" (Jona.3:8-10).**	We can now obtain the mercy of God. We need God to have mercy upon us because we have sinned against Him. We have done everything imaginable against God... • ignored Him • neglected Him • rebelled against Him • disobeyed Him • rejected Him • denied Him • cursed Him God will forgive our sins; He will have mercy upon us. But we must come to the throne of grace and ask for mercy. We must humble ourselves and fully acknowledge that mercy comes only through Christ Jesus. **"Who is a God like unto thee, that pardoneth iniquity, and passeth by the transgression of the remnant of her heritage? he retaineth not his anger for ever, because he delighteth in mercy" (Mi.7:18).**

PROPHET	TIME/PLACE GIVEN	MAIN MESSAGE	PRACTICAL APPLICATION
JOSEPH (He has added) **Known Facts** 1. Was the son of Jacob (Ge.29:22-24). 2. Was persecuted and sold into slavery by his brothers (Ge.37:4; 23-28). 3. Was forced to live in Egypt, a slave to Potiphar, falsely accused by his master's wife (39:1-2; 11-17). 4. Remained faithful to God (39:21-23). 5. Raised up after many years in prison to the throne of Egypt, second only to Pharaoh (Ge.41:39-41). 6. Had a gift from God for interpreting dreams (Ge.40:6-22). **Predictions and Messages** 1. Pharaoh's butler would be restored to his position (Ge.40:9-13). 2. Pharaoh's baker would be executed (Ge.40:16-19). 3. Seven years of bountiful harvest would come to Egypt, but they would be followed by seven years of terrible famine (Ge.41:25-32). **Scripture References** Ge.40:1-23; 41:1-32	**Time** *1900–1885 B.C., during Joseph's reign as secondary only to Pharaoh of Egypt.* **Place** *Ancient Egypt, during the time of the Pharaohs.*	God is in complete control, and He carries out His plan regardless of the evil intentions of mankind. Joseph had all kinds of evil done against him. He was… • hated and persecuted by his brothers • sold into slavery • reported dead to his father • tempted by an immoral woman • falsely accused of adultery • imprisoned for twenty years Despite all of these awful experiences, God's purpose for Joseph was not stopped, not even hindered. At just the right time, God lifted Joseph up to be the second highest ranking official in Egypt, second only to Pharaoh himself. Even then Joseph did not take credit for himself. He gave all honor and praise to God for the interpretation of the dreams of Pharaoh. Through dreams, God delivered Joseph out of all his troubles and used him in a mighty way to save lives of multiplied thousands. **"Yet within three days shall Pharaoh lift up thine head, and restore thee unto thy place and thou shalt deliver Pharaoh's cup into his hand, after the former manner when thou wast his butler" (Ge.40:13).** **"Yet within three days shall Pharaoh lift up thy head from off thee, and shall hang thee on a tree; and the birds shall eat thy flesh from off thee" (Ge.40:19).** **"Behold, there come seven years of great plenty throughout all the land of Egypt: And there shall arise after them seven years of famine; and all the plenty shall be forgotten in the land of Egypt; and the famine shall consume the land" (Ge.41:29-30).** **"And for that the dream was doubled unto Pharaoh twice; it is because the thing is established by God, and God will shortly bring it to pass" (Ge.41:32).** **"But as for you, ye thought evil against me; but God meant it unto good, to bring to pass, as it is this day, to save much people alive" (Ge.50:20).**	God's plans overrule man's opposition. God's counsel controls the evil of men, subjecting and using even the wickedness of men to work all things out for good and to achieve His will for the earth. Not even rulers, no matter how powerful they are, can stop or hinder the hand of God. People do all kinds of evil, trying to control situations, trying to rule over someone or to exert some authority beyond their position. Just think for a moment of the terrible evil things people in the world do every day. They … • hate • steal • murder • destroy • commit immorality • encourage others to sin • revile those who will not take part in their sin • persecute believers • even attempt to stamp out the gospel and the church But no matter what people do, they cannot stop the will of God and His plan. They will fail, for God has a plan and He will overrule and carry out His plan. Kings and rulers stand up and rally against God and His Christ, the Messiah. They stand against, stand in opposition to and in hostility toward Christ, foolishly thinking that they always have and always will overthrow God's plan. But they will fail. God's great plan of salvation will continue to march triumphantly down through the ages of history. Despite the railings of the devil and all his forces, God's church will go forward, will grow and conquer more and more. God rules and will continue to rule over all the evil plans of men. It is critical to know that God not only has a plan for the world, but for every person. The believer can rest assured that nothing can stop the plan God has for his life. **"The LORD bringeth the counsel of the heathen to nought: he maketh the devices of the people of none effect. The counsel of the LORD standeth for ever, the thoughts of his heart to all generations" (Ps.33:10-11).** **"Consider the work of God: for who can make that straight, which he hath made crooked?" (Ec.7:13).**

PROPHET	TIME/PLACE GIVEN	MAIN MESSAGE	PRACTICAL APPLICATION
MALACHI **(My messenger)** **Known Facts** 1. Prophesied after the captivity in Judah. 2. Lived in the time of Nehemiah. 3. Was the last of the Old Testament writers. **Predictions and Messages** 1. The declaration that God has always loved Israel (Mal. 1:1-5). 2. The declaration that worship must be sincere (Mal.1:6-14). 3. The declaration that failing to honor the LORD results in a curse (Mal.2:1-9). 4. The declaration that marriage is holy before the LORD (Mal. 2:10-16). 5. The call to return to the LORD (Mal.2:17–3:7). 6. The declaration that a person must not rob God of His tithes and offering, not if the person wishes to be blessed by God. (Mal. 3:8-12). 7. The prophecy concerning the judgment of the wicked—they will not be spared (Mal.3:13-18). 8. The declaration that the righteous will triumph (Mal.4:1-3). 9. The prophecy that one like Elijah (John the Baptist) will come as a forerunner to the Messiah (Mal.4:4-6; Mt. 11:12-15; 17:10-13). **Scripture References** The book of *Malachi*	**Time** *430 B.C., about one hundred years after the Temple had been rebuilt under the direction of Haggai and Zechariah. Malachi was the last of the prophets to appear until Christ was born.* **Place** *Jerusalem, the capital city of the Southern Kingdom of Judah.*	Many of Malachi's listeners had participated in the great revivals of Ezra and Nehemiah and had fully committed their lives to the LORD. But now, just a few years later, they had slipped away from the LORD, turning back to a life of sin and neglecting the worship of the LORD and their duty to support the House of God (1:6-14; 3:6-12). The people were apathetic, complacent, only half-heartedly committed to the LORD. They needed to be called back to God. Thus God raised up Malachi to preach the utter necessity of repentance. In scathing sermon after scathing sermon, he pointed out the seriousness of Israel's sin. He called the people to return to the true worship of God. **"For from the rising of the sun even unto the going down of the same my name shall be great among the Gentiles; and in every place incense shall be offered unto my name, and a pure offering: for my name shall be great among the heathen, saith the LORD of hosts" (Mal.1:11).** **"Even from the days of your fathers ye are gone away from mine ordinances, and have not kept them. Return unto me, and I will return unto you, saith the LORD of hosts" (Mal.3:7).**	True worship means more than ceremony, ritual and form. True worship must be sincere in heart, completely genuine. True worship, worship which truly draws us closer to the LORD must be five things: ➢ Worshipping the only living and true God, the worship of Him and Him alone. ➢ Approaching and seeking God's acceptance exactly as He says through the substitute sacrifice of the Lord Jesus Christ. ➢ Living for God by following the Lord Jesus Christ and obeying His holy Word. ➢ Hoping in the resurrection and not holding on to this world, but looking to the next. ➢ Always seeking to have a pure conscience. This means… • struggling, even to the point of pain, to keep a pure conscience • struggling to be *void of offense*—to keep from stumbling and from causing others to stumble • struggling to have a clear conscience toward both God and men **"There shall no strange god be in thee; neither shalt thou worship any strange god" (Ps.81:9).** **"But the hour cometh, and now is, when the true worshippers shall worship the Father in spirit and in truth: for the Father seeketh such to worship him" (Jn.4:23).** **"That ye may approve things that are excellent; that ye may be sincere and without offence till the day of Christ" (Ph.1:10).**

PROPHET	TIME/PLACE GIVEN	MAIN MESSAGE	PRACTICAL APPLICATION
MICAH **(Who is like Jehovah/Yahweh?)** **Known Facts** 1. Lived in Moresheth (Mi.1:1). 2. Wrote the book of *Micah* (Mi.1:1). 3. Ministered only a few years, but prophesied to both the Northern and Southern Kingdom (Mi.1:1). 4. Prophesied with Isaiah (Mi.1:1; Je.26:18; see Is.36-39). **Predictions and Messages** 1. The prophecy of God's judgment against Samaria and Jerusalem for idolatry (Mi.1). 2. The prophecy that judgment will come against social injustice (Mi.2:1-11). 3. The prophecy that there will be restoration for those remaining (Mi.2:12-13). 4. The prophecy that wicked leaders will be judged (Mi.3). 5. The prophecy of the promise of peace and purity of worship (Mi.4:1-5). 6. The prophecy that Israel will be made strong (Mi.4:6–5:1). 7. The prophecy that Christ will be born in Bethlehem (Mi.5:2-6; Mt.2:5-6). 8. The prophecy that Israel will be pure from the idolatry of the world (Mi.5:7-15). 9. A sermon about what God requires of a person (Mi.6). 10. A sermon concerning the terrible corruption among the people (Mi.7:1-6). 11. A prayer of repentance (Mi.7:7-11). 12. The prophecy about Israel's future restoration (Mi.7:12-20). **Scripture References** The book of *Micah*; Je.26:18; Mt. 2:5-6	**Time** *735-725 B.C., dur-ing the reigns of Jotham, Ahaz, and Heze-kiah.* **Place** *Judea, Jerusalem, and Samaria.*	In Micah's day, the Assyrians were just a few years away (722 B.C.) from conquering Samaria, the capital of the Northern Kingdom of Israel. The Assyrians would be within easy striking distance of Jerusalem. Although Micah sternly warned Judah that a terrible situation was coming for the nation, the religious leaders would not believe it. Micah preached that not even God's holy mountain would be spared. But the leaders assumed that since the temple and God's Holy Place was in Jerusalem, the foreign invasion was impossible. Their pride would lead to their downfall. Micah warned the people: The LORD absolutely requires justice, mercy and humility. No matter how much we do in the name of the LORD, without these three things, we cannot hope to be acceptable before God. Without living the way God requires, judgment will come, terrible judgment. But if we walk humbly before people, showing mercy and executing justice, and truly worshipping the LORD, the LORD will accept us. For He accepts all who obey His Word and walk humbly before Him. **"Wherewith shall I come before the LORD, and bow myself before the high God? shall I come before him with burnt offerings, with calves of a year old? Will the LORD be pleased with thousands of rams, or with ten thousands of rivers of oil? shall I give my firstborn for my transgression, the fruit of my body for the sin of my soul? He hath showed thee, O man, what is good; and what doth the LORD require of thee, but to do justly, and to love mercy, and to walk humbly with thy God? The LORD's voice crieth unto the city, and the man of wisdom shall see thy name: hear ye the rod, and who hath appointed it" (Mi.6:6-9).**	God is to be feared, for He resists and stands opposed to the proud. The very thing we do not want to be is prideful. For the only way to escape the judgment of God's hand is to humble ourselves under His mighty hand. If we stand up to His hand, we will be stricken down; but if we humble ourselves under His hand, we will be protected and lifted up, exalted forever and ever. God is going to exalt the humble. The day is coming when the humble will be exalted in all the glory and majesty of Christ. They will be exalted to live with Christ, ruling and reigning with Him and serving Him throughout the entire universe. They will be with Christ, worshipping and serving Him forever and ever. **"Humble yourselves therefore under the mighty hand of God, that he may exalt you in due time" (1 Pe.5:6).** **"Humble yourselves in the sight of the Lord, and he shall lift you up" (Js.4:10).** **"But thou, O God, shalt bring them down into the pit of destruction: bloody and deceitful men shall not live out half their days; but I will trust in thee" (Ps.55:23).**

THE PROPHETS

PROPHET	TIME/PLACE GIVEN	MAIN MESSAGE	PRACTICAL APPLICATION
MICAIAH (Who is like Jehovah/Yahweh?) **Known Facts** 1. Was the son of Imlah (1 K.22:8-9). 2. Suffered persecution for speaking the Word of the LORD (1 K. 22:24). **Predictions and Messages** 1. The prophecy that King Ahab of Israel and King Jehoshaphat of Judah would meet with disaster if they tried to battle the Aramean (Syrian) army (2 Chr.18:16). 2. The declaration that the LORD had allowed a lying spirit to influence the false prophets so that Ahab would be enticed into battle and to his doom (1 K.22:19-23; 2 Chr.18:18-22). **Scripture References** 1 K.22:1-37; 2 Chr.18:1-34	**Time** *853 B.C., at the end of the reign of King Ahab.* **Place** *Samaria, the capital of the Northern Kingdom.*	The battle at Ramoth-Gilead would be a disaster. Micaiah gave this prophetic message to King Ahab of Israel and King Jehoshaphat of Judah, who were planning to attack the Arameans (Syrians). Even though an attendant of the king warned Micaiah not to give a negative message to King Ahab, he advised that everyone go home and not fight the Arameans (Syrians) at this time. But the LORD had allowed a lying spirit to influence the false prophets to speak in unison so that Ahab would go against what the LORD had truly said. Because of his terribly wicked life and rule, God's longsuffering with Ahab had run its course. Now, it was time for Ahab to face the judgment of God. **"Then he said, I did see all Israel scattered upon the mountains, as sheep that have no shepherd: and the LORD said, These have no master; let them return therefore every man to his house in peace" (2 Chr.18:16).** **"Now therefore, behold, the LORD hath put a lying spirit in the mouth of all these thy prophets, and the LORD hath spoken evil concerning thee" (1 K.22:23).**	We must guard ourselves against false prophets and false teachers, for the world is full of both. Far too often, the pulpits of the world are filled with false prophets who preach a doctrine other than the doctrine of Christ and His Holy Word. Their focus is not the Word of God but some other religious literature or some feel-good message. Ignoring the truth of God's Word, they seek the approval of their congregations by tickling their ears with messages of positive thinking and self-esteem or by placing too much emphasis on healing and miracles or a particular spiritual gift. These subjects are important, for they are each a part of God's Word. But the whole counsel of God's Word is to be proclaimed—both negative and positive. False prophets seek merely to captivate or pacify us, giving us messages they feel will secure our approval and enhance their own honor and recognition. We must guard against false teachers, wherever they come from, whatever position they have. False teachers mislead us into half-truths, lies and serious doctrinal error, which will lead to destruction. **"Beware of false prophets, which come to you in sheep's clothing, but inwardly they are ravening wolves" (Mt.7:15).**

PROPHET	TIME/PLACE GIVEN	MAIN MESSAGE	PRACTICAL APPLICATION
## Moses (Drawn out) **Known Facts** 1. Was the only prophet of Old Testament times with whom God spoke face-to-face (Ex.33:11). 2. Was born into the tribe of Levi (Ex. 6:16-20). 3. Was the son of Amram and Jochebed (Ex.6:20). 4. Was raised as an Egyptian (Ex.2:1-10; He.11:26-27). 5. Ran from Egypt to escape from a murder charge (Ex.2:11-15). 6. Heard God speak from the burning bush where God revealed His Name to him (Ex.3:1-14). 7. Led the people of Israel out of bondage (Ex.14:21-31). 8. Performed many miraculous signs (Ex. 4:30; 7:20; 8:6, 17; 9:10, 23; 10:13, 22; 14:21, 27). 9. Received the Law from God on Mt. Sinai (Ex.19:1–24:18). 10. Received the instructions for the Tabernacle from God on Mt. Sinai (Ex.25:1–31:18). 11. Was prevented from entering the promised land because he disobeyed God (De.34:4). 12. Wrote the Penteteuch, the first five books of the Bible. **Predictions and Messages** 1. The prophecy of the coming Messiah, the Savior of the world (De.18:15-18). 2. The Song of Moses: a prophecy concerning the future of Israel (De.32:1-43). 3. The Blessing of Moses: a prophecy concerning the future of each of the twelve tribes of Israel (De.33:1-29). (cont. on next page)	**Time** *1405 B.C., near the end of Moses' life.* **Place** *Across the Jordan from the promised land, in the Arabah, the dry desert land east of the Jordan River.*	Throughout his final forty years, Moses proclaimed the holiness and sovereignty of the LORD. During this time of leading the Israelites from the exodus from Egypt to the promised land of blessing, Moses wrote the first five books of the Bible (which is really one great book called *the Law* or *the Instruction* or *the Pentateuch*). In these Scriptures are found: 1. The beginnings of the world and the Israelite nation (*Genesis*). 2. The account of Israel's Exodus from Egypt, their escape from bondage: A type of escaping from the bondage of sin (*Exodus*). 3. The Law of God which Moses received on Mt. Sinai (*Exodus*). 4. The instructions for the Tabernacle, the place of worship: A picture of heaven (*Exodus*). 5. The instructions for the sacrifices, showing how man can approach God and be acceptable to God: The sacrifices foreshadowed Jesus Christ and His sacrifice as a sin offering. Through His sacrifice a person can be saved from sin, death and hell (*Leviticus*). 6. The journeys of the Israelite people: powerful lessons on following God (*Numbers*). 7. The sermons of Moses: the first studies concerning the nature and character of God and how people can follow and live for God (*Deuteronomy*). Thus the Mosaic Covenant, the law of God, lays the groundwork for all that follows in the Old Testament and in the Bible. For the Law points out that we need a Savior and that we must humbly come to God on His terms, offering the Sacrifice that He demands. The Law also points out that the believer must be separated from the world, refusing to live like the world and not being conformed to the world. The Law of Moses proclaims the very same message the entire Bible proclaims, that we need the salvation provided in Jesus Christ, God's Son. Moses preached his series of sermons (found in the book of *Deuteronomy*) as the children of Israel were getting ready to enter the promise Land. At the end of his life, he warned Israel not to forget the LORD, not to go astray as they had in the past.	The greatest commandment is clear: we must love God with all our heart, soul and strength. We must know that "the LORD our God *is* one LORD" (De.6:4). Note these three vital facts about this great declaration: ➢ God is the *only* living and true God, the only God Who can save, deliver and redeem. ➢ The Lord is our God. We have a personal relationship with the Lord. It is a daily experience. We are His people, the sheep of His pasture. Therefore, we should love, adore and worship Him. ➢ The Lord is one Lord. There is no other. The many false gods of the world exist only in the imaginations of people. Look at how great God is! No wonder the Scripture commands us to love God with our whole being, with all of our heart, soul, mind and strength. We are to love Him thoroughly, fully, completely—in every way for the rest of our lives. **"And he said unto them, Set your hearts unto all the words which I testify among you this day, which ye shall command your children to observe to do, all the words of this law. For it is not a vain thing for you; because it is your life: and through this thing ye shall prolong your days in the land, whither ye go over Jordan to possess it" (De.32:46-47).** **"For the law was given by Moses, but grace and truth came by Jesus Christ" (Jn.1:17).** **"Hear, O Israel: The LORD our God is one LORD: And thou shalt love the LORD thy God with all thine heart, and with all thy soul, and with all thy might" (De.6:4-5).**

PROPHET	TIME/PLACE GIVEN	MAIN MESSAGE	PRACTICAL APPLICATION
MOSES (cont.) **Scripture References** The books of *Genesis, Exodus, Leviticus, Numbers,* and *Deuteronomy;* Jos.8:31-32; 1 S.12:8; 1 K.8:56; 2 K.23:23-25; 1 Chr.22:13; Ps.90; Is.63:11-12; Mt.17:1-3		As he preached, Moses also broke out into song and prophesied of the future of Israel. Most importantly, Moses told of One Who would rise later, One Who would be similar to Moses. Moses spoke of the Messiah, Jesus Christ. Just as Moses spoke the words God gave him to speak so Jesus Christ spoke and did what the Father spoke and directed Him to do. Just as Moses delivered God's people from the bondage of Egypt so Christ delivers God's people from the bondage of sin. **"The LORD thy God will raise up unto thee a Prophet from the midst of thee, of thy brethren, like unto me; unto him ye shall hearken … I will raise them up a Prophet from among their brethren, like unto thee, and will put my words in his mouth; and he shall speak unto them all that I shall command him" (De.18:15, 18).** **"Give ear, O ye heavens, and I will speak; and hear, O earth, the words of my mouth. My doctrine shall drop as the rain, my speech shall distil as the dew, as the small rain upon the tender herb, and as the showers upon the grass: Because I will publish the name of the LORD: ascribe ye greatness unto our God" (De.32:1-3).** **"And this is the blessing, wherewith Moses the man of God blessed the children of Israel before his death. And he said, The LORD came from Sinai, and rose up from Seir unto them; he shined forth from mount Paran, and he came with ten thousands of saints: from his right hand went a fiery law for them. Yea, he loved the people; all his saints are in thy hand: and they sat down at thy feet; every one shall receive of thy words" (De.33:1-3).**	

PROPHET	TIME/PLACE GIVEN	MAIN MESSAGE	PRACTICAL APPLICATION
NAHUM **(Comfort)** **Known Facts** 1. Lived in Elkosh (Na. 1:1). 2. Prophesied about Nineveh, just as Jonah did, but the Ninevites did not listen to Nahum, and they were destroyed (Na.2:8-13). 3. Wrote the book of *Nahum* (Na.1:1). **Predictions and Messages** 1. A poem about God's zeal for justice—His goodness and protection for those who take refuge in Him and His fierce wrath that falls upon the wicked (Na.1:2-8). 2. The doom of the Ninevites, who will be destroyed even though they have many weapons (Na.1:9-2:13). 3. A funeral poem about Nineveh, the greedy and violently wicked city (Na.3:1-19). **Scripture References** The book of *Nahum*; Is.52:7	**Time** *663–612 B.C., during the reign of Manasseh, Amon and Josiah.* **Place** *Judah, the Southern Kingdom and Nineveh, the capital city of Assyria, hundreds of miles from Jerusalem.*	The outcry of evil from Nineveh, the capital city of the Assyrians, reached up to God, calling out for judgment. And swift judgment was on the way. The Ninevites thought that they were unstoppable, too mighty to even be slowed down. For the small country of Judah, Nineveh personified the word terror. But Nahum had a message from God: the LORD is zealous, avenging His people and pouring out wrath upon His enemies. About one hundred years earlier, Nineveh had repented under conviction of Jonah's preaching to them. But now, the city had returned to its wicked and brutal ways, caring only about conquest and plunder, power and wealth. Nahum preached a message of total destruction. This time, the Ninevites did not repent and the judgment of God fell on the entire city. Tragically, the Ninevites had felt all powerful, so powerful that nothing or no one could harm their large fortified city. But when God pronounced judgment on them, nothing and no one could save them. Nineveh was destroyed in 663 B.C. **"God is jealous, and the LORD revengeth; the LORD revengeth, and is furious; the LORD will take vengeance on his adversaries, and he reserveth wrath for his enemies. The LORD is slow to anger, and great in power, and will not at all acquit the wicked: the LORD hath his way in the whirlwind and in the storm, and the clouds are the dust of his feet"** (Na.1:2-3). **"There is no healing of thy bruise; thy wound is grievous: all that hear the bruit [report] of thee shall clap the hands over thee: for upon whom hath not thy wickedness passed continually?"** (Na.3:19).	God is going to rectify all the injustices of the world. God's judgment is going to fall upon every person who has mistreated others. All unjust behavior of men will bear the terrible judgment of God, all the... • killing • stealing • mocking • fighting • cursing • prejudice • cheating • bitterness • abusing • hatred The list could go on and on, but the point is this: much of the world's behavior is evil and unjust. God *must judge* the world, for judgment is the righteous and just penalty for evil. All the injustices of the world must be corrected. God is going to judge the world. He is just and righteous Himself; therefore, His very nature demands that all the injustices and wrongs that men have inflicted upon others be judged and punished. God will execute justice and avenge His people. God sees the great need of His people, and God alone can meet their need. Therefore God, the just Judge of the universe, will avenge them of their adversaries (spiritual as well as human). Even now, when His people pray, continually bringing their case before God, He hears their plea, and He delivers them. And when the time comes, justice will be executed against the persecutors of His people. **"Shall not the Judge of all the earth do right?"** (Ge.18:25). **"And shall not God avenge his own elect, which cry day and night unto him, though he bear long with them? I tell you that he will avenge them speedily"** (Lu.18:7-8). **"So that a man shall say, Verily there is a reward for the righteous: verily he is a God that judgeth in the earth"** (Ps.58:11).

NATHAN
(He has given)

Known Facts

1. Ministered during the time of the united kingdom under King David and King Solomon (2 S.7:1-5; 1 Chr. 17:1-4).
2. Named David's son Jedidiah (who later became known as Solomon) (2 S.12:25).
3. Stood with David against Adonijah the rebel, helping establish Solomon on the throne (1 K.1:8-46).
4. Wrote the history of the kingship of David and Solomon (1 Chr. 9:29; 2 Chr.29:25).

Predictions and Messages

1. The prophecy that Israel would have a permanent dwelling place (2 S.7:4-10; 1 Chr.17:3-9).
2. The prophecy that God would establish David's family on the throne forever—that the Messiah, the King of kings, would come through David's family (2 S.7:11-17; 1 Chr.17:10-15).
3. The parable of the poor sheep owner—the exposure of David's sin of adultery (2 S.12:1-9; Ps.51:1).
4. The prophecy that David's household would be filled with death and violence (2 S.12:10).
5. The prophecy that David's secret sin of adultery would be punished by a public sin of adultery against him (2 S.12:11-12).

Time

1003-931 B.C., during the reigns of King David and King Solomon when the kingdom of Israel was still united and strong.

Place

Jerusalem, the capital of Israel and the city chosen by God to place the temple.

Through all the messages sent by God through Nathan the prophet, this one theme stands out: the LORD will greatly bless and defend all who honor Him.

King David had a burning desire to build a temple for the LORD. Nathan had encouraged David to build the temple; but that very night God corrected Nathan, reversing his counsel to David.

Nonetheless, God was very pleased with David and blessed David greatly because David honored Him with his whole heart. Note the tremendous blessings that Nathan predicted would be given to David by God:

➢ David would be given a position of astounding royalty and power.
➢ David would have the blessing of God's presence and guidance through the years.
➢ David would be given the power to conquer his enemies.
➢ David would be given an honorable name and reputation.
➢ David was assured that the promised land would be given to Israel.
➢ David was assured that he would receive future rest from all his enemies.
➢ David would receive a never ending dynasty.
➢ David would receive a Promise Seed raised up by God Himself.
➢ David would receive a kingdom established by God Himself.
➢ David was given the promise that the temple would be built by his son.
➢ David was given the promise of a descendant Who would be God's own Son.
➢ David was given the promise that the same descendant would be punished for sin.

Although David did not build the temple, he honored God by his burning desire to build it. God greatly blessed David because he had a heart that longed to give honor to God.

God is good, and His goodness is overwhelming. But we live in a wicked world, a world where evil men roam and commit acts of terror, violence and lawlessness. In addition to evil men, the world is full of misfortune and hardship, temptation and trial. Yet in the midst of all the difficulties and problems of life, God's goodness shines through. For if we trust the Lord, He promises to save and deliver us and to meet our every need. No matter what the terrible circumstance, God will pour out His goodness upon us, strengthening and helping us to walk through any problem or difficulty. God is good, and He longs for us to trust Him. And if we trust Him, His goodness pours out the riches promises to us, promises that assure us of the most victorious and fruitful life imaginable. This is the wonderful promise of the incredible goodness of God.

"And he said unto him, Why callest thou me good? there is none good but one, that is, God: but if thou wilt enter into life, keep the commandments" (Mt. 19:17).

"The LORD is my strength and my shield; my heart trusted in him, and I am helped: therefore my heart greatly rejoiceth; and with my song will I praise him" (Ps.28:7).

"Thou art good, and doest good; teach me thy statutes" (Ps.119:68).

"The LORD is good, a strong hold in the day of trouble; and he knoweth them that trust in him" (Na.1:7).

PROPHET	TIME/PLACE GIVEN	MAIN MESSAGE	PRACTICAL APPLICATION
NATHAN (cont.) 6. The declaration that God had seen David's repentance and had forgiven him of his adultery (2 S.12:13). 7. The prophecy that David and Bathsheba son, born from their adulterous relationship, would die (2 S. 12:14). **Scripture References** 2 S.7:1-17; 1 K.1; 1 Chr.17		"And it came to pass that night, that the word of the LORD came unto Nathan, saying, Go and tell my servant David, Thus saith the LORD, Shalt thou build me an house for me to dwell in? Whereas I have not dwelt in any house since the time that I brought up the children of Israel out of Egypt, even to this day, but have walked in a tent and in a tabernacle. In all the places wherein I have walked with all the children of Israel spake I a word with any of the tribes of Israel, whom I commanded to feed my people Israel, saying, Why build ye not me an house of cedar? Now therefore so shalt thou say unto my servant David, Thus saith the LORD of hosts, I took thee from the sheepcote, from following the sheep, to be ruler over my people, over Israel: And I was with thee whithersoever thou wentest, and have cut off all thine enemies out of thy sight, and have made thee a great name, like unto the name of the great men that are in the earth. Moreover I will appoint a place for my people Israel, and will plant them, that they may dwell in a place of their own, and move no more; neither shall the children of wickedness afflict them any more, as beforetime, And as since the time that I commanded judges to be over my people Israel, and have caused thee to rest from all thine enemies. Also the LORD telleth thee that he will make thee an house. And when thy days be fulfilled, and thou shalt sleep with thy fathers, I will set up thy seed after thee, which shall proceed out of thy bowels, and I will establish his kingdom. He shall build an house for my name, and I will stablish the throne of his kingdom for ever. I will be his father, and he shall be my son. If he commit iniquity, I will chasten him with the rod of men, and with the stripes of the children of men: But my mercy shall not depart away from him, as I took it from Saul, whom I put away before thee. And thine house and thy kingdom shall be established for ever before thee: thy throne shall be established for ever" (2 S.7:4-17).	

PROPHET	TIME/PLACE GIVEN	MAIN MESSAGE	PRACTICAL APPLICATION
NOAH **(Rest)** **Known Facts** 1. Was the son of Lamech (Ge.5:28-29). 2. Found favor in the sight of God (Ge. 6:5-8). 3. Was a righteous man (Ge.6:9). 4. Received instruction from God to build an ark to preserve his family and some of each living animal (Ge.6:13-21). 5. Entered into a covenant with God to be saved (Ge.6:18). 6. Built the ark (Ge. 6:22). 7. Called a preacher of righteousness by the Scripture (2 Pe.2:5). 8. Was saved by following God's instructions (Ge.7:1-24). **Predictions and Messages** 1. Preached righteousness to a wicked generation (2 Pe.2:5). 2. Prophesied about the future of his three sons and their descendants (Ge.9:25-27). **Scripture References** Ge.5–8	**Time** *Unknown, but at least seven generations after Adam.* **Place** *The center of civilization, before the tower of Babel.*	Noah was a preacher of righteousness, warning people that the judgment of God was coming upon the whole world. What did he preach? Simply what God had told him—there is a consequence for sin. God would eventually withdraw his Spirit: His Spirit would not always strive with man, not forever. If man did not repent, the consequences of his sin would come upon him. Through the preaching of Noah, the Spirit of God was doing just what He does with people today when they hear the Word of God preached and taught in the power of God. He was convicting them of sin and of coming judgment. But the people were resisting and quenching the convictions of the Spirit. They were not listening to the voice of God struggling within their hearts. They wanted to live like they wanted, to do their own thing. Consequently, God had no choice. God had to give man a final warning: if man did not repent, God would withdraw His Spirit and let judgment fall upon the ungodliness and unrighteousness of men. **"And the LORD said, My spirit shall not always strive with man, for that he also is flesh: yet his days shall be an hundred and twenty years....And the LORD said, I will destroy man whom I have created from the face of the earth" (Ge.6:3, 7).** **"And he said, Cursed be Canaan; a servant of servants shall he be unto his brethren. And he said, Blessed be the LORD God of Shem; and Canaan shall be his servant. God shall enlarge Japheth, and he shall dwell in the tents of Shem; and Canaan shall be his servant" (Ge.9:25-27).** **"[God] spared not the old world, but saved Noah the eighth person, a preacher of righteousness, bringing in the flood upon the world of the ungodly" (2 Pe. 2:5).**	Judgment for sin is coming. Yet, people act as if the world will go on undisturbed. People act as if tomorrow will be just like today. The world continues in sin, foolishly rushing here and there, living as if there is no consequence for sin. Think how much our society is like the first society of earth. Think of the cult of beauty and sex, the power given to the immoral, the sin that runs wild all through society. But it will not continue forever. Just like Noah's day, eventually God will withdraw His Spirit and judgment will fall. The terrible wrath of God will be made known to the sinner, either when he dies, or when the judgment of God falls upon the entire world. A person simply cannot live an immoral and wicked life and hope that God will not notice. There are consequences for sin, serious consequences. **"But as the days of Noe were, so shall also the coming of the Son of man be. For as in the days that were before the flood they were eating and drinking, marrying and giving in marriage, until the day that Noe entered into the ark, and knew not until the flood came, and took them all away; so shall also the coming of the Son of man be" (Mt.24:37-39).** **"Now the works of the flesh are manifest, which are these; Adultery, fornication, uncleanness, lasciviousness, Idolatry, witchcraft, hatred, variance, emulations, wrath, strife, seditions, heresies, Envyings, murders, drunkenness, revellings, and such like: of the which I tell you before, as I have also told you in time past, that they which do such things shall not inherit the kingdom of God" (Ga.5:19-21).**

PROPHET	TIME/PLACE GIVEN	MAIN MESSAGE	PRACTICAL APPLICATION
OBADIAH **(Servant of Jehovah/Yahweh)** **Known Facts** 1. Wrote the book of *Obadiah* (Ob.1). 2. Ministered to Judah, the Southern Kingdom of Israel (Ob.16-17). **Predictions and Messages** 1. The prophecy of the doom of the nation of Edom (Ob.1-16). 2. The prophecy that Judah will overpower Edom, taking away Edom's territory and ending the evil nation's violence against Judah (Ob.17-21). **Scripture References** The book of *Obadiah*; 2 K.8:20-22; 2 Chr.21:8-20	**Time** *845 B.C., during the reign of King Jehoram of Judah.* **Place** *Judah, the Southern Kingdom of Israel.*	Edom will be overthrown because of her pride, a pride which led to a lifestyle of wickedness, and savage brutality, and violence against the Israelites down through the centuries. The Edomites were the descendants of Esau and were actually related to Judah. Because of their ancient relationship, the Edomites should have been good neighbors to Judah, but instead they were hostile, brutal and savage. Now, God would make them pay for their arrogance. Edom would suffer one invasion after the other over the next several centuries. Eventually, just as predicted, in the second century B.C., the Maccabees, who were Jewish zealots, finally conquered the Edomites and subjected them under the heel of Judah's authority. **"The vision of Obadiah. Thus saith the Lord GOD concerning Edom; We have heard a rumour from the LORD, and an ambassador is sent among the heathen, Arise ye, and let us rise up against her in battle" (Ob.1).** **"Though thou exalt thyself as the eagle, and though thou set thy nest among the stars, thence will I bring thee down, saith the LORD" (Ob.4).** **"But thou shouldest not have looked on the day of thy brother in the day that he became a stranger; neither shouldest thou have rejoiced over the children of Judah in the day of their destruction; neither shouldest thou have spoken proudly in the day of distress" (Ob.12).** **"For the day of the LORD is near upon all the heathen: as thou hast done, it shall be done unto thee: thy reward shall return upon thine own head" (Ob.15).**	All boasting and arrogance, pride and conceit is wrong. It is wrong to elevate ourselves above others, to think that we are *better* or *higher* than anyone else. God will severely judge all pride. **"Therefore pride compasseth them about as a chain; violence covereth them as a garment" (Ps.73:6).** **"And he shall spread forth his hands in the midst of them, as he that swimmeth spreadeth forth his hands to swim: and he shall bring down their pride together with the spoils of their hands" (Is.25:11).**

PROPHET	TIME/PLACE GIVEN	MAIN MESSAGE	PRACTICAL APPLICATION
PAUL (Small, little) **Known Facts** 1. Lived in Tarsus (Ac. 9:11; 21:39). 2. Was an apostle "born out of due time" (1 Co.15:8). 3. Was originally named *Saul* (Ac.13:9). 4. Persecuted the Christians, fiercely persecuted them (Ac.8:1–9:2). 5. Was converted in a dramatic confrontation with Christ (Ac. 9:3-9). 6. Became just as zealous for Christ as he had been for Judaism (2 Co.12:15). 7. Made many missionary journeys, taking the gospel to the world (Ac.13:1–28:31). 8. Was taken prisoner by the Roman empire (Ac.21:11-13; 25:14). 9. Wrote much of the New Testament. 10. Was martyred for the cause of Christ (by Nero in A.D. 64, according to church history). **Predictions and Messages** 1. A prophecy given to Paul by an angel—that all on board the ship caught in a storm would live (Ac.27:12-26). 2. A prophecy that Christ will return to the earth (Ph.3:20; 1 Th. 4:16). 3. A prophecy that the world will become very evil in the last times, with some saints even falling away (2 Th.2:3; 2 Ti. 3:1-7). 4. A prophecy that the saints of God will be resurrected (1 Co. 15:50-57; Ph.3:21; 1 Th.4:13-18). (cont. on next page)	**Time** *A.D. 35–64, all the years of Paul's life after his conversion.* **Place** *Various churches, homes and prisons, north and east of the Mediterranean Sea.*	If the message of Paul can be summed up in a few words, it can only be done in his own words: **"For I am not ashamed of the gospel of Christ: for it is the power of God unto salvation to every one that believeth; to the Jew first, and also to the Greek. For therein is the righteousness of God revealed from faith to faith: as it is written, The just shall live by faith" (Ro.1:16-17).** **"For though I preach the gospel, I have nothing to glory of: for necessity is laid upon me; yea, woe is unto me, if I preach not the gospel!" (1 Co.9:16).** What greater example could be set before us than the life of Paul, other than the life of Christ? The Apostle Paul was the apex of dedication and service, surpassed only by Christ Himself. Paul exhausted himself preaching and teaching the gospel, finally giving his life as a martyr. In all the preaching and prophecies of Paul, there was one clear point, one unmistakable focus: the gospel of Jesus Christ, the good news that Christ paid the price for sin on Calvary. Every person who accepts this, calling on the name of the Lord, can be saved from his sins. This person can become acceptable to God and be given a wonderful entrance into heaven, the place of eternal reward and receive the Spirit of God into his heart and life. With the presence of God's Spirit in his life, the believer has the power to live a conquering triumphant life through all the trials and temptations of life. No matter what the believer faces—even if it is the terrible evil of the last days—God empowers the believer to be "more than a conqueror" (Ro.8:37-39). Think, when the believer comes face-to-face with death, quicker than the eye can blink, the Lord transfers him to heaven, the place of eternal reward.	The hope of salvation—the forgiveness of sins, a victorious and conquering life and the gift of eternal life—all this has been entrusted into the hands of Paul and to all other believers. Note exactly what the Bible teaches: God's Word and the teaching of God's Word have been committed to men by the commandment of God. God's Word and the preaching of His Word are not an option. God commands that we take care of His Word, that we be good stewards of the truth of the gospel, that we preach and teach it to the whole world. **"Go ye therefore, and teach all nations, baptizing them in the name of the Father, and of the Son, and of the Holy Ghost: Teaching them to observe all things whatsoever I have commanded you: and, lo, I am with you alway, even unto the end of the world" (Mt.28:19-20).** **"And he said unto them, Go ye into all the world, and preach the gospel to every creature" (Mk. 16:15).** **"Then said Jesus to them again, Peace be unto you: as my Father hath sent me, even so send I you" (Jn.20:21).**

PROPHET	TIME/PLACE GIVEN	MAIN MESSAGE	PRACTICAL APPLICATION
PAUL (cont.) 5. A prophecy of the antichrist—that the man of sin will be revealed in the end time (2 Th.2:1-5). 6. A prophecy that Christ will receive those who are His into heaven and their eternal reward (1 Co.1:8). 7. A prophecy that death will be destroyed (1 Co.15:24-26). **Scripture References** Ac.8:1–28:31, the books of *Romans, 1 & 2 Corinthians, Galatians, Ephesians, Philippians, Colossians, 1 & 2 Thessalonians, 1 & 2 Timothy, Titus, Philemon*		"Nay, in all these things we are more than conquerors through him that loves us. For I am persuaded, that neither death, nor life, nor angels, nor principalities, nor powers, nor things present, nor things to come, Nor height, nor depth, nor any other creature, shall be able to separate us from the love of God, which is in Christ Jesus our Lord" (Ro. 8:37-39). "And the Lord shall deliver me from every evil work, and will preserve *me* unto his heavenly kingdom: to whom *be* glory for ever and ever. Amen" (2 Ti.4:18).	

PROPHET	TIME/PLACE GIVEN	MAIN MESSAGE	PRACTICAL APPLICATION
SAMUEL **(God hears)** **Known Facts** 1. Dedicated to God from birth (1 S.1:11; 2:18). 2. Was favored highly with God and man (1 S.2:26). 3. Was given prophecies from God even as a boy (1 S.3:1-18). 4. Was recognized as a prophet to all Israel (1 S.3:20). 5. Lived in Ramah (1 S.7:17). 6. Appointed his sons as judges, but they were wicked (1 S.8:3). 7. Anointed Saul as king (1 S.10:1). 8. Recorded events of David's reign and the regulations to govern the king and control his power (1 S.10:25; 1 Chr.29:29). 9. Faithfully served as a judge all his days (1 S.12:1-5). 10. Called down rain and thunder during the dry season—a sign that Samuel was God's spokesman (1 S. 12:16-18). 11. Anointed David as king over Israel (1 S. 16:1, 13). **Predictions and Messages** 1. The prophecy that judgment would fall on the family of Eli, the priest, because of his evil sons (1 S. 3:11-14; 4:17-22). 2. The prophecy that if Israel would get rid of their false gods, the LORD would help Israel defeat the Philistines (1 S.7:3). 3. The prophecy that when Israel cried out to the LORD because of the severe rule of the king they had insisted on, the LORD would not hear them (1 S.8:10-18). (cont. on next page)	**Time** *1095-1015 B.C., about forty years before King Saul and during most of his reign.* **Place** *In the center regions of Israel, serving as judge to the entire nation. In order to hear all the cases and judge Israel rightly, Samuel traveled on a regular yearly circuit all his life from Bethel to Gilgal to Mizpeh and back to his home in Ramah (1 S. 7:15-17).*	The messages, ministry and life of Samuel the prophet can be summed up in three words: "Serve the LORD." With this simple message, Samuel guided and judged the people of Israel for eighty years. Samuel encouraged the people: 1. To serve the LORD with all their heart (1 S.12:20, 24). 2. To serve the LORD and not to turn aside (1 S.12:20). 3. To serve the LORD in truth (1 S.12:24). 4. To serve the LORD, considering what great things He had done for them (1 S.12:24). Samuel's testimony is one of the strongest records of faithfulness ever lived. In Samuel's lifetime, he witnessed some of the most horrifying evil and wickedness ever committed upon the face of the earth, even by the leadership of Israel. For example, Eli, the priest who reared and trained him, would not control his own wicked sons. They committed the most vile acts of immorality imaginable—at the very tabernacle itself, the worship center of Israel (1 S.2;22). Saul, whom God had raised up to serve as king, turned out to be a great disappointment. Despite Samuel's great trust in him, Saul disobeyed God time and time again, until God finally had to remove him from the kingship and instruct Samuel to anoint another (David). But Samuel was faithful, faithful to the end. Through all the years he stayed true to the LORD despite all the horrifying evil of society.	Just imagine the impact Samuel's life and ministry had. There was no one, not a single person who could accuse Samuel of wrongdoing. he had lived a righteous life and served faithfully throughout all the years, throughout all the days of his life. What a testimony! What a dynamic, living example for us. We must live righteous lives, keeping all the commandments of God, obeying Him in all that He says. We must be faithful and diligent in all that we do. This is the strong declaration of God's Holy Word: **"Moreover it is required in stewards, that a man be found faithful" (1 Co.4:2).** **"Therefore, my beloved brethren, be ye stedfast, unmoveable, always abounding in the work of the Lord, forasmuch as ye know that your labour is not in vain in the Lord" (1 Co.15:58).** **"As every man hath received the gift, even so minister the same one to another, as good stewards of the manifold grace of God" (1 Pe. 4:10).** **"These shall make war with the Lamb, and the Lamb shall overcome them: for he is Lord of lords, and King of kings: and they that are with him are called, and chosen, and faithful" (Re.17:14).** **"Let your heart therefore be perfect with the LORD our God, to walk in his statutes, and to keep his commandments, as at this day" (1 K.8:61).**

PROPHET	TIME/PLACE GIVEN	MAIN MESSAGE	PRACTICAL APPLICATION
SAMUEL (cont.) 4. The declaration that Saul's donkeys had been found (1 S.9:20). 5. The prophecy that God would change Saul into a different man so that he could serve as king (1 S.10:6). 6. The sermon of the history of Israel—a strong message that God would be with Israel so long as they faithfully obeyed Him (1 S.12:6-15). 7. The prophecy that the LORD would take Israel out of the promised land if they did evil (1 S.12:24-25). 8. The declaration that God had rejected Saul and chosen another (David) to be king (1 S.13:13-14; 15:17-29; 28:16-17). 9. The message from God to Samuel, that God was sorry he had made Saul king, because Saul had been so disobedient (1 S.15:10-11). 10. The prophecy that Saul and Jonathan would die the next day in battle (1 S. 28:18-19). **Scripture References** 1 S.1:1-25:1; 28:8-20; Je.15:1		"If ye will fear the LORD, and serve him, and obey his voice, and not rebel against the commandment of the LORD, then shall both ye and also the king that reigneth over you continue following the LORD your God: But if ye will not obey the voice of the LORD, but rebel against the commandment of the LORD, then shall the hand of the LORD be against you, as it was against your fathers....And Samuel said unto the people, Fear not: ye have done all this wickedness: yet turn not aside from following the LORD, but serve the LORD with all your heart; And turn ye not aside: for then should ye go after vain things, which cannot profit nor deliver; for they are vain. For the LORD will not forsake his people for his great name's sake: because it hath pleased the LORD to make you his people. Moreover as for me, God forbid that I should sin against the LORD in ceasing to pray for you: but I will teach you the good and the right way: Only fear the LORD, and serve him in truth with all your heart: for consider how great things he hath done for you. But if ye shall still do wickedly, ye shall be consumed, both ye and your king" (1 S.12:14-15, 20-25). "And Samuel said, Hath the LORD as great delight in burnt offerings and sacrifices, as in obeying the voice of the LORD? Behold, to obey is better than sacrifice, and to hearken than the fat of rams. For rebellion is as the sin of witchcraft, and stubbornness is as iniquity and idolatry" (1 S. 15:22-23).	

PROPHET	TIME/PLACE GIVEN	MAIN MESSAGE	PRACTICAL APPLICATION
SHEMAIAH (Jehovah/Yahweh hears) **Known Facts** 1. Recorded the history of Rehoboam (2 Chr. 11:15). 2. Ministered to Judah, the Southern Kingdom (1 K.12:22; 2 Chr.12:5). **Predictions and Messages** 1. The message to King Rehoboam that the rebellion of Jeroboam and the northern tribes of Israel was the will of God and that Rehoboam should not try to stop the uprising (1 K.12:22-24; 2 Chr.11:2-4). 2. The prophecy that Jerusalem would be given into the hand of Egypt's King Shi-shak because the people had been unfaithful, forsaking the Law of the LORD (2 Chr.12:5). 3. The prophecy that the people would become servants of Shishak, but Jerusalem would not be destroyed, because the people had repented at the LORD's first message (see #2; 2 Chr.12:7-8). **Scripture References** 1 K.12:22-24; 2 Chr.11:2-4; 12:5-8, 15	**Time** *926 B.C., the fifth year of the reign of Rehoboam, king of Judah.* **Place** *Jerusalem, the capital of Judah, the Southern kingdom of Israel.*	Shortly after the ten northern tribes had revolted and formed the Northern Kingdom, Rehoboam mobilized an army of 180,000 soldiers to put down the rebellion. His purpose was to invade the northern tribes and permanently subject them under his rule. But while marching north to attack, God's prophet Shemaiah confronted Rehoboam. God's prophet had a stark warning for the king and the leaders of Judah (vv.2-4). They were not to fight against their brothers, the Israelites. Rather they were to return home, for the ruptured, divided kingdom was of God, the work of His hands. Hearing this stern warning from the prophet, the king and the people obeyed the LORD and returned home. But five years later when the scene refocuses upon Rehoboam and Judah, tragic differences are seen in the life of the king and people. They have turned away from the LORD, disobeying His Word and committing apostasy against Him. The hearts of Rehoboam and the people have wandered away from the LORD. As a result Shemaiah, the prophet, had another message for the king and people: Shishak, the Egyptian king was going to destroy Jerusalem. Upon hearing this message, the leaders quickly humbled themselves before the LORD. Thus God sent Shemaiah back with an amended message: Shishak would still attack and some of the people would be taken away as slaves, but the city of Jerusalem would remain. Note: the more severe judgment of God was averted because the people repented, but they still suffered the consequences for their sin. **"But the word of God came unto Shemaiah the man of God, saying, Speak unto Rehoboam, the son of Solomon, king of Judah, and unto all the house of Judah and Benjamin, and to the remnant of the people, saying, Thus saith the LORD, Ye shall not go up, nor fight against your brethren the children of Israel: return every man to his house; for this thing is from me. They hearkened therefore to the word of the LORD, and returned to depart, according to the word of the Lord" (1 K.12:22-24).**	God demands obedience, a lifetime of obedience. We are to always obey God's Holy Word, His commandments. Obeying God today and disobeying Him tomorrow does not make us acceptable to God. A life of inconsistency—obeying this week and disobeying next week—exposes a heart of insincerity and hypocrisy, a heart of dishonesty before God. A true profession of Christ means that we keep God's Word, obey His holy commandments. When we keep some commandments now and break other commandments later and continue a path of inconsistency, this is a life of deception and duplicity. Professing to be a follower of the LORD and consistently breaking His commandments is living a double life. It is attempting to establish a relationship with the LORD that is phony, double-dealing, shifty—a fake life that professes to obey God by living an unfaithful, untruthful life—a hypocritical life. **"Not every one that saith unto me, Lord, Lord, shall enter into the kingdom of heaven; but he that doeth the will of my Father which is in heaven. Many will say to me in that day, Lord, Lord, have we not prophesied in thy name? and in thy name have cast out devils? and in thy name done many wonderful works? And then will I profess unto them, I never knew you: depart from me, ye that work iniquity" (Mt.7:21-23).** **"Ye are my friends, if ye do whatsoever I command you" (Jn.15:14).** **"O that there were such an heart in them, that they would fear me, and keep all my commandments always, that it might be well with them, and with their children for ever!" (De.5:29).** **"Draw nigh to God, and he will draw nigh to you. Cleanse your hands, ye sinners; and purify your hearts, ye double minded" (Js.4:8).**

(cont. on next page)

PROPHET	TIME/PLACE GIVEN	MAIN MESSAGE	PRACTICAL APPLICATION
SHEMAIAH (cont.)		"Then came Shemaiah the prophet to Rehoboam, and to the princes of Judah, that were gathered together to Jerusalem because of Shishak, and said unto them, Thus saith the LORD, Ye have forsaken me, and therefore have I also left you in the hand of Shishak. Whereupon the princes of Israel and the king humbled themselves; and they said, The LORD is righteous. And when the LORD saw that they humbled themselves, the word of the LORD came to Shemaiah, saying, They have humbled themselves; therefore I will not destroy them, but I will grant them some deliverance; and my wrath shall not be poured out upon Jerusalem by the hand of Shishak. Nevertheless they shall be his servants; that they may know my service, and the service of the kingdoms of the countries" (2 Chr.12:5-8).	

PROPHET	TIME/PLACE GIVEN	MAIN MESSAGE	PRACTICAL APPLICATION
The UNNAMED PROPHET who prophesied total victory for King Ahab of Israel over the Arameans (Syrians) **Known Facts** Delivered a message from God to King Ahab (1 K. 20:28). **Predictions and Messages** The entire Aramean (Syrian) army would be given into the hand of King Ahab. **Scripture References** 1 K.20:26-30	**Time** *855 B.C., during the reign of Ahab of Israel and during the ministry of Elijah the prophet.* **Place** *Samaria, the capital of the Northern Kingdom of Israel.*	The LORD sent His prophet to King Ahab once more to announce that He would deliver the vast army of the Arameans (Syrians) into the hands of the Israelites. Through the victory Ahab was to learn a great truth: The LORD is sovereign; His power is not partial or limited, but absolute. The LORD was going to prove that He was not just one god among many, not just a god of the hills as the Syrians falsely believed. He alone is the LORD (Jehovah/Yahweh), the only true and living God. **"And there came a man of God, and spake unto the king of Israel, and said, Thus saith the LORD, Because the Syrians have said, The LORD is God of the hills, but he is not God of the valleys, therefore will I deliver all this great multitude into thine hand, and ye shall know that I am the LORD" (1 K.20:28).**	The lesson for us is a much needed one: The LORD's sovereignty (His power) is not limited or partial, but absolute. The LORD is sovereign everywhere, throughout the entire universe. He is sovereign over all nations and kingdoms upon earth and in heaven. No limitation whatsoever hampers God's sovereignty or power. God controls all events and all happenings. And His sovereign power will eventually end all evil. **"For he must reign, till he hath put all enemies under his feet" (1 Co.15:25).** **"The LORD shall reign for ever and ever" (Ex.15:18).** **"The LORD hath prepared his throne in the heavens; and his kingdom ruleth over all" (Ps. 103:19).**

PROPHET	TIME/PLACE GIVEN	MAIN MESSAGE	PRACTICAL APPLICATION
The UNNAMED PROPHET who prophesied a victory for King Ahab of Israel over the Arameans (Syrians) **Known Facts** Delivered two messages from God to King Ahab (1 K.20:13, 22). **Predictions and Messages** 1. The prophecy that the LORD would deliver the Arameans (Syrians) into the hand of King Ahab (1 K. 20:13-15). 2. The prophecy that the Arameans would attack again the next year (1 K.20:22). **Scripture References** 1 K.20:1-25	**Time** *856 B.C., during the reign of Ahab of Israel and during the ministry of Elijah the prophet.* **Place** *Samaria, the capital of the Northern Kingdom of Israel.*	The LORD sent His prophet to King Ahab with a very special message during a very difficult time. The massive Syrian army was surrounding Ahab's capital city of Samaria. The situation seemed utterly hopeless. But the LORD longed to reach the heart of Ahab, longed for Ahab to stop Jezebel's savage purge of God's prophets and the worship of the LORD. Thus the LORD sent an unnamed prophet to Ahab, announcing that God was going to give a miraculous victory to the king for one specific purpose: to prove that He alone is God, the only true and living God. Ahab followed the battle instructions given him and achieved a great victory. Later, after the battle, the prophet came again and warned Ahab that the Arameans would attack again the next year. Now note this fact: even this warning should have aroused Ahab to repent, for God was still reaching out to him in compassion, patiently longing for him to turn from his wickedness, to acknowledge the one and only true God. But Ahab's heart was stubborn and unyielding. **"Thus saith the LORD, Hast thou seen all this great multitude? behold, I will deliver it into thine hand this day; and thou shalt know that I am the LORD. And Ahab said, By whom? And he said, Thus saith the LORD, Even by the young men of the princes of the provinces. Then he said, Who shall order the battle? And he answered, Thou. Then he numbered the young men of the princes of the provinces, and they were two hundred and thirty two: and after them he numbered all the people, even all the children of Israel, being seven thousand" (1 K.20:13-15).** **"Go, strengthen thyself, and mark, and see what thou doest: for at the return of the year the king of Syria will come up against thee" (1 K.20:22).**	God's purpose for helping us in times of trouble is to prove that He alone is God. There is only one true and living God, only one Creator, only one Sovereign LORD and Majesty of the universe. All other gods are false, deceivers that mislead and entrap human beings and capture their loyalty. And the terrible tragedy is this: if we are deceived into following and worshipping false gods, we condemn and doom ourselves. When hardships and misfortunes fall upon us, there is no living God to help us; for we are following false gods that are lifeless and powerless to help. We must recognize the LORD, the only true God. We must trust in the only One Who can help us in time of trouble. **"Thou, even thou, art LORD alone; thou hast made heaven, the heaven of heavens, with all their host, the earth, and all things that are therein, the seas, and all that is therein, and thou preservest them all; and the host of heaven worshippeth thee" (Neh.9:6).** **"Of old hast thou laid the foundation of the earth: and the heavens are the work of thy hands" (Ps.102:25).** **"I make a decree, That in every dominion of my kingdom men tremble and fear before the God of Daniel: for he is the living God, and stedfast for ever, and his kingdom that which shall not be destroyed, and his dominion shall be even unto the end" (Da.6:26).** **"But the salvation of the righteous is of the LORD: he is their strength in the time of trouble" (Ps.37:39).**

PROPHET	TIME/PLACE GIVEN	MAIN MESSAGE	PRACTICAL APPLICATION
The UNNAMED PROPHET who rebuked Eli and his house for profaning the temple of the LORD **Known Facts** Delivered a message to Eli the priest (1 S.2:27-34). **Predictions and Messages** 1. The prophecy that each generation of Eli's family would be stricken so that all the men would die in the prime of life (1 S. 2:27-33; esp. v.31). 2. The prophecy that Eli's sons would both die in the same day—a sign that the prophecy concerning Eli's family would come true (1 S.2:34). 3. The prophecy that the LORD would raise up a faithful priest in place of Eli (1 S.2:35-36). **Scripture References** 1 S.2:12-36	**Time** *1085 B.C., when Eli, the priest, was an old man.* **Place** *Shiloh, the central place of worship in Israel prior to the rule of the kings.*	An unnamed prophet was sent by God to pronounce the terrifying judgment against the priestly family of Eli. All three of his sons who were priests, would soon die, and the priesthood of Eli's family was to be transferred to the family of a faithful priest. The unnamed prophet declared three things: 1. He challenged Eli and his sons to remember the history of the priesthood. He pointed out what a privilege it was for priests to approach God and present the offerings to him. For the offerings symbolized the redemption of God's people through the blood of the sacrifice. 2. He pronounced the charge of God against Eli and his sons— that they had scorned the holy things of God and committed immorality. 3. He pronounced the judgment of God against Eli and his sons. The wickedness of Eli and his sons had been so horrible that God was left with no choice. He had to cut them off as priests. **"And there came a man of God unto Eli, and said unto him, Thus saith the LORD,...Wherefore kick ye at my sacrifice and at mine offering, which I have commanded in my habitation; and honourest thy sons above me, to make yourselves fat with the chiefest of all the offerings of Israel my people? Wherefore the LORD God of Israel saith,...Behold, the days come, that I will cut off thine arm, and the arm of thy father's house, that there shall not be an old man in thine house....And this shall be a sign unto thee, that shall come upon thy two sons, on Hophni and Phinehas; in one day they shall die both of them. And I will raise me up a faithful priest, that shall do according to that which is in mine heart and in my mind: and I will build him a sure house; and he shall walk before mine anointed for ever. And it shall come to pass, that every one that is left in thine house shall come and crouch to him for a piece of silver and a morsel of bread, and shall say, Put me, I pray thee, into one of the priests' offices, that I may eat a piece of bread" (1 S.2:27, 29-31, 34-36).**	Judgment upon the immoral and wicked of this world will definitely take place. This is the strong prophetic message of God's Word. Just when the judgment of God is going to fall upon this world is unknown. Just when each of us is going to stand before God, even the minister, is unknown. But the day is definitely coming. The only sure thing that we know about our lives is this: we will die and after that will be the judgment. Judgment is sure, definite, and absolutely certain. Judgment is coming. **"And as it is appointed unto men once to die, but after this the judgment" (He.9:27).** **"When the Son of man shall come in his glory, and all the holy angels with him, then shall he sit upon the throne of his glory: And before him shall be gathered all nations: and he shall separate them one from another, as a shepherd divideth his sheep from the goats: And he shall set the sheep on his right hand, but the goats on the left" (Mt.25:31-33).**

PROPHET	TIME/PLACE GIVEN	MAIN MESSAGE	PRACTICAL APPLICATION
The UNNAMED PROPHET who rebuked Israel for fearing the false gods of the Amorites **Known Facts** Delivered a message to the Israelites (Jud.6:8-10). **Predictions and Messages** The message that Israel had been disobedient because they were in fear of the Amorites (Jud.6:8-10). **Scripture References** Jud.6:7-10	**Time** *Approximately 1210 B.C., during the oppression of the Israelites by the Amorites.* **Place** *The southern regions of Israel.*	The LORD raised up a prophet to rebuke the Israelites because the Israelites needed to be warned as never before. For generations, the Israelites had been failing God, turning back time and again to the sins and evil of their neighbors and engaging in their false worship. The prophet rebuked Israel for four specific sins or evils: ➢ The Israelites had forgotten God's salvation, His wonderful deliverance from Egyptian slavery. ➢ The Israelites had forgotten God's deliverance down through the centuries from their oppressors and forgotten His gift of the promised land. ➢ The Israelites had forsaken God, engaging in false worship or idolatry. ➢ The Israelites had refused to listen to God, disobeying Him and breaking His commandments. **"The LORD sent a prophet unto the children of Israel, which said unto them, Thus saith the LORD God of Israel, I brought you up from Egypt, and brought you forth out of the house of bondage; And I delivered you out of the hand of the Egyptians, and out of the hand of all that oppressed you, and drave them out from before you, and gave you their land; And I said unto you, I am the LORD your God; fear not the gods of the Amorites, in whose land ye dwell: but ye have not obeyed my voice" (Jud.6:8-10).**	If we continue in sin—walk day by day disobeying God—a strong rebuke and correction are needed. We need to be awakened, stirred, aroused out of our slumber and hardness of sin. When we sincerely confess our sins and repent, God will deliver us. But we need to learn one truth: we are not to return to our sin. The sin is to be forsaken or left behind, and we are to walk forward, growing more and more in the righteousness of God. If we return to the same sin time and again, continuing in sin, we deserve to be rebuked. **"And Jesus said unto him, No man, having put his hand to the plough, and looking back, is fit for the kingdom of God" (Lu. 9:62).** **"And have no fellowship with the unfruitful works of darkness, but rather reprove them" (Ep. 5:11).** **"Them that sin rebuke before all, that others also may fear" (1 Ti.5:20).**

PROPHET	TIME/PLACE GIVEN	MAIN MESSAGE	PRACTICAL APPLICATION
The UNNAMED PROPHET who rebuked King Ahab of Israel for sparing Ben-Hadad, the evil king of Aram (Syria) **Known Facts** 1. Belonged to the school of the prophets (1 K.20:35). 2. Delivered a message to King Ahab (1 K.20:39-42). 3. Was known as a prophet (1 K.20:41). **Predictions and Messages** 1. The prophecy that a fellow prophet would be killed by a lion (1 K.20:36). 2. The message that King Ahab had done evil by sparing Ben-Hadad, the evil king of Aram (1 K.20:39-42). **Scripture References** 1 K.20:31-43	**Time** *855 B.C., during the reign of Ahab of Israel and during the ministry of Elijah the prophet.* **Place** *Samaria, the capital of the Northern Kingdom of Israel.*	Under God's instructions, an unnamed prophet sought to disguise himself in order to confront King Ahab. The unnamed prophet ordered a fellow prophet to strike him so that he would appear to be a wounded soldier when he confronted the king. But the fellow prophet refused. As a result, the unnamed prophet predicted the other prophet's death. The next man obeyed and struck the unnamed prophet, wounding him so that his disguise would not be questioned. Disguised as a wounded soldier, the unnamed prophet waited by the road for the king. When Ahab finally arrived and was passing by, the unnamed prophet cried out for a pardon. He told the king that he was in trouble because he had let a prisoner escape. Ahab demonstrated his hard heart by condemning the man. As soon as Ahab had issued his verdict, the prophet stripped off his disguise and pronounced God's condemnation upon Ahab for letting Ben-Hadad, the evil king of Syria, go free. Ahab's life would be demanded in place of the life of Ben-Hadad. **"Then said he unto him, Because thou hast not obeyed the voice of the LORD, behold, as soon as thou art departed from me, a lion shall slay thee. And as soon as he was departed from him, a lion found him, and slew him" (1 K.20:36).** **"And as the king passed by, he cried unto the king: and he said, Thy servant went out into the midst of the battle; and, behold, a man turned aside, and brought a man unto me, and said, Keep this man: if by any means he be missing, then shall thy life be for his life, or else thou shalt pay a talent of silver. And as thy servant was busy here and there, he was gone. And the king of Israel said unto him, So shall thy judgment be; thyself hast decided it" (1 K.20:39-40).**	The lesson we need to learn is that disobedience has consequences. If we disobey God, we stand condemned and will bear the hand of God's judgment. In giving the commandments, God intended good for us. The commandments tell us how to live good, honorable and productive lives that are victorious and conquering. Through obedience, we can live lives that prove to be successful and that bring a sense of fulfillment and satisfaction to the human heart. **"And to you who are troubled rest with us, when the Lord Jesus shall be revealed from heaven with his mighty angels, In flaming fire taking vengeance on them that know not God, and that obey not the gospel of our Lord Jesus Christ: Who shall be punished with everlasting destruction from the presence of the Lord, and from the glory of his power" (2 Th.1:7-9).** **"But if ye will not obey the voice of the LORD, but rebel against the commandment of the LORD, then shall the hand of the LORD be against you, as it was against your fathers" (1 S.12:15).** **"And a curse, if ye will not obey the commandments of the LORD your God, but turn aside out of the way which I command you this day, to go after other gods, which ye have not known" (De.11:28).**

PROPHET	TIME/PLACE GIVEN	MAIN MESSAGE	PRACTICAL APPLICATION
The **UNNAMED PROPHET** who rebuked **King Amaziah of Judah for his idolatry** **Known Facts** Delivered a message to King Amaziah of Judah. **Predictions and Messages** 1. The rebuke of King Amaziah for foolishly worshipping the gods of the Edomites (2 Chr.25:15). 2. The prophecy that King Amaziah would be destroyed because he would not listen to the message of the prophet (2 Chr.25:16). **Scripture References** 2 Chr.25:14-16	**Time** *767 B.C., the last year of the reign of King Amaziah of Judah.* **Place** *Jerusalem, the capital of the Southern Kingdom of Judah.*	Almost unbelievably and certainly tragically, Amaziah committed the terrible sin of false worship. As part of the plunder from his victory, the king brought back the idols of Edom, set them up and worshipped them. Why would King Amaziah commit such folly, turning away from the LORD to false idols? Perhaps King Amaziah began to think that he actually had the support of these false gods so he began to worship them in thanksgiving for the victory he had achieved. The anger of the LORD was aroused and burned against Amaziah. God sent a prophet to warn the king by asking him a question: why had the king worshipped false gods, gods that could not save their own people from the hand of Amaziah? Reacting in rage, the king rejected the prophetic warning and threatened the prophet if he continued issuing his message of rebuke. But fearlessly, the prophet issued a final warning: God would judge and destroy the king for his sin and for not heeding the warning. **"Wherefore the anger of the LORD was kindled against Amaziah, and he sent unto him a prophet, which said unto him, Why hast thou sought after the gods of the people, which could not deliver their own people out of thine hand? And it came to pass, as he talked with him, that the king said unto him, Art thou made of the king's counsel? forbear; why shouldest thou be smitten? Then the prophet forbare, and said, I know that God hath determined to destroy thee, because thou hast done this, and hast not hearkened unto my counsel" (2 Chr.25:15-16).**	Believers must guard and keep themselves from idols. What does this mean? An idol is anything that takes first place in a person's life, anything that a person puts before God. An idol is anything that consumes man's focus and concentration, anything that consumes his energy and efforts more than God. A person can make an idol out of anything in this world; a person can take anything and worship it before God; he can allow it to consume his mind and thoughts and life: ⇒ houses ⇒ cars ⇒ lands ⇒ boats ⇒ job ⇒ sports ⇒ position ⇒ money ⇒ spouse ⇒ comfort ⇒ children ⇒ television ⇒ sex ⇒ possessions ⇒ food ⇒ pleasures ⇒ power ⇒ recreation But idols are not gods, no matter what their worshipers may think. There is no other God but One. It is true that people call out to gods, but... • they are gods of their own minds and imaginations, ideas and notions. • they are gods of wood and stone. • they are gods and lords of their own creation. • they have no power to save or deliver. **"Little children, keep yourselves from idols" (1 Jo.5:21).** **"Professing themselves to be wise, they became fools, and changed the glory of the uncorruptible God into an image made like to corruptible man, and to birds, and four-footed beasts, and creeping things" (Ro.1:22-23).**

PROPHET	TIME/PLACE GIVEN	MAIN MESSAGE	PRACTICAL APPLICATION
The UNNAMED PROPHET who rebuked **King Jeroboam I** for his idolatry **Known Facts** 1. Lived in Judah (1 K. 13:1). 2. Prayed for King Jeroboam and the king's withered hand was healed (1 K.13:6). 3. Commanded by God not to delay—not even to eat or drink—while on his mission (1 K. 13:9). 4. Broke the command of God by visiting and having a meal with an old prophet (1 K.13:19). 5. Was killed by a lion because he disobeyed God's command (1 K.13:24). **Predictions and Messages** 1. The prophecy that a king named Josiah would execute all the false prophets on the altar at Bethel which King Jeroboam had set up for idolatry (1 K.13:2). 2. The prophecy that the altar at Bethel would split apart (1 K.13:3). **Scripture References** 1 K.13:1-25; 2 K.23:15-20	**Time** *931 B.C., the first year of the reign of King Jeroboam I, when the country of Israel had just split into two nations, the Northern Kingdom of Israel and the Southern Kingdom of Judah.* **Place** *Bethel, just north of Jerusalem.*	Just as King Jeroboam was standing by the altar he had set up at Bethel, getting ready to present a false sacrifice, he was suddenly confronted by a young unnamed prophet. The young man prophesied against the altar of false worship established by Jeroboam. The altar and its priests would be destroyed by a future descendant of David named Josiah. To prove that this event would take place, the young prophet gave Jeroboam a sign. The altar would immediately be split apart by the power of God Himself and the ashes would pour out. And so it happened. Pointing to the young man, Jeroboam ordered his guards to arrest him. Instead, another shocking sign happened, which abruptly interrupted the arrest. Jeroboam's hand immediately withered. Terrified, Jeroboam pleaded with the prophet for help. The prophet prayed for the king and his hand was restored. **"And he cried against the altar in the word of the LORD, and said, O altar, altar, thus saith the LORD; Behold, a child shall be born unto the house of David, Josiah by name; and upon thee shall he offer the priests of the high places that burn incense upon thee, and men's bones shall be burnt upon thee. And he gave a sign the same day, saying, This is the sign which the LORD hath spoken; Behold, the altar shall be rent, and the ashes that are upon it shall be poured out" (1 K.13:2-3).**	The lesson for us is strikingly clear: idolatry and false worship do not please the LORD. God totally opposes idolatry and false worship. Idols are not just images made out of wood, stone, metal or some other material. We can make an idol out of anything, for idols are anything that captures our heart more than God. Whatever captivates our hearts, whatever the focus of our hearts is, whatever we give our hearts to, that person or thing becomes our god, our idol. For that person or thing possesses our hearts, our primary interest and attention. As a result, God is denied, ignored or forgotten. **"For the wrath of God is revealed from heaven against all ungodliness and unrighteousness of men, who hold the truth in unrighteousness;…Who changed the truth of God into a lie, and worshipped and served the creature more than the Creator, who is blessed for ever. Amen" (Ro.1:18, 25).** **"Thou shalt not make unto thee any graven image, or any likeness of any thing that is in heaven above, or that is in the earth beneath, or that is in the water under the earth" (Ex.20:4).** **"Take heed to yourselves, that your heart be not deceived, and ye turn aside, and serve other gods, and worship them" (De.11:16).**

PROPHET	TIME/PLACE GIVEN	MAIN MESSAGE	PRACTICAL APPLICATION
The **UNNAMED PROPHET** who warned **King Amaziah of Judah not to hire the army of Israel** **Known Facts** Delivered a message to King Amaziah. **Predictions and Messages** 1. The warning that King Amaziah of Judah will meet with disaster if he deploys the troops of Israel into battle (2 Chr. 25:7-8). 2. The message that God has the power to help or to bring defeat (2 Chr.25:8). 3. The message that God is able to supply far more than anything ever lost (2 Chr.25:9). **Scripture References** 2 Chr.25:5-10	**Time** *767 B.C., the last year of the reign of King Amaziah of Judah.* **Place** *Jerusalem, the capital of the Southern Kingdom of Judah.*	King Amaziah of Judah was preparing for war against the age-old enemy of Israel, the Edomites. Amaziah had just hired the armies of Israel to assist him in his battles. But before he could deploy these troops, Amaziah was confronted by a prophet of the LORD who issued a strong warning to the king. The prophet told King Amaziah that he must not allow Israel's mercenary troops to march with him. For the LORD was not with Israel. Living wicked lives and engaging in false worship, the people of the Northern Kingdom had rejected the LORD and were no longer placing their hope in the eternal covenant given to David. They had abandoned the LORD; consequently, the LORD had abandoned them. Still speaking to Amaziah, the prophet continued his warning. If the king marched into battle with the Israelite mercenary soldiers, he would be defeated. Even if he fought courageously against the Edomites, the LORD would make sure he was defeated. For the LORD has the power to help or to overthrow an army. The prophet further assured King Amaziah that God would provide far more plunder—more than enough—to cover his losses if he would just discharge the unbelieving troops. **"But there came a man of God to him, saying, O king, let not the army of Israel go with thee; for the LORD is not with Israel, to wit, with all the children of Ephraim. But if thou wilt go, do it, be strong for the battle: God shall make thee fall before the enemy: for God hath power to help, and to cast down. And Amaziah said to the man of God, But what shall we do for the hundred talents which I have given to the army of Israel? And the man of God answered, The LORD is able to give thee much more than this"** (2 Chr.25:7-9).	Believers are to turn away from evil associations. Close associations always influence us. If we fellowship with godly people, we will be influenced by godliness. But if we fellowship with ungodly people, their ungodliness will influence us. It is impossible to escape the influence of close associations. We all influence each other; and the more closely we are associated, the more we are influenced. If a believer associates with the wicked, eventually the wicked will encourage the believer to join him in his sinful behavior. A godly person is always pulled down, influenced negatively by close associations with those who smoke, take drugs, get drunk, or engage in immoral behavior. No matter who we are or how strong we may be, we will be strongly influenced to participate in the sinful behavior. For this reason the LORD commands us to live lives of *spiritual separation*. Believers are not to fellowship nor become closely associated with the wicked and evil of this earth. We are to be spiritually separated. Living upon the earth, we are to be friends with everyone, unbeliever as well as believer. And we are to be kind, caring, and helpful to everyone. But we are not to form close alliances, associations, or bonds with the wicked and evil of this earth. **"But now I have written unto you not to keep company, if any man that is called a brother be a fornicator, or covetous, or an idolater, or a railer, or a drunkard, or an extortioner; with such an one no not to eat"** (1 Co.5:11). **"Thou shalt not follow a multitude to do evil; neither shalt thou speak in a cause to decline after many to wrest judgment"** (Ex. 23:2).

PROPHET	TIME/PLACE GIVEN	MAIN MESSAGE	PRACTICAL APPLICATION
URIJAH **(Jehovah/Yahweh is a Light)** **Known Facts** 1. Was the son of Shemaiah (Je.26:20). 2. Lived in Kiriath-Jearim (Je.26:20). 3. Prophesied in Judah (Je.26:20-21). 4. Fled to Egypt to escape execution by King Jehoiakim (Je. 26:21). 5. Was brought back from Egypt by the king's men and slain (Je.26:22-23). 6. Given the burial of a common criminal (Je.26:23). **Predictions and Messages** Preached messages similar to those of Jeremiah the prophet (Je.26:20). **Scripture References** Je.26:20-23	**Time** *608 B.C., at the beginning of the reign of Jehoiakim, king of Judah.* **Place** *Jerusalem, the capital city of Judah, in the palace of the king.*	All that is known about the messages of Urijah is that they were similar to those of Jeremiah, the prophet. By this one fact, we can know something of what Urijah prophesied. First, Urijah was bound to be a true prophet, proclaiming the messages given him by God. He was not speaking the popular, conscience-soothing messages of the false prophets of that time. Second, Urijah was courageous, warning both king and citizen to repent of their wickedness and false worship or else face the judgment of God. Otherwise, why would the king be so angry and determined to have Urijah executed? Third, we can be sure that Urijah preached the truth of God's Word right up until the day of his martyrdom. **"And there was also a man that prophesied in the name of the LORD, Urijah the son of Shemaiah of Kirjathjearim, who prophesied against this city and against this land according to all the words of Jeremiah" (Je. 26:20).**	The preacher must not compromise the Word of God. He must say exactly what God gives him to say. After all, the message is not his, but God's. It is not his to change or alter in the least. Even if it means death, the man of God must not give another message or a watered down version of the truth. He must not seek to say what is popular or more acceptable to his listeners. He must preach the whole counsel of God without regard to circumstances or popular opinion. He must say exactly what God gives him to say. **"And he said unto them, Go ye into all the world, and preach the gospel to every creature" (Mk. 16:15).** **"And daily in the temple, and in every house, they ceased not to teach and preach Jesus Christ" (Ac.5:42).** **"But we preach Christ crucified, unto the Jews a stumblingblock, and unto the Greeks foolishness" (1 Co.1:23).** **"For though I preach the gospel, I have nothing to glory of: for necessity is laid upon me; yea, woe is unto me, if I preach not the gospel! (1 Co.9:16).** **"Preach the word; be instant in season, out of season; reprove, rebuke, exhort with all longsuffering and doctrine" (2 Ti.4:2).**

PROPHET	TIME/PLACE GIVEN	MAIN MESSAGE	PRACTICAL APPLICATION
ZECHARIAH (Jehovah/Yahweh has brought to mind), the son of Jehoiada **Known Facts** 1. Was the son of Jehoiada, the priest (2 Chr.24:20). 2. Was stoned to death because of his message (2 Chr.24:21). **Predictions and Messages** The message that the LORD had forsaken the people of Judah because they had forsaken the LORD and his commandments by their false worship and idolatry (2 Chr. 24:20). **Scripture References** 2 Chr.24:17-22; Mt. 23:34-39; Lu.11:47-51	**Time** *797 B.C., a year before the death of Joash, king of Judah.* **Place** *Jerusalem, the capital city of Judah.*	After the death of Jehoiada, the priest, King Joash, who had led a tremendous revival and spiritual reformation in his younger years, slipped away from the LORD and committed terrible apostasy. Joash listened and gave in to wicked, influential leaders who were false worshipers. Because of their terrible apostasy of turning away to false worship, they stood guilty before the LORD and aroused His anger. God sent prophet after prophet to warn the king, but the king and people stubbornly rejected the prophets of God, refusing to listen to their warnings and refusing to repent. In mercy, however, the LORD made one last attempt to get Joash and the people to repent. The Spirit of the LORD came upon Zechariah with a very special message for the king and the people. They had disobeyed God's commandments and forsaken Him; consequently, the LORD had now forsaken them. But in the depth of their stubborn, stiff-necked rebellion, they still did not repent. Instead, they actually murdered the prophet Zechariah. Furious over the pronouncement of judgment against them, Joash ordered the prophet stoned to death in the very courtyard of the temple itself. Looking up into the eyes of the king as he lay dying, Zechariah pronounced a divine curse upon the king and the people. They were to soon face God's vengeance. The next year, the Arameans (Syrians) attacked and overran the countryside. Joash was killed in battle. **"And the Spirit of God came upon Zechariah the son of Jehoiada the priest, which stood above the people, and said unto them, Thus saith God, Why transgress ye the commandments of the LORD, that ye cannot prosper? because ye have forsaken the LORD, he hath also forsaken you" (2 Chr.24:20).**	How many people have a wonderful beginning in life but a terrible ending? Think of people who have walked through many years of life with upright characters, living honest, moral, and just lives. Yet in the latter years of their lives their character has declined, deteriorated. Some have become immoral and dishonest, even cheating other people. Others are no longer kind and gracious but, rather, unkind, mean-spirited, and reactionary, sometimes even cursing or assaulting those who love and care for them. Whereas they used to live righteous lives and profess to be followers of the LORD, they are now backsliding, living carnal, fleshly lives. They not only ignore the LORD but they also deny Him. They curse His name, use profanity, and tell off-colored jokes. They no longer worship the LORD or are faithful in church attendance. Instead of setting the example that we must listen to the Word of God being taught, they slip into immorality, tearing out the hearts of parents, wives, husbands, children, former pastors, and teachers. Far too many who begin with Christ eventually turn away from Him, committing terrible apostasy against Him. **"And because iniquity shall abound, the love of many shall wax cold" (Mt.24:12).** **"They on the rock *are they,* which, when they hear, receive the word with joy; and these have no root, which for a while believe, and in time of temptation fall away" (Lu.8:13).** **"But now, after that ye have known God, or rather are known of God, how turn ye again to the weak and beggarly elements, whereunto ye desire again to be in bondage" (Ga.4:9).** **"Harden not your hearts, as in the provocation, in the day of temptation in the wilderness: When your fathers tempted me, proved me, and saw my works forty years. Wherefore I was grieved with that generation, and said, They do alway err in their heart; and they have not known my ways. So I sware in my wrath, They shall not enter into my rest.) Take heed, brethren, lest there be in any of you an evil heart of unbelief, in departing from the living God" (He.3:8-12).**

PROPHET	TIME/PLACE GIVEN	MAIN MESSAGE	PRACTICAL APPLICATION
ZECHARIAH (Jehovah/Yahweh has brought to mind), the son of Berechiah **Known Facts** 1. Was the son of Berechiah, the priest (Zec. 1:1). 2. Was the grandson of Iddo, the priest (Ezr. 6:14). 3. Ministered at the same time as Haggai, the prophet (Ezr.5:1; 6:14). 4. Prophesied in Jerusalem after the return from captivity (Zec. 1:1; Ezr.6:16). 5. Helped to restore the temple (Ezr.6:14-15). 6. Saw startling visions of the end times (Zec. 1:7-6:8). **Predictions and Messages** 1. The sermon that the people needed to repent and turn to the LORD (Zec.1:2-6). 2. The vision of the horseman beside the myrtle trees—the promise of restoration of the temple and to Jerusalem (Zec.1:7-17). 3. The vision of the four horns and the four craftsmen—the prophecy of future world powers (Zec.1:18-21). 4. The vision of a man with a measuring line—the prophecy of divine protection for Jerusalem (Zec.2). 5. The vision of Joshua the High Priest being accused and slandered by Satan—a prophecy of the redemption for all Israel (Zec.3). 6. The prophecy of the Messiah, the Savior of the world, the Righteous Branch Who would take away the sins of the land and bring peace (Is.11:1; Zec.3:8-10; Mt.2:23). (cont. on next page)	**Time** *520-518 B.C., during the reign of Darius the Mede, when the Israelites had returned from captivity.* **Place** *Jerusalem, the capital city of the remnant of Israel.*	The people of Israel had just come out of foreign captivity and badly needed to have a strong sense of direction. Zechariah, along with Haggai, the prophet, immediately pointed them to God, greatly encouraging the people to restore the temple so that it might be worthy to be used to worship the LORD. Now it was not just a building project that Zechariah was leading. As a spiritual leader of thousands of exiles who had just returned from captivity, Zechariah realized the great importance of quickly calling the people to genuine worship. He had to ground them firmly in the LORD right away. And so Zechariah encouraged the people time and again to turn to the LORD with their whole heart, to worship the Great Shepherd of their souls. Zechariah helped to lead a very great revival. His many visions and prophecies emphasized the love of a sovereign God for His people, and His desire to uphold them and work in their behalf. For those who were determined to serve God wholeheartedly, they would be supported and sustained by the LORD. He would bring about marvelous things in their future. **"Therefore say thou unto them, Thus saith the LORD of hosts; Turn ye unto me, saith the LORD of hosts, and I will turn unto you, saith the LORD of hosts" (Zec.1:3).** **"Thus saith the LORD of hosts; Let your hands be strong, ye that hear in these days these words by the mouth of the prophets, which were in the day that the foundation of the house of the LORD of hosts was laid, that the temple might be built" (Zec.8:9).**	God is sovereign. He rules over the entire universe. But a person should not think that God is far off in outer space someplace. Coming out of terrible tragedy, it is easy for a person to feel that God is a billion miles away. After a tragedy, it is difficult to have a sense of direction. But it is during hardship that a person needs to seek God like never before and to draw close to Him for understanding, for God cares about our problems. We must always be aware that God is not an unconcerned observer of the world He created. He truly cares about every struggle we go through, and He longs to move in our lives to make the future better, much better than our past. God did not just create the world, wind it up and leave it on its own to fly throughout space with man making out the best he can. God is interested and concerned with the world—so much so that He came to earth in human flesh to show how vitally concerned He is. God would not leave man to grope and grasp in the dark. His call to repentance is not for the purpose of pushing man down but to bring him up, to show man that there is a bright future ahead for those who determine to wholeheartedly serve the LORD. **"Jesus saith unto him, I am the way, the truth, and the life: no man cometh unto the Father, but by me" (Jn.14:6).** **"In my distress I called upon the LORD, and cried to my God: and he did hear my voice out of his temple, and my cry did enter into his ears" (2 S.22:7).** **"When thou art in tribulation, and all these things are come upon thee, even in the latter days, if thou turn to the LORD thy God, and shalt be obedient unto his voice; (For the LORD thy God is a merciful God;) he will not forsake thee, neither destroy thee, nor forget the covenant of thy fathers which he sware unto them" (De.4:30-31).**

PROPHET	TIME/PLACE GIVEN	MAIN MESSAGE	PRACTICAL APPLICATION
ZECHARIAH (cont.) 7. The vision of a golden lampstand and two olive trees—the prophecy of continual anointing for Zerubbabel, who was a type of Christ (Zec.4). 8. The vision of a flying scroll—a declaration that wickedness will be purged from the land (Zec.5:1-4). 9. The vision of a woman in a basket—the prophecy of the rebellion of Babylon in the end times (Zec. 5:5-11). 10. The vision of four chariots—the declaration of God's sovereignty over all nations (Zec.6:1-8). 11. A sermon about the proper attitude for religious ceremony (Zec. 7:4-7). 12. A sermon about loving your neighbor (Zec.7:8-14). 13. The prophecy of God's favor coming upon Jerusalem and Judah (Zec.8:1-17). 14. The prophecy of the salvation of the Gentiles (Zec.8:18-23). 15. The prophecy of God's judgment upon Judah's enemies (Zec. 9:1-10). 16. The prophecy of the Christ's kingly declaration—that the Messiah, the Savior of the world, would enter Jerusalem riding on a young donkey (Zec.9:9; Mt.21:1-11). (Cont. in col.3) **Scripture References** The book of *Zechariah*; Ezr.5:1; 6:14; 8:3, 11, 16		**Predictions and Messages** (cont. from col.1) 17. The prophecy of restoration to all Israel (Zec.9:11-10:12). 18. The illustration of two shepherds' staffs—a prophecy of the rejection of the Messiah, the Great Shepherd (Zec.11). 19. The prophecy that the Messiah, the Savior of the world, would be betrayed for thirty pieces of silver (Zec.11:13). 20. The prophecy that Israel will never again abandon the LORD (Zec.12:1-13:9). 21. The prophecy that the Jews will recognize Jesus Christ as the true Messiah, as their true Savior, in the last days (Zec.12:10-14). 22. The prophecy that in the end times, the LORD will be the only king on the earth (Zec.14).	

PROPHET	TIME/PLACE GIVEN	MAIN MESSAGE	PRACTICAL APPLICATION
ZEPHANIAH (Jehovah/Yahweh is darkness or God hides) **Known Facts** 1. Was the son of Cushi (Zep.1:1). 2. Was a descendant of the righteous King Hezekiah (Zep.1:1). 3. Prophesied to Judah, the Southern Kingdom, helping to lead the way for the religious reforms of Josiah (Zep.1:1). **Predictions and Messages** 1. The prophecy of the coming judgment against Judah and Jerusalem (Zep.1:2-18). 2. The sermon about seeking the LORD to escape His wrath (Zep. 2:1-3). 3. The prophecy of the coming judgment against the Philistines (Zep.2:4-7). 4. The prophecy of the coming judgment against Moab and Ammon (Zep.2:8-11). 5. The prophecy of the coming judgment against Cush (Zep. 2:12). 6. The prophecy of the coming judgment against Assyria (Zep. 2:13-15). 7. The prophecy of the coming judgment against Jerusalem (Zep.3:1-7). 8. The prophecy of the purity of Israel in the last days (Zep.3:8-13; Re.14:1-5). 9. The prophecy of the restoration of Israel and Jerusalem (Zep. 3:14-20). **Scripture References** The book of *Zephaniah*	**Time** *640-609 B.C., during the entire reign of Josiah, king of Judah, who led the last great revival before the fall of Jerusalem in 586 B.C.* **Place** *Judah, the Southern Kingdom of Israel and Jerusalem, the capital city.*	After Manasseh and Amon, two of the most wicked kings in all of Judah's history, God raised up a godly king—Josiah. It was at the tender age of eight that Josiah was crowned king. Obviously, some consistent and righteous believers had a strong, spiritual influence upon young Josiah, for he lived a righteous life in the sight of the LORD. In fact, Scripture says that he followed the godly example of David, never deviating from the righteous example set by the ancient king (2 K.22:2). During his reign, Josiah had one major concern: the restoration of the temple and the true worship of the LORD, the only living and true God (2 K.22:3-7). No doubt, the prophet Zephaniah was one of the people who had a strong spiritual influence on Josiah. Zephaniah called the people to repent and to turn back to God. They had acted no better than their evil neighbors, and the wrath of God was about to be poured out. But there was still a ray of hope if only the people would repent and change their evil ways. Scripture reveals to us that the nation did listen to Zephaniah and the other prophets of that time and that the invasion of Babylon was delayed because of their change of heart (2 Chr.34:27-28). As a result of the messages of Zephaniah and others, Josiah started one of the two great revivals in Israel's history. (The other was by Hezekiah, the ancestor of Zephaniah.) Zephaniah's message announced the coming terrible judgment of God, in very dark words. But there was also promised blessing and a bright future ahead for those who turned to God. **"Gather yourselves together, yea, gather together, O nation not desired; Before the decree bring forth, before the day pass as the chaff, before the fierce anger of the LORD come upon you, before the day of the LORD's anger come upon you. Seek ye the LORD, all ye meek of the earth, which have wrought his judgment; seek righteousness, seek meekness: it may be ye shall be hid in the day of the LORD's anger" (Zep.2:1-3)**	Deep concern for righteousness and for true worship should grip our hearts. For righteousness and true worship determine our destiny, both individually and corporately, as a society and nation. Righteousness builds a character of integrity within people, and righteous individuals build up a nation. If a person is righteous, he is honest, just, true, moral and law-abiding. He keeps the laws of the land and works diligently at his job in order to make a significant contribution to society. Righteousness builds the character of morality and integrity. And when there are enough of us with righteous characters, we build a nation of righteousness, a nation of enormous strength. This can be the experience of any of us. True worship also determines our destiny. If we truly worship the true and living God with a humble and repentant attitude, accepting the sacrifice of His Son, then He will accept us. Think about this glorious truth: The LORD God of the universe, Who sent His Son to die for our sins, is the true and living God who loves us. It is He who is to be worshipped, and He alone. There is a bright future for anyone who turns from sin, lives a righteous life, and truly worships God. **"Awake to righteousness, and sin not; for some have not the knowledge of God: I speak this to your shame" (1 Co.15:34).** **"Teaching us that, denying ungodliness and worldly lusts, we should live soberly, righteously, and godly, in this present world; Looking for that blessed hope, and the glorious appearing of the great God and our Saviour Jesus Christ" (Tit.2:12-13).** **"By the blessing of the upright the city is exalted: but it is overthrown by the mouth of the wicked" (Pr.11:11).**

(cont. on next page)

PROPHET	TIME/PLACE GIVEN	MAIN MESSAGE	PRACTICAL APPLICATION
ZEPHANIAH (cont.)		"I will gather them that are sorrowful for the solemn assembly, who are of thee, to whom the reproach of it was a burden. Behold, at that time I will undo all that afflict thee: and I will save her that halteth, and gather her that was driven out; and I will get them praise and fame in every land where they have been put to shame. At that time will I bring you again, even in the time that I gather you: for I will make you a name and a praise among all people of the earth, when I turn back your captivity before your eyes, saith the LORD" (Zep. 3:18-20).	

TYPES, SYMBOLS, AND PICTURES
THE BOOK OF 2 KINGS

ALPHABETICAL OUTLINE

What is a biblical type or symbol? Simply put, a *biblical type* is a *foreshadowing* of what was to come at a later time in history. Through a person, place, or thing, a biblical type points toward a New Testament fulfillment.

In addition to biblical types, there are what we may call *biblical pictures*. A biblical picture is a lesson that we can see in the Scriptures *without distorting the truth*. The study of biblical types and pictures is a valuable tool in that it helps us apply the truth of the Scripture in our lives. Scripture itself tells us this:

"Now all these things happened unto them for examples: and they are written for our admonition, upon whom the ends of the world are come" (1 Co.10:11).
"For whatsoever things were written aforetime were written for our learning, that we through patience and comfort of the scriptures might have hope" (Ro.15:4).

PERSON/PLACE/THING	SCRIPTURE, OUTLINE AND DISCUSSION
AMAZIAH *Life of. Somewhat righteous, but did not remove all the false worship. A picture of half-hearted commitment.*	2 K.14:1-6
Reign of. His determination to use his power to battle Israel. A picture of losing an opportunity to serve.	2 K.14:1-22
Unwise declaration of war by. Upon Israel. A picture of boastful pride and arrogance.	2 K.14:8-16
ARROW. *Of Jehoash. A symbol of victory over the enemy.*	2 K.13:14-19
ATHALIAH *Murderous rampage of royal heirs by. A picture of self-exaltation and murder.*	2 K.11:1
Overthrow of and the establishment of Joash on the throne. A picture of renewal and recommitment to the LORD.	2 K.11:4-21
BAAL and ASHTORETH. *False worship of. A symbol of the desire for fertile crops through sexual acts.*	2 K.23:6-7
CLOTHING. *Tearing of and wearing sackcloth. A symbol of repentance and grief.*	2 K.19:1
CORPSE. *Raising of to life. By touching the bones of Elisha. A symbol of the great resurrection in the end times.*	2 K.13:20-21
ELIJAH *Ascension of. A type of Christ's ascension.*	2 K.2:1-12
A type of the resurrection of all believers.	2 K.2:1-12
Mantle of. Passing to Elisha. A symbol of God's equipping His servants.	2 K.2:13-25

TYPES, SYMBOLS, AND PICTURES
ALPHABETICAL

PERSON/PLACE/THING	SCRIPTURE, OUTLINE AND DISCUSSION
ELISHA *Parting the Jordan River. A symbol of God's power to guide the believer through any difficulty.*	2 K.2:14
Staff of. A symbol of God's power to perform miracles.	2 K.4:29
Transfer of Elijah's ministry to. A picture of total commitment to God and of God's power.	2 K.2:1-25
FIRE. Soldiers who tried to arrest Elijah. Consumed by. *A picture of God's protection of His servants.*	2 K.1:9-12
GEDALIAH. Appointment of. As king of the land. *A picture of despair.*	2 K.25:22-26
HEZEKIAH *His foolish entertainment of the Babylonian ambassadors. A picture of pride.*	2 K.20:12-21
Life of. A picture of total devotion and commitment.	2 K.18:1-12
IDOLS. Ashes of. Scattering of. By Josiah. *A symbol of God's rejection of false worship.*	2 K.23:4-6
ISRAEL. Fall of. Reason for. *A picture of the tragic consequences of sin.*	2 K.17:7-41
JEHOIACHIN. Release of. From prison. *A picture of hope, of being freed from captivity.*	2 K.25:27-30
JEROBOAM II. Reign of. *A picture of God's mercy and patience despite wickedness.*	2 K.14:23-29
JERUSALEM. Total destruction of. *A picture of the final judgment.*	2 K.25:1-21
JOASH. Hiding and training of. *A picture of godly training.*	2 K.11:2-3
LEPERS. Spoils of war found by and shared with a starving city. *A powerful picture of evangelism.*	2 K.7:10-20
PASSOVER. Celebration of. *A symbol of God's deliverance of His people from Egypt and from the bondage to sin (a symbol of enslavement to the world).*	2 K.23:21-23
PEKAHIAH. Reign of. *A picture of greed and covetousness for political power.*	2 K.15:23-26
PROPHETS. School of. Building of. Doing the work themselves. *A picture of diligent labor.*	2 K.6:1-4
SIEGE. On Samaria. By Syria. *A picture of utter hopelessness.*	2 K.6:24-33
TEMPLE. *A symbol of God's presence and of the need to worship and praise Him.*	2 K.25:9
ZECHARIAH. Reign of and assassination of. *A picture of God's faithfulness in fulfilling His promises.*	2 K.15:8-12

TYPES, SYMBOLS, AND PICTURES
THE BOOK OF 2 KINGS

CHRONOLOGICAL OUTLINE

What is a biblical type or symbol? Simply put, a *biblical type* is a *foreshadowing* of what was to come at a later time in history. Through a person, place, or thing, a biblical type points toward a New Testament fulfillment.

In addition to biblical types, there are what we may call *biblical pictures*. A biblical picture is a lesson that we can see in the Scriptures *without distorting the truth*. The study of biblical types and pictures is a valuable tool in that it helps us apply the truth of the Scripture in our lives. Scripture itself tells us this:

> "Now all these things happened unto them for examples: and they are written for our admonition, upon whom the ends of the world are come" (1 Co.10:11).
> "For whatsoever things were written aforetime were written for our learning, that we through patience and comfort of the scriptures might have hope" (Ro.15:4).

PERSON/PLACE/THING	SCRIPTURE, OUTLINE AND DISCUSSION
FIRE. *Soldiers who tried to arrest Elijah. Consumed by. A picture of God's protection of His servants.*	2 K.1:9-12
ELISHA. *Transfer of Elijah's ministry to. A picture of total commitment to God and of God's power.*	2 K.2:1-25
ELIJAH *Ascension of.* *A type of Christ's ascension.*	2 K.2:1-12
A type of the resurrection of all believers.	2 K.2:1-12
Mantle of. Passing to Elisha. A symbol of God's equipping His servants.	2 K.2:13-25
ELISHA *Parting the Jordan River. A symbol of God's power to guide the believer through any difficulty.*	2 K.2:14
Staff of. A symbol of God's power to perform miracles.	2 K.4:29
PROPHETS. *School of. Building of. Doing the work themselves. A picture of diligent labor.*	2 K.6:1-4
SIEGE. *On Samaria. By Syria. A picture of utter hopelessness.*	2 K.6:24-33
LEPERS. *Spoils of war found by and shared with a starving city. A powerful picture of evangelism.*	2 K.7:10-20
ATHALIAH. *Murderous rampage of royal heirs by. A picture of self-exaltation and murder.*	2 K.11:1
JOASH. *Hiding and training of. A picture of godly training.*	2 K.11:2-3
ATHALIAH. *Overthrow of and the establishment of Joash on the throne. A picture of renewal and recommitment to the LORD.*	2 K.11:4-21
ARROW. *Of Jehoash. A symbol of victory over the enemy.*	2 K.13:14-19

PERSON/PLACE/THING	SCRIPTURE, OUTLINE AND DISCUSSION
CORPSE. *Raising of to life. By touching the bones of Elisha. A symbol of the great resurrection in the end times.*	2 K.13:20-21
AMAZIAH *Life of. Somewhat righteous, but did not remove all the false worship. A picture of half-hearted commitment.*	2 K.14:1-6
Reign of. His determination to use his power to battle Israel. A picture of losing an opportunity to serve.	2 K.14:1-22
Unwise declaration of war by. Upon Israel. A picture of boastful pride and arrogance.	2 K.14:8-16
JEROBOAM II. *Reign of. A picture of God's mercy and patience despite wickedness.*	2 K.14:23-29
ZECHARIAH. *Reign of and assassination of. A picture of God's faithfulness in fulfilling His promises.*	2 K.15:8-12
PEKAHIAH. *Reign of. A picture of greed and covetousness for political power.*	2 K.15:23-26
ISRAEL. *Fall of. Reason for. A picture of the tragic consequences of sin.*	2 K.17:7-41
HEZEKIAH. *Life of. A picture of total devotion and commitment.*	2 K.18:1-12
CLOTHING. *Tearing of and wearing sackcloth. A symbol of repentance and grief.*	2 K.19:1
HEZEKIAH. *His foolish entertainment of the Babylonian ambassadors. A picture of pride.*	2 K.20:12-21
IDOLS. *Ashes of. Scattering of. By Josiah. A symbol of God's rejection of false worship.*	2 K.23:4-6
BAAL *and* **ASHTORETH.** *False worship of. A symbol of the desire for fertile crops through sexual acts.*	2 K.23:6-7
PASSOVER. *Celebration of. A symbol of God's deliverance of His people from Egypt and from the bondage to sin (a symbol of enslavement to the world).*	2 K.23:21-23
JERUSALEM. *Total destruction of. A picture of the final judgment.*	2 K.25:1-21
TEMPLE. *A symbol of God's presence and of the need to worship and praise Him.*	2 K.25:9
GEDALIAH. *Appointment of. As king of the land. A picture of despair.*	2 K.25:22-26
JEHOIACHIN. *Release of. From prison. A picture of hope, of being freed from captivity.*	2 K.25:27-30

THE
OUTLINE & SUBJECT INDEX

REMEMBER: When you look up a subject and turn to the Scripture reference, you have not just the Scripture but also an outline and a discussion (commentary) of the Scripture and subject.

This is one of the GREAT FEATURES of *The Preacher's Outline & Sermon Bible*®. Once you have all the volumes, you will have not only what all other Bible indexes give you, that is, a list of all the subjects and their Scripture references, but in addition you will have...

- an outline of every Scripture and subject in the Bible
- a discussion (commentary) on every Scripture and subject
- every subject supported by other Scripture, already written out or cross referenced

DISCOVER THE UNIQUE VALUE for yourself. Quickly glance below to the first subject of the Index. It is:

ACCOUNTABILITY
    By God.
        Rulers are held **a**. by God. 9:1-13, Thgt. 1
        We will reap what we sow. 9:1-13, Thgt.1

Turn to the first reference. Glance at the Scripture and the outline, then read the commentary. You will immediately see the TREMENDOUS BENEFIT of the INDEX of *The Preacher's Outline & Sermon Bible*®.

OUTLINE AND SUBJECT INDEX

ACCOUNTABILITY
By God.
  Rulers are held **a**. by God. 9:1-13, Thgt. 1
  We will reap what we sow. 9:1-13, Thgt.1

ACCUSATIONS (See **PERSECUTION**)

AHAB (See also 1 Kings)
Death of. Noted. 1:1; 3:5
Family.
  Father.
    Of Ahaziah. 1:1-8
    Of Joram. 3:1
    Of seventy sons. 10:1
  Husband. Of Jezebel. 9:7
  Known for their evil deeds. 8:18, 27
Influence of. Evil. Influenced his son and his son-in-law to do evil. 1:18; 8:27
Judgment upon.
  Executed by Jehu. 9:7-10:17
  Prophesied by Elijah. 9:36; 10:10
Sins of.
  Murder.
    Of God's servants. 9:7
    Of Naboth. 9:26
  Worshipped Baal. 10:18; 21:3

AHAZ
Character. Very Depraved. 16:2, 12-16
False worship of.
  Brought a foreign altar into the temple of God. 16:12-15
  Of Molech. 16:3
  Used God's altar for pagan divining rituals. 16:15
King. Of Judah. 16:1-20

Sins of.
  Listed. 16:1-20
  Profaning the priesthood. 16:16
  Profaning the temple. 16:12-15

  Trusted in earthly kings instead of God. 16:7-9
  Worshipped false gods. 16:3-4
Son. Of Jotham. 16:1

AHAZIAH (King of Israel)
Death of.
  Cause. **A** sinned by seeking a false god. 1:6, 16
  Prophesied. By Elijah. 1:6, 16
Evil reign. 1:1-8
Family.
  Brother of Joram. 3:1
  Son of Ahab. 3:1
Influence. Of Parents. **A**. was evil like Ahab and Jezebel. 1:1-18
Judgment upon.
  Cause. Sought false gods. 1:2, 6
  Died.
    Because of his sin. 1:16-17
    Childless. 1:16-18
King. Of Israel. 1:1-18
Problems of.
  Accident. 1:2
  Revolt. 1:1
  Turned against God. 1:2, 6
Sins of. Attempted to arrest Elijah. 1:9-15

AHAZIAH (King of Judah)
Character. Evil like his parents. 8:26-27
Influence of. **A**. acted evil like his parents. 8:26-27
Reign.
  Evil. 8:27
  Only one year. 8:26
Wars of. Joined Joram to fight against Syria. 8:28

ALLIANCE
Evil.
  Jehoram married Joram's sister, making an evil **a**. 8:18
  Result of. Will eventually cause us to commit spiritual adultery. 8:16-24, Thgt.1

AMAZIAH
Death of. Assassinated. 14:19-20
King. Of Judah. 14:1-22
Pride of. **A**. was filled with pride after he defeated the Edomites. 14:7-16
Reign of.
  Prideful. Ended up in exile after a foolish battle. 14:8-16
  Second. Returned from exile, but did nothing. 14:17-22
Wars of.
  Losses. Against Jehoash. 14:8-16
  Victories. Against Edom. 14:7

AMON
Assassinated. By his servants. 21:23
Character. Evil. 21:20
Influence on. **A**. followed the evil example of his parents. 21:20-21

ANGELS
Protection by. Elisha was protected from Syria by **a**. 6:15-23
Seen.
  Appeared as an army of horses and chariots. 6:17
  Example. Elisha prayed and his attendant saw the protecting **a**. all around. 6:17

ANGER
Of God. (See **GOD**, Anger)

INDEX

CULT
Of Jeroboam I. Influence of. Many kings of Israel followed the **c.** of Jeroboam I. 3:3; 9:9; 10:29-31; 13:2; 15:9

CURSE
Example. Gehazi and his descendants were **c.** with leprosy because of his greed. 5:26-27

DEATH
Cause of. Sin. 1:16-18, Thgt.1
Escape from. Example. Elijah went directly to heaven in a whirlwind. 2:11

DEBT
Duty.
In ancient times. To pay or become a slave to the creditor. 4:1
Of the believer. To pay debts owed. 4:1-7

DECEPTION (See **PLOTTING**)

DEDICATION (See **COMMITMENT**)
Example. Amaziah. **D.** to God, but not with his whole heart like David. 14:1-7

DEFENSE
Of God. Example. Elisha knew ahead of time where the Ara-means were going to attack. 6:8-23

DELIVERANCE (See **SALVATION**)
Assurance of. Example. Given to Hezekiah by Isaiah. 19:1-13
From crisis. Discussed. 19:1-37, Intro.
Of God.
From hopelessness. God **d.** by His great power. 6:24-7:20, Intro.
From the enemy.
God **d.** Israel from Syria. 6:8-23; 13:4-5
God **d.** Judah from the Assyrians. 19:20-36
God **d.** Samaria from starvation and hopelessness. 7:3-9
Seeking. Example. Hezekiah sought God for **d.** from the Assyrians. 19:14-19
Promised. Example. Hezekiah was promised **d.** by God. 19:20-37
Source. God's promises. 7:1-2

DEPRAVITY
Cause of. Sinful man's reaction to bad circumstances. 6:24-33
Example.
Ahaz. Profaned the worship of God by bringing a foreign altar. 16:12-15
Cannibalism. During the siege, a woman boiled her son and ate him. 6:28-29
Proof of. 21:1-26, Intro.

DESPAIR
Answer. Prayer. 19:14-19
Causes. Discussed. 18:1-37, Intro.
Example. Those left in Jerusalem after the fall were in **d.** 25:22-26
Experiences of.
Described. 4:1-44, Intro.
Listed. 2:1-25, Intro.

DETERMINATION (See **STEADFASTNESS; PERSEVERANCE**)

DEVOTION (See **COMMITMENT; DEDICATION**)
Example. Hezekiah. Was greatly **d.** to God. 18:3-6

DILIGENCE (See **FAITHFULNESS; PERSEVERANCE**)
Duty. We must be **d.** 6:1-7, Thgt.1
Example. The student in the school of the prophets worked with **d.** 6:1-7

DISAPPOINTMENT
Cause. Shame.
Of having an evil example. 8:1-29, Intro.
Of sin. 8:1-29, Intro.

DISCIPLES (See **BELIEVERS**)

DISCIPLINE (See **CHASTISEMENT**)

DISCOURAGEMENT
Causes. Discussed. 18:1-37, Intro.
Example. Those left in Jerusalem after the fall were **d.** 25:22-26

DISCRETION
Example. Elisha showed **d.** by not accepting a payment from Naaman. 5:16

DISEASES
Deadly.
Boil. Of Hezekiah. 20:1
Leprosy.
Cured. Naaman was healed of his **d.** of leprosy. 5:14
Curse of. Gehazi was cursed with leprosy, because of his greed and deception. 5:20, 25-27
Example.
Azariah. 15:1-7
Four men. Who discovered the abandoned camp of the Syrians and saved the entire city of Samaria. 7:3-9
Gehazi, Elisha's servant. 5:27
Naaman, the Syrian commander. 5:1

DISOBEDIENCE (See **REBELLION**)
Example. Jehu **d.** God by worshipping the golden calf of Jeroboam. 10:31

DISTRESS
Answer. Prayer. 19:14-19

DIVISION
Cause. Disorder. 15:8-31, Intro.

DOUBLE-MINDEDNESS
Example. Joram removed an idol but still engaged in false worship. 3:2-3

DUTY
Of believers. (See **BELIEVERS**, Duty)
Shunning. Example. Jehoiachin did not try to defend Jerusalem. 24:7-16

EDOM
Tribute of. Paid tribute to Israel since King David. 8:20-22
Wars of.
Gained freedom when Jehoram reigned Judah. 8:20-24
With Amaziah. Completely defeated. 14:7

EGYPT
Conquest by. Of Judah. 23:31-33

EKRON
False worship. Of Baal-Zebub. 1:1-6
Philistine city. 1:1-8

ELIJAH (See also 1 Kings)
Ascension. 2:1-12
Confrontations by.
With Ahaziah. Because he sought a false god. 1:3-8
With three army divisions. 1:9-16
Last day on earth. Taken up to heaven in a whirlwind. 2:1-12
Ministry. Well-known. **E.** was recognized by his clothes. 1:5-8
Miracles. Called fire down from heaven. 1:10, 12
Prophecy. That King Ahaziah would die from his injury. 1:6, 16
Taking of.
In a whirlwind. 2:11
Reason for.
To challenge people to seek God. 2:1-12, Thgt. 2
To demonstrate the reality of heaven and eternal life. 2:1-12, Thgt. 2

ELISHA
Calling.
E. was called by God to take the place of Elijah. 2:13-25
Proofs.
Appearance of water. 3:16-18
Cursing of the threatening gang. 2:23-25
Dividing of the Jordan River. 2:14
Fallen cloak of Elijah. 2:13
Purifying of the waters of Jericho. 2:19-22
Verification of **E.** word. 2:15-18

INDEX

Character. Strong. **E.** was steadfast to the end. 13:14-20

Commitment. **E.** showed great commitment to Elijah. 2:1-12

Compassion of.
  Seen in his many miracles. (See, **ELISHA**, Miracles of)
  Wept. About the coming destruction to Israel. 8:11-12

Death of. 13:20

Message. Final. To King Jehoash. 13:14-19

Ministry.
  Anointing by. **E.** instructed one of the prophets to anoint Jehu as king. 9:1-3

Miracles.
  Caused an ax head to float. 6:1-7
  Healed a leper. 5:1-14
  Multiplied supplies.
    Bread to feed one hundred men. 4:42-44
    Widow's oil. 4:1-7
  Parted the Jordan River. 2:13-14
  Purified a pot of poison food. 4:38-41
  Raised people from the dead.
    Corpse which touch **E.** bones. 13:21
  Supplied water overnight. 3:13-20
  Shunammite's son. 4:32-37
  Sweetened bitter water. 2:19-22

Predictions.
  Food would be multiplied. 4:43
  Gehazi and his descendants would be struck with leprosy. 5:26-27
  Great famine would end in one day. 7:1
  Israel would defeat Syria three times. 13:14-19
  Jehu would become king and kill the entire family of Ahab. 9:6-8
  King's official would see famine end, but not eat any of the food. 7:2
  Spring would be purified. 2:21
  Water would miraculously appear. 3:17

Records of. 2:2-13:21

Political influence.
  Had audience with the king of Israel. 8:1-6
  Sought by Ben-Hadad, king of Syria, for a word from God. 8:7-15

Protection of. Attackers were blinded. 6:18-20

ENDURANCE (See **DILIGENCE; FAITHFULNESS; PERSEVERANCE**)

ENEMY
Works of. Threats and oppression. 18:13-37

ENTHUSIASM (See **COMMITMENT**)

ETERNAL LIFE
Choice of. We must walk with God to have eternal life. 1:16-18, Thgt.1

EVANGELISM (See **WITNESSING**)

EVIL (See **SIN; WICKEDNESS**)
Acts. Listed. 21:1-26, Intro.
Duty. Not to follow. 21:19-26, Thgt.1

EVIL-MERODACH
Kindness of. To Jehoiachin. A picture of hope. 25:28-30
King. Of Babylon. 25:27

EXAMPLE
Evil. Example.
  Ahab and Jezebel upon their son and son-in-law (both named Azariah). 1:1-18; 8:26-27
  Athaliah upon her son, Azariah 8:26-27
Godly.
  Duty.
    To be a godly **e.** all our lives. 12:1-16, Thgt. 1
    To look for godly **e.** to follow. 12:1-16, Thgt.1
  Need for. 8:1-29, Intro.
  Rejecting. Of parents. 21:1-18
  Very important to set a godly **e.** 8:1-6, Thgt.1
Importance. **E.** we set affects the kind of life we will have. 8:1-6, Thgt.1

EXPECTATION (See **HOPE**)

FAILURE
Cause. 23:31-24:20, Intro.
Examples of. 23:31-24:20
Feelings of.
  Cause. 23:31-24:20, Intro.
  Problem. 23:31-24:20, Intro.

FAITH
Evidence of. Perseverance. 13:14-25, Thgt.1
Kinds of.
  Great. The widow of the prophets had great **f.** 4:1-7
  Persistent. The Shunammite's persistent **f.** was rewarded. 4:21-37
  Reward for. Example. The Shunammite's persistent **f.** was rewarded. 4:21-37

FAITHFULNESS (See **DILIGENCE; PERSEVERANCE**)
In worship. Jotham **f.** worshipped God. 15:34
Of God. Fulfills His promises. 15:12

FALSE GOD (See **GODS, FALSE**)

FALSE RELIGION (See **IDOLATRY; GODS, FALSE WORSHIP, FALSE**)

FALSE WORSHIP (See **WORSHIP,** False)

FAMINE
Cause of. Siege. 6:24-31
Judgment of God. 8:1

FAVOR (See **BLESSING**)

FEAR
Causes. Discussed. 18:1-37, Intro.

FIGHTING (See **WAR**)

FLESH
Fact. Is corruptible and decays. 20:1-21, Intro.
Needs of. Discussed. 20:1-21, Intro.

FORGIVENESS
Asked for. Example. Naaman asked for **f.** since he was forced to participate in false worship. 5:18

FREEDOM
From captivity.
  Example. Jehoiachin. 25:27
  Picture of hope. 25:27-30

GEDALIAH
Appointed. By Nebuchadnezzar. 25:22

GEHAZI
Greed of. Tried to get a reward from Naaman after Elisha had refused it. 5:21-23
Repentance. **G.** apparently repented because he came back to serve Elisha. 8:1-6, Cf.6:15
Servant to Elisha. 5:20; 8:1-6

GLORY (See **WORSHIP**)

GOD
Anger of. Cause.
  Disobedience. 22:13
  Wickedness. 24:17-20, Thgt.1
Compassion of. Is seen in that He meets our needs. 4:1-7, Thgt.1
Deliverance by. Example. God delivered Samaria from starvation. 7:3-9
False. (See **GOD, FALSE**)
Names-Titles.
  Creator. 1:1-18, Intro.
  Defense. 6:8-23, Thgt.1
  Fortress. 6:8-23, Thgt.1
  Hiding Place. 6:8-23, Thgt.1
  Living God. 1:1-18, Intro.
  Lord and Majesty of the universe. 1:1-18, Intro.
  Lord God Almighty. 1:1-18, Intro.
  One and only God 1:1-18, Intro.

Joash. 11:17-12:21
Josiah. 21:26-23:30
Jotham. 15:32-38
Manasseh. 20:21-21:18
Uzziah. 14:21-22; 15:1-7
Zedekiah. 24:18-25:21
Queen of.
Athaliah. 11:1-20
Wars of.
Against Assyria.
Delivered by the power of God. 19:20-36
Severely oppressed. 18:13-37
Against Edom. By Jehoram. Could not put down the revolt. 8:20-24
Against Egypt. Josiah was wounded and killed in the battle with Pharaoh Neco. 23:28-30
Against Libnah. By Jehoram. Revolted when Edom gained their freedom. 8:22

JUDGMENT (See **JUSTICE**)
Cause of.
Sin. 1:16-18, Thgt.1; 23:26-30, Thgt.1; 24:17-20, Thgt.1
Rejecting God's warnings. 23:34-24:6, Thgt.1
Unbelief. 7:1, 17-20
Example. Of Judah. 25:1-21
Fact.
Will be just. 25:1-30, Intro.
Will be perfect. 25:1-30, Intro.
Final. Is inevitable. 25:1-21, Thgt. 1
Fulfilled. Upon Judah. 25:1-21
Of Israel. Was eventually taken captive because they would not end their idolatry and wickedness. 15:27-31, Thgt. 1
Of Judah. Predicted. 23:26-27
Surety of. 25:1-30, Intro.
Ahab's family was completely wiped out, just as Elijah had prophesied. 9:6-8; 10:17
Ahaziah died just as Elijah had prophesied. 1:16-17
King's official was trampled by the people because he did not believe God's promise of provision. 7:17-20
Time of. Unknown. 15:27-31, Thgt.1; 17:5-6, Thgt.1

JUSTICE (See **JUDGMENT**)
Of Rulers. Duty. To administer **j**. 9:1-13
Execution. Example. Amaziah executed the servants who had murdered his father. 14:5
Results. Protects the people. 9:1-10:36, Intro.

KILLING (See **MURDER**)

KINDNESS (See **COMPASSION**; **MERCY**)
Example. Evil-Merodach treated Jehoiachin with **k**. 25:28-30

KINGS (See **LEADERS**)
Appointment of. Jehu was chosen by God to be **k**. 9:1-3
Foreign.
Mesha. Of Moab. 3:4
Of Israel.
Ahaziah. 1:1-18
Hoshea. 17:1-23
Jehoahaz. 13:1-9
Jehoash. 13:9-25; 14:8-16
Jehoram. 1:17; 3:1-8:15
Jehu. 9:1-10:36
Jeroboam II. 14:23-29
Menahem. 15:16-22
Pekah. 15:27-31
Pekahiah. 15:23-26
Shallum. 15:13-15
Zechariah. 15:8-12
Of Judah.
Ahaz. 15:38-16:20
Ahaziah. 8:25-29; 9:27-29
Amaziah. 14:1-20
Athaliah. 11:1-16
Gedaliah (appointed). 25:22-26
Hezekiah. 18:1-20:21
Jehoachin. 24:8-17; 25:27-30
Jehoakim. 23:34-24:7
Jehoaz. 23:31-33
Jehoram. 8:16-24
Joash. 11:17-12:21
Josiah. 21:26-23:30
Jotham. 15:32-38
Manasseh. 20:21-21:18
Uzziah. 14:21-22; 15:1-7
Zedekiah. 24:18-25:21

LABOR
Duty. We must be hardworking at our **l**. 6:1-7, Thgt.1
Example. Students in the prophets schools **l**. to make their own lodging. 6:1-7

LAW
Of God.
Disobedience to. Example. Jehu disobeyed God's L. by worshipping the golden calf at Bethel. 10:31
Obedience to. Amaziah did not execute the sons of his father's murderers, according to the L. 14:6

LEADER
Corrupt. Results. The people suffer. 11:1-21, Intro.
Evil. Example. King Zedekiah. 24:17-20
Strong. Needed. 13:1-25, Thgt.1

LEGACY
Duty. To leave a good **l**. 13:10-13, Thgt.1
Evil. Example.
Jehoash. Named his son after an idolater. 13:13
Jehu. Left a terrible **l**. of disobedience to God. 10:29-36, Thgt.1

LEPROSY (See **DISEASES**)

LIBNAH
Tribute of. Paid tribute to Israel. 8:20-22
Wars of. Gained their freedom when Jehoram reigned in Judah. 8:20-24.

LIFE
Dignity of. Is preserved by justice. 9:1-10:36, Intro.
Duty in. To be a godly example and to look for godly examples to follow. 12:1-16, Thgt.1
Ending of. People often become unkind in later years. 12:17-21, Thgt.1
Failure in. Cause. 23:31-24:20, Intro.

LONGSUFFERING
Of God.
Example. Had mercy on Israel because of their pitiful situation. 14:23-29
Great. He waits with great **l**. for us to repent. 14:23-29, Thgt.1
Limit. God's patience and **l**. has a limit. 17:5-6, Thgt.1

LOYALTY (See **OBEDIENCE**)

LUKEWARM (See **HALF-HEARTEDNESS**)

LYING (See **PLOTTING**)

MANKIND
Fallen nature of. Proof. 21:1-26, Intro.
Goodness of. Evidence. 22:1-20, Intro.

MANASSEH
Character. Very evil. 21:2
False worship of.
Abominations of the nations. 21:2
Influenced Judah to do evil. 21:9
Worshipped Molech. 21:6
Influence of. Evil. 21:9
King. Of Judah. 21:1
Murdered. Many innocent people 21:16
Parents. Example. Rejected. 21:1-18
Reign. 21:1-18
Wickedness of.
Discussed. 20:1-18
More wicked than the Amorites. 21:11

MARRIAGE
Of an unbeliever. The **m**. of Jehoram was into the wicked family of Ahab. 8:18

MATERIALISM
Defined and discussed. 3:1-27, Intro.
Example. Gehazi was filled with g. at the thought of a reward. 5:20-27

Seeking of. By the world. Through many vain philosophies. 3:1-27, Intro.

TURNING AWAY

From God. Example. Ahaziah turned away from the only living and true God to a false god. 1:2, 6

UNBELIEF

Example. King's official did not believe God's promise of miraculous provision. 7:1. Results. Death. 7:17-20

UNBELIEVERS

Alliances with. Will eventually cause us to commit spiritual adultery. 8:16-24, Thgt.1

Duty. We must not be unequally yoked with **u**. 8:16-24, Thgt.1

UZZIAH (See **AZARIAH**)

VICTORY

Of Israel. Over Moab. 3:20-27
Promised. By God.
To Israel and Judah when they went to fight Moab. 3:18-19
To Israel when they would fight Syria. Three **v**. were promised. 13:19

VOW (See **PROMISES**)

WALK

Spiritual. Duty. To **w**. with God all our lives. 12:1-16, Thgt.1

WAR (See **CONQUEST**)

Of Israel. By Joram. Against Moab. 3:4-19
Of Syria. Against Israel.
Siege. Syria besieged the city of Samaria. 6:24-33
Strategy of Syria was revealed to Elisha beforehand. 6:8-14
Strategy.
Example. Jehoshaphat had the **s**. of circling behind the enemy. 3:8
Siege. Syria against Samaria. 6:24-33

WARNING

Against false worship.
To the believer. 17:24-41
To the reader of Scripture. 17:24-41
Of God. Rejected. Results. Judgment will fall. 23:34-24:6, Thgt.1

WICKEDNESS (See **EVIL**; **SIN**)

Contrasted. With righteousness. 16:1-20, Intro.
Example.
Ahaz. Profaned the worship of God by bringing a foreign altar. 16:12-15
Athaliah. Murdered all the royal heirs to take the throne. 11:1
Hazael. Murdered Ben-Hadad I in order to take the throne. 8:15
Jeroboam II. Worshipped in the cult of Jeroboam I. 14:24
Of Israel. Became very great. 17:7-23

WIDOW

Needs met. Example. Oil was miraculously multiplied after she followed the counsel of Elisha. 4:3-7
Poor. Example. Wife of one of the prophets

WITNESS

Duty.
Of every believer. To proclaim the gospel. 7:10-20, Thgt. 1
Power of. Is in the message, not the messenger. 7:10-20, Thgt. 1
To believe in the power of God to deliver as we have heard **w**. 5:1-7, Thgt.1
Example. A young slave girl **w**. of the power of God to heal Naaman the leper. 5:3
Godly. Needed. 8:1-29, Intro.
Of Life. Results. Woman who **w**. of God's goodness was blessed further. 8:1-6

WORD OF GOD

Discovered. By Josiah. 22:8
Duty toward.
Every believer should proclaim the Word of God 3:4-19, Thgt.1
Every minister should proclaim the Word of God 3:4-19, Thgt.1
To study and know the Word of God so that we can obey His commandments. 22:8-20, Thgt.1
Reading. In worship. By Josiah. 23:1-3
Surety of.
Example.
Ahaziah died just as Elijah prophesied. 1:16-17
King's official saw the provision of food, but did not get any of it, just as Elisha had predicted. 7:2, 17-20
(See also **GOD**, Promises of)

WORLD

Fallen nature of. Proof. 21:1-26, Intro.
Is beautiful and good. Evidence of. 22:1-20, Intro.

WORLD HISTORY

Power shift. From Assyria to Babylon. 22:1-20, Intro.

WORLDLINESS

Example. Gehazi was filled with **w**. at the thought of a reward. 5:20-27

WORSHIP

Faithful. Example. Jotham. Worship God as Uzziah, his father had done. 15:34
False. (See **GODS, FALSE; IDOLATRY**)
Example. Joram clung to the sins and false **w**. of Jeroboam I. 3:2-3
Of the golden calves. Set up by Jeroboam. Followed by many kings. 3:3, 9:9, 10:29-31; 13:2; 15:9
Of Molech. Worshippers of **M**. would sacrifice their children by fire. 3:27; 23:10
Of Rimmon.
By Naaman master. 5:18
By the Syrians. 5:18
Trait. Of people. 23:1-30, Intro.
Services. Reading of God's Word. 23:1-3
True.
Determines our destiny. 22:1-7, Thgt.1
Must approach God exactly as He instructs. 15:32-38, Thgt. 1

WRATH OF GOD (See **GOD**, Wrath of)

ZECHARIAH

Assassinated. By Shallum. 15:10
Character. Evil. 15:9
King. Of Israel. 15:8-12
Reign of. Short. 15:8
Son. Of Jeroboam II. 15:8

ZEDEKIAH

Character. Evil. 24:19
Example. Of parents. Was evil. 24:19
Reign. 24:18-20

LEADERSHIP MINISTRIES WORLDWIDE

PURPOSE STATEMENT

LEADERSHIP MINISTRIES WORLDWIDE exists to equip ministers, teachers, and laypersons in their understanding, preaching, and teaching of God's Word by publishing and distributing worldwide *The Preacher's Outline & Sermon Bible*® and derivative works to reach & disciple all people for Jesus Christ.

MISSION STATEMENT

1. To make the Bible so understandable – its truth so clear and plain – that men and women everywhere, whether teacher or student, preacher or hearer, can grasp its message and receive Jesus Christ as Savior, and…

2. To place the Bible in the hands of all who will preach and teach God's Holy Word, verse by verse, precept by precept, regardless of the individual's ability to purchase it.

The Preacher's Outline & Sermon Bible and derivative works been given to LMW as LMW Resources for printing and distribution worldwide at/below cost, by those who remain anonymous. One fact, however, is as true today as it was in the time of Christ:

THE GOSPEL IS FREE, BUT THE COST OF TAKING IT IS NOT

LMW depends on the generous gifts of believers with a heart for Him and a love for the lost. They help pay for the printing, translating, and distributing of LMW Resources into the hands of God's servants worldwide, who will present the Gospel message with clarity, authority, and understanding beyond their own.

LMW was incorporated in the state of Tennessee in July 1992 and received IRS 501 (c)(3) non-profit status in March 1994. LMW is an international, nondenominational mission organization. All proceeds from USA sales, along with donations from donor partners, go directly to underwrite translation and distribution projects of LMW Resources to preachers, church and lay leaders, and Bible students around the world.

LMW Resources

This material, like similar works, has come from imperfect man and is thus susceptible to human error. We are nevertheless grateful to God for both calling us and empowering us through His Holy Spirit to undertake this task. Because of His goodness and grace, *The Preacher's Outline & Sermon Bible*® New Testament and the Old Testament volumes have been completed.

LMW Resources include *The Minister's Personal Handbook, The Believer's Personal Handbook,* and other helpful resources available in printed form as well as electronically on various digital platforms.

God has given the strength and stamina to bring us this far. Our confidence is that as we keep our eyes on Him and remain grounded in the undeniable truths of the Word, we will continue to produce other helpful resources for God's dear servants to use in their Bible study and discipleship.

We offer this material, first, to Him in whose name we labor and serve and for whose glory it has been produced and, second, to everyone everywhere who studies, preaches, and teaches the Word.

Our daily prayer is that each volume will lead thousands, millions, yes even billions, into a better understanding of the Holy Scriptures and a fuller knowledge of Jesus Christ the Incarnate Word, of whom the Scriptures so faithfully testify.

You will be pleased to know that Leadership Ministries Worldwide partners with Christian organizations, printers, and mission groups around the world to make LMW Resources available and affordable in many countries and foreign languages. It is our goal that *every* leader around the world, both clergy and lay, will be able to understand God's holy Word and present God's message with more clarity, authority, and understanding—all beyond his or her own power.

Leadership Ministries Worldwide
1928 Central Avenue • Chattanooga, TN 37408
1(800) 987-8790
Email: info@lmw.org
lmw.org

11/22

LEADERSHIP MINISTRIES WORLDWIDE

Product Listing

THE PREACHER'S OUTLINE & SERMON BIBLE® (POSB)   *Available in KJV (44 vols) & NIV (40 vols)*

OLD TESTAMENT

- Genesis I: Chs. 1–11
- Genesis II: Chs. 12–50
- Exodus I: Chs. 1–18
- Exodus II: Chs. 19–40
- Leviticus
- Numbers
- Deuteronomy
- Joshua
- Judges, Ruth
- 1 Samuel
- 2 Samuel
- 1 Kings
- 2 Kings
- 1 Chronicles
- 2 Chronicles
- Ezra, Nehemiah, Esther
- Job
- Psalms I: Chs. 1-41
- Psalms II: Chs. 42-106
- Psalms III: Chs. 107-150
- Proverbs
- Ecclesiastes, Song of Solomon
- Isaiah I: Chs. 1-35
- Isaiah II: Chs. 36-66
- Jeremiah I: Chs. 1-29
- Jeremiah II: Chs. 30-52, Lamentations
- Ezekiel
- Daniel, Hosea Joel, Amos, Obadiah, Jonah, Micah, Nahum
- Habakkuk, Zephaniah, Haggai, Zechariah, Malachi

NEW TESTAMENT

- Matthew I: Chs. 1–15
- Matthew II: Chs. 16–28
- Mark
- Luke
- John
- Acts
- Romans
- 1 & 2 Corinthians
- Galatians, Ephesians, Philippians, Colossians
- 1 & 2 Thessalonians, 1 & 2 Timothy, Titus, Philemon
- Hebrews, James
- 1 & 2 Peter, 1, 2, & 3 John, Jude
- Revelation
- Master Outline & Subject Index

Handbooks

- **What the Bible Says to the Believer** — The Believer's Personal Handbook
  11 Chapters. – Over 500 Subjects, 300 Promises, & 400 Verses Expounded - Gift leatherette or paperback options

- **What the Bible Says to the Minister** — The Minister's Personal Handbook
  12 Chapters. - 127 Subjects - 400 Verses Expounded - Gift leatherette or paperback options

- **What the Bible Says to the Business Leader**—The Business Leader's Personal Handbook
  12 Chapters – Over 100 topics plus hundreds of scriptural values for conducting business in a 21st-century world — Paperback

- **What the Bible Says About Series** — Various Subjects

everyWORD

Scripture, Outline, Commentary of the Gospels with ESV Scripture

- everyWORD: Matthew 1–16:12

- everyWORD: Matthew 16:13–28:20

- everyWORD: Mark

- everyWORD: Luke 1–13:21

- everyWORD: Luke 13:22–24:53

- everyWORD: John

- **The Teacher's Outline & Study Bible™** - Various New Testament Books
  Complete 30 - 45 minute lessons – with illustrations and discussion questions
- *Practical Illustrations — Companion to the POSB Arranged by topic and Scripture reference*
- *LMW Resources on various digital platforms Learn more on our website at lmw.org*
- *Contact for resources in other languages*

Contact Us

LEADERSHIP MINISTRIES WORLDWIDE
1928 Central Avenue • Chattanooga, TN 37408
1(800) 987-8790 • E-mail - info@lmw.org
Order online at lmw.org

Made in the USA
Columbia, SC
31 January 2025

52864680R00189